Handbook of Research on Web Information Systems Quality

Coral Calero Muñoz
University of Castilla–La Mancha, Spain

Mª Ángeles Moraga
University of Castilla–La Mancha, Spain

Mario Piattini
University of Castilla–La Mancha, Spain

INFORMATION SCIENCE REFERENCE

Hershey · New York

Acquisitions Editor:	Kristin Klinger
Development Editor:	Kristin Roth
Senior Managing Editor:	Jennifer Neidig
Managing Editor:	Sara Reed
Copy Editor:	Lanette Ehrhardt, Susanna Svidunovich
Typesetter:	Michael Brehm
Cover Design:	Lisa Tosheff
Printed at:	Yurchak Printing Inc.

Published in the United States of America by
Information Science Reference (an imprint of IGI Global)
701 E. Chocolate Avenue, Suite 200
Hershey PA 17033
Tel: 717-533-8845
Fax: 717-533-8661
E-mail: cust@igi-global.com
Web site: http://www.igi-global.com

and in the United Kingdom by
Information Science Reference (an imprint of IGI Global)
3 Henrietta Street
Covent Garden
London WC2E 8LU
Tel: 44 20 7240 0856
Fax: 44 20 7379 0609
Web site: http://www.eurospanonline.com

Library of Congress Cataloging-in-Publication Data

Handbook of research on Web information systems quality / Coral Calero, Mª Ángeles Moraga, and Mario Piattini, editors.

p. cm.

Summary: "This book integrates invaluable research on the models, measures, and methodologies of Web information systems, software quality, and Web engineering into one practical guide to Web information systems quality, making this handbook of research an essential addition to all library collections"--Provided by publisher.

Includes bibliographical references and index.

ISBN 978-1-59904-847-5 (hardcover) -- ISBN 978-1-59904-848-2 (ebook)

1. World Wide Web--Handbooks, manuals, etc. 2. Information technology--Handbooks, manuals, etc. 3. Computer software--Quality control--Handbooks, manuals, etc. 4. Application software--Development--Handbooks, manuals, etc. 5. Web services--Handbooks, manuals, etc. I. Calero, Coral, 1968- II. Moraga, Mª Ángeles, 1979- III. Piattini, Mario, 1966-

TK5105.888.H362 2008

004.67'8--dc22

2007032032

British Cataloguing in Publication Data
A Cataloguing in Publication record for this book is available from the British Library.

All work contributed to this book set is original material. The views expressed in this book are those of the authors, but not necessarily of the publisher.

Editorial Advisory Board

Table of Contents

Section I
Effort and Quality Assessment

Chapter I

Emilia Mendes, The University of Auckland, New Zealand

Chapter II

Emilia Mendes, University of Auckland, New Zealand
Silvia Abrahão, Valencia University of Technology, Spain

Chapter III

Pankaj Kamthan, Concordia University, Canada

Chapter IV

Rosemary Stockdale, Massey University, New Zealand
Chad Lin, Curtin University of Technology, Australia

Chapter V

May Haydar, Université de Montréal, Canada
Ghazwa Malak, Université de Montréal, Canada
Houari Sahraoui, Université de Montréal, Canada
Alexandre Petrenko, Centre de recherche informatique de Montréal (CRIM), Canada
Sergiy Boroday, Centre de recherche informatique de Montréal (CRIM), Canada

Section III
Metadata, MDE, Metamodels, and Ontologies

Section IV
Search Engine and Information

Detailed Table of Contents

Section I
Effort and Quality Assessment

This section is related to effort and quality assessment and is composed of eight chapters. The first two chapters deal with Web development effort estimation. The other six are related to several aspects of Web quality such as context of use, pragmatic quality, effectiveness of small and medium size business Web sites, anomaly detection, and quality evaluation and assessment. Also, two chapters are included where quality models for Web portals and data portal quality are presented.

This chapter presents a survey literature of size measures (attributes) that have been proposed for Web effort estimation. These measures are classified according to a proposed taxonomy. In addition, the authors discuss ways in which Web companies can devise their own size measures.

The objective of this chapter is to introduce the concepts related to Web effort estimation and effort estimation techniques. It also details and compares, by means of a case study, three effort estimation techniques, chosen for this chapter because they have been to date the ones mostly used for Web effort estimation: multivariate regression, case-based reasoning, and classification and regression trees.

The chapter emphasizes the significance of approaching Web information systems (WIS) from an engineering viewpoint. A methodology for deploying patterns as means for improving the quality of WIS as perceived by their stakeholders is presented.

This chapter discusses and analyses the effectiveness of SME business to business Web sites from a user perspective, under the premise that an effective method of evaluating a Web site can contribute to the development of more quality Web sites and greater realization of benefits.

This chapter addresses the problem of Web application quality assessment from two perspectives. First, it shows the use of model checking of properties formulated in LTL to detect anomalies in Web applications. Second, the chapter explains how probabilistic models (Bayesian Networks) can be built and used to evaluate quality characteristics. The two proposed approaches are evaluated and a discussion on how they complement each other is presented.

This chapter presents the most prominent systems and prototypes implemented for the automatic quality assessment for Internet pages, and analyzes the knowledge sources exploited for these approaches.

Chapter VII

Mª Ángeles Moraga, University of Castilla—La Mancha, Spain
Julio Córdoba, University of Alicante, Spain
Coral Calero, University of Castilla—La Mancha, Spain
Cristina Cachero, University of Alicante, Spain

In this chapter, several portal quality models are presented and compared. Authors have adapted one of the best portal quality models proposed in the literature to the e-banking context. In addition, the new e-banking portal quality model has been compared with the original portal quality model, as well as with the main portal quality characteristics.

Chapter VIII

Angélica Caro, University of Bio Bio, Chile
Coral Calero, University of Castilla-La Mancha, Spain
Mario Piattini, University of Castilla-La Mancha, Spain

The chapter proposes a model for data quality in Web portals (PDQM) built on the foundation of three key aspects: (1) a set of Web data quality attributes identified in the literature in this area, (2) data quality expectations of data consumers on the Internet, and (3) the functionalities that a Web portal may offer its users.

Section II
Accessibility and Usability

This section is divided into two main topics. The first chapter works on both topics. The next three chapters deal with accessibility, one of them from a general point of view, another one comparing approaches to Web accessibility assessment, and the last one about maximizing Web accessibility. The other three chapters are about usability from the point of view of ergonomic criteria as part of the development of Web applications or as an important aspect for the construction of business process driven Web applications.

Chapter IX

Marta Fernández De Arriba, University of Oviedo, Spain
Eugenia Díaz, University of Oviedo, Spain
Jesús Rodríguez Pérez, University of Oviedo, Spain

This chapter is presented in the structure of an index, which serves as support that allows the development team to create the specification of the context of use document for the development of Web applications, bearing in mind characteristics of usability and accessibility.

This chapter studies the Web accessibility issue from the perspective of Web information systems quality. In addition, the closed relation between accessibility and standard Web technologies is explained.

In this chapter the importance of Web accessibility assessment is discussed and 15 different approaches found in literature are compared.

The user interface is the place where users can interact with the information by using their minds. Users with special needs can acquire information by using a human centered user interface. This chapter highlights the need to investigate the relationship between cognition and user interface.

This chapter proposes a quality model that focuses on quality in use or usability for the product characterization of the World Wide Web.

This chapter surveys the most emergent usability evaluation models to be adopted during the whole lifecycle of Web information systems for promoting usability. For each evaluation method, the main features, as well as the emerging advantages and drawbacks, are illustrated.

Chapter XV

In this chapter, the authors gather a set of guidelines provided by experts in Web usability and present the solution designed in a particular Web engineering method that follows a model driven development approach

Section III
Metadata, MDE, Metamodels, and Ontologies

Section III is related to Metadata, MDE, metamodels, and ontologies. The first four chapters are focused on Metadata issues. In concrete, the former presents a proposal annotated-based to portletizing existing Web application, the second one uses metada evolution for adaptive Web, and the last two are related to information. The next chapter presents a proposal for developing quality Web information systems through precise model driven development. In the next three chapters, different metamodels oriented to Web requirements, development of Web applications, and Web exploration are shown. Finally, an ontology for WSRP standard is presented and a philosophy of architecture design in Web Information Systems.

Chapter XVI

This chapter focuses on "portletizing" existing Web applications, that is, wrapping them as portlets, without requiring any modification. After providing some background on portlet technology, they discuss two kinds of approaches to portletization: automatic and annotation-based.

Chapter XVII

The authors survey techniques for ontology evolution. The authors detail the various existing languages and techniques devoted to Web data evolution, with particular attention to Semantic Web concepts, and how these languages and techniques can be adapted to evolving data in order to improve the quality of web information systems applications.

Chapter XVIII

In this chapter, the importance of using ontologies to represent database schemas is highlighted. The representation of the fuzzy data in fuzzy databases management systems (FDBMS) has certain special requirements, and these characteristics must be explicitly defined to enable this kind of information to be accessed.

This chapter addresses those issues by proposing a Web metadata-based model to evaluate and recommend Web pages based on their information quality, as predicted by their metadata.

This chapter presents one WIS development methodology (MIDAS) that has been completed with the definition of a strategy for the formal specification of its models with V&V objectives.

This chapter presents NDT (navigational development techniques), a Web methodological approach to deal with requirements, based on model-driven engineering. The proposal is composed of a set of procedures, techniques, and models to assure the quality of results in the Web requirements treatment.

Chapter XXII

Cristina Cachero Castro, Universidad de Alicante, Spain
Coral Calero, University of Castilla-La Mancha, Spain
Yolanda Marhuenda García, Universidad Miguel Hernández de Elche, Spain

This chapter introduces the necessity to consider quality management activities as part of the Web engineering (WE) process to improve the final quality of Web applications with respect to creative practices.

Chapter XXIII

Sergej Sizov, University of Koblenz-Landau, Germany
Stefan Siersdorfer, University of Sheffield, UK

This chapter addresses the problem of automatically organizing heterogeneous collections of Web documents for generation of thematically focused expert search engines and portals. As a possible application scenario for the presented techniques, the authors show a Web crawler that aims to populate topics of interest by automatically categorizing newly fetched documents.

Chapter XXIV

Mª Ángeles Moraga, University of Castilla-La Mancha, Spain
Ignacio García-Rodríguez De Guzmán, University of Castilla-La Mancha, Spain
Coral Calero, University of Castilla-La Mancha, Spain
Mario Piattini, University of Castilla-La Mancha, Spain

This chapter presents an ontology for WSRP standard. The aim of this standard is to provide a common interface in order to allow the communication between portal and portlets. Bearing this in mind, in this work the authors propose an ontology for the WSRP standard. The ontology offers an understandable summary of the standard.

Chapter XXV

Tony C. Shan, Bank of America, USA
Winnie W. Hua, CTS Inc., USA

This chapter defines a comprehensive set of guiding principles—philosophy of architecture design (PAD)—as a means of coping with the architecture design complexity and managing the architectural assets of Web information systems in a service-oriented paradigm.

Section IV
Search Engine and Information

This section is focused on two main topics: search engine and information. Among the chapters classified in this section, four of them are related to the first topic, whereas the last two are related to the second one. The chapters focused on search engine deal with the following issues: improve the quality of Web search, enhance Web search engine performance, and Web search engine architectures. Regarding the chapters which are focused on information, we can highlight that one of them proposes a model for evaluating Web retrieval systems in non English queries, and the other one presents Web information resources vis-à-vis traditional information services.

In this chapter, the authors propose the improvement of the quality of Web search by combining meta-search and self-organizing maps. This can help users both in locating interesting documents more easily and in getting an overview of the retrieved document set.

In this chapter, some past research in Web search and current trends focusing on how to improve the search quality in different perspectives of "what," "how," "where," "when," and "why" are discussed.

The objectives of the chapter are to review the theories and technologies pertaining to Web search, helping in the understanding of how Web search engines work, and how to use the search engines more effectively and efficiently.

The purpose of this chapter is to describe the methods and the criteria used for evaluating search engines, and proposes a model for evaluating the searching effectiveness of Web retrieval systems in non English queries.

Chapter XXX

John D'Ambra, The University of New South Wales, Australia
Nina Mistilis, The University of New South Wales, Australia

The chapter proposes that visitor information centres are analogous to a general information system and that centre user experience can partially be explained by their perception of the information resource quality.

Preface

Web information systems are rapidly growing, and the increasing demand of that software has made the quality a discriminator factor becoming a key factor for their success.

Advances in technology and the use of Internet have favored the appearance of a great variety of Web software applications. As a result, over the past decade the number of organizations which make use of Web applications has grown dramatically. These Web applications are used by different companies with the aim of giving several services to their clients. From the user's point of view, Web applications are used to make deals. In both cases, the quality is relevant. In the first case, it is fundamental the quality of Web applications in order to give a good service and assure the loyalty of users. In the second case, the quality is important in order that users can achieve their objectives in a proper way.

Therefore, it is essential not only to develop new Web information systems, but also to take into account their quality. With regard to this, new methodologies and models are being developed to improve and assess the quality of Web information systems. In such an ever-evolving environment, Web engineers, software quality managers, software engineers, software architects, MSc. Students, and university-level professors of the discipline need access to the most current information about the models, measures, and methodologies in this emerging field.

The Web age has modified our society, and new business models have appeared, while others have been modified. In addition, the relationships between the different actors have changed.

It may be worth emphasizing that Web Technologies have become very important in information systems. Web Technologies are essential for organizations. Currently, it is indispensable that the developed Web products, such as Web pages, Web applications, Web portals, and so forth, achieve a minimum level of quality.

According to Offutt 2002[1], several factors inherent to Web development affect to the quality:

1. Developers build Web-based software systems by integrating numerous diverse components from disparate sources, including custom built special-purpose applications, customized off-the-shelf software components, and third-party products.
2. Much of the new complexity found with Web-based applications also results from how the different software components are integrated. Not only is the source unavailable for most of the components, the executables might be hosted on computers at remote, even competing organizations. To ensure high quality for Web systems composed of very loosely coupled components, we need novel techniques to achieve and evaluate these components' connections.
3. Finally, Web-based software offers the significant advantage of allowing data to be transferred among completely different types of software components that reside and execute on different computers. However, using multiple programming languages and building complex business applications complicates the flow of data through the various Web software pieces.

The *Handbook of Research on Web information systems Quality* provides comprehensive coverage of the most important issues, such as: effort and quality assessment, accessibility, usability, metadata, MDE, metamodels, ontologies search engine, and information. All of them focus on Web information systems.

The handbook is divided into four sections that cover the main tendencies on the Web information systems research and gives a clear vision of the main actual lines of work and also the topics where more effort is being developed.

The first section is on quality assessment, where different approaches, whose central point is quality, are presented. The second is on accessibility and usability, perhaps two of the most important factors related to Web information systems and where more research and development efforts are deployed from the beginning of this discipline. The third section approaches the technological point of view with chapters about metadata, MDE, metamodels, and ontologies. Finally, the last section works on Web engines and information on the Web.

As we have already mentioned, the first section is related to effort and quality assessment and is composed of eight chapters. The first chapter presents a survey literature of size measures (attributes) that have been proposed for Web effort estimation. These measures are classified according to a proposed taxonomy. In addition, the authors discuss ways in which Web companies can devise their own size measures. The objective of the second chapter is to introduce the concepts related to Web effort estimation and effort estimation techniques. It also details and compares, by means of a case study, three effort estimation techniques.

Chapter III emphasizes the significance of approaching Web information systems (WIS) from an engineering viewpoint. A methodology for deploying patterns as means for improving the quality of WIS as perceived by their stakeholders is presented. The fourth chapter discusses and analyses the effectiveness of SME business to business Web sites from a user perspective under the premise that an effective method of evaluating a Web site can contribute to the development of more quality Web sites and greater realization of benefits. In Chapter V, the problem of Web application quality assessment is assessed from two perspectives.

Chapter VI presents the most prominent systems and prototypes implemented for the automatic quality assessment for Internet pages and analyzes the knowledge sources exploited for these approaches. In Chapter VII several portal quality models are presented and compared. Authors have adapted one of the best portal quality model proposed in the literature to the e-banking context.

Finally, the section ends with a chapter that proposes a model for data quality in Web portals (PDQM) built upon the foundation of three key aspects: (1) a set of Web data quality attributes identified in the literature in this area, (2) data quality expectations of data consumers on the Internet, and (3) the functionalities that a Web portal may offer its users.

The second section of the book is divided into two main topics and is composed of seven chapters. The first works on both topics. The three next chapters deal with accessibility, one of them from a general point of view, another one comparing approaches to Web accessibility assessment, and the last one about maximizing Web accessibility. The other three chapters are about usability from the point of view of ergonomic criteria as part of the development of Web applications or as an important aspect for the construction of business process driven Web applications.

Concretely, Chapter IX is presented in the structure of an index, which allows the development team to create the specification of the context of use document for the development of Web applications, bearing in mind characteristics of usability and accessibility.

Chapter X studies the Web accessibility issue from the perspective of Web information systems Quality. In addition, the closed relationship between accessibility and standard Web technologies is explained. In the eleventh chapter, the importance of Web accessibility assessment is discussed and 15 different approaches found in literature are compared.

The user interface is the place where users can interact with the information by using their minds. Users with special needs can acquire information by using a human centred user interface. Chapter XII highlights the need to investigate the relationship between cognition and user interface.

Chapter XIII proposes a quality model that focuses on quality in use or usability for the product characterization of the World Wide Web, and Chapter XIV surveys the most emergent usability evaluation models to be adopted during the whole lifecycle of Web information systems, for promoting usability.

In the last chapter of this section, the authors gather a set of guidelines provided by experts in Web usability and present the solution designed in a particular Web engineering method that follows a model driven development approach.

The third section is related to metadata, MDE, metamodels, and ontologies. The first four chapters focus on metadata issues. In the next three chapters, different metamodels oriented to Web requirements, development of Web applications, and Web exploration are shown. Finally, an ontology for WSRP standard is presented and a philosophy of architecture design in Web information systems.

The section starts with Chapter XVI, focused on "portletizing" existing Web applications, that is, wrapping them as portlets, without requiring any modification. After providing some background on portlet technology, they discuss two kinds of approaches to portletization: automatic and annotation-based. In Chapter XVII, the authors survey techniques for ontology evolution. The authors detail the various existing languages and techniques devoted to Web data evolution, with particular attention to Semantic Web concepts, and how these languages and techniques can be adapted to evolving data in order to improve the quality of Web information systems applications.

In Chapter XVIII, the importance of using ontologies to represent database schemas is highlighted. The representation of the fuzzy data in fuzzy databases management systems (FDBMS) has certain special requirements, and these characteristics must be explicitly defined to enable this kind of information to be accessed. Chapter XIX addresses those issues by proposing a Web metadata-based model to evaluate and recommend Web pages based on their information quality, as predicted by their metadata.

Chapter XX presents one WIS development methodology (MIDAS) that has been completed with the definition of a strategy for the formal specification of its models with V&V objectives, and chapter XXI presents NDT (navigational development techniques), a Web methodological approach to deal with requirements, based on model-driven engineering. The proposal is composed of a set of procedures, techniques and models to assure the quality of results in the Web requirements treatment.

Chapter XXII introduces the necessity to consider quality management activities as part of the Web engineering (WE) process to improve the final quality of Web applications with respect to creative practices.

The problem of automatically organizing heterogeneous collections of Web documents for generation of thematically focused expert search engines and portals is the focus of Chapter XXIII. As a possible application scenario for the presented techniques, the authors show a Web crawler that aims to populate topics of interest by automatically categorizing newly fetched documents.

An ontology for WSRP standard is presented in Chapter XXIV. The aim of this standard is to provide a common interface in order to allow the communication between portal and portlets. Bearing this in mind, in this work the authors propose an ontology for the WSRP standard that offers an understandable summary of the standard.

Closing this section, Chapter XXV provides a comprehensive set of guiding principles—philosophy of architecture design (PAD)—as a means of coping with the architecture design complexity and managing the architectural assets of Web information systems in a service-oriented paradigm.

The last section of the book focuses on two main topics: search engine and information. Among the chapters classified in this section, four of them are related to the first topic, whereas the last two are related to the second one.

The section starts with Chapter XXVI, where the authors propose the improvement of the quality of Web search by combining meta-search and self-organizing maps. This can help users both in locating interesting documents more easily and in getting an overview of the retrieved document set.

In Chapter XXVII, some past research in Web search and current trends focusing on how to improve the search quality in different perspectives of "what," "how," "where," "when," and "why" are discussed.

The objectives of Chapter XXVIII are to review the theories and technologies pertaining to Web search, helping in the understanding of how Web search engines work, and how to use the search engines more effectively and efficiently.

The purpose of the Chapter XXIX is to describe methods and criteria used for evaluating search engines. The chapter also proposes a model for evaluating the searching effectiveness of Web retrieval systems in non English queries.

Finally, the last chapter of the book proposes that visitor information centres are analogous to a general information system and that centre user experience can partially be explained by their perception of the information resource quality.

Due to the variety of topics and the different aspects related to the research on quality for Web information systems, this handbook can be used by software engineering researchers and practitioners (professors, PhD, and postgraduate students, industrial R&D departments, etc.) for helping in the understanding of the topic, knowing about the main current tendencies of research and the future lines of research on Web information systems quality.

ENDNOTE

[1]   Offutt, A. J. (2002). Quality attributes of Web software applications. *IEEE Software, 19*(2), 25-32.

Acknowledgment

The editors would like to acknowledge the help of all involved in the collation and review process of the handbook, without whose support the project could not have been satisfactorily completed.

Most of the authors of chapters included in this handbook also served as referees for chapters written by other authors. Also, other important international researchers have collaborated as reviewers of our handbook. We want to thank all of them for their great work and constructive and comprehensive reviews.

Special thanks also go to the publishing team at IGI Global, whose contributions throughout the whole process from inception of the initial idea to final publication have been invaluable. Thanks in particular to Kristin Roth and Jessica Thompson, who continuously prodded via e-mail for keeping the project on schedule, and to Michelle Potter, whose enthusiasm motivated me to initially accept her invitation for taking on this project.

Special thanks go to Spanish Ministry of Education that financed this work, under the research projects ESFINGE (TIN2006-15175-C05-05) and CALIPSO (TIN2005-24055-E).

In closing, we wish to thank all of the authors for their insights and excellent contributions to this handbook.

Dra. Coral Calero

Dra. Mª Ángeles Moraga

Dr. Mario Piattini

Ciudad Real, Spain
June 2007

Section I
Effort and Quality Assessment

Chapter I
Sizing Web Applications for Web Effort Estimation

Emilia Mendes
The University of Auckland, New Zealand

ABSTRACT

Surveying and classifying previous work on a particular field brings several benefits, which are: 1) to help organise a given body of knowledge; 2) to provide results that can help identify gaps that need to be filled; 3) to provide a categorisation that can also be applied or adapted to other surveys; and 4) to provide a classification and summary of results that may benefit practitioners and researchers who wish to carry out meta-analyses. This chapter presents a survey literature of size measures (attributes) that have been proposed for Web effort estimation. These measures are classified according to a proposed taxonomy. We also discuss ways in which Web companies can devise their own size measures.

INTRODUCTION

The purpose of estimating effort is to predict the necessary amount of labour units to accomplish a given task, based on knowledge of previous similar projects and other project characteristics that are believed to be related to effort. Project characteristics are the input, and effort is the output we wish to predict.

A task to be estimated can be as simple as developing a single function (e.g., creating a Web form with 10 fields) or as complex as developing a large application, and the one input always found to have the strongest influence on effort is size. Thus, using an adequate size measure is fundamental to building adequate and accurate effort estimation models.

One of the main challenges in Web effort estimation is to determine what is/are the best measure(s) to be used to size an application. There are no standards and throughout industry and academia different size measures are used.

Since 1998, numerous size measures have been proposed for Web effort estimation and it is important that such body of knowledge be structured and made available such that practitioners may look at existing measures and assess whether or not they are applicable to their own environment; in addition, researchers may use this body of knowledge as a starting point to understand trends in sizing Web applications.

The literature to date has published three surveys on Web measures (Calero, Ruiz, & Piattini, 2004; Dhyani, Ng, & Bhowmick, 2002; Mendes, Counsell, & Mosley, 2005). Of these, only Mendes et al. (2005) has included measures that are applicable for Web effort estimation.

Each survey is briefly described below:

- Dhyani et al. (2002) concentrates on measures that belong to one of the following six categories:
  - **Web graph properties:** measures that quantify structural properties of the Web on both macroscopic and microscopic scales.
  - **Web page significance:** measures used to assess candidate pages in response to a search query and have a bearing on the quality of search and retrieval on the Web.
  - **Usage characterization:** measures that quantify user behavior aiming at improving the content, organization, and presentation of Web sites.
  - **Web page similarity:** measures that quantify the extent of association between Web pages.
  - **Web page search and retrieval:** measures for evaluating and comparing the performance of Web search and retrieval services.
  - **Information theoretic:** measures that capture properties related to information needs, production, and consumption.
- Calero et al. (2004) provides a survey where Web measures are classified into three dimensions, all related to Web quality:
  - **Web features dimension:** incorporates content, navigation, and presentation measures.

  - **Quality characteristics dimension:** incorporates functionality, reliability, efficiency, portability, and maintainability measures.
  - **Life cycle processes dimension:** Process measures related to a Web development life cycle.

In addition to the above classification, Calero et al. (2004) also assess the surveyed measures according to an additional criteria:

  - **Granularity level:** whether the measure's scope is a "Web page" or "Web site."
  - **Theoretical validation:** whether or not a measure has been validated theoretically.
  - **Empirical validation:** whether or not a measure has been empirically validated.
  - **Automated support:** whether or not there is a support tool that facilitates the calculation of the measure.
- Mendes et al. (2005) provided a survey and taxonomy of hypermedia and Web size measures based on literature published since 1992. The criteria they used to classify measures will be detailed in the next section because this is the same criteria we use in this chapter. A taxonomy represents a model that is used to classify and understand a body of knowledge.

This chapter's objectives are twofold: first, to complement Mendes et al.'s work by focusing further on size measures for Web effort estimation. We employ the same taxonomy proposed in Mendes et al. (2005) to classify the existing body of knowledge; second, to make recommendations to Web companies on how to define their own size measures, whenever that seems applicable.

The remainder of this chapter is organised as follows: First, it introduces the taxonomy we employ, explaining terms and definitions that are part of this classification. Second, it presents our literature review, which was based on 10 papers. Note that we only included in our literature review papers that proposed a new set of measures, that is, if two or more papers used the same set of size measures we included only the first one published. Third, it applies the taxonomy to classify each of the papers from our literature review. Fourth, it discusses the change in trends that have occurred in the area of Web sizing. Fifth, it details the necessary steps to be used by a Web company to derive its own size measures. Finally, it presents its conclusions.

SIZE MEASURES TAXONOMY

The taxonomy that was proposed by Mendes et al. (2005) uses as its basis software measurement concepts 0 and literature in software size measures and measurement (Briand & Wieczorek, 2002). It originally comprises nine categories, which are applied to each size measure identified in the literature. We will only use eight of these categories, which are as follows:

- **Harvesting time**
- **Measure foundation**
- **Class**
- **Entity**
- **Measurement scale**
- **Computation**
- **Validation**
- **Model dependency**

Each is detailed below.

Harvesting Time

The harvesting time category describes when, in a project's development life cycle, the measure should be obtained (measured). Whenever a measure has to be obtained early on in a project's development life cycle it is very likely that it will need to be estimated. Otherwise, it may be directly

measured. The main motivation for including this category to classify the size measures in this chapter is that measures for effort estimation should ideally all be gathered early in a project's development life cycle, and thus we want to also assess to what extent what has been proposed in the literature complies with this premise. This category can have simple values such as "early size measure" or "late size measure;" however, a longer description can also be given whenever necessary (e.g., "late size measure to be measured after the implementation is finished").

Measure Foundation

The measure foundation category describes whether the size measure is a problem-orientated measure or a solution-orientated measure (Briand & Wieczorek, 2002):

- **Problem-orientated measure:** a problem-orientated measure assumes that an application's size corresponds directly to the size of the problem to be solved in order to deliver a corresponding application. Therefore, the greater the problem, the greater the size. In this context, the problem to be solved is denoted by the functionality of the application to be developed. Problem-orientated size measures generally take the form of surrogate measures of functionality. These measures can be extracted from the specification or design documents (e.g., use case diagrams 0, data flow diagrams (DeMarco, 1982), or entity-relationship models (Mendes et al., 2002)). An example of a common problem-oriented metric is function points, which aims to measure the size of an application in terms of the amount of functionality within the application, as described by its proposed specification 01997).
- **Solution-orientated measure:** in contrast, a solution-orientated measure assumes that an application's size corresponds to the

3

actual delivered size of an application. A frequently used size measure is lines of code (LOC), which measures the size of a given software implementation. This measure has been frequently criticised for its difficulty in being measured consistently (Jones, 1998) and for being a difficult measure to estimate early in the development life cycle. Finally, another source of criticism is that LOC is a measure that is highly dependent on the programming paradigm, language and style employed (Briand & Wieczorek, 2002).

Class

The class category allows for the classification of size measures into either of three possible classes: length, complexity, and functionality (Fenton & Pfleeger, 1997):

- **Length:** measures the physical size of an application;
- **Functionality:** measures the functions and features supplied by the application to the user; and
- **Complexity:** measures the structural complexity of an application, where the application's structure is represented by the way in which nodes (e.g., Web pages) are interconnected via links. The assumption behind complexity size measures is that by analysing the application's structure, the application's development (authoring) can be improved to create more comprehensible structures. These therefore improve the application's usability, as they enable users to better traverse (navigate) the application. More comprehensible structures also reduce the disorientation caused by traversing a complex structure.

According to the descriptions given above, we can say that the foundation for both length and complexity measures is "solution-orientated,"

whereas the foundation for a functionality size measure is "problem-orientated."

Entity

The entity category represents the product to which the size measure is associated. Within the context of this chapter, there are six different types of products, which are: Web hypermedia application, Web software application, Web application, media, program/script, and Web application design model. Each is described below:

- **Web hypermedia application** (Christodoulou, Zafiris, & Papatheodorou, 2000): a nonconventional application characterised by the authoring of information using nodes (chunks of information), links (relations between nodes), anchors, access structures (for navigation), and delivery over the Web. Technologies commonly used for developing such applications are HTML, XML, JavaScript, and multimedia. In addition, typical developers are writers, artists, and organisations who wish to publish information on the Web or CD-ROM without the need to know programming languages such as Java. These applications have unlimited potential in areas such as software engineering, literature, education, and training.
- **Web software application** (Christodoulou et al., 2000): a conventional software application that relies on the Web or uses the Web's infrastructure for execution. Typical applications include legacy information systems such as databases, booking systems, knowledge bases, and so forth. Many e-commerce applications fall into this category. Typically, they employ development technologies (e.g., DCOM, ActiveX, etc.), database systems, and development solutions (e.g., J2EE). Developers are in general young programmers fresh from a Computer Science or Software Engineering degree course, managed by a few more senior staff.

- **Web application:** an application delivered over the Web that combines characteristics of both Web hypermedia and Web software applications.
- **Media:** a multimedia component, for example, graphic, audio, video, animation, and photograph.
- **Program/Script:** code employed to add functionality to an application (e.g., Perl scripts, javascript).
- **Web application design model:** a conceptual representation of a Web application. Such representations are characterised by models, for example, navigation model and presentation model. These models are abstractions that later are translated into an implementation of the Web application.

Measurement Scale Type

To understand the measurement scale type category it is first important to understand what measurement means. Measurement represents a process by which numbers or symbols are assigned to attributes (measures) of entities in the real world such that these entities can be described according to clearly defined rules. For example, in relation to an entity "Person," the attributes (measures) *height*, *weight*, and *gender* are used as characteristics of "Person." Each attribute (measure) can be measured using one of five different measurement scale types. Each scale type represents a set of characteristics associated with a measure that help interpret this measure and also determine what sort of manipulations can be applied to it. The five scale types are Nominal, Ordinal, Interval, Ratio, and Absolute (Fenton & Pfleeger, 1997), and their descriptions are as follows:

- **Nominal:** Defines classes or categories, and places entities in a particular class or category, based on the value of the attribute. Let's suppose we wish to measure the attribute *application type* for the entity "Web

application," and that the types of application considered were:
  - **Academic**
  - **Corporate**
  - **E-commerce**
  - **E-trading**
  - **Educational**
  - **Entertainment**
  - **Multimedia Presentation**
  - **News and Information**
  - **Nonprofit**
  - **Online community/forum**
  - **Personal**
  - **Political**
  - **Promotional**
  - **Virtual marketplace (B2B)**
  - **Other**

  Each Web application would then be placed within one of the classes that represent the attribute *application type*. Note that there is no notion of ordering between the classes. This means that, even if we had used instead of symbols, numbers from 1 to 15, they would not represent any notion of ranking between numbers. The same also applies to symbols, that is, an application of type "News and Information" is not more or less important than an application of type "Personal."

- **Ordinal:** Augments the nominal scale with information about an ordering of classes or categories. This means that entities belong to classes that are ordered with respect to the attribute. Let's suppose we wish to measure the attribute *application structural complexity* for the entity "Web application," and that structural complexity is measured using the following classes:
  - **Very high**
  - **High**
  - **Average**
  - **Low**
  - **Very low**

  Each Web application would then be placed within one of the classes that represent the

attribute *application structural complexity.*
Here, there is a notion of ordering (ranking)
between the classes. This means that applications that belong to class "Very high" have
greater structural complexity than those that
belong to class "High," and so forth. Classes
can be represented by numbers or symbols;
however, it is important to note that even if
we had used number (e.g., 1 to 5) to represent
classes, these numbers would only represent
ranking, so addition, subtraction, and other
arithmetic operations have no meaning.

- **Interval:** Augments the ordinal scale with
information about the size of the intervals
that separate the classes. Thus, the ranking
between classes is preserved, however, now
the interval between two classes is constant.
For example, the difference between 20°C
- 10°C is the same as that for 30°C - 20°C.
However, it does not make sense to say
that 20°C is twice as hot as 10°C. Another
example of an interval scale is relative time,
for example, the number of calendar days
since the start of a given Web project. The
difference between two consecutive calendar days is always the same. Note that this
measurement scale type does not have a
natural zero representing the complete absence of a class. Addition and subtraction are
acceptable operations between two classes,
but **not** multiplication and division.

- **Ratio:** Preserves ordering, the size of intervals between classes, and ratios between
classes. People's heights and weights are
typical ratio-scale measures. It is meaningful
to say that someone who has a height of 180
cm is twice as tall as someone who has a
height of 90 cm, and this holds true regardless of whether height is being measured in
centimetres, meters, or yards. All arithmetic operations are acceptable between two
classes.

- **Absolute:** The measure always takes the
form "number of occurrences of x in the
entity E." For example, to measure the size

of a "Web application" using as measure the
number of new Web pages uses an absolute
scale because there is only one choice here
which is to count the number of new Web
pages. This scale type is very often used
to measure software and Web application
attributes.

Computation

The computation category describes whether a size
measure can be measured *directly* or *indirectly*
(Fenton & Pfleeger, 1997). *Indirect* measurement
means that the measure is computed based on other
measures. Conversely, *direct* measurement means
that the size measure does not rely on other measures in order to be measured. For example, assume
the three size measures presented below:

- **Page count:** Number of HTML or SHTML
files.
- **Connectivity:** Number of internal links, not
including dynamically generated links.
- **Connectivity density:** Computed as *Connectivity* divided by *page count*.

Page count and *connectivity* are both *direct*
measures because they can be measured without
using other measures. However, *connectivity
density* is an *indirect* measure because to be
computed it uses other two measures: *connectivity*
and *page count*.

Validation

The validation category describes whether a size
measure has been validated. To be validated
means that evidence has been gathered regarding the measure's usefulness to measure what it
purports to measure. Validations can be carried
out empirically, where generally data is used to
provide evidence of a measure's usefulness; or
theoretically, where the measurement principles
associated with a proposed measure are checked
to make sure that they are in line with the mea-

surement theory that supports the definition of that measure.

Possible values for the validation category are "validated empirically," "validated theoretically," "both," and "none." This is similar to one of the criterion suggested by Calero et al. (2004).

Model Dependency

This represents whether a size measure requires the use of a specific Web methodology or model in order to be measured. For example, as will be discussed later, Mangia and Paiano (2003) proposed size measures to estimate effort to develop Web applications that have been modeled using the W2000 methodology. This means that unless Web companies use the W2000 methodology to design and model their Web applications they are unlikely to find the size measures proposed by Mangia and Paiano (2003) useful for their own context. On the other hand, Mendes, Mosley, and Counsell (2003) has proposed size measures that are applicable to measure the size of any Web application, where applications can be designed using the W2000 methodology or not. The two possible values that this category takes are "Specific" and "Nonspecific."

LITERATURE REVIEW OF WEB SIZE MEASURES

This section presents a literature review of Web size measures proposed since 1998, described in chronological order.

1998, 2000: Size Measures by Cowderoy

Cowderoy, Donaldson, and Jenkins (1998) and Cowderoy (2000) organised their proposed measures into four distinct categories: Web application, Web page, media, and program. The sets of measures within each category are presented below:

Web Application

- **Web pages:** Measures the number of Web pages in a Web application.
- **Home pages:** Measures the number of major entry points to the Web application.
- **Leaf nodes:** Measures the number of Web pages, in a Web application, that have has no siblings.
- **Hidden nodes:** Measures the number of Web pages excluded from the main navigation buttons.
- **Depth:** Measures the number of Web pages on the second level that have siblings.
- **Application Paragraph count:** Measures the number of *Page paragraph count* (described later) for all Web pages in a Web application.
- **Delivered images:** Measures the number of unique images used by a Web application.
- **Audio files:** Measures the number of unique audio files used in a Web application.
- **Application movies:** Measures the number of *Page movies* (described later) for all the Web pages in an application.
- **3d objects:** Measures the number of files (including 3D objects) used in a Web application.
- **Virtual worlds:** measures the number of files (including virtual worlds) used in a Web application.
- **External hyperlinks:** Measures the number of unique URLs in a Web application.

Web Page

- **Actions:** Measures the number of independent actions by use of Javascript, Active X, and so forth.
- **Page paragraph count:** Measures the number of paragraphs in a Web page.
- **Word count:** measures the number of words in a Web page.

- **Navigational structures:** Measures the number of different structures in a Web page.
- **Page movies:** Measures the number of movie files used in a Web page.
- **Interconnectivity:** Measures the number of URLs that link to other pages in the same application.

Media

- **Image size (IS):** Measures the size of an image, computed as width * height.
- **Image composites:** Measures the number of layers from which the final image was created.
- **Language versions:** Measures the number of image versions that must be produced to accommodate different languages or different cultural priorities.
- **Duration:** Measures the summed duration of all sequences within an audio file.
- **Audio sequences:** Measures the number of sequences within the audio file.
- **Imported images:** Measures the number of graphics images imported into an audio file.

Program

- **Lines of source code:** Measures the number of lines of code in a program/script.
- **McCabe ciclomatic complexity:** Measures the structural complexity of a program/script.

2000, 2001: Size Measures by Mendes et al.

Mendes, Counsell, and Mosely (2000) and Mendes, Mosely, and Counsell (2001) organised their proposed size measures into five distinct categories: hypermedia application, Web application, Web page, media, and program. The sets of measures proposed for each category are presented below:

Web Application

- **Page count:** Measures the total number of HTML or SHTML files that a Web application has.
- **Media count:** Measures the total number of unique media files that a Web application has.
- **Program count:** Measures the total number of CGI scripts, JavaScript files, and Java applets that a Web application has.
- **Total page allocation:** Measures the total amount of space (Mbytes) allocated for all the HTML or SHTML pages of a Web application.
- **Total media allocation:** Measures the total amount of space (Mbytes) allocated for all media files used by a given Web application.
- **Total code length:** Measures the total number of lines of code for all the programs in a given Web application.
- **Reused media count:** Measures the total number of reused or modified media files that a given Web application has.
- **Reused program count:** Measures the total number of reused or modified programs that a given Web application has.
- **Total reused media allocation:** Measures the total amount of space (Mbytes) allocated for all reused media files that belong to a given Web application.
- **Total reused code length:** Measures the total number of lines of code for all reused programs that belong to a given Web application.
- **Code comment length:** Measures the total number of comment lines in all the programs that belong to a given Web application.
- **Reused code length:** Measures the total number of reused lines of code in all the

programs that belong to a given Web application.

- **Reused comment length:** Measures the total number of reused comment lines in all the programs that belong to a given Web application.
- **Total page complexity:** Measures the average number of different types of media used, excluding text, for a given Web application.
- **Connectivity:** Measures the total number of internal links, not including dynamically generated links, for a given Web application.
- **Connectivity density:** Computed as Connectivity divided by page count. Measures the average number of links per Web page for a given Web application
- **Cyclomatic complexity:** Computed as Connectivity - page count) + 2. Measures the cyclomatic complexity for a given Web application.

Web Page

- **Page allocation:** Measures the total allocated space (Kbytes) of a HTML or SHTML file.
- **Page complexity:** Measures the total number of different types of media used on a Web page, not including text.
- **Graphic complexity:** Measures the total number of graphics media on a Web page.
- **Audio complexity:** Measures the total number of audio media on a Web page.
- **Video complexity:** Measures the total number of video media on a Web page.
- **Animation complexity:** Measures the total number of animations on a Web page.
- **Scanned image complexity:** Measures the total number of scanned images on a Web page.
- **Page linking complexity:** Measures the total number of links on a Web page.

Media

- **Media duration:** Measures the total duration (minutes) of audio, video, and animation.
- **Media allocation:** Measures the total size (Kbytes) of a media file.

Program

- **Program Code length:** Measures the total number of lines of code in a program.

2000: Size Measures by Rollo

Although Rollo (2000) did not suggest any new size measures we have included his work here because he was the first, as far as we know, to investigate the issues of measuring functionality of Web applications specifically aiming at cost estimation, using numerous function point analysis methods:

- **Functional size:** Measures the total number of function points associated with a Web application. Function points were measured using COSMIC-FFP, Mark II, and Albrecht (Rollo, 2000).

Later, other studies have also employed the COSMIC full function points method to size Web applications (Mendes et al., 2002; Umbers, & Miles, 2004). These studies are not described here as the size measure employed is the same one used by Rollo.

2000: Size Measures by Cleary

Cleary (2000) proposed size measures organised into three categories: Web hypermedia application, Web software application, and Web page. Each measure is detailed below:

Web Hypermedia Application

- **Nontextual elements:** Measures the total number of unique nontextual elements within a Web hypermedia application.
- **Externally sourced elements:** Measures the total number of externally sourced elements. Being externally sourced means that such elements were not developed by the development team responsible for developing the given Web hypermedia application. They can be developed within the same company by a different group of developers, or even developed by third party.
- **Customised infrastructure components:** Measures the total number of customised infrastructure components. Such components would not have been developed from scratch for the given Web hypermedia application, but rather, reused from elsewhere and adapted to the given application.
- **Total Web points:** Measures the total size of a Web hypermedia application in Web points. The Web points measure computes size by taking into account the complexity of the Web pages contained within an application. Complexity of a page is a function of the number of words this page contains, number of existing links, and number of nontextual elements. Once the complexity of a page is measured, it leads to a number of Web points for that page (Abrahao, Poels, & Pastor, 2004).

Web Software Application

- **Function points:** measures the functionality of a Web software application using any existing function points measures (e.g., IFPUG, Mark II, COSMIC).

Web Page

- **Nontextual elements page:** Measures the total number of nontextual elements in a Web page.
- **Words Page:** Measures the total number of words in a Web page.
- **Web points**: Measures the total length of a Web page. This measure uses an ordinal scale with scale points "low," "medium," and "high." Each point is attributed a number of Web points, previously calibrated to a specific dataset of Web projects data.
- **Number of links into a Web page:** Measures the total number of incoming links (internal or external links). Incoming links are links that point to a given Web page.
- **Number of links out of a Web page:** Measures the total number of outgoing links (internal or external links). Outgoing links are links that have their origin at the given Web page and destination elsewhere.
- **Web page complexity:** Measures the complexity of a Web page based upon its *number of words*, and combined *number of incoming* and *outgoing links*, plus the *number of nontextual elements*.

2000: Size Measures by Reifer

Reifer (2000) proposed a single size measure to be used to estimate effort to develop Web applications:

- **Web objects:** Measures the total number of Web Objects in a Web application using Halstead's equation for volume, tuned for Web applications. The equation is as follows:

$$V = N \log_2(n) = (N_1 + N_2) \log_2(n_1 + n_2) \qquad (1)$$

where:

N = number of total occurrences of operands and operators

n = number of distinct operands and operators

N_1 = total occurrences of operand estimator

N_2 = total occurrences of operator estimators

n_1 = number of unique operands estimator

n_2 = number of unique operators estimators

V = volume of work involved represented as Web objects

Operands are comprised of the following measures:

- **Number of building blocks:** Measures the total number of components in a Web application, for example, Active X, DCOM, and OLE.
- **Number of COTS:** Measures the total number of COTS components (including any wrapper code) in a Web application.
- **Number of multimedia files:** Measures the total number of multimedia files, except graphics files, in a Web application.
- **Number of object or application points** (Cowderoy et al., 1998; Cowderoy, 2000): Measures the total number of object/application points, and so forth, in a Web application.
- **Number of Lines:** Measures the total number of xml, sgml, html, and query language lines in a Web application.
- **Number of Web components:** Measures the total number of applets, agents, and so forth, in a Web application.
- **Number of graphics files:** Measures the total number of templates, images, pictures, and so forth, in a Web application.
- **Number of scripts:** Measures the total number of scripts for visual language, audio, motion, and so forth, in a Web application.

2003: Size Measures by Mendes et al.

Mendes et al. (2003) proposed size measures, organised as follows:

Web Application

- **Web pages:** Measures the total number of Web pages in a Web application.
- **New Web pages:** Measures the total number of Web pages created from scratch in a Web application.
- **Customer Web pages:** Measures the total number of Web pages, provided by the customer, in a Web application.
- **Outsourced Web pages:** Measures the total number of outsourced Web pages in a Web application.
- **Text pages:** Measures the total number of text pages (A4 size), part of a Web application, which had to be typed.
- **Electronic text pages:** Measures the total number of reused text pages, part of a Web application, which are in electronic format.
- **Scanned text pages:** Measures the total number of reused text pages, part of a Web application, which had to be scanned with OCR.
- **New images:** Measures the total number of new images/photos/icons/buttons created from scratch for a given Web application.
- **Electronic images:** Measures the total number of reused images/photos, contained in a given Web application, which are in electronic format.
- **Scanned images:** Measures the total number of reused images/photos, contained in a given Web application, which need to be scanned.
- **External images:** Measures the total number of images, contained in a given Web application, which were obtained from an image/photo library or outsourced.

- **New animations:** Measures the total number of new animations (Flash/gif/3D, etc.), contained in a given Web application, which were created from scratch.
- **External animations:** Measures the total number of reused animations (Flash/gif/3D etc.) contained in a given Web application.
- **New audio:** measures the total number of new audio/video clips created from scratch for a given Web application.
- **External audio:** Measures the total number of reused audio/video clips contained in a given Web application.
- **High Fots:** Measures the total number of High-effort features off-the-shelf (FOTS) contained within a given Web application. Features off-the-shelf are features that have been reused as they are, without any adaptation. High effort represents the minimum number of hours to develop a single function/feature by one experienced developer that is considered high (above average). This number is currently set to 15 hours based on collected data from industrial Web projects.
- **High FotsA:** Measures the total number of High-effort FOTS contained in a Web application, which were reused and adapted to local circumstances. High effort here represents the minimum number of hours to adapt a single function/feature by one experienced developer that is considered high (above average). This number is currently set to 4 hours based on collected data from industrial Web projects.
- **High new:** Measures the total number of new High-effort Feature/Functionality contained in a Web application, which was developed from scratch.
- **Fots:** Measures the total number of Low-effort FOTS contained in a Web application.
- **FotsA:** Measures the total number of Low-effort FOTS contained in a Web application,

which were adapted to local circumstances.
- **New:** Measures the total number of Low-effort Feature/Functionality contained in a Web application, which were developed from scratch.

Examples of feature/functionality are as follows:

- **Auction/Bid utility**
- **Bulletin Boards**
- **Discussion Forum/Newsgroups**
- **Chat Rooms**
- **Database creation**
- **Database integration**
- **Other persistent storage integration (e.g., flat files)**
- **Credit Card Authorization**
- **Member login**
- **Online Secure Order Form**
- **Charts**
- **File upload/download**
- **Traffic Statistics**
- **Search Engine**
- **User Guest book**
- **Visitor statistics**

2003: Size Measures by Mangia and Paiano

Mangia and Paiano (2003) proposed size measures to be used to estimate the necessary effort to develop Web applications that have been modeled according to the W2000 methodology.

Web Application

- **Macro:** Measures the total number of macrofunctions in a Web application, which are required by the user.
- **DEI:** Measures the total number of input data for each operation.
- **DEO:** Measures the total number of output data for each operation.
- **Entities:** Measures the total number of information entities that model the database conceptually.

12

- **AppLimit:** Measures the total application limit of each operation.
- **LInteraction:** Measures the total level of interaction that various users of the application have in each operation.
- **Compatibility:** Measures the total compatibility between each operation and an application's delivery devices.
- **TypeNodes:** Measures the total number of types of nodes that constitute the navigational structure.
- **Acessibility:** Measures the total number of accessibility associations and pattern of navigation between node types.
- **NavCluster:** Measures the total number of navigation clusters.
- **ClassVisibility:** Measures the total visibility that classes of users have of a Web application's navigational structure.
- **DeviceVisibility:** Measures the total visibility that delivery devices have of a Web application's navigational structure.

2003: Size Measures by Baresi et al.

Baresi, Morasca, and Paolini (2003) proposed size measures to estimate the effort required to design Web applications that have been designed according to the W2000 methodology. Their size measures were organised according to the three different types of design models that result from using W2000: information model, navigation model, and presentation model. These measures are detailed below:

Information Model

- *entities*: Measures the total number of entities in the model
- *components*: Measures the total number of components in the model
- *infoSlots*: Measures the total number of slots in the model

- *slotsSACenter*: Measures the average number of slots per semantic association center
- *slotsCollCenter*: Measures the average number of slots per collection center in the model
- *componentsEntity*: Measures the average number of components per entity
- *slotsComponent*: Measures the average number of slots per component
- *SAssociations*: Measures the number of semantic associations in the model
- *SACenters*: Measures the number of semantic association centers in the model
- *segments*: Measures the number of segments in the model

Navigation Model

- *nodes*: Measures the total number of nodes in the model
- *navSlots*: Measures the total number of slots in the model
- *nodesCluster*: Measures the average number of nodes per cluster
- *slotsNode*: Measures the average number of slots per node
- *navLinks*: Measures the total number of links in the model
- *clusters*: Measures the total number of clusters in the model

Presentation Model

- *pages*: Measures the total number of pages in the model
- *pUnits*: Measures the total number of publishing units in the model
- *prLnks*: Measures the total number of links in the model
- *sections*: Measures the total number of sections in the model

2006: Size Measures by Costagliola et al. (2006)

Costagiola, Di Martino, Ferruci, Gravino, Tortoro, and Vitiello (2006) organised their size measures into two separate categories: length and functional.

Web Application

- **Wpa:** Measures the total number of Web pages
- **N_Wpa:** Measures the number of new Web pages
- **Me:** Measures the number of multimedia elements
- **N_Me:** Measures the number of new multimedia elements
- **CSAPP:** Measures the number of client side scripts and applications
- **SSApp:** Measures the number of server side scripts and applications
- **IL:** Measures the number of internal links
- **EL:** Measures the number of external references
- **EI:** Measures the number of external inputs
- **EO:** Measures the number of external outputs
- **EQ:** Measures the number of external queries
- **ILF:** Measures the number of internal logical files
- **EIF:** Measures the number of external interface files
- **WBB:** Measures the number of Web building blocks
- **MMF:** Measures the number of multimedia files
- **Scr:** Measures the number of scripts
- **Lin:** Measures the number of links

APPLICATION OF TAXONOMY TO SURVEYED SIZE MEASURES

This section discusses the literature review presented in the previous section in light of the taxonomy presented previously. In order to provide a more effective discussion, we present the detailed findings in Table 1, followed by a summary of the main findings from the literature review in Table 2. The literature review was based on 10, where 144 measures were proposed in total.

Out of the 144 measures proposed for effort estimation, 47 measures (33%) are *early* measures; of these, 10 measures (21%) can only be obtained after a Web application has been designed. These results therefore show that, of the 144 measures proposed for Web effort estimation only 37 (26%) can be gathered very early on in the development life cycle, even before a detailed requirements stage. These 47 measures were proposed by only three studies (Costagliola et al., 2006; Mangia & Paiano, 2003; Mendes et al., 2003).

Most of the proposed measures are solution-orientated (71%) and length (69%) measures. Twenty (77%) measures, out of a total of 26 functionality measures, measure functionality using some of the function points analysis methods, and the remaining six base their measurement on a list of features/functions to be provided to customers at the start of the development (Mendes et al., 2003).

A large number of the proposed size measures (74.4%) relate to the entities Web application or Web application design model, which suggests they can be used for static as well as dynamic Web applications.

Only 31 size measures (22%) are bottom-up measures, allowing for the measurement of "parts" of an application (e.g., Web page, media). The remaining size measures (78%) target at the whole application, where application can be represented as Web hypermedia (3%), Web software (0.6%), Web (52.2%), or also represented as a conceptual abstraction using a Web design model (22.2%).

Table 1. Taxonomy applied to all 144 measures

Measure	Harvesting Time	Metric Foundation	Class	Entity	Measurement Scale	Computation	Validation	Model Dependency
Cowderoy								
Web pages	Late	Solution orientated	Length	Web application	Ratio	Direct	None	Non-specific
Home pages	Late	Solution orientated	Length	Web application	Ratio	Direct	None	Non-specific
Leaf nodes	Late	Solution orientated	Length	Web application	Ratio	Direct	None	Non-specific
Hidden nodes	Late	Solution orientated	Length	Web application	Ratio	Direct	None	Non-specific
Depth	Late	Solution orientated	Length	Web application	Ratio	Direct	None	Non-specific
Application Paragraph count	Late	Solution orientated	Length	Web application	Ratio	Indirect	None	Non-specific
Delivered images	Late	Solution orientated	Length	Web application	Ratio	Direct	None	Non-specific
Audio files	Late	Solution orientated	Length	Web application	Ratio	Direct	None	Non-specific
Application movies	Late	Solution orientated	Length	Web application	Ratio	Indirect	None	Non-specific
3d objects	Late	Solution orientated	Length	Web application	Ratio	Direct	None	Non-specific
Virtual worlds	Late	Solution orientated	Length	Web application	Ratio	Direct	None	Non-specific
External hyperlinks	Late	Solution orientated	Complexity	Web application	Ratio	Direct	None	Non-specific
Actions	Late	Problem orientated	Functionality	Web page	Ratio	Direct	None	Non-specific
Page paragraph count	Late	Solution orientated	Length	Web page	Ratio	Direct	None	Non-specific
Word count	Late	Solution orientated	Length	Web page	Ratio	Direct	None	Non-specific
Navigational structures	Late	Solution orientated	Complexity	Web page	Ratio	Direct	None	Non-specific
Page movies	Late	Solution orientated	Complexity	Web page	Ratio	Direct	None	Non-specific
Interconnectivity	Late	Solution orientated	Complexity	Web page	Ratio	Direct	None	Non-specific
Image size	Late	Solution orientated	Length	Media	Ratio	Indirect	None	Non-specific
Image composites	Late	Solution orientated	Length	Media	Ratio	Direct	None	Non-specific
Language versions	Late	Solution orientated	Length	Media	Ratio	Direct	None	Non-specific
Duration	Late	Solution orientated	Length	Media	Ratio	Indirect	None	Non-specific
Audio sequences	Late	Solution orientated	Length	Media	Ratio	Direct	None	Non-specific
Imported images	Late	Solution orientated	Length	Media	Ratio	Direct	None	Non-specific
Lines of source code	Late	Solution orientated	Length	Program/Script	Ratio	Direct	None	Non-specific

continued on following page

Table 1. continued

Measure	Harvesting Time	Metric Foundation	Class	Entity	Measurement Scale	Computation	Validation	Model Dependency
McCabe ciclomatic complexity	Late	Solution orientated	Length	Program/Script	Ratio	Indirect	None	Non-specific
Mendes et al.								
Page count	Late	Solution orientated	Length	Web application	Ratio	Direct	Empirically	Non-specific
Media count	Late	Solution orientated	Length	Web application	Ratio	Direct	Empirically	Non-specific
Program count	Late	Solution orientated	Length	Web application	Ratio	Direct	Empirically	Non-specific
Total page allocation	Late	Solution orientated	Length	Web application	Ratio	Indirect	Empirically	Non-specific
Total media allocation	Late	Solution orientated	Length	Web application	Ratio	Indirect	Empirically	Non-specific
Total code Length	Late	Solution orientated	Length	Web application	Ratio	Indirect	Empirically	Non-specific
Reused media count	Late	Solution orientated	Length	Web application	Ratio	Direct	Empirically	Non-specific
Reused program count	Late	Solution orientated	Length	Web application	Ratio	Direct	Empirically	Non-specific
Total reused media allocation	Late	Solution orientated	Length	Web application	Ratio	Indirect	Empirically	Non-specific
Total reused code Length	Late	Solution orientated	Length	Web application	Ratio	Direct	Empirically	Non-specific
Code comment Length	Late	Solution orientated	Length	Web application	Ratio	Direct	Empirically	Non-specific
Reused code Length	Late	Solution orientated	Length	Web application	Ratio	Direct	Empirically	Non-specific
Reused comment Length	Late	Solution orientated	Length	Web application	Ratio	Direct	Empirically	Non-specific
Total page complexity	Late	Solution orientated	Length	Web application	Ratio	Indirect	Empirically	Non-specific
Connectivity	Late	Solution orientated	Complexity	Web application	Ratio	Indirect	Empirically	Non-specific
Connectivity density	Late	Solution orientated	Complexity	Web application	Ratio	Indirect	Empirically	Non-specific
Cyclomatic complexity	Late	Solution orientated	Complexity	Web application	Ratio	Indirect	Empirically	Non-specific
Page allocation	Late	Solution orientated	Length	Web page	Ratio	Direct	Empirically	Non-specific
Page complexity	Late	Solution orientated	Length	Web page	Ratio	Direct	Empirically	Non-specific
Graphic complexity	Late	Solution orientated	Length	Web page	Ratio	Direct	Empirically	Non-specific
Audio complexity	Late	Solution orientated	Length	Web page	Ratio	Direct	Empirically	Non-specific

continued on following page

Table 1. continued

Measure	Harvesting Time	Metric Foundation	Class	Entity	Measurement Scale	Computation	Validation	Model Dependency
Video complexity	Late	Solution orientated	Length	Web page	Ratio	Direct	Empirically	Non-specific
Animation complexity	Late	Solution orientated	Length	Web page	Ratio	Direct	Empirically	Non-specific
Scanned image complexity	Late	Solution orientated	Length	Web page	Ratio	Direct	Empirically	Non-specific
Page Linking complexity	Late	Solution orientated	Complexity	Web page	Ratio	Direct	Empirically	Non-specific
Media duration	Late	Solution orientated	Length	Media	Ratio	Direct	Empirically	Non-specific
Media allocation	Late	Solution orientated	Length	Media	Ratio	Direct	Empirically	Non-specific
Program Code Length	Late	Solution orientated	Length	Program/Script	Ratio	Direct	Empirically	Non-specific
Rollo								
Functional size	Late	Problem orientated	Functionality	Web application	Ratio	Indirect	None	Non-specific
Cleary								
Non-textual elements	Late	Solution orientated	Length	Web Hypermedia application	Ratio	Direct	Empirically	Non-specific
Externally sourced elements	Late	Solution orientated	Length	Web Hypermedia application	Ratio	Direct	Empirically	Non-specific
Customised infra-structure components	Late	Solution orientated	Length	Web Hypermedia application	Ratio	Direct	Empirically	Non-specific
Total Web points	Late	Solution orientated	Length	Web Hypermedia application	Ratio	Indirect	Empirically	Non-specific
Function points	Late	Problem orientated	Functionality	Web software application	Ratio	Indirect	None	Non-specific
Non-textual elements page	Late	Solution orientated	Length	Web page	Ratio	Direct	Empirically	Non-specific
Words Page	Late	Solution orientated	Length	Web page	Ratio	Direct	Empirically	Non-specific
Web points	Late	Solution orientated	Length	Web page	Ordinal	Direct	Empirically	Non-specific
Number of Links into a Web page	Late	Solution orientated	Complexity	Web page	Ratio	Direct	Empirically	Non-specific
Number of Links out of a Web page	Late	Solution orientated	Complexity	Web page	Ratio	Direct	Empirically	Non-specific
Web page complexity	Late	Solution orientated	Complexity	Web page	Ordinal	Direct	Empirically	Non-specific
Reifer								
Web Objects	Late	Solution orientated	Length	Web application	Ratio	Indirect	None	Non-specific

continued on following page

Table 1. continued

Measure	Harvesting Time	Metric Foundation	Class	Entity	Measurement Scale	Computation	Validation	Model Dependency
Number of building blocks	Late	Solution orientated	Length	Web application	Ratio	Direct	None	Non-specific
Number of multimedia files	Late	Solution orientated	Length	Web application	Ratio	Direct	None	Non-specific
Number of object or application points	Late	Problem orientated	Functionality	Web application	Ratio	Indirect	None	Non-specific
Number of Lines	Late	Solution orientated	Length	Web application	Ratio	Direct	None	Non-specific
Number of Web components	Late	Solution orientated	Length	Web application	Ratio	Direct	None	Non-specific
Number of graphics files	Late	Solution orientated	Length	Web application	Ratio	Direct	None	Non-specific
Number of scripts	Late	Solution orientated	Length	Web application	Ratio	Direct	None	Non-specific
Mendes et al. ('03)								
Web Pages	Early	Solution orientated	Length	Web application	Ratio	Indirect	Empirically	Non-specific
New Web Pages	Early	Solution orientated	Length	Web application	Ratio	Direct	Empirically	Non-specific
Customer Web Pages	Early	Solution orientated	Length	Web application	Ratio	Direct	Empirically	Non-specific
Outsourced Web pages	Early	Solution orientated	Length	Web application	Ratio	Direct	Empirically	Non-specific
Text Pages	Early	Solution orientated	Length	Web application	Ratio	Direct	Empirically	Non-specific
Electronic Text Pages	Early	Solution orientated	Length	Web application	Ratio	Direct	Empirically	Non-specific
Scanned Text Pages	Early	Solution orientated	Length	Web application	Ratio	Direct	Empirically	Non-specific
New Images	Early	Solution orientated	Length	Web application	Ratio	Direct	Empirically	Non-specific
Electronic Images	Early	Solution orientated	Length	Web application	Ratio	Direct	Empirically	Non-specific
Scanned Images	Early	Solution orientated	Length	Web application	Ratio	Direct	Empirically	Non-specific
External Images	Early	Solution orientated	Length	Web application	Ratio	Direct	Empirically	Non-specific
New Animations	Early	Solution orientated	Length	Web application	Ratio	Direct	Empirically	Non-specific
External Animations	Early	Solution orientated	Length	Web application	Ratio	Direct	Empirically	Non-specific
New Audio	Early	Solution orientated	Length	Web application	Ratio	Direct	Empirically	Non-specific
External Audio	Early	Solution orientated	Length	Web application	Ratio	Direct	Empirically	Non-specific
High Fots	Early	Problem orientated	Functionality	Web application	Ratio	Direct	Empirically	Non-specific

continued on following page

Table 1. continued

Measure	Harvesting Time	Metric Foundation	Class	Entity	Measurement Scale	Computation	Validation	Model Dependency
High FotsA	Early	Problem orientated	Functionality	Web application	Ratio	Direct	Empirically	Non-specific
High New	Early	Problem orientated	Functionality	Web application	Ratio	Direct	Empirically	Non-specific
Fots	Early	Problem orientated	Functionality	Web application	Ratio	Direct	Empirically	Non-specific
FotsA	Early	Problem orientated	Functionality	Web application	Ratio	Direct	Empirically	Non-specific
New	Early	Problem orientated	Functionality	Web application	Ratio	Direct	Empirically	Non-specific
Mangia and Paiano								
Macro	Early	Problem orientated	Functionality	Web application design model	Ratio	Direct	None	Specific
DEI	Early	Problem orientated	Functionality	Web application design model	Ratio	Direct	None	Specific
DEO	Early	Problem orientated	Functionality	Web application design model	Ratio	Direct	None	Specific
Entities	Early	Problem orientated	Functionality	Web application design model	Ratio	Direct	None	Specific
AppLimit	Early	Problem orientated	Functionality	Web application design model	Ratio	Direct	None	Specific
LInteraction	Early	Problem orientated	Functionality	Web application design model	Ratio	Direct	None	Specific
Compatibility	Early	Problem orientated	Functionality	Web application design model	Ratio	Direct	None	Specific
TypeNodes	Early	Problem orientated	Complexity	Web application design model	Ratio	Direct	None	Specific
Acessibility	Early	Problem orientated	Complexity	Web application design model	Ratio	Direct	None	Specific
NavCluster	Early	Problem orientated	Complexity	Web application design model	Ratio	Direct	None	Specific
ClassVisibility	Early	Problem orientated	Complexity	Web application design model	Ratio	Direct	None	Specific
DeviceVisibility	Early	Problem orientated	Complexity	Web application design model	Ratio	Direct	None	Specific
Baresi et al.								
entities	Early	Problem orientated	Length	Web application design model	Ratio	Direct	Empirically	Specific

continued on following page

Table 1. continued

Measure	Harvesting Time	Metric Foundation	Class	Entity	Measurement Scale	Computation	Validation	Model Dependency
components	Early	Problem orientated	Length	Web application design model	Ratio	Direct	Empirically	Specific
infoSlots	Early	Problem orientated	Length	Web application design model	Ratio	Direct	Empirically	Specific
slotsSACenter	Early	Problem orientated	Length	Web application design model	Ratio	Indirect	Empirically	Specific
slotsCollCenter	Early	Problem orientated	Length	Web application design model	Ratio	Indirect	Empirically	Specific
componentsEntity	Early	Problem orientated	Length	Web application design model	Ratio	Indirect	Empirically	Specific
slotsComponent	Early	Problem orientated	Length	Web application design model	Ratio	Indirect	Empirically	Specific
SAssociations	Early	Problem orientated	Complexity	Web application design model	Ratio	Direct	Empirically	Specific
SACenters	Early	Problem orientated	Length	Web application design model	Ratio	Direct	Empirically	Specific
segments	Early	Problem orientated	Length	Web application design model	Ratio	Direct	Empirically	Specific
nodes	Late	Problem orientated	Length	Web application design model	Ratio	Direct	Empirically	Specific
navSlots	Late	Problem orientated	Length	Web application design model	Ratio	Direct	Empirically	Specific
nodesCluster	Late	Problem orientated	Length	Web application design model	Ratio	Indirect	Empirically	Specific
slotsNode	Late	Problem orientated	Length	Web application design model	Ratio	Indirect	Empirically	Specific
navLinks	Late	Problem orientated	Complexity	Web application design model	Ratio	Direct	Empirically	Specific
clusters	Late	Problem orientated	Length	Web application design model	Ratio	Direct	Empirically	Specific
pages	Late	Problem orientated	Length	Web application design model	Ratio	Direct	Empirically	Specific
pUnits	Late	Problem orientated	Length	Web application design model	Ratio	Direct	Empirically	Specific

continued on following page

Table 1. continued

Measure	Harvesting Time	Metric Foundation	Class	Entity	Measure- ment Scale	Computa- tion	Validation	Model Dependency
prLnks	Late	Problem orientated	Complexity	Web application design model	Ratio	Direct	Empirically	Specific
sections	Late	Problem orientated	Length	Web application design model	Ratio	Direct	Empirically	Specific
Costagiola et al.								
Wpa	Early	Solution orientated	Length	Web application	Ratio	Direct	Empirically	Non-specific
N_Wpa	Early	Solution orientated	Length	Web application	Ratio	Direct	Empirically	Non-specific
Me	Early	Solution orientated	Length	Web application	Ratio	Direct	Empirically	Non-specific
N_Me	Early	Solution orientated	Length	Web application	Ratio	Direct	Empirically	Non-specific
CSAPP	Late	Solution orientated	Length	Web application	Ratio	Direct	Empirically	Non-specific
SSApp	Late	Solution orientated	Length	Web application	Ratio	Direct	Empirically	Non-specific
IL	Late	Solution orientated	Length	Web application	Ratio	Direct	Empirically	Non-specific
EL	Late	Solution orientated	Length	Web application	Ratio	Direct	Empirically	Non-specific
EI	Late	Solution orientated	Functionality	Web application	Ratio	Direct	Empirically	Non-specific
EO	Late	Solution orientated	Functionality	Web application	Ratio	Direct	Empirically	Non-specific
EQ	Late	Solution orientated	Functionality	Web application	Ratio	Direct	Empirically	Non-specific
ILF	Late	Solution orientated	Functionality	Web application	Ratio	Direct	Empirically	Non-specific
EIF	Late	Solution orientated	Functionality	Web application	Ratio	Direct	Empirically	Non-specific
WBB	Late	Solution orientated	Functionality	Web application	Ratio	Direct	Empirically	Non-specific
MMF	Late	Solution orientated	Functionality	Web application	Ratio	Direct	Empirically	Non-specific
Scr	Late	Solution orientated	Functionality	Web application	Ratio	Direct	Empirically	Non-specific
Lin	Late	Solution orientated	Functionality	Web application	Ratio	Direct	Empirically	Non-specific

continued on following page

Table 2. Summary of literature review findings

Category	Values	studies	%
Harvesting Time	Early	47	33%
	Late	97	67%
Measure foundation	Problem-orientated	42	29%
	Solution-orientated	102	71%
Class	Length	99	69%
	Functionality	26	18%
	Complexity	19	13%
Entity	Web software application	1	0.6%
	Web hypermedia application	4	3%
	Web application	76	52.2%
	Web page	20	14%
	Media	8	6%
	Program/Script	3	2%
	Web application design model	32	22.2%
Measurement Scale	Nominal	0	0%
	Ordinal	2	1%
	Interval	0	0%
	Ratio	122	99%
	Absolute	0	0%
Computation	Direct	119	83%
	Indirect	25	17%
Validation	Empirically	96	67%
	Theoretically	0	0%
	Both	0	0%
	None	48	33%
Model Dependency	Specific	32	22%
	Nonspecific	112	78%

The large majority of measures are measured on a ratio scale (99%), not surprising given that most measures are solution-orientated. This is also reflected on the number of measures that can be computed directly (83%), as opposed to indirectly (17%). A comparatively high number of measures have been proposed without either empirical or theoretical validation (33%), which unfortunately makes their corresponding studies "advocacy research." Empirical or theoretical validations are fundamental to building our scientific knowledge 0.

CHANGE IN TRENDS

Out of the six studies published within the period from 1998 to 2000, proposing size measures for Web cost estimation, five were by industry practitioners (Cowderoy et al., 1998; Cowderoy, 2000; Cleary, 2000; Rollo, 2000; Reifer, 2000). Except for Cleary (2000) what the remaining studies from practitioners had in common was that proposed measures had not been validated empirically or theoretically. Even Cleary (2000) used a very small data set to illustrate his approach, thus, their findings may not be of wide benefit to other practitioners and to researchers. Since 2000, all remaining size measures were all proposed by researchers.

Except for Baresi (2003), Mangia and Paiano (2003), and Mendes et al. (2003) all size measures were related to implemented Web applications, represented predominantly by solution-orientated size measures. This suggests that some of the more recent proposals are more geared toward problem-oriented measures, thus pointing out a change in trends.

Some of the most recent studies have also focused on size measures that are applied to Web application design models. This was a change in trends. The downside is that such measures may be too dependent on a particular development methodology, hindering their use by those who do not employ that particular methodology.

Also interesting to note that until 2003 hardly any size measures were classified as functionality measures. The small amount of previous work using functionality size measures may be explained by the fact that until recently the highest volume of Web applications developed used solely static pages, written in HTML, with graphics and Javascript. Therefore, both researchers and practitioners would have focused on size measures that were adequate for this type of Web application.

DEFINING YOUR OWN SIZE MEASURE

Different organisations use software and measures with different aims. If your organisation's aim is to improve the way effort is estimated for your software projects, then this section may be of help. The first step would be to look at the size measures that have been proposed in the past to assess whether or not they can be reused within your organisation's context. Table 1 and the section presenting the literature review will provide the necessary details for you to decide what to reuse. It is also important to decide if the Web applications developed by your organisation can be measured using a single size measure, or if a combination of size measures will be necessary. Previous work has provided size measures that represent both situations. For example, Mendes et al. (2003) proposed a set of size measures that can be gathered at a project's bidding stage; Reifer (2000) proposed a single size measure that can be obtained once an application's implementation details have been defined. An option can also be to use different size measures at different points in an application's development life cycle. An organisation may start using early size measures such as those proposed by Mendes et al. (2003), and then use Reifer's size measure (Reifer, 2000) once the application's physical design is complete. Another option is to use Mendes et al.'s measures (Mendes et al., 2003) very early on, followed by measures that can be applied to an application's conceptual design (see Baresi et al., 2003; Mangia & Paiano, 2003), and finally to use Reifer's measure applied to the application's physical design.

The use of different sets of size measures at different stages in the development life cycle is only applicable if late measures provide more precise effort estimates.

The choice of size measures is also related to how well-structured your current Web development processes are. For example, if you use an in-house or third-party development methodology you can propose size measures that take into account all the deliverables produced using the development methodology, thus an approach to proposing size measures similar to the one used by Baresi et al. (2003) would be suitable. There are also other constraints that may need to be taken into account, such as the amount of time it may take to manually gather the necessary data. This may be a decisive point determining the number of size measures to use.

CONCLUSION

This chapter presented a survey literature of Web size measures published in the literature since 1998, and classified the surveyed studies according to the taxonomy proposed by Mendes et al. (2005).

The main findings from the survey were the following:

*   Most size measures are harvested late in the development life cycle.
*   Most measures were solution-orientated and measured length.
*   Most measures measured attributes of Web applications or Web application design models, and were measured directly using a ratio scale.
*   A large number of the proposed measures have been validated empirically; however 33% have not been validated at all.

As for the change in trends, we have observed that initially most size measures were proposed by practitioners, and since 2001 this trend shifted to the proposal of size measures by researchers only. Also, initially hardly any proposed measures were validated, and this trend changed since 2001. Functionality measures did not seem to be used early on, however, recently they are often proposed. Finally, recently measures have been proposed associated with specific design models, which suggest the move toward measures that can be gathered from specification and design documents. Although this is a positive sign it is also important to point out that measures that are model-specific can only be employed by those who use that particular model, thus there is a trade-off here between flexibility and benefits.

REFERENCES

Abrahao, S., Poels, G., & Pastor, O. (2004). Evaluating a functional size measurement method for Web applications: An empirical analysis. In Proceedings of the 10th International Symposium on Software metrics, (pp. 358-369).

Baresi, L., Morasca, S., & Paolini, P. (2003, September 3-5). Estimating the design effort of Web applications. In Proceedings of the Ninth International Software Measures Symposium, (pp. 62-72).

Briand, L.C., & Wieczorek, I. (2002). In J.J. Marciniak (Ed.), Software resource estimation. *Encyclopedia of Software Engineering*, (Vol. 2, P-Z, 2nd ed., pp. 1160-1196). New York: John Wiley & Sons.

Calero, C., Ruiz, J., & Piattini, M. (2004). A Web measures survey using WQM. In *Proceedings of the ICWE04*, LNCS 3140, (pp. 147-160).

Christodoulou, S.P., Zafiris, P.A., & Papatheodorou, T.S. (2000). WWW2000: The developer's view and a practitioner's approach to Web engineering. In *Proceedings of the 2nd ICSE Workshop Web Engineering*, (pp. 75-92).

Cleary, D. (2000). Web-based development and functional size measurement. In *Proceedings of the IFPUG 2000 Conference*.

Costagliola, G., Di Martino, S., Ferruci, F., Gravino, C., Tortora, G., & Vitiello, G. (2006). Effort estimation modeling techniques: A case study for Web applications. In *Proceedings of the ICWE 2006*, (pp. 9-16).

Cowderoy, A.J.C. (2000). Measures of size and complexity for Web site content. In *Proceedings*

of the 11th ESCOM Conference, Munich, Germany, (pp. 423-431).

Cowderoy, A.J.C., Donaldson, A.J.M., & Jenkins, J.O. (1998). A measures framework for multimedia creation. In *Proceedings of the 5th IEEE International Software Measures Symposium*, Maryland, USA.

DeMarco, T. (1982). *Controlling software projects: Management, measurement and estimation*. New York: Yourdon Press.

Dhyani, D., Ng, W.K., & Bhowmick, S.S. (2002). A survey of Web measures. *ACM Computing Surveys, 34*(4), 469-503.

Fenton, N.E., & Pfleeger, S.L. (1997). Software measures: A rigorous & practical approach (2nd ed.). Boston: PWS Publishing Company and International Thomson Computer Press.

Jones, T.C. (1998). *Estimating software costs*. New York: McGraw-Hill.

Kitchenham, B.A., Hughes, R.T., & Linkman, S.G. (2001). Modeling software measurement data. *IEEE Transactions on Software Engineering, 27*(9), 788-804.

Mangia, L., & Paiano, R. (2003). MMWA: A software sizing model for Web applications. In *Proceedings of the WISE'03*, (pp. 53-61).

Mendes, E., Counsell, S., & Mosley, N. (2000, June). Measurement and effort prediction of Web applications. In *Proceedings of the 2nd ICSE Workshop on Web Engineering*, Limerick, Ireland, (pp. 57-74).

Mendes, E., Counsell, S., & Mosley, N. (2005). Towards a taxonomy of hypermedia and Web application size metrics. In *Proceedings of the ICWE'05 Conference*, Springer LNCS 3579, (pp. 110-123).

Mendes, E., Mosley, N., & Counsell, S. (2001). Web measures—estimating design and authoring effort. *IEEE Multimedia, Special Issue on Web Engineering, 8*(1), 50-57.

Mendes, E., Mosley, N., & Counsell, S. (2002a). The application of case-based reasoning to early Web project cost estimation. In *Proceedings of the IEEE COMPSAC*, (pp. 393-398).

Mendes, E., Mosley, N., & Counsell, S. (2002b, June). Comparison of Web size measures for predicting Web design and authoring effort. *IEE Proceedings Software*, *149*(3), 86-92.

Mendes, E., Mosley, N., & Counsell, S. (2003). Investigating early Web size measures for Web costimation. In *Proceedings of the EASE'2003 Conferenc*e, Keele University.

Reifer, D.J. (2000). Web development: Estimating quick-to-market software. *IEEE Software*, *17*(6), 57-64.

Rollo, T. (2000). Sizing e-commerce. In *Proceedings of ACOSM 2000*, Sydney, Australia.

Umbers, P., & Miles, G. (2004, September 14-16). Resource estimation for Web applications. In Proceedings of the10th International Symposium on Software Metrics, (pp. 370-381).

KEY TERMS

Effort Estimation: To predict the necessary amount of labour units to accomplish a given task, based on knowledge of previous similar projects and other project characteristics that are believed to be related to effort. Project characteristics are the input, and effort is the output we wish to predict.

Size Measure Class: Classifies size measures into either of three possible classes: Length, Complexity, and Functionality. Length measures the physical size of an application; Functionality measures the functions and features supplied by the application to the user; and Complexity measures the structural complexity of an application, where the application's structure is represented by the way in which nodes (e.g., Web pages) are interconnected via links.

Web Application: An application delivered over the Web that combines characteristics of both Web hypermedia and Web software applications.

Web Application Design Model: A conceptual representation of a Web application. Such representations are characterised by models, for example, navigation model or presentation model. These models are abstractions that later are translated into an implementation of the Web application.

Web Hypermedia Application (Christodoulou et al., 2000): A nonconventional application characterised by the authoring of information using nodes (chunks of information), links (relations between nodes), anchors, access structures (for navigation), and delivery over the Web. Technologies commonly used for developing such applications are HTML, XML, JavaScript, and multimedia.

Web Size Measure: A measure used to forecast the size of a developed Web application. The size measure may assume that application's size corresponds directly to the size of the problem to be solved in order to deliver a corresponding application, or it may assume that an application's size corresponds to the actual delivered size of an application.

Web Software Application (Christodoulou et al., 2000): A conventional software application that relies on the Web or uses the Web's infrastructure for execution. Typical applications include legacy information systems such as databases, booking systems, knowledge bases, and so forth. Many e-commerce applications fall into this category. Typically, they employ development technologies (e.g., DCOM, ActiveX, etc.), database systems, and development solutions (e.g., J2EE).

Chapter II
Web Development Effort Estimation:
An Empirical Analysis

Emilia Mendes
University of Auckland, New Zealand

Silvia Abrahão
Valencia University of Technology, Spain

ABSTRACT

Effort models and effort estimates help project managers allocate resources, control costs and schedule, and improve current practices, leading to projects that are finished on time and within budget. In the context of Web development and maintenance, these issues are also crucial, and very challenging, given that Web projects have short schedules and a highly fluidic scope. Therefore, the objective of this chapter is to introduce the concepts related to Web effort estimation and effort estimation techniques. In addition, this chapter also details and compares, by means of a case study, three effort estimation techniques, chosen for this chapter because they have been to date the ones mostly used for Web effort estimation: Multivariate regression, Case-based reasoning, and Classification and Regression Trees. The case study uses data on industrial Web projects from Spanish Web companies.

INTRODUCTION

The Web is used as a delivery platform for numerous types of Web applications, ranging from complex e-commerce solutions with back-end databases to online personal static Web pages (Mendes, Mosley, & Counsell, 2005a). With the sheer diversity of Web application types and technologies employed, there are a growing number of Web companies bidding for as many Web projects as they can accommodate. As usual, in order to win the bid, companies estimate unrealistic schedules, leading to applications that are rarely developed within time and budget (Mendes & Mosley, 2005).

The purpose of estimating effort is to predict the necessary amount of labour units to accomplish a given task, based on knowledge of previous similar projects and other project characteristics that are believed to be related to effort. Project characteristics (independent variables) are the input, and effort (dependent variable) is the output we wish to predict (see Figure 1). For example, a given Web company may find that to predict the effort necessary to implement a new Web application, it will require the following input: *estimated number of new Web pages, total number of developers who will help develop the new Web application, developers' average number of years of experience with the development tools employed, main programming language used, the number of functions/features* (e.g., shopping cart) *to be offered by the new Web application.* Of these variables, *estimated number of new Web pages* and *the number of functions/features to be offered by the new Web application* are size variables (size measures); the other three, *total number of developers who will help develop the new Web application, developers' average number of years of experience with the development tools employed,* and *main programming language used,* are not used to "size" the "problem to be solved" (Web application), but they are believed to influence the amount of effort necessary to develop a Web application, and in this sense are related to effort. Therefore, they are also considered input, and jointly named "cost drivers."

The challenge in estimating effort is to obtain an estimate that is similar to the real amount of effort necessary to develop an application. Thus, research in this field aims to quantify and to determine the factors necessary to derive an estimate, such that the process of estimating effort can be fully understood, and can be repeated. In addition, it also uses and compares effort estimation techniques, looking for the technique(s) that provides most accurate effort estimates.

Figure 1. Deriving an effort estimate

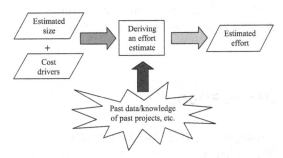

A task to be estimated can be as simple as developing a single function (e.g., creating a Web form with 10 fields) or as complex as developing a large application, and in general the one input (independent variable) assumed to have the strongest influence on effort is size. Cost drivers are also influential.

It is also often the case where knowledge about past projects, or even data on past finished projects, is also used to help derive an effort estimate (see Figure 1). The effort estimation techniques described later in this chapter all use data on past projects; however, many Web companies use as basis for their estimations solely knowledge on past projects, estimated size, and cost drivers.

Cost and effort are often used interchangeably within the context of effort estimation (prediction) because effort is taken as the main component of project costs. However, given that project costs also take into account other factors such as contingency and profit (Kitchenham, Pickard, Linkman, & Jones, 2003) we will use the word "effort" and not "cost" throughout this chapter.

The remainder of this chapter is structured as follows: Section 2 presents an introduction to Web effort estimation techniques, and a literature review and comparison of previous work in Web effort estimation. Section 3 presents a case study where a data set of industrial Web projects is used with three different effort estimation techniques to obtain effort estimates for these projects. This section also compares the prediction accuracy between the techniques. Section 4 discusses the necessary steps that need to be carried out in order to determine which is the best effort estimation technique. Finally, conclusions and a discussion on future trends in this field are given in Section 5.

BACKGROUND

Categories of Effort Estimation Techniques

Effort estimation techniques fall into three general categories, which are described in the next section (Shepperd & Kadoda, 2001):

- Expert-based effort estimation;
- Algorithmic models; and
- Artificial intelligence techniques.

Expert-Based Effort Estimation

Expert-based effort estimation represents the process of estimating effort by subjective means, and is often based on previous experience from developing/managing similar projects. This is by far the most used technique for Web effort estimation. Within this context, the attainment of accurate effort estimates relies on the competence and experience of individuals (e.g., project manager, developer).

The drawbacks of expert-based estimation are the following:

1. It is very difficult to quantify and to determine those factors that have been used to derive an estimate, making it difficult to repeat.
2. When a company finally builds up its expertise with developing Web applications using a given set of technologies, other technologies appear and are rapidly adopted (mostly due to hype), thus leaving behind the knowledge that had been accumulated.

3. Obtaining an effort estimate based on experience with past similar projects can be misleading when projects vary in their characteristics. For example, knowing that a Web application containing 10 new static pages using HTML, 10 new images, and developed by one person took 40 person hours does not mean that a similar application developed by two people will also use 40 person hours. Two people may need additional time to communicate, and may also have different experiences with using HTML. In addition, another application eight times its size is unlikely to take exactly eight times longer.
4. Developers and project managers are known for providing optimistic effort estimates (DeMarco, 1982). Optimistic estimates lead to underestimated effort, and the consequences are projects over budgeted and over time.

The problems related to expert-based effort estimation lead to the proposal of other techniques for effort estimation, namely algorithmic and artificial intelligence techniques.

Algorithmic Techniques

Algorithmic techniques are the most popular techniques described in the Web and software effort estimation literature. Such techniques attempt to build models that precisely represent the relationship between effort and one or more project characteristics via the use of algorithmic models. Such models assume that application size is the main contributor to effort; thus in any algorithmic model the central project characteristic used is usually taken to be some notion of application size (e.g., the number of lines of source code, function points, number of Web pages, number of new images). The relationship between size and effort is often translated as an equation such as that shown by equation 1, where a and b are constants, S represents the estimated size of an application, and *E* represents the estimated effort required to develop an application of size *S*.

$$E = a\,S^{b} \qquad (1)$$

In Equation 2, when *b* < 1 we have economies of scale, that is, larger projects use less effort, comparatively, than smaller projects. The opposite situation (*b* > 1) gives diseconomies of scale, that is, larger projects use more effort, comparatively, than smaller projects. When *b* is either > or < 1, the relationship between *S* and *E* is non linear. Conversely, when *b* = 1 the relationship is linear.

However, size alone is unlikely to be the only contributor to effort. Other project characteristics, such as developer's programming experience, tools used to implement an application, maximum/average team size, are also believed to influence the amount of effort required to develop an application. These variables are known in the literature as *cost drivers*.

Therefore, an algorithmic model should include not only size but also the cost drivers believed to influence effort. This set of cost drivers will vary from company to company and will be determined on a case to case basis. In summary, effort is determined mainly by size; however, its value is adjusted taking into account cost drivers (see Equation 2).

$$E = a\,S^{b} CostDrivers \qquad (2)$$

Different proposals have been made as to the exact form such algorithmic models should take.

The type of algorithmic model that has been used the most in the software and Web engineering literatures is regression analysis. Regression analysis, used to generate regression-based algorithmic models, provides a procedure for determining the "best" straight-line fit (see Figure 1) to a set of project data that represents the relationship between effort (response or dependent variable) and cost drivers (predictor or independent variables) (Schofield, 1998). Figure 2 shows an example of a regression line, using real data that describes the relationship between log (Effort) and log (totalWebPages). In this example the original variables *Effort* and *totalWebPages* have been transformed using the natural logarithmic scale in order to comply more closely with the assumptions of the regression analysis techniques. Note that variables are not always transformed and this decision will depend on the type of data available at the time the analysis is being carried out. The Equation represented by the regression line presented in Figure 1 is as follows:

$$\log Effort = \log a + b \log totalWebPages \quad (3)$$

where,

log *a* is the point in which the regression line intercepts the *Y*-axis. This is also known simply as the *intercept*.

b represents the slope of the regression line, that is, its inclination.

Equation 3 shows a linear relationship between log (*Effort*) and log (*totalWebPages*). However, since the original variables have been transformed before the regression technique was employed, this equation needs to be transformed back such

Figure 2. Example of a regression line

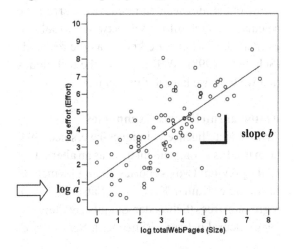

Equations 6 and 7.

$$EstimatedEffort = C + a_0 EstSizeNewproj + a_1 CD_1 + \cdots + a_n CD_n \qquad (6)$$

$$(7)$$
$$EstimatedEffort = C\, EstSizeNewproj^{a_0}\, CD_1^{a_1} \cdots CD_n^{a_n}$$

where,

C is the regression line's intercept, a constant denoting the initial estimated effort (assuming size and cost drivers to be zero).

$a_0 \ldots a_n$ are constants derived from past data.

$CD_1 \ldots CD_n$ are cost drivers that have an impact on effort.

that it uses the original variables. The resultant equation is:

$$Effort = a\, totalWebPages^b \qquad (5)$$

Other examples of equations representing regression lines are given in Equations 6 and 7.

Regarding the regression analysis itself, two of the most widely used techniques are multiple regression (MR) and stepwise regression (SWR). The difference between both is that MR obtains a regression line using all the independent variables at the same time, whereas SWR is a technique that examines different combinations of independent variables, looking for the best grouping to explain the greatest amount of variation in effort. Both use least squares regression, where the regression line selected is the one that reflects the minimum values of the sum of the squared errors. Errors are calculated as the difference between actual and estimated effort and are known as the residuals (Schofield, 1998). SWR is one of the techniques that we will use later in this chapter.

Artificial Intelligence Techniques

Artificial intelligence techniques have, since 1994, been used as a complement to, or as an alternative to, the previous two categories. Examples include fuzzy logic (Kumar, Krishna, & Satsangi, 1994), regression trees (Schroeder, Sjoquist, & Stephan, 1986), neural networks (Shepperd, Schofield, &

Kitchenham, 1996), and case-based reasoning (Shepperd & Kadoda, 2001). We chose to introduce case-based reasoning (CBR) and regression trees (CART) because they have to date been the two most popular machine learning techniques employed for Web effort estimation, and these are two of the three techniques that will be used later on in this chapter. A useful summary of numerous machine learning techniques can also be found in (Gray & MacDonell, 1997).

Case-based reasoning (CBR) uses the assumption that similar problems provide similar solutions. It provides estimates by comparing the characteristics of the current project to be estimated against a library of historical information from completed projects with a known effort (case base). It involves the following steps (Angelis & Stamelos, 2000):

1.   Characterising a new project p, for which an estimate is required, with variables (features) common to those completed projects stored in the case base. In terms of Web and software effort estimation, features represent size measures and cost drivers which have a bearing on effort. This means that if a Web company has stored data on past projects where the data represents, for example, features *effort*, *size*, *development team size*, and *tools used*, the data used as input to obtaining an effort estimate will also need to include these same features.

2. Using this characterisation as a basis for finding similar (analogous) completed projects, for which effort is known. This process can be achieved by measuring the "distance" between two projects at a time (project p and one finished project), based on the features' values, for all features (k) characterising these projects. Each finished project is compared to project p, and the finished project presenting the shortest distance overall is the "most similar project" to project p. Although numerous techniques can be used to measure similarity, nearest neighbour algorithms using the unweighted Euclidean distance measure have been the most widely used to date in Web and software engineering.

3. Generating a predicted value of effort for project p based on the effort for those completed projects that are similar to p. The number of similar projects to take into account to obtain an effort estimate will depend on the size of the case base. For small case bases (e.g., up to 90 cases), typical values are to use the most similar finished project, or the two most similar finished projects, or the three most similar finished projects (1, 2, and 3 closest neighbours/analogues). For larger case bases no conclusions have been reached regarding the best number of similar projects to use. The calculation of estimated effort is obtained using the same effort value as the closest neighbour, or the mean effort for two or more closest neighbours. This is the common choice in Web and software engineering.

When using CBR there are six parameters to consider (Selby & Porter, 1998):

- **Feature subset selection:** Involves determining the optimum subset of features that yields the most accurate estimation. This feature is not promptly available in CBR tools.

- **Similarity measure:** Measures the level of similarity between different cases, with several similarity measures proposed in the literature (e.g., Unweighted Euclidean distance, weighted Euclidean distance, maximum distance). Various similarity measures are described in Angelis and Stamelos (2000).

- **Scaling:** Scaling (also known as standardisation) represents the transformation of feature values according to a defined rule, such that all features present values within the same range and hence have the same degree of influence on the results (Angelis & Stamelos, 2000).

- **Number of analogies:** Refers to the number of most similar cases that will be used to generate an effort estimate.

- **Analogy adaptation:** The choice of number of most similar projects to be used to obtain estimated effort for a new project, and (in case of more than one) how their efforts will be aggregated (e.g., average effort, median effort).

- **Adaptation rules:** Used to adapt the estimated effort, according to a given criterion, such that it reflects the characteristics of the target project (new project) more closely.

Classification and regression trees (CART) (Brieman, Friedman, Olshen, & Stone, 1984)

Classification and regression trees (CART) are techniques where independent variables (predictors) are used to build binary trees where each leaf node either represents a category to which an estimate belongs to, or a value for an estimate. The former situation occurs with *classification trees* and the latter occurs with *regression trees*, that is whenever predictors are categorical (e.g., Yes/No) the CART tree is called a *classification tree* and whenever predictors are numerical the CART tree is called a *regression tree*. In order to obtain an estimate one has to traverse tree nodes from root to leaf by selecting the nodes that represent the category or value for the independent variables associated with the case to be estimated.

The data used to build a CART model is named *learning sample*. Once the tree has been built it can be used to estimate effort for new projects.

A CART model constructs a binary tree by recursively partitioning the predictor space (set of all values or categories for the independent variables judged relevant) into subsets where the distribution of values or categories for the dependent variable (e.g., effort) is successively more uniform. The partition (split) of a subset *S1* is decided on the basis that the data in each of the descendant subsets should be "purer" than the data in *S1*. Thus node "impurity" is directly related to the amount of different values or classes in a node, that is, the greatest the mix of classes or values, the higher the node "impurity." A "pure" node means that all the cases (e.g., Web projects) belong to the same class, or have the same value. The partition of subsets continues until a node contains only one class or value. Note that not necessarily all the initial independent variables are used to build a CART model, that is, only those variables that are related to the dependent variable are selected by the model. This means that a CART model can be used not only to produce a model that can be applicable for effort prediction, but also to obtain insight and understanding into the factors that are relevant to estimate a given dependent variable.

PREVIOUS WORK ON WEB EFFORT ESTIMATION

This section presents a survey of Web effort estimation models proposed in the literature. Each work is described and finally summarised in Table 1.

First Study: Measurement and Effort Prediction for Web Applications (Mendes, Counsell, & Mosely, 2000)

Mendes et al. (2000) investigated the use of case-based reasoning, linear regression, and stepwise regression techniques to estimate development effort for Web applications developed by experienced or inexperienced students. The case-based reasoning estimations were generated using a freeware tool—ANGEL—developed at the University of Bournemouth, UK. The most similar Web projects were retrieved using the unweighted Euclidean distance using the "leave one out" cross-validation. Estimated effort was generated using either the closest analogue or the mean of two or three analogues. The two datasets (HEL and LEL) employed had data on Web applications developed by second-year Computer Science students and had 29 and 41 data points, respectively. HEL represented data from students with high experience in Web development, whereas LEL had data from inexperienced students. The size measures collected were Page Count (total number of HTML pages created from scratch), Reused Page Count (total number of reused HTML pages), Connectivity (total number of links in the application), Compactness (Botafogo, Rivlin, & Shneiderman, 1992) (scale from 1 to 5 indicating the level of interconnectedness in the application. One represents no connections and 5 represented a totally connected application), Stratum (Botafogo et al., 1992), (scale from 1 to 5 indicating how "linear" the application is. 1 represents no sequential navigation and 5 represents totally sequential navigation) and structure (topology of the application's backbone, being either sequential, hierarchical, or network). Prediction accuracy was measured using MMRE and MdMRE. Results for the HEL group were statistically significantly better than those for the LEL group. In addition, case-based reasoning showed the best results overall.

Second Study: Web Development: Estimating Quick-To-Market Software (Reifer, 2000)

Reifer (2000) proposed a Web cost estimation model—WEBMO—which is an extension of the COCOMO II model. The WEBMO model has nine cost drivers and a fixed effort power law, instead of seven cost drivers and variable effort power law as used in the COCOMO II model. Size is measured in Web Objects, which are calculated by applying Halstead's formula for volume. They are based on subcomponents such as: # of building blocks (Active X, DCOM, OLE, etc.), # of COTS components (includes any wrapper code), # of multimedia files, except graphics files (text, video, sound, etc.), # of object or application points (Cowderoy, 2000) or others proposed (# server data tables, # client data tables, etc.), # of xml, sgml, html, and query language lines (# lines including links to data attributes), # of Web components (applets, agents, etc.), # of graphics files (templates, images, pictures, etc.), # of scripts (visual language, audio, motion, etc.) and any other measures that companies find suitable. Reifer allegedly used data on 46 finished industrial Web projects and obtained predictions which are "repeatable and robust." However, no information is given regarding the data collection nor any summary statistics for the data.

Third Study: Web Metrics: Estimating Design and Authoring Effort (Mendes, Mosely, & Counsell, 2001)

Mendes et al. (2001) investigated the prediction accuracy of top-down and bottom-up Web cost estimation models, generated using Linear and Stepwise multiple regression models. They employed one dataset with data on 37 Web applications developed by Honours and postgraduate Computer Science students. Gathered measures were organised into five categories: length size, reusability, complexity size, effort, and confounding factors (factors that, if not controlled, could influence the validity of the evaluation), and are associated to one of the following entities: Application, Page, Media and Program. Prediction models were generated for each entity and prediction accuracy was measured using the MMRE measure. Results showed that the best predictions were obtained for the entity Program, based on nonreused program measures (code length and code comment length).

Fourth Study: Measurement, Prediction and Risk Analysis for Web Applications (Fewster & Mendes, 2001)

Fewster and Mendes (2001) investigated the used of proposed a Generalised Linear Model (GLM) for Web cost estimation. Generalised linear models provide a flexible regression framework for predictive modeling of effort. The models allow nonlinear relationships between response and predictor variables, and they allow for a wide range of choices for the distribution of the response variable (e.g., effort).

Fewster and Mendes (2001) employed the same dataset used in Mendes et al. (2001); however, they reduced the number of size measures targeting at only the entity type Application. These measures were organised into five categories: effort metrics, structure metrics, complexity metrics, reuse metrics, and size metrics.

In addition to proposing a prediction model, they also investigate the use of the GLM model as a framework for risk management. They did not measure prediction accuracy but relied on the model fit produced for the model. However, a model with a good fit to the data is not the same as a good prediction model.

Fifth Study: The Application of Case-based Reasoning to Early Web Project Cost Estimation (Mendes, Mosely, & Counsell, 2002a)

Most work on Web cost estimation proposes models based on late product size measures, such as number of HTML pages, number of images, and so forth. However, for the successful management of software/Web projects, estimates are necessary throughout the whole development life cycle. Preliminary (early) effort estimates in particular are essential when bidding for a contract or when determining a project's feasibility in terms of cost-benefit analysis. Mendes et al. (2002a) focus on the harvesting of size measures at different points in the Web development life cycle, to estimate development effort, and their comparison based on several prediction accuracy indicators. Their aim was to investigate how different cost predictors are, and if there are any statistically significant differences between them. Their effort estimation models were generated using case-based reasoning, where several different parameters were used: Similarity measure; Scaling; Number of closest analogues; Analogy adaptation; and Feature Subset Selection. Their study was based on data from 25 Web applications developed by pairs of postgraduate Computer Science students. The measures of prediction accuracy employed were the MMRE, MdMRE, Pred(25), and Boxplots of residuals. Contrary to the expected, late measures did not show statistically significant better predictions than early measures.

Sixth Study: A Comparison of Development Effort Estimation Techniques for Web Hypermedia Applications (Mendes et al., 2002b)

An in depth comparison of Web cost estimation models is presented in Mendes et al. (2002b), where they: i) compare the prediction accuracy of three CBR techniques to estimate the effort to develop Web applications; and ii) compare the prediction accuracy of the best CBR technique, according to their findings, against three commonly used prediction models, namely multiple linear regression, stepwise regression, and regression trees. They employed one dataset of 37 Web applications developed by honours and postgraduate Computer Science students and the measures used are: Page Count (Number of html or shtml files used in the application), Media Count (Number of media files used in the application), Program Count (Number of JavaScript files and Java applets used in the application), Reused Media Count (Number of reused/modified media files), Reused Program Count (Number of reused/modified programs), Connectivity Density (Total number of internal links divided by Page Count), Total Page Complexity (Average number of different types of media per page) and Total Effort (Effort in person hours to design and author the application). Note that Subjects did not use external links to other Web hypermedia applications. All the links pointed to pages within the original application only. Regarding the use of case-based reasoning, they employed several parameters, as follows: three similarity measures (unweighted Euclidean, weighted Euclidean and Maximum), three choices for the number of analogies (1, 2 and 3), three choices for the analogy adaptation (mean, inverse rank weighted mean and median) and two alternatives regarding the standardisation of the attributes ("Yes" for standardised and "No" for not standardised). Prediction accuracy was measured using MMRE, MdMRE, Pred(25), and boxplots of residuals. Their results showed that different measures of prediction accuracy gave different results. MMRE and MdMRE showed better prediction accuracy for Multiple regression models, whereas boxplots showed better accuracy for CBR.

Seventh Study: Cost Estimation for Web Applications (Ruhe, Jeffrey, & Wieczorek, 2003)

The aim of Ruhe et al.'s study (2003) was to assess whether the COBRA™ (Cost Estimation Benchmarking and Risk Analysis) method was adequate for estimating Web development effort accurately using data from a small Web company. COBRA is a registered trademark of the Fraunhofer Institute for Experimental Software Engineering (IESE), Germany, and is a method that aims to develop an understandable cost estimation model based on a company-specific dataset. It uses expert opinion and data on past projects to estimate development effort and risks for a new project. The size measure employed was Web Objects (Reifer, 2000), measured for each one of the 12 finished Web applications used in this study. The prediction accuracy obtained using COBRA™ was compared to those attained employing expert opinion and linear regression, all measured using MMRE and Pred(25), giving COBRA the most accurate results.

Eighth Study: Do Adaptation Rules Improve Web Cost Estimation? (Mendes, Mosely, & Counsell , 2003a)

This study (Mendes et al., 2003a) compared several methods of CBR-based effort estimation, investigating the use of adaptation rules as a contributing factor for better estimation accuracy. They used two datasets, where the difference between these datasets was the level of "messiness" each had. "Messiness" was evaluated by the number of outliers and the amount of collinearity (Shepperd & Kadoda, 2001). The dataset which was less "messy" than the other presented a continuous "cost" function, translated as a strong linear relationship between size and effort. The "messiest" dataset, on the other hand, presented a discontinuous "cost" function, where there was no linear or log-linear relationship between size and effort. Both datasets represented data on Web applications developed by students. Two types of adaptation were used, one with weights and another without weights (Mendes et al., 2003a). None of the adaptation rules gave better predictions for the "messier" dataset; however, for the less "messy" dataset one type of adaptation rule (no weights) gave good prediction accuracy. Prediction accuracy was measured using MMRE, Pred(25), and Boxplots of absolute residuals.

Ninth Study: Estimating the Design Effort of Web Applications (Baresi, Morasca, Paolini, 2003)

Baresi et al. (2003) investigated the relationship between a number of size measures obtained from W2000 design artefacts and the total effort needed to design Web applications. Their size measures were organised in categories and presented in detail in Table 1. The categories employed were Information Model, Navigation Model, and Presentation Model. They identified a few attributes that may be related to the total design effort. In addition, they also carried out a finer-grain analysis, studying which of the used measures have an impact on the design effort when using W2000. Their dataset comprised 30 Web applications developed by students.

Tenth Study: Effort Estimation Modeling Techniques: A Case Study for Web Applications (Costagliola et al., 2006)

Costagliola et al. (2006) carried out an empirical investigation where, using data from 15 industrial Web projects, they compare two sets of size measures (length: number of pages, number of media types, number of client and server side scripts, and so forth, and functionality: external inputs, external outputs, external queries, etc.), using several effort estimation techniques, namely linear regression, regression trees, case-based reasoning, a combination of Regression Trees and Linear Regression, and a combination of Regression Trees and Case-based reasoning. Their results showed that, at least for the dataset employed, length measures were the best effort predictors, in particular the number of server-side scripts/applications. Regression trees and case-based reasoning provided the best results when length measures were employed; otherwise, linear regression provided the best results, when used in combination with functionality measures.

Discussion

Table 1 summarises the ten studies presented previously using the following criteria (Mendes & Mosley, 2005)

- **Study:** Identification of study and reference.
- **Study type:** If the study was a case study, experiment, or survey.
- **# Datasets (#datapoints):** Number of datasets employed and for each, also its number of datapoints.
- **Subjects:** Range of subjects who participated in the study (e.g., students, professionals).
- **Size measure(s):** Size measure(s) that was/ were used to estimated effort.
- **Prediction technique(s):** Effort estimation technique(s) that was/were used to estimate effort.
- **Best technique(s):** Effort estimation technique(s) that presented the best effort estimates.
- **Measure(s) prediction accuracy:** Measure(s) used to assess the prediction accuracy of an effort estimation technique.

Table 1 suggests the following trends:

- Linear regression is the mostly used prediction technique;

Table 1. Summary of previous work on Web effort estimation

Study	Study Type	# datasets (#datapoints)	Subjects	Size Measure(s)	Prediction technique(s)	Best technique(s)	Measure(s) Prediction Accuracy
1st	Case study	2 (29 and 41)	2nd year CS students	Page Count, Reused Page Count, Connectivity, Compactness, Stratum, Structure	Case based reasoning, Linear regression, Stepwise regression	Case based reasoning for high experience group	MMRE
2nd	Case study	1 (46)	professionals	Web objects	WEBMO (parameters generated using linear regression)	—	Pred(n)
3rd	Case study	1 (37)	honours and postgraduate CS students	Length size, Reusability, Complexity, Size	Linear regression Stepwise regression	Linear Regression	MMRE
4th	Case study	1 (37)	honours and postgraduate CS students	Structure metrics, Complexity metrics, Reuse metrics, Size metrics	Generalised Linear Model	—	Goodness of fit
5th	Case study	1 (25)	honours and postgraduate CS students	Requirements and Design measures, Application measures	Case-based reasoning		MMRE, MdMRE, Pred(25), Boxplots of residuals

continued on following page

Table 1. continued

Study	Study Type	# datasets (#data-points)	Subjects	Size Measure(s)	Prediction technique(s)	Best technique(s)	Measure(s) Prediction Accuracy
6th	Case study	1 (37)	honours and postgraduate CS students	Page Count, Media Count, Program Count, Reused Media Count, Reused Program Count, Connectivity Density, Total Page Complexity	Case-based reasoning, Linear regression, Stepwise regression, Classification and Regression Trees	Linear/ stepwise regression or case-based reasoning (depends on the measure of accuracy employed)	MMRE, MdMRE, Pred(25), Boxplots of residuals
7th	Case study	1 (12)	professionals	Web Objects	COBRA, Expert opinion, Linear regression	COBRA	MMRE, Pred(25), Boxplots of residuals
8th	Case study	2 (37 and 25)	honours and postgraduate CS students	Page Count, Media Count, Program Count, Reused Media Count (only one dataset) Reused Program Count (only one dataset), Connectivity Density, Total Page Complexity	Case-based reasoning	—	MMRE, Pred(25), Boxplots of absolute residuals
9th	experiment	1 (30)	CS students	Information model measures, Navigation model measures, Presentation model measures	Linear regression	—	—
10th	Case study	1 (15)	professionals	Number of web pages, Number of new web pages, Number of multimedia elements, Number of new multimedia elements, Number of Client side Scripts and Applications, Number of Server side Scripts and Applications, Number of Internal Links, Number of External References, Number of External Inputs, Number of External Outputs, Number of External Queries, Number of Internal Logical Files, Number of External Interface Files, Number of Web Building Blocks, Number of Multimedia Files, Number of Scripts, Number of Links	linear regression, regression trees, case-based reasoning, a combination of Regression Trees and Linear Regression, and a combination of Regression Trees and Case-based reasoning	Regression trees and case-based reasoning provided the best results when length measures were employed; otherwise, linear regression provided the best results, when used in combination with functionality measures.	MMRE, MdMRE, Pred(25)

- MMRE and Pred(25) are the mostly employed measures of prediction accuracy;
- The sizes of the datasets employed are relatively small and not greater than 46 data points;
- Only three studies have employed datasets with industrial Web projects, two of which using small datasets with 12 and 15 projects, respectively.
- Although five studies (50%) have compared effort estimation techniques results did not converge; in addition, only one of these five studies had a clear best technique.
- The size measures used in the various studies were not constant throughout, indicating the lack of standards to sizing Web applications.

In addition to the trends presented above, another perspective in which we can look at previous work is determining what type of Web applications were used in the empirical studies, classified as Web hypermedia applications, Web software applications, or Web applications (Christodoulou, Zafiris, & Papatheodorou, 2000). A Web hypermedia application is a nonconventional application characterised by the authoring of information using nodes (chunks of information), links (relations between nodes), anchors, access structures (for navigation) and its delivery over the Web. A typical type of application in this category is a Web Museum where information about paintings and artists is accessed through links and access structures such as indexes or guided tours. Technologies commonly used for developing such applications are HTML, JavaScript and multimedia resources. In addition, typical developers are writers, artists and organisations that wish to publish information on the Web and/or CD-ROMs without the need to use programming languages such as Java. Conversely, a Web software application represents conventional software applications that depend on the Web or use the Web's infrastructure for execution. Typical applications

Table 2. Types of Web applications used in the 10 Web cost estimation studies surveyed

Study	Type of Web application
1st	Web hypermedia applications
2nd	Not documented
3rd	Web hypermedia applications
4th	Web hypermedia applications
5th	Web hypermedia applications
6th	Web hypermedia applications
*7th	Web software applications
8th	Web software applications
9th	Web hypermedia applications
*10th	Web software applications

include legacy information systems such as databases, booking systems, knowledge bases and so forth. Many e-commerce applications fall into this category. Typically they employ technology such as Components off-the-shelf, components such as DCOM, OLE, ActiveX, XML, PHP, dynamic HTML, databases, and development solutions such as J2EE. Developers are young programmers fresh from a Computer Science or Software Engineering degree, managed by more senior staff. Finally, a Web application incorporates characteristics of both Web hypermedia and Web software applications. This category combines the behaviour of complex Web software applications with complex navigational structures, which are present in Web hypermedia applications. Table 2 applies the classification aforementioned to the studies previously presented, indicating that, out of the 10 papers referenced in this section, 6 (60%) have used datasets of Web hypermedia applications (i.e., static Web applications), and another 3 (30%) have used Web software applications. Two of the most recent studies have employed datasets representing Web software applications, suggesting the change in the type of Web applications currently developed. Another observation is that, of the three studies that employed datasets representing Web software applications, two used datasets containing data on industrial Web projects, thus supporting the view that Web applications currently developed seem to be mostly Web software applications; however, we cannot generalise this observation since the datasets used in those studies do not represent random samples from the observed population.

EMPIRICAL STUDY

Introduction

This section presents a case study on Web effort estimation using data from real industrial projects. The Web company that volunteered the data is a Spanish company where five people work in Web development. This company was established in 1993, so it is more than 10 years old. All the data that was volunteered were Web applications. This company did not follow a defined and documented development process; its development team was not involved in a process improvement programme and was not part of a software metrics programme.

The volunteered data that is used in our analyses employed the same variables as those for the Tukutuku database (Mendes, Mosley, & Counsell, 2005b), which are described in Table 3.

Within the context of the Tukutuku project for a new feature/function to be considered high-effort it should employ at least 15 hours to be developed by one experienced developer. And for an adapted feature/function to be considered high-effort it should employ at least 4 hours to be adapted by one experienced developer. These values are based on collected data.

Applying Multivariate Regression to Building a Web Effort Estimation Model

The following sections describe our data analysis procedure using multivariate regression:

1. Data validation
2. Variables and model selection
3. Extraction of effort equation
4. Model validation

The results using Multivarate regression were obtained using the statistical software SPSS 12.0.1 for Windows, and the significance level for all statistical tests employed was set at 95% ($\alpha = 0.05$).

Data Validation

Data validation (DV) performs the first screening of the collected data. It generally involves understanding what the variables are (e.g., purpose, scale type) and also uses descriptive statistics (e.g., mean, median, minimum, maximum) to help identify any missing or unusual cases.

In relation to our dataset, its variables have already been presented in Table 3. The descriptive statistics for the dataset's numerical variables are presented in Table 4.

None of the numerical variables seem to exhibit unusual values, although this requires careful examination. Except for EstEff, none exhibits missing values. HFots, HFotsA, and Hnew all seem not to have any values other than zero for all the volunteered projects. However, this is perfectly possible whenever there are no features/functions that have employed more than the minimum number of hours necessary to make it high effort.

Once we have checked the numerical variables our next step is to check the categorical variables using their frequency tables as a tool. However, this is not necessary for this dataset given that all projects did not follow a defined and documented process, development teams were not involved in a process improvement programme or part of a software metrics programme. In regard to the company's effort recording procedure, it was also the same for all projects, and indicates the use of a poor recording procedure of effort values because

Table 3. Variables for the Tukutuku database

Variable Name	Scale	Description
Company data		
Country	Categorical	Country company belongs to.
Established	Ordinal	Year when company was established.
nPeopleWD	Ratio	Number of people who work on Web design and development.
Project data		
TypeProj	Categorical	Type of project (new or enhancement).
nLang	Ratio	Number of different development languages used
DocProc	Categorical	If project followed defined and documented process.
ProImpr	Categorical	If project team involved in a process improvement programme.
Metrics	Categorical	If project team part of a software metrics programme.
Devteam	Ratio	Size of project's development team.
Teamexp	Ratio	Average team experience with the development language(s) employed.
totEff	Ratio	Actual total effort used to develop the Web application.
estEff	Ratio	Estimated total effort necessary to develop the Web application.
Accuracy	Categorical	Procedure used to record effort data.
Web application		
TypeApp	Categorical	Type of Web application developed.
TotWP	Ratio	Total number of Web pages (new and reused).
NewWP	Ratio	Total number of new Web pages.
TotImg	Ratio	Total number of images (new and reused).
NewImg	Ratio	Total number of new images created.
HFots	Ratio	Number of reused high-effort features/functions without adaptation.
HFotsA	Ratio	Number of reused high-effort features/functions adapted.
Hnew	Ratio	Number of new high-effort features/functions.
Fots	Ratio	Number of reused low-effort features without adaptation.
FotsA	Ratio	Number of reused low-effort features adapted.
New	Ratio	Number of new low-effort features/functions.

no timesheets were used by the development teams to record effort.

Once the data validation is complete, we are ready to move on to the next step, namely variables and model selection.

Variables and Model Selection

The second step in our data analysis methodology is subdivided into two separate and distinct phases: preliminary analysis and model building.

Preliminary analysis allows us to choose which variables to use, discard, modify, and, where necessary, sometimes create. Model building determines an effort estimation model based on our data set and variables.

Preliminary Analysis

This important phase is used to create variables based on existing variables, discard unnecessary variables, and modify existing variables (e.g.,

Table 4. Descriptive statistics for numerical variables

Variable	Number of points		Mean	Median	Std. Deviation	Minimum	Maximum
	Valid	Missing					
nPeopleWD	12	0	5.00	5.00	0.00	5	5
nLang	12	0	5.50	5.00	1.00	5	8
DevTeam	12	0	2.50	2.00	1.38	1	5
TeamExp	12	0	6.75	6.50	1.29	4	8
TotEff	12	0	867.00	27.50	1417.16	6	4000
EstEff	4	8	2590.00	1120.00	2940.00	1120	7000
Accuracy	12	0	1.00	1.00	0.00	1	1
TotWP	12	0	71.08	23.50	76.25	3	200
NewWP	12	0	6.83	3.50	9.50	0	30
TotImg	12	0	34.00	5.00	64.76	1	230
NewImg	12	0	20.00	0.00	57.05	0	200
HFots	12	0	0.00	0.00	0.00	0	0
HFotsA	12	0	0.00	0.00	0.00	0	0
Hnew	12	0	0.00	0.00	0.00	0	0
Fots	12	0	7.50	7.50	2.61	5	10
FotsA	12	0	3.00	0.00	5.72	0	20
New	12	0	6.08	4.50	5.48	0	15

joining categories). The net result of this phase is to obtain a set of variables that are ready to use in the next phase, model building. Because this phase will construct an effort model using stepwise regression, we need to ensure that the variables comply with the assumptions underlying regression analysis, which are (Mendes, Mosely, & Counsell, 2005c):

1. The input variables (independent variables) are measured without error. If this cannot be guaranteed, then these variables need to be normalised.
2. The relationship between dependent and independent variables is linear.
3. No important input variables have been omitted. This ensures that there is no specification error associated with the data set. The use of a prior theory-based model justifying the choice of input variables ensures this assumption is not violated.
4. The variance of the residuals is the same for all combinations of input variables (i.e., the residuals are homoscedastic rather than heteroscedastic).
5. The residuals must be normally distributed.
6. The residuals must be independent, that is, not correlated.
7. The independent variables are not linearly dependent, that is, there are no linear dependencies among the independent variables.

The first task within the preliminary analysis phase is to examine the entire set of variables and check if there is a significant amount of missing values (> 60%). If yes, they should be automatically discarded as they prohibit the use of imputation methods and will further prevent the identification of useful trends in the data. Imputation methods are methods used to replace missing values with estimated values.

Only one variable presents missing values—EstEff, and this variable was gathered simply to have a benchmark against which to compare the estimated effort obtained using different estimation techniques. Seven variables do not exhibit missing values, however each presents a single value for all projects, thus hindering its usefulness as predictors—Typeproj, DocProc, ProImpr, Metrics, HFots, HFotsA, and Hnew. They are all discarded from further analysis. Therefore the variables used in the remaining of this chapter are: nLang, DevTeam, TeamExp, TotWP, NewWP, TotImg, NewImg, Fots, FotsA, and New.

Next, we present the analyses for numerical variables first, followed by the analyses for categorical variables.

Numerical Variables: Looking for Symptoms

Our next step is to look for symptoms (e.g., skewness, heteroscedasticity, and outliers) that may suggest the need for variables to be normalised, that is, having their values transformed such that they resemble more closely a normal distribution. This step uses histograms, boxplots, and scatter plots. Skewness measures to what extent the distribution of data values is symmetrical about a central value; Heteroscedasticity represents unstable variance of values; Outliers are unusual values.

Histograms, or bar charts, provide a graphical display, where each bar summarises the frequency of a single value or range of values for a given variable. They are often used to check if a variable is normally distributed, in which case the bars are displayed in the shape of a bell-shaped curve.

Histograms for all the numerical variables are presented in Figure 3, and indicate that most variables do not present skewed distributions, however histograms alone are not enough to rule out the need to transform the data.

Next, we use boxplots (see Figure 4) to check the existence of outliers. Boxplots use the median, represented by the horizontal line in the middle of the box, as the central value for the distribution.

The box's height is the interquartile range, and contains 50% of the values. The vertical (whiskers) lines up or down from the edges contain observations which are less than 1.5 times interquartile range. Outliers are taken as values greater than 1.5 times the height of the box. Values greater than 3 times the box's height are called extreme outliers (Kitchenham, MacDonell, Pickard, & Shepperd, 2001).

When upper and lower tails are approximately equal and the median is in the centre of the box, the distribution is symmetric. If the distribution is not symmetric the relative lengths of the tails and the position of the median in the box indicate the nature of the skewness. The length of the box relative to the length of the tails gives an indication of the shape of the distribution. So, a boxplot with a small box and long tails represents a very peaked distribution, whereas a boxplot with a long box represents a flatter distribution (Kitchenham et al., 2001).

The boxplots for numerical variables (see Figure 4) indicate the presence of some outliers, which may indicate a nonnormal distribution. When this situation arises it is common practice to normalise the data, that is, to transform the data trying to approximate the values to a normal distribution. A common transformation is to take the natural log (ln), which makes larger values smaller and brings the data values closer to each other (Maxwell, 2002). However, before transforming the data a statistical test can be used to confirm if the data is not normally distributed. This statistical test is called the One-Sample Kolmogorov-Smirnov Test. It compares an observed distribution to a theoretical distribution. Significance values equal to or smaller than 0.05 indicate that the observed distribution differs from the theoretical distribution. After applying the K-S one variable needed to be transformed, NewImg. Because this variable had zeroes, we added 1 to it before applying the natural log transformation. The new variable created, containing the transformed values, is called LNewImg.

Figure 3. Histograms for numerical variables

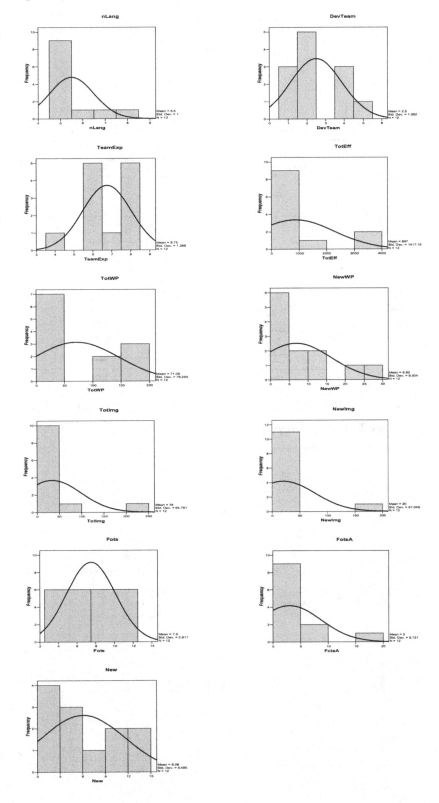

Figure 4. Boxplots for numerical variables

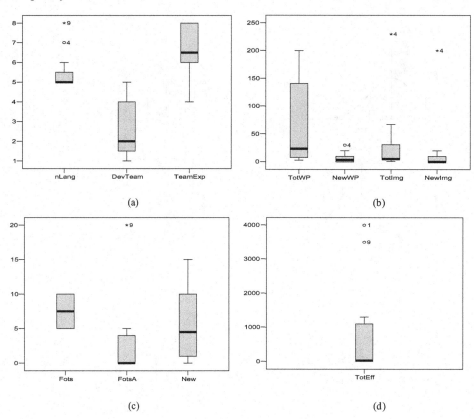

(a)   (b)

(c)   (d)

Figure 5. Scatterplots for TotEff and independent variables

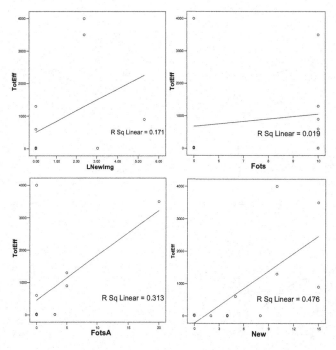

The last part of the preliminary analysis is to check if the relationship between the dependent variable (TotEff) and the independent variables is linear. The tool used to check such relationships is a scatter plot.

Numerical Variables: Relationship with Total Effort

Scatter plots are used to explore possible relationships between numerical variables (see Figure 5). They also help to identify strong and weak relationships between two numerical variables.

A strong relationship is represented by observations (data points) falling very close to or on the trend line. Examples of such relationships are shown in Figure 5(a). A weak relationship is shown by observations that do not form a clear pattern, which in our case is a straight line. And example of such a relationship is shown in Figure 5(f).

We can also say that a relationship is positively associated when values on the y-axis tend to increase with those on the x-axis (e.g., Figure 5(a)–(h)). When values on the y-axis tend to decrease as those on the x-axis increase, we say that the relationship is negatively associated.

Figure 5 shows that all variables present a positive relationship with TotEff.

Our preliminary analysis for numerical variables is finished. Because there are no categorical variables to be used further in our analysis, out next step is to build the effort model using a two-step process. The first step is to use a manual stepwise regression based on residuals to select the numerical variables that jointly have a statistically significant effect on the dependent variable, TotEff. The second step is to use these selected variables to build the final effort model using multivariate regression, that is, linear regression using more than one independent variable.

Building the Model Using a Two-Step Process

This section describes the use of a manual stepwise regression based on residuals to build the effort model. This technique, proposed by Kitchenham (1998), enables the use of information on residuals to handle relationships among independent variables. In addition, it only selects the input variables that jointly have a statistically significant effect on the dependent variable, thus avoiding any multicollinearity problems.

The input variables to use are those selected as a result of our preliminary analyses, which are: nLang, DevTeam, TeamExp, TotWP, NewWP, TotImg, LNewImg, Fots, FotsA, and New.

The manual stepwise technique comprises the following steps (Kitchenham, 1998):

Step 1.   Construct the single variable regression equation with effort as the dependent variable using the most highly (and significantly) correlated input variable (IV1).

Step 2.   Calculate the residuals (Res1).

Step 3.   Correlate the residuals with all the other input variables.

Step 4.   Any input variables that were initially significantly correlated with effort but are not significantly correlated with the residual are significantly correlated with IV1 and offer no additional information about the dependent variable. They can therefore be eliminated from the stepwise regression.

Step 5.   Construct a single variable regression with the residuals (Res1) as the dependent variable and the variable (IV2), of the remaining input variables, which is the most highly (and significantly) correlated with Res1.

Step 6.   Calculate residuals Res2.

Step 7.   Correlate the residuals Res2 with the remaining input variables. Any variables that were correlated with Res1 in step 5 but are not correlated with Res2 are eliminated from the analysis. They are variables that are highly correlated with IV2.

Step 8.   Continue in this way until there are no more input variables available for inclusion in the model or none of the remaining variables are significantly correlated with the current residuals.

Step 9.   The simplest way to construct the full regression model is then to use simple multivariate regression with only the selected input variables.

We have set the statistical significance at $\alpha = 0.05$. In Tables 5 and 6 any variables with p values greater than 0.05 are identified as "n.s."

We also need to verify the stability of the regression model. This involves identifying large residual and high-influence data points (i.e., projects), and also checking whether residuals are homoscedastic and normally distributed. Several types of plots (e.g., residual, leverage, probability) and statistics are available in most statistics tools to accomplish such tasks. The ones we have employed here are:

- A residual plot showing residuals vs. fitted values to investigate if the residuals are random and normally distributed. The plotted data points should be distributed randomly about zero. They should not exhibit patterns such as linear or nonlinear trends, or increasing or decreasing variance.

- A normal P–P plot (probability plots) for the residuals. Normal P–P plots are generally employed to verify whether the distribution of a variable is consistent with the normal distribution. If the distribution is Normal, the data points are close to linear.

- Cook's D statistic to identify projects that exhibited jointly a large influence and large residual (Maxwell, 2002). Any projects with D greater than $4/n$, where n represents the total number of projects, are considered to have high influence on the results. When there are high-influence projects the stability of the model needs to be tested by removing these projects, and observing the effect their removal has on the model. If the coefficients remain stable and the adjusted R^2 increases, this indicates that the high-influence projects

Table 5. Results for the first cycle in the stepwise procedure

Variable	Effect	Adj. R²	Significance
nLang	+	0.458	p < 0.01
DevTeam	+	0.320	p = 0.032
TeamExp	-	0.095	Ns
TotWP	+	0.435	p < 0.01
NewWP	+	0.279	p = 0.045
TotImg	-	0.029	Ns
LNewImg	+	0.088	Ns
Fots	-	0.079	Ns
FotsA	+	0.244	Ns
New	+	0.423	p < 0.01

Table 6. Results for the second cycle in the stepwise procedure

Variable	Effect	Adj. R²	Significance
nLang	+	0.458	p < 0.01
DevTeam	+	0.032	ns *
TeamExp	-	0.092	Ns
TotWP	+	0.166	ns *
NewWP	-	0.069	ns *
TotImg	+	0.031	Ns
LNewImg	-	0.084	Ns
Fots	+	0.073	Ns
FotsA	-	0.098	Ns
New	-	0.069	ns *

are not destabilising the model and therefore do not need to be removed.

First Cycle

Table 5 shows the results of applying the manual stepwise procedure to the numerical variables. This is the first cycle in the stepwise procedure. The numerical variable nLang is the most significant, becausee it presents the highest adjusted R^2 of 0.458.

The single variable regression equation with TotEff as the dependent/response variable and nLang as the independent/predictor variable gives an adjusted R^2 of 0.458. Two projects are identified with Cook's D > 0.33; however, their removal did not seem to destabilise the model, that is, after their removal the coefficients remained stable and the adjusted R^2 increased. The residuals resulting from the linear regression are used for the second cycle in the stepwise procedure.

Second Cycle

Table 6 shows that DevTeam, TotWP, NewWP and New have no further statistically significant effect on the residuals obtained in the previous cycle. Therefore they can all be eliminated from the stepwise procedure. Because there are no other variables that are significantly correlated with TotEff the stepwise procedure finishes.

Finally, our last step is to construct the effort estimation model using a multivariate regression analysis with only the input variable selected using the manual stepwise procedure. The coefficients for the effort model are presented in Table 7. Its adjusted R^2 is 0.458 suggesting that nLang

can explain 45.8% of the variation in TotEff. No other variables were selected from the manual stepwise procedure, suggesting that either there are problems with the data that has been obtained, or that other variables that are also important to predict effort have been omitted from the data collection.

Once the residuals and the stability of the regression model have been checked, we are in a position to extract the equation that represents the model.

Extraction of Effort Equation

The equation that is obtained from Table 7 is the following:

$$TotEff = -4682 + 1008.909nLang \qquad (8)$$

Obtaining a model that can explain, sometimes to a large degree, the variation in the dependent variable is not enough to assume this model will provide good effort predictions. To assess whether a model is a good prediction model, it also needs to be validated.

Model Validation

To validate a model we need to carry out the following steps:

Step 1. Divide the original dataset d into a training set t and a validation set v.

Step 2. Use t to produce an effort estimation model te (if applicable).

Table 7. Coefficients for the effort model

Variable	Coeff.	Std. error	T	P>|t|
(Constant)	-4682.00	1756.955	-2.665	0.024
nLang	1008.909	314.714	3.206	0.009

Table 8. Coefficients for the effort model built using the training set

Variable	Coeff.	Std. error	t	P>|t|
(Constant)	-5081.714	972.333	-5.226	0.002
nLang	1072.714	177.894	6.030	0.001

Table 9. Prediction accuracy measures using model-based estimated effort

Measure	%
MMRE	1,465.111
MdMRE	598.519
Pred(25)	0

Step 3.   Use *te* to predict effort for each of the projects in *v*, as if these projects were new projects for which effort was unknown.

This process is known as cross-validation. For an *n*-fold cross-validation, *n* different training/validation sets are used. In this section we will show the cross-validation procedure using a one-fold cross-validation, with a 66% split. This split means that 66% of our project data will be used for model building, the remaining 34% to validate the model, that is, the training set will have 66% of the total number of projects and the validation set will have the remaining 34%.

Our initial dataset had 12 projects. At step 1 they are split into training and validation sets containing 8 and 4 projects, respectively. Generally, projects are selected randomly.

As part of step 2 we need to create an effort model using the 8 projects in the training set. We will create an effort model that only considers the variable that has been previously selected and presented in Equation 8, which is nLang. Here we do not perform the residual analysis or consider Cook's D because it is assumed these have also been done using the generic equation, Equation 8. The training model's coefficients are presented in Table 8, and its corresponding Equation as Equation 9. Its adjusted R^2 is 0.835.

$$TotEff = -5081.714 + 1072.714 nLang \quad (9)$$

To measure the model's prediction accuracy we obtain the MMRE, MdMRE, and Pred(25)

for the validation set. The model presented as Equation 9 is applied to each of the 4 projects in the validation set to obtain estimated effort, and MRE is computed. Having the calculated estimated effort and the actual effort (provided by the Web company), we are finally in a position to calculate MRE for each of the 4 projects, and hence MMRE, MdMRE, and Pred(25) for the entire 12 projects.

Table 9 shows the measures of prediction accuracy, calculated from the validation set, and is assumed to represent the entire set of 12 projects.

If we assume a good prediction model has an MMRE less than or equal to 25% and Pred(25) greater than or equal to 75%, then the values presented in Table 9 suggest that the accuracy of the effort model used is very poor. We also had the real estimated effort for two of the projects in the validation set, which give an MMRE and MdMRE of 49.7, and a Pred(25) of 50%. This indicates that the model obtained using regression analysis is much worse than the company's own effort estimates, and thus the company should be very cautious when using an effort model based on the dataset employed in this chapter. Obviously, we cannot generalise these results outside the scope of this case study because the dataset used does not represent a random sample of Web projects. We feel that it is also important to mention that the accuracy of the effort values that were provided was 1, which indicates that no timesheets were recorded by the development team, and it is likely that the effort values provided were close to guess.

Applying Case-Based Reasoning to Building a Web Effort Estimation Model

The following sections describe our data analysis procedure using CBR:

1. Data validation
2. Variables selection
3. Obtaining Effort Estimates & Model Validation

The results using Case-based Reasoning were obtained using the CBR tool CBR-Works version 4.2.1, which is a commercial tool. In addition, for all statistical tests employed, we have set the significance level at 95% ($\alpha = 0.05$).

Data Validation

The Data validation (DV) phase here is the same as that previously presented, and thus it is not going to be repeated here. Once the data validation is complete, we are ready to move on to the next step, namely variables selection.

Variables Selection

This phase, Variables and model selection, is very similar to the one described earlier, where we create variables based on existing variables, discard unnecessary variables, and modify existing variables (e.g., joining categories). However, it adds another step, which is used to identify which variables are significantly associated with effort. This step is carried out in order to simulate the "features subset selection" parameter in CBR and will use the input variables selected as a result of our preliminary analyses, which are: nLang, DevTeam, TeamExp, TotWP, NewWP, TotImg, LNewImg, Fots, FotsA, and New.

Because all variables, except for NewImg, were normally distributed, we measured their association with TotEff using a parametric test called Pearson's correlation test. This test measures the direction and the strength of the relationship between two variables measured at least on an interval scale. In regard to NewImg, we measured its association with TotEff using a nonparametric test called Spearman's correlation test. It measures the strength and the direction of

the relationship between two variables that were measured on an ordinal scale. The attributes found significantly correlated with TotEff are: nLang, DevTeam, TotWP, NewWP, and New. These will be the attributes that we will use with the CBR tool to obtain effort estimates.

Obtaining Effort Estimates & Model Validation

When using CBR there is not a model per se that is built, simply the retrieval of the most similar cases to the one being estimated. Therefore, there is not also a generic model, such as that presented in Equation 8. We have estimated effort for the same 4 projects that were used as validation set previously, and the remaining 8 projects as the case base. This means that the same step (obtaining effort) is also being used to validate the CBR "model."

In relation to the six CBR parameters we employed the following:

- **Feature Subset Selection:** No feature subset selection was used. What we have done was to only use in the CBR procedure those attributes that were significantly correlated with TotEff.
- **Similarity Measure:** The similarity measure used in this section was the Unweighted Euclidean distance.
- **Scaling:** Scaling was automatically done by the CBR tool employed.
- **Number of Analogies:** Effort estimates were generated based on the most similar case.
- **Analogy Adaptation:** There was no adaptation per se, as we used as estimated effort the same effort obtained from the most similar case.
- **Adaptation Rules:** No adaptation rules were employed.

Table 10 shows the prediction accuracy obtained for the validation set when employing CBR to estimate effort. They present estimation accuracy worse than the accuracy associated with expert's own estimates (49.7%).

It is important to understand that we have used a very simple set of CBR parameters and it is possible that a different combination of CBR parameters could have led to better results. For example, previous studies have often used 1, 2 and 3 analogies (not only 1 as we did), and also different analogy adaptations and adaptation rules. We have not employed different CBR parameters because it was not the purpose of this section to compare different CBR results, but to show one possible way to use CBR.

Applying Classification and Regression Trees to Building a Web Effort Estimation Model

The following sections describe our data analysis procedure using CART:

1. Data validation
2. Variables selection
3. Obtaining effort estimates & model validation

The results using CART were obtained using a commercial classification and regression tree tool called AnswerTree 3.1.The statistical results presented were obtained using the statistical software SPSS 12.0.1 for Windows, where the significance level was set at 95% ($\alpha = 0.05$).

Table 10. Prediction accuracy measures using CBR

Measure	%
MMRE	59.65
MdMRE	63.33
Pred(25)	0

Data Validation

This step, Data Validation, is the same one employed with CBR and Multivariate regression, and thus we will not repeat the same analysis here.

Variables Selection

This step, Variables Selection, was exactly the same as that used with CBR, and thus we will not repeat the same analysis here.

Obtaining Effort Estimates & Model Validation

When using CART the model that is built is a binary tree, which in our case is a regression tree, to be used to obtain effort estimates for the projects that have not being used to build that tree. Within the scope of our case study, our CART tree will be built using the same training set used with CBR and regression. Later, we use the same validation set employed with CBR and Regression to validate the CART tree (model). With CART we could have initially built a tree using the entire subset of 12 projects, however we chose not to do so as this step is not necessary here. It would make sense to do so if we were to use the entire dataset to build a tree, and later use this tree to estimate effort for other projects belonging to the same company or other companies (projects that have not been used to build the tree).

We have estimated effort for the same 4 projects that were used as validation set previously, and the remaining 8 projects to build the tree. This means that the model validation step is intertwined with the model building step, similar to what we observed when applying CBR.

In relation to the CART settings in AnswerTree we employed the following:

- Maximum Tree Depth equal to 5. This depth represents the number of levels below the root node.

Figure 6. Regression Tree using 8 projects

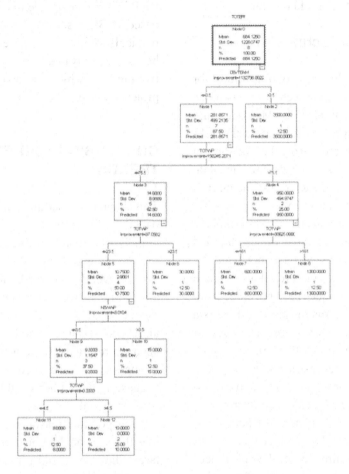

- Minimum number of cases in the parent node equal to 2; minimum number of cases in the child node equal to 1.

The regression tree obtained is presented in Figure 6, which shows that the predictor variables that were used were DevTeam, TotWP, and NewWP. To obtain estimated effort for each of the four projects in the validation set we simply have to traverse the tree using each project's data, until we reach a leaf node. Then, we use as estimated effort the value indicated beside the word "Predicted."

Table 11 shows the prediction accuracy obtained for the validation set when employing CART to estimate effort. They present estimation accuracy much worse than the accuracy associated with expert's own estimates (49.7%).

The prediction accuracy obtained using CART seems much worse than that obtained using Regression or CBR. It could be that the projects were too different from one another, making it difficult to obtain leaf nodes that are balanced. It

Table 11. Prediction accuracy measures using CART

Measure	%
MMRE	18,044.79
MdMRE	6,966.667
Pred(25)	0

could also be that the sample size was too small to be used effectively to build the tree.

What is the Best Technique?

We have measured the prediction accuracy for particular effort estimation techniques using as measures of accuracy MMRE, MdMRE, and Pred(25). However, when you are comparing techniques, in addition to measuring their prediction accuracy, you also need to verify if the absolute residuals obtained using each of the techniques being compared have come from the same distribution. In case they have, what this means is that the differences in absolute residual values obtained using different techniques have occurred by chance. However, if the absolute residuals obtained using each of the techniques have not come from the same distribution, this means that there is a legitimate difference between absolute residuals obtained using these different techniques, which implies that the differences in prediction accuracy that have been observed have not occurred by chance, and are statistically significant. The choice to use absolute residuals, and not simply residuals, is motivated by the fact that we are not interested in the direction of the differences between actual and estimated efforts, but rather in the absolute differences themselves.

In order to compare the absolute residuals, we employed the One-Sample Kolmogorov-Smirnov Test to check if the distributions of residuals were normally distributed or not. Because they were not, we employed Kendall's W Test to compare regression-based residuals to CBR-based residuals and CART-based residuals. Kendall's W test is a nonparametric test that checks whether K related samples come from the same population. We found that all residuals came from the same population. Results showed that all three sets of residuals came from the same population, which means that, despite their differences in MMRE and MdMRE values, estimations obtained using regression are similar to those obtained using

CBR, and both are similar to those obtained using CART. We were unable to compare Regression-based, CBR-based, and CART-based absolute residuals to those from expert-based predictions because we only had expert-based predictions for two projects, which was a very small number of projects to use.

CONCLUSION AND FUTURE TRENDS

This chapter has used an industrial dataset to compare three different effort estimation techniques, namely Multivariate Regression, Case-based reasoning, and Classification and Regression Trees. Overall, the predictions obtained using all techniques were very poor both compared to expert-based estimates and also baseline MMRE and Pred(25) values. In addition, when comparing absolute residuals, there were no statistical differences among the three techniques employed, suggesting that either would lead to similar absolute residuals.

One possible reason for the poor results is that the size of the data set is small, and thus larger data sets could provide different results. In addition, the size measures used in this study are early size measures based on the Tukutuku database. We also need to investigate other size measures for Web applications based on function points such as Internet Points (Cost Xpert Group, 2001) and OOmFPWeb (Abrahão, 2004) in order to assess to what extent the Tukutuku measures are adequate for Web effort estimation.

Another possible reason for the poor result of all three estimation techniques is that the Web company that volunteered the project data did not follow a defined and documented development process. In addition, it also presented poor effort recording procedures because no timesheets were recorded by the development team. In the past we have built accurate effort models using industrial data, however such data presented high levels of correctness, in particular for the recorded effort. To address the problem related to poor effort recording, we are currently analysing a set of Web projects developed using a systematic development process based on a model-driven development paradigm to assess to what extent the effort estimation models obtained in this context improve current industry practices.

REFERENCES

Abrahão S. (2004, October). *On the functional size measurement of object-oriented conceptual schemas: Design and evaluation issues*. Unpublished doctoral dissertation, Department of Information Systems and Computation, Valencia University of Technology, 410.

Angelis, L., & Stamelos, I. (2000). A simulation tool for efficient analogy based cost estimation. *Empirical Software Engineering, 5*, 35-68.

Baresi, L., Morasca, S., & Paolini, P. (2003, September 3-5). Estimating the design effort of Web applications. In *Proceedings of the Ninth International Software Measures Symposium*, (pp. 62-72).

Boehm, B. (1981). *Software engineering economics*. Englewood Cliffs, NJ: Prentice Hall.

Boehm, B. (2000). COCOMO II. Retrieved October 11, 2007, from The University of Southern California Web site: http://sunset.usc.edu/research/COCOMOII/Docs/modelman.pdf

Boehm, B., Abts, C., Brown, A., Chulani, S., Clark, B., Horowitz, E., et al. (2000). *Software cost estimation with Cocomo II*. In B. Boehm (Ed.). Pearson Publishers.

Botafogo, R., Rivlin, A.E., & Shneiderman, B. (1992). Structural analysis of hypertexts: Identifying hierarchies and useful measures. *ACM Transactions on Information Systems, 10*(2), 143-179.

Briand, L.C., El-Emam, K., Surmann, D., Wieczorek, I., & Maxwell, K.D. (1999). An assessment and comparison of common cost estimation modeling techniques. In *Proceedings of ICSE 1999*, Los Angeles, USA, (pp. 313-322).

Briand, L.C., Langley, T., & Wieczorek, I. (2000). A replicated assessment and comparison of common software cost modeling techniques. In *Proceedings of ICSE 2000*, Limerick, Ireland, (pp. 377-386).

Brieman, L., Friedman, J., Olshen, R., & Stone, C. (1984). *Classification and regression trees*. Belmont: Wadsworth.

Christodoulou, S. P., Zafiris, P. A., & Papatheodorou, T. S. (2000). WWW2000: The developer's view and a practitioner's approach to Web engineering. In *Proceedings of the 2nd ICSE Workshop on Web Engineering*, (pp. 75-92).

Costagliola, G., Di Martino, S., Ferrucci, F., Gravino, C., Tortora, G., & Vitiello, G. (2006). Effort estimation modeling techniques: A case study for Web applications. In *Proceedings of the 6th International Conference on Web Engineering*, (pp. 9-16).

Cost Xpert Group Inc. Estimating Internet Development. Retrieved October 11, 2007, from http://www.costxpert.com/resource_center/articles/software_development/pg3.html

Cowderoy, A.J.C. (2000). Measures of size and complexity for Web site content. In *Proceedings of the 11th ESCOM Conference*, Munich, Germany, (pp. 423-431).

DeMarco, T. (1982). *Controlling software projects: Management, measurement and estimation*. New York: Yourdon Press.

Fewster, R.M., & Mendes, E. (2001). Measurement, prediction and risk analysis for Web Applications. In *Proceedings of the IEEE METRICS Symposium*, (pp. 338-348).

Finnie, G.R., Wittig, G.E., & Desharnais, J-M. (1997). A comparison of software effort estimation techniques: Using function points with neural networks, case-based reasoning and regression models. *Journal of Systems and Software. 39*, 281-289.

Gray, A., & MacDonell, S. (1997a). Applications of fuzzy logic to software metric models for development effort estimation. In *Proceedings of the IEEE Annual Meeting of the North American Fuzzy Information Processing Society - NAFIPS*, Syracuse, NY, USA, (pp. 394-399).

Gray, A.R., & MacDonell, S.G. (1997b). A comparison of model building techniques to develop predictive equations for software metrics. *Information and Software Technology, 39*, 425-437.

Gray, R., MacDonell, S.G., & Shepperd, M.J. (1999). Factors systematically associated with errors in subjective estimates of software development effort: The stability of expert judgement. In *Proceedings of the 6th IEEE Metrics Symposium*, (pp. 216-226).

Hughes, R.T. (1997). *An empirical investigation into the estimation of software development effort.* Unpublished doctoral dissertation, Department of Computing, University of Brighton.

Jeffery, R., Ruhe, M., & Wieczorek, I. (2000). A comparative study of two software development cost modeling techniques using multiorganizational and company-specific data. *Information and Software Technology, 42*, 1009-1016.

Jeffery, R., Ruhe, M., & Wieczorek, I. (2001). Using public domain metrics to estimate software development effort. In *Proceedings of the 7th IEEE Metrics Symposium,* London, (pp. 16-27).

Jørgensen, M., & Sjøberg, D. (2001). Impact of effort estimates on software project work. *Information and Software Technology, 43*, 939-948.

Kadoda, G., Cartwright, M., Chen, L., & Shepperd, M.J. (2000). Experiences using case-based reasoning to predict software project effort. In *Proceedings of the EASE 2000 Conference,* Keele, UK.

Kemerer, C.F. (1987). An empirical validation of software cost estimation models. *Communications of the ACM, 30*(5), 416-429.

Kitchenham, B.A. (1998, April). A procedure for analyzing unbalanced datasets. *IEEE Transactions on Software Engineering, 24*(4), 278-301.

Kitchenham, B.A., MacDonell, S.G., Pickard, L.M., & Shepperd, M.J. (2001). What accuracy statistics really measure. *IEE Proceedings Software, 148*(3), 81-85.

Kitchenham, B.A., Pickard, L.M., Linkman, S., & Jones, P. (2003, June). Modelling software bidding risks. *IEEE Transactions on Software Engineering, 29*(6), 542-554.

Kok, P., Kitchenham, B.A., & Kirakowski, J. (1990). The MERMAID approach to software cost estimation. In *Proceedings of the ESPRIT Annual Conference,* Brussels, (pp. 296-314).

Kumar, S., Krishna, B.A., & Satsangi, P.S. (1994). Fuzzy systems and neural networks in software engineering project management. *Journal of Applied Intelligence, 4*, 31-52.

Maxwell, K. (2002). *Applied statistics for software managers.* Prentice Hall PTR.

Mendes, E., Counsell, S., & Mosley, N. (2000, June). Measurement and effort prediction of Web applications. In *Proceedings of the 2nd ICSE Workshop on Web Engineering,* Limerick, Ireland, (pp. 57-74).

Mendes, E., & Mosley, N. (2005). Web cost estimation: Principles and applications. In M. Khosrow-Pour & J. Travers (Eds.), *Web engineering—principles and techniques* (pp. 182-202). Hershey, PA: Idea Group.

Mendes, E., Mosley, N., & Counsell, S. (2001). Web measures—estimating design and authoring effort. *IEEE Multimedia*, Special Issue on Web Engineering, *8*(1), 50-57.

Mendes, E., Mosley, N., & Counsell, S. (2002a). The application of case-based reasoning to early Web project cost estimation. In *Proceedings of the IEEE COMPSAC*, (pp. 393-398).

Mendes, E., Mosley, N., & Counsell, S. (2003a). Do adaptation rules improve Web cost estimation?. In *Proceedings of the ACM Hypertext Conference 2003*, Nottingham, UK, (pp. 173-183).

Mendes, E., Mosley, N., & Counsell, S. (2003b). A replicated assessment of the use of adaptation rules to improve Web cost estimation. In *Proceedings of the ACM and IEEE International Symposium on Empirical Software Engineering*. Rome, Italy, (pp. 100-109).

Mendes, E., Mosley, N., & Counsell, S. (2005a). The need for Web engineering: An introduction. In E. Mendes & N. Mosley (Eds.), *Web engineering* (pp. 1-26). Springer-Verlag.

Mendes, E., Mosley, N., & Counsell, S. (2005b, August). Investigating Web size metrics for early Web cost estimation. Journal of Systems and Software, 77(2), 157-172.

Mendes, E., Mosley, N., & Counsell, S. (2005c). Web effort estimation. In E. Mendes & N. Mosley (Eds.), *Web engineering* (pp. 29-73). Springer-Verlag.

Mendes, E., Watson, I., Triggs, C., Mosley, N., & Counsell, S. (2002b, June). A comparison of development effort estimation techniques for Web hypermedia applications. In *Proceedings of the IEEE Metrics Symposium*, Ottawa, Canada, (pp. 141-151).

Reifer, D.J. (2000). Web development: Estimating quick-to-market software. *IEEE Software*, *17*(6), 57-64.

Ruhe, M., Jeffery, R., & Wieczorek, I. (2003). Cost estimation for Web applications. In *Proceedings of the ICSE 2003*, Portland, USA, (pp. 285-294).

Schofield, C. (1998). *An empirical investigation into software estimation by analogy.* Unpublished doctoral dissertation, Department of Computing, Bournemouth University.

Schroeder, L., Sjoquist, D., & Stephan, P. (1986). *Understanding regression analysis: An introductory guide, No. 57.* Newbury Park: Sage Publications.

Selby, R.W., & Porter, A.A. (1998). Learning from examples: Generation and evaluation of decision trees for software resource analysis. *IEEE Transactions on Software Engineering, 14*, 1743-1757.

Shepperd, M.J., & Kadoda, G. (2001). Using simulation to evaluate prediction techniques. In *Proceedings of the IEEE 7th International Software Metrics Symposium*, London, UK, (pp. 349-358).

Shepperd, M.J., & Schofield, C. (1997). Estimating software project effort using analogies. *IEEE Transactions on Software Engineering, 23*(11), 736-743.

Shepperd, M.J., Schofield, C., & Kitchenham, B. (1996). Effort estimation using analogy. In *Proceedings of the ICSE-18*, Berlin, (pp. 170-178).

Vliet, H.V. (2000). *Software engineering: Principles and practice* (2nd ed.). New York: John Wiley & Sons.

KEY TERMS

Algorithmic Techniques: Attempt to build models that precisely represent the relationship between effort and one or more project characteristics via the use of algorithmic models. Such models assume that application size is the main contributor to effort thus in any algorithmic model the central project characteristic used is usually taken to be some notion of application size (e.g., the number of lines of source code, function points, number of Web pages, number of new images). The relationship between size and effort is often translated as an equation.

Case-Based Reasoning: Assumes that similar problems provide similar solutions. It provides estimates by comparing the characteristics of the current project to be estimated against a library of historical information from completed projects with a known effort (case base).

Classification and Regression Trees (CART) (Brieman et al., 1984): Techniques where independent variables (predictors) are used to build binary trees where each leaf node either represents a category to which an estimate belongs to, or a value for an estimate. In order to obtain an estimate one has to traverse tree nodes from root to leaf by selecting the nodes that represent the category or value for the independent variables associated with the case to be estimated.

Cross-Validation: Process by which an original dataset d is divided into a training set t and a validation set v. The training set is used to produce an effort estimation model (if applicable), later used to predict effort for each of the projects in v, as if these projects were new projects for which effort was unknown. Accuracy statistics are then obtained and aggregated to provide an overall measure of prediction accuracy.

Effort Estimation: To predict the necessary amount of labour units to accomplish a given task, based on knowledge of previous similar projects and other project characteristics that are believed to be related to effort. Project characteristics (independent variables) are the input, and effort (dependent variable) is the output we wish to predict.

Expert-Based Effort Estimation: Represents the process of estimating effort by subjective means, and is often based on previous experience from developing/managing similar projects. This is by far the mostly used technique for Web effort estimation. Within this context, the attainment of accurate effort estimates relies on the competence and experience of individuals (e.g., project manager, developer).

Mean Magnitude of Relative Error: Calculates the Mean Magnitude of Relative Error (MRE), which measures for a given project the difference between actual and estimated effort relative to the actual effort. The mean takes into account the numerical value of every observation in the data distribution, and is sensitive to individual predictions with large MREs.

Prediction at Level l: Also known as Pred(l). It measures the percentage of estimates that are within l% of the actual values.

Chapter III
Patterns for Improving the Pragmatic Quality of Web Information Systems

Pankaj Kamthan
Concordia University, Canada

ABSTRACT

The significance of approaching Web information systems (WIS) from an engineering viewpoint is emphasized. A methodology for deploying patterns as means for improving the quality of WIS as perceived by their stakeholders is presented. In doing so, relevant quality attributes and corresponding stakeholder types are identified. The role of a process, feasibility issues, and the challenges in making optimal use of patterns are pointed out. Examples illustrating the use of patterns during macro- and micro-architecture design of a WIS, with the purpose of the improvement of quality attributes, are given.

INTRODUCTION

The Web information systems (WIS) (Holck, 2003) have begun to play an increasingly vital role in our daily activities of communication, information, and entertainment. This evidently has had an impact on how WIS have been developed and used over the last decade (Taniar & Rahayu, 2004).

The development environment of WIS is constantly facing technological and social challenges posed by new implementation languages, variations in user agents, demands for new services, and user classes from different cultural backgrounds, age groups, and capabilities. This motivates the need for a *methodical* approach toward the development life cycle and maintenance of "high-quality" WIS.

In this chapter, we address the quality of WIS as viewed by the stakeholders by considering WIS as end-products of a pattern-oriented engineering process. The purpose of this chapter is to motivate the use of patterns (Alexander, 1979) within a systematic approach to the development of WIS and to point out the benefits and challenges in doing so.

The rest of the chapter is organized as follows. We first outline the background and related work necessary for the discussion that follows and state our position. This is followed by the presentation of the pragmatic quality framework for representations in WIS, discussion of patterns as means for addressing the granular quality attributes in the framework, and examples. Next, challenges and directions for future research are outlined and, finally, concluding remarks are given.

BACKGROUND

In this section, we present a synopsis of Web engineering, quality in Web Applications, and patterns.

For the purpose of this chapter, we view the WIS as a specialized class of Web Applications. The need for managing increasing size and complexity of Web Applications and the necessity of a planned development led to the discipline of *Web Engineering* (Ginige & Murugesan, 2001; Powell, Jones, & Cutts, 1998), which has been treated comprehensively in recent years (Kappel, Proll, Reich, & Retschitzegger, 2006; Mendes & Mosley, 2006).

That WIS exhibit "high-quality" is critical for all stakeholders involved. If unaddressed, there is a potential for a resource in WIS to be rendered unreadable on a user agent of a customer, be inaccessible to someone who is visually impaired, or be prohibitive to adaptive maintenance by an engineer.

There have been various initiatives for addressing the quality of WIS: listing, organizing, and discussing relevant quality attributes (Brajnik, 2001; Dustin, Rashka, & McDiarmid, 2001; Hasan & Abuelrub, 2006; Offutt, 2002), including in some cases from a user's perspective (Ross, 2002), providing a means for evaluation (Mich, Franch, & Gaio, 2003; Olsina & Rossi, 2002). However,

these efforts are limited by one of more of the following issues: although quality attributes relevant to WIS are given, the means of addressing them are either suggested informally or not at all, or the focus is less on assurance (prevention) and more on evaluation (cure).

Patterns were formally introduced in the urban planning and architecture domain (Alexander, 1979; Alexander, Ishikawa, & Silverstein, 1977). A pattern is a proven solution to a recurring problem in a given context. The existence of *proven* and *rationalized* solutions based on established principles (Ghezzi, Jazayeri, & Mandrioli, 2003), that are specific to problems in a given *context* in a structured form, often makes patterns more practical in their applicability compared to other means for quality improvement, such as guidelines (Wesson, Cowley, 2003).

Formally, a pattern is typically described (Meszaros & Doble, 1998) using an ordered list of elements labeled as (pattern) *name, author, context, problem, forces, solution, example,* and *related patterns*. At times, the labels may vary across a community, and optional elements, such as those related to metadata, may be included to enrich the description. In the rest of the chapter, the elements of a pattern are highlighted in italics.

Over the last decade, patterns have been discovered in a variety of domains of interest including those that are applicable to the development of WIS: navigation design (Gillenson, Sherrell, & Chen, 2000; Rossi, Schwabe, & Lyardet, 1999); hypermedia design (German & Cowan, 2000; Rossi, Lyardet, & Schwabe, 1999); and Web Applications in general and electronic commerce in particular (Montero, Lozano, & González, 2002; Rossi & Koch, 2002; Van Duyne, Landay, & Hong, 2003).

There are some patterns available specifically for addressing maintainability concerns of Web Applications (Weiss, 2003). However, in some cases the *solutions* are highly technology-specific and the integration of patterns into any development process is not mentioned. There are also patterns available for specifically for addressing usability (Graham, 2003; Perzel & Kane, 1999) concerns of Web Applications. However, usability is viewed as an atomic (nondecomposable) concept and the integration of patterns into any user-centered development process is not shown unequivocally.

It has been shown that patterns can be successfully applied to the development of electronic commerce applications such as a shopping cart (Montero, López-Jaquero, & Molina, 2003) and other Web Applications (Garzotto, Paolini, Bolchini, & Valenti, 1999). However, in these cases, the relation of patterns to the underlying development process or to the improvement of quality is not discussed explicitly.

A PATTERN DEPLOYMENT METHODOLOGY FOR THE PRAGMATIC QUALITY OF WEB INFORMATION SYSTEMS

In this section, we propose a methodology for addressing the quality of WIS consisting of the following interrelated steps:

1. Conducting a Feasibility Study;
2. Selecting the Development Process Model;
3. Identifying and Organizing Quality Concerns from a Stakeholder Viewpoint;
4. Selecting Suitable Patterns; and
5. Applying Patterns.

Figure 1 provides an abstract view of this approach. We now discuss each of these aspects in detail.

Conducting a Feasibility Study

From a practical standpoint, it is desirable that the WIS development process, pragmatic quality concerns, and means for addressing them all be

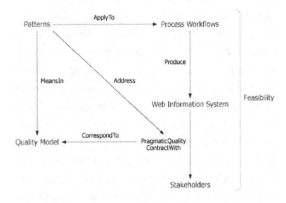

Figure 1. A high-level view of pattern-oriented, stakeholder-quality-centric, and feasibility-sensitive engineering for WIS

feasible. The feasibility study could be a part of the overall WIS project management planning activity.

Feasibility of Development Process

The process model for the development of a WIS will evidently depend on the organizational process maturity. This in turn involves several factors, including flexibility (agility), emphasis on quality, entry-exit conditions among workflows, and available tool support.

Feasibility of Quality Attributes

The expectations of improving the quality attributes of a WIS must be feasible in order to be practical.

We contend that the pragmatic quality attributes (discussed later) in Table 1 cannot (at least mathematically) be *completely* satisfied. For example, an a priori guarantee that a WIS will be usable to *all* users at *all* times in *all* task-specific or computing environment-specific situations that the users can find themselves in, is simply unrealistic.

Feasibility of Patterns

The adoption and subsequent deployment of patterns must also be viable. One of the benefits of pattern solutions is *conceptual* reuse. However, reuse of any knowledge, including the use of patterns in the development of WIS, is neither automatic, nor free. There is a cost in terms of time, effort, and resources of learning and adaptation involved in any reuse (Boehm, Abts, Brown, Chulani, Clark, Horowitz et al., 2001). For example, there is a learning curve involved in aspects such as understanding the pattern description at large, checking if and how accurately the *context* of the pattern matches with that of the *problem* of the WIS under development at hand, and the constraints under which the solution suggested by the pattern exists. The trade-offs and consequences associated with the proposed solution can help determine the suitability of the solution with respect to the required time and effort.

For an adoption of a pattern-based approach to the development of WIS, it is important that there be design and implementation patterns that can sufficiently "map" the solution space. There is no *a priori* guarantee that for every quality related problem, there will be pattern(s) available to solve it.

The issue of feasibility is evidently related to decision making. decision trees, analytical hierarchy process (AHP), and quality function deployment (QFD) are some of the commonly used techniques for tackling with the issue of decision support in general and prioritization in particular. Further discussion of this aspect is beyond the scope of this chapter.

Selecting the Development Process Model

The inclusion of patterns in the development of WIS cannot be ad-hoc or an afterthought. The deployment of patterns in the development of WIS must be carried out in lieu of the process model followed.

Because WIS are interactive, any selection and adoption of a process model must especially be sensitive to the users. A human-centric process whether linear or nonlinear for developing WIS will typically address aspects of both the analysis and the synthesis. During analysis, an understanding and specification of the problem domain will take place, leading to artifacts such as the domain model and use model, and based on them, the requirements specification. During synthesis, an understanding and specification of the solution domain will take place, leading to artifacts for the macroarchitecture design and microarchitecture design, followed by the implementation source code and data.

Extreme programming (XP) (Beck & Andres, 2005) is a broadly-used and well-tested agile methodology (Highsmith, 2002) for software development. The unified process (UP) (Jacobson, Booch, & Rumbaugh, 1999), which is a process *framework* that can be customized to produce a process model such as the rational unified process (RUP) (Kruchten, 2004). Both XP (Wallace, Raggett, & Aufgang, 2002) and RUP (Kappel et al., 2006) have been "tailored" to Web applications such as WIS. Patterns play an integral role in both these process initiatives.

Identifying and Organizing Quality Concerns from a Stakeholder Viewpoint

For the purpose of this chapter, we focus on the semiotic quality of WIS. Among the proposed approaches for quality in information systems (Eppler, 2001), we adopt and extend past treatments (Lindland, Sindre, & Sølvberg, 1994; Shanks, 1999). Our construction is as follows:

1. From a semiotics (Stamper, 1992) perspective, we can view a WIS on six interrelated levels: physical, empirical, syntactic, semantic, pragmatic, and social. Our focus in this chapter is only on the pragmatic level,

which is responsible for the relation of signs to their interpreters.

2. We contend that pragmatic quality is a multidimensional concept, and decompose it into granular levels that consist of known attributes that can be addressed directly or indirectly (Fenton & Pfleeger, 1997). For the definitions of these quality attributes, we adopt the IEEE Standard 1061-1998 (IEEE, 1998) and the ISO/IEC 9126-1 Standard (ISO, 2001).

3. We assign patterns as means for improving the quality attributes.

Table 1 summarizes this construction.

We contend that the quality attributes in Table 1 are necessary, however, we make no claim of their sufficiency.

The quality attributes within the same tier in Table 1 are not necessarily mutually exclusive. For example, the steps taken toward improving reliability (say, fault tolerance) may lead to redundant source code or data (that can be unfavorable to maintainability) and a sacrifice of ease-of-use (that can be unfavorable to usability).

The quality attributes in Tier 2 depend on that in Tier 1. For example, if a user cannot comprehend

Table 1. A model for the pragmatic quality of WIS

Semiotic Level	Quality Attributes	Means for Quality Assurance
Social Quality Concerns		
Pragmatic	[Tier 2] Maintainability, Reusability, Usability	Patterns
	[Tier 1] Comprehensibility, Performance, Reliability	
Physical, Empirical, Syntactic, and Semantic Quality Concerns		

the information in a WIS, he/she cannot use the WIS to its full potential.

The Stakeholder-Quality Attribute Mapping

We view pragmatic quality as a *contract* between a WIS and a stakeholder. For the sake of simplicity, we will limit ourselves to the discussion of (not necessarily mutually exclusive) stakeholders of the type *end-user* and *engineer*. The relevance of quality attributes in Table 1 varies with respect to stakeholder types:

- The quality attributes of direct concern to an end-user at the level Pragmatic-Tier 1 are comprehensibility, performance, and reliability.
- The quality attributes of direct concern to an engineer at the level Pragmatic-Tier 1 is comprehensibility.
- The quality attributes of direct concern to an end-user at the level Pragmatic-Tier 2 is usability. We will view accessibility as a special case of usability (Mendes & Mosley, 2006).
- The quality attributes of direct concern to an engineer at the level Pragmatic-Tier 2 are maintainability. We will consider modifiability, portability, and reusability as special cases of maintainability (Buschmann et al., 1996).

Finally, we note that the significance and priority of quality attributes will likely vary across different types of WIS. For example, the quality needs of a Campus Wide Information System (CWIS) or a shopping portal will vary from that of a WIS that provides tourist information.

Selecting Suitable Patterns

In general, the relationship between a quality attribute and a pattern is many-to-many (as, for example, is evident from Table 2). This leads to the need for selection of patterns. The underlying problem at hand along with the context in which it occurs will play a crucial role in selecting desirable patterns. Although there are preliminary results on automation such as an expert system-based decision analysis (McPhail & Deugo, 2001), the selection of patterns appropriate for a task largely remains a manual process.

The challenges in the patterns' selection process stem from a variety of factors:

- There are some patterns that have similar or same names but semantically different functionality, or patterns in different collections with similar intent or functionality but with different names. These patterns may have been (re)discovered independently. For example, STRUCTURED ANSWER from one collection (Lyardet, Rossi, & Schwabe, 1999) is similar to ORGANIZED SEARCH RESULTS from another collection (Van Duyne, Landay, & Hong, 2003).

- There are some patterns that may be classified into familiar categories (like "structural" or "behavioral") while others may be presented as a linear and loosely related informal collection. These collections may be only print-based, be only electronically-based, but may only rarely be a combination thereof. This could adversely impact locating desirable patterns (Segerståhl & Jokela, 2006).

- There are some patterns that are better documented than others. For example, some patterns may have gone through a comprehensive review process (or "shepherding") while others may have not.

- Often, patterns do not exist in isolation and are part of an overall vocabulary (or pattern "language") that attempts to solve a larger problem than an individual pattern could. Indeed, due to the context-driven relationships among them, the use of one pattern

can lead to the requirement of using other pattern(s). That means that the decision of selecting patterns cannot be singular; it must take into account the application of patterns as a collective.

- It is crucial that the team responsible for the WIS must have the knowledge and skills to be able to understand the constraints of a pattern, including the *forces* that must be overcome to implement a pattern in the available technologies-of-choice.

Applying Patterns

There are two main nonmutually exclusive concerns in the application of patterns: the understanding of the pattern description and the order in which patterns are applied.

The understanding of the underlying *problem*, the *context* in which it occurs, and the trade-offs and consequences of the proposed *solution*, is imperative. The appropriate use of patterns depending on the context of use is particularly critical. A pattern applied to an inappropriate *context* can compromise the benefit it offers (and give the appearance of an "antipattern"). For example, patterns that suggest some form of a graphical solution will not be applicable in situations where the underlying browser is text-based (such as in case of visually impaired users).

In the design phase, the patterns for high-level design are applied first, followed by the patterns for low-level design. A well-documented pattern description will have *context* and *related patterns* elements that may give an indication of the order of application of patterns. The patterns that precede the pattern under consideration will usually be mentioned in the *context* element and the patterns that succeed the pattern under consideration will usually be mentioned in the *related patterns* element.

In the following, we will limit ourselves to addressing the role of patterns in the design phase. It is not our intention in this chapter to provide a definitive list of patterns or point out every single pattern for a given quality attribute. Our selection of patterns is based on their generality, neutrality with respect to any specific application domain, broad availability, parity to the quality attribute at hand, suitability of the *context* and the *forces* (where available), and the credibility of the authors.

In order to distinguish the patterns from the main text, their names are listed in uppercase.

Macroarchitecture Design of WIS

The macroarchitecture design is the place where high-level design decisions, independent of any implementation paradigm or technology, are made. The patterns applicable to the macroarchitecture of WIS are the CLIENT-SERVER (Schmidt et al., 2000) and the MODEL-VIEW-CONTROLLER (MVC) (Buschmann et al., 1996).

The CLIENT-SERVER pattern supports maintainability. For example, a server or resources on the server-side could be modified without impacting the client. The CLIENT-SERVER pattern also supports reusability. For example, a single server can support multiple clients simultaneously, or a client could make simultaneous requests for resources residing on multiple servers. For instance, an Extensible Markup Language (XML) document could be located on one server while an Extensible Style Sheet Language Transformations (XSLT) style sheet on another server.

The MVC pattern supports maintainability. The separation of structure of content in a markup document from its presentation is one of the principles of Web Architecture (Jacobs & Walsh, 2004). By adopting this principle and an appropriate use of MVC, leads to a separation of semantically-different aspects into three components, namely model, view, and controller, and a minimization of coupling between those components. Thus, modifications to one component are localized and lead to minimal propagation of changes to other components. This improves

maintainability of a WIS. The MVC pattern also supports reusability. The same model in a MVC could be used with multiple views. For example, the same information could be transformed and delivered based upon different browser environments or user needs.

In spite of several implementations of MVC available in a variety of programming languages such as Java and application frameworks like Ajax (Mahemoff, 2006), we note that a true separation of model, view, and controller at the macroarchitecture level alone is hard to realize in practice. It is with the help of, say, object-oriented microarchitecture design patterns (Gamma et al., 1995) such as OBSERVER, COMPOSITE, and STRATEGY, that a separation is achieved.

Microarchitecture Design of WIS

The microarchitecture design is the place where low-level design decisions that must be implementable are cast. In the following, we will focus only on the design aspects that impact pragmatic quality. As such, our attention is geared more toward client-side rather than server-side concerns.

Interaction design (Preece, Rogers, & Sharp, 2002) is an approach to design that focuses on the human as well as the computer aspects, to make both the content and the user interface useful, easy-to-use, and enjoyable. Many of the patterns available for interaction design in general (Tidwell, 2005) are also applicable to the WIS.

We now consider three of the most critical interaction design aspects of the WIS, namely information design, navigation design, and search design:

- **Information design:** The classification of information is a conventional approach by humans to understanding information. The information organization patterns (Van Duyne, Landay, & Hong, 2003) contribute toward the information architecture of a WIS and, when use appropriately, aid comprehensibility and usability. For example, the WHAT'S NEW PAGE pattern that provides newly added information to a WIS could include the CHRONOLOGICAL ORGANIZATION pattern. A document in a WIS that contains a list of countries in the United Nations could be based on the ALPHABETICAL ORGANIZATION pattern. The users of a WIS can vary in their capabilities and preferences, and may find one view of information to be more usable than another. The MIRRORWORLD pattern (German & Cowan, 2000) provides two or more views of the same information. Now, documents in a WIS may contain images for presenting some information such as the corporate logo or product pictures. The FAST-DOWNLOADING IMAGES pattern suggests creation of images optimized for color and size in an appropriate format, and thus aids accessibility and performance. The REUSABLE IMAGES pattern suggests caching images that appear at multiple places in a WIS, and thereby aids performance.

- **Navigation design:** Navigation is traversal in information space for some purpose such as casual or targeted browsing for information or complementing a reading sequence (like in electronic books). Intra- and inter-document navigation within the context of WIS is realized by the use of hypermedia (German & Cowan, 2000). There are various patterns for navigating through WIS proposed over the years (Lyardet & Rossi, 1998; Van Duyne, Landay, & Hong, 2003). The navigation patterns, when use appropriately, aid usability. For example, the BREADCRUMBS pattern could be used to inform the user of his/her location and the FLY-OUT MENU pattern could be used to present content organized in a "compound" menu where each menu item itself has a submenu. The CLEAR ENTRY POINTS

pattern presents only a few entry points into the interfaces, which can restrict the navigation to a specific category and make it task-oriented. Any interaction design must take exceptional behavior into consideration to support usability. The MISSING LINK pattern (German & Cowan, 2000) informs the user that certain hyperlink does not exist and suggests alternatives. There are navigation design patterns that aid comprehensibility (Tidwell, 2005). For example, the WIZARD pattern leads the user through the interface step by step for carrying out tasks in a prescribed order. The RESPONSIVE DISCLOSURE pattern starts with a very minimal interface, and guides a user through a series of steps by showing more of the interface as the user completes each step. These two patterns could, for example, be used for carrying out a registration process.

- **Search design:** The goal of searching is finding information. Searching is not native to WIS, but has become ever more challenging as the amount of information to be searched through increases. There are various patterns for searching WIS proposed over the years (Lyardet, Rossi, & Schwabe, 1999; Van Duyne, Landay, & Hong, 2003). The searching patterns, when used appropriately, support comprehensibility and performance. The use of STRAIGHTFORWARD SEARCH FORMS pattern with a SIMPLE SEARCH INTERFACE pattern, that requires minimal technical background on part of the user, will contribute toward comprehensibility. The use of SELECTABLE SEARCH SPACE pattern that can restrict the search to a specific category, SELECTABLE KEYWORDS pattern that based on the past experience can suggest keywords for improving subsequent search results, and ORGANIZED SEARCH RESULTS pattern that present a summary of

Figure 2. An organized assembly of interaction design patterns in the development of WIS

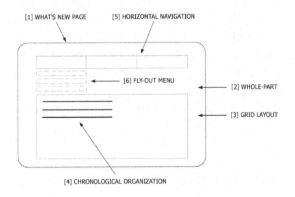

Table 2. Pragmatic quality attributes of a WIS and correspondingly rated patterns

Pragmatic Quality Attribute	Pattern(s)
Comprehensibility	ALPHABETICAL ORGANIZA-TION(+), CHRONOLOGICAL ORGANIZATION(+), RESPONSIVE DISCLOSURE(+), SIMPLE SEARCH INTERFACE(+), STRAIGHTFOR-WARD SEARCH FORMS(+), WIZ-ARD(+)
Maintainability	CLIENT-SERVER(+), INTRODUCE REDUNDANCY(−), MODEL-VIEW-CONTROLLER(+)
Performance	FAST-DOWNLOADING IMAGES(+), ORGANIZED SEARCH RESULTS(+), SELECTABLE KEYWORDS(+), SE-LECTABLE SEARCH SPACE(+)
Reliability	FAILURE NOTIFICATION(+), IN-TRODUCE REDUNDANCY(+)
Reusability	CLIENT-SERVER(+), MODEL-VIEW-CONTROLLER(+)
Usability	BREADCRUMBS(+), CLEAR ENTRY POINTS(+), FAST-DOWNLOADING IMAGES(+), FLY-OUT MENU(+), MISSING LINK(+), MIRROR-WORLD(+), WHAT'S NEW PAGE(+)

the most relevant search results, improve the effectiveness of the searching activity.

For addressing reliability (specifically, availability) concerns, the microarchitecture design of server-side components of a WIS could use a number of patterns (Ahluwalia & Jain, 2006). For example, extra measures (unrelated to the functionality of the WIS) could be included by using the INTRODUCE REDUNDANCY pattern, and if and when the need arises, a failure message could be relayed using the FAILURE NOTIFICATION pattern. Evidently, any redundancy increases maintenance responsibilities.

Figure 2 gives an abstract illustration of some of the interaction design patterns mentioned previously. The numbers indicate the order of application and the FLY-OUT MENU items are shown in dashed lines to exemplify nonpermanence.

Table 2 summarizes the patterns mentioned in this section. A symbol of (+) adjacent to a pattern name implies a positive impact on the corresponding quality attribute, whereas a (−) implies a negative impact. As mentioned earlier, the list of patterns is by no means complete and is subject to evolution.

FUTURE TRENDS

The work presented in this chapter can be extended in a few different directions, which we now briefly outline.

A possible extension of the model presented in Table 1 is the use of patterns for improving the quality of other, particularly higher-level, semiotic quality concerns. For example, one extension of interest would be addressing the social quality concerns, namely credibility, privacy, and security. (We note that not all issues pertaining to these attributes, such as those related to underlying platform or operating system, are within the purview of the development of WIS.) Although there is an apparent lack of patterns for credibility, patterns for privacy (Hafiz, 2006) and security (Schumacher, 2003; Schumacher et al., 2006) have been recently proposed, and some of these could be used in the development of WIS. We note that such extensions would require that the aspects of microarchitecture design to which the patterns are applied be different than those dealt with in this chapter.

In this chapter, it was assumed that the microarchitecture design is being created from scratch. Refactoring (Fowler et al., 1999) involves structural transformations with the aim of improving *existing* designs by eradicating the undesirable(s) from an artifact while preserving its behavioral semantics. Refactoring has been adopted as one of the core practices in XP. There are patterns available that serve as a guide for carrying out refactorings of existing object-oriented designs to patterns (Kerievsky, 2005), which when used appropriately, can lead to reduction of structural complexity (thereby improving the potential for comprehensibility), reduce redundancy (and thus resource utilization, thereby improving efficiency), and offer better prospects for reusability. An extension of the notion of refactoring to the improvement of interaction designs of WIS where they could be steered to well-known patterns would be of interest.

It is known that standards provide a common ground based on consensus and, when applied well (Schneidewind & Fenton, 1996), can contribute toward improvement of productivity and communicability across project teams. There exist initiatives for standardizing the development of Web Applications such as the IEEE Standard 2001-2002 (IEEE, 2003). For a widespread acceptance of patterns in the development of WIS, the adoption of patterns in such standards efforts will be crucial.

Finally, the chapter focused on the improvement of the *product* quality. Investigating the impact of patterns on *process* quality would also be of interest. Indeed, as patterns are increasingly used and get entrenched in an organizational environment, they can become a *lingua franca* of teams. In due course, teams' experience that certain patterns are used more frequently than others, and this collection converges to a common-to-all cohesive set that acts like a *handbook* for guidance and reference. Whether the existence and use of this pattern "handbook" leads to a visible improvement in productivity (such as savings in time or effort) could be a subject of potential research.

CONCLUSION

A disciplined and methodical approach toward the development of large-scale WIS is necessary for their longevity and for acceptance by their stakeholders. Integral to this is a systematic and lasting view toward pragmatic quality and means for addressing it.

Patterns provide one such practical means when they are located, adopted, and applied with care taking feasibility issues into consideration. However, for patterns to continue being useful as entities of knowledge (Garzas & Piattini, 2005; May & Taylor, 2003) within the Zachman Framework for Enterprise Architecture (Zachman, 1987), they must be adequately described and documented, readily available and findable, and evolve with the needs of the WIS. In other words, the quality of WIS will intimately depend on the quality of patterns themselves.

In conclusion, an initial investment toward a pattern-oriented approach toward quality improvement can benefit the organizations hosting WIS in the long-term. Like with other products, embracing any change requires a reflection and reexamination of the current state of the development of WIS. It also requires considering nonfunctional aspects of WIS as first-class concerns. For such a change to come to a realization, the current culture (Wiegers, 1996) in the organizations will need to evolve.

REFERENCES

Ahluwalia, K. S., & Jain, A. (2006, October 21-23). High availability design patterns. In *Proceedings of the Thirteenth Conference on Pattern Languages of Programs (PLoP 2006)*, Portland, USA.

Alexander, C. (1979). *The timeless way of building*. Oxford University Press.

Alexander, C., Ishikawa, S., & Silverstein, M. (1977). *A pattern language: Towns, buildings, construction*. Oxford University Press.

Beck, K., & Andres, C. (2005). *Extreme programming explained: Embrace change* (2nd ed.). Addison-Wesley.

Boehm, B. W., Abts, C., Brown, A. W., Chulani, S., Clark, B. K., Horowitz, E., et al. (2001). *Software cost estimation with COCOMO II*. Prentice Hall.

Brajnik, G. (2001, June 4-6). Towards valid quality models for Web sites. In *Proceedings of the Seventh Conference on Human Factors and the Web (HFWeb 2001)*, Madison, USA.

Buschmann, F., Meunier, R., Rohnert, H., Sommerlad, P., & Stal, M. (1996). Pattern oriented software architecture: *A system of patterns* (Vol. 1). John Wiley and Sons.

Dustin, E., Rashka, J., & McDiarmid, D. (2001). *Quality Web systems: Performance, security, and usability*. Addison-Wesley.

Eppler, M. J. (2001). The concept of information quality: An interdisciplinary evaluation of recent information quality frameworks. *Studies in Communication Sciences, 1*(2), 167-182.

Fenton, N. E., & Pfleeger, S. L. (1997). *Software metrics: A rigorous & practical approach*. International Thomson Computer Press.

Fowler, M., Beck, K., Brant, J., Opdyke, W., & Roberts, D. (1999). *Refactoring: Improving the design of existing code*. Addison-Wesley.

Gamma, E., Helm, R., Johnson, R., & Vlissides, J. (1995). *Design patterns: Elements of reusable object-oriented software*. Addison-Wesley.

Garzas, J., & Piattini, M. (2005). An ontology for microarchitectural design knowledge. *IEEE Software, 22*(2), 28-33.

Garzotto, F., Paolini, P., Bolchini, D., & Valenti, S. (1999, November 15-18). "Modeling-by-Patterns" of Web applications. In *Proceedings of the International Workshop on the World Wide Web and Conceptual Modeling (WWWCM 1999)*, Paris, France.

German, D. M., & Cowan, D. D. (2000, January 4-7). Towards a unified catalog of hypermedia design patterns. In *Proceedings of the Thirty Third Hawaii International Conference on System Sciences (HICSS 2000)*, Maui, USA.

Ghezzi, C., Jazayeri, M., & Mandrioli, D. (2003). *Fundamentals of software engineering* (2nd ed.). Prentice-Hall.

Gillenson, M., Sherrell, D. L., & Chen, L. (2000). A taxonomy of Web site traversal patterns and structures. *Communications of the AIS, 3*(4).

Ginige, A., & Murugesan, S. (2001). Web engineering: An introduction. *IEEE Multimedia, 8*(1), 14-18.

Graham, I. (2003). *A pattern language for Web usability*. Addison-Wesley.

Hafiz, M. (2006, October 21-23). A collection of privacy design patterns. In *Proceedings of the Thirteenth Conference on Pattern Languages of Programs (PLoP 2006)*, Portland, USA.

Hasan, L. R., & Abuelrub, E. (2006, June 19-21). Criteria for evaluating quality of Web sites. In *Proceedings of the Sixth IBIMA Conference on Managing Information in Digital Economy*, Bonn, Germany.

Highsmith, J. (2002). *Agile software development ecosystems*. Addison-Wesley.

Holck, J. (2003, January 6-9). Perspectives on Web information systems. *In Proceedings of the Thirty Sixth Annual Hawaii International Conference on System Sciences (HICSS 2003)*, Island of Hawaii, USA.

IEEE. (1998). IEEE Standard 1061-1998. IEEE Standard for a Software Quality Metrics Methodology, *IEEE Computer Society.*

IEEE. (2003). IEEE Standard 2001-2002. IEEE Recommended Practice for the Internet - Web Site Engineering, Web Site Management, and Web Site Life Cycle. Internet Best Practices Working Group, *IEEE Computer Society.*

ISO. (2001). ISO/IEC 9126-1:2001. Software Engineering -- Product Quality -- Part 1: Quality Model. *International Organization for Standardization (ISO).*

Jacobs, I., & Walsh, N. (2004). Architecture of the World Wide Web (Vol. 1). W3C recommendation. *World Wide Web Consortium (W3C).*

Jacobson, I., Booch, G., & Rumbaugh, J. (1999). *The unified software development process.* Addison-Wesley.

Kappel, G., Pröll, B., Reich, S., & Retschitzegger, W. (2006). *Web engineering.* John Wiley and Sons.

Kerievsky, J. (2005). *Refactoring to patterns.* Addison-Wesley.

Kruchten, P. (2004). *the rational unified process: An introduction* (3rd Edition). Addison-Wesley.

Lindland, O. I., Sindre, G., & Sølvberg, A. (1994). Understanding quality in conceptual modeling. *IEEE Software, 11*(2), 42-49.

Lyardet, F., & Rossi, G. (1998, August 11-14). Patterns for designing navigable information spaces. In *Proceedings of the Fifth Conference on Pattern Languages of Programs (PLoP 1998)*, Monticello, USA.

Lyardet, F., Rossi, G., & Schwabe, D. (1999, July 8-10). Patterns for adding search capabilities to Web information systems. In *Proceedings of the Fourth European Conference on Pattern Languages of Programming and Computing (EuroPLoP 1999)*, Irsee, Germany.

Mahemoff, M. (2006). *Ajax design patterns.* O'Reilly Media.

May, D., & Taylor, P. (2003). Knowledge management with patterns. *Communications of the ACM, 46*(7), 94-99.

McPhail, J. C., & Deugo, D. (2001, June 4-7). Deciding on a pattern. In *Proceedings of the Fourteenth International Conference on Industrial and Engineering Applications of Artificial Intelligence and Expert Systems (IEA/AIE 2001)*, Budapest, Hungary.

Mendes, E., & Mosley, N. (2006). *Web engineering.* Springer-Verlag.

Meszaros, G., & Doble, J. (1998). A pattern language for pattern writing. In R. C. Martin, D. Riehle, & F. Buschmann (Eds.), *Pattern languages of program design 3* (pp. 529-574. Addison-Wesley.

Mich, L., Franch, M., & Gaio, L. (2003). Evaluating and designing Web site quality. *IEEE Multimedia, 10*(1), 34-43.

Montero, F., López-Jaquero, V., & Molina, J. P. (2003, September 1-2). Improving e-shops environments by using usability patterns. In *Proceedings of the Second Workshop on Software and Usability Cross-Pollination*, Zürich, Switzerland.

Montero, F., Lozano, M., & González, P. (2002, August 5-7). Designing Web sites by using design patterns. In *Proceedings of the Second Latin American Conference on Pattern Languages of Programming (SugarLoafPLoP 2002)*, Rio de Janeiro, Brazil.

Offutt, J. (2002). Quality attributes of Web software applications. *IEEE Software, 19*(2), 25-32.

Olsina, L., & Rossi, G. (2002). Measuring Web application quality with WebQEM. *IEEE Multimedia, 9*(4), 20-29.

Powell, T. A., Jones, D. L., & Cutts, D. C. (1998). *Web site engineering.* Prentice Hall.

Perzel, K., & Kane, D. (1999, August 15-18). Usability patterns for applications on the World Wide Web. In *Proceedings of the Sixth Conference on Pattern Languages of Programs (PLoP 1999),* Monticello, USA.

Preece, J., Rogers, Y., & Sharp, H. (2002). *Interaction design: Beyond human-computer interaction.* John Wiley and Sons.

Ross, M. (2002). Quality in Web design for visually impaired users. *Software Quality Journal, 10*(4), 285-298.

Rossi, G., & Koch, N. (2002, July 3-7). Patterns for adaptive Web applications. In *Proceedings of the Seventh European Conference on Pattern Languages of Programs (EuroPLoP 2002),* Irsee, Germany.

Rossi, G., Lyardet, F. D., & Schwabe, D. (1999). Developing hypermedia applications with methods and patterns. *ACM Computing Surveys, 31*(4es).

Rossi, G., Schwabe, D., & Lyardet, F. (1999, May 11-14). Improving Web information systems with navigational patterns. In *Proceedings of the Eighth International World Wide Web Conference (WWW8),* Toronto, Canada.

Schmidt, D. C., Stal, M., Rohnert, H., & Buschmann, F. (2000). *Pattern-oriented software architecture: Patterns for concurrent and networked objects* (Vol. 2). John Wiley and Sons.

Schneidewind, N. F., & Fenton, N. E. (1996). Do standards improve product quality? *IEEE Software, 13*(1), 22-24.

Schumacher, M. (2003). *Security engineering with patterns: Origins, theoretical models, and new applications.* Springer-Verlag.

Schumacher, M., Fernandez-Buglioni, E., Hybertson, D., Buschmann, F., & Sommerlad, P. (2006). *Security patterns: Integrating security and systems engineering.* John Wiley and Sons.

Segerståhl, K., & Jokela, T. (2006, April 22-27). Usability of interaction patterns. In *Proceedings of the CHI 2006 Conference on Human Factors in Computing Systems,* Montréal, Canada.

Shanks, G. (1999, September 29). Semiotic approach to understanding representation in information systems. In *Proceedings of the information systems Foundations Workshop,* Sydney, Australia.

Stamper, R. (1992, October 5-8). Signs, organizations, norms and information systems. In *Proceedings of the Third Australian Conference on information systems,* Wollongong, Australia.

Taniar, D., & Rahayu, J. W. (2004). *Web information systems.* Hershey, PA: Idea Group.

Tidwell, J. (2005). *Designing interfaces: Patterns for effective interaction design.* O'Reilly Media.

Van Duyne, D. K., Landay, J., & Hong, J. I. (2003). *The design of sites: Patterns, principles, and processes for crafting a customer-centered Web experience.* Addison-Wesley.

Wallace, D., Raggett, I., & Aufgang, J. (2002). *Extreme programming for Web projects.* Addison-Wesley.

Weiss, M. (2003, September 8-12). Patterns for Web applications. In *Proceedings of the Tenth Conference on Pattern Languages of Programs (PLoP 2003),* Urbana, USA.

Wesson, J., & Cowley, L. (2003, September 1-2). Designing with patterns: Possibilities and pitfalls. In *Proceedings of the Second Workshop on Software and Usability Cross-Pollination*, Zürich, Switzerland.

Wiegers, K. (1996). *Creating a software engineering culture*. Dorset House.

Zachman, J. A. (1987) A framework for information systems architecture. *IBM Systems Journal*, *26*(3), 276-292.

KEY TERMS

Agile Development: A philosophy that embraces uncertainty, encourages team communication, values customer satisfaction, vies for early delivery, and promotes sustainable development.

Pattern: A proven solution to a recurring problem in a given context.

Pattern Language: A set of interrelated patterns that forms a gestalt in which each of its patterns collaborate to solve a more fundamental problem that is not explicitly addressed by any individual pattern.

Quality: The totality of features and characteristics of a product or a service that bear on its ability to satisfy stated or implied needs.

Quality Model: A set of characteristics and the relationships between them that provide the basis for specifying quality requirements and evaluating quality of an entity.

Semiotics: The field of study of signs and their representations.

Software Process: A set of activities, methods, practices, and transformations that are used to develop and maintain software and its associated products.

Web Engineering: A discipline concerned with the establishment and use of sound scientific, engineering and management principles and disciplined and systematic approaches to the successful development, deployment, and maintenance of high-quality Web Applications.

Chapter IV
Evaluation of the Effectiveness of Small and Medium Sized Businesses Web Sites in a Business to Business Context

Rosemary Stockdale
Massey University, New Zealand

Chad Lin
Curtin University of Technology, Australia

ABSTRACT

Many small and medium sized businesses (SMEs) have set up their own Web sites, as part of their business strategies, to improve their competitiveness and responsiveness. Careful evaluation and adoption of Web sites by SMEs can assist them in improving the effectiveness of their venture into e-commerce. This chapter discusses and analyses the effectiveness of SME business to business Web sites from a user perspective. An effective method of evaluating a Web site can contribute to the development of more quality Web sites and greater realization of benefits. Therefore, an established evaluation instrument (eQual) is used to assess 80 Web sites in terms of usability, information quality, and interaction and service. The analysis shows that although a significant number of sites reflect little understanding of the attributes of good design or potential benefits to be gained from Web sites, there are examples of competent and effective Web site use.

INTRODUCTION

The importance of e-commerce to small and medium sized businesses (SMEs) is growing as globalization and rapid technological changes have brought new opportunities as well as risks, via e-commerce, to the business environment. For example, SMEs play a crucial role in national economies and are estimated to account for 80% of global economic growth (Jutla, Bodorik, & Dhaliqal, 2002). One aspect of SME e-commerce activity that is acknowledged but rarely examined is their use of Web sites. Web sites are a "critical component of the rapidly growing phenomenon of e-commerce" (Loiacono, Watson, & Goodhue, 2002, p. 4) and their successful design and use can alter the effectiveness of an SME's venture into e-commerce. However, SMEs are still lagging behind larger organizations in the adoption and evaluation of their e-commerce activities despite the benefits it offers (Lin, Cripps, & Bode, 2005). Understanding the factors used by customers to evaluate Web site quality can serve as a basis for creating and improving Web sites (Webb & Webb, 2004).

Numerous studies have been conducted to examine the effectiveness of the Web sites in general (Hong & Kim, 2004; Shiels, McIvor, & O'Reilly, 2003; Tsai & Chai, 2005). There have been calls for more extensive work into the analysis and evaluation of Web sites in the business to business context in particular (Chakraborty, Lala, & Warren, 2002; Ellinger, Lynch, Andzulis, & Smith, 2003; Loiacono et al., 2002). However, relatively few studies have been conducted in SMEs. Therefore, the objectives of the chapter are to: (1) present and discuss the current Web site evaluation literature on SMEs in general; and (2) assess the quality of Web sites within the small business sector of one regional area within Australia, using an established quality evaluation instrument, eQual (Barnes & Vigden, 2002). This chapter contributes to a better understanding of how SMEs are addressing the constructs of Web site development identified in the literature. These constructs have been incorporated into eQual and tested in other environments (Barnes & Vigden, 2001, 2002, 2003). A deeper understanding of SME Web sites and where areas for improvement lie will enable development of support frameworks to improve SMEs' recognition and realization of benefits from their Web sites; a prerequisite for encouraging e-commerce adoption (Poon & Swatman, 1999).

BACKGROUND

Web Sites for SMEs

Several initiatives have been launched to improve electronic adoption rates and e-competencies (Jones Donald Strategic Partners, 2000; NOIE, 2002), but many SMEs are failing to achieve the levels of e-commerce abilities required to benefits from Internet based business (Lin, Cripps et al., 2005; Walker, Bode, Burn, & Webster, 2003). Smaller businesses are often caught between the need to understand the dynamic and frequently intimidating electronic environment and the need to respond to the many calls to conduct more business online (Goode, 2002; Walker et al., 2003). Their subsequent attempts to trade online results in e-commerce activity that is unproductive such as launching ineffective Web sites, ignoring customer e-mails, and failing to efficiently fulfill online orders. Where smaller businesses turn to consultants to overcome their own lack of expertise, results often fall short of expectations as SMEs do not have sufficient knowledge to judge the effectiveness of a consultant's work prior to implementation (Bode & Burn, 2001).

One highly visible aspect of e-commerce activity that is often seen as the first step toward online trading is the launch of a Web site. Statistics show that 36% of small and 82% of medium-sized businesses in Australia have established a Web site (ABS, 2003). Two thirds of SMEs believe that their

Web site enhances their business effectiveness, by increasing visibility and accessibility, improving communications, and increasing sales (ABS, 2003). This accords with Loiacono et al's (2002, p. 4) view that Web sites "play a significant role in the overall marketing communication mix." The implementation of B2B Web sites is seen as an important stage in e-commerce development (Ellinger et al., 2003) and a crucial part of a firm's use of the Internet for communicating, entertaining, and interaction with stakeholders (Chakraborty et al., 2002).

Despite the statistics and the frequent mention of the use of Web sites in much of the research on SME e-commerce adoption (Bode & Burn, 2001; Daniel, Wilson, & Myers, 2002; Korchak & Rodman, 2001; Tsao, Lin & Lin, 2004), the quality of such Web sites and the need to determine their function is rarely addressed (Manuel, 2004). Auger (2005) discusses the impact of design sophistication and level of interactivity in increasing the number of visitors and the impact on overall performance. While design sophistication was not found to necessarily positively affect performance, interactivity is an important asset. Fry, Tyrall, Pugh, and Wyld (2004) examine the elements of accessibility and visibility among the increasing number of sites on the Web. They note however, that government targeting of small businesses in this field tends to overly emphasize the technical rather than business aspects of Web site use. There are numerous online sources offering, often conflicting, advice and help on setting up a Web site while business organizations and government sources continue to encourage smaller businesses to launch Web sites. The proliferation of sites has increased the imperative for businesses to have some knowledge of what they intend their site to achieve.

That many of these sites are subsequently deemed ineffective by their owners is often due to an uncertainty over the role of the site and a lack of understanding of how to integrate Internet strategies into an existing business. Indecision and lack of knowledge leads to ineffective sites and consequent disappointment in recognizable benefits (Ellinger et al., 2003; Stockdale & Standing, 2004). Therefore, it is critical for these SMEs to understand customer requirements and to enhance their Web accordingly. A SME with a Web site that is difficult to use and understand can weaken the firm's presence on the Internet (Barnes & Vidgen, 2002). According to Turban and Gehrke (2000), there are significant discrepancies between factors identified in various academic publications and those rated in consumer surveys. Therefore, there is a need to identify critical success factors for effective Web site usage by SMEs both from the customers' viewpoint and from the designer and owner perspective. Such factors can contribute to the ability of SMEs to improve their Web sites over time, then benchmark against competitors and best practice in any industry (Barnes & Vidgen, 2002).

Evaluation

Evaluation is a complex but critical function of any business. The need to justify expenditure, to judge the effectiveness of a project or to measure academic achievement are common faces of evaluation. Calls for more holistic evaluations have been echoed in the field of information systems where the growth of electronic commerce has emphasized the need for more effective evaluations of IT (Stockdale & Standing, 2006). However, evaluation is not often carried out. For example, investigation by Lin and Pervan (2003), found that nearly 35% of large Australian organizations did not evaluate their IT and 67% did not determine whether expected benefits were being achieved. For those who have evaluated, evaluations have often been used to justify economic outlay and strategic achievements, with the required definitive outcomes such as a pass-or-fail/ yes-or-no judgment (Love, Irani, Standing, Lin & Burn, 2005; Smithson & Hirschheim, 1998). These evaluation processes often lead to inaccurate and mechanistic methods and overly concrete outcomes (Lin, Pervan, & McDermid, 2005; Smithson & Hirschheim, 1998). As a result, organizations are under increasing pressure to find a way to evaluate the contribution of their IT to business performance, as well as to find reliable ways to ensure that the business benefits from IT are actually realized (Lin & Pervan, 2003).

The purpose of an evaluation is a key factor in planning how it should be carried out. Where definitive measurements are available and a judgment required on the success of a system, then an objective assessment is possible. Where an understanding of how users perceive the usefulness of a Web site or what makes them repeat their visits is required, more holistic methods are needed. The subjectivity the user brings to the Web site must be reflected in the evaluation if understanding is to be achieved. The subjectivity inherent in such evaluations should not be seen as a weakness of the evaluation but rather as a strength. Although these methods reduce an evaluator's ability to find "generalizable truths," it does allow for a local solution or local meaning to be identified (House, 1980). In the context of Web sites this is an important step toward achieving real benefits from an evaluation. Understanding of the local solution, in this case the Web site, is preferable to a generalizable judgment.

Web Site Evaluation

Many B2B Web sites have emerged from the rapid development of the Internet. As the number of Web sites has increased, it becomes critical to evaluate their effectiveness. This requires systemized evaluation criteria (Hong & Kim, 2004), constant assessment, careful management, frequent updates (Albert, Goes, & Gupta, 2004), and ongoing innovation (Reichheld, Markey, Jr., & Hopton, 2000). Indeed, Web site evaluation is the assessment of the effectiveness of the online trading in fulfilling or meeting business goals. It is an important way of ensuring that the Web site meets the

business requirements of SMEs as well as the needs of their users. It has a range of potential advantages such as: (a) reduction of the risk of budget or scope blow-out; (b) refinement of the target and the scope of Web site activities (e.g., redevelopment and site marketing); and (c) identification and realization of the benefits at an acceptable cost (van der Merwe & Bekker, 2003).

Effective Web sites are usually dynamic, and subject to constant update, innovation, and management (Albert et al., 2004). To evaluate a Web site as a static object loses meaning, and sets the evaluation into Walsham's (1993) category of ritualistic measurement to reinforce existing judgments rather than as a means to achieve improvement. Web site evaluation has developed in an ad hoc way using a variety of criteria and methods. Mich, Franch, and Gaio (2003) have developed a model based on the use of Cicero's rhetoric to gain complete coverage of evaluation. This model takes the criteria of who, what, when, where, and how that are familiar in the Content, Context, and Process evaluation framework originally developed by Symons (1991). In contrast, Zhang and von Dran (2002) develop their arguments from Kano's model of customer expectations for feature categorization and also apply the nature of quality changes over time.

The underlying concept of these different models arises from the consideration of what is being evaluated and for what purpose the evaluation is being carried out. This affects the different way that Web site elements are considered in evaluations, such as domains, the ongoing of time and even cultural differences (Aladwani & Palvia, 2002; Mich et al., 2003; Schubert, 2003; Zhang & von Dran, 2002). Such elements are not of equal importance and have to be assessed by weighting according to the nature of the evaluation.

The advantages of evaluating multiple Web sites regularly are significant in the context of assessing these features. In contrast, to get an in-depth impression from a user perspective and a more complete understanding of user behavior requires an individual approach (Ivory, Sinha, & Hearst, 2001). An individual approach is necessary for improving human interfaces, although it can also provide some basic and objective measurements. Mich et al. (2003) contribute by calling for consideration of the stakeholders' views within the evaluation. The stakeholders vary according to the reason for the evaluation. For example, users hold a central stake when user satisfaction is under consideration, but developers may have a greater influence on evaluations of Web site design. In both cases, users and designers are stakeholders in the Web site. Intention to use a Web site can be considered as a contribution to the assessment of a Web site from the user satisfaction perspective (Chiu, Hsieh, & Kao, 2005). User satisfaction has long been a significant measure of information systems success (DeLone & McLean, 1992) and this is echoed in the many evaluations that take this perspective. An evaluation instrument that is adaptable to a variety of uses requires that the instrument be easy to use, parsimonious to enable adaptation, and flexible enough to allow evaluator insights to be recorded (Barnes & Vigden, 2002; Mich et al., 2003).

RESEARCH DESIGN AND FINDINGS

To assess the quality of Web sites within the small business sector of one regional area within Australia, an established quality evaluation instrument, eQual (version 4), is used (Barnes & Vigden, 2002). The instrument was designed and tested over several years (Barnes & Vigden, 2001, 2002, 2003) as a method for assessing the quality of a firm's e-commerce offerings through its Web site. EQual (formerly known as WebQual) has been under development at the University of Bath since 1998. When using the instrument, Web site users are asked to rate target sites against a range of qualities using a seven point scale. The range of qualities have evolved through an iterative process, drawing on

literature from mainstream IS research, service quality literature in marketing and e-commerce, and usability research from the human-computer interaction literature. Workshops and empirical research have been used to further refine the range of qualities contained in the questionnaire (Barnes & Vigden, 2001, 2002, 2003). EQual enables Web site quality to be judged through three dimensions: usability, information quality, and service interaction quality. In developing the instrument, Barnes and Vigden (2002) identified five factors of importance that are encompassed within the three dimensions: usability, design, information, trust, and empathy.

This research examines the Web sites of 80 SMEs based in Western Australia (WA). The region appears particularly suited to the development of e-commerce. WA has a high percentage of SMEs in the private sector that employ over 47% of nonagricultural workers (ABS, 2003). It is a technologically well developed region with a strong exporting economy. The use of e-commerce applications is well suited to its geographical isolation both within the state and from its export destinations. B2B e-commerce is the most profitable sector of online trading (Ellinger et al., 2003), although it has been insufficiently addressed in Web site evaluation research (Loiacono et al., 2002). This research targets B2B SMEs, but includes firms that also trade B2C. Purely B2C firms are not addressed in this research.

Data Collection and Analysis

Eighty SMEs trading in Western Australia have been identified through Web searches, use of online directories, Yellow Pages, and local knowledge. SMEs are defined according to the Australian Bureau of Statistics as firms employing less than 200 full time equivalent workers and that are not subsidiaries, public companies, or incorporated bodies (ABS, 2003).

An initial analysis of 10 Web sites was made by the authors to test eQual 4.0, the research instrument. This also enabled them to make a preliminary assessment of the range of SME Web sites in WA. The evaluation of the remaining 70 Web sites was then carried out by two businessmen and six research assistants under the guidance of the authors. The research instrument consists of 23 questions with a Likert scale of 1 to 7. After the initial analysis, the authors added a comment area for each question to collect further data on the evaluators' responses to each Web site. The qualitative nature of the additional responses enables the context of each Web site to be considered and supports greater understanding of the "why" behind identified patterns in the survey data (Barnes & Vigden, 2003).

Analysis of the data involved the assessment of each Web site within the three instrument dimensions of usability, information quality, and interaction and service quality. The researchers evaluated each of the Web sites using a Likert scale where the anchors are 1="strongly disagree" and 7="strongly agree" in each of the three instrument dimensions. The results were analysed using a statistical software package, SPSS. The evaluators' comments were analysed by coding the texts using the research instrument to construct the units of analysis. These were based around the three dimensions of the instrument and with particular reference to the five factors of usability, design, information, trust, and empathy as identified by Barnes and Vigden (2002).

Research Findings

Of the 80 SME Web sites evaluated, 46.9% were assessed as above average for overall quality, while a third (37.0%) was rated as below average for quality. The mean scores for the 23 eQual 4.0 questions are listed in Table 1. The findings are presented within the three dimensions of the research instrument.

Usability

In terms of Web site usability, most SME Web sites were easy to learn to operate (56.8%) and to use (65.5%). These Web sites had also conveyed a sense of competency (59.2%). However, only 49.4% of the Web sites examined reportedly created a positive experience for the users. Moreover, it appears that a positive experience was the most important usability factor for determining the overall view of the Web sites (correlation=0.858). Of those Web sites that had scored an overall positive rating, 76.3% of them had also scored positive ratings for conveying a sense of competency. Overall, the average score for the usability dimension was 4.39 out of a possible 7 points.

Usability in the context of this evaluation addresses how a user interfaces and reacts to a Web site: the emphasis is on the user and not on the designer or the software of the site (Barnes & Vigden, 2002). Ease of use of a Web site is seen as a prerequisite for visitor use (Barnes & Vigden, 2002) and has a positive influence on customer responsiveness (Dadzie, Cherlariu, & Winston, 2005). A Web site that is easy to use also enhances the ability of visitors to learn to navigate around the site and to find the facilities that they seek.

In a B2B situation it is to be expected that visitors will have at least some level of competency in electronic business, although this assumption should not be taken for granted. Therefore, Web sites should have high usability in order to attract visitors of all types. Design is an integral part of usability and influences both the evaluators' perceptions of ease of use, and of the sense of competence. Appropriate design was one of the lowest rated factors in the usability section.

Evaluation of a Web site must be necessarily subjective, but there was some consensus displayed by the evaluators on the ease with which visitors could learn how to use the sites and how

Table 1. Mean score for eQual 4.0 questions

eQual 4.0 questions	Mean	Sum	Standard Deviation
I find the site easy to learn to operate	4.52	366	0.823
My interaction with the site is clear and understandable	4.41	357	0.997
I find the site easy to navigate	4.51	365	0.976
I find the site easy to use	4.54	368	0.923
The site has an attractive appearance	4.48	363	1.256
The design is appropriate to the type of site	4.26	345	1.302
The site conveys a sense of competency	4.54	368	1.582
The site creates a positive experience for me	3.93	318	1.439
The site provides accurate information	4.20	340	1.487
The site provides believable information	4.49	364	1.518
The site provides timely information	4.14	335	1.498
The site provides relevant information	4.26	345	1.481
The site provides easy to understand information	4.20	340	1.249
The site provides information at the right level of detail	3.85	312	1.606
The site presents the information in an appropriate format	3.91	317	1.535
The site has a good reputation	4.22	342	1.533
It feels safe to complete transactions	3.93	318	1.464
My personal information feels secure	3.79	307	1.498
The site creates a sense of personalization	4.04	327	1.495
The site conveys a sense of community	4.12	334	1.426
The site makes it easy to communicate with the organization	4.93	399	1.170
I feel confident that goods/services will be delivered as promised	4.32	350	1.540
My overall view of this Web site	4.17	338	1.539

easy they were to use. However, it is worth noting that nearly a third of the Web sites did not rate as easy to use; a significant number in terms of potential users visiting and remaining to use the site. Web site users have low levels of tolerance and will move Web sites if they cannot find the information they need quickly (Shuster, 2000).

Information Quality

In terms of information quality, content is considered as the most important element of Web sites and is seen to be directly related to Web site success. Most B2B Web sites provided believable information (54.3%) but failed to provide information at the right level of detail (only 39.5%) as well as in an appropriate format (only 42.0%). Providing believable information to users was the most important information quality factor for determining the overall view of the Web sites (correlation=0.841). Of those Web sites that had scored an overall positive rating, almost all (97.4%) had scored highly for providing believable information. The average score for the information quality dimension was also 4.16 out of 7 points.

An acceptable level of detail was visible in less than half the sites evaluated and some vital elements of information were missing from these sites. For example, information on products and services was found to be scant in many areas with the apparent assumption that the site visitor had sufficient knowledge to understand the variations of the product range. In contrast, one of the highly recommended sites had detailed information on the practical applications of each item in its product range linked to the catalogue entry, thereby providing levels of information to suit all customers.

A second important area where information was found to be lacking was in the provision of company details. This is considered a crucial element of a business Web site (Shuster, 2000) and is a necessary source of information for visitors searching for new suppliers. Again the highly rated sites had detailed company information that gave the history, business aims, location and sometimes testimonials from satisfied suppliers. In one case, the names, photograph, contact details, and area of expertise of each of the company's sales force were presented. This level of contact detail was rare and sites provided only an e-mail address or a telephone number. In one case the only content information was a map from which the customer could infer the address and in another the Web site consisted only of contact details rather like a telephone book entry.

The refreshment of content is seen to be an important element of Web sites to keep up interest levels and show that the company is maintaining the site (Shuster, 2000), but few of the Web sites showed evidence of current input. In at least half of the sites the last update or date of creation was unknown. In 12% of cases, the Web site had not been altered since before 2004 and only three sites actually gave a date of less than a month since the last upgrade. In the more highly rated sites, information was seen to be well organized, timely, and relevant. This led to the perception

of accurate and believable information being presented. Some sites provided extensive information that was not found to be useful. For example, one company using natural products displayed encyclopedia extracts explaining the nature of the product, but had no prices or catalogue showing the product range on offer. The site had the appearance of an educational site rather than a commercial venture. The lack of prices on some transactional sites was somewhat of a puzzle and was recorded as insufficient information in the evaluation. In at least one case, prices may be visible through a passworded extranet, although it was not possible to verify this.

Interaction and Service Quality

In terms of interaction and service quality, most SMEs' Web sites made it easy for users to communicate with them (72.9%). However, only 39.5% of the Web sites evaluated made users' personal information feel secure and 42.0% made users feel it was safe to complete transactions. In fact, only three of the SME Web sites evaluated actually transacted online through secure sites. Moreover, the users' confidence in the delivery of goods/services as promised was the important interaction quality factor for determining the quality of the Web sites (correlation=0.889). Of those Web sites that had scored an overall positive rating, all had scored positively for making users feel confident that goods/services will be delivered as promised. In addition, the average score for interaction and service quality dimension was also 4.21 out of 7 points.

Channels for communication were offered by all sites in at least one form, although the use of e-mail did not predominate. There was also little evidence of multichannel communication on offer, with many sites offering either telephone or e-mail, or in some cases only a postal address. The three Web sites with fully functional secure transactional sites rated highly in all areas. In two other firms offering online purchase, the Web sites offered a form into which visitors were invited to enter their credit card details, although no security precautions were evident. Other companies used intermediaries such as PayPal to host their transactions. Only one site offered a range of payment options within a secure site. Surprisingly, none of the sites discussed electronic invoicing or payment terms more in keeping with B2B transactions. The majority ran brochure sites only and invited potential customers to contact the firm to discuss things further. While this is an acceptable measure, the sites did not make it easy for potential customers to properly ascertain if they wished to progress with their enquiries; for example, by offering complete product lists, prices, delivery details, invoicing details, and so forth. Confidence in the delivery of goods received a 100% rating from firms considered to have very good sites, but was not relevant in the majority of cases where only brochure or catalogue sites were used.

DISCUSSION

The majority of Web sites examined were brochure and catalogue sites, with only 15 of the 80 sites selling online. The result accords with Albert et al.'s (2004) findings that while many visitors are comfortable conducting transactional activities online, the primary activity remains information and communication based.

The purpose of the majority of sites was held to be informational, either for existing customers or to attract visitors seeking to broaden their supplier base. In the transactional sites, online selling was primarily an addition to an informational site and only three sites had developed the secure transaction mechanisms necessary for online trading. These three sites displayed the attributes of full transactional sites, including delivery options, online tracking, and secure payment methods.

Users should have a positive experience when visiting a Web site (Barnes & Vigden, 2002; Turban & Gehrke, 2000). In a highly competitive commercial environment, a negative view of the overall experience might easily lead to a user searching for new suppliers. Where an established partner is concerned, it may be that they prefer not to use the site, thereby losing opportunities for realising the benefits of e-commerce. A positive experience for the user was found in only half of the Web sites evaluated. Despite higher ratings in the usability section of the analysis, half of the SMEs were rated as below standard overall. This reflects the evaluators' comments that although the Web sites were easy to use and good to look at, they did not enable the visitor to find what they wanted. This aspect of usability is strongly influenced by the Web site design. Good Web site design must fulfil customers' needs for information or transaction capabilities (Heldal, Sjovold, & Heldal, 2004). The evaluators rated the more complex Web sites, incorporating graphics, animation, and sound, as low on usability. The same sites also had lower ratings on information and interaction. The Web sites appeared designed to please the owner (or designer) rather than provide appropriate information to the visitor; a finding that supports the view that a designer's desire for artistry often supersedes the users' needs (Heldal et al., 2004). Because the designer viewpoint is rarely the same as the users', the dimension of service interaction quality can be affected by failure to address the customers and their needs.

The research instrument devotes a number of questions to ascertaining the quality of information, which is regarded as a major contributor to the success of a Web site. Consideration of the quality of the content presented is considered of primary importance when using a Web site (Turban & Gehrke, 2000). Specifically, comprehensive product information is vital if prospective customers are to develop an interest in the site and returning customers are to maintain loyalty (Dadzie et al., 2005). Product information was found to be incomplete or not included in a quarter of the Web sites evaluated. This has significant implications for attracting and retaining customers who may find it preferable to search for information elsewhere rather than consider contacting the company for more details. Where product information was given, there were some innovative ideas with well structured pages to enable the visitor to choose the depth of information required.

A further concern in this area is the lack of company information, including contact details. Nielsen argues that the home page of a site is the online equivalent of the reception area. The impression created will often influence whether a visitor remains on the site or leaves immediately (in Shuster, 2000). The homepage should contain basic information about the company, together with an address, an e-mail, and a telephone number to support multiple communication options. The lack of such fundamental information creates an unprofessional appearance to visitors and does not provide the necessary introduction to those searching for new suppliers.

Clear concise text in an appropriate format gives a positive feel to a Web site (Turban & Gehrke, 2000) and this was one area in which performance was high with rare examples of inappropriate text or layout. However, the overall assessment of the Web sites were lower than indicated by this section as although the text was clear and well laid out, it did not provide the information that visitors were seeking. Also, the appearance of more timely text would benefit the majority of the Web sites, particularly where dates of homepage creation or last update were over a year old. While it was known that these firms are still operating, visitors from further afield may doubt their continuing existence and search elsewhere. It was possible to see some examples where the site had been created by Web consultants and subsequently left untended, probably through lack of in-house skills; a

scenario well recorded in the literature (Bode & Burn, 2001; van Akkeren & Cavaye, 1999) and a problem for many smaller businesses dependent on the advice and expertise of consultants.

Concerns of empathy and trust are key factors of the service interaction quality (Barnes & Vigden, 2002). The evaluators' comments confirmed the correlation between users' confidence in the delivery of goods and an overall positive assessment of the site. This supports the concepts of trust and empathy as a key feature of Web site interaction. While high user confidence implies empathy and trust, the notion of trust did not appear to be associated with security. This may arise from the low number of the firms actually trading online. The issue of security is seen as a significant concern in the business press, although it is interesting to note that in Turban and Gehrke's (2000) determinants of e-commerce sites, experts did not rank security highly and concentrated on network security, copyright, and confirmation of purchase. In contrast, consumers ranked security as of first importance in an e-commerce situation. Only three sites rated highly for confidence in security from a transactional perspective. These sites also rated highly in regard to protection of customer information. Those firms that are transacting through the use of downloadable forms for credit card details did not rate highly from either perspective. It also appeared to the evaluators that these firms were not supporting significant levels of online trading.

What emerged from the examination of these sites is that few of the firms are prepared to trade online. This finding is well supported by the literature (Saban & Rau, 2005). Although some SMEs have the ability to develop Web sites that function at a high level of e-commerce, the majority retain an informational perspective. Several of the evaluated sites have been in existence for a number of years but have not progressed beyond the brochure or catalogue format. This would imply either that the site owners are gaining no benefits from the site and have no motivation to improve or update them, or that they are satisfied with the level of custom being generated. Alternatively, the Web site may have been created as a result of peer group convention or perceived business wisdom to give the appearance of legitimacy (Grewal, Comer, & Mehta, 2001). In such cases owner expectations are usually low and lack of strategy means that the realization of benefits remains very low and interest in the Web site is abandoned (Stockdale & Standing, 2004). Resource constraints are another factor that influences more complex adoption, not least the industry sector and the IT skills within the firm (Poon & Swatman, 1999; van Akkeren & Cavaye, 1999). Higher than anticipated costs for developing and maintaining a highly functional Web site can also stall progressive development of an informational site (Saban & Rau, 2005).

The customer-centric sites discussed by Albert et al. (2004) are clearly beyond the scope of the SMEs discussed in this evaluation. Differentiating the design of nontransactional and transactional Web sites to reflect the goals and experiential requirements (Albert et al., 2004) implies a level of strategy development that is rare in smaller businesses. Nevertheless, the evaluated firms have dedicated resources to building Web sites, many have taken steps towards online trading and there were excellent examples of how even the smallest businesses could effectively use the Internet for business purposes.

CONCLUSION

User perceptions of the Web sites evaluated varied across the three dimensions used to assess them. The effectiveness of the Web sites was evident in specific areas; ease of use, attractiveness, and navigation were highly rated, as was providing believable information and conveying a sense of competence. The results in these areas are encouraging. Significant numbers of smaller businesses are managing to project themselves online and present Web sites that attract and encourage visitors.

Where problems can occur is in meeting visitors' subsequent needs. Users perceived that their needs were not met in regard to levels of information detail, and trust in the secure handling of both personal and transactional information. The inability to provide the right level of information and security seriously hinders the progression of e-commerce for these sites and affects the positive experience of the visitor. SMEs too often have little recognition of the benefits of a Web site and the adverse effect that an incomplete or untended site can have as an advertisement for ineffectiveness.

It is perhaps natural to emphasize the failings found in the evaluation and to overlook the number of smaller firms that are presenting competent and well designed Web sites to potential customers. Although in global terms the sites are not highly visible, within the regional market there is encouraging evidence of firms gaining benefits from their e-commerce activities and presenting effective Web sites to potential and existing customers. To extend the number of SMEs in this category, firms must be encouraged to develop the information and service quality dimensions of their Web sites and to gain an understanding of visitors' needs. Finally, a weakness of the study is the omission of the perspective of the Web site owners. A future development of this study could include, for example, their views on the effectiveness of the type and range of services and information that were offered on their Web sites.

FUTURE TRENDS

Several studies have found that SMEs are likely to increase the use of their Web sites in the future (e.g., Burns-Howell, Hemming, Gilbert, & Burns-Howell, 2004). Therefore, it is envisaged that SMEs' Web sites will play a vital role in attracting potential customers and in influencing purchasing decision as more and more businesses are beginning to conduct more and more of their business via their Web sites. However, unless SMEs can see the benefits of using their Web sites, they are unlikely to continue investing and evaluating in their Web sites (Burns-Howell et al., 2004). Therefore, it becomes critical for the SMEs to understand customer requirements, to continuously assess the effectiveness of their Web sites, and to enhance their Web accordingly. In addition, to fully utilize the effectiveness of the Web sites, the design will need to be more business oriented than technical focused. Moreover, the Web sites will need to serve to the needs and business goals of the SMEs.

Furthermore, producing high quality functionality and information for a wide range of services and products may still be beyond the resources of many SMEs in the future. It may be more appropriate, for example, to simply provide links to the manufacturer's Web sites. However, SMEs are starting to leverage on business to business electronic commerce through their Web sites in gaining competitive advantage with the trend toward increased functionality supported by improved future Internet technology. The great challenge for the SMEs is to find the incentives and motivation to pour in more resources into updating and maintaining their Web sites, evaluating the impact of their Web sites, and then refining their services on a regular basis.

REFERENCES

ABS. (2003). *Business use of information technology*. Canberra: Australian Bureau of Statistics.

Aladwani, A. M., & Palvia, P. C. (2002). Developing and validating an instrument for measuring user-perceived Web quality. *Information and Management, 39*(6), 467-476.

Albert, T., Goes, P., & Gupta, A. (2004). GIST: A model for design and management of content and interactivity of customer-centric Web sites. *MIS Quarterly, 28*(2), 161-182.

Auger, P. (2005). The impact of interactivity and design sophistication on the performance of commercial Web sites for small business. *Journal of Small Business Management, 43*(2), 119-137.

Barnes, S., & Vigden, R. (2001). An evaluation of cyber-bookshops: The WebQual method. *International Journal of Electronic Commerce, 6*(1), 11-30.

Barnes, S., & Vigden, R. (2002). An integrative approach to the assessment of e-commerce quality. *Journal of Electronic Commerce Research, 3*(3), 114-127.

Barnes, S., & Vigden, R. (2003). Measuring Web site quality improvements: A case study of the forum on strategic management knowledge exchange. *Industrial Management & Data Systems, 103*(5), 297-309.

Bode, S., & Burn, J. M. (2001). Web site design consultants, Australian SMEs and electronic commerce success factors. *International Journal of Business Studies, 9*(1), 73-85.

Burns-Howell, T., Hemming, M., Gilbert, S., & Burns-Howell, J. (2004, March). *Supporting SMEs in dealing with e-business risks*. A study conducted on behalf of Walsall, Wolverhampton and South Staffordshire Regeneration Zone. Retrieved October 16, 2007, from www.futurefoundations.org.uk

Chakraborty, G., Lala, V., & Warren, D. (2002). An empirical investigation of antecedents of B2B Web sites' effectiveness. *Journal of Interactive Marketing, 16*(4), 51-72.

Chiu, H-C., Hsieh, Y-C, & Kao, C-Y. (2005). Web site quality and customers' behavioural intention: An exploratory study of information asymmetry. *Total Quality Management, 16*(2), 185-197.

Dadzie, K., Chelariu, C., & Winston, E. (2005). Customer service in the Internet-enabled logistics supply chain: Web site design antecedents and loyalty effects. *Journal of Business Logistics, 26*(1), 53-78.

Daniel, E., Wilson, H., & Myers, A. (2002). Adoption of e-commerce by SMEs in the UK. *International Small Business Journal, 20*(3), 253-269.

DeLone, W. H., & McLean, E. R. (1992). Information systems success: The quest for the dependent variable. Information Systems Research, *3*(1), 60-95.

Ellinger, A., Lynch, D., Andzulis, J., & Smith, R. (2003). B-to-B e-commerce: A content analytical assessment of mot carrier Web sites. *Journal of Business Logistics, 24*(1), 199-221.

Fry, J., Tyrrall, D., Pugh, G., & Wyld, J. (2004). The provision and accessibility of small business Web sites: A survey of independent UK breweries. *Journal of Small Business and Enterprise Development, 11*(3), 302-314.

Goode, S. (2002). Management attitudes toward the World Wide Web in Australian small business. *Information Systems Management, Winter,* 45-48.

Grewal, R., Comer, J. M., & Mehta, R. (2001). An investigation into the antecedents of organizational participation in business-to-business electronic markets. *Journal of Marketing, 65*(3), 17-33.

Heldal, F., Sjovold, E., & Heldal, A. F. (2004). Success on the Internet - optimizing relationships through the corporate site. *International Journal of Information Management, 24,* 115-129.

Hong S., & Kim, J. (2004) Architectural criteria for Web site evaluation – conceptual framework and empirical validation. *Behaviour & Information Technology, 23*(5), 337-57.

House, E. R. (1980). *Evaluating with validity.* London: Sage.

Ivory, M. Y., Sinha, R. R., & Hearst, M. A. (2001). Empirically validated Web page design metrics. *Paper presented at the ACM SIGCHI'01,* Seattle, WA, USA.

Jones Donald Strategic Partners. (2000). *Taking the plunge 2000, sink or swim? Small business attitudes to electronic commerce.* Commonwealth of Australia: National Office for the Information Economy.

Jutla, D., Bodorik, P., & Dhaliqal, J. (2002). Supporting the e-business readiness of small and medium-sized enterprises: Approaches and metrics. *Internet Research: Electronic Networking Applications and Policy, 12*(2), 139-164.

Korchak, R., & Rodman, R. (2001). eBusiness adoption among U.S. small manufacturers and the role of manufacturing extension. *Economic Development Review, 17*(3), 20-25.

Lin, C., & Pervan, G. (2003). The practice of IS/IT benefits management in large Australian organizations. *Information and Management, 41*(1), 13-24.

Lin, C., Cripps, H., & Bode, S. (2005, June 6-8). Electronic commerce projects adoption and evaluation in Australian SMEs: Preliminary findings. In *Proceedings of the 18th Bled eConference (Bled 2005),* Bled, Slovenia, (pp. 1-14).

Lin, C., Pervan, G., & McDermid, D. (2005). IS/IT investments evaluation and benefits realization issues in Australia. *Journal of Research and Practices in Information Technology, 37*(3), 235-251.

Loiacono, E., Watson, R., & Goodhue, D. (2002). *WebQual™: A measure of Web site quality.* Retrieved October 16, 2007, from http://www.terry.uga.edu/cisl/includes/pdf/webqual.pdf

Love, P.E.D., Irani, Z., Standing, C., Lin, C., & Burn, J. (2005). The enigma of evaluation: Benefits, costs and risks of IT in small-medium sized enterprises. *Information and Management, 42*(7), 947-964.

Manuel, N. (2004). Wizzy Web sites can make SMEs look like world-beaters. *Financial Times, 18.*

Mich, L., Franch, M., & Gaio, L. (2003). Evaluating and designing the quality of Web sites: The 2QCV3Q metamodel. *IEEE Multimedia, 10*(1), 34-43.

NOIE. (2002). *E-business strategy for small business.* Retrieved October 16, 2007, from www.noie.gov.au/projects/ebusiness

Poon, S., & Swatman, P. (1999). An exploratory study of small business Internet commerce issues. *Information and Management, 35,* 9-18.

Reichheld, F., Markey, Jr, R., & Hopton, C. (2000). E-customer loyalty - applying the traditional rules of business for online success. *European Business Journal, 12*(4), 173-179.

Saban, K., & Rau, S. (2005). The functionality of Web sites as export marketing channesl for small and medium enterprises. *Electronic Markets, 15*(2), 128-135.

Schubert, P. (2002-03). Extended Web assessment method (Ewam) - evaluation of e-commerce applications from the customer's viewpoint. *International Journal of Electronic Commerce, 7*(2 (Winter)), 51-80.

Shiels, H., McIvor, R., & O'Reilly, D. (2003). Understanding the implications of ICT adoption: Insights from SMEs. *Logistics Information Management, 16*(5), 312-326.

Shuster, L. (2000). Designing a Web site. *Civil Engineering, 70*(2), 64-65.

Smithson, S., & Hirschheim, R. (1998). Analysing information systems evaluation: Another look at an old problem. European Journal of Information Systems, 7, 158-174.

Stockdale, R., & Standing, C. (2004). Benefits and barriers of electronic marketplace participation: An SME perspective. *Journal of Enterprise Information Management, 17*(4), 301-311.

Stockdale, R., & Standing, C. (2006). An interpretive approach to evaluating information systems: A content, context, process framework. *European Journal of Operational Research, 173*(3), 701-1188.

Symons, V. J. (1991). A review of information systems evaluation: Content, context and process. *European Journal of Information Systems, 1*(3), 205-212.

Tsai, S., & Chai, S. (2005). Developing and validating a nursing Web site evaluation questionnaire. *Journal of Advanced Nursing, 49*(4), 406-413.

Tsao, H., Lin, K. H., & Lin, C. (2004). An investigation of critical success factors in the adoption of B2BEC by Taiwanese companies. *The Journal of American Academy of Business, Cambridge, 5*(1/2), 198-202.

Turban, E., & Gehrke, D. (2000). Determinants of e-commerce Web sites. *Human Systems Management, 19,* 111-120.

van Akkeren, J., & Cavaye, A. L. M. (1999). Factors affecting entry-level Internet technology adoption by small business in Australia - evidence from three cases. *Journal of Systems and Information Technology, 3*(2), 33-48.

Van der Merwe, R. & Bekker, J. (2003). A framework and methodology for evaluating e-commerce Web sites. *Internet Research, 13*(5), 330-341.

Walker, E. A., Bode, S., Burn, J. M., & Webster, B. J. (2003, September 29-30). Small business and the use of technology: Why the low uptake? In *Proceedings of the SEAANZ Conference,* Ballarat.

Walsham, G. (1993). *Interpreting information systems in organizations.* Chichester: John Wiley.

Webb, H. W., & Webb, L. A. (2004). SiteQual: An integrated measure of Web site quality. *The Journal of Enterprise Information Management, 17*(6), 430-440.

Zhang, P., & von Dran, G. (2002). User expectations and rankings of quality factors in different Web site domains. *International Journal of Electronic Commerce*, 6(2), 9-33.

KEY TERMS

B2BEC: Business-to-business electronic commerce. Business conducted through the Internet between companies.

Information Quality Dimension: This dimension considers content as the most important element of Web sites and is seen to be directly related to Web site success.

Service Quality Dimension: The dimension allows for examination of the role of service provider within organizations. This is particularly important in the context of e-commerce where the end user is the customer and not the employee.

SMEs: Small to medium enterprises. The European Commission has defined SMEs as organizations which employ less than 250 people.

Usability Dimension: This dimension addresses how a user interfaces and reacts to a Web site: the emphasis is on the user and not on the designer or the software of the site.

Web site: A place on the World Wide Web where an organization's homepage is located. It is a collection of Web pages, that is, HTML/XHTML documents accessible via HTTP on the Internet.

Web Site Evaluation: This is the weighing up process to rationally assess the effectiveness and benefits of Web sites which are expected to improve organizations' business value.

Web Site Quality: This refers to the elements of a Web site that affect the end user in the way they interact and use a business Web site.

Chapter V
Anomaly Detection and Quality Evaluation of Web Applications

May Haydar
Université de Montréal, Canada

Ghazwa Malak
Université de Montréal, Canada

Houari Sahraoui
Université de Montréal, Canada

Alexandre Petrenko
Centre de recherche informatique de Montréal (CRIM), Canada

Sergiy Boroday
Centre de recherche informatique de Montréal (CRIM), Canada

ABSTRACT

This chapter addresses the problem of Web application quality assessment from two perspectives. First, it shows the use of model checking of properties formulated in LTL to detect anomalies in Web applications. Anomalies can be derived from standard quality principles or defined for a specific organization or application. The detection is performed on communicating automata models inferred from execution traces. Second, the chapter explains how probabilistic models (Bayesian networks) can be built and used to evaluate quality characteristics. The structure of the networks is defined by refinement of existing models, where the parameters (probabilities and probability tables) are set using expert judgment and fuzzy clustering of empirical data. The two proposed approaches are evaluated and a discussion on how they complement each other is presented.

INTRODUCTION

The Internet has reshaped the way people deal with information. A few years ago, simple Web sites existed, where the components were text documents interconnected through hyper links. Nowadays, the Internet and the Web affect daily life in many ways. They are used to run large-scale software applications relating to almost all aspects of life, including information management/gathering, information distribution, e-commerce (business-to-customer, business to business), software development, learning, education, collaborative work, and so forth. According to Offut (2002), diversity is a key description of Web applications (WA) in many aspects that led to the notion of "Web engineering." Web applications are developed with cutting edge technologies and interact with users, databases, and other applications. They also use software components that could be geographically distributed and communicate through different media. Web applications are constructed of many heterogeneous components, including plain HTML files, mixtures of HTML, XML, and programs, scripting languages (CGI, ASP, JSP, PHP, servlets, etc.), databases, graphical images, and complex user interfaces. These diversities led to the need for large teams of Web developers who do not share the same skills, experience, and knowledge. These include programmers, usability engineers, data communications and network experts, database administrators, information layout specialists, and graphic designers [38]. With such a diversity of Web applications developers, quality is a primary concern. Unlike traditional software, Web applications have an extremely short development and evolution life cycle and have to meet stringent time to market requirements. Web applications often have a large number of untrained users, who often experiment with the Web applications unpredictably. The success of Web applications solely depends on their users and their satisfaction. Hence, a low quality of these applications can be very costly; as an example, the 4-day outage of Microsoft Money in 2004 was caused by a server glitch that prevented users from accessing their online personal finance files (Pertet & Narasimhan, 2005). Microsoft Money's servers were unable to recognize usernames and passwords through the Microsoft's Passport authentication and log-in service. Therefore, thorough analysis and verification of WA is indispensable to assure their high quality.

There exist at least two different perspectives for dealing with quality of Web applications. The first one concentrates on detecting and correcting anomalies and the second viewpoint focuses on building their quality models. In this chapter, two approaches are described, and both perspectives are elaborated, namely detecting anomalies using model checking of execution traces and quality evaluation using probabilistic quality models.

One approach uses formal methods for the analysis and validation of Web applications. The idea is to observe the executions of a given Web application from which its automata-based models are inferred. Using existing quality and usability rules that assess Web application's design and implementation, properties in linear temporal logic (LTL) are formulated; for more details on LTL, see Clarke, Grumberg, and Peled (2000). The model and properties are fed to the model checker Spin that verifies if the model satisfies those properties. The model checker then provides a counter example in case the property is not satisfied in the model. Counter example information helps in the evaluation and correction of Web applications.

Another approach relies on a probabilistic quality model involving Bayesian networks and fuzzy logic to assess the quality of Web applications. Web applications quality criteria, proposed in the literature Olsina (1998), Nielsen (2000), and Koyani, Bailey, and Nall (2003), are collected along with a list of the existing guidelines and recommendations. The list is extended by considering additional criteria that are also significant in the evaluation process of different aspects, such as usability, functionality, and so forth. A Bayesian Network with those criteria is built. Then, to define the parameters of the Network nodes, a probability distribution is determined using expert judgments with the help of fuzzy logic. When introducing the measured values of the entry nodes, for a given Web application, the Bayesian Network provides an estimation of the quality of this application.

The flow of the chapter is as follows. In Section 2, the literature on existing work in verification, testing, and quality evaluation of Web applications, is reviewed. Section 3 describes the approach and framework of model checking Web applications with few examples on temporal properties translated from existing quality rules and verified within the described framework. Section 4 illustrates the approach for quality assessment of Web applications using Bayesian Networks, applied to the Navigability design Network fragment. Section 5 is dedicated to the evaluation of the proposed approaches and to a discussion on how they complement each other. Finally, a conclusion is given in Section 6.

EXISTING WORK ON WEB QUALITY

Focusing on Anomaly Detection

Formal modeling and validation of Web applications is a relatively new research direction. Related work on the topic includes modeling approaches that target the verification of such applications (de Alfaro, 2001a; de Alfaro, Henziger, & Mang, 2001b; Stotts & Cabarrus, 1998; Stotts & Navon, 2002). Several results have also been achieved in Web applications testing (Benedikt, Freire, & Godefroid, 2002; Conallen, 1999; Ricca & Tonella, 2001; Tonella & Ricca, 2002; Wu & Offutt, 2002).

In de Alfaro (2001a) and de Alfaro et al. (2001b), a static Web site is modeled as a directed graph. A node in the graph represents a Web page, and the edges represent links clicked. If the page contains frames, the graph node is then a tree, whose tree nodes are pages loaded in frames, and tree edges are labeled by frame names. This model is used to verify properties of Web sites with frames. However, only static pages are considered in this work, concurrent behavior of multiple windows is not modeled, and all the links, whose targets could create new independent windows, are treated as broken links. Also, the proposed model is inadequate for representing the concurrent behavior inherent in multiwindow applications. In Stotts and Cabarrus (1998) and Stotts and Navon (2002), the authors present a model based on Petri nets to model check static hyperdocuments and framed pages, respectively. Perti nets are translated into the automata specification language, accepted by a model checker. De Alfaro (2001), Stotts and Cabarrus (1998), and Stotts and Navon (2002) do not tackle the modeling and verification of multiwindow applications or dynamic pages resulting from submitting forms. Benedict et al. (2002) introduce VeriWeb, a tool that automatically explores Web site execution paths, while automatically navigating through dynamic components of Web sites. When forms are encountered, they are automatically populated using user specified sets of attribute-value pairs, during Web site exploration. This approach contributes to the functional and regression testing of dynamic components of Web applications, but it does not address concurrent behavior of multiframe/window applications. Also, due to the limited features of the state exploration tool used, the graph is traversed only up to a certain predefined depth. The work in Conallen (1999), Ricca and Tonella (2001), and Tonella and Ricca (2002) focuses on inferring a UML model of a Web application for the static analysis (HTML code inspection and scanning, data flow analysis), and semiautomatic test case generation. The model does not address multi-frames/windows behavior and, Ricca and Tonella (2001) and Tonella and Ricca (2002), deals only with GET method-based forms. In Wu and Offut (2002), a modeling technique for Web applications is presented based on regular expressions for the purpose of functional testing. Each of the above related work concentrates on some aspects and do not offer a solution which could address a wide range of properties of Web applications.

Focusing on Quality Models

In order to assess, control, and improve Web applications quality, many studies have been conducted. Some organizations (IEEE, 2001; W3C, 1999) and authors (Koyani et al., 2003; Nielsen, 2000) suggest principles, guidelines, and recommendations to help developers in the design of Web applications. Most of these proposals focus exclusively on Web application usability aspects. However, the other quality characteristics are at least as important as usability to improve the overall quality of Web applications.

In the quality measurement domain, a wide range of metrics is developed (Olsina 1998; Ivory, 2001) and classified (Dhyani, NG, & Bhowmick, 2002). Nevertheless, as usual in emerging paradigms, there is little consensus among the proposed metrics (Calero, Ruiz, & Piattini, 2004). Several tools are available on the Internet to test Web applications usability and accessibility. Other tools are also developed to automate, partially, the usability evaluation process (Olsina, 1998; Ivory, 2001; Shubert & Dettling, 2002). However, several criteria considered in these tools are subjective, and the quality models are simple (Brajnik, 2001).

Other work focuses on the development of quality models in the form of trees (Albuquerque & Belchior, 2002; Olsina, 1998). Both projects propose hierarchical models constrained by the fact that any criterion must be classified under a unique characteristic. A graphical model is more tailored for representing different types of relationships that can exist between these criteria.

Analyzing the evolution of the research in this field, one can notice that a common vision on the quality of Web applications is absent and a solid foundation is lacking, on which this research can further evolve. As argued in a previous work (Malak, Badri, Badri, & Sahraoui, 2004), it is recognized that there is no common standard followed by the authors, and quality factors do not totally comply with the ISO/IEC 9126 standard (ISO/IEC, 2001). Existing literature includes work that proposes hierarchical models, while few studies deal with uncertainty, inaccuracy, and subjectivity problems inherent to the Web field.

ANOMALY DETECTION USING MODEL CHECKING

Motivation

In recent years, the software community has started accepting formal methods as a practical and reliable solution to analyze various applications.

In particular, model checking techniques (Clarke et al., 2000) have increasingly been used and in many cases preferred over testing and simulation, because model checking can perform an exhaustive exploration of all possible behaviors of a given system. Indeed, testing and simulation methods are not exhaustive and deal with a part of the system leaving the unexplored behaviors of the system unchecked. Model checking is fully automatic, and in case the design does not satisfy a given property, the model checker produces a counter example that points out to the behavior that violates the property.

Model checking is supported by multiple commercial and free tools, used for several years, if not decades, in industry and academia. Such tools allow the specification of general properties using temporal logic and solving a wider range of problems related to Web applications. These tools have undergone years of development, enhancement, and upgrades solving many of the scalability problems related to the state explosion problem (Clarke et al., 2000).

Approach Overview

A modeling approach is developed (Haydar, Petrenko, & Sahraoui, 2004; Haydar, Boroday, Petrenko, & Sahraoui, 2005a; Haydar, Boroday, Petrenko, & Sahraoui, 2005b) to produce a communicating automata model tuned to features of WA that have to be validated, while delegating the task of property verification to an existing model checker. To build such a model according to such a dynamic (black-box based) approach, one executes a given application and uses only the observations of an external behavior of the application. Thus, its behavior is analyzed without having access to server programs or databases. The observations are provided by a monitoring tool, a proxy server (SOLEX, 2004) or an off-the-shelf network monitoring tool (Orebaugh, Morris, Warnicke, & Ramirez, 2004), where HTTP requests and responses are logged. The resulting model is a system of communicating automata representing all windows and frames of the application under test. The existence of frames and windows reflects concurrent behavior of the Web application under test (WAUT), where these objects affect each other behaviors via links and forms with specified targets. Therefore, the use of a system of communicating automata is a suitable and natural modeling technique, which leaves the burden of building a global state graph of the model to a model checker. As opposed to the existing approaches, not only static pages are modeled, but also dynamic pages generated with GET and POST forms, frames, multiple windows, and their concurrent behavior. Generally speaking, one could build a special Web-oriented model checker, as in de Alfaro et al. (2001b) to verify Web properties. Developing an efficient model checker might be a daunting task, which may take years of work of qualified experts. Building a front-end to an existing model checker, such

Figure 1. Framework for formal analysis of Web applications

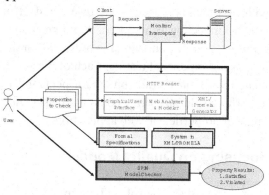

as Spin (Holzmann, 2003), could be easier. In this case, models of Web applications should be described with an input language of the model checker. In case of Spin, the input language is Promela, a C-like language to specify automata based models.

Figure 1 illustrates the framework developed for the formal analysis and verification of Web applications (Haydar et al., 2004).

From Traces to Automata

An observed behavior of a WAUT, called a *browsing session*, is a sequence of Web pages that have the same domain name intermittent with the corresponding requests.

Browsing Sessions

An observed browsing session represents the behavior of the communicating entities of the WA, namely, browser's main and independent windows and frames. Therefore, given the browsing session, first *local browsing sessions*, which correspond to local behaviors of the entities in the browsed part of the WA, are determined. These entities affect each other's behavior through target names associated with links and forms. Frames and windows are initially assumed to be inactive.

They are activated (created) through link clicks or form submissions with target names in case of windows, or frame source URIs in case of frames. Frames/framesets are deactivated (destroyed), whenever a link/form is clicked/submitted and targets a parent of these frames of framesets. Whenever an explored link/form targets an active entity, the entity, where the link/form was triggered does not change its display, while the targeted entity changes its display.

Automata Model of a Browsing Session

A browsing session is modeled by a system of communicating automata, such that each window, frame, and frameset is represented by an automaton. This is achieved by converting each of the local browsing sessions into an automaton as follows. Initially, the automaton is in the start state, which is inactive state. All the response pages in the local session are converted into states of the automaton. Page attributes that are of interest to the user represent the state attributes, or atomic propositions, that are true in the states and used for model checking. The set of events include the set of all the links, form actions (along with submitted data values), frame source URIs present in all the pages displayed in the corresponding

entity, as well as all the requests in the local session. Each request in the local session defines a transition from the state/page, where the request was triggered to the state/page that is the response of the request. Each explored form or link in a page loaded in the entity and repeated in another page defines a transition from the state, where it occurs, to the state that corresponds to the response of the submitted filled form or clicked link. Each unexplored link or unexplored form defines a transition from the state representing the page, where it exists to a state called *trap* that represents the unexplored part of the WA and whose attributes are undefined.

Communications between automata occur in the following three cases. (1) A request for a link/form in an entity targets another entity. (2) Frames are created (displayed in a window). (3) A link/form in a frame/frameset targets a parent entity. Haydar et al. (2004) presented the algorithms that convert a browsing session into communicating automata, which communicate by rendezvous.

Box 1 is a fragment of a browsing session of the Web application of a research center (www.crim. ca) representing 18 Web pages actually visited, and Figure 2(a) shows the automaton that represents the browsing session, where state s_5 is a deadlock

Box 1.

```
 GET http://www.crim.ca HTTP/1.0
Host: www.crim.ca
Accept: application/vnd.ms-excel, application/msword, application/vnd.ms-
powerpoint, image/gif, image/x-xbitmap, image/jpeg, image/pjpeg, */*
User-Agent: Mozilla/4.0 (compatible; MSIE 6.0; Windows NT 4.0)
Accept-Language: en-us
-----------------------END OF HTTP REQUEST--------------------------------
HTTP/1.1 200 OK
Content-Type: text/html
Content-Length: 18316
Server: Apache/1.3.9 (Unix) mod_perl/1.21 mod_ssl/2.4.9 OpenSSL/0.9.4
<HTML>
<HEAD>
<LINK rel="stylesheet" href="/styles.css">
<TITLE> CRIM</TITLE></HEAD> ...
...<a href="/rd/"> recherche-développement </a> ...
</HTML>
-----------------------END OF HTTP RESPONSE--------------------------------
```

Figure 2. (a) Example of a session automaton; (b) Snapshot of prototype tool with a session automaton

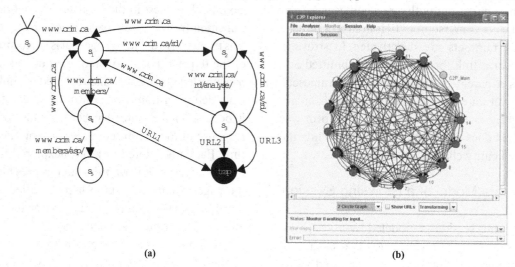

Figure 2. (a) Example of a session automaton; (b) Snapshot of prototype tool with a session automaton

(a) (b)

state representing an error page, whose status code is 404. URL1, URL2, and URL3 (named as such for simplicity) represent few unexplored links that label transitions to the trap state. Figure 2(b) shows a snapshot of a prototype tool visualizing an inferred automaton from a browsing session, where state C2P_Main is the inactive state. The automaton includes 17 states and 171 transitions. For simplicity, the transition labels (links URIs) are not included, and unexplored links to the trap state are omitted.

Figure 3 shows a fragment of a communicating automata model, which represents three entities, the *browser window*, *Frame1*, and *Frame2*. These entities are modeled by three automata, A_1, A_2, and A_3, respectively, which communicate by common events (rendezvous). Initially, the three automata are in their inactive states s_0, u_0, and v_0, respectively. The event a is a link, clicked by the user, which makes A_1 to move to state s_1 that represents the frameset document containing URIs of *Frame1* and *Frame2*. The events f_1 and f_2 are from the browser window received by the two frames, respectively, represent the browser triggered requests for frames source pages. A_2 and A_3 are then active, while A_1 remains in s_1. In *Frame1*, the user can click the link b so that

A_1 moves to state u_2 by executing the transition labeled by action b. In *Frame2*, the user can click the link c, whose target is _top, such that the corresponding page is loaded in the full window, thus canceling the two frames. In this case, c is a multirendezvous of A_3, A_1, and A_2; as a result, A_2 and A_3 move to their inactive states u_0 and v_0, and A_1 moves to state s_2.

Figure 3. (a) A_1 for Browser Window, (b) A_2 for Frame1, (c) A_3 for Frame2

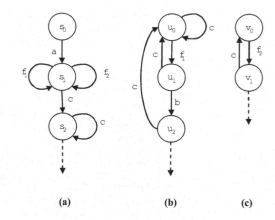

(a) (b) (c)

From Anomalies to LTL Properties

The Web community over the years has developed numerous rules and good practices that assess the usability and quality of Web applications.

Hundreds of rules and several alternative taxonomies related to quality, usability, and good practices for the development and design of Web applications are suggested by various quality and usability groups (Olsina, 1998; Ivory, 2001; OPQUAST; IBM). As mentioned above, these rules concern general ergonomic, technical, and functional features of Web applications. Many of them could be translated into LTL, to specify properties (rules) that can be verified over a given Web application model using model checking techniques. LTL extends the classical propositional logic with several temporal operators, such as the *Always* operator, denoted G, and *Weak Until* operator *W*. G*p* means that the formula *p* holds at every state on the path. (*p* W *q*) means that *p* holds either in all the states of the path, or at least until *q* becomes true. While properties of Web pages could be expressed in propositional logic, temporal operators allow us address (navigational) paths of a given WA. The properties are expressed as LTL formulae that use page attributes in their atomic propositions.

Few examples of quality and usability rules that can be translated into LTL are as follows:

1. *Promotions of certain products are only present either on the Home page or on Shopping pages and, for each page, the number of promotions does not exceed 2.*

This property is used to ensure that a promoted product is not oversold. Though this property may seem local to each page, in case of multiframe applications, model checking is justified because it validates the property on all the different and possible interleavings of states (combinations of frames) which may not have been explored by the user.

The property could be formulated in LTL as follows,

$$G\,(\,(((\neg Home \wedge \neg Shopping) \rightarrow (Promotions = 0)) \wedge ((Home \vee Shopping) \rightarrow (Promotions \leq 2))\,)$$

Home and *Shopping* are Boolean attributes that designate the home page and the shopping pages. *Promotions* is an integer attribute that counts the number of promotions in each page.

2. *Secure pages are not reachable from regular pages without going through authorization pages.*

This property is a typical security requirement. It states that certain pages with secure information are only accessible via an authorization process. Property can be expressed in LTL as follows:

$$G(Regular \wedge \neg Secure \rightarrow (\neg Secure \text{ W } (Authorization \wedge \neg Secure)))$$

Similar to the previous property, *Regular*, *Secure*, and *Authorization* are Boolean attributes that identify regular, secure, and authorization pages.

Note that some of the usability and quality rules referred in this section are not addressed in the framework. Examples of such rules are as follows: *"the user should receive an e-mail containing purchase transactions information within 60 minutes,"* and *"the user should receive an electronic receipt of his purchase within 3 days."*

QUALITY ASSESSMENT USING PROBABILISTIC MODELS

Motivation

A quality model is essentially a set of criteria that are used to determine whether a Web application reaches a certain level of quality (Brajnik, 2001). However, some quality criteria are subjective (Nielsen, 2000; Olsina, 1998), and it is hard to define realistic threshold values for many others (Ivory, 2001). On the other hand, balancing criteria is important because of the variety of application domains (Malak et al., 2004) and subcriteria weight assignment adds a new subjective dimension to the quality evaluation. Furthermore, the same criterion can affect simultaneously several criteria. These interdependences are difficult to represent in a hierarchical way. Thus, selecting a particular grouping (hierarchy) means that some relationships have to be ignored.

To be useful, a Web quality model must take into account the inherent subjectivity, uncertainty, and complexity of the quality factors, their measures and their relationships. Both theory and experience have shown that probabilities are powerful tools for modeling uncertainty (Baldi, Frasconi, & Smyth, 2003). In the context of quality models, reasoning with probabilities allows weighting criteria and handling uncertainty issues. Moreover, a graphical model provides an intuitive means for representing interacting sets of criteria (Naim, Wuillemin, Leray, Pourret, & Becker, 2004), particularly using the Bayesian Networks (BNs). With BNs it is possible to represent the interrelations between criteria in an intuitive and explicit way by connecting causes to effects. Also, BNs resolve the problems of subjectivity of several criteria, regrouping and weighting them by using probabilities.

Approach Overview

In previous work, Malak et al. (2004) attempted to collect Web applications quality criteria proposed by several authors. The obtained list is extended, and refined by applying GQM (Goals, Questions, Metrics) paradigm (Basili, Caldiera, & Rombach, 1994), and retained criteria are classified hierarchically on the basis of the characteristics and subcharacteristics definitions in ISO 9126

standard (ISO/IEC, 2001).

Following the probabilistic approach, the hierarchically gathered criteria are represented in the form of a Bayesian Network (BN). Considering the big number of criteria and subcriteria gathered the resulting BN model is large and complex. However, according to Neil, Fenton, & Nielson (2000), BNs can be built starting from semantically meaningful units called network "fragments" to decrease the complexity when dealing with large systems. A fragment is a set of related random variables that could be constructed and reasoned about separately from other fragments (Laskey & Mahoney, 1997).

Although the ultimate objective is to elaborate a comprehensive BN model for Web applications quality, this chapter concentrates on the definition of navigability design fragment to illustrate the approach. In fact, in recent years, several researches recognize the navigability design as an important quality criterion for Web applications (Koyani, et al., 2003; Olsina, 2000; Zhang, Zhu, & Greenwood, 2004). According to several definitions (Koyani et al., 2003; Nielsen, 2000; W3C, 1999), navigability design in a Web application can be determined as follows: the facility, for a given user, to recognize his position in the application and to locate and link, within suitable time, required information; this can be done via the effective use of hyperlinks towards the destination pages. Moreover, various studies address specifically Web navigation quality (Koyani et al., 2003; Nielsen, 2000; W3C, 1999). Authors propose many design elements, control points, directives, and guidelines to ensure the quality of navigability design. This criterion can be assessed at the page level. Thereafter, the methodology can be extended to assess several pages or all the pages of a given application.

The first step in the approach consists in gathering, from existing work, all the suggested criteria, guidelines and directives that influence the quality of navigability design in a Web page. Then, following a top-down process, these criteria are refined by determining subcriteria that may characterize them. This is done with the perspective of improving the evaluation. The refinement process is done using the GQM paradigm. It allows the reorganization, extension, improvement, and validation of the model and the determination of metrics for some important criteria. Results are summarized in Table 1.

Table 1 illustrates well the limitations mentioned previously. Indeed, it is noticed that: (1) a same subcriterion (e.g., *Links number)* characterizes different super-criteria at the same time, (2) the evaluation of some criteria is subjective (e.g.,

Locate, Access, Revisit), and (3) the majority of subcriteria can be captured by a binary metric (Yes/No).

Considering these limitations, building the BN for the navigability design at the page level is done in two steps:

1. **Build the graph structure:** Criteria are considered as random variables and represent the nodes of the BN. Criteria affecting the same criterion should be independent variables.

2. **Define the node probability tables for each node of the graph:** A conditional probability function models the uncertain relationship between each node (subcriterion) and its parents (Neil et al., 2000). As all BNs, probability tables are built using a mixture of empirical data and expert judgments.

BN Structure Definition

The Navigability design at the level of a Web page can be assessed by the presence of some design elements and mechanisms that allows the users to:

- locate themselves and recognize easily the page where they are,
- find within the page the required information,
- have the possibility to access this information directly via hyper links, and
- have the possibility to return easily to this page, with a suitable time.

For a selected Web page, it is supposed that:

- **NavigabilityDesignP:** The variable representing the navigability design criterion at a Web page level.
- **Locate:** The variable representing the facility, for a given user, to know in which page of the application he or she is and to localize the required information within the page.

Table 1. Navigability design criteria refined using the GQM paradigm

1.	Navigability Design criteria	Metrics
1.1	**Locate the position**	Subjective
1.1.1	Current position label	Y/N
1.1.2	Breadcrumbs	Y/N
1.1.3	Relative URLs	Y/N
1.1.4	Navigation elements	Y/N
1.1.5	Search mechanism	Y/N
1.1.6	Site map	Y/N
1.1.7	Link text significant	Measure
1.1.8	Link title	Y/N
1.1.9	Visited link color	Y/N
1.2	**Access or link to the information**	Subjective
1.2.1	Hypertext links	Subjective
1.2.1.1	Links number (page)	Measure
1.2.1.2	Breadcrumb	Y/N
1.2.1.3	Navigation elements	Y/N
1.2.2	Site map	Y/N
1.2.3	Back button always active	Y/N
1.2.4	Link to home	Y/N
1.3	**Revisit the page**	Subjective
1.3.1	Back button always active	Y/N
1.3.2	Page download time	Measure
1.3.3	Link to home	Y/N
1.3.4	Breadcrumbs	Y/N
1.3.5	Navigation elements	Y/N
1.3.6	Links number (page)	Measure

- **Access:** The variable representing the facility, for a given user, to access to the required information in the destination page from the selected page.
- **Revisit:** The variable representing the facility, for a given user, to return to the selected page with a suitable time.

Thus, *NavigabilityDesignP, Locate, Access* and *Revisit* are variables, represented by four nodes (Figure 4). Because there is a definition relation between these variables, the node *NavigabilityDesignP* is defined in terms of the three other nodes (Neil et al., 2000). The direction of the edges indicates the direction, in which a subcriterion defines a criterion, in combination with the other subcriteria.

The obtained structure is recursively refined. The same process is followed to construct the subnetworks for *Locate, Access,* and *Revisit* nodes. To ensure to "*return easily to this page, with a*

suitable time," the presence of many design elements (as shown in Figure 5) can help user return to the page (Koyani et al., 2003; Nielsen, 2000). Also, the presence of many design elements suggests that the user is able to revisit the page (back button, Link to home, Breadcrumbs) (Koyani et al., 2003; W3C, 1999). Moreover, the presence of navigational elements and a fast download time support the return to the page. Subsequently, the relationship that exists between *Revisit* and its parents is causal and not definitional, as shown in Figure 4. However, with numerous parents, a reorganization of this network is needed to avoid the combinatory explosion during the preparation of the probability tables. To achieve this, some nodes are grouped together whenever possible. The introduction of new nodes (meaningful or synthetic) gathering some parents' nodes and decreasing their number help defining probability tables. According to existing definitions (Koyani et al, 2003; W3C, 1999), the synthetic nodes can

Figure 4. BN sub network of NavigabilityDesignP

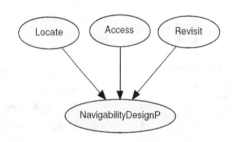

Figure 5. BN subnetwork of Revisit subcriterion criterion

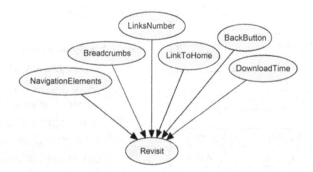

Figure 6. Final Revisit BN

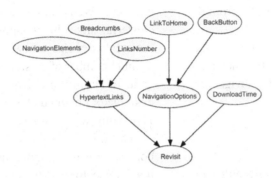

Figure 7. Final Navigability design BN at Web page level

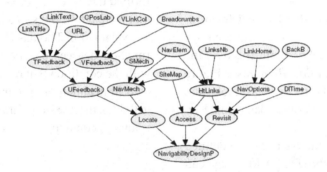

Figure 8. Revisit NPT with values determined by expert judgments

Revisit

NavigationOr	Good				Bad			
HypertextLink	Good		Bad		Good		Bad	
DownloadTin	Low	High	Low	High	Low	High	Low	High
Good	0.99	0.8	0.7	0.5	0.5	0.3	0.2	0.01
Bad	0.01	0.2	0.3	0.5	0.5	0.7	0.8	0.99

Figure 9. Fuzzy clusters of "DlTime"

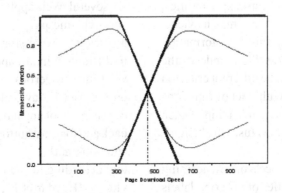

be added by grouping other nodes, when the presence of these nodes is independent from the others (Figure 6).

After constructing the subnetworks for "Locate" and "Access" nodes, all the fragments are put it together to obtain the BN of the Navigability design at a page level (Figure 7).

Parameter Definition

The NPTs (node probability tables) are built using a mixture of empirical data and expert judgments. Yet, the assignment of probabilities is performed differently depending on whether the variable is an intermediate or input node.

Intermediate nodes of the BN are defined/influenced by their parents. For example, the node *NavigationOptions* is defined/influenced by the nodes *LinkToHome* and *BackButton* (see Figure 6). These nodes are not directly measurable, and their probability distribution is determined by expert judgments.

In an initial phase, the NPTs can be defined using expert judgments (Figure 8). They can be adjusted using automatic learning from data samples or from processed cases.

Input nodes of the BN are criteria considered as measurable variables that do not have parents. Most of these criteria are binary (present or not). The other input variables have measurable numerical values. As the number of possible values can be infinite, they have to be transformed into discrete variables with a limited number of values. This is done to ease the definition of probabilities. According to Sahraoui, Boukadoum, Chawiche, Mai, and Serhani (2002), this transformation can be achieved using fuzzy logic. Indeed, the fuzzification process takes the different criterion values and replaces them with a set of functions that represent the degree of membership of each value to different fuzzy labels (usually, "High," "Medium," and "Low").

More specifically, the process of transforming crisp values into probabilities of criterion labels is as follows. First, the criterion value for a large number of Web pages is measured. Then, a fuzzy clustering algorithm is applied on them to specify the number of classes (two or three classes). The optimal number of clusters is determined by the value of Dunn coefficient. Figure 9 provides an example of obtained clusters for the criteria *Dl-Time* with two classes.

The third step consists in defining cluster boundaries using an approximation method (drawing intersecting lines segments tangent to the curves of clusters (Figure 9). Finally, when using the BN for assessing the quality of a particular page, the measure of the input criteria is transformed into a set of probabilities which indicate that the page belongs to a label/class. Note that, as explained in Thomas (1981), the membership function degrees can be used as probabilities with the condition that both the fuzzy clustering algorithm and the approximation method adhere to the fact that the sum of the membership degrees is always equal to one.

EVALUATION AND DISCUSSION

Two approaches for quality assessment of Web applications are presented: detecting anomalies via model checking and using probabilistic quality models. In this section, first their evaluation is described and then a discussion on how they complement each other is presented.

With the model checking approach (Section 3), several Web applications that include static and dynamic pages were tested, eight of those applications were single window and five were multiframe/window applications. The aim was at verifying properties of Web applications based on the user behavior focusing on browsing independently of any navigational aids, such as the back and forward buttons or the browser's history and bookmarks. Using the developed prototype tool according to the framework described previously (Haydar et al., 2004), automata models

Table 2. Some results for a rapid evaluation of several Web pages

Web applications	Navigability design quality at page level (PL)	Web applications	Navigability design quality PL
Winner of *Webby Awards*	85.44 %	The *Worst of the Web* or *The Webby Worthy*	59.24 %
	85.09 %		51.22 %
	80.96 %		74.33 %
	84.83 %		57.88 %

Table 3. Correlation between Calculated and users evaluation values

Calculated Values / User Evaluation Values	NavigabilityDesignP
Perceived Navigability	0.7432
Experienced Navigability	0.7227

were constructed from executions of those Web applications. An open source crawler was used to exhaustively navigate through many static applications and build complete automata models, where the number of states reached 500 and the number of transitions exceeded 20,000. The tool then exported those models into Promela. A set of properties over those models was verified. The properties included reachability properties, frame related properties, and properties translated from the usability and quality rules discussed previously. Examples of properties are:

- Home page is reachable from every other page.
- Secure pages are not reachable without authentication process.
- Combination of words cannot be present in certain pages (this property is checked in frame based Web applications).
- Number of links is balanced (in multiframe/window applications).
- In e-commerce applications, promotions of certain products are only present either on the Home page or on Shopping pages and, for each page, the number of promotions does not exceed 2.

For the approach using probabilistic quality models (Section 4), two types of evaluation were performed. In a first experiment, two groups of Web pages were selected, respectively, from *Top 100 of Webby Awards* and *Worst of the Web or Webby Worthy*. The BN was applied on each page of each group and the probability of the label "good" of navigability design was collected. The goal of the evaluation was to see whether the assessment would not contradict the status of each group. As shown in Table 2, a good score for the pages of *Webby Awards* and low scores for the ones of the *Worst of the Web or Webby worthy* were obtained. This score gives a first indication that the selected and evaluated criteria allow to reach the same conclusions as known ratings.

In a second phase, a controlled experiment was conducted to demonstrate the validity of the approach. The *NavigabilityDesignP* was evaluated for a number of Web pages using the described model. In parallel, users were asked to evaluate the quality of the navigability design for the same pages. The users gave two different evaluations: a subjective one (perceived Navigability) and task-based one, that is, after performing specific tasks using the Web applications (Experienced Navigability). The goal is to compare the model-based assessment with that of the users. As the compared variables are of different natures (respectively, probabilities of "good" navigability design vs. a score on a 10 point scale), correlation-based comparison was used. The results given in Table 3 show a good positive correlation between the model estimations and user evaluation values.

We conclude by aligning two approaches for quality assessment of Web applications, detecting anomalies via model checking, and using probabilistic quality models into a unique perspective. Indeed, they address the problem of quality assessments from two different perspectives and, thus, are complementary in several ways. On one hand, the probabilistic approach has the advantage of evaluating a given Web application, as a whole, based on probabilistic data collected by checking quality criteria in individual Web pages. It allows one to see whether a Web application has a good quality, and thus promotes standard quality criteria and usability rules. Therefore, it offers probabilistic answers and does not give precise refactoring suggestions. On the other hand, the model checking approach has the advantage of detecting precise violations of general or specific quality properties in Web applications. The violations can easily be corrected. However, correcting a set of anomalies does not necessarily guarantee the global quality of the Web applications.

Advantages of one approach are, in fact, limitations of another. For this reason, the use of both approaches allows taking the best from both worlds. More specifically, during the Web application development life cycle, the probabilistic approach can be used prior and during the development to produce quick evaluations of a given Web application, while the formal approach can be used after the development is completed.

From another perspective, properties in the model checking approach that are frequently violated can be modeled as fragments of the BN model and conversely, some fragments in the BN model of the probabilistic approach can be modeled as properties that can be formally verified. The cross fertilization will significantly increase, on one side, the effectiveness of the probabilistic model and, on the other side, the spectrum of properties that can be formally checked.

A final remark that the two approaches use different kinds of information from Web applications: the anomaly detection approach uses mainly execution traces (dynamic analysis), and the probabilistic approach uses measures (static analysis). One can, thus, expect that their joint use provide a more profound quality assessment than each of them separately.

CONCLUSION

In this chapter, the problem of quality assessment of a Web application is addressed from two different, but complementary, perspectives. One approach uses formal methods for the analysis and validation of Web applications. The framework, in which communicating automata models are inferred from execution traces of Web applications, is described. Using Web quality and usability rules, properties are formulated in LTL and verified against the inferred models using Spin model checker. In case a property is not satisfied in a given model, the model checker provides a counter example that helps in pointing out to the problem in the Web application under test. Note that properties verified are not limited to Web quality rules, but also include generic and global properties that can be specific to certain Web applications.

Another approach for quality assessment is based on a probabilistic quality model using Bayesian networks and fuzzy logic. The model built is based on criteria gathered from several existing studies. It is validated using the GQM paradigm. Input parameters are set using fuzzy clustering on a large-size data sample collected on hundreds of Web applications.

The two approaches have been experimentally evaluated. The obtained results are encouraging, although there is room for improvement. Indeed, in the future, the two approaches can further be integrated together. The results of property verification on Web application models using model checking could be used as a basis for reliable statistics in the probabilistic model as new BN nodes to further evaluate the quality level of Web applications. On the other hand, existing nodes in the BN model can be used to formulate properties to be verified on existing Web applications using the first approach.

CONTRIBUTION OF AUTHORS

The first author, as well as the last two authors, contributed mainly to the part related to the model checking approach, the second author contributed to the part related to the probabilistic approach, and the third author to the whole chapter.

REFERENCES

Albuquerque, A. B., & Belchior, A. D. (2002). E-commerce Web sites: A qualitative evaluation. In *Proceedings of the 11th International WWW Conference*. Honolulu, Hawaii.

Baldi, P., Frasconi, P., & Smyth, P. (2003). *Modeling the Internet and the Web: Probabilistic methods and algorithms*. John Wiley.

Basili, V. R., Caldiera, G., & Rombach, H. D. (1994). The goal question metric approach. *Encyclopedia of software engineering*. Retrieved October 16, 2007, from ftp://ftp.cs.umd.edu/pub/sel/papers/gqm.pdf

Benedikt, M., Freire, J., & Godefroid, P. (2002). VeriWeb: Automatically testing dynamic Web sites. In *Proceedings of the 11th International World Wide Web Conference*. Honolulu, Hawaii.

Brajnik, G. (2001). Towards valid quality models for Web sites. In *Proceedings of the 7th Conference on Human Factors and the Web*, Madison, Wisconsin.

Calero, C., Ruiz, J., & Piattini, M. (2004). A Web metrics survey using WQM. In *Proceedings of the International Conference on Web Engineering*, Munich, Germany, (pp. 147-160).

Clarke, E. M., Grumberg, O., & Peled, D. A. (2000). *Model checking*. MIT Press.

Conallen, J. (1999). Modeling Web application architectures, with UML. *Communications of the ACM, 2*(10), 63-70.

De Alfaro, L. (2001a). Model checking the World Wide Web. In G. Berry, H. Comon, & A. Finkel (Eds.), *Proceedings of the 13th International Conference on Computer Aided Verification* (Vol. 2102, pp. 337-349). Paris, France: Lecture Notes in Computer Science.

De Alfaro, L., Henziger, T. A., & Mang, F. Y. C. (2001b). MCWEB: A model-checking tool for Web site debugging. In *Proceedings of the 10th World Wide Web Conference* (pp. 86-87). Hong Kong.

Dhyani, D., NG, W. K., & Bhowmick, S. S. (2002). A survey of Web metrics. *ACM Computing Surveys, 34*(4), 469-503.

Haydar, M., Boroday, S., Petrenko, A., & Sahraoui, H. (2005a). Properties and scopes in Web model checking. In *Proceedings of the 20th IEEE/ACM International Conference on Automated Software Engineering*, Long Beach, CA, (pp. 400-404).

Haydar, M., Boroday, S., Petrenko, A., & Sahraoui, H. (2005b). Propositional scopes in linear temporal logic. In *Proceedings of the 5th International Colloquium on Nouvelles Technologies de la Repartition*, Gatineau, Quebec, (pp. 163-173).

Haydar, M., Petrenko, A., & Sahraoui, H. (2004). Formal verification of Web applications modeled by communicating automata. In *Proceedings of the 24th IFIP WG 6.1 IFIP International Conference on Formal Techniques for Networked and Distributed Systems*, Madrid, Spain, (Vol. 3235, pp. 115-132).

Holzmann, G. J. (2003). *The spin model checker, primer and reference manual*. Addison-Wesley.

IBM (n.d.). *Ease of use – e-commerce topics*. Retrieved October 16, 2007, from http://www-03.ibm.com/easy/page/611

IEEE. (2001). *Web publishing guide*. Retrieved October 16, 2007, from http://www.ieee.org/web/developers/style/

ISO/IEC. (2001). ISO/IEC 9126. (2001). "Software Engineering—Product Quality—Part 1: Quality model"

Ivory, M. (2001). *An empirical foundation for automated Web interface evaluation*. Doctoral dissertation, Berkeley, California: UC Berkeley, Department of Computer Science.

Koyani, S. J., Bailey, R. W., & Nall, J. R. (2003). *Research-based Web design & usability guidelines*. National Institutes of Health.

Laskey, K. B., & Mahoney, S. M. (1997). Network fragments: Representing knowledge for constructing probabilistic models. In *Proceedings of the 13th Annual Conference on uncertainty in Artificial Intelligence*. San Francisco, CA: Morgan Kaufman.

Malak, G., Badri, L., Badri, M., & Sahraoui H. (2004). Towards a multidimensional model for Web- based applications quality assessment. In *Proceedings of the 5th International Conference on E-Commerce and Web Technologies*, Spain, (LNCS Vol. 3182, pp. 316-327). Springer-Verlag.

Naïm, P., Wuillemin, P. H., Leray, P., Pourret, O., & Becker, A. (2004). *Réseaux Bayésiens*. Eyrolles.

Neil, M., Fenton, N. E., & Nielsen, L. (2000). Building large-scale Bayesian Networks. *The Knowledge Engineering Review*, *15*(3), 257-284.

Nielsen, J. (2000). *Designing Web usability: The practice of simplicity*. New Riders Publishing.

Offutt, J. (2002). Web software applications quality attributes. *Quality engineering in software technology* (pp. 187-198). Nuremberg, Germany.

Olsina, L. (1998). Web site quality evaluation method : A case study on museums. In *Proceedings of the ICSE 99 – 2nd Workshop on Software Engineering over the Internet*.

OPQUAST: Bonne pratique qualité pour les services en ligne. (n.d.). Retrieved October 16, 2007, from http://www.opquast.com/

Orebaugh, A., Morris, G., Warnicke, E., & Ramirez, G. (2004). *Ethereal packet sniffing*. Syngress Publishing.

Pertet, S., & Narasimhan, P. (2005). *Causes of failure in Web applications (*Tech. Rep. No. CMU-PDL-05-109). Parallel Data Laboratory. Pittsburgh, PA: Carnegie Mellon University.

Ricca, F., & Tonella, P. (2001). Analysis and testing of Web applications. In *Proceedings of the International Conference on Software Engineering*, Toronto, Canada, (pp. 25-34).

Sahraoui, H., Boukadoum, M., Chawiche, H. M., Mai, G., & Serhani, M. A. (2002). A fuzzy logic framework to improve the performance and interpretation of rule-based quality prediction models for object-oriented software. In *Proceedings of the 26th Computer Software and Applications Conference* (pp. 131-138), Oxford.

Shubert, P., & Dettling, W. (2002). Extended Web assessment method (EWAM): Evaluation of electronic commerce applications from the customer's viewpoint. In *Proceedings of the 35th Hawaii International Conference on System Sciences* (51-80).

SOLEX. (2004). *Web application testing with Eclipse*. Retrieved October 16, 2007, from http://solex.sourceforge.net/

Stotts, P. D., & Cabarrus, C. R. (1998). Hyperdocuments as automata: Verification of trace-based browsing properties by model checking. *ACM Transactions on Information Systems*, *16*(1), 1-30.

Stotts, P. D., & Navon, J. (2002). Model checking CobWeb Protocols for verification of HTML frames behavior. In *Proceedings of the 11th WWW Conference* (pp. 182-190). Hawaii, USA.

Thomas, S. F. (1981). Possibilistic uncertainty and statistical inference. In *Proceedings of the ORSA/TIMS Meeting,* Houston, Texas.

Tonella, P., & Ricca, F. (2002). Dynamic model extraction and statistical analysis of Web applications. In *Proceedings of the International Workshop on Web Site Evolution*, Montreal, Canada, (pp. 43-52).

W3C Recommendation (1999). *Web content accessibility guidelines 1.0*. Retrieved October 16, 2007, from http://www.w3.org/TR/WAI-WEB-CONTENT/

Wu, Y., & Offutt, J. (2002). *Modeling and testing Web-based applications* (Tech. Rep. No. ISE-TR-02-08). GMU ISE Technical.

Zhang, Y., Zhu, H., & Greenwood, S. (2004). Web site complexity metrics for measuring navigability. In *Proceedings of the 4ᵗʰ International Conference on Quality Software* (pp. 172-179).

KEY TERMS

Formal Verification: The use of formal methods to ensure that a set of properties are valid in a given system under test.

GQM: A goal-driven method for developing and maintaining a meaningful measurement program that is based on three levels, goals, questions, and metrics.

Measurement: The determination of the dimensions, in whatever types of units, of an object, product, or process.

Quality: The totality of features and characteristics of a product or service that bear on its ability to satisfy stated or implied needs.

Usability: A set of attributes that bear on the effort needed for use, and on the individual assessment of such use, by a stated or implied set of users (ISO/IEC 9126).

Web Analysis: The process to analyze the behavior of Web applications for the purpose of verification and validation.

Web Application: An application providing interactive services by rendering Web resources in the form of Web pages.

Chapter VI
Automatic Quality Assessment for Internet Pages

Thomas Mandl
Universität Hildesheim, Germany

ABSTRACT

Automatic quality assessment of Web pages needs to complement human information work in the current situation of an information overload. Several systems for this task have been developed and evaluated. Automatic quality assessments are most often based on the features of a Web page itself or on external information. Promising results have been achieved by systems learning to associate human judgments with Web page features. Automatic evaluation of Internet resources according to various quality criteria is a new research field emerging from several disciplines. This chapter presents the most prominent systems and prototypes implemented so far and analyzes the knowledge sources exploited for these approaches.

INTRODUCTION

Many definitions for the quality of information products have been discussed in the research literature. Content and user interface are inseparable on the Web and as a consequence, their evaluation cannot always be separated easily. As a consequence, content and interface are usually considered to form two aspects of quality and they are jointly assessed for Web pages. Many researchers in the area of automatic quality assessment agree that an objective notion of quality cannot be found. Nevertheless, quality can be treated as independent of relevance. Relevance describes the situational value of a page in a search setting. Quality describes aspects of pages independent of any current information need. Consequently, the user should be able to assign quality independent of a concrete information need and its pragmatic parameters.

It is not well understood how humans assess the overall quality of Web pages. However, experiments show that layout and design aspects are very important for human quality and also trust decisions. In several experiments, well designed pages were preferred by users over other pages with comparable content (Dhamija, Tygar, & Hearst, 2006). The assignment of quality to Web pages does not seem to be universally constant. Design and content features which humans consider important for their quality decisions are culturally dependent.

BACKGROUND

Many lists of criteria for the quality of Web pages have been developed from the perspective of library and information science. These lists intend to support the user during quality decision processes (Cooke, 1999). From the perspective of automatic quality assessment, however, these lists are of little help. Their criteria are often vague and it is often not clear whether a rule indicates high or low quality. Lists of quality criteria from several countries proved to partially contain different criteria and to assign different importance to the same criteria. An exemplary survey of over 300 Internet users in Peru and Germany revealed great differences as well. It showed that guidelines for the evaluation of Web sites differ from culture to culture. The typical criteria appearing in many lists from several cultures are arranged in substantially different rankings. This shows that there is no global culture of the Internet and that local cultures still dominate the behavior of Web users. The correlation between the lists is on average between 0.5 and 0.8 (measured by the Spearman Correlation Coefficient, which has a maximum of 1.0). That means that the correlation is only of medium strength (Mandl & de la Cruz, 2006).

QUALITY ASSESSMENT ON THE WEB

Assessing the quality of individual Web pages is the aim of many approaches. The following sections review sources for quality decisions, analyzed features, and implemented systems.

Sources for Human Judgments

The methods which are presented below use the following knowledge sources for quality decisions. Link analysis regards the decisions of Web page authors. A link to a page is considered as a positive quality vote for that page. This source is the one most widely used. It has some disadvantages which will be discussed below. Another source is Web log-files which show which pages have been visited more often than others. Such approaches are limited to a small number of sites which are willing to provide the log-files. Moreover, it is not clear whether users visited the page because of its high quality or whether they evaluated it negatively during their visit. Nevertheless log data from search engines, which is called click-through data, is commonly used as knowledge source for relevance decisions (Shen, Tan, & Zhai, 2005). Relevance assessment from information retrieval can also be used (Kamps, 2005; Wang, Liu, Zhang, & Ma, 2005).

Many explicit decisions are available in quality controlled Internet directories or clearinghouses for which humans jurors or editors judge sites and decide whether they are worthy of being included. Explicit decisions for a limited number of Web sites are available in recommendations and reviews. Very important for large scale systems are the content and code of pages which can be interpreted in various ways for quality assumptions (Mandl & de la Cruz, 2007). One needs to be aware that the subjective judgment of the individual user is often highly correlated with the visual aspects of a page (Rachna, Tygar, & Hearst, 2006).

Typical Criteria for Page Quality Measures

One of the first automatic quality assessment systems originated in Web engineering and performed HTML syntax checking and validation. Syntax checkers and validation programs for HTML and other Web standards analyze the quality of Web pages from the perspective of software engineering (Brajnik, 2004). These tools test the proper use of HTML and report errors like missing closing tags or other syntax errors. These errors might remain unnoticed for viewers of the page. These systems can recognize issues for cross browser compatibility and accessibility.

Beyond syntax, these systems consider issues of information presentation and optimal use of HTML. For example, the use of an alternative text for an image is highly recommended by most Web design guidelines. Such a text can be displayed while the image is still loading or provide additional information even when the image is being shown. The proper use of the tag is not necessary but it improves the human-computer interaction. Systems like Weblint (Bowers, 1996) check if this alternative text is included. These systems might also check the proper organization of the information by controlling page organization. They report whether the headline tags are used in proper order. For example, a third level headline should be preceded by a secondary headline. Other tools check the use of meta tags.

Recently, syntax checking tools have become more elaborate and emphasize aspects of accessibility. A comprehensive service like WebXACT (Watchfire, 2006) reports quality problems like HTML elements missing height and width attributes and browser compatability.

Several studies which implemented an automatic quality assessment used machine learning algorithms to associate human judgments on quality with atomic features extracted from pages. The following section focuses on the features used. Some systems use only one single feature of a page as a quality indicator. In the Digester system, the expected utility of a Web page is measured as a function of its size. The smaller a page is, the higher its utility for the user is estimated (Bickmore & Schilit, 1997). Size is a property that is also analyzed (Kamps, 2005). Kamps considered the pages out of a large Web collection which were identified as relevant by humans for information retrieval tasks.

Temporal aspects are also often exploited. The freshness of a page can be seen from the modification date and the number of dead links on a page is an indicator for the quality of the maintenance (Spinellis, 2003). The decay of a page can even be interpreted as the number of dead links encountered when following subsequent links of the page (Bar-Yossef, Kumar, Broder, & Tomkins, 2004).

Some researchers relied on more than one feature when developing their systems. In one study, six features of Web pages were manually derived and compared to usage data. The initial hypotheses was, that pages which follow popular Web design guidelines might attract more viewers than other pages. The judges looked for the dominant color, the presence of advertisement, logos, animations and frames, and the frequency of links and graphics (Bucy, Lang, Potter, & Grabe, 1999). Some of the features were better predictors for the high usage of the pages than others.

The approach implemented by Zhu and Gauch (2000) automatically extracts six criteria for the quality of Web pages: *currency, availability, information–to–noise ratio, authority, popularity,* and *cohesiveness.* These criteria are used to influence the ranking of documents in a retrieval system. In retrieval experiments, it was shown that the average precision of the rankings, including quality measures, outperformed those which relied solely on traditional information retrieval measures in some cases. However, this evaluation does not take the quality of the results into account, but only the relevance of the pages in the result list. An appropriate evaluation needs to investigate whether the average quality of the result list has increased. In order to do that, test users need to be asked to judge the results pages according to their subjective quality perception.

Amento, Terveen, and Hill (2000) also stress the importance of a distinction between relevance and quality. An experiment involving some 1000 pages suggests that the human perception of the quality of Web pages can be predicted equally well by four formally defined features. These four features include link analysis measures like the PageRank value and the total number of in-links. Simple features like the number of pages on a site and the number of graphics on a page correlated highly with the human judgments (Amento et al., 2000).

The system WebTango extracts more than 150 atomic and simple features from a Web page and tries to reveal statistical correlations to a set of sites rated as excellent (Ivory, Sinha, & Hearst, 2001). The extracted features are based on the design, the structure, and the HTML code of a page. WebTango includes the ratings of the Weblint syntax checking software. The definition of the features is based on hypotheses on the effect of certain design elements on usability. As a consequence, the approach is restricted by the validity of these assumptions. The data was extracted form an Internet design award for popular pages. Pages assigned the award were considered to be of high quality. The collection contained 5400 pages. They were distributed over the categories good, average, and poor. Classifiers could learn this mapping between quality decisions and features with high accuracy (Ivory et al., 2001).

An experiment which focused on the quality aspect in the user test considered 113 features extracted from the Web pages (Mandl, 2006). The following list shows the categories and gives a few examples for each category:

- **File measures:** Number of elements, length of URL, length of HTML title, file size.
- **Frequency of important HTML tags:** H1, H2, H3, layer, table, frameset, frequency of a set of text style tags.
- **Measures based on HTML lists:** number of lists, average, median, and deviation of the number of li tags per list.
- **Measures based on HTML tables:** Number of embedded tables, number of tables divided by file size, average, median, and deviation of the number of tr and td tags per table.

- **Colors:** Number of colors, number of unique colors, RGB values of most frequent color, text color, background color.
- **Language features:** Number of words, number of unique words, number of stop-words, number of sentence markers, relation between words and stopwords.
- **Calculated measures and relations between atomic measures:** Number of out-links to file size, number of graphics to DOM elements, number of graphics to text length, number of words to DOM elements.

Many features capture in some way the complexity of the page. The structural complexity is correlated, for example, to the number of DOM elements encountered. Several features intend to measure the level of balance in a page with respect to several aspects. Balance is an important aspect in graphic design. Good design needs to find a tradeoff between a high level of structure and a high level of complexity. Structure is emphasized, for example, through symmetry. Highly symmetric pages appear well structured; however, too much symmetry or too simple forms of symmetry may lead to a lack of visual stimuli which might ultimately cause boredom. High visual complexity can be caused by a lack of symmetry or by many symmetry axes.

Other features capture in some way the graphic design of the page. These include the number of graphics on a page, the number of links to graphics, the relation between the number of graphics, and the file size. The language features and especially the number of stopwords and file size and some relations calculated based on these atomic features try to capture the information to noise ratio of a Web page. These measures are motivated by the information to noise ratio proposed by Zhu and Gauch (2000), and extend it to language features.

The experiments reported in Mandl (2006) showed that the perceived quality of the pages in the results set increased when the quality model was applied. In the experiment, a standard search engine was used within a metasearch service. The metasearch sent the user query to a search engine and collected the result pages. These pages were analyzed according to their quality by the model which was trained off-line. The ranking was modified in order to assign higher ranks to high quality pages. The experiments counterbalanced ranking fusion methods and base Web search engines. Among the first 10 or 20 documents, more high quality pagers were encountered if the quality ranking was applied compared to a random ranking or the original search engine ranking. The quality models were further analyzed in order to identify highly relevant features of Web pages. Surprisingly, several language factors were among the most important ones (Mandl, 2006).

Content: The Quality of Text

If systems for assessing the quality of text succeed, they will play an important role for human-computer interaction. The readability of text is an important issue for the usability of a page. Good readability leads to a fast and more satisfying interaction. The prototypes developed so far are focused on the application of teacher assistance for essay grading; however, the use of such systems for Web resources will soon be debated. The automatic evaluation of the quality of text certainly poses many ethical questions and will raise a lot of debate once it is implemented on a larger scale.

Two approaches are used in prototypes for the automatic evaluation of texts. The first approach is to measure the coherence of a text and use it as a yardstick. The second typical approach is to calculate the similarity of the texts to sample texts which have been evaluated and graded by humans. The new texts are then graded according to their similarity to the already graded texts.

A different application domain is addressed by the Intelligent Essay Assessor, which is based on Latent semantic indexing (LSI) (Foltz, Klintsch,

& Landauer, 1999). LSI is a reduction technique. In text analysis, usually each word is used for the semantic description of the text resulting in a large number of descriptive elements. LSI analyzes the dependencies between these dimensions and creates a reduced set of artificial semantic dimensions. The Intelligent Essay Assessor considers a set of essays graded by humans. For each essay, it calculates the similarity of the essay to the graded essays using text classification methods. The grade of the most similar cluster is then assigned to the essay. For 1200 essays, the system reached a correlation of 0.7 to the grades assigned by humans. The correlation between two humans was not higher than that (Foltz et al., 1999). The Intelligent Essay Grader could be modified for the Web and used to evaluate the text on pages. Such systems still need to be adapted to the domain texts on the Web. They would be dependent on the language for which they were developed.

Site Design

In an early effort, the design of sites was analyzed quantitatively. The approach of Botafogo, Rivlin, and Shneiderman (1992) evaluated the balance and structure of the hypergraph of a site were analyzed with newly developed graph based measures. The degree of compactness of a hypergraph is measured as the degree to which pages are linked to each other. Another measure called stratum captures the degree of linearity of the site structure. This measure is low for fully hierarchically organized. However, site structure is merely one aspect of Web quality and does not seem to be a sufficient indicator for a quality search engine. The number of incoming links is also related to the structure of a Web page (Mandl, 2007).

External features: Link Analysis

The most prominent knowledge source using information encountered outside the Web page itself is link analysis. It exploites merely the link structure and the links between Web pages to analyse the quality of these pages. The basic assumption of link analysis is that the number of links which point to a Web page are a measure for the popularity and consequently for the quality of a page. These links which refer to a page are often called in- or back-links of that page. A popular algorithm is PageRank (Borodin, Roberts, Rosenthal, & Tsaparas, 2005; Langville & Meyer, 2004). PageRank assigns an authority value to each Web page which is primarily a function of its back links. Additionally, it assumes that links from pages with high authority should be weighed higher and should result in a higher authority for the receiving page. To account for the different values each page has to distribute, the algorithm runs out iteratively until the result converges to a fairly stable result. Information retrieval in Web search engines is the most important application of link analysis.

Link analysis has several disadvantages. The assignment of links by Web authors to pages is a social process which globally leads to stable distribution patterns. Most importantly, the number of in-links for Web pages follows a power law distribution (Borodin et al., 2005). A power law distribution is an extremely unequal distribution of some good in which the median value is much lower than the average. This means, that many pages have few in-links, while few pages have an extremely high number of in-links. This finding indicates that Web page authors choose the Web sites they link to without a thorough quality evaluation. Much rather, they act according to economic principles and invest as little time as possible for their selection. As a consequence, authors as social actors in networks rely on the preferences of other actors. Another reason for setting links is thematic similarity. The number of incoming links to a Web page depends to a large extent on the structural position of a Web page within a site. Homepages are more likely to attract many links than other pages deeply in a site structure (Mandl, 2007).

Definitely, quality considerations are not the only reason for setting a link.

The popularity of link analysis and the assumptions about its role in search engine rankings has led to great efforts by search engines optimization professionals. Many links are set only to gain influence on the ranking of certain pages. These so called link spamming efforts occur in a large scale.

An alternative approach using external knowledge can be found in social network analysis. One example for a system uses some 130.000 users which requires only a few trust decisions by each member and manages to propage trust over several links formed by social ties (Guha, Kumar, Raghavan & Tomkins, 2004).

FUTURE TRENDS

In the future, many real world systems for automatic quality control need to be developed in order to support users in their information work when confronted with the information overload on the Internet. More complex quality models based on more features will be developed and fusion systems integrating different quality definitions will be established. Link analysis will become a part of such integrated models. Natural language processing will gain more importance in the quality assessment. Models will be different for domains and user needs.

More research should be dedicated to empirical Web design which analyses the design of many pages by Web mining techniques. That way, more knowledge on the design of sites present on the Web could be derived. Some examples for studies have been published. Web Design Mining (Eibl & Mandl, 2005) should become a new field of Web mining.

CONCLUSION

Information search has been delegated to machines and information retrieval has become a key technology in the information society. Currently, other aspects of knowledge work are being delegated fully or partly to machines. Automatic quality assessment of Web pages has been implemented in link analysis at a large scale and more elaborated systems are reaching maturity. These systems use properties of Web pages which can be extracted automatically and they are associated with machine learning algorithms to human quality judgments.

REFERENCES

Amento, B., Terveen, L., & Hill, W. (2000). Does "authority" mean quality? Predicting expert quality ratings of Web documents. In *Proceedings of the Annual International ACM Conference on Research and Development in Information Retrieval (SIGIR 2000),* Athens, (pp. 296-303). ACM Press.

Bar-Yossef, Z., Kumar, R., Broder, A., & Tomkins, A. (2004). Sic transit gloria telae: Towards an understanding of the Web's decay. In *Proceedings of the International WWW Conference*, New York, USA, (pp. 328-337).

Bickmore, T., & Schilit, B. (1997). Digestor: Device-independent access to the World Wide Web. *Computer Networks and ISDN Systems, 29*(8-13), 1075-1082.

Botafogo, R., Rivlin, E., & Shneiderman, B. (1992). Structural analysis of hypertexts: Identifying hierarchies and useful metrics. *ACM Transactions on Information Systems, 10*(2), 142-180.

Borodin A., Roberts, G., Rosenthal, J., & Tsaparas, P. (2005). Link analysis ranking: Algorithms, theory, and experiments. *ACM Transactions on Internet Technology (TOIT), 5*(1), 231-297.

Bowers, N. (1996). Weblint: Quality assurance for the World Wide Web. *Computer Networks and ISDN Systems, 28*(7), 1283-1290.

Brajnik, G. (2004, June). Using automatic tools in accessibility and usability assurance. In C. Stephenidis (Ed.), Proceedings of the 8th ERCIM UI4ALL Workshop, Vienna, Austria. Springer-Verlag [LNCS].

Bucy, E., Lang, A., Potter, R., & Grabe, M. (1999). Formal features of cyberspace: Relationships between Web page complexity and site traffic. *Journal of the American Society for Information Science, 50*(13), 1246-1256.

Cooke, A. (1999). Authoritative guide to evaluating information on the Internet. New York & London: Neal-Schuman.

Dhamija, R., Tygar, J. D., & Hearst, M. (2006, April 22-27). Why phishing works. In *Proceedings of the SIGCHI Conference on Human Factors in Computing Systems CHI '06*, Montréal, Québec, Canada, (pp. 581-590). New York: ACM Press. DOI= http://doi.acm.org/10.1145/1124772.1124861

Eibl, M., & Mandl, T. (2005). An empirical assessment of colour use on the WWW. In Proceedings of the 11th International Conference on Human-Computer Interaction (HCI Intl.), Las Vegas, (Vol. 2, The management of information: E-business, the Web, and mobile computing). Mahwah, NJ; London: Lawrence Erlbaum Associates.

Foltz, P., Klintsch, W., & Landauer, T. (1998). The measurement of textual coherence with latent semantic analysis. Discourse Processes, 25(2&3), 285-307.

Guha, R., Kumar, R., Raghavan, P., & Tomkins, A. (2004, May 17-20). Propagation of trust and distrust. In *Proceedings of the 13th international Conference on World Wide Web WWW ,04*, New York, NY, USA, (pp. 403-412). New York: ACM Press. DOI= http://doi.acm.org/10.1145/988672.988727

Ivory, M., Sinha, R., & Hearst, M. (2001). Empirically validated Web page design metrics. In *Proceedings of the SIGCHI Conference on Human factors in Computing Systems*, (pp. 53-60).

Kamps, J. (2005) Web-centric language models. In Proceedings of the 14th ACM international Conference on Information and Knowledge Management (CIKM), (pp. 307-308).

Langville, A., & Meyer, C. (2004). A survey of eigenvector methods of Web information retrieval. SIAM review. *Journal of the Society for Industrial and Applied Mathematics, 47*, 135.

Mandl, T. (2006). Implementation and evaluation of a quality based search engine. In Proceedings of the 17th ACM Conference on Hypertext and Hypermedia (HT '06), Odense, Denmark (pp. 73-84). ACM Press.

Mandl, T. (2007). The impact of site structure on link analysis. *Internet Research, 17*(2), *196-206.*

Mandl, T., & de la Cruz, T. (2007). International differences in Web page evaluation guidelines. *International Journal of Intercultural Information Management (IJIIM), 1*(2). To appear.

Rachna, D., Tygar, J., & Hearst, M. (2006). Why phishing works. In *Proceedings of the ACM SIG-CHI Conference on Human Factors in Computing Systems*, (pp. 581-590).

Shen, X., Tan, B., & Zhai, C. (2005). Context-sensitive information retrieval using implicit feedback. In Proceedings of the 28th Annual International ACM SIGIR Conference on Research and Development in Information Retrieval (SIGIR '05), (pp. 43-50).

Spinellis, D. (2003). The decay and failures of Web references. *Communications of the ACM, 46*(1), 71-77.

Wang, C., Liu, Y., Zhang, M., & Ma, S. (2005). Data cleansing for Web information retrieval using query independent features. In *Proceedings of the Information Retrieval Technology, 2nd Asia Information Retrieval Symposium (AIRS 2005)*, Jeju Island, Korea [LNCS 3689], (pp. 516-521).

Watchfire. (2006). WebXACT system. Retrieved October 16, 2007, from http://www.webxact.com/

Zhu, X., & Gauch, S. (2000). Incorporating quality metrics in centralized/distributed information retrieval on the World Wide Web. In *Proceedings of the ACM Conference on Research and Development in Information Retrieval (SIGIR 2000)*, Athens, (pp. 288-295).

KEY TERMS

Accessibility: Accessibility is a subfield of human-computer interaction and deals with users with deficiencies. These deficiencies mostly lie in the perception capabilities. For example, users who cannot see or hear as well as other require special consideration during the implementation of user interfaces.

Human-Computer Interaction: HCI deals with the optimization of interfaces between human users and computing systems. Technology needs to be adapted to the properties and the needs of users. The knowledge sources available for this endeavor are guidelines, rules, standards and results from psychological research on the human perception and cognitive capabilities. Evaluation is necessary to validate the success of interfaces.

Information Retrieval: Information retrieval is concerned with the representation and knowledge and subsequent search for relevant information within these knowledge sources. Information retrieval provides the technology behind search engines.

Latent Semantic Indexing: LSI is a dimensionality reduction technique for objects which are represented by large and sparsely populated vectors. The original vector space is formally transformed into a space with less but artificial dimensions. The new vector space has fewer dimensions and is an approximation of the original space.

Link Analysis: The links between pages on the Web are a large knowledge source which is exploited by link analysis algorithms for many ends. Many algorithms similar to PageRank determine a quality or authority score based on the number of incoming links of a page. Furthermore, link analysis is applied to identify thematically similar pages, Web communities and other social structures.

Machine Learning: Machine learning is a subfield of artificial intelligence which provides algorithms for the discovery of relations or rules in large data sets. Machine learning leads to functions which can automatically classify or categorize objects based on their features. Inductive learning from labeled examples is the most well known application.

Quality: In the context of information systems, quality describes the degree to which a product or service fulfills certain requirements. Quality measures the excellence of a product or system quality is usually is context dependent.

Chapter VII
A General View of Quality Models for Web Portals and a Particularization to E–Banking Domain

Mª Ángeles Moraga
University of Castilla—La Mancha, Spain

Julio Córdoba
University of Alicante, Spain

Coral Calero
University of Castilla—La Mancha, Spain

Cristina Cachero
University of Alicante, Spain

ABSTRACT

The success of Web portals has increased over time, in such a way that a portal user can choose among a wide variety of portals. Therefore, the presence of a Web portal in Internet will depend on its quality. In this chapter, several portal quality models are presented and compared. Moreover, one of the best portal quality model previously proposed has been adapted to the e-banking context. Finally, the new e-banking portal quality model has been compared with the original portal quality model, as well as with the main portal quality characteristics.

INTRODUCTION

A portal is a Web presence that consolidates a variety of information and services for example, searching, news, e-mail, discussion groups, and e-commerce (Ma, Bacon, Petridis, & Windall, 2006). The aim of Web portals is to select, organize, and distribute content (information, or other services and products) in order to satisfy its users/customers (Domingues, Soares, & Jorge, 2006).

Although the term was initially used to refer to general purpose Web sites such as Yahoo, it is increasingly being used to refer to vertical Web sites that feature personalization/customization, cross-platform usability, distributed access, management, and security of information and services within a particular enterprise/industry, and thus the so-called enterprise, corporate, or vertical portals (Ma et al., 2006).

Over the past years, the number of Web portals has grown, in such a way that nowadays a wide variety of portals are offered. Consequently, portal users have to choose one portal among several hundred possibilities. Therefore, the success of a portal depends on customers using and returning to their sites, because if a new portal puts up a competitive site of higher quality, customers will almost immediately shift their visits to the new site once they discover it (Offutt, 2002). As more people use Web portals, the quality of Web portals has become an important issue for owners to satisfy their users.

Bearing all that in mind, it can be concluded that portal existence depends on its quality. Portal quality must be assessed in accordance with a *"quality model"* that makes it possible to determine the quality level that a Web portal reaches.

In general, quality models should consider criteria that satisfy the needs of the developers, maintainers, buyers, and end users (ISO/IEC, 2001). Quality models can be split into two different types, general quality models, which can be adopted as-is and specify what has to be measured and how (Brajnik, 2001), and specific models. Specific models, which are only valid for a concrete context, can stem from a generic model that has been tailored for such concrete context.

This chapter discusses related literature review on general quality models for Web portals. In addition, the chapter makes an attempt to contribute to the literature by proposing a specific quality model for e-banking context. In concrete, section 2 presents a brief overview of general models for portal quality, whereas in section 3 the specific quality model for e-banking context is shown. Moreover, in this section a comparative among the different models of the literature and the proposed model is presented. Finally, the last section outlines the main conclusions as well as the principal areas of future work.

GENERAL MODELS FOR PORTAL QUALITY

In this section, we are going to present some proposals of portal quality models and a comparative study made with them. This study is explained deeply in Moraga, Calero, and Piattini (2006).

PQM: A Portal Quality Model: Moraga, Calero, and Piattini (2004)

In Moraga et al. (2004) a model for portals, namely PQM (Portal Quality Model) is proposed. This model has been made using as a basis the SERVQUAL model, presented by Parasuraman, Zeithami, and Berry (1998) and the GQM (Goal Question Metric) method (Basili, Caldiera, & Rombach, 1994).

The different dimensions of the SERVQUAL model have been adapted to the portal context and some of them are split up into subdimensions, in order to create a quality model for Web portals. As a final result, the dimensions identified for the PQM model are:

- **Tangible:** Characteristic of the portal that indicates whether it contains all the software and hardware infrastructures needed, according to its functionality. The subcharacteristics are:
  - **Adaptability:** Ability of the portal to be adapted to different devices (for instance PDA's, PCs, mobile phones, etc.).
  - **Transparent access:** Ability of the portal to provide access to the resources, while at the same time isolating the user from their complexity.
- **Reliability:** Ability of the portal to perform its functionality accurately. In addition, this characteristic will be affected by:
  - **Fault tolerance:** Capability of the portal to maintain a specified level of performance in the event of software faults (e.g., a fault during the sending of information or the execution of a job).
  - **Resource utilization:** Capability of the portal to offer its resources to the user according to his profile or particular role or privileges.
  - **Availability:** Capability of the portal to be always operative, so that users may be able to access it and use it anywhere, anytime.
  - **Search Quality:** Appropriateness of the results that the portal provides when undertaking a search/request made by the user.
- **Responsiveness:** Willingness of the portal to help and provide its functionality in an immediate form to the users. In this characteristic, the subcharacteristics are:
  - **Scalability:** Ability of the portal to adapt smoothly to increasing workloads which come about as the result of additional users, an increase in traffic volume, or the execution of more complex transactions.
  - **Speed:** Ability of the portal to remain within the response time boundaries tolerated by portal users.
- **Empathy:** Ability of the portal to provide caring and individual attention. This dimension has the following subcharacteristics:
  - **Navigation:** Simplicity and intuitiveness of the navigation paths provided by the portal.
  - **Presentation:** Clarity and uniformity of the interface.
  - **Integration:** Degree of global portal coherence achieved after the inclusion of the components that make up the portal. All the components of the portal must be integrated in a coherent form.
  - **Personalization:** The portal's capability to adapt to the user's priorities.
- **Data quality (DQ):** This characteristic is defined as the quality of the data contained in the portal. It has four subcharacteristics:
  - **Intrinsic DQ:** Degree of care taken in the creation and preparation of information.
  - **Representation DQ:** Degree of care taken in the presentation and organization of information for users.
  - **Accessibility DQ:** Degree of freedom that users have to use data, define or refine the manner in which information is input, processed or presented to them.
  - **Contextual DQ:** Degree to which the information provided meets the needs of the users.
- **Security:** Capability of the portal to prevent, reduce, and respond to malicious attacks adequately. Its subcharacteristics are:
  - **Access control:** Capability of the portal to allow access to its resources only to authorized people. Thus, the portal must be able to identify, authenticate, and authorize its users.

Figure 1. PQM

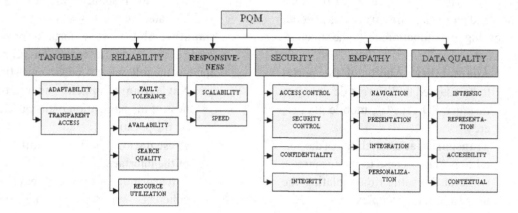

Security control: Capability of the portal to carry out auditing of security and to detect attacks. The auditing of security shows the degree to which security personnel are enabled to audit the status and use of security mechanisms by analyzing security-related events. In addition, attack detection seeks to detect, record, and notify attempted attacks as well as successful attacks.

○ Confidentiality: Ability to guard the privacy of the users.

○ Integrity: Capability of the portal to protect components (of data, hardware, and software) from intentional or unauthorized modifications.

In Figure 1, a summary of the PQM characteristics and subcharacteristics is shown.

An Instrument to Measure User Perceived Service Quality: Yang, Cai, Zhou, and Zhou (2004)

The objective of Yang et al. (2004) is to develop and validate an instrument to measure user-perceived overall service quality of IP Web portals (Information Presenting Web portal). This in-

formation is useful for researchers and for portal managers.

According to (Eisenmann & Pothen, 2000) an IP Web portal is "a site that provides users with online information and information-related services, such as search functions, community building features, commerce offerings, personal productivity applications, and a channel of communication with the site owner and peer users."

The authors adopt the technology adoption model (TAM) and consider that an IP Web portal is an information system (IS). For these reasons, the following conceptual foundations are taken into account (Figure 2):

• Information quality (IQ): Web-based information is defined as "users' perception of the quality of information presented on a Web site." Under this point, the dimensions are classified into:

○ Usefulness of content: Value, reliability, currency, and accuracy of information.

○ Adequacy of information: Extent of completeness of information.

• System quality (SQ): This refers to customers' perception of a Web site's performance in information retrieval and delivery. Factors are categorized into four dimensions:

Figure 2. Proposed conceptual foundations and quality dimensions of information presenting Web portals (Yang et al., 2004).

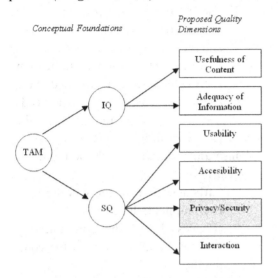

Usability: This is related to user friendliness. Here, various factors have been identified: content layout and classification, Web site structure, user interface, Web site appearance and visual design, intuitiveness, readability/comprehension/clarity, search facilities, and ease of navigation.

○ **Accessibility:** Customers expect the Web-based services to be available at all times and they also desire speedy log-on access, search, and Web page download. This dimension involves two aspects: availability and responsiveness.

○ **Privacy/Security:** Some frequently-used measures are: to include vendor guarantees of protection of personal information, confidence resulting from promises on the site, and the reputation of the organization.

○ **Interaction:** Although using an IP Web portal is primarily a self-served process, users may still expect to receive personalized or customized services

from a knowledgeable, responsive, and caring contact person.

A Flexible Evaluation Framework for Web Portals: Sampson and Manouselis (2004)

Sampson and Manouselis (2004) present an evaluation framework for addressing the multiple dimensions of Web portals that can affect user satisfaction.

As a first step, the authors defined several dimensions related to the main satisfaction factors:

- **Web portal content:** The dimensions were:
  ○ **Satisfaction from content organization:** This aspect refers to the categorization of information so as to enable efficient search and retrieval.
  ○ **Satisfaction from content credibility:** This aspect refers to the trust and reliability of the information and the content provider and has multiple facets, such as the accuracy and clarity of the content and the trustworthiness, recognition and reputation of the content author or provider.
  ○ **Satisfaction from content usefulness:** This aspect concerns the focus of the content, the use of appropriate language, and the usefulness of information according to the needs of the audience to whom it is directed.
  ○ **Satisfaction from content integration:** This aspect concerns all content services related with the integration of external sources of information and the provision of links to external resources.
- **Design of a Web portal:**
  ○ **Satisfaction from information architecture:** It is closely related to the

organization of content. In this context, however, it is approached rather from the system design perspective, and it can therefore be considered independent.

○ **Satisfaction from usability:** Addresses all issues related to the interaction and navigation of the user in the portal.

○ **Satisfaction from graphical design:** The Web portal design should be subject to periodical revisions and redesigns from time to time, with the minimum possible effect to the portal operation.

○ **Satisfaction from technical integrity/performance:** The dimension concerned with proper operation of the Web portal services and the satisfactory performance of the overall services.

• **Personalization:**

○ **Satisfaction from the personalization of navigation:** All issues related to the adjustment of the navigation mechanism and functions to the needs of individual users.

○ **Satisfaction from the personalization of information/content:** All issues related to notifying users about new relevant content and providing them with information tailored to their needs and preferences.

○ **Satisfaction from the personalization of interface:** All issues related to the adaptation of the interface to the needs and preferences of the users and the properties of their equipment.

• **Community support:** With the following dimensions:

○ **Satisfaction from the communication support:** It refers to tools and services related to the communication between the members of a virtual community.

○ **Satisfaction from the collaboration support:** Related to the tools and services allowing effective and efficient collaboration between users.

In Figure 3, the evaluation framework proposed by Sampson and Manouselis (2004) is summarized.

Figure 3. Evaluation framework for Web portals proposed by Sampson and Manouselis (2004)

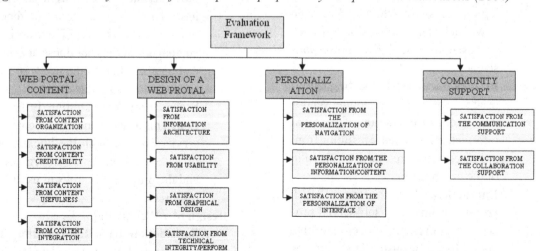

The authors then presented a methodology to assess the strong and weak points of a Web portal. This methodology is composed of three steps: in the first step, a set of criteria and subcriteria upon which the different dimensions of user satisfaction from a Web portal are defined; in the second step, the integration of the results collected is carried out and partial satisfaction indicators are obtained; in the third step, techniques for the analysis of the evaluation results are put into operation. Following, the authors presented an evaluation process so this methodology could be integrated into a generic evaluation procedure. As a result, a framework was formulated.

Drivers of Web Portal Use: Telang and Mukhopadhyay (2004)

Telang and Mukhopadhyay (2004) tried to explore how Internet users choose portals. In order to do so, the authors relied on the cognitive psychology and human computer interaction (HCI) literature, along with marketing literature, in an attempt to understand the drivers of Web portal use.

Firstly, the authors affirmed that a successful portal needs users who repeatedly come back to the same portal on a frequent basis for extended periods of use. This is because portal services are given away for free, and users have access to multiple providers. So they defined three measures of portal use:

- **Repeat use:** No portal can be financially viable without a significant fraction of its users coming back to the site repeatedly.
- **Stickiness:** Portal site operators want the users to spend more time per visit.
- **Frequency:** Users must return to the site frequently to increase the viability of the portal business model.

Secondly, they developed a conceptual model of portal use made up of three components:

- **A model of repeat use:** This model examines the effect of repeated use, demographics and other variables on portal choice.
- **A model of stickiness:** This model on stickiness concerns the length of user visits.
- **A model of use frequency:** This model examines the frequency of portal use.

For each one of the previous models, a set of independent and dependent variables were defined (Table 1).

After that, the authors estimated each one of the models using:

Table 1. Independent and dependent variables in each model

Model	Dependent variable	Independent variables
Repeat use model	Choice variable (1 for the portal visited, o for others)	Repeat use (RU), advertisement (Ad), cumulative negative experience (CNE), demographic variables (Demo), five portal level dummies. They create three RU variables for each task, RU_S (for search), RU_I (for information) and RU_PS (for personal)
Stickiness model	Number of minutes spent on a portal	Repeat use (RU), cumulative negative experience (CNE), demographic variables (Demo), six portal level dummies. They create three dummy variables (one for each task) and S (for search), I (for information) and PS (for personal)
Frequency model	Count of number of visits to all portals in a week. Count of number of visits to all portals in a week for each task.	Repeat use (RU), trend (T), previous week's count (Count_Lag), demographic variables (Demo). They add three lag variables, one for each task. Lag_S (Lag of search task), Lag_I (Lag of Information task), Lag_PS (Lag of Personal task)

- Multinomial logic for estimating the repeat use model.
- Fixed effect OLS regression for estimating the stickiness model.
- Negative binomial regression for estimating the frequency model.

To estimate these models, the authors collected Internet navigation data for 102 demographically diverse Internet users for six major portals over a period of 1 year. They analysed the results and found that there existed a connection between the selection of a particular portal and use of information and personal services, the quality of the search services, and so forth.

Comparing the Models

In this section, we attempt to compare the models presented previously. In Table 2, the main characteristics of the models set out in the previous section are shown.

From the previous table, the following main conclusions can be inferred:

- The (Telang et al., 2004) proposal focuses on studying how different factors affect portal use but it does not study portal quality
- The instrument developed by Yang et al. (2004) focuses on a specific type of portals, namely IP Web portals, and as such it is not a generic model.
- The (Sampson et al., 2004) proposal has not been validated.

Table 2. A comparative among the different models

Characteristics	Model			
	PQM	**Yang**	**Sampson**	**Telang**
Objective	Develop and validate a portal quality model	Develop and validate an instrument to measure user perceived overall service quality of IP Web portals	Develop an evaluation framework for addressing the multiple dimensions of Web portals that can affect users' satisfaction	Try to explore how Internet users choose portals.
Background	SERVQUAL model	The technology adoption model (TAM)	(Winkler, 2001), (Nielsen, 2000) (Lacher, Koch, & Woerndl, 2001), etc.	Cognitive psychology and human computer interaction literature along with marketing literature
Type of portal	All portals	IP Web portals	All portals	All portals
Number of dimensions	Six	Six	Thirteen	None
Methodology	GQM	Methodology proposed by (Churchill, 1979)	No	No
Measures	No	No	Yes	Repeat use, stickiness and frequency
Validation	No	They conducted a principal component factor analysis, and a confirmatory factor analysis.	No	It is based on Internet navigation data of 102 demographically diverse users for six major portals over a period of one year
Application	It has been applied to a Spanish regional portal	It has been applied to a IP Web portal of Hong Kong	It has been applied to the Go-Digital Portal	No
Tools	No	No	No	No

Table 3. Dimensions proposed by Yang et al. (2004) vs. dimensions of PQM

Dimensions proposed by Yang et al. (2004)	PQM dimensions
Usefulness of content	Contextual Data Quality
Adequacy of information	Intrinsic Data Quality
Usability	Navigation, Presentation, Confidentiality
Accessibility	Availability, speed
Interaction	Personalization

- The PQM model has not defined measures yet.

In Table 2, we specify the number of dimensions that have been observed in each model proving that PQM has taken into account more portal dimensions than the others. Hence, we compare the dimensions of the rest of the models with respect to the dimensions proposed in the PQM model. In Table 3, we compare the dimensions identified by Yang et al. (2004) with PQM dimensions and in Table 4, the dimensions proposed by Sampson and Manouselis (2004) and the corresponding ones in the PQM model are shown.

From this comparative we can conclude that:

- PQM takes into account all the dimensions of the model proposed by Yang et al. (2004) and also the following ones: tangible, scalability, integration, personalization (from the point of view of the portal), representation data quality, and accessibility (although they have defined a dimension called accessibility, the meaning of this term is different).
- Although Sampson and Manouselis (2004) identify more dimensions than PQM, all the aspects considered by them are considered in PQM as well. Also, we can see that only in PQM the tangible dimension exist. And moreover, the following subdimensions has been proposed in PQM and they do not appear in the model proposed by Sampson and Manouselis (2004): availability, search quality, scalability, speed, and confidentiality.

We can thus infer from the previous tables that the dimensions which have been set out in all models are:

Table 4. Dimensions proposed by Sampson et al. (2004) vs. dimensions of PQM

Dimensions proposed by Sampson et al. (2004)	PQM dimensions
Satisfaction from content organization	Representation
Satisfaction from content creditability	Intrinsic data quality
Satisfaction from content usefulness	Intrinsic data quality
Satisfaction from content integration	Integration
Satisfaction from information architecture	Representation
Satisfaction from usability	Navigation
Satisfaction from graphical design	Presentation
Satisfaction from technical integrity/performance	Integration
Satisfaction from the personalization of navigation	Personalization
Satisfaction from the personalization of information/content	Personalization
Satisfaction from the personalization of interface	Personalization
Satisfaction from the communication support	Personalization
Satisfaction from the collaboration support	Personalization

- Navigation
- Presentation
- Personalization
- Intrinsic data quality

So researchers give special attention to the empathy subdimensions (i.e., navigation, presentation, integration, and personalization) and to the intrinsic data quality (related to the creation and presentation of information for user). To this end, all models attach great importance to visual aspects.

The dimensions which have been exclusively considered in PQM are:

- Tangible
- Search quality
- Scalability
- Accessibility

As a result from this comparative study we can conclude that PQM seems to be the most complete model for portal quality.

PARTICULARIZING A GENERAL MODEL TO A SPECIFIC DOMAIN: THE E-BANKING PORTAL QUALITY MODEL

Developing a quality-assured Web portal is important for those organizations aiming at providing services through the Web; this fact is especially

relevant for e-banking Web portals. The reason is threefold:

- Firstly, as a banking channel, the Internet has certainly experienced strong growth in customer uptake in recent years. This banking channel competes in importance with actual physical branches and call centres.
- Secondly, banks acquired a competitive advantage by being the first to market with Internet banking services before there was widespread availability of these. This fact served as a useful marketing tool to attract more technologically-aware consumers. Banks are forced to give their services some features that make them different, by using quality "hooks," such as enhanced functionalities and effective Web design.
- Thirdly, certain bank quality characteristics are bound up with the core of the business itself. For example, the conditions under which some kinds of operations are performed are regulated by tight requirements and governmental laws, so the developers must be sure that they are enforced in the application.

BPQM attempts to meet all these needs. This model used expert consultation to extract which of the general portal quality characteristics, gathered mainly from PQM were relevant for the e-banking domain.

Figure 4. BPQM (Banking Portal Quality Model)

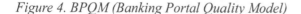
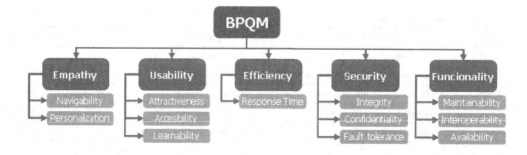

Next, the model was completed with a set of new characteristics/subcharacteristics, not present in any of the sources. Finally, the quality model was validated through a survey performed on 168 e-banking users.

So, BPQM can be considered as a particularization of PQM. However, in order to detect gaps in the model for considering their inclusion in future versions of BPQM a comparative study has been done. The complete comparison study can be found in Calero, Cachero and Cordoba (2007).

The BPQM model

The characteristics that compose BPQM are:

- **Empathy:** Capacity of the portal to provide personalised help and attention. Within this characteristic we would highlight:
  - **Navigability:** Capacity of the portal to offer users an intuitive and easy-to-use navigation system.
  - **Personalisation:** Capacity of the portal to allow users to customise their services so that user effort is reduced and client satisfaction is increased.
- **Usability:** Capacity of a software product to be understood, learned and used, as well as to be attractive, always bearing in mind regulations and usability guides. Within this characteristic the following subcharacteristics are found:
  - **Degree of attractiveness:** The portal must be able to satisfy the wishes of users, not only in terms of visual appearance, but also through its services and the degree of satisfaction achieved in its deployment.
  - **Accessibility:** This refers to the freedom of users when using data, by defining or refining the manner by which the information is entered, processed, or presented to them.
  - **Learning capacity:** It focuses on the amount of effort needed by the user to learn how to use services and functionalities that are available in the portal.
- **Efficiency:** Capacity of a software product to provide an appropriate performance which takes into account the amount of resources used and which is adaptable to specific conditions. This characteristic includes:
  - **Response time:** It focuses on the response times after a user request. There are various important response times for a banking portal: the time that elapses between when the solution indicates to the user that it is processing a request (state bar or progress bar) and the time taken by the solution in delivering a final response, whether positive or negative, the latter through an error message.
- **Security:** It represents the "capacity of the software product to avoid unauthorised access, either accidental or deliberate, to programs and data." For this characteristic we point out:
  - **Integrity:** The portal must protect the data and information in such a way that no deliberate or unauthorised modifications take place.
  - **Confidentiality:** The main focus is on preserving the privacy of users.
  - **Fault tolerance:** It refers to the capacity of offering a clear response to the user when faults, errors, or attacks occur. The portal must, at all times, recover in the shortest period of time and affect user services as little as possible.
- **Functionality:** It refers to the "capacity of a software product to satisfy the established functional requirements and the implicit needs of users." It includes:
  - **Maintainability:** The portal must be built in such a way that it facilitates the easy and rapid solution of any type of

error, as well as the maintenance and updating of information.

- ○ **Interoperability:** It focuses on the ability of the portal to interact with other systems and services.
- ○ **Available services:** The portal must have the maximum amount of services, which should be available 24 hours a day.

COMPARING BPQM WITH PQM

In this section the comparative study of PQM and BPQM is explained. Table 5 shows the comparison made between both models. Black cells mean equality in the sub characteristic in both models. Dark grey cells mean some kind of similarity (partial coverage of a sub characteristic, same meaning but different name, etc.) while rows or columns in grey imply that there is not any kind

Table 5. PQM subcharacteristics vs. BPQM subcharacteristics

PQM		BPQM Empathy: Navigability	Personalization	Usability: Attractiveness	Accessibility	Learnability	Efficiency: Response time	Security: Integrity	Confidentiality	Fault tolerance	Functionality: Maintainability	Interoperability	Availability
Tangibility	*Adaptability*												
	Transparent access					▨							
Reliability	*Fault tolerance*									■			
	Availability												■
	Search Quality												
	Resource utilization	▨											
Responsiveness	*Scalability*						▨			▨			
	Speed						▨						
Empathy	*Navigation*	■											
	Presentation			▨									
	Integration			▨									
	Personalization		■										
Data Quality	*Intrinsic DQ*												
	Representation DQ												
	Accessibility DQ				■								
	Contextual DQ												
Security	*Access control*								■				
	Security control												
	Confidentiality								■				
	Integrity							■					

of coincidence. In the next subsections, the results of the study are explained.

As shown in Table 1 above, there are 10 subcharacteristics that are common to both models:

1. Fault tolerance
2. Availability
3. Navigation
4. Personalization
5. Confidentiality
6. Integrity
7. Accessibility DQ
8. Access control
9. Speed
10. Transparent access

Most of these characteristics are mainly related to the comfort of the user when using the portal (2, 3, 4, 7, 9, 10) and to security aspects, which are very relevant when the portal is used as part of the user activities (1, 5, 6, 8). These aspects coincide with the definition of a portal given by (Collins, 2001): "a working environment where users can easily navigate to find the information they specifically need to make decisions and to perform their operational or strategic functions quickly." From these characteristics, transparent access (covered by learnability in BPQM) plays a dominant role in e-banking applications. Transparent access involves isolating the user from the application complexity. However, in e-banking applications, other learnability aspects are also important. Notably, given that (1) bank customers are not Internet experts and that (2) e-banking applications are a service channel, in BPQM special regard is given to training clients in the use of the Internet as a channel of access to banking services. Also, it must be noted that BPQM considers access control as an integral part of confidentiality and that personalization includes both static and dynamic techniques.

There are three subcharacteristics of PQM that are partially supported in BPQM:

1. Presentation (with attractiveness)
2. Integration (with attractiveness)
3. Scalability (with response time and fault tolerance).

BPQM provides a single subcharacteristic, attractiveness, to refer to all the issues related with the presentation and integration of the application (1, 2), under the assumption that users are not aware of components, and therefore they are not actually concerned about whether their comfort problems with the application are being caused by a poor integration of components or simply by a poor design of the interface.

Last but not least, there are seven characteristics in PQM that have been not considered in BPQM:

1. Adaptability
2. Scalability
3. Intrinsic DQ
4. Representational DQ
5. Contextual DQ
6. Search quality
7. Security control

As far as adaptability (1) is concerned, so far we have not found interest on this topic among the users interviewed. The lack of concerns about adaptability (support for different devices) might be due to the fact that the impact of some channels on the way of accessing e-banking services, such as mobile devices, hasn't been up to the expectations, and therefore their support has remained very minor. We think that, with the continuous advances in technology and the increasing number of technology-aware consumers, this tendency may change in the future, and therefore banks should start getting ready to meet this need.

Regarding scalability (2) the situation is different; whether there are 10 or 10,000 users, accessing the e-banking solution is not something the user knows or cares about; they just care about whether the application is answering their demands quickly and accurately.

PQM includes a whole section devoted to quality of data (3, 4, 5) which, in the case of BPQM, is not covered completely. One reason for this fact may be that most data are very specific or directly come from databases (e.g., account states) or external sources (e.g., stock prices) and so authoring of content was not considered to be a significant activity during e-banking portal development. Nevertheless, the fact that the e-banking survey showed that help mechanisms (most of them data-intensive) are necessary, makes this section a suitable candidate for its inclusion in the BPQM model.

Regarding search quality (6) an interesting issue arose during the survey that led to the construction of BQPM. In this survey, while 65% of users showed interest in having search facilities in bank portals, 38% didn't even know whether his portal offered him such facilities, and also around 40% could not evaluate how good the search results were. These results suggest that providing searching facilities is an underused feature in bank portals, and a feature that users scarcely use, although they regard it as a good idea. One reason may be that kind of services most likely to require from searching facilities (e.g., looking for a mortgage, managing their stocks, etc.) are services that are still mostly done in branches, and not through Internet. Therefore a question arises: would the provision of better searching facilities, even crossing bank boundaries, increase the use of banking portals for complex services? Our guess is yes, although it remains an issue of further investigation. If this is the case, then searching capabilities should definitely become part of BPQM.

Last, the lack of interest for security control (7) showed by e-banking users is the most outstanding result. Even if during the survey bank users showed concern for physical security (e.g., while withdrawing money), they did not seem concerned about how the bank monitors attacks and audits the status and use of security mechanisms. We do believe that this situation is partly due to an audience that is little aware of the technology is-

sues that may hamper the security of their data. E-banking users simply believe that the bank is taking care of such issues; otherwise they simply would not use the e-banking solution. We do not expect such a situation to change in the near future, so we have dismissed this characteristic as being relevant for BPQM.

The third group of subcharacteristics is made up of those that are included in BPQM but not considered in PQM:

1. Maintainability
2. Interoperability

Users expect e-banking applications to have a high maintainability. This means that they expect the bank to maintain the accuracy of the data provided and to respond rapidly to any problems encountered or to any lack of functionality detected during use (1). In addition, users require the e-banking portals to provide the possibility of interconnecting with different applications. Because a bank is a financial operator, the interoperability (2) with third parties is vital for users, as 90% stated in our survey.

As result of the study, we obtained that the BPQM includes 50% of PQM subcharacteristics completely and that an additional 15% of the PQM subcharacteristics have been tailored to better reflect the banking user concerns that were gathered by our empirical study. The remaining 35% subcharacteristics are not hitherto considered in BPQM. From them, security control and scalability (10%) have been definitely dismissed, while the remaining 25% (adaptability, various forms of data quality and search quality) pose a challenge for the future of e-banking portals. We do believe that their inclusion in BPQM could be useful as quality indicators to evaluate how well the e-banking application has foreseen changes in the way bank service types and user access devices may evolve in the future. Last, BPQM has detected two new subcharacteristics (maintainability and interoperability) that are important for e-banking portals even if they haven't up to now

Table 6. BPQM vs. general quality characteristics

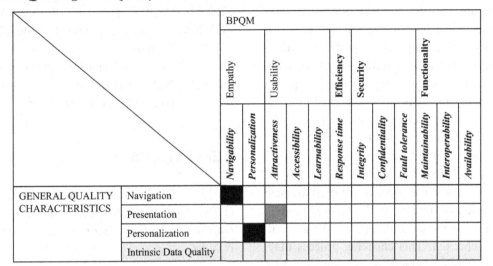

been taken into account in e-banking applications. As an example, around 60% of the bank users think that there is plenty of room for improvement regarding the number of third parties with which the application is able to interact.

From the point of view of PQM, some issues have also arisen. First, the refinements done in BPQM on the concepts of presentation, integration, and resource utilization based on the survey results should be further considered in a future revision of PQM, as some of our findings could be also useful for general-purpose portals. Also, we need to further give consideration to whether scalability and security control should be regarded as characteristics of PQM. On one hand, our survey has shown that from a user perspective, scalability is related to fault tolerance and speed. Both of these characteristics are already included in PQM, so scalability could be redundant. Regarding security control, it seems that users are not interested in how security personnel audit information as long as the control is confidential and shows integrity (these characteristics are also present in PQM). Finally, the two new e-banking subcharacteristics (maintainability and interoperability) may be also suitable candidates to be part of the PQM quality model.

Comparing BPQM with the Main Portal Quality Characteristics

Another interesting comparison can be made among BPQM characteristics and these that have been found as common of all the studied general models. Table 6 shows this comparison.

Again, there is not a complete coverage of these characteristics in BPQM. Concretely:

- navigation and personalization are completely covered,
- presentation is only partially covered, and finally
- intrinsic data quality is not included at all in BPQM.

Again, from these results we can conclude that it is necessary to made more validations with BPQM in order to determine if this tendency is correct or if it is not and these characteristics must to be considered.

CONCLUSION

Quality of service is vital for a portal success. In order for the organizations to assess such quality, they need to be provided with quality models. For some domains, it suffices with general portal quality models, while for others (such as e-banking applications) it is convenient to perform a tailoring process over these general models in order to better reflect the user needs. Tailoring a given general model instead of creating a brand new one provides us with several advantages: (1) the use of a general model as a guidance helps to make sure that no important aspect is being dismissed, (2) the experience gained with the application of the general model may be directly used to back some of the assumptions of the tailored model, and (3) during the tailoring process the general model is checked, This checking process may end up with new characteristics being added to the general model.

In this chapter, we have presented a comparison of some of the most relevant general quality models for Web portals. This comparison has shown that, despite their differences, all of them share a significant amount of characteristics. Also, we have presented an example of how a general model such as PQM can be tailored to fit the specific needs of a particular domain, in our case the e-banking domain. The result of this tailoring process is BPQM, which was made up taking into account expert opinions and a survey filled in by 168 e-banking users.

The subsequent comparison made between PQM and BPQM shows that, in spite of the empirical research that backs the BPQM model, PQM still provides some additional aspects that seem suitable candidates for their inclusion in future versions of BPQM. Conversely, the gathered empirical evidence has also introduced two new characteristics that could be relevant for general portals.

ACKNOWLEDGMENT

This chapter has been supported by the MEC Spanish Ministry projects CALIPSO (TIN20005-24055-E), MEC-FEDER (TIN2004-03145), ESFINGE (TIN2006-15175-C05-05), METASIGN (TIN2004-00779), and DSDM (TIN2005-25866-E)). Also, it is part of the DADASMECA project (GV05/220), financed by the Valencia Government and DIMENSIONS (PBC-05-012-1) financed by the Castilla-La Mancha Government.

REFERENCES

Basili, V. R., Caldiera, C., & Rombach, H. D. (1994). Goal question metric paradigm. *Encyclopedia of Software Engineering, 1, John Wiley & Sons.*

Brajnik, G. (2001). Towards valid quality models for web sites. *Paper presented at the 7th Human Factors and the Web Conference.* Retrieved October 16, 2007, from http://users.dimi.uniud.it/~giorgio.brajnik/papers/hfweb01.html

Calero, C., Cachero, C., & Córdoba, J. (2007). PQM vs. BPQM: Studying the tailoring of a general quality model to a specific domain. *Paper presented at the QOIS Workshop into the ER2007 Conference*, Auckland.

Churchill, G. A. (1979). A paradigm for developing better measures of marketing constructs. *Journal of Marketing Research, 16*(1), 64-73.

Collins, H. (2001). *Corporate portals*. New York: Amacom.

Domingues, M. A., Soares, C., & Jorge, A. M. (2006). *A Web-based system to monitor the quality of meta-data in Web portals. Paper presented at the IEEE/WIC/ACM International Conference on Web Intelligence and Intelligent Agent Technology (WI-IAT 2006 Workshops)(WI-IATW'06)*, (pp. 188-191).

Eisenmann, T., & Pothen, S. T. (2000). Online portals. *Case Number 9-801-305, Harvard Business School, Boston, MA*, 1-29.

ISO/IEC. (2001). *ISO/IEC 9126. Software engineering-product quality. Parts 1 to 4*: International Organization for Standardization/International Electrotechnical Commission.

Lacher, M. S., Koch, M., & Woerndl, W. (2001). *A framework for personalizable community Web portals*. Paper presented at the Proceedings of the Human-Computer Interaction International Conference.

Ma, C., Bacon, L., Petridis, M., & Windall, G. (2006). *Towards the design of a portal framework for Web services integration*. Paper presented at the Advanced International Conference on Telecommunications and International Conference on Internet and Web Applications and Services (AICT-ICIW'06), (pp. 163-170).

Moraga, M. Á., Calero, C., & Piattini, M. (2004). *A first proposal of a portal quality model*. Paper presented at the IADIS International Conference. E-society 2004. ISBN: 972-98947-5-2, Ávila, Spain. (pp. 630-638).

Moraga, M. Á., Calero, C., & Piattini, M. (2006). Comparing different quality models for portals. *Online Information Review, 30*(5), 555-568.

Nielsen, J. (2000). *Designing Web usability*. Indianapolis, IN: New Riders.

Offutt, A. J. (2002). Quality attributes of Web software applications. *IEEE Software, 19*(2), 25-32.

Parasuraman, A., Zeithami, V. A., & Berry, L. L. (1998). SERVQUAL: A multi-item scale for measuring consumer perceptions of service quality. *Journal of Retailing, 67*(4), 420-450.

Sampson, D., & Manouselis, N. (2004). *A flexible evaluation framework for Web portals based on multicriteria analysis*. In A. Tatnall (Ed.), *Web portals- the new gateways on Internet information and services*. Hershey, PA: Idea Group.

Telang, R., & Mukhopadhyay, T. (2004). Drivers of Web portal use. *Electronic Commerce Research and Applications, 4*(2005), 49-65.

Winkler, R. (2001). *The all-in-one Web supersites: Features, functions, definition, taxonomy. SAP Design Guild* (ed. 3). Retrieved October 16, 2007, from http://www.sapdesignguild.org/editions/edition3/overview_edition3.asp

Yang, Z., Cai, S., Zhou, Z., & Zhou, N. (2004). Development and validation of an instrument to measure user perceived service quality of information presenting Web portals. *Information and Management, 42*(2005), 575-589.

KEY TERMS

E-Banking: Online service provides by a bank company which facilitates bank management, such as check your account balance, bank transfers, and so on.

E-Banking Portals: A special type of Web portal whose aim is to provide different services related to the bank context.

Portal Quality: Degree to which a portal achieves a certain degree of quality for the different characteristic which affect to portal quality.

Portal Quality Model: Set of characteristics and subcharacteristics which affect the quality of a portal.

Portal Reliability: Ability of the portal to perform its functionality accurately.

Security: Capability of the portal to prevent, reduce, and respond to malicious attacks adequately.

Tangible: Characteristic of the portal that indicates whether it contains all the software and hardware infrastructures needed, according to its functionality.

Chapter VIII
A Data Quality Model for Web Portals

Angélica Caro
University of Bio Bio, Chile

Coral Calero
University of Castilla-La Mancha, Spain

Mario Piattini
University of Castilla-La Mancha, Spain

ABSTRACT

Web portals are Internet-based applications that provide a big amount of data. The data consumer who uses the data given by these applications needs to assess data quality. Due to the relevance of data quality on the Web together with the fact that DQ needs to be assessed within the context in which data are generated, data quality models specific to this context are necessary. In this chapter, we will introduce a model for data quality in Web portals (PDQM). PDQM has been built upon the foundation of three key aspects: (1) a set of Web data quality attributes identified in the literature in this area, (2) data quality expectations of data consumers on the Internet, and (3) the functionalities that a Web portal may offer its users.

INTRODUCTION

In recent years, Web portals have risen in popularity as a way of aggregating, organizing, and presenting content in a highly uniform, customizable, and personalized way. In simplest terms, a portal is a Web site that provides content and application functionality in a way that is both useful and meaningful to the end user (Secrist 2003).

In general, Web portals provide users with access to different data sources (providers)

(Mahdavi, Shepherd, Benatallah, 2004), as well as to online information and information-related services (Yang, Cai, Zhou, & Zhou, 2004). Moreover, they create a working environment where users can easily navigate in order to find the information they specifically need to quickly perform their operational or strategic tasks and make decisions (Collins, 2001). So, users or data consumers aimed at using the data offered by these applications need to ensure that these data are appropriate for the use they need, being fundamental to assess the quality of data.

Data and information quality (DQ hereafter) is often defined as "fitness for use," that is, the ability of a data collection to meet user requirements (Strong, Lee, & Wang 1997; Cappiello, Francalanci, & Pernici, 2004). This definition suggests the relativity of this concept because data considered appropriate for a specific use may not be appropriate for another. Even more, this definition involves understanding DQ from the user's point of view and, consequently, understanding that the quality of data cannot be assessed independently of the people who use data (Wang & Strong, 1996).

Due to the relevance of DQ on the Web together with the fact that DQ needs to be assessed within the context of its generations (Knight & Burn, 2005), in the last years the research community started studying the subject of DQ in the Web context (Gertz, Ozsu, Sattke, & Sattler, 2004). However, despite the sizeable body of literature available on DQ and the different domains studied on the Web, we have found no works on DQ that address the particular context of Web portals. Likewise, except for a few works in the DQ area, such as (Wang & Strong, 1996; Burgess, Fiddian, & Gray, 2004; Cappiello et al., 2004), most of the contributions target quality from the data producers' or data custodians' perspective and not from the data consumers' perspective (Burgess, et al., 2004). The last perspective differs from the two others in two important aspects: (1) data consumers have no control over the quality of available

data and (2) the aim of consumers is to find data that match their personal needs, rather than provide data that meet the needs of others.

So, consequently to this situation, the aim of our research work is the creation of a Data Quality Model for Web Portals (PDQM). The objective of this chapter is to present the definition of PDQM. This model is focused on the data consumer's perspective and as key pieces in its definition we have taken: (1) a set of Web DQ attributes identified in the literature, (2) the DQ expectations of data consumers on the Internet described by Redman (Redman, 2000) and (3) the functionalities that a portal Web may offer its users (Collins, 2001).

BACKGROUND

Data Quality and the Web

Research on DQ began in the context of information systems (Strong et al., 1997; Lee, 2002) and it has been extended to contexts such as cooperative systems, data warehouses or e-commerce, among others. Due to the particular characteristics of Web applications and their differences from the traditional information systems, the research community started to deal with the subject of DQ on the Web (Gertz et al., 2004). In fact, the particular nature of the Internet has forced to pay attention to a series of particular issues of this context that can affect or influence the quality of data. We have summarized some of them in Table 1.

In the last years, based on the previous Web issues and others, frameworks and models to deal with DQ in different domains in the Web context have been proposed. Among them we can highlight those shown in Table 2.

Concerning Table 2, we can make two important observations. First, the frameworks proposed tackle different domains on the Web. This reasserts the idea that DQ needs to be assessed within the context of the data source (Knight & Burn,

Table 1. Particular issues of Web context that can affect DQ

Issues	Description	Authors
Data Quality from the User's Perspective	It implies that DQ cannot be assessed independently of the people who use data.	(Strong, et al., 1997; Cappiello et al., 2004; Gertz et al., 2004; Knight & Burn, 2005)
Demand for realtime services	Web applications interact with different external data sources whose workload is not known. This situation can drastically influence response times, affecting DQ in aspects such as opportunity or updatedness.	(Amirijoo, Hansson, & Son, 2003).
Development of electronic commerce	DQ is essential to achieve the development of e-commerce on the Web as well as to win customer's trust.	(Lim & Chin, 2000; Davydov, 2001; Haider & Koronios, 2003).
Dynamism on the Web	The dynamism with which data, applications and sources change can affect DQ.	(Pernici & Scannapieco, 2002; Gertz et al., 2004)
Integration of structured and non-structured data	The use of nonstructure data (e-mails, work documents, manuals, etc.) and their integration with structured data is an important challenge because both of them contain knowledge of great value for organizations.	(Finkelstein & Aiken, 1999)
Integration of data from different sources	The access to diverse data sources that probably do not have the same level of DQ can damage the DQ of the product of this integration that is given to users.	(Naumann & Rolker, 2000; Zhu & Buchmann, 2002; Angeles & MacKinnon, 2004; Gertz et al., 2004; Winkler, 2004)
Need to understand data and their quality	A common language that facilitates communication between people, systems and programs is essential and to be able to evaluate DQ, it is necessary to understand data and the criteria used for determining their quality.	(Finkelstein & Aiken, 1999; Gertz et al. 2004)
Typical problems of a Web page	Un-updated information, publication of inconsistent information, obsolete links and so on.	(Eppler & Muenzenmayer 2002).
Users' Loyalty	This involves the need of an appropriate management of the data of each user or type of user, data fitness for users, and the permanent data output that keeps the interest and loyalty of users.	(Davydov, 2001)

2005). Second, for Web portals we have not found specific DQ frameworks.

During the past decade, an increasing number of organizations have established Web portals to complement, substitute, or widen existing services to their clients. In general, portals provide users with access to different data sources (providers) (Mahdavi, et al., 2004), as well as to online information and information-related services (Yang et al., 2004).

In the same way, the amount of people that access these applications grows every day. They use them from business to education and entertainment. In each case, people need to make operations related to data and they need that these data are appropriate for the use they need. For example, if the purpose is to obtain the cinema billboard to

find out the movie's schedule, users will hope to receive the appropriate data to plan what movie to watch and at what time, and all this performed in accord with their plans. So, they need data to be valid, correct, believable, accessible, and so forth. That is, they need data with quality.

Nowadays, DQ is a critical factor of success for Web applications (Schaupp, Fan, & Belanger, 2006). Web portals owners need to know the DQ needs of data consumers as a way to ensure their loyalty. Data consumers aimed at using the data offered by these applications need to ensure that the obtained data are appropriate for the use they need.

The challenge of our research is to develop a DQ model for Web portals that meets these needs. So, the first step to achieve this objective

Table 2. Summary of Web DQ frameworks in the literature

Author	Domain	Framework structure
(Katerattanakul & Siau, 1999)	Personal Web sites	4 categories and 7 constructors
(Naumann & Rolker, 2000)	Data integration	3 classes and 22 quality criterion
(Aboelmeged, 2000)	e-commerce	7 stages to modeling DQ problems
(Katerattanakul & Siau, 2001)	e-commerce	4 categories associated with 3 categories of data user requirements.
(Pernici & Scannapieco, 2002)	Web information systems (data evolution)	4 categories, 7 activities of DQ design and architecture to DQ management.
(Fugini, Mecella et al., 2002)	e-service cooperative	8 dimensions
(Graefe, 2003)	Decision making	8 dimensions and 12 aspects related to (providers/consumers)
(Eppler, Algesheimer, & Dimpfel, 2003)	Web sites	4 dimensions and 16 attributes
(Gertz et al., 2004)	DQ on the Web	5 dimensions
(Moustakis, Litos et al., 2004)	Web sites	5 categories and 10 sub-categories
(Melkas, 2004)	Organizational networks	6 stages to DQ analysis with several dimensions associated with each of them
(Bouzeghoub & Peralta, 2004)	Data integration	2 factors and 4 metrics
(Yang et al., 2004)	Web information portals	2 dimensions within the global model

is to define, in a theoretical way, a model that supports the DQ perspective of data consumers and identifies a set of DQ attributes that allow the assessment of DQ in Web portals. The next section will describe the process developed to obtain this model.

DEFINING A DQ MODEL

To produce the PDQM model we defined the process shown in Figure 1. This process is divided into two parts. The first one, presented in this chapter, consists of the theoretical definition of PDQM and the second one, now in progress, consists of the preparation of PDQM to be used in evaluation processes.

The first part is composed by four phases. During the first phase, we have recompiled Web DQ attributes from the literature, which we believe should be applicable to Web portals. In the second phase we have built a matrix for the classification of the attributes obtained in the previous phase. This matrix reflects two basic aspects considered in our model: the data consumer's perspective and the basic functionalities which a data consumer uses to interact with a Web portal. In the third phase we have used the obtained matrix to analyse the applicability of each Web DQ attribute in a Web portal. The fourth phase (not essential), corresponds to the validation of the selected set of DQ attributes. The theoretical model generated in this part will be used as an input for the second part into the general process. In next subsections we will describe each phase developed to define our model.

Figure 1. Development process of PDQM

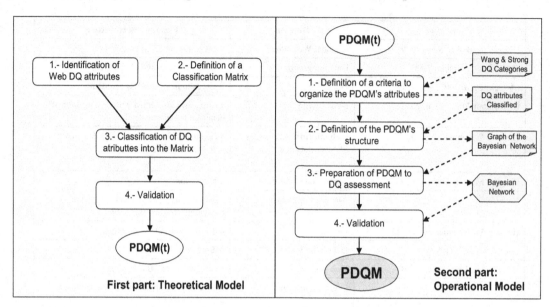

Foundations of PDQM

PDQM is a data quality model for Web portals focused on the data consumer's perspective. For the theoretical definition we have considered three key elements:

- **Data consumer's point of view:** When data management is conceptualized as a production process (Strong et al., 1997), we can identify three important roles in this process: (1) data producers (who generate data), (2) data custodians (who provide and manage resources for processing and storing data), and (3) data consumers (who access and use data for their tasks). The data consumer's perspective differs from the data producer's and the data custodian's perspectives in two important aspects (Burgess et al., 2004):
- Data consumers have no control over the quality of available data.
- The aim of consumers is to find data that match their personal needs, rather than provide data that meet the needs of others.

In other words, data consumers expect to find in a Web portal, or by means of it, the data that "meet their requirements." So, to consider the data consumer's perspective in our model we have used the DQ expectations of the data consumer on the Internet, proposed in (Redman, 2000). These expectations are organized into six categories: privacy, content, quality of values, presentation, improvement, and commitment:

- **Web Data Quality Attributes:** As shown in Table 2, different DQ models have been proposed in the literature for different domains in the Web context. With the idea of taking advantage of work already carried out in this context we have decided to study these works and consider their application to the specific domain of Web portals. Specifically, our intention is to identify Web DQ attributes that can be used in our model.
- **Web portal functionalities:** Web portals present basic software functionalities to data consumers deploying their tasks. Under our perspective, consumers judge data by using

application functionalities. So, we used the Web portal software functions that Collins proposes (Collins, 2001) considering them as basic in our model. These functions are as follows: Data Points and Integration, Taxonomy, Search Capabilities, Help Features, Content Management, Process and Action, Collaboration and Communication, Personalization, Presentation, Administration, and Security. Behind these functions, the Web portal encapsulates the producer-custodian role.

Once having defined these aspects, we carry out the first part of the development process to generate PDQM. In the next subsections we will explain each phase.

Phase 1. Identification of Web Data Quality Attributes

The first phase in the development of our model consisted of a systematic review of the relevant literature (Kitchenham, 2004). With this task we aimed at identifying DQ attributes which had been proposed for different domains in the Web context (Web sites (Katerattanakul & Siau, 1999; Eppler

et al., 2003; Moustakis et al., 2004), data integration (Naumann & Rolker, 2000; Bouzeghoub & Peralta, 2004), e-commerce (Katerattanakul & Siau, 2001), Web information portals (Yang et al., 2004), cooperative e-services (Fugini et al., 2002), decision making (Graefe, 2003), organizational networks (Melkas, 2004) and DQ on the Web (Gertz et al., 2004)). The idea was to take advantage of work already carried out in the Web context and apply it to Web portals.

In this review we studied 55 works, published between 1995 and 2004. From the studied work we selected the projects in which DQ attributes applicable to the Web context were proposed. Thus, we obtained a total of 100 Web DQ attributes. Our objective was to reduce this number, having also detected certain synonymous among the attributes identified. Those attributes were combined including the ones which had similar name and meaning, obtaining a final set of 41 attributes. Table 3 shows these attributes, pointing out for each attribute the work where they were put forward, as well as the total number of pieces of work where they can be found referred to. In addition, the symbols × and ⊗ were used to

Table 3. Web data quality attributes 1-41

Author	Year	Accessibility	Accuracy	Amount of data	Applicability	Attractiveness	Availability	Believability	Completeness	Concise Representation	Consistent Representation	Cost Effectiveness	Customer Support	Currency	Documentation	Duplicates	Ease of operation	Expiration	Flexibility	Granularity	Interactive	Internal Consistency	Interpretability	Latency	Maintainable	Novelty	Objectivity	Ontology	Organization	Price	Relevancy	Reliability	Reputation	Response time	Security	Specialization	Source's Information	Timeliness	Traceability	Understand ability	Validity	Value-added	Number of Attributes
Nauman and Rolker	2000		×	×			×	×	×	×	×		×		×								×	×		×					×	×	×	×	×	×			×	⊗	×		×	22
Katerattanakul and Siau	1999, 2001	×	⊗		×																				×											×					⊗		6
Eppler	2001	×	×		×				×	⊗	⊗			×			⊗				×	⊗			×										⊗	×				×	×	⊗	16
Fugini et al	2002		⊗		×		⊗	×															×								⊗				⊗			×					8
Pernici and Scannapieco	2002		×						×												×												⊗										4
Graefe	2003	⊗					⊗	×															×		×						⊗										⊗	⊗	8
Bouzeghoub and Peralta	2004													×																								×					2
Gertz	2004											×		×	×				×						×										×								5
Melkas	2004	×	×	⊗			×	×	×	×	×						×		×				×			×					×		×	⊗	×			×	×	×		×	20
Moustakis	2004			⊗			⊗																										⊗			×							4
Yang et al.	2004		×				⊗	×							×																		⊗										5
Number of references		4	7	2	3	1	1	6	7	3	3	1	1	4	1	1	2	1	1	1	2	3	1	1	1	2	1	1	1	6	2	2	3	4	1	1	5	3	4	1	3	

represent how they were combined (× indicates the same name and meaning and ⊗ marks the fact that only the meaning is the same).

From this set of DQ attributes we will determine which of them can be applicable to the Web portal context.

Phase 2. Definition of a Classification Matrix

In the second phase we defined a matrix which would allow us to perform a preliminary analysis of how applicable the previously identified attributes were to the domain of Web portals. The matrix was defined basing on the relationship that

Figure 2. Matrix for the classification of attributes of Web data quality

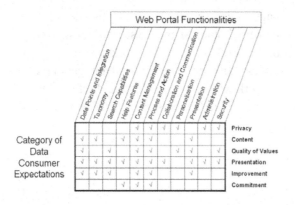

exists between: (1) The functionalities of a Web portal (Collins, 2001): data points and integration, taxonomy, search capabilities, help features, content management, processes and actions, communication and collaboration, personalization, presentation, administration and security; and (2) The data quality expectations of Internet data consumers as stated in (Redman, 2000): privacy, content, quality of values, presentation, improvement, and commitment.

In this matrix we carried out an analysis of which expectations were applicable to each of the different functionalities that a portal offers to a data consumer. This is represented in Figure 2 with a "√" mark.

The description of each one of these relationships (functionality, expectation) is shown in Appendix A.

Phase 3. Classification of Data Quality Attributes into the Matrix

The third phase of the development process of the PDQM model (see Figure 1), consisted of classifying the Web data quality attributes (shown in section 2) into each one of the relationships (functionality, expectation) established in the classification matrix created in phase 2 (and presented in the previous subsection). In Table 4, we will

Table 4. Data quality attributes for functionality

Functionalities	Accessibility	Accuracy	Amount of data	Applicability	Attractiveness	Availability	Believability	Completeness	Concise Representation	Consistent Representation	Cost effectiveness	Customer support	Currency	Documentation	Duplicates	Ease of operation	Expiration	Flexibility	Granularity	Interactive	Internal consistency	Interpretability	Latency	Maintainable	Novelty	Objectivity	Ontology	Organization	Price	Relevancy	Reliability	Reputation	Response time	Security	Specialization	Source's Information	Timeliness	Traceability	Understand ability	Validity	Value-added	Total of Attributes
Data Points and Integration	✓	✓	✓			✓		✓	✓		✓		✓	✓			✓								✓					✓	✓							✓	✓	✓		15
Taxonomy	✓		✓			✓		✓					✓			✓														✓	✓							✓	✓	✓		11
Search Capabilities	✓		✓			✓	✓	✓					✓	✓			✓								✓					✓	✓								✓	✓		13
Help Features	✓		✓					✓					✓				✓														✓								✓	✓		8
Content Management	✓		✓	✓		✓	✓	✓	✓				✓	✓	✓	✓	✓					✓			✓	✓		✓		✓	✓	✓		✓	✓	✓		✓	✓	✓	✓	24
Process and Action	✓	✓	✓	✓		✓	✓	✓	✓				✓			✓	✓					✓			✓					✓	✓	✓		✓	✓			✓	✓	✓		21
Collaboration and Communication						✓							✓									✓								✓				✓					✓			6
Personalization		✓						✓					✓			✓																						✓	✓	✓		7
Presentation			✓		✓		✓						✓	✓	✓		✓													✓	✓			✓				✓	✓	✓		15
Administration		✓						✓	✓				✓																					✓						✓		6
Security	✓	✓	✓				✓	✓					✓				✓																	✓					✓	✓		10
Number of References	7	4	9	2	1	3	6	5	9	1	0	8	5	1	1	8	4	1	0	0	0	5	0	0	3	2	0	1	0	7	7	2	0	5	3	1	0	7	11	8	1	

set out a summary of the attributes applicable to each portal functionality.

As it can be seen in Table 4, there are some DQ attributes which were not classified into the matrix. This is basically due to the fact that they could no be assessed by data consumers, for example, ontology and latency.

As a result of this phase we obtained a set of 34 DQ attributes that can be used to assess DQ in a Web portal (see Appendix B).

Phase 4. Validation

The fourth phase consisted of the validation of the set of DQ attributes selected. The method selected for this validation was the development of a survey. In this survey, users of Web portals were asked about the importance they gave to the DQ attributes considered in PDQM.

As a starting point, we performed a partial survey to validate the DQ attributes assigned to the data points and integration functionality. The questionnaire contained four questions. The aim of the first two questions (open questions) was to obtain from the respondents the attributes they considered important for the functionality under study. The results showed that the most mentioned attributes were: accessibility, accuracy, understandability, currency, consistent representation, and relevance (all considered in our model for the functionality under study), organization, source's information, and response time (all considered in our model but not for this functionality).

In the third question (also open question) we showed all the attributes considered in our model for the functionality and we asked data consumers for other attributes that they consider necessary. As a result, the most-proposed attributes were Attractiveness with 22%, Security with 12%, and source's information, response time and easy of operation with 10%. All of them were considered in our model but not classified within this functionality.

Finally, in the fourth question (close question), the participants had to assign a degree of importance between levels 1 and 7 (1 not important and 7 very important) to each attribute. The attributes that had at least 70% of preferences (adding the percentages of level 6 and 7) will be considered as important for data consumers. Among the 15 attributes assigned to this functionality, 10 of them appeared to be relevant (with more of a 70% of preferences) for the subjects. This result showed a coincidence with the subjects of at least 66%, for the asked functionality.

Considering this experience and the results obtained from this partial validation of PDQM, we decided to develop a new survey to validate the complete model. The purpose of this new survey was to collect ratings of the importance of each one of the 34 DQ attributes of PDQM. The survey questionnaire was composed of 34 questions, one for each DQ attribute. Each question was measured by using a 5-point Lickert scale where 1 means "Not Important" and 5 "Very Important."

We used a sample of student subjects (convenience sampling) for our survey. A group of 70 Master students in the final-year (fifth) of Computer Science was enrolled (from a software engineering class). The total effective sample was 54, or 77% of the subjects that had initially been enrolled.

We decided that DQ attributes that had a mean of 3 or more (considering the choices "moderately important," "important," and "very important") would be kept in the PDQM. All the others are rejected. Regarding the results of the survey, 33 DQ attributes obtained a mean of 3 or more (97 %). These 33 attributes made up the new version of PDQM. The DQ attribute Source's Information was eliminated because their mean was 2.56 (see in Table 5 the row marked).

Table 5 shows the retained DQ attributes list and descriptive statistics about them. A detailed description of the validation process can be found in Caro et al. (2007).

Table 5. Final set of DQ attributes of PDQM

Attribute	Mean	Min	Max	Attribute	Mean	Min	Max
Attractiveness	4.06	2	5	Interactivity	3.19	1	5
Accessibility	4.52	3	5	Interpretability	3.87	2	5
Accuracy	4.28	2	5	Novelty	3.67	2	5
Amount of Data	3.96	2	5	Objectivity	3.50	1	5
Applicability	4.00	2	5	Organization	3.94	2	5
Availability	4.60	3	5	Relevancy	4.09	2	5
Believability	4.15	2	5	Reliability	4.15	2	5
Completeness	3.85	2	5	Reputation	3.46	2	5
Concise Representation	3.63	2	5	Response Time	4.30	2	5
Consistent Representation	3.63	2	5	Security	4.22	2	5
Currency	4.54	3	5	Source's Information	2.56	1	5
Customer Support	3.54	1	5	Specialization	3.61	2	5
Documentation	3.31	1	5	Timeliness	4.06	2	5
Duplicates	3.00	1	5	Traceability	3.63	1	5
Ease of Operation	3.72	2	5	Understandability	4.02	2	5
Expiration	3.28	1	5	Validity	3.57	1	5
Flexibility	3.26	2	5	Value added	3.98	1	5

FUTURE WORK

As a result of our work, so far, we have defined a theoretical DQ model for Web portals. Our future work will be centred in the development of the second part of the development process of PDQM, that is, we will convert PDQM into an operational model. This means that we need to define a structure where we can organize DQ attributes and associate measures and criteria for them.

Considering the uncertainty inherent in quality perception, we have decided to use a probabilistic approach (Bayesian network and Fuzzy logic) to structure, refine, and represent the 33 DQ attributes. The construction of a BN for a particular quality model can be carried out in two stages (Malak, Sahraoui, Badri, & Badri, 2006). At the first one, the graph structure is built. This graphical approach is essential in order to establish the appropriate relationships among DQ attributes and it provides us with a generic structure for

our model. At the second stage it is necessary to define the node probability tables for each node of the graph. This stage must be developed according to the evaluation context (Shankar & Watts, 2003).

After the generation of the structure of PDQM and its preparation for DQ evaluation in a specific context, the validation process will be conducted. This validation will be used for the adjustment of our model with the judgments of data consumers for a specific context.

One of the advantages of our framework will be its flexibility. Indeed, the idea is to develop a global framework that can be adapted for both the goal and the context of evaluation. From the goal's perspective, the user can choose the subnetwork that evaluates the characteristics he or she is interested in. From the context's point of view, the parameters (probabilities) can be changed to consider the specific context of the evaluated portal. This operation can be performed by using available historical data from the organization.

CONCLUSION

Web portals are applications that have been positioned like information sources or means of accessing information over the last decade. On the other hand, those who need to use information from these portals must be sure; somehow, that this information is suitable for the use they wish. In other words, they really need to assess the level of the quality of the obtained data.

In the literature, there are no specific proposals for data quality models for Web portals. In this chapter we have presented the first part of the development of a Data Quality Model for Web portals (PDQM) that considers the consumers' point of view. This model has been built upon three fundamental aspects: a set of Web data quality attributes found in the relevant literature, data quality expectations of data consumers on the Internet, and the functionalities which a Web portal may offer its users.

The main contribution of this work is the identification, based on the data consumer's perspective, of a set of 33 DQ attributes that can be used for DQ evaluation in Web portals. This work has generated a theoretical model that will be used to generate an operational model that could be used in different contexts and processes of DQ evaluation in Web portals.

ACKNOWLEDGMENT

This research is part of the following projects: CALIPSO (TIN20005-24055-E) supported by the Ministerio de Educación y Ciencia (Spain), DIMENSIONS (PBC-05-012-1) supported by FEDER, and by the "Consejería de Educación y Ciencia, Junta de Comunidades de Castilla-La Mancha" (Spain), and COMPETISOFT (506AC0287), financed by CYTED.

REFERENCES

Aboelmeged, M. (2000). A soft system perspective on information quality in electronic commerce. In *Proceedings of the Fifth Conference on Information Quality,* (pp. 318-319).

Amirijoo, M., Hansson, J., & Son, S. (2003). Specification and management of QoS in imprecise real-time databases. In *Proceedings of the Seventh International Database Engineering and Applications Symposium,* (pp. 192-201).

Angeles, P., & MacKinnon, L. (2004). Detection and resolution of data inconsistencies, and data integration using data quality criteria. *QUATIC'2004,* (pp. 87-93).

Bouzeghoub, M. & Peralta, V. (2004). A framework for analysis of data freshness. In *Proceedings of the International Workshop on Information Quality in Information Systems, (IQIS2004),* ACM, Paris, France, (pp. 59-67).

Burgess, M., Fiddian, N., & Gray, W. (2004). Quality measures and the information consumer. In *Proceedings of the Ninth International Conference on Information Quality,* (pp. 373-388).

Cappiello, C., Francalanci, C., & Pernici, B. (2004). Data quality assessment from the user's perspective. In *Proceedings of the International Workshop on Information Quality in Information Systems, (IQIS2004),* ACM, Paris, France, (pp. 68-73).

Caro, A., Calero, C., Caballero, I., & Piattini, M. (2007). A Proposal for a set of attributes relevant for Web portal data quality, *Software Quality Journal*, to appear.

Collins, H. (2001). *Corporate portal definition and features.* AMACOM.

Davydov, M. (2001). *Corporate portals and e-business integration.* McGraw-Hill.

Eppler, M., Algesheimer, R., & Dimpfel, M. (2003). Quality criteria of content-driven Web sites and their influence on customer satisfaction and loyalty: An empirical test of an information quality framework. In *Proceedings of the Eighth International Conference on Information Quality,* (pp. 108-120).

Eppler, M., & Muenzenmayer, P. (2002). Measuring information quality in the Web context: A survey of state-of-the-art instruments and an application methodology. In *Proceedings of the Seventh International Conference on Information Quality,* (pp. 187-196).

Finkelstein, C., & Aiken, P. (1999). *XML and corporate portals. Wilshire Conferences.*

Fugini, M., Mecella, M., Plebani, P., Pernici, B., & Scannapieco, M. (2002). *Data quality in cooperative Web information systems.*

Gertz, M., Ozsu, T., Saake, G., & Sattler, K.-U. (2004). Report on the Dagstuhl Seminar "Data Quality on the Web". *SIGMOD Record, 33*(1), 127-132.

Graefe, G. (2003). Incredible information on the Internet: Biased information provision and a lack of credibility as a cause of insufficient information quality. In *Proceedings of the Eighth International Conference on Information Quality,* (pp. 133-146).

Haider, A., & Koronios, A. (2003). Authenticity of information in cyberspace: IQ in the Internet, Web, and e-business. In *Proceedings of the Eighth International Conference on Information Quality,* (pp. 121-132).

Katerattanakul, P., & Siau, K. (1999). Measuring information quality of Web sites: Development of an instrument. In *Proceedings of the 20th International Conference on Information System,* (pp. 279-285).

Katerattanakul, P., & Siau, K. (2001). Information quality in Internet commerce design. In M. Piattini & C. Calero, & M. Genero (Ed.), *Information and database quality.* Kluwer Academic Publishers.

Kitchenham, B. (2004). *Procedures for performing systematic reviews.*

Knight, S. A., & Burn, J. M. (2005). "Developing a framework for assessing information quality on the World Wide Web." *Informing Science Journal* 8, 159-172.

Lee, Y. (2002). "AIMQ: A methodology for information quality assessment." *Information and Management. Elsevier Science*, 133-146.

Lim, O., & Chin, K. (2000). An investigation of factors associated with customer satisfaction in Australian Internet bookshop Web sites. In *Proceedings of the 3rd Western Australian Workshop on Information Systems Research,* Autralia.

Mahdavi, M., Shepherd, J., & Benatallah, B. (2004). A collaborative approach for caching dynamic data in portal applications. In *Proceedings of the Fifteenth Conference on Australian Database,* (pp. 181-188).

Malak, G., Sahraoui, H., Badri, L., & Badri, M. (2006). Modeling Web-based applications quality: A probabilistic approach. In *Proceedings of the 7th International Conference on Web Information Systems Engineering*, Wuhan, China, (pp. 398-404). Springer LNCS.

Melkas, H. (2004). Analyzing information quality in virtual service networks with qualitative interview data. In *Proceedings of the Ninth International Conference on Information Quality,* (pp. 74-88).

Moustakis, V., Litos, C., Dalivigas, A., & Tsironis, L. (2004). Web site quality assesment criteria. In *Proceedings of the Ninth International Conference on Information Quality,* (pp. 59-73).

Naumann, F., & Rolker, C. (2000). Assesment methods for information quality criteria. In *Proceedings of the Fifth International Conference on Information Quality,* (pp. 148-162).

Pernici, B., & Scannapieco, M. (2002). Data quality in Web information systems. In *Proceedings of the 21st International Conference on Conceptual Modeling,* (pp. 397-413).

Redman, T. (2000). *Data quality: The field guide.* Boston: Digital Press.

Schaupp, C., Fan, W., & Belanger, F. (2006). Determining success for different Web site goals. In *Proceedings of the 39th Hawaii International Conference on Systems Science (HICSS-39 2006)* (p. 107.2). Kauai, HI. USA: IEEE Computer Society.

Secrist, M. (2003). Portalise It! Dev2Dev.

Shankar, G., & Watts, S. (2003). A relevant, believable approach for data quality assessment. In *Proceedings of the Eighth International Conference on Information Quality (IQ2003),* (pp. 178-189).

Strong, D., Lee, Y., & Wang, R. (1997). Data quality in context. *Communications of the ACM, 40*(5), 103-110.

Wang, R., & Strong, D. (1996). Beyond accuracy: What data quality means to data consumers. *Journal of Management Information Systems; Armonk; Spring, 12*(4), 5-33.

Winkler, W. (2004). Methods for evaluating and creating data quality. *Information Systems, 29*(7), 531-550.

Yang, Z., Cai, S., Zhou, Z., & Zhou, N. (2004). Development and validation of an instrument to measure user perceived service quality of information presenting Web portals. *Information and Management. Elsevier Science, 42,* 575-589.

Zhu, Y., & Buchmann, A. (2002). Evaluating and selecting Web sources as external information resources of a data warehouse. In *Proceedings of the 3rd International Conference on Web Information Systems Engineering,* (pp. 149-160).

KEY TERMS

Data Quality: Data has quality when it has "fitness for use," that is, when it meets user requirements.

Data Consumer: Person who uses data for a specific purpose and can be affected by its quality.

Data Quality Attribute: Characteristics or properties of data that are relevant in a specific context.

Data Quality Model: A defined set of relevant attributes and relationships between them, which provides a framework for specifying data quality requirements and evaluating data quality.

Evaluation: The activity of assessing the quality of a system or the data it contains.

Portal Functionalities: Basic software functions in Web portals that are used for users to interact with a Web portal.

Web Portals: Internet-based applications that enable access to different sources (providers) through a single interface which provides personalization, single sign on, content aggregation from different sources and which hosts the presentation layer of Information Systems.

APPENDIX A

Functionality	Privacy	Categories of DQ Expectations of Data Consumers on Internet				
		Content	Quality of Values	Presentation	Improvement	Commitment
Data Points and Integration. They provide the ability to access information from a wide range of internal and external data sources and display the resulting information at the single point-of-access desktop.		Data Consumers need a description of portal areas covered, use of published data, etc.	Data consumers should expect the result of searches to be correct, up-to-date and complete	Formats, language, and other aspects are very important for easy interpretation	Users want to participate with their opinions in the portal improvements and know what the results of applying them are	
Taxonomy. It provides information context (including the organization-specific categories that reflect and support the organization's business).		Data consumers need a description of what data are published and how they should be used, as well as easy-to-understand definitions of every important term, etc.		Formats and language in the taxonomy are very important for easy interpretation; users should expect to find instruc-tions when reading data	Users should expect to convey their comments on data in the taxonomy and know what the result of improvements are	
Search Capabilities. This provides several services for Web portal users and needs to support searches across the company, the WWW, and into search engine catalogs and indexes.			Data consumers should expect the result of searches to be correct, up-to-date and complete	Formats and language are important for consumers, both for searching and for easy interpretation of results	Consumers should expect to convey their comments on data in the taxonomy and be aware of the result of improvements	
Help Features. These provide help when using a Web portal.				Formats, language, and other aspects are very important for easy interpretation of help texts		Consumers should be able to ask and obtain answers to any question regarding the proper use or meaning of data, update schedules, etc., easily.
Content Management. This function supports content creation, authorization, and inclusion in (or exclusion from) Web portal collections.	A privacy policy for all consumers to manage, access sources and guarantee Web portals data should exist	Consumers need a description of data collections	A consumer should expect all data values to be correct, up-to-date and complete	Formats and language should be appropriate for easy interpretation	Consumers should expect to convey their comments on contents and their management and be aware of the result of improvements	Consumers should be able to ask any question regarding the proper use or meaning of data, etc

continued on following page

Appendix A. continued

Function						
Process and Action. This function enables Web portal users to initiate and participate in a business process of a portal owner.	Data consumer should expect that there is a privacy policy to manage the data about the business in a portal	Consumers should expect to find descriptions about the data published for this function, their uses, etc.	All data associated with this function must be correct, up-to-date and complete	Formats and other aspects are very important in order to interpret data	Consumers should expect to convey their comments on contents and their management and know the results of improvements	Consumer should be able to ask and obtain an answer to any question
Collaboration and Communication. This function facilitates discussion, locating innovative ideas, and recognizing resourceful solutions.	Consumers should expect that there is a privacy policy for all consumers that participate in activities of this function					A consumer should be able to ask and have any question answered regarding the proper use or meaning of data for this function.
Personalization. This is a critical component in creating a working environment that is organized and configured specifically for each user.	Consumers should expect privacy and security regarding their personalized data, profile, etc.		Data about the user's profile should be correct and up-to-date			
Presentation. It provides the web portal user with both the knowledge desktop and the visual experience that encapsulate all of the portal's functionality.		The presentation of a Web portal should include data about areas covered, appropriate and inappropriate uses, definitions, etc.	Data of this function should be correct, up-to-date and complete.	Formats, language, and other aspects are very important for the easy interpretation and appropriate use of data.	Consumers should expect to convey their comments on contents and their management	
Administration. This function provides a service for deploying maintenance activities or tasks associated with the Web portal system.	Data consumers need security for data about the portal administration		Data about tasks or activities of administration should be correct and complete			
Security. It provides a description of the levels of access that each user is allowed for each application and software function included in the Web portal.	Consumers need a privacy policy regarding the data of the levels of access.		Data about the levels of access should be correct and up-to-date	Data about security should be in a format and language for easy interpretation		

APPENDIX B

	Attribute	Definition
1	Accessibility	The extent to which the Web portal provides enough navigation mechanisms so that visitors can reach their desired data faster and easier.
2	Accuracy	The extent to which data are correct, reliable, and certificated as free of error.
3	Amount of Data	The extent to which the quantity or volume of data delivered by the portal is appropriate
4	Applicability	The extent to which data are specific, useful and easy applicable for the target community.
5	Attractiveness	The extent to which the Web portal is attractive for their visitors.
6	Availability	The extent to which data are available by means the portal.
7	Believability	The extent to which data and their source are accepted as correct.
8	Completeness	The extent to which data, provides for a Web portal, are of sufficient breadth, depth, and scope for the task at hand.
9	Concise Representation	The extent to which data are compactly represented without superfluous or not related elements
10	Consistent Representation	The extent to which data are always presented in the same format, compatible with previous data and consistent with other sources.
11	Customer Support	The extent to which the Web portal provides on-line support by means text, e-mail, telephone, etc.
12	Documentation	Amount and usefulness of documents with meta information.
13	Duplicates	The extent to which data delivered for the portal contains duplicates.
14	Ease of Operation	The extent to which data are easily managed and manipulate (i.e., updated, moved, aggregated, etc.)
15	Expiration	The extent to which the date until which data remain current is known
16	Flexibility	The extent to which data are expandable, adaptable, and easily applied to other needs.
17	Interactivity	The extent to which the way which data are accessed or retrieved can be adapted to one's personal preferences through interactive elements.
18	Interpretability	The extent to which data are in language and units appropriate for the consumer capability.
19	Novelty	The extent to which data obtained from the portal influence the knowledge and the new decisions.
20	Objectivity	The extent to which data are unbiased and impartial.
21	Organization	The organization, visual settings or typographical features (colour, text, font, images, etc.) and the consistent combinations of these various components.
22	Relevancy	The extent to which data are applicable and helpful for users' needs.
23	Reliability	The extent to which users can trust the data and their source.
24	Reputation	The extent to which data are trusted or highly regarded in terms of their source or content.
25	Response Time	Amount of time until complete response reaches the user.
26	Security	Degree to which information is passed privately from user to information source and back.
27	Specialization	Specificity of data contained and delivered for a Web portal
28	Source's Information	The extent to which information about the author/owner of Web portal is delivered to the data consumers
29	Timeliness	The availability of data on time, that is, within the time constrains specified by the destination organization
30	Traceability	The extent to which data are well-documented, verifiable, and easily attributed to a source.
31	Understandability	The extent to which data are clear, without ambiguity, and easily comprehensible
32	Currency	The extent to which the Web portal provides not obsolete data.
33	Validity	The extent to which users can judge and comprehend data delivered by the portal.
34	Value added	The extent to which data are beneficial and provide advantages from their use.

Section II
Accessibility and Usability

Chapter IX
Specification of the Context of Use for the Development of Web–Based Applications

Marta Fernández de Arriba
University of Oviedo, Spain

Eugenia Díaz
University of Oviedo, Spain

Jesús Rodríguez Pérez
University of Oviedo, Spain

ABSTRACT

This chapter presents the structure of an index which serves as support so allowing the development team to create the specification of the context of use document for the development of Web applications, bearing in mind characteristics of usability and accessibility, each point of the index being explained in detail. A correct preparation of this document ensures the quality of the developed Web applications. The international rules and standards related to the identification of the context of use have been taken into account. Also, the functionality limitations (sensorial, physical, or cognitive) which affect access to the Web are described, as well as the technological environment used by disabled people (assistive technologies or alternative browsers) to facilitate their access to the Web content. Therefore, following the developed specification of the context of use, usable and accessible Web applications with their corresponding benefits can be created.

INTRODUCTION

ISO (International Organization for Standardization) defines usability in the document "ISO 9241-11" (ISO, 1998) as "the extent to which a product can be used by specified users to achieve specified goals with effectiveness, efficiency and satisfaction in a specified context of use."

On the other hand, the international standard "ISO/IEC 9126-1" (ISO, 2001a) employs the term "quality in use" to indicate "the capability of the software product to enable specified users to achieve specified goals with effectiveness, productivity, safety, and satisfaction in **specified contexts of use**."

Also included within the international standard "ISO 13407" (ISO, 1999) as one of the four activities of human-centred design is to understand and **specify the context of use**.

Lastly, the standard "ISO/TS 16071" (ISO, 2003) defines accessibility in relation to usability as "the usability of a product, service, environment, or facility by people with the widest range of capabilities."

Therefore, in order to ensure the quality of Web sites, it is necessary that they comply with a series of characteristics of usability, with the identification of the context of use being paramount. The details of the characteristics of the users, their objectives and tasks as well as the environment within which they carry out their tasks, provide important information which is necessary in order to be able to correctly identify all the requirements of the product and, in particular, the requirements related to usability and accessibility.

There are standard published guidelines related to general usability (see Usability Standards in Figure 1), as well as general accessibility (see accessibility standards in Figure 1) and specific to Web-based applications accessibility (see W3C-World Wide Web Consortium- Guidelines in Figure 1), but there are no guidelines that unify usability and accessibility features. Furthermore, some standards specify a great number of rules to

Figure 1. Regulation associated to the context of use

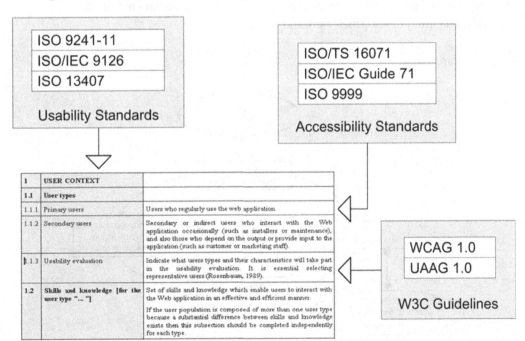

be followed, making their application very difficult for the development team members.

This chapter details how to specify the context of use, bearing in mind both the guidelines and also usability and accessibility standards at an international level for the development of Web applications.

The rest of the chapter is organized as follows. In the next section an overview of the ISO 13407 model is described. The following section presents the structure of the specification of the context of use document for the development of Web applications. In the section "Users with special needs and technological environment" functionality limitations which affect the access to Web content and the technological environment used by persons with disabilities are detailed. Finally, conclusions are drawn, including the benefits of a usable and accessible Web design.

USER-CENTERED DESIGN

A design centred on the user proposes that the designers comprehend the context of use. That is to say that they must understand the users and the environment in which they develop their work and

the tasks that they need to carry out. The aim is to obtain systems which are more usable, favouring their effectiveness and efficiency, improving the human working conditions and reducing the possible adverse effects of their use on health, safety, and functional characteristics.

The International Standard "ISO 13407" (ISO, 1999) establishes the principals of the design of systems centred on the user. This standard is presented as a complement to existing design methods, in such a way that it can be integrated and used with any Software Engineering methodology, within the lifecycle of the project.

A human-centred approach is characterized by:

1. The active involvement and implication of users in all stages of the development process from the beginning, so requirements and user tasks can be identified to include them in the system specifications.
2. An appropriate allocation of the functions between users and technology.
3. A process of iterative design whereby a prototype of the future system is designed, evaluated, and modified.

Figure 2. ISO 13407 model

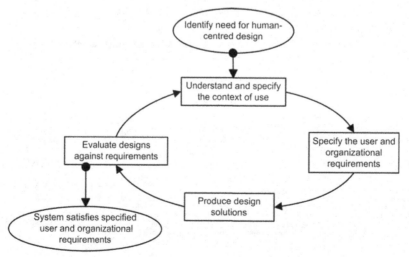

4. A multidisciplinary team composed of experts in human factors and technology, end-users, designers, and system developers.

ISO 13407 describes four human-centred design activities which need to be integrated during a system development project. These activities must be repeated iteratively, as can be seen in Figure 2, until the system satisfies all the proposed requirements.

STRUCTURE OF THE SPECIFICATION OF THE CONTEXT OF USE DOCUMENT

International Standard "ISO 9241-11: Guidance on Usability" (ISO, 1998) indicates that context of use should be identified in the following terms:

- Significant characteristics of the *users,* such as knowledge, skills, competences, experience, education, training, motivation, attitude, physical attributes, and motor and sensory capabilities.
- Description of *tasks* that users should perform to achieve a goal, detailing characteristics which may imply risks or influence usability, for example, the frequency and the duration of performance.
- *Environment* of the system, including relevant characteristics of the technical environment (equipment and software), as well as characteristics of the physical environment (workplace), and the social and cultural environment (work practices, organisational structure, and attitudes).

ISO 9241-11 Annexe A provides an example of how the context of use can be specified in terms of attributes which may be relevant to usability. On the other hand, Thomas and Bevan (1996) present a practical method for documenting contextual factors which affect usability, and for ensuring that these factors are represented when systems are evaluated and Maguire (1998) describes the RESPECT framework for user requirements specification.

Taking into account all these works and adapting them to the specific context of Web applications development, we define a new index where the different points include a brief explanation about how to create the specification of the context of use document. It has to be borne in mind that some of these points may not appear in all the documents because it depends on the features of each application developed.

Users

This section compiles information regarding different user types for Web-based applications. Nevertheless, because distinguishing between users' categories is a laborious task, it is advisable to differentiate only when substantial differences between their skills and knowledge exist, or when differences exist in their personal characteristics, or when different Web functionalities were used by different users.

The user context information will permit the establishment of many user profiles as different user groups have been identified by the development team (see Table 1).

Tasks

Tasks are the activities undertaken by users to achieve the specified goal. In the context of use, task features that may influence usability should be described.

It is fundamental to identify all the tasks involved in a Web application, distinguishing the distribution of functions between those performed by humans and those performed by the technology (see Table 2).

Technical Environment

This section specifies the software features, equipment, and reference material in which the Web application is used. If several technical environments have to be provided for different user groups then all technical alternatives must be included. Subsequently, the section "Impairment produced by the environment or technology" will provide further information related with certain technical conditions that affect user accessibility in Web contents access (see Table 3).

Physical Environment

This section describes the relevant physical characteristics of the workplace in which the Web application is used and which could affect the performance of the user or the hardware and the safety and health of the user. If several physical

Table 1.

1	User Context	
1.1	**User types**	Users of the Web-based application.
1.1.1	Primary users	Users that usually use the Web application.
1.1.2	Secondary users	Indirect users (such as installers or maintenance) that interact with the Web application occasionally. Also, those users (such as customers or marketing staff) that have to provide input data to the application or are affected by the application outputs.
1.1.3	Usability evaluation	The user types and their characteristics that will be considered in the usability evaluation have to be indicated. The selection of representative users (ISO, 1999; Rosenbaum, 1989) is essential.
1.2	**Skills and knowledge [for the user type "... "]**	Set of skills and knowledge which enable users to interact with the Web application in an effective and efficient manner. If the user population is composed by more than one user type (due to a substantial difference between skills and knowledge) then this subsection should be independently completed for each user type.
1.2.1	Knowledge and experience with the system	The training with processes and tasks that the Web application supports (either manual or by means of another product) and the experience obtained when using other programs with similar functions have to be indicated.
1.2.2	Information Technology experience	Computer literacy should distinguish between: General knowledge about computer based systems (Operating Systems, desktop applications, ...). Knowledge and training using Web browsers (customization of the browser options, experience with style sheets, ...) Knowledge and training using Web pages (experience with forms, frames, toolbars, file downloading, navigation shortcuts, ...) Ability to use input and output devices, such as the use of keyboard (typing skills), mouse or touch screen.
1.2.3	Linguistic ability	Level in the language knowledge used in the Web application.
1.2.4	Educational and general knowledge	Background knowledge (not necessarily formal or as a qualification result) that is useful for the user tasks performance in the Web application.
1.3	**Personal characteristics [for the user type "... "]**	This subsection will be filled out independently for each user type if more than one user type has been identified (due to the existence of significant differences in their personal characteristics).
1.3.1	Age	The typical age ranges of the users have to be identified. This point is especially important when a significant proportion of the users are aging beause most functional abilities decrease in elderly people. Further on, section "Disabilities and barriers on the Web" will provide more information concerned with the influence of ageing on human abilities which affect Web application access.

continued on following page

Table 1. continued

1.3.2	Physical limitations and disabilities	User characteristics that produce an immediate impact on the successful use of Web applications include: Sensory abilities such as sight (people who are blind, with low vision or colour-blindness) and hearing (people who are deaf or hard of hearing). Physical abilities such as dexterity and manipulation. Cognitive abilities such as intellectual disability, memory impairment, or attention deficit disorder. The details of different limitations of sensory, physical, or cognitive abilities that affect Web-based application access will be tackled in section "Disabilities and barriers on the Web."
1.3.3	Attitude and motivation	Perceived enjoyment and attitude of the users related to the information technologies and Web applications in general, to their organization, their job, as well as to using the new system.
1.4	**Job features [for the user type "..."]**	This subsection will be filled out independently for each user type when more than one user type has been identified (because of the existence of significant differences in their job features -set of tasks-).
1.4.1	Job function	The general purpose, the main goals and the job responsibilities have to be detailed.
1.4.2	List of tasks	List of all tasks that the user type "..." performs when using the Web application.
1.4.3	Hours of work	Total working hours and their percentage when using the Web application.
1.4.4	Tasks/user types matrix	If different user groups have been identified, each task has to be related with user's type. A functionality matrix can be used to make a cross reference between the type of user and the tasks that will be used.

Table 2.

2	**Task Context**	
2.1	**Task name**	Task identifier.
2.2	**Task goals**	To explain the main objectives of carrying out the task and: The task breakdown, that is, the activities that need to be performed in order to complete the task. The task output, detailing the information and the means in which the task is produced and, which depends on the task results.
2.3	**Task execution**	To describe the variables that affect the way in which the task can be performed, such as: The execution type. It indicates if the task is carried out by human or by technology. Task dependencies: information, technology, or resources that are required in order to perform the task. Task flexibility. It indicates whether or not the task must be completed following a predefined order. Task duration. It represents how long it will generally take the user to complete the task. Task frequency. It refers to how often the task will normally be performed.
2.4	**Physical and mental demands**	To include any relevant factor that could make the task require too much physical or mental effort (e.g., the users can only perform the task using a voice input device or making decisions quickly) and how is its demand in relation with other tasks.
2.5	**Linked tasks**	List of the tasks that must precede or follow the current task (if the task is carried out concurrently with other tasks).
2.6	**Safety**	To indicate if the task has negative feedback for the health or well-being of the user or other persons (and to specify who is affected).
2.7	**Effects resulting from errors**	To include all possible adverse side effects that can occur as the result of carrying out the task erroneously (e.g., the loss of large amounts of money).
2.8	**Usability evaluation**	To show if the task will be used as part of the usability evaluation. The selection of realistic tasks is fundamental (Rosenbaum, 1989) as well as those problematic tasks that are critical because they can imply risks or usability problems.

Table 3.

3	Technical Environment	
3.1	Software environment	To describe the necessary software to run the Web application on the client's side and the software required to install the Web server.
3.1.1	Operating System (OS)	To indicate whether or not it is mandatory to use a specific OS (Microsoft Windows, UNIX-like, etc.).
3.1.2	Web browser	To detail the Web browser that the user must have installed in his computer equipment for a correct operation of the Web application. If the Web site is compatible with any browser, it must be explicitly indicated. See section "Web browsers" for more information.
3.1.3	Additional software	To include all Web browser plug-ins that must be installed in the computer equipment for the Web application operations to work correctly. For example: Compressor and decompressor needed for downloading files. Readers of specific file types (for instance, multimedia or PDF files). Java Virtual Machine to run Java applets. Furthermore, this point has to include any assistive software technology that must be installed in the computer equipment of disabled users. Consult section "Computer based assistive technology" for detailed information.
3.2	Computer hardware	This subsection is concerned with the hardware environment required to run the Web application on the client's side and the system requirements to host the Web application (in the server).
3.2.1	Mainboard	The speed of the microprocessor and the main memory size required.
3.2.3	External storage	The minimum amount of hard disk space or other storages required (floppy disk, CD, DVD, USB Flash, or ZIP drive).
3.2.4	Input and output devices	Specific peripheral devices (monitor, sound card, keyboard, mouse, etc.) and assistive technology hardware (special keyboards and mouse, Braille display, etc.) used by people with disabilities (will be thoroughly covered in section "Computer based assistive technology").
3.2.5	Network infrastructure	To describe the type of network connection required (network card -DSL/cable- or modem) to determine the average transfer speed needed.
3.3	Reference documents	To include all reference material that help users perform tasks in the Web application (e.g., user manual, online help facilities, etc).

Table 4.

4	Physical Environment	
4.1	Laws and standards	To include relevant legislative documents that may affect safety and health due to the physical environment conditions e.g., conforming to European Directive 90/270/EEC (European Commission, 1990), which establishes the minimum safety and health requirements for work with display screen equipment.
4.2	Location type	The type of setting such as an office, home, laboratory, or kiosk.
4.3	Environmental conditions of the workplace	Conditions of the workplace which may affect performance of user or hardware such as: Atmospheric conditions (e.g., air quality, humidity, etc.) Auditory environment, loud noise, or sound which could distract the user, cause stress, or prevent from hearing relative sounds of the Web application. Thermal environment. To indicate if there are high/low temperatures and air conditioning or heating. Visual conditions could make it difficult to see visual content such as bad lighting (too much darkness/brightness), glare on the user screen, or smoky environments. Environmental instability, such as the effects of vibration or any other movement of the workplace. Furthermore, section "Impairment produced by the environment or technology" will provide information related to several environment conditions that affect user accessibility to the Web contents.

continued on following page

Table 4. continued

4.4	Workplace design	
4.4.1	Space and furniture	To describe the amount of available space, layout, and furniture in the workplace.
4.4.2	User posture	The physical posture adopted by the users while using the Web application (standing, sitting, etc).
4.4.3	Location	The application location in relation to the user workplace and, where the workplace is located regarding work colleagues, customers, resources, and user's home.
4.5	Safety and health	
4.5.1	Health hazards	Workplace or environment conditions that may affect the user's health and safety (e.g., industrial accidents, loss of vision, etc.).
4.5.2	Protective clothing and equipment	To describe any protective clothing or safety equipment that the user must wear in the workplace (e.g., gloves, face mask, etc.).

Table 5.

5	Social and Organisational Environment	
5.1	General structure	
5.1.1	Working groups	To indicate if the user carries out the tasks alone or in collaboration with other people. In the latter case, the other people's roles and their relationship with the user have to be specified.
5.1.2	Assistance received	The availability of assistance from expert staff using the Web application. It is independent that the aid comes from colleagues or from an external organization.
5.1.3	Interruptions	To include the frequency and nature of any interruptions in the user's operating of the Web application that can have repercussions in the usability. For example, the average number of interruptions due to telephone calls.
5.1.4	Management structure	Relationships and responsibilities of the organization staff with respect to the users who carry out the tasks.
5.1.5	Communications structure	To describe the main communication methods between persons inside and outside the organisation and the relationships between these people.
5.2	Attitudes and culture	
5.2.1	Policy on the use of computers	To indicate the attitudes of the organization and its employees toward the introduction, acquisition, and use of a technological information system.
5.2.2	Support policy on the use of Web application	Specification of the assistance that will be needed by each user group, including training courses and staff to be involved (expert colleagues or external company).
5.2.3	Organisational aims	To indicate the goals and objectives that the organization aims to achieve using the Web application.
5.2.4	Industrial relations	To describe the nature of the existing relations between different individuals of the organization. For example: include the relations between the employees and the management.
5.3	Worker control	
5.3.1	Performance monitoring	To indicate the process and methods used to gather up data, to evaluate them and to assure the quality and speed of the users work.
5.3.2	Performance feedback	To describe how users receive feedback about the quality and speed of their work.

environments have to be provided for different groups, then all physical alternatives should be included (see Table 4).

Social and Organisational Environment

This section includes descriptions of the organisational structures within the environment in which the Web application will be run. It should also include the company's attitude and culture towards computers and their related products, as well as factors that affect the productivity and quality of the Web-based application (see Table 5).

USERS WITH SPECIAL NEEDS AND TECHNOLOGICAL ENVIRONMENT

With the purpose of facilitating the specification of the context of use according to accessibility, in this section the information related to the user characteristics of people with any given disability and the technological environment they usually use to access the Web content (assistive technologies and alternative browsers) is detailed.

Disabilities and Barriers on the Web

Disabled people can suffer different types of difficulties for using the Web as a result of combining the barriers to access the computer hardware (physical input/output devices), the software (browsers or plug-ins) and the Web pages content. This subsection tackles the different sensory, physical, and cognitive limitations that affect Web access and the disabilities that are caused by the environment and the technology used.

When making an accessible Web site for all types of users, a set of accessibility principles must be taken into account. Nowadays, the only standards that refer to accessible Web page creation are the "Web Content Accessibility Guidelines 1.0" (W3C, 1999). On the other hand,

International Standard "ISO/IEC Guide 71" (ISO, 2001b) facilitates a list of requirements that should be considered when developing products for the different disabilities. Although this guide only provides requirements that are very general, it is useful as a starting point for classifying the different existing disabilities.

Visual Impairments

Sight (or vision) relates to the ability to sense the presence of light and to sense the form, size, shape, and colour of visual stimuli (ISO, 2001b). The incidence and severity of visual impairment increase with age and, among others, it can appear as:

- Loss of visual acuity
- Loss of near or distance vision, as well as inability to see things to the side (tunnel vision)
- Colour perception deficits

The main barrier for blind users is how to obtain, identify, and navigate between information exclusively presented in a visual display. To make their access to the Web easier, developers will provide alternative text for any visual content (images, videos, frames), and they will mark up tables appropriately. Also, many persons with blindness use screen readers (assistive software that reads the textual information and describes the graphic objects of the interface), so it is very difficult or impossible for them to attend to auditory outputs that occur while their screen reader is reading.

People who have low vision usually have problems distinguishing text or images, carrying out tasks that require hand and eye coordination (such as the precise control of a mouse), as well as many of the problems described for blind people (depending on the type and extent of visual limitation). To access the Web pages, they may need to use their personal style sheet (increasing the size of text, customizing the contrast between text and background colours) and activate the objects with keyboard equivalents of mouse commands.

Lastly, colour blindness is a lack of sensibility to certain colours. Sometimes it results in the inability to see any colour (achromatopsia). Their access to the Web content can be facilitated providing sufficient colour contrast between text and background, allowing them to use their own style sheets, as well as showing information that does not rely exclusively on colour.

Hearing Impairments

Hearing functions relate to sensing the presence of sounds and discriminating the location, pitch, loudness, quality, and comprehension of sounds (ISO, 2001b). As people age, they tend to lose the ability to detect sounds.

A deaf person cannot perceive amplified speech even with a hearing aid. A common definition of "deaf" is the inability to hear sound below 90 dB (ISO, 2003). People who are profoundly deaf are traditionally divided into two categories:

- People who have prelingual deafness. They lost their hearing before learning to speak so they may have difficulty understanding written and spoken language because, for most of these people, their primary language is usually sign language and not the native tongue spoken in their environment. Furthermore, they are not usually able to produce speech recognizable by voice-input systems.
- People who have post lingual deafness, losing their hearing after they have acquired a basic spoken language.

When interacting with Web applications, deaf users will encounter problems if important information is presented only in audio form since they need captions for audio content. Furthermore, barriers that users who suffer from prelingual deafness may encounter on the Web include the use of complex or technical language, lack of content-related images in pages full of text and requirements for voice input on Web sites.

Finally, users who are hard of hearing may or may not use electronic hearing aids, depending on the nature of their hearing impairment (ISO, 2003). They may have trouble hearing sounds of certain frequencies or low volume, and thus it is fundamental to allow them sounds customization.

Physical Impairments

Physical impairments with an impact on the use of ICT include dexterity and manipulation:

- Dexterity is related to activities where hands and arms are used, especially coordinated actions of handling objects, manipulating, and carrying them out using the fingers and a hand (ISO, 2001b).
- Manipulation relates to activities of carrying and moving objects. It can be impaired by an inability to use both hands when carrying out an activity. It is also affected when joint movement, particularly of the hands or arms, is restricted. Speed of manipulation also declines in old age as a result of slower reaction time and slower movement (ISO, 2001b).

People with involuntary uncoordinated movements have problems carrying out tasks that require precise movements (such as moving a mouse or pressing the keys of the keyboard) or timing, as well as doing complex keyboard manipulation (pressing a combination of keys simultaneously).

To benefit users who have motor disabilities affecting the hands or arms with their access to Web, include accessibility features (access key to links and form elements), avoid the use of time-limited response options and do not automatically open new windows.

Cognitive Impairments

Cognition is the understanding, integrating and processing of information. People with a cognitive impairment may have trouble learning new things, making generalizations and associations, expressing themselves through spoken and written language, as well as the reduced ability to concentrate on a task (ISO, 2001b).

Cognitive impairments, related to access to the Web contents, can be distinguished as follows:

- Users with intellectual impairment. Intellect is the capacity to know, understand and reason (ISO, 2001b). As people get older, they keep their basic intellectual abilities but they require more time to perform most tasks. Individuals with impairments of intelligence may learn more slowly, or have difficulty with abstract concepts (W3C, 2005a). To use the Web, these users may take more time on a Web site, may rely more on graphics to enhance understanding of a site, may benefit if the level of language is clear and simple, and may rely on a consistent design and consistent navigation options throughout the Web pages. Also, to make it easier for them to be able to use different search options.
- People with memory impairments. Memory relates to specific mental functions of registering and storing information and retrieving it as needed. As people get older, failing memory affects people's ability to recall and learn new things (ISO, 2001b). To use the Web this type of users may rely on a consistent content and navigational structure throughout the site.
- Individuals with attention deficit disorder. They may have difficulty focussing on information and in continuing to pay attention to a task. This problem is very frequent in elderly people (ISO, 2001b). For this type of users to use the Web, it helps to be able

to freeze the animated objects and to find a clear and consistent organization of Web sites.

- Users with dyslexia have difficulties in reading text that is presented in written form and difficulties in producing written text (ISO, 2003). They may need to access the Web to find the content in multiple modalities simultaneously (alternative text and captions for audio), they should not find an unnecessarily complex language for the site's content and they should be able to use multiple search options.
- Finally, some types of epilepsy are triggered by visual flickering or audio signals at a certain frequency (W3C, 2005a). To use the Web, these users may need to turn off animations, blinking text, or certain frequencies of audio. Avoidance of these visual or audio frequencies in Web sites helps prevent the triggering of seizures.

Impairment Produced by the Environment or Technology

It should be taken into account that disability is not the only limitation that hinders content accessibility. There are other limitations derived from the use context and the access device (hardware or software) used by the users.

Vanderheiden (2000) establishes a parallelism between all possible impairments and the situational constraints which would provide the same access problems:

- Lack of vision. It affects both blind users and people whose eyes are busy (e.g., driving a car) or are in darkness/brightness environments. This limitation is also damaging to users who have not installed a plug-in to show the graphic information.
- Low vision. The same effect as users with partial visual impairment can be common for people who use a small display or who

work in a smoky environment or undertake an excessive number of visual tasks.

- Colour blindness. Users with a monochrome display share the same problems as users with colour vision deficiency.
- Lack of hearing. It restricts both deaf users and any user in contexts where sound is masked by background noise or whose ears are busy (e.g., a telephone operator) or where sound cannot be used (e.g., a library). This limitation also affects users that do not have a sound card in their computer equipment or who have not installed a plug-in to reproduce the auditory information.
- Limited hearing. Users hard of hearing share the same problem as people who are in noisy environments.
- Limited manual dexterity. This limitation has an adverse effect on people who have motor disabilities affecting their hands or arms, and users who use gloves or who are in an unstable environment.
- Limited cognition. Persons with cognitive impairments have the same problems as users who are distracted or frightened or under the influence of alcohol.
- Unable to read. It affects users with intellectual impairment and dyslexia, users who have not learned to read this language, and also people who have left their reading glasses behind.

Therefore, there are environments that may produce disabilities and technological disabilities when the appropriate technology does not exist.

Furthermore, in the context of Web–based applications, one of the problems when using HTML (Hypertext Markup Language) is the lack of compatibility between the language versions supported by the different browsers that translate their own labels and not those officially published as standard by the W3C. This problem obliges Web developers to keep different versions of the same document or to use a label subset (with a loss of functionality) to guarantee access to the greatest possible number of users.

The language has another problem: the continuous and quick evolution (not within the published W3C standards) and the proliferation of new languages and implementation techniques of Web documents. This problem forces a constant updating of the browser's versions to assure access to the new documents. These versions are not always available to all users, especially in the case of browsers for users with disabilities (see section "Computer based assistive technology").

Web Browsers

Software used by users to display and interact with Web page content are referred to as "user agents" by the W3C (1999), including desktop graphical browsers, text-only browsers, voice browsers, mobile phones, multimedia players, plug-ins, and some software assistive technologies used in conjunction with browsers (see section "Computer based assistive technology").

The Web Accessibility Initiative has developed the "User Agent Accessibility Guidelines (UAAG) 1.0" (W3C, 2002). These guidelines constitute a set of recommendations for designing HTML browsers and other types of software that lower barriers to Web accessibility for people with disabilities (visual, hearing, physical, cognitive, and neurological). Although these guidelines are devised to design accessible user agents, they can be used as a tool for evaluation, checking the level of accessibility that any Web browser accomplishes. The output will allow us to conclude if it is interesting or not to use a particular browser.

Browsers can be roughly divided into two types, although there is not a well-defined borderline between both types because more and more standard browsers include accessibility features that allow users with special needs to access the Web pages in alternative formats:

- Standard browsers, developed by the main software companies, are the most used. They have their own accessibility features and they can be used in combination with assistive technologies.
- Alternative browsers, specially developed for people with disabilities, present the information of the Web pages in a different way to the traditional mouse-and-screen-based browsers (W3C, 2005b), including:
  - Text-only browsers that show the textual content exclusively.
  - Voice browsers which allow voice-driven navigation.
  - Text-to-speech browsers that use synthesized speech to offer the Web page content.

Computer Based Assistive Technology

Frequently, users with functionality limitations (sensorial, physical, or cognitive) are not able to access Web content only using browsers. This happens because browsers and Web content are developed without regard to all people or possible circumstances, making the new technology inaccessible.

International Standard "ISO 9999" (ISO, 2002) defines technical aids as "any product, instrument,

Table 6. Assistive technology related to type of impairment

Type of impairment	Assistive technology (H: Hardware, S: Software)
Severe visual impairment	Voice synthesizer (H)
	Braille keyboard (H)
	Braille display (H)
	Braille writing devices (H)
	Voice recognition (S y H)
	Screen reader (S)
Partial visual impairment	Enlarged screens (H)
	Voice synthesizer (H)
	Voice recognition (H y S)
	Screen magnifier (H y S)
	Screen reader (S)
	Accessibility in graphic environment (S)
Severe or partial hearing loss	Programming sound (S)
	Sonorous warnings (S)
Physical difficulties (hands and arms)	Adaptations to standard keyboard (H)
	Special keyboard or mouse (H)
	Universal switch (H)
	Voice recognition (H y S)
	Programming keyboard or mouse (S)
	Virtual keyboard or mouse (S)
Cognitive difficulties	Voice synthesizer (H)
	Voice recognition (S y H)
	Screen reader (S)

equipment or technical system used by a disabled person to prevent, compensate, relieve or neutralize an impairment, disability or handicap."

Assistive technology is used by disabled users to enable them to carry out tasks using the computer that they were formerly unable to accomplish, or had great difficulty accomplishing. It is useful both for people with disabilities, and for people using computers in environments that may produce disabilities, helping them to overcome their impairments.

The following table relates software or hardware assistive technologies that can operate in conjunction with browsers to improve the access to Web-based applications to users with any type of impairment.

BENEFITS OF A USABLE AND ACCESSIBLE WEB DESIGN

Making Web applications more usable produces the following benefits (ISO, 1999; Henry, 2002):

- Reduce production and maintenance costs, because user involvement into the design process, over design is minimized.
- Reduce training and support costs because they are easier to understand and use.
- Reduce errors produced by a wrong use of the product.
- Increase user satisfaction since discomfort and stress are reduced. Moreover, it allows users to manage a greater variety of tasks.
- Improve the productivity of users and therefore the operational efficiency of organizations.
- Improve product quality and its attractiveness for end-users. This can provide a competitive advantage in the market.

Guaranteeing accessibility, as well as directly benefiting the disabled or elderly, presents other social, legal, technical, commercial, and economical advantages:

- The increase of the potential audience of the Web site since:
  - The World Health Organization (2006) estimated that around 600 million people live with disabilities, that is 10% of the world's population. Furthermore, according to the survey carried out by Graphic, Visualization & Usability Center (1998), 9.2% of the users connected to the Internet have some form of disability or impairment.
  - It helps users with low literacy levels and people whose primary language is different from that of the Web page.
  - It helps young users that have not acquired much knowledge yet.
  - It improves the results of site search engines.
  - It facilitates the ability of content generation for multiple formats or devices. This facilitates the access from any of them (e.g., cellular phones, PDAs, and GPS car navigation systems) and widens the range of browsers that can access the content.
  - It provides support for Semantic Web.
- Economical benefits derived from the increase of the number of possible consumers (ISO, 2001b). Moreover, Intranets can increase the number of possible employees.
- According to the legislation of many countries. More and more governments demand accessibility in Web sites, considering it a civilian right. As Loughborough (1999) stated, "Accessibility is right, not privilege." In European Union (http://europa.eu.int), the accessibility aspects that Web pages have to fulfil are compiled in the e-Europe action plans where the "Web Content Accessibility Guidelines 1.0" (W3C, 1999) are considered

- a de facto standard for the design of accessible Web sites.
- Reduction of maintenance costs as a consequence of the improvement in the general design and implementation.
- Reduction of the Web servers load.
- Demonstration of a social responsibility and improvement of the company corporate image.

CONCLUSION

This chapter proposes the structure of an index explaining in detail how to create the specification of the context of use in terms of attributes which may be relevant to usability, as well as the characteristics of people with special needs, significant barriers that they may encounter when interacting with Web applications and the technological environment that they usually use to access the Web content. The outcome is a documented set of user requirements, task requirements, and environmental requirements (technical, physical, social, and organisational) which may have a significant influence on usability and accessibility of Web-based applications.

Understanding and specifying the context of use is the first activity in the user-centred design process. A design centred on the user proposes that the designers comprehend the context of use with the goal of obtaining more usable systems. On the Web, usability is fundamental because if a Web site is difficult to use, people leave (Nielsen, 2003).

This chapter facilitates for the development team members the task of generating the specification of the context of use of Web-based applications with a special attention on the synergy between factors which affect usability and accessibility. When applications are usable and accessible, the benefits obtained are greater than the addition of both approaches. The reason is that the improvement of accessibility for people

with disabilities can improve the usability for all people and vice versa. Furthermore, a correct preparation of the specification of the context of use document ensures the quality of the developed Web applications.

REFERENCES

European Commission. (1990, June 21). Minimum safety and health requirements for work with display screen equipment. Directive (90/270/EEC). *Official Journal of the European Communities, No. L 156*, 0014-0018.

Graphic, Visualization & Usability Center. (1998). *GVU's tenth WWW user survey: Disability*. Retrieved October 16, 2007, from http://www.gvu.gatech.edu/user_surveys/survey-1998-10/graphs/general/q12.htm

Henry, S. (2002). Understanding Web accessibility. In Glasshaus (Ed.), *Constructing accessible Web sites* (pp. 7-31). Birmingham: Peer Information Link.

ISO. (1998). *ISO 9241-11: Ergonomic requirements for office work with visual display terminals (VDTs). Part 11: Guidance on usability*. Geneva, Switzerland: International Organization for Standardization.

ISO. (1999). *ISO 13407: Human-centred design processes for interactive systems*. Geneva, Switzerland: International Organization for Standardization.

ISO. (2001a). *ISO/IEC 9126-1:2001. Software engineering. Product quality. Part 1: Quality model*. Geneva, Switzerland: International Organization for Standardization.

ISO. (2001b). *ISO/IEC Guide 71:2001. Guidelines for standards developers to address the needs of older persons and persons with disabilities*. Geneva, Switzerland: International Organization for Standardization.

ISO. (2002). *ISO 9999:2002. Technical aids for persons with disabilities. Classification and terminology.* Geneva, Switzerland: International Organization for Standardization.

ISO. (2003). *ISO/TS 16071:2003. Ergonomics of human-system interaction. Guidance on accessibility for human-computer interfaces.* Geneva, Switzerland: International Organization for Standardization.

Loughborough, W. (1999). An accessibility guarantee plan. *WWW8 Developer's Day.* Retrieved October 16, 2007, from http://www.utoronto.ca/ian/www8/loughborough.html

Maguire, M. C. (1998). *User-centred requirements handbook, versión 3.3.* Loughborough/UK: HUSAT Research Institute.

Nielsen, J. (2003). Alertbox. *Usability 101: Introduction to usability.* Retrieved October 16, 2007, from http://www.useit.com/alertbox/20030825.html

Rosenbaum, S. (1989). Selecting appropriate subjects for documentation usability testing. In Elsevier (Ed.), *Third International Conference on Human-Computer Interaction, on Work with Computers: Organizational, Management, Stress and Health Aspects* (Vol. 1, pp. 620-627). Boston.

Thomas, C., & Bevan, N. (1996). *Usability context analysis—a practical guide, v4.04.* Tendington/UK: NPL Usability Services.

Vanderheiden, G. (2000). Fundamental principles and priority setting for universal usability. In ACM Press (Ed.), *Conference on Universal Usability*, Arlington, VI, USA, (pp. 32-37).

W3C. (1999). *Web content accessibility guidelines 1.0.* W3C Recommendation REC-19990505. Retrieved October 16, 2007, from http://www.w3.org/TR/WAI-WEBCONTENT/

W3C. (2002). User agent accessibility guidelines 1.0. W3C Recommendation REC-UAAG10-20021217. Retrieved October 16, 2007, from http://www.w3.org/TR/UAAG10/

W3C. (2005a). How people with disabilities use the Web. Retrieved October 16, 2007, from http://www.w3.org/WAI/EO/Drafts/PWD-Use-Web/Overview.html

W3C. (2005b). Alternative Web browsing. Retrieved October 16, 2007, from http://www.w3.org/WAI/References/Browsing

World Health Organization. (2006). World report on disability and rehabilitation. Retrieved October 16, 2007, from http://www.who.int/disabilities/publications/dar_world_report_concept_note.pdf

KEY TERMS

Accessibility: Usability of a product, service, environment, or facility by people with the widest range of capabilities.

Assistive Technology: Hardware or software products used by disabled users to enable them to carry out tasks using the computer that they were formerly unable to accomplish, or had great difficulty accomplishing.

Context of Use: Users, tasks, equipment (hardware, software and materials), and the physical and social environments in which a product is used.

Disability: Impairment that interferes with the customary manner in which a task is performed or that requires accommodation in order to perform a task.

Quality in Use: The capability of the software product to enable specified users to achieve specified goals with effectiveness, productivity, safety, and satisfaction in specified contexts of use.

Usability: Extent to which a product can be

used by specified users to achieve specified goals with effectiveness, efficiency, and satisfaction in a specified context of use.

Usability Evaluation: The process of testing whether software meets a predetermined and quantifiable level of usability.

Chapter X
Web Accessibility

Carlos García Moreno
Indra, Spain

ABSTRACT

This chapter faces the Web accessibility issue from the perspective of Web Information Systems Quality, which is the main topic of the handbook. The closed relation between both issues (and also standard Web technologies) will be explained. It will be proven that Web accessibility does not imply any extra effort; it is a consequence of good development and design practices. In order to achieve this objective the basic topics related to Web accessibility will be defined and necessary introductory information will be exposed, in order to set the basis for the understanding of the points of discussion, which form the main content of the chapter. Also, some benefits of Web accessibility will be proven and the myths related to Web accessibility will be refuted. By the end of the chapter, the future trends and the newest standard Web technologies that have been designed, taking into account Web accessibility needs, will be introduced.

INTRODUCTION

Web accessibility is an issue that can be faced from different perspectives. As the purpose of this handbook is to provide comprehensive coverage of the most important issues, concepts, models, measures, and methodologies related to Web information systems quality, this chapter will be focused on the relation between Web accessibility and the Web information systems quality.

The most important thing that must be taken into account within this context is that Web accessibility is not an extra step in the creation process of a Web information system, but it should be present in all steps of the process. We could say that if a Web site has been since the beginning designed and developed using quality criteria a reasonable accessibility level is almost fully guaranteed. On the other hand, an accessible Web site is always a high-quality Web site in terms of design and development. This is the main concept of this chapter.

Along the chapter it will be shown that the most important issues in the accessibility of a Web site are neither special nor innovative; the appropriate use of the existing standard Web technologies is enough to ensure the accessibility of a Web site in a high percentage of the cases. This is the reason why most references in this chapter have been extracted from the W3C Web site. If the last HTML (HyperText Markup Language) specification is "truly" known it is not necessary to learn anything else to develop reasonably accessible Web information systems.

Another important goal will be to demonstrate, contrarily to the common thought, that Web accessibility not only benefits users with disabilities. The truth is that almost 100% users have enjoyed (or will enjoy) the benefits of Web accessibility.

There are also a lot of controversial issues when talking about Web accessibility. As it will be explained, the origin of this controversy is, mainly, a wrong work methodology, and the answer to it is to face the design and the development of Web information systems following a quality criteria.

So, the main objectives of this chapter are:

- To place Web accessibility into the creation process of a Web site and to show the relation between Web accessibility and the Quality of a Web information system.
- To show the relation between standard Web technologies and Web accessibility.
- To face the controversial matters related to Web accessibility and to demonstrate that the answer to these matters is in the appropriate use of standard Web technologies and in the observance of quality criteria during the whole process.
- To show the benefits of Web accessibility not only for users with disabilities, but also for all kind of users.

BACKGROUND

This section aims at introducing some concepts that will set the basis for the future contents of the chapter. In this section some points of future discussion will also be introduced.

The Basis

What is Web Accessibility?

According to W3C (World Wide Web Consortium):

Web accessibility means that people with disabilities can use the Web. More specifically, Web accessibility means that people with disabilities can perceive, understand, navigate, and interact with the Web, and that they can contribute to the Web. Web accessibility also benefits others, including older people with changing abilities due to aging." (Lawton & participants of the Education and Outrech Working Group, 2005)

The last sentence is a first approximation of how Web accessibility can benefit all of us, at least in the future.

What is Disability?

According to the Disability Discrimination Act (1995) a person has a disability if he has a *"physical or mental impairment which has a substantial and long-term adverse effect on his ability to carry out normal day-to-day activities" (Disability Discrimination Act, 1995)*. The term *"disabled person"* means a person who has a disability.

This is the definition of disability from a governmental point of view. But if the expression "long-term" is suppressed it is easy to realize that all of us have been (or will be) disabled persons sometime in our life. This concept will be further explained while introducing the list of the main disabilities.

List of Disabilities

This is one of the numerous existing lists of disabilities. It has been extracted form the "The Individuals with Disabilities Education Act (IDEA)" (National Dissemination Center for Children with Disabilities, 2002), which is a United States federal law to ensure "a free appropriate public education" for students with disabilities, in the Least Restrictive Environment. This is the list in alphabetic order:

• Autism
• Deaf-blindness
• Emotional disturbance
• Hearing impairment (including deafness)
• Mental retardation
• Multiple disabilities
• Orthopedic impairment
• Other health impairment
• Specific learning disability
• Speech or language impairment
• Traumatic brain injury
• Visual impairment (including blindness)

When reading the list someone could wonder how a Web document could be accessible for all these kinds of disabilities. According to the previous definition, these are the actions that a user should be able to carry out when accessing a Web document: perceive, understand, navigate and interact. If we were strict the answer to the question should be NO. For example: could a user suffering a traumatic brain injury understand a scientific Web document? Probably he could not. But, does it really mean the Web site is not accessible? NO, of course, it could be accessible. Think about this: would you be able to understand all scientific Web documents?

The right way to interpret this definition is to think that a Web document is accessible if IT HAS NO OBSTACLES for a user to perceive, understand, navigate and interact with it. For example: a wrong markup could be an obstacle to the perception of the Web document, an unclear design could be an obstacle for the navigation and a wrong selection or use of the technologies could be an obstacle for the interaction.

But, what about the problem of understanding? Most Web documents are not understandable for some users. But we have the same problem, for example with books. Well, we must assume that there are different contents for different kind of users. So we should not find the understanding obstacles in the content. The real obstacles are those that could make us not to understand a content that is suitable for us. These obstacles could be, for example, an unclear composition or grammatical and syntactical errors.

Assistive Technologies

There is a very common question regarding Web accessibility: How can a blind user read a Web page?

This question shows that a lot of people not only think that Web accessibility is only for disabled users (which is a big mistake), but they also think that Web accessibility is only for blind users (which is a bigger mistake). Let's see which technologies are used by people with disabilities to access the Web, according to the appendix of the WCAG 2.0 (Web content accessibility guidelines 2.0). (Caldwell et al., 2006b)

User Agents

A user agent is any software that retrieves and renders Web content for users. For example: Web browsers, media players, plug-ins, and other programs (including assistive technologies) that help in retrieving and rendering Web content.

Assistive Technologies

The next is a list of relevant (in the context of Web accessibility) assistive technologies, according to W3C:

- Screen magnifiers, which are used by people with visual disabilities to enlarge and change colors on the screen to improve the visual readability of rendered text and images.
- Screen readers, which are used by people who are blind or have reading disabilities to read textual information through synthesized speech or Braille displays.
- Voice recognition software, which may be used by people who have some physical disabilities.
- Alternative keyboards, which are used by people with certain physical disabilities to simulate the keyboard.
- Alternative pointing devices, which are used by people with certain physical disabilities to simulate mouse pointing and button activations.

The Controversy

The Myths

There are several polemic issues, wrong concepts and myths regarding Web accessibility. Some of them have been already briefly discussed. The surprising thing is that most of these myths have been created and spread by Web developers (which is very dangerous, because it can make other people think that these myths are true). They have spread the idea that accessible Web sites are:

- **Expensive:** It is common to think about Web accessibility as an extra issue, and added value, the final (and annoying) step in the creation process of a Web information system. In most cases what Web developers do is to modify the final version of the Web site, in order to get the desired accessibility level. The objective is to satisfy some guidelines and checkpoints using any accessibility evaluation tool. Of course, this approach means more work and an additional capital investment.

- **Useless:** As it has been exposed before, it is also very usual in the Web developers community to think that Web accessibility only benefits disabled users, and that it is a too reduced audience to be worthwhile to make the corresponding effort. The only incentive for developing accessible Web sites is when clients (mainly public organizations) insist on it.
- **Ugly:** Mainly graphic designers (but also Web developers) usually think that an accessible Web site is always ugly. They use to think that Web accessibility implies a lot of restrictions that are against appearance.

As it will be proven during the chapter, the main cause of these thoughts is that people who have promoted them are used to "bad practices" when designing and developing. As Web accessibility is a consequence of "good practices," it implies an extraordinary effort for these developers. All these myths will be refuted in the next sections of the chapter.

The Problems

There are also some polemic technologies, regarding Web accessibility. These technologies are:

- **Frames**
- **JavaScript**
- **Flash**

Is their use allowed? Are these technologies against Web accessibility? In this case, does Web accessibility imply losing some features? Or is there any alternative?

All these questions will be answered along the chapter.

The Rules

Although the objectives of Web accessibility are clear, a set of guidelines is necessary in order to avoid mistakes while trying to ensure the accessibility in a Web development. It is also necessary to involve in the development of these guidelines most of the people and organizations related with this subject. It would be very important that these guidelines become a widely accepted standard.

The development process of these guidelines has been led by the Web accessibility Initiative (WAI). The WAI belongs to the W3C, which is the organization in charge of the Web standardization.

According its Web site (W3C, 1994-1996), the W3C "*develops interoperable technologies (specifications, guidelines, software, and tools) to lead the Web to its full potential.*" And, as Tim Berners-Lee (W3C Director and inventor of the World Wide Web) said "*the power of the Web is in its universality. Access by everyone regardless of disability is an essential aspect.*"

This information shows that there should be a close relation between Web accessibility and standard Web technologies.

WAI

According W3C Web site, the WAI is the section of W3C that works with organizations around the world to develop strategies, guidelines, and resources to help make the Web accessible to people with disabilities (Lawton, 2006).

All these products are possible thanks to the participation of volunteers from around the world that are included in the different working groups.

The WAI develops its work through W3C's consensus-based process, involving different stakeholders in Web accessibility. These include industry, disability organizations, government, accessibility research organizations, and more. WAI, in partnership with these organizations, pursues accessibility of the Web through five primary activities (Lawton & Brewer, 2006):

- Ensuring that core technologies of the Web support accessibility.
- Developing guidelines which are widely regarded as the international standard for Web accessibility: Web content, user agents, and authoring tools. Facilitating development of evaluation and repair tools for accessibility.
- Conducting education and outreach. Developing support materials to help understand and implement Web accessibility.
- Coordinating with research and development that can affect future accessibility of the Web.

The following are the most important sets of guidelines developed by the WAI:

- Web content accessibility guidelines (WCAG) (Lawton, 2005a)
- Authoring tool accessibility guidelines (ATAG) (Lawton & May, 2005a)
- User agent accessibility guidelines (UAAG) (Lawton & May, 2005b)

In this chapter, the most interesting set of guidelines for us is the WCAG, because it is focused on the Web content, whose accessibility is what we should ensure when developing a Web information system. According to WCAG 2.0 (Caldwell et al., 2006b) "content" is information to be communicated to the user by means of a user agent, and Web "content" generally refers to the information in a Web page or Web application, including text, images, forms, sounds, and such. So content is information and the objective of information is to reach as many people as possible. So "information" and "inaccessible" are words that don't go well together.

WCAG

The WCAG (Lawton, 2005a) explains how to make Web content accessible to people with disabilities.

WCAG is primarily intended for:

- Web content developers (page authors, site designers, etc.)
- Web authoring tool developers
- Web accessibility evaluation tool developers

The current version of the WCAG is WCAG 1.0. This version was approved in May 1999, and is the stable and referenceable version.

A new version (WCAG 2.0) is being developed to apply to different Web technologies, be easier the use and understanding, and to be more precisely testable. WCAG 2.0 was supposed to be completed in 2006 but, because of the nature of the W3C specification development process, WAI cannot be certain when the final version will be available. WCAG 1.0 will remain the latest approved version until WCAG 2.0 is complete. In the "Future Trends" section the main features of WCAG 2.0 will be put forward.

WCAG 1.0 (Chisholm et al., 1999)

In this section only the guidelines organization will be exposed, not the full list of guidelines. Along the chapter some of them will be explained in relation to the HTML specification or to a determined polemic point.

The WCAG 1.0 includes 14 guidelines. Each guideline has several checkpoints that explain how they apply in typical content development scenarios. Each checkpoint is intended to be specific enough so that someone reviewing a page or site may verify that it has been satisfied.

Each checkpoint has a priority level assigned by the Working Group based on its impact on accessibility.

- **Priority 1:** A Web content developer must satisfy this checkpoint. Otherwise, one or more groups will find it impossible to access information in the document.

- **Priority 2:** A Web content developer should satisfy this checkpoint. Otherwise, one or more groups will find it difficult to access information in the document.
- **Priority 3:** A Web content developer may address this checkpoint. Satisfying this checkpoint will improve access to Web documents.

There are also three conformance levels, which are closely related to the priority levels:

- Conformance Level "A" (all Priority 1 checkpoints are satisfied).
- Conformance Level "Double-A" (all Priority 1 and 2 checkpoints are satisfied).
- Conformance Level "Triple-A" (all Priority 1, 2, and 3 checkpoints are satisfied).

When having developed a Web page the developer can add one of the next logos to indicate the Web page conformance level.

In general, if a Web page satisfies all Priority 2 checkpoints, we could say that it is reasonably accessible.

Legislation

(Lawton, 2005b) According to W3C, there is a growing body of national laws and policies which address accessibility of information and communications technology (ICT), including the Internet and the Web. There is also a great variety of approaches among these laws and policies: some take the approach of establishing a human or civil right to ICT; others the approach that any ICT purchased by government must be accessible; others that any ICT sold in a given market must be accessible; and there are still other approaches.

In this section only two of these approaches will be exposed: The U.S. legislation (that FORCES Federal agencies to guarantee the access and use of information and data to individuals with disabilities who are Federal employees) and the EU resolutions (that only EMPHASISES the need of public sector Web sites to be accessible).

U.S.: The Rehabilitation Act Amendments (Section 508) (United States Access Board, 1973)

On August 7, 1998, President Clinton signed into law the Rehabilitation Act Amendments of 1998 which covers access to federally funded programs and services. The law strengthens section 508 of the Rehabilitation Act and requires access to electronic and information technology provided by the Federal government. The law applies to all Federal agencies when they develop, procure, maintain, or use electronic and information technology.

...Individuals with disabilities who are Federal employees to have access to and use of information and data that is comparable to the access to and use of the information and data by Federal employees who are not individuals with disabilities. (Requirements for Federal departments and agencies. 1—accessibility. A—Development, procurement, maintenance, or use of electronic and information technology)

The law also forces each Federal departments or agencies to incorporate new standards.

Not later than 6 months after the Access Board publishes the standards required under paragraph (2), the Federal Acquisition Regulatory Council shall revise the Federal Acquisition Regulation and each Federal department or agency shall revise the Federal procurement policies and directives under the control of the department or agency to incorporate those standards (Requirements for Federal departments and agencies, 3 —Incorporation of standards).

EU: Communications and resolutions (Skaalum et al., 2002)

The next are the main actions carried out by EU institutions:

- Commission Communication of September 2001
- Council Resolution of March 2002
- Parliament Resolution of June 2002
- Committee of the Regions Opinion (May-June 2002)
- Economic and Social Committee Opinion (February 2002)
- Commission Communication of September 2001

These resolutions and communications specify that Public sector Web sites and their content in Member States and in the European institutions must be designed to be accessible to ensure that citizens with disabilities can access information and take full advantage of the potential for e-government. And these actions should have been executed by the European Institutions and the European Union Member States through the adoption of the WCAG for public Web sites by the end of 2001:

Organizations receiving public funding to be encouraged to make their Web sites accessible.

...within the framework of the eEurope Action Plan, Member States should encourage not only national public Web sites but also local and regional public Web sites to comply with the Guidelines.

Encourages the Member States and the Commission to take account of the need for digital content to be accessible, for example by, when funding development of Web sites, requiring those Web sites to implement the Guidelines.

MAIN FOCUS OF THE CHAPTER

In this section the previously exposed polemic issues will be clarified, the myths will be refuted and, as it is the main objective, it will be proved the fact that Web accessibility and Web information systems quality are closely related subjects.

Standard Web Technologies and Web Accessibility

In the "Introduction" section it was emphasized that Web accessibility is a consequence of good development practices, which includes using standard Web technologies. The best way to understand it is using some examples.

HTML is Semantic

HTML is semantic, and this fact is very useful for Web accessibility. Every tag in an HTML document means something, not only its content.

For example, the heading elements (H1 to H6) represent the hierarchical structure of the document, so *<H1>Main focus of the chapter</H1>* not only means "main focus of the chapter," but also "Level 1 section: Main focus of the chapter." User agents may use heading information, for example, to automatically build a table of contents of a document. So a disabled (or not disabled) user could browse directly to the desired section or subsection of the document.

It is only one example (there are lots of them) of how user agents use the semantic of the HTML markup to tell the user the real meaning of the content and to make its navigation easier and more comfortable.

The next sample shows two visually equivalent fragments of code:

```
<h1>Main focus of the chapter</h1>
```

```
<p style="font-size:32px; font-weight:
bold;">Main focus of the chapter</p>
```

It's clear that the second code is wrong, although the appearance is the same, because it does not express its real meaning.

This simple example can help us to start refuting some myths:

- **Web accessibility implies additional effort and cost:** Think what would happen if you want, for example, to modify the color of the headings. There are two options:
  - Writing *"h1{color:#0000ff;}"* in the style sheet.
  - Modify ALL appearances of the tag adding the color information *"<p style="font-size:32px; font-weight: bold; color:#0000ff;">"*. It could happen a lot of times in your whole Web site.

So, which of the two options requires a greater effort? It seems clear that separating content from presentation make maintenance easier, and also improves device independence and faster downloads (smaller documents).

- **Web accessibility only benefits disabled users:** Imagine you are accessing the Internet using a mobile device. Mobile devices have a very small screen. You want to read the third section of the document and you don't want to wait while the content goes down the screen till the desired point. Which markup would let you browse directly to the third section? A right markup can improve, for example, device independence.

We have discovered, without reading any accessibility guideline, two important things that we should always do when developing Web content:

- Markup documents using the proper structural elements.
- Control presentation using style sheets rather than presentation elements and attributes.

This is the third accessibility guideline, but we already knew that it is the right way to write HTML documents, because we work using quality criteria.

HTML is Accessible

Perhaps the more representative example is the alternative text for images. Imagine a blind user accessing a Web document through a screen reader. The screen reader will synthesize the content of the document. This is easy to understand when talking about textual content. But, what will happen with nontextual content, for example images?

Well, the Web developer should provide a textual description for this image. HTML provides a way to include this information: the attribute "alt."

Let's analyze this simple code:

```
<img src="url" alt="short description">
```

Is this an accessible image? It depends on the description. According to the HTML 4.01 specification (Raggett et al., 1999a) the description should be relevant and meaningful. Imagine it is descriptive enough. Is it an accessible image then? Yes, but this is not its main characteristic. This is simply a CORRECT image. An image without an alternative text is not a correct image, as it is specified in the HTML 4.01 dtd (Raggett et al., 1999b) (and the specification forces the alternative text to be relevant and meaningful).

```
<!ELEMENT IMG - O EMPTY -- Embedded
image -->
<!ATTLIST IMG
  %attrs; -- %coreattrs, %i18n, %events –
  src %URI; #REQUIRED -- URI of image to
  embed –
  alt %Text; #REQUIRED -- short description
  –
  ...
```

But, once again, this attribute is mandatory not only to benefit disabled users, but also text-browsers users, or those who have configured their graphical user agents not to display images, or those using devices that does not support graphics. But the most benefited person is the developer, because search engines will find the image when a search is made using that description. This shows an economic benefit of Web accessibility.

So, it is an example of how knowing the HTML specification let you develop accessible Web sites without learning any accessibility guideline. As in the previous case, the first accessibility guideline says *"Provide equivalent alternatives to auditory and visual content."* (Chisholm et al., 1999), but we don't need to know it in order to develop Accessible Web sites because we already know the current HTML specification.

Historical Perspective

(Axelsson et al., 2006) According to W3C, HTML has been in use by the World Wide Web (WWW) global information initiative since 1990. The purpose of HTML was to be a simple markup language used to create platform independent hypertext documents.

So, According to Steven Pemberton works (more info in the next section) HTML was originally designed as a structure description language, not a presentational language (Pemberton, 2002a), and the very first version of HTML was designed to represent the structure of a document, not its presentation. Even though presentation-oriented elements were later added to the language by browser manufacturers, HTML is at heart a document structuring language. (Axelsson et al., 2006).

HTML 2.0 specification was closed in 1996. It sets the standard for core HTML features based upon current practice in 1994 (Pemberton, 2002b).

The next significant specification was HTML 3.2 (1996) (Raggett, 2002). The presentation features of computers were growing, and CSS had just been born, so it added some representation elements (BASEFONT, BIG, CENTER, FONT, STRIKE and U). It also provided widely-deployed features such as tables, maps, applets, scripts, text-flow around images, superscripts and subscripts. Although it provided backwards compatibility with the existing HTML 2.0 standard, some elements were suppressed (LISTING, PLAINTEXT, XMPI). It also added some semantic elements like phrase elements (EM, STRONG, DFN, CODE, SAMP, KBD, VAR, CITE, ABBR, and ACRONYM), Structural elements (DIV), and also added the possibility to separate presentation from content.

As we can see, the beginnings were a bit confusing. The spirit of HTML (a structure description language) was there but, on the other hand, the progress could not wait, generating sometimes mistakes and contradictions.

HTML 4.01 is the current HTML specification (Raggett et al., 1999c). It is a revision of the HTML 4.0 Recommendation first released on December 18, 1997. HTML4.X added some improvements to tables and forms. They also added a useful structural element (SPAN), and deprecated several presentation elements (BASE-FONT, CENTER, FONT, S, STRIKE and U), but, incomprehensibly, they maintained others (I, B, BIG and SMALL).

This version of the specification encourages the separation between presentation and content. At that point Web accessibility was possible; as we already know, in 1999 the first version of the accessibility guidelines WCAG 1.0 was approved.

HTML 4.01 (and also XHTML 1.0 (The members of the W3C HTML Working Group, 2000)) is specified in three variants, each one has its own DTD, which sets out the rules for using HTML in a succinct and definitive manner. The three variants are: HTML 4.01 Strict, HTML 4.01 Transitional and HTML 4.0 Frameset. From the perspective of good practices and, consequently, of Web accessibility, the only valid variant is HTML

4.01 Strict, because it means cleaning structural markup. HTML 4.01 Transitional uses markup associated with layout and HTML 4.01 Frameset uses frames, which is not advisable, as it will be explained in later sections.

XHTML 1.0 is the W3C's first Recommendation for XHTML. The first version of XHTML 1.0 recommendation was released in 2000. It is a reformulation of HTML 4.01 in XML, and combines the strength of HTML 4 with the power of XML.

XHTML 1.0 brings the rigor of XML to Web pages and is the keystone in W3C's work to create standards that provide richer Web pages on an ever increasing range of browser platforms including cell phones, televisions, cars, wallet sized wireless communicators, kiosks, and desktops.

XHTML 1.0 reformulates HTML as an XML application. This makes it easier to process and to maintain. XHTML 1.0 borrows elements and attributes from W3C's earlier work on HTML 4, and can be interpreted by existing browsers.

The newest version of XHTML (XHTML 2.0 (Axelsson et al., 2006)) is also a great change. XHTML 2.0 takes HTML back to these roots, by removing all presentation elements, and subordinating all presentation to style sheets. This gives greater flexibility, greater accessibility, more device independence, and more powerful presentation possibilities, because style sheets can do more than the presentational elements of HTML ever did. XHTML 2.0 will be more detailed in the "Future Trends" section.

Refuting Myths

Web Accessibility is Expensive

As it has already been explained, Web accessibility can be expensive if a Web project has not been faced taking into account quality criteria. In this case, if the Web developer wants to reach a specific accessibility level the only solution is to modify the final version of the Web site in order to satisfy the guidelines. As it has also been explained, this approach means extra effort and cost.

Web accessibility can also be expensive if an alternative version (usually a text version) is included. We have seen that if standard Web technologies are used during the design and development process the product will be accessible to screen readers, PDA and all standard browsers.

As HTML includes accessibility there is no additional cost in building an accessible Web site from the beginning. What is expensive is to modify a nonaccessible site. As it has been also proven, an accessible Web site can save costs, because its maintenance is easier and cheaper.

The only situation that could mean an additional cost is to include subtitles in video-clips, but it is not a very common case, and it will also imply benefits (satisfied users, multidevice support, search engine positioning, etc.).

Web Accessibility is Useless

As it has been said before, it is very common to think that Web accessibility only benefits disabled users. At this point it has been proven enough that it is not right. Web accessibility also benefits users of PDAs, mobile phones or nontraditional browsers, and so forth.

We should also take into account that all of us can suffer a temporary physical disability. It means that 100% of the population is a hypothetical audience of accessible Web sites. Moreover, all of us want to become ancient, it will imply suffering some kind of physical disability, for example reduced vision.

With regard to this example, there is a very useful and easy to apply accessibility checkpoint:

3.4 Use relative rather than absolute units in markup language attribute values and style sheet property values. [Priority 2] For example, in CSS, use "em" or percentage lengths rather than "pt" or "cm," which are absolute units. If absolute units are used, validate that the rendered content is usable (Chisholm et al., 1999).

The application of this checkpoint is very helpful for users with reduced vision or, simply, tired users that don't want to read small texts. If the font-size attribute is specified using relative values the user could resize the text of the document (Chisholm et al., 2000).

Example
Use em to set font sizes, as in:
  H1 { font-size: 2em }
rather than:
  H1 { font-size: 12pt }

Almost every site I go to fails my three-second accessibility test—increasing the size of the type (Krug, 2005).

The corresponding standard specification is not very strict about it. There is only one reference to this requirement:

There are two types of length units: relative and absolute. Relative length units specify a length relative to another length property. Style sheets that use relative units will more easily scale from one medium to another (e.g., from a computer display to a laser printer) (Bos et al., 2006).

If these reasons are not enough, let's try with an economic reason: Your most important user is blind; can you guess its name?

Your most important user is blind. Half of your hits come from Google, and Google only sees what a blind user can see. If your site is not accessible, you will get fewer hits. End of story (Pemberton, 2005a).

It is a quotation from Steven Pemberton. He chaired the European WWW Working Group W4G. As a consequence he became involved with CSS and HTML. Nowadays, he is chair of the W3C Working Group developing the next generation of XHTML (XHTML 2.0) (Pemberton, 2006).

He has also written other interesting sentences regarding economic benefits of Web accessibility (Pemberton, 2005b):

There are more browsers on phones now than on desktops.

Device independence, accessibility and usability are surprisingly closely related.

Even though Web site builders may not yet know it, device independence, accessibility and usability have a major economic argument in their favour. Spread the word!

Web Accessibility is Ugly

The last exposed accessibility requirement (use relative units) is one of the reasons for Web developers, and mainly graphic designers, to think that an accessible Web site is always ugly. They usually claim that Web accessibility implies a lot of restrictions that are against appearance.

Often, the real reason for this is that graphic designers think in a Web design like a picture instead of like content. So any possibility of resizing content means an outrage against good taste. The same happens with the possibility of replacing the style of the document, which is possible thanks to the separation of content and appearance. It is very useful for users with reduced vision, because they can provide sufficient contrast between foreground and background if the developer has not done it. This is the accessibility checkpoint 2.2:

2.2 Ensure that foreground and background color combinations provide sufficient contrast when viewed by someone having color deficits or when viewed on a black and white screen. [Priority 2 for images, Priority 3 for text] (Chisholm et al., 1999).

Another reason for thinking that Web accessibility implies a too simple design or a poor appearance is the existence of separate text versions of the Web pages. It has been already proven that it is not necessary at all, while on the contrary it implies a more expensive maintenance of the Web site.

Solving Problems

Frames

The XFrames working draft (Pemberton, 2002c) clearly explains the problems associated to the use of frames.

Frames were firstly included into HTML 4.0. They added a manner of composing several HTML documents into a single view to create an application-like interface.

However, Frames introduced several accessibility and usability problems. So, Web site builders should avoid them at all costs:

- It causes dysfunction in some browser buttons. For example, the "back" button works unintuitively, the "reload" action is unpredictable and the "page up" and "page down" are often hard to do.
- You cannot be sure whether the document you want to bookmark is the frame where you are placed or the container window.
- Searching finds HTML pages, not framed pages, so search results usually give you pages without the navigation context that they were intended to be in.
- There are security problems caused by the fact that it is not visible to the user when different frames come from different sources.
- Although frames are not fully inaccessible, there are also accessibility problems, because frames cause disorientation in screen readers (or other assistive devices) users.

Sometimes users can also get trapped in a frameset.

As we can see, the problems associated with frames are not only related to accessibility. But a functionality problem is more serious for a disable user than for anyone using a nonconventional browser.

However, frames have also some advantages, like the application-like interface and the reuse of code. So an alternative is needed.

One possible solution will be XFrames. It allows similar functionality to HTML Frames, with fewer usability problems, principally by making the content of the frameset visible in its URI.

But XFrames are still not working on browsers, so the best alternative by now is the dynamic inclusion of content, using a server scripting language like JSP or PHP to reuse code. Then, the application-like interface is easy to get through, of course, CSS.

JavaScript

Regarding JavaScript and accessibility, there are two myths:

- Using JavaScript implies that your Web site is inaccessible.
- Not using JavaScript implies loosing functionality in your Web site.

Neither of these myths is fully true. The WCAG 1.0 gives the rules to build accessible Web pages using JavaScript (Chisholm et al., 1999):

6.3 Ensure that pages are usable when scripts, applets, or other programmatic objects are turned off or not supported. If this is not possible, provide equivalent information on an alternative accessible page. [Priority 1]

For example, ensure that links that trigger scripts work when scripts are turned off or not supported

(e.g., do not use "javascript:" as the link target). If it is not possible to make the page usable without scripts, provide a text equivalent with the NOSCRIPT element, or use a server-side script instead of a client-side script.

6.4 For scripts and applets, ensure that event handlers are input device-independent. [Priority 2]

The first test you should make is turning off the JavaScript in your browser and then reloading the page. If the content is still there and all the functionality works, your page is accessible. In other case, you should use the NOSCRIPT tag to include the lost content.

You must also ensure that your event-handlers are input device-independent (for example "onfocus" instead of "onmouseover"), so anyone using an input device different from a mouse can also interact.

The truth is that JavaScript is rarely necessary or, at least, its functionality (e.g., forms validation) can be developed using a nonintrusive technology, like server side scripting. Another alternative option is the use of XForms (more info in the next section).

Flash

Flash is a nonstandard technology. It has several accessibility problems, mainly due to the fact that Flash content is not textual content, but it is a compiled object. So any user accessing with a nonvisual device will have problems. It is also important the fact that it is a proprietary product, which needs an extra software installation.

Some work is being done to improve Flash accessibility, this is true. But it is not an easy to achieve goal, and it always implies an extra effort for Web developers.

One sign of this is that in the "accessibility on Adobe.com" Web page, if you use an assistive device you are invited to go to the HTML version of the site (Adobe Systems Incorporated, 2006).

How To Access This Site With Assistive Devices
Please click the button below for the site version you'd like to access. If you use assistive devices, the HTML version of Adobe.com may be easiest to navigate.

If you really need to use Flash there is a simple way to include alternative content to the Flash object without having to browse to an alternative page. The solution is including the accessible content inside the OBJECT tag where you have defined the Flash data. If the browser cannot play the Flash animation (maybe the plug-in is not installed) the alternative content will be shown. Of course, your Flash object must be accessible if the browser can render it.

FUTURE TRENDS

WCAG 2.0 (Caldwell et al., 2006a)

As it has been exposed, WCAG 2.0 is under development and WAI cannot be certain when the final version will be available.

The objective of this new version of the guidelines is to be easier to use and understand, and to be more precisely testable. In order to achieve this purpose the WCAG 2.0 Guidelines (instead of the 14 guidelines of WCAG 1.0) are organized around the following four principles:

1. Content must be perceivable.
2. Interface components in the content must be operable.
3. Content and controls must be understandable.
4. Content should be robust enough to work with current and future user agents (including assistive technologies).

WCAG 2.0 includes several important new terms:

- **Web unit:** It refers to any collection of information, consisting of one or more resources, intended to be rendered together, and identified by a single Uniform Resource Identifier. For example, a Web page containing several images and a style sheet is a typical Web unit.
- **Programmatically determined:** This means that the author is responsible for ensuring that the content is delivered in such a way that software can access it.
- **Baseline:** This term allows WCAG 2.0 to adapt to changing technologies and to the needs of different countries and environments.

It is important to emphasize (in order to keep the calm) that the WCAG 2.0 does not mean a substantial change respecting WCAG 1.0. So an accessible Web page will continue being accessible when the new version of the guidelines come into effect.

XHTML 2.0 (Pemberton, 2002a)

The objectives of XHTML 2.0 show that its aim is to continue with (and to advance in) the progresses achieved in the previous version. These objectives are closely related to good design and development practices:

- As generic XML as possible.
- Less presentation, more structure: All only-presentation markup will be removed and more semantically oriented markup will be added in order to make documents richer.
- Less scripting: Taking into account how scripting is currently used some changes are being made to try to cover 80% of this functionality. For example, replacing current Forms with XForms. XForms includes client-side checking, more data types, returns XML instance, and separates form controls markup from data-types and returned values.

- More usability: For example, replacing current frames with XFrames.
- More accessibility: As we can see the specification is trying to preserve quality criteria in the whole Web building process, so accessibility and device independence will also be improved.

The next example shows how structure (semantic) has been improved by replacing the current set of heading tags (H1 to H6) with the combination of two new tags (H and SECTION):

```
<section>
<h>Future trends</h>
....
   <section>
   <h>WCAG</h>
   ...
   </section>
</section>
```

All new tags have been listed in the "Historical Perspective" section.

CONCLUSION

At this point we know a bit more about Web accessibility. We know something about disability and how people with disabilities access Internet. We know the organizations promoting Web accessibility and the guidelines that can help us to achieve it. We know the relation between Web accessibility and standard Web technologies, and their evolution. We know the controversy that has arisen over Web accessibility and the available solutions to it. We have discovered the benefits of Web accessibility. And the most important point: we have learned all these things from the perspective of Web information systems quality, and we have realized that there is a strong relationship between Web accessibility and Web information systems quality.

After having dealt with Web accessibility in depth, we can affirm that:

- Web accessibility does not only benefit disabled users.
- Standard Web technologies are very important in Web information systems quality and, consequently, in Web accessibility.
- The future trends and newest standard Web technologies confirm the previous assertion and ensure the continuity of this design and development philosophy.
- Web accessibility does imply neither extra effort nor extra cost. On the contrary, Web accessibility saves development and maintenance time (and money) because it means that good practices have been used in the whole process.
- Web accessibility is a consequence of including quality criteria in the design and development process.

REFERENCES

Adobe Systems Incorporated (2006). *accessibility on Adobe.com.* Retrieved October 18, 2007, from http://www.adobe.com/help/accessibility.html

Axelsson, J., Birbeck, M., Dubinko, M., Epperson, B., Ishikawa, M., McCarron, S., et al. (2006, July). *Introduction to XHTML 2.0.* Retrieved from http://www.w3.org/TR/xhtml2/introduction.html.

Berners-Lee, T., & Connolly, D. (1995). *HTML 2.0 Materials.* Retrieved from http://www.w3.org/MarkUp/html-spec/.

Bos, B., Çelik, T., Hickson, I., & Wium, H. (2006, April). *Cascading Style Sheets, level 2 revision 1. (CSS 2.1) Specification.* Retrieved from http://www.w3.org/TR/CSS21.

Caldwell, B., Chisholm, W., Slatin, J., & Vanderheiden, G. (2006a, April). *Web Content accessibility Guidelines 2.0.* Retrieved from http://www.w3.org/TR/WCAG20

Caldwell, B., Slatin, J., & Vanderheiden, G. (2006b). *Web Content accessibility Guidelines 2.0. Appendix A: Glossary (Normative)*. Retrieved from http://www.w3.org/TR/WCAG20/appendixA.html

Chisholm, W., Vanderheiden, G. & Jacobs, I. (1999). *Web Content accessibility Guidelines 1.0*. Retrieved from http://www.w3.org/TR/WCAG10

Chisholm, W., Vanderheiden, G., & Jacobs, I. (2000). *CSS Techniques for Web Content accessibility Guidelines 1.0*. Retrieved from http://www.w3.org/TR/WCAG10-CSS-TECHS

Disability Discrimination Act 1995 (c. 50). (1995). *Chapter 50* from http://www.opsi.gov.uk/acts/acts1995/95050--a.htm

Krug, S. (2005). *Don't make me think: A Common sense approach to web usability* (2nd Edition). New Riders.

Lawton, S. (2005a). *Web Content accessibility Guidelines (WCAG) Overview* from http://www.w3.org/WAI/intro/wcag.php.

Lawton, S. (2005b). *Policies Relating to Web accessibility* from http://www.w3.org/WAI/Policy/

Lawton, S. (2006). *About WAI - Links to Documents* from http://www.w3.org/WAI/about-links.html

Lawton, S., & Brewer, J. (2006). *WAI Mission and Organization* from http://www.w3.org/WAI/about.html

Lawton, S., & May, M. (2005a). *Authoring Tool accessibility Guidelines (ATAG) Overview* from http://www.w3.org/WAI/intro/atag.php

Lawton, S., & May, M. (2005b). *User Agent accessibility Guidelines (UAAG) Overview* from http://www.w3.org/WAI/intro/uaag.php

Lawton, S., & participants of the Education and Outreach Working Group. (2005). *Introduction to Web accessibility* from http://www.w3.org/WAI/intro/accessibility.php.

National Dissemination Center for Children with Disabilities. (2002). *General Information about Disabilities: Disabilities That Qualify Infants, Toddlers, Children, and Youth for Services under the IDEA*. Retrieved from http://www.nichcy.org/pubs/genresc/gr3.htm

Pemberton, S. (2002a). *XHTML, XForms and Device Independence* (Talk 2002) form http://www.w3.org/Talks/2002/04/11-pemberton

Pemberton, S. (2002b). *HyperText Markup Language (HTML) Home Page*. Previous Versions of HTML from http://www.w3.org/MarkUp/#previous

Pemberton, S. (2002c). *XFrames (Working Draft 6 August 2002)* from http://www.w3.org/TR/2002/WD-xframes-20020806

Pemberton, S. (2005a). *Ineluctable Modality of the Visible (talk 2005)* from http://www.w3.org/2005/Talks/0121-steven-ineluctable

Pemberton, S. (2005b). *Usability, accessibility and Markup (talk 2005)* from http://www.w3.org/2005/Talks/11-steven-usability-accessibility

Pemberton, S. (2006). *Steven Pemberton at CWI*. 2006 from http://homepages.cwi.nl/~steven/

Raggett, D. (2002). *HTML 3.2 Reference Specification* (Recommendation 14-Jan-1997) from http://www.w3.org/TR/REC-html32

Raggett, D., Le Hors, A., & Jacobs, I. (1999a). *HTML 4.01 Specification* (W3C Recommendation 24 December 1999). Objects, Images, and Applets. alt attribute from http://www.w3.org/TR/REC-html40/struct/objects.html#adef-alt

Raggett, D., Le Hors, A., & Jacobs, I. (1999b). *HTML 4.01 Strict DTD* from http://www.w3.org/TR/html4/strict.dtd

Raggett, D., Le Hors, A., & Jacobs, I. (1999c). *W3C*

HTML 4.01 Specification (Recommendation 24 December 1999). Index of Elements from http://www.w3.org/TR/REC-html40/index/elements.html, http://www.w3.org/TR/REC-html40/index/elements.html

Skaalum, P., Monteiro, M., Placencia-Porerro, I., Junique, F., & Lobell, R. (2002, December). *eEurope Action Plan 2002/eaccessibility. WAI contents guidelines for public Web sites in the EU* (Final Progress Report—December 2002) from http://ec.europa.eu/employment_social/knowledge_society/docs/eacc_wai.pdf

The members of the W3C HTML Working Group. (2000). *XHTML™ 1.0 The Extensible HyperText Markup Language (Second Edition).* A Reformulation of HTML 4 in XML 1.0 (Recommendation 26 January 2000, revised 1 August 2002) from http://www.w3.org/TR/xhtml1

United States Access Board. (1973). Section 508 of the Rehabilitation Act of 1973, as amended from http://www.access-board.gov/sec508/guide/act.htm.

W3C. (1994-2006). *World wide Web Consortium home page* from http://www.w3.org

KEY TERMS

Assistive Technologies: Technologies that provides greater independence for people with disabilities by enabling them to perform tasks that they were formerly unable to accomplish, or had great difficulty accomplishing, by providing enhancements to or changed methods of interacting with the technology needed to accomplish such tasks. The most relevant assistive technologies are: screen magnifiers, screen readers, voice recognition software, alternative keyboards and alternative pointing devices.

Disability: Physical or mental impairment which has an adverse effect on the ability to carry out normal day-to-day activities. The term is often used to refer to individual functioning, including physical impairment, sensory impairment, cognitive impairment, intellectual impairment or mental health issue.

Section 508: Section of the Rehabilitation Act focused in "Electronic and Information Technology." Section 508 requires Federal agencies to make their electronic and information technology accessible to people with disabilities. It was enacted to eliminate barriers in information technology, to make available new opportunities for people with disabilities, and to encourage development of technologies that will help achieve these goals. The law applies to all Federal agencies when they develop, procure, maintain, or use electronic and information technology.

W3C: The World Wide Web Consortium (W3C) is an international consortium where Member organizations, a full-time staff, and the public work together to develop Web standards. W3C's mission is to lead the World Wide Web to its full potential by developing protocols and guidelines that ensure long-term growth for the Web.

WAI: The Web Accessibility Initiative (WAI) is the section of W3C that works with organizations around the world to develop strategies, guidelines, and resources to help make the Web accessible to people with disabilities. All these products are possible thanks to the participation of volunteers from around the world that are included in the different working groups.

WCAG: The Web Content Accessibility Guidelines (WCAG) are general principles of accessible design. The current version is WCAG 1.0, which has 14 guidelines; each one has one or more checkpoints that explain how the guideline applies in a specific area. WCAG 2.0 is nowadays being developed to apply to different Web technologies, be easier to use and understand, and be more precisely testable.

Web accessibility: Web accessibility means that everybody can access and use (perceive, understand, navigate, and interact with) the Web, regardless of disability.

XForms: XForms is W3C's name for a specification of Web forms that can be used with a wide variety of platforms including desktop computers, hand-helds, information appliances, and even paper. XForms started life as a subgroup of the HTML Working Group, but has now been spun off as an independent Activity.

XFrames: XFrames is an XML application for composing documents together, replacing HTML Frames. By being a separate application from XHTML, it allows content negotiation to determine if the user agent accepts frames; by encoding the "population" of frames in the URI, it allows framesets to be bookmarked. XFrames allows similar functionality to HTML Frames, with fewer usability problems, principally by making the content of the frameset visible in its URI.

XHTML 2.0: XHTML 2 is a general purpose markup language designed for representing documents for a wide range of purposes across the World Wide Web. To this end, it does not attempt to be all things to all people, supplying every possible markup idiom, but to supply a generally useful set of elements, with the possibility of extension using the class and role attributes on the span and div elements in combination with style sheets, and attributes from the metadata attributes collection.

Chapter XI
Comparing Approaches to Web Accessibility Assessment

Adriana Martín
Universidad Nacional del Comahue, Argentina

Alejandra Cechich
Universidad Nacional del Comahue, Argentina

Gustavo Rossi
Universidad Nacional de La Plata and Conicet, Argentina

ABSTRACT

Web accessibility is one facet of Web quality in use, and one of the main actors upon which the success of a Web site depends. In spite of these facts, surveys repeatedly show that the accessibility at the Web for people with disabilities is disappointingly low. At the Web, most pages present many kinds of accessible barriers for people with disabilities. The former scenario encouraged research communities and organizations to develop a large range of approaches to support Web accessibility. Currently, there are so many approaches available that comparisons have emerged to clarify their intent and effectiveness. With this situation in mind, this chapter will discuss the importance of Web accessibility assessment and compare 15 different approaches found in literature. To do so, we provide an evaluation framework, WAAM, and instantiate them by classifying the different proposals. The aim of WAAM is to clarify from an evaluation and classification perspective the situation at the accessibility arena.

INTRODUCTION

The World Wide Web (Web), originally conceived as an environment to allow for sharing of information, has proliferated to different areas like e-commerce, m-commerce, and e-business. Over the last few years, the Web has literally bloomed and the continuous evolution of its purpose has introduced a new era of computing science. A Web application, as any other interactive software system, must to face up to quality properties such as Usability, which ensures the effectiveness, efficiency, and satisfaction with which specified users achieve specified goals in particular environments. Particularly, defining methods for ensuring usability and studying its impact on software development is at the present one of the goals that has captured more attention from the research community (Matera, Rizzo, & Toffetti Carughi, 2006; Rafla, Robillard, & Desmarais, 2006). Among these matters, Web accessibility is one facet of Web quality in use, and one of the main actors upon which the success of a Web site depends. An accessible Web site is a site that can be perceived, operated, and understood by individual users despite their congenital or induced disabilities (Irwin & Gerke, 2004; Paciello, 2000). It means having a Web application usable to a wide range of people with disabilities, including blindness and low vision, deafness and hearing loss, learning difficulties, cognitive limitations, limited movement, speech difficulties, photosensitivity and combinations of these. In short, we can say that Accessibility addresses a universal Usability.

Web browsers and multimedia players play a critical role in making Web content accessible to people with disabilities. The features available in Web browsers determine the extent to which users can orient themselves and navigate the structure of Web resources. The notion of travel and mobility on the Web was introduced to improve the accessibility of Web pages for visually impaired and other travelers by drawing an analogy between virtual travel and travel in the physical world (Harper, Goble, & Stevens, 2003). Travel is defined as the confident navigation and orientation with purpose, ease and accuracy navigation within an environment (Yesilada, Harper, Goble, & Stevens, 2004), that is to say, the notion of travel extends navigation and orientation to include environment, mobility and purpose of the journey. Mobility is defined as the easy movement around Web pages supported by visual navigational objects (Yesilada et al., 2004). However, traveling upon the Web is difficult for visually impaired users because the Web pages are designed for visual interaction (Goble, Harper, & Stevens, 2000). Visually impaired users usually use screen readers to access the Web in audio. However, unlike sighted users, screen readers cannot see the implicit structural and navigational knowledge encoded within the visual presentation of Web pages.

Today, many countries are discussing or putting into practice diverse initiatives to promote Web accessibility (HKSAR, 2001; CLF, 2001; European Union, 2002; HREOC, 2003; Cabinet Office, 2003). In spite of these facts, surveys repeatedly show that the accessibility at the Web for people with disabilities is disappointingly low.

The Web Accessibility Initiative (WAI)[1] has developed a set of accessibility guidelines called Web Content Accessibility Guidelines (WCAG 1.0, 1999). The (WCAG 1.0, 1999) recommendations are the established referent for Web accessibility, but there are many other initiatives --e.g. (Section 508, 2003; Stanca Law, 2004; PAS 78, 2006). Table1, borrowed from Loiacono (2004), summarizes a study conducted over 100 American corporations' home pages to specifically examine how well they dealt with the issue of Web accessibility. This study revealed that most of the corporate home pages fail to meet criteria, presenting many kinds of accessible barriers for people with disabilities.

During the last years a large range of approaches have become available to support Web accessibility (Paciello, 2000; Takagi, Asakawa, Fukuda, & Maeda, 2004; Xiaoping, 2004; Yesilada et al., 2004; Plessers, Casteleyn, Yesilada, De Troyer, Stevens, Harper, & Goble, 2005; Leporini, Paternò, & Scorcia, 2006). Tools are useful to assist Web authors at developing accessible content for the Web. Such tools include (Petrie & Weber, 2006): (i) authoring tools that provide guidance on accessibility; (ii) tools that can be used to check for specific accessibility issues, although they were not designed for this purpose; (iii) tools that were developed to visualize specific accessibility issues; (iv) tools that provide easy access to a range of specific checking capabilities; (v) automated evaluation and evaluation and repair tools that evaluate the conformance to some of the standards or guidelines; (vi) testing Web resources with assistive technologies, such as screen readers for blind users and software for dyslexic users, to check how they are rendered in these technologies, and (vii) testing Web resources with disabled Web users to ensure that these groups can easily use the resources. In spite of this diversity, tools for the integration of automatic testing with user and manual testing are still in their initial states of development (Petrie & Weber, 2006). To alleviate these problems, the use of best practices and the application of multiple and different tools must be ensured (Ragin, 2006). However, the heterogeneity of users with different requirements is not yet supported by either automatic tool or tools for manual testing (Benavídez, Fuertes, Gutiérrez, & Martínez, 2006). Actually, there are so many tools currently available that comparisons have emerged to clarify their intent and effectiveness (Brajnik, 2004). Furthermore, a proliferation of organizations is focusing on different aspects of Web accessibility --e.g. WAI, SIDAR[2], CAST[3], AWARE[4], WebAIM[5], ATRC[6], CTIC[7], and so forth.

In this context, this chapter discusses the importance of Web accessibility assessment and compares 15 different approaches found in literature. We provide an evaluation framework and instantiate them by classifying the different proposals. Our accessibility assessment model differentiates three *dimensions*, each one address-

ing a different concern. The assessment criteria dimension allows distinguishing among the evaluations that can be applied by an approach. While, the assessment deliverables dimension allows categorizing the assessment results characteristics. Finally, the supporting tool dimension considers if the approach counts with specific tool support or not. In Section 3, we describe how to weigh up these concerns when classifying each approach at the resulting grid. In short, the main idea is to make available a method to analyze most relevant aspects of accessibility approaches.

RELATED WORK

There are different approaches to evaluate Web pages accessibility. We discuss some of the most important research works in this area.

Ivory, Mankoff, and Le (2003) have presented a survey of automated evaluation and transformation tools in the context of the user abilities they support. The work discusses the efficacy of a subset of these tools based on empirical studies, along with ways to improve existing tools and future research areas. It aims at evaluating quality of use in three steps: (1) showing a review of automated tools, characterizing the types of users they currently support, (2) given an empirical study of automated evaluation tools showing that the tools themselves are difficult to use and, furthermore, suggesting that the tools did not improve user performance on information-seeking tasks, and (3) describing ways to expand and improve the automated transformation tools in such a way that they make the Web more usable by users with diverse abilities.

Brajnik (2004) has worked on a comparison over a pair of tools that takes into account correctness, completeness and specificity in supporting the task of assessing the conformance of a Web site with respect to established guidelines. The goal of this work is to illustrate a method for comparing different tools that is (1) useful to pinpoint strengths and weakness of tool in terms

Table 1. Relative frequency of barriers/failures on 100 Corporate Home Pages (Loiacono, 2004)

Priority 1: A Web content developer must satisfy this criterion*	Fortune 100 corporate home pages failing to meet criteria
Provide alternate text for all images.	77
Provide alternate text for all image-type buttons in forms.	19
Provide alternate text for all image map hot-spots (AREAs).	17
Give each frame a title.	4
Provide alternate text for each applet.	3
Priority 2: A Web coentent developer should satisfy this criterion.*	
Use relative sizing and positioning (% values) rather than absolute (pixels).	96
Explicitly associate form controls and their labels with the LABEL element.	71
Make sure event handlers do not require the use of a mouse.	63
Use a public text identifier in a DOCTYPE statement.	62
Do not use the same link phrase more than once wehn the links point to different URLs.	46
Do not cause a page to refresh automatically.	8
Create link phrases taht make sense when read out of context.	4
Include a document TITLE	2
Provide a NOFRAMES section when using FRAMEs.	1
Nest headings properly.	1
Avoid scrolling text created with MARQUEE element	0
Priority 3: A Web content developer may address this criterion.*	
Provide a summary for tables.	93
Identify the language of the text.	92
Include default, place-holding characters in edit boxes and text areas.	61
Separate adjacent links with more than white space.	59
Client side image map contains a link not presented elsewhere on this page.	22
Include a document TITLE.	1
Use a public text identifier in a DOCTYPE statement.	1
Section 508	
Provide alternative text for all images.	71
Provide alternate text for all image map hot-spots (AREAs)	26
Explicitly associate form controls and their labels with the LABEL element.	23
Give each frame a title.	10
Provide alternative text for each APPLET	8
Provide alternative text for all image-type button in forms.	8
Include default place-holding characters in edit boxes and text areas	0
Identify the language of the text	0

of their effectiveness, (2) viable in the sense that the method can be applied with limited resources, and (3) repeatable in the sense that independent applications of the method to the same tools should lead to similar results. These properties of the method are partly demonstrated by results derived from a case study using the *Lift* machine and *Bobby* (see these tools in Section3.2).

Bohman and Anderson (2005) have developed a conceptual framework, which can be used by tool developers to chart future directions of development of tools to benefit users with cognitive disabilities. The framework includes categories of functional cognitive disabilities, principles of cognitive disability accessibility, units of Web content analysis, aspects of analysis, and realms of responsibility. The authors stated that if tools capable of identifying at least some of the access issues for people with cognitive disabilities are available, developers might be more inclined to design Web pages content accordingly. So, with this vision on mind, the work addresses the next generation of tools with deeper commitment from tool developers to review the underlying structure of the content, the semantic meaning behind it, and the purpose for which it exist: to communicate information to users.

The works cited above agreed on the fact that currently exist fairly abundant accessibility approaches to analyze Web pages' and sites' accessibility. The aim of our work is to provide an accessibility evaluation framework to help clarify the state-of-the-art at the accessibility arena. Differently from the ones cited here, our model—named Web accessibility Assessment Model—is not for classifying approaches from a quality of use perspective (like Ivory's) or from correctness, completeness, and specificity perspective (like Brajnik's), neither it is specifically oriented to tool developers (like Bohman and Anderson's). As an alternative to the former works, we developed a space for comparison, addressing those concerns that we considered most relevant to our purpose of providing a handy accessibility evaluation framework. In this sense,

our framework can accomplish and reinforce from an evaluation and classification perspective the former efforts made at the accessibility area.

A SPACE FOR CLASSIFICATION

This section introduces the Web accessibility assessment model (or WAAM for short), a framework for classifying Web accessibility assessment approaches. The organization of WAAM was influenced by our previous work in software quality component models (Cechich & Piattini, 2002), and some related work in quality models for databases (Piattini, Calero, & Genero, 2002) and Web systems (Ruiz, Calero, & Piattini, 2003; Matín-Albo, Bertoa, Calero, Vallecillo, Cechich, & Piattini, 2003). However, we found out that the situation for Web accessibility was fairly more complicated than those cases, because many different dimensions were identified, each one addressing a different concern. Finally, we decided to distinguish between *dimensions* and *factors*. The first ones classify Web accessibility assessment approaches according to the assessment criteria, the assessment deliverables, and the degree of automation through supporting tools. Factors are characteristics that further describe particular aspects of the different dimension's values, such as report style of the assessment

Figure 1. WAAM framework (2007, Adriana Martín. Used with permission.)

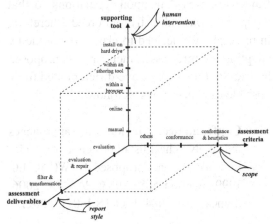

deliverables; human intervention required by the supporting tools; and scope of the assessment criteria. WAAM defines three dimensions, which are shown in Figure 1:

- The *assessment criteria* that addresses the way in which the different approaches assess accessibility.
- The *assessment deliverables* that characterizes the results of applying an approach.
- The *supporting tool* that provides space to classify the degree of automation.

WAAM Dimensions

This section covers the three *dimensions* of the framework and their associated features, as depicted in Figure 1. We explicitly detail these *dimensions* showing their respective categories. Also, we explain the *factors* mentioned above and why and how we decided to assign each one to a different *dimension*.

Assessment Criteria

In the analysis we conducted, it was easy to distinguish among approaches applying the rules and guidelines from those applying heuristics or some other evaluations. This is a clear distinction; however, it can cause a great confusion to a potential user of the approaches. As a matter of fact, we discovered that this confusion was present in some cases in which an assessment framework was built upon regulations so that compliance was indirectly reinforced. Therefore, in principle, we decided to clarify this issue by adapting the three assessment criteria proposed by Brajnik (2004). We have differentiated three possible categorizations as follows:

- **Conformance:** It includes the approaches that apply a checklist of principles or guidelines like the ones proposed by (WCAG 1.0, 1999; Section 508, 2003; PAS 78, 2006; Stanca Law, 2004; ISO/TS 16071, 2002).

- **Conformance & Heuristics:** it classifies those approaches that use heuristics in the interpretation and extension of the conformance criteria. These approaches also apply standards but the analysis includes the product's context of use and in some cases other usability properties like user effectiveness, productivity and satisfaction. Examples of this kind of assessment criteria are proposed (ISO/DIS 9241-11, 1994; ISO/IEC 9126-4, 2005; Brajnik, 2006).

- **Others:** These approaches perform evaluations with no direct reference and appliance to accessibility principles and guidelines (WCAG 1.0, 1999; Section 508, 2003; PAS 78, 2006; Stanca Law, 2004; ISO/TS 16071, 2002). It states that the approaches can apply any "other" practice—for example, using an ontology, an heuristic, a markup framework, and so forth, to analyze and treat Web page accessibility and to generate an accessible Web page version.

These three types of *assessment criteria* can produce widely dissimilar results. Most of the available approaches are based on "conformance" criteria, but depending on the applied reference guidelines and in the way they are applied, the results can also be broadly different.

Additionally, as Figure 1 shows, we also took into account a *scope* factor like the one proposed by WebAIM (2006) to examine the *assessment criteria* dimension. In this sense, an approach can be:

- **Simple and limited:** That is, it evaluates just one page at a time and it is often an accessibility evaluation tool available online and as a part of a browser;
- **Very specific:** That is, it focuses on just one element of a Web site, it demonstrates what the site looks like to someone who is blind or has low vision, and it is commonly found in a tool available online and as a part of a browser; or

- **Site-wide:** That is, it examines large sites and checks for a variety of errors, it is an accessibility evaluation tool that usually requires additional software installation.

Assessment Deliverables

In general, there is no consensus on how to define and categorize assessment results characteristics. In our approach, we will follow as much as possible the distinction proposed by the Binghamton University (2001), which identifies three alternative sets: *evaluation, evaluation & repair*, and *filter & transformation*. Our value definition is as follows.

- **Evaluation:** These approaches perform a static analysis of Web pages or sites regarding their accessibility, and return a report or a rating.
- **Evaluation & repair:** These approaches perform an evaluation too, but additionally they guide the repairing process by assisting the author in making the pages more accessible.
- **Filter & transformation:** These approaches assist Web users rather than authors to either modify a page or supplement an assisting technology or browser. A filter & transformation process is performed by transcoders that produces a built-in or customized transformed page version. A build-in page version is a consequence of transformations that remove contents or change structure and layout; while a customized page version is a consequence of transformations driven by annotations.

As Figure 1 shows, we also inspect the *assessment deliverables* dimension taking into account the *report style* that the approach produces. In first place, we use here the classification proposed by WebAIM (2006) where the style can be:

- Text-based report, which lists the specific guideline used to scan the page and the instances of each type of accessibility error (some approaches also returns the source code of the Web page where the error occurs);
- Graphic/icon-based report, which uses special icons to highlight accessibility errors and manually checks issues on a Web page (these icons are integrated into the Web page's graphical user interface next to the item on the page with an accessibility issue);
- Evaluation and reporting language (EARL) report, which is a machine readable report; and
- Adaptation-based report. A consideration related to the documents that "filter & transformation" approaches lead us to include this kind of report. As we explained before, a transcoder generates an adapted Web page version and, in general, an intermediate document to drive this Web page adaptation is used during the process. In our framework, these intermediate documents will be considered as adaptation-based reports.

Supporting Tool

This dimension indicates whether the approach has an associated tool support or not. In the former case, this dimension allows a distinction based on where the tool is meant to be available, that is, it functions as a stand along software or embedded into another software or application. On this dimension, we define five supporting tool criteria. Again, we follow the classification proposed by WebAIM (2006) as follows.

- **Manual:** It refers approaches without any supporting tool.
- **Online:** These tools ask the visitor to input the URL of a Web page, choose from a set of evaluation options, and then select a

"Go" button for initializing the accessibility evaluation.

- **Within a browser:** These tools provide accessibility extensions to evaluate the page that is currently at an Internet browser, that is, Internet Explorer, Netscape, Mozilla, and so forth.

- **Within an authoring tool:** These tools function as part of a Web authoring tool, that is, Macromedia Dreamweaver or Microsoft FrontPage, allowing Web developers to examine their content for accessibility in the same environment they are using to create this content.

- **Install on hard drive:** These tools are the most powerful and require their installation on a hard drive or server, like other pieces of software.

As Figure 1 shows, we decided to weight the *supporting tool* criteria with a *human intervention* factor. We apply here a classification that uses the concepts of "automatic test" and "manual test" proposed by Brajnik (2004). An "automatic test" flags only issues that are true problems, while a "manual test" flags issues that are potential problems which cannot be automatically assessed. We named these categories as *none* and *fully,* respectively.

At this point we have to be aware about the limitations of no human intervention. A useful approach must highlight issues that require human evaluation to determine whether they are false positive. That is the reason why we propose another category—*medium*—to represent the case in which the test flags both kind of issues.

Again, some extra considerations related to the human intervention factor for "filter & transformation" approaches are required. In this case, we will use the same classification proposed above for human intervention but with a slightly different implication. Human intervention for "filter & transformation" approaches will refer to the human evaluation needed to mark up issues

that require transformations driven by filtering or annotations; while in the former case, human intervention refers to the human evaluation needed to assess issues flagged by the test.

HOW TO USE WAAM

Once the WAAM *dimensions* and *factors* have been defined, this section describes how the WAAM model can be used. Since WAAM defined three dimensions, we will informally refer to the resulting grid as the WAAM *cube*.

Please, note that some approaches have more than one value in each dimension (for instance, there are approaches that can have more than one kind of supporting tool). Thus, we cannot think of the WAAM model as a "taxonomy" for Web accessibility assessments. Rather, each cell in the cube contains a set of approaches: those that are assigned to the cell because the approach applies to the values of the cell's coordinates.

By studying the population of the cube we can easily identify gaps (i.e., empty cells), and also collisions (i.e., overpopulated cells, which means that too many approaches follows similar criteria). Additionally, a given user of the WAAM model who is interested in certain number of characteristics (cells) may quickly obtain the set of approaches that are related to his or her concern.

As mentioned in the introduction, we are currently witnessing a proliferation of approaches for Web accessibility assessment. For the present study, we surveyed the existing literature on these topics, looking for approaches that could provide interesting information for designing and assessing accessibility. For filling the cells of the cube, we iterated over the list of approaches assigning the dimension's values after considering their characteristics. Figure 2 shows the resulting classification, and rationale behind our choices is briefly described below. It is included to clarify the assignment to a particular cell of the cube.

Figure 2. Classification of fifteen web accessibility approaches (2007, Adriana Martín. Used with permission)

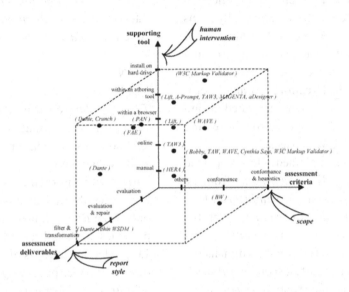

Bobby

Bobby has been in the accessibility arena for several years. It was initially developed in 1996 by CAST and it was freely available; now it is operated by WatchFire[8] and has changed their Web site to WebXACT[9]. *Bobby* is an accessibility tool designed to expose possible barriers to Web site use by those with disabilities. *Bobby* checks a Web page and evaluates it to determine how well it addresses the Section 508 standards of the US Rehabilitation Act (Section 508, 2003) and the W3C Web Content Accessibility Guidelines (WCAG 1.0, 1999). The tool can also be configured to complaint one of the three official levels of WCAG 1.0 guidelines (ACompliance—AACompliance—AAACompliance). *Bobby* checks one page at a time and provides a text-based report that lists the specific guideline used to scan the page and the instances of each type of accessibility error. The report highlights issues that are true problems but also issues that are potential problems, so a medium human intervention is required. Due to the reasons explained below we

placed *Bobby* in the following cell: *conformance* from the assessment criteria dimension, *online* from the supporting tool dimension and *evaluation* from the assessment deliverables dimension. Finally, we said that *Booby's* test scope is *simple and limited*, *Booby's* human intervention is *medium* and *Booby's* report style is *text-based* report style is text-based.

Lift

Lift was developed by Usablenet[10]. It assists not only to the evaluation process but also the repairing process. *Lift* is an enterprise-wide Web site testing solution that centralizes accessibility and usability management, and like *Bobby*, it allows to test and monitor for compliance with US Section 508 standards (Section 508, 2003), and W3C's Web Content Accessibility Guidelines (WCAG 1.0, 1999). As another similarity with *Bobby*, *Lift* also requires human intervention to check the reported issues. However, there are some differences between the two tools. Firstly, *Lift* generates a variety of Web-based reports to highlight accessibility errors on Web site pages for both executives and individual content creators. Secondly, *Lift* can be a server-based application installed on a hard drive that automatically scans internal and external Web sites. In addition, *Lift* can be an extension to different Web page design applications, for instance, within an authoring tool like Macromedia Dreamweaver and Microsoft Front Page. *Lift* offers an integrated design assistant that guides developers through creating accessible and usable Web pages.

Due to the reasons explained below we placed *Lift* in the cell identified by *conformance* from the assessment criteria dimension, *within an authoring tool* but also *install on hard drive* from the supporting tool dimension and *evaluation & repair* from the assessment deliverables dimension. Finally, we say that *Lift's* test scope is *site-wide oriented*, *Lift's* human intervention is *medium* and *Lift's* report style is *graphic/icon-based*.

A-Prompt

A-Prompt was developed by the University of Toronto at the Adaptive Technology Resource Centre (ATRC). Like *Bobby*, *A-Prompt* evaluates a Web page at a time to identify barriers to accessibility for people with disabilities. But differently from *Bobby* and *Lift*, *A-Prompt* evaluation is aimed to determine the conformance with W3C's Web Content Accessibility Guidelines (WCAG 1.0, 1999) only. Similarly to *Lift*, *A-Prompt* provides the Web author with a fast and easy way to make decisions and to make the necessary repairs. It requires to be installed on hard disk and it runs under Windows 95/98/NT/2000/XP. *A-Prompt* displays a report with dialog boxes and guides the user to fix the problem. Many repetitive tasks are automatically repaired, such as the addition of ALT-text or the replacement of server-side image maps with client-side image maps. Due to the reasons explained bellow, we placed *A-Prompt* in the following cell: *conformance* from the assessment criteria dimension, *install on hard drive* from the supporting tool dimension and *evalua-*

tion & repair from the assessment deliverables dimension. Finally, we say that *A-Prompt's* test scope is *simple and limited*, *A-Prompt's* human intervention is *medium,* and *A-Prompt's* report style is *graphic/icon-based*.

TAW

TAW was developed by the Centre for the Development of Information and Communication Technologies foundation from Spain (CTIC). *TAW* evaluates a Web site to identify accessibility barriers in conformance with W3C's Web Content Accessibility Guidelines (WCAG 1.0, 1999) only. Like *Bobby*, it takes into account the three priorities and the three official levels of WCAG 1.0 guidelines. *TAW* is aimed for Web masters, developers, Web page designers, and so forth. It is a family of free available products[11]: *TAW* online; downloadable *TAW3*; *TAW3 Web Start* and *TAW3 in one click*. The online version has the same properties and functionality as *Bobby*. Downloadable *TAW3* is a desktop application that analyses individual pages or complete Web sites and brings assistance to decision and reparation processes. It has to be installed on a hard disk, it is multiplatform, and it runs over different operating systems like Windows, Mac OS, Unix, and their family, that is, Linux, Solaris, and so forth. Downloadable *TAW3* generates three kinds of report styles of our dimension: text-based, graphic/icon-based and EARL reports. While *TAW3 Java Web Start* has the same functionality as downloadable *TAW3*, its goal is automating the installation process and running a Java-based application with just a click on the Web browser. *TAW3 in one click* is an extension for Firefox browser.

Due to the reasons explained below we have to make a distinction between the *TAW* versions. We place *TAW online* at the same cell as *Bobby*, but in the case of *TAW3*, at the following cell: *conformance* from the assessment criteria dimension, *install on hard drive* and *within a browser* from the supporting tool dimension; and *evaluation & repair* from the assessment deliverables dimension. We say that *TAW online* test scope and the human intervention report style is the same as *Bobby*. Finally, we say that *TAW3's* test scope is *site-wide oriented, TAW3's* human intervention is *medium,* and *TAW3's* report style is *text-based, graphic/icon-based* and *EARL*.

HERA

HERA is a multilingual online tool developed by SIDAR Foundation that, like *Bobby* and *TAW,* performs an automatic analysis of as many checkpoints as possible in conformance with W3C's Web Content Accessibility Guidelines (WCAG 1.0, 1999). But, in spite of been an online tool[12], *HERA* supports manual verification and repair assistance, providing extensive help, modified views of the Web page for the evaluation of some checkpoints and storage of evaluation scores and commentaries (Benavídez et al., 2006). *HERA* provides a report generation module that produces two kinds of report styles: text-based and EARL. *.HERA 1.0* was the first version of the tool freely available online to the public in 2003. This version is browser-dependent and uses a set of style sheets written in Cascading Style Sheets (CSS)[13] in order to identify and highlight Web page issues. It allows the evaluator to examine the different issues without having to inspect the source code. *HERA 2.0* is the second version of the tool launched in 2005 to overcome some weaknesses of the previous version. Instead of using CSS to highlight the Web page issues, this new version is browser-independent modified page views because it uses PHP[14] server-side technology.

Due to the reasons explained below, we place *HERA* in the following cell: *conformance* from the assessment criteria dimension, *online* from the supporting tool dimension and *evaluation & repair* from the assessment deliverables dimension. Finally, we say that *HERA's* test scope is *simple and limited, HERA's* human intervention is *medium,* and *HERA's* report style is *text-based* and *EARL*.

Dante (Yesilada et al., 2004)

Dante was developed in the Department of Computer Science of the University of Manchester. *Dante* is a semiautomated tool for the support of travel and mobility for visually impaired Web users. The main concept is that travel support could be improved if the objects that support travel are presented in a way that they can fulfill their intended roles and ease the travel. The tool is classified as semiautomatic because the travel analysis is a subjective process, therefore it cannot be fully automated to give as high-quality results as human analysis. That is why a Web page is semiautomatically analyzed an annotated by the tool. *Dante* analyzes Web pages toward semiautomatically: (i) identify travel objects; (ii) discover their roles; (iii) annotate the identified objects by using an ontology; and (iv) transform the Web page with respect to these annotations. To enhance the mobility of visually impaired Web travelers, *Dante* annotates pages with the Web Authoring for Accessibility (WAfA) tool, formerly known as the Travel Ontology (Yesilada et al., 2004), which aims to encapsulate rich structural and navigational knowledge about the travel objects. The tool can be implemented and used on both the server side and the client side. It is more likely that it will be implemented on the client side. In *Dante*, the Mozilla plug-in version of COHSE[15] is used for annotation and the prototype transformation part of *Dante* is also implemented as a plug-in to Mozilla. By using a plug-in approach, the transformer and the annotator can access the DOM[16] object built by the browser and they can base the transformations and annotations on this intermediate document. In (Plessers et al., 2005), the *Dante* annotation process is integrated into the Web Site Design Method (WSDM) that allows Web sites and Web applications to be developed in a systematic way. The annotations are generated from explicit conceptual knowledge captured during the design process by means of WSDM's modeling concepts. These WSDM's modeling concepts used in the different phases are described in WSDM ontology. To generate code that is annotated with concepts from the WAfA ontology, a relationship between the concepts in the WSDM ontology and the WAfA ontology is established. By using these mapping rules, we can establish a transformation process that takes the conceptual design models as input and generates a set of annotations as a consequence. The transformation process consists of two annotation steps: authoring and mobility, which resemble the original annotation process of the Dante approach. The difference is that the authoring annotation in Dante is manual and based on the HTML source code of the Web site.

Due to the reasons explained below, we decided to differentiate between *Dante* and *Dante within WSDM*. We classify *Dante* as *others* from the assessment criteria dimension, *within a browser* but also *install on hard drive* from the supporting tool dimension and *filter & transformation* from the assessment deliverables dimension. We say that *Dante's* test scope is *simple and limited, Dante's* human intervention is *medium* and *Dante's* report style is *adaptation-based*. We classify *Dante within WSDM* as *others* from the assessment criteria dimension, *manual* from the supporting tool dimension and *filter & transformation* from the assessment deliverables dimension. We say that *Dante within WSDM's* test scope is *site wide, Dante within WSDM's* human intervention is *fully* and *Dante within WSDM's* report style is *adaptation-based*.

PAN

Personalizable accessible navigation (*PAN*) (Iaccarino, Malandrino, & Scarano, 2006) was developed in the Informatics and Applications Department of the University of Salerno. *PAN* is a set of edge services designed to improve Web page accessibility and developed on the top of a programmable intermediary framework, called SISI: Scalable Infrastructure for Edge Services (Colajanni, Grieco, Malandrino, Mazzoni, &

Scarano, 2005). The main goal of *PAN* is to provide efficient adaptation services, that is, services that are able to apply different types of on-the-fly transformations on Web pages in order to meet different users' preferences/needs/abilities. To use *PAN's* set of accessibility services, users have to install the SISI framework that is available as raw source code for Unix/Linux platforms and in a precompiled version for Windows. The installation and the deployment of *PAN* are accomplished by simply using the deployment mechanism provided by the SISI framework. The services provided by *PAN* are grouped into four main categories depending on whether they act on text, links, images or other objects on the HTML page—such as pop-up windows—according to the classification implicitly provided by the Web Content Accessibility Guidelines (WCAG 1.0, 1999). The text-based edge services adapt Web pages by taking into account the rules suggested by W3C to improve accessibility and to enhance, in general, the navigation of Web pages and, more specifically of Cascading Style Sheets (CSS) files. The link-based edge services act on links of Web pages in order to make Web pages more readable when users use assistive technologies such as speech synthesizers, screen readers, and so forth. The filter images edge services remove any image embedded in a Web page by replacing it with a link to it. The GIF animated images are also replace with a static one, by showing its first frame. The easy and smooth navigation service removes advertisements, banners, pop-ups in Javascripts and HTML, and so forth. This service also removes useless and redundant code, white spaces, HTML comments, and so forth.

Due to the reasons explained below, we place *PAN* at the following cell: *conformance* from the assessment criteria dimension, *install on hard drive* from the supporting tool dimension and *filter & transformation* from the assessment deliverables dimension. We say that *PAN's* test scope is *site-wide, PAN's* human intervention is *none,* and *PAN's* report style is *adaptation-based*.

Barrier Walkthrough

The *BW: Barrier Walkthrough* (Brajnik, 2006) was developed in the Mathematics and Informatics Department of the University of Udine. *BW* is a heuristic walkthrough method based on barriers[17]. This work defines a barrier as any condition that makes it difficult for people to achieve a goal when using the Web site through specified assistive technology. A barrier is a failure mode of the Web site, described in terms of (i) the user category involved, (ii) the type of assistive technology being used, (iii) the goal that is being hindered, (iv) the feature of the pages that raise the barrier, and (v) further effects of the barrier. Barriers to be considered are derived by interpretation of relevant guidelines and principles (WCAG 1.0, 1999; Section 508, 2003; PAS 78, 2006). To apply *BW* a number of different scenarios need to be identified. A scenario is defined by user characteristics, settings, goals, and possibly tasks of users who belong to given categories. At least categories involving blind users of screen readers, low-vision users of screen magnifiers, motor-disable users of normal keyboard or mouse, deaf users, and cognitive disabled users should be considered (Brajnik, 2006). In the *BW* method, user goals and tasks can be defined only referring the site being tested. For a Web application, one should consider some of the possible goals and tasks usually documented in use cases and cross these goals with user categories to obtain the relevant scenarios. For the information of a Web site, a sample of possible information needs can be considered and crossed with user categories. In this way, each user goal/task will be associated to different sets of pages to test, and these will be crossed to user categories (Brajnik, 2006). Evaluators then analyses these pages by investigating the presence of barriers that are relevant to the particular user category involved in the scenario. Cross-checking a barrier to a set of pages in the context of a scenario enables evaluators to understand the impact of this barrier with respect to the user goal and how often that barrier shows up when those users try to achieve the goal (Brajnik, 2006). Finally, using the *BW* evaluator produces a list of problems associated to a barrier in a given scenario, to a severity level, and possibly to performance attributes that are affected, that is, effectiveness, productivity, satisfaction, safety. The *BW* tries to assist the evaluator in filling the gap created by guidelines for conformance testing, because they often are very abstract to be directly applicable to Web sites.

Due to the reasons explained below, we place *BW* at *conformance & heuristics* from the assessment criteria dimension, *manual* from the supporting tool dimension and *evaluation & repair* from the assessment deliverables dimension. We say that *BW's* test scope is *simple and limited*, *BW's* human intervention is *fully*, and *BW's* report style is *text-based*.

WAVE

Web accessibility Versatile Evaluator (*WAVE*) is a free, Web-based tool to help Web developers make their Web content more accessible. *WAVE* was developed by WebAIM in conjunction with the Temple University Institute on Disabilities[18]. *Wave* facilitates evaluation by exposing many kinds of accessibility errors in the content, as well as possible errors, accessibility features, semantic elements, and structural elements. Like *Bobby*, *WAVE* evaluates pages against guidelines (WCAG 1.0, 1999; Section 508, 2003) and displays instances of different types of errors on the page. *WAVE* is an online service but it can be a tool within a browser too. *WAVE* checks one page at a time and provides a graphic/icon-based report and also an EARL report. These reports list the specific guideline being used to scan the page and the instances of each type of accessibility error. Like *Bobby*, the *WAVE* report highlights issues that are true problems but also issues that are potential problems, so a medium human intervention is required.

Due to the reasons explained below we place *WAVE* at *conformance* from the assessment criteria dimension, *online* but also *within a browser* from the supporting tool dimension and *evaluation* from the assessment deliverables dimension. Finally, we say that *WAVE's* test scope is *simple and limited, WAVE's* human intervention is *medium,* and *WAVE's* report style is *graphic/icon-based* and also *EARL.*

FAE

Functional accessibility evaluator (FAE) with the *Web accessibility visualization tool* and the *HTML Best Practices* (Rangin, 2006) were developed by the University of Illinois at Urbana/Champaign (UIUC)[19]. The goal of accessibility at UIUC is to make Web resources more functionally accessible to people with disabilities by improving the navigational structure or ability of users to restyle content for their own needs. The tools support developers in using accessible markup by estimating the use of best practices, and help developers visualize the accessibility of their resources. The tools use the following functional accessibility requirements defined in five major topics: (i) navigation and orientation, (ii) text equivalents, (iii) scripting, (iv) styling, and (v) standards. UIUC developed a set of *HTML Best Practices* that translates the requirements of guidelines (Section 508, 2003; WCAG 1.0, 1999) into markup requirements for implementing common Web page features. This translation of requirements into markup requirements is substantially different from conventional assessment tools like *Lift*, since *FAE* works over the *HTML Best Practices* document instead of over the accessibility principles and guidelines. *FAE* provides a means to estimate the functional accessibility of Web resources by analyzing Web pages and estimating their use of best practices. The test results are linked to both the *HTML Best Practices* document and the *Web accessibility Visualization Tool* for Web developers to find out more information about the results. The *Web accessibility Visualization Tool* is a visualization tool that provides graphical views of functional Web accessibility issues based on the *HTML Best Practices.*

Due to the reasons explained below we place *FAE* with the *Web accessibility Visualization Tool* and the *HTML Best Practices* at *others* from the assessment criteria dimension, *within an authoring tool* from the supporting tool dimension and *evaluation & repair* from the assessment deliverables dimension. Finally, we say that *FAE's* test scope is *simple and limited, FAE's* human intervention is *medium* and *FAE's* report style is *graphic/icon-based.*

Crunch

Crunch (Gupta & Kaiser, 2005) is a tool for preprocessing inaccessible Web pages to make them more accessible. *Crunch* is developed as a Web proxy usable with essentially all browsers, for the purpose of content extraction (or clutter reduction). It operates sending the Web browser's URL request to the appropriate Web server, and then applying its heuristic filter to the retrieved Web page before returning the content extracted from that Web page to the browser or other HTTP client. The first step in Crunch's analysis of the Web page is to pass it through a conventional HTML parser, which corrects the markup and creates a Document Object Model (DOM) tree. *Crunch's* heuristic manipulates the DOM representation in terms of tree transformation and pruning operations, rather than working with HTML text. This enables *Crunch* to perform its analysis at multiple granularities walking up and down the tree (Gupta & Kaiser, 2005). One of the limitations of the framework is that *Crunch* could potentially remove items from the Web page that the user may be interest in, and may present content that the user is not particularly interested in. *Crunch* partially addresses this problem by offering two ways. The first one is providing an administrative console, whereby an individual user can adjust the "settings" of each heuristic in order to produce what that user deems the "best" results for a given Web page. But, this manual procedure can be tedious and not appropriate for most users. So, the second one, is automating analogous tweaking by employing another set of heuristics to try to determine whether the DOM-pruning collection of heuristics mentioned above are properly narrowing in on the content. In short, *Crunch* is a Web proxy that utilizes a collection of heuristics, essentially tuneable filters operating on the DOM representation of the HTML Web page, with, among other goals, that the resulting Web page be accessible even if the original was not (Gupta & Kaiser, 2005).

Due to the reasons explained below we place *Crunch* at *others* from the assessment criteria dimension, *install on hard drive* from the supporting tool dimension and *filter & transformation* from the assessment deliverables dimension. Finally, we say that *Crunch's* test scope is *simple and limited*, *Crunch's* human intervention is *medium* and *Crunch's* report style is *adaptation-based*. Note that in spite of *Dante* and *Crunch* share the same classification space, there is a difference between them. While the former applies transformations by annotations using an ontology, *Crunch* applies filtering by pruning using a heuristic framework.

MAGENTA

Multi-Analysis of Guidelines by an Enhanced Tool for Accessibility (MAGENTA) with GAL: guidelines abstraction language and GE: guideline editor (Leporini et al., 2006) is an environment for defining, handling, and checking guidelines for the Web. The goal of such an environment is to support developers and evaluators in flexibly handling multiple sets of guidelines, which can be dynamically considered in the evaluation process. The *MAGENTA* tool has been developed with the intent to check whether a Web site is accessible and usable and to provide support to

improve it. Currently, *MAGENTA* supports three sets of guidelines for the Web: a set of guidelines for visually-impaired users (Leporini & Paternò, 2004), the guidelines from the (WCAG 1.0, 1999) and the guidelines associated with the (Stanca Law, 2004). The tool is not limited to checking whether the guidelines are supported but, in case of failure, it also provides support for modifying the implementation in order to make the resulting Web site more usable and accessible. *MAGENTA* has been developed considering the limitations of most current tools, in which the guidelines supported are specified in the tool implementation. In this work the aim is to provide a tool independent from the guidelines to check. The solution is based on the definition of a language for specifying guidelines that are stored externally to the tool. As guideline specification, the XML-based *Guideline Abstraction Language (GAL)* is proposed. In order to facilitate this process, a graphical editor has been designed and added to the *MAGENTA* tool, thus enabling people not particularly expert in handling languages such as X/HTML[20] and CSS to specify the desired guidelines. The *Guideline Editor (GE)* has been designed for assisting developers in handling single as well as groups of guidelines. The tool supports new guidelines definition and various types of editing (Leporini et al., 2006).

Due to the reasons explained below we place *MAGENTA* with *GAL* and *GE* at *conformance* from the assessment criteria dimension, *install on hard drive* from the supporting tool dimension and *evaluation & repair* from the assessment deliverables dimension. Finally, we say that *MAGENTA's* test scope is *site-wide*, *MAGENTA's* human intervention is *medium*, and *MAGENTA's* report style is *graphic/icon-based*. Note that in spite of *MAGENTA* share the same classification space with *Lift*, *TAW*, and *A-Prompt*, there is a difference between them. While *MAGENTA* is a tool independent from the guidelines to check, the other tools are predefined to test and monitor for compliance with (WCAG 1.0, 1999) guidelines or with (Section 508, 2003) standards.

Cynthia Says

Cynthia Says was developed by the International Centre for Disability Resources on the Internet (ICDRI)[21] in collaboration with Hi-Software[22]. It is an automated accessibility checker that can be used to test one Web page per minute. It can generate a report based on (Section 508, 2003) standards or on (WCAG 1.0, 1999) checkpoints, with and additional evaluation of the quality of alternative texts. This evaluation looks at the page for some common authoring tool errors or alt text creation errors. *Cynthia Says* is an online automatic tool available only in English that does not check all the checkpoints and provides no support, beyond a checklist for manual evaluation (Benavídez et al., 2006).

Due to the reasons explained below we place *Cynthia Says conformance* from the assessment criteria dimension, *online* from the supporting tool dimension and *evaluation* from the assessment deliverables dimension. Finally, we say that like *Bobby*, *Cynthia Says's* test scope is *simple and limited*, *Cynthia Says's* human intervention is *medium*, and *Cynthia Says's* report style is *text-based*.

aDesigner

aDesigner (Takagi et al., 2004) was developed in collaboration with alphaWorks Services[23] from IBM research and development labs. *aDesigner* is a disability simulator that helps Web designers ensure that their pages are accessible and usable by the visually impaired. Web developers can use *aDesigner* to test the accessibility and usability of Web pages for low-vision and blind people. The tool looks at such elements as the degree of color contrast on the page, the ability of users to change the font size, the appropriateness of alternate text for images, and the availability of links in the page to promote navigability. The tool also checks the page's compliance with accessibility guidelines. The result of this analysis is a report listing the

problems that would prevent from accessibility and usability to visually impaired users. In addition, each page is given an overall score. With this information, Web developers get immediate feedback and can address these obstacles before the pages are published. The platform requirements to install *aDesigner* is Windows 2000 or XP operating systems and Internet Explorer 6.0 or above. Once *aDesigner* is installed on hard drive it performs two kinds of accessibility checks. The first one, checks regulations and guidelines such as (Section 508, 2003; WCAG 1.0, 1999) but also checks the Japan Industrial Standard (JIS)[24] and the IBM's checklist[25]. They call such items to be checked as "compliance items." The second one checks usability problems faced by people with visual impairments, going beyond compliance. An author can experience how low vision users see the Web pages by using "low vision simulation" modes, and an author can also understand how blind users listen to and navigate through the pages by using "blind visualization." *aDesigner* aims at providing Web designers an environment to gain experiences in how low-vision people see a Web page, and how blind people access a Web page by using voice browsers. In short, aDesigner is an assistive authoring tool that aims at simulating disabilities to check the pages real usability while authoring.

Due to the reasons explained below we place *aDesigner* at *conformance* from the assessment criteria dimension, *install on hard drive* from the supporting tool dimension and *evaluation & repair* from the assessment deliverables dimension. Finally, we say that *aDesigner's* test scope is *very specific*, *aDesigner's* human intervention is *medium*, and *aDesigner's* report style is *graphic/ icon-based*. Note that *aDesigner* share the same classification space with *Lift*, A-*Prompt*, *TAW3*, and *MAGENTA*. However, the difference among these accessibility tools is that *aDesigner* tries not only to evaluate compliance but goes beyond compliance too.

Table 2. The assessment criteria dimension weigh with the scope factor

Scope factor ✓ simple and limited		Assessment criteria						
~ very specific		others			conformance			confor-mance & heuristics
✗ site-wide		Ontology	Markup	Heuristic	WCAG	Section 508	Another standard / specifica-tion	BW over WCAG
Accessibility approach	Bobby				✓	✓		
	Lift				✗	✗		
	A-Prompt				✓			
	TAW				✓ ✗			
	HERA				✓			
	Dante	✓						
	Dante within WSDM	✗						
	PAN				✗			
	BW							✓
	WAVE				✓	✓		
	FAE					·		
	Crunch			✓				
	MAGENTA				✗		✗	
	Cynthia Says				✓	✓		
	aDesigner				~	~	~	
	W3C MVS						✓	

Figure 3. Analysis of the population at the assessment criteria dimension (2007, Adriana Martín. Used with permission.)

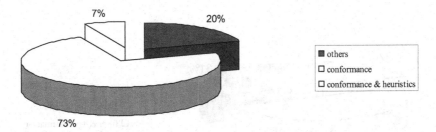

- ■ others — 20%
- ☐ conformance — 73%
- ☐ conformance & heuristics — 7%

Table 3. The assessment deliverables dimension weigh with the report style factor

Report Style factor		evaluation	evaluation & repair	filter & transformation	
✓	text-based			**Assessment deliverables**	
~	graphic/icon-based			build-in page version transformations by removing contents or changing structure and layout	customized page version transformations driven by annotations
✗	EARL				
✧	adaptation-based				
Accessibility approach	Bobby	✓			
	Lift		~		
	A-Prompt		~		
	TAW	✓	✓ ~ ✗		
	HERA		✓ ✗		
	Dante				✧
	Dante within WSDM				✧
	PAN			✧	
	BW		✓		
	WAVE	~ ✗			
	FAE		~		
	Crunch			✧	
	MAGENTA		~		
	Cynthia Says	✓			
	aDesigner		~		
	W3C MVS	✓			

Figure 4. Analysis of the population at the assessment deliverables dimension (2007, Adriana Martín. Used with permission.)

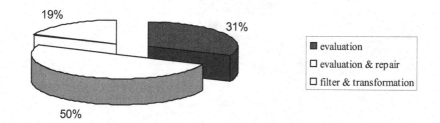

Table 4. The supporting tool dimension weigh with the human intervention factor

Human Intervention factor		manual	online	within a browser	within an authoring tool	install on hard drive
~	none					
✓	medium					
✗	fully					
Accessibility approach	Bobby		✓			
	Lift				✓	✓
	A-Prompt					✓
	TAW		✓	✓		✓
	HERA		✓			
	Dante			✓		✓
	Dante within WSDM	✗				
	PAN					~
	BW	✗				
	WAVE		✓	✓		
	FAE				✓	
	Crunch					✓
	MAGENTA					✓
	Cynthia Says		✓			
	aDesigner					✓
	W3C MVS		✓			✓

Figure 5. Analysis of the population at the supporting tool dimension (2007, Adriana Martín. Used with permission.)

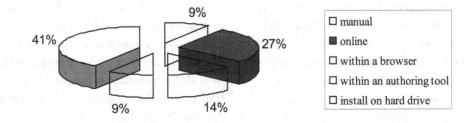

9%

41%

27%

9%

14%

☐ manual
■ online
☐ within a browser
☐ within an authoring tool
☐ install on hard drive

W3C Markup Validation Service

W3C markup validation service was created and maintained by Gerald Oskoboiny under the auspices of the quality assurance activity[26]. Most Web documents are written using markup languages, such as HTML or XHTML. *W3C Markup validator* is an online free service that helps check the validity of these Web documents for conformance to W3C recommendations[27] and other standards. These markup languages are defined by technical specifications, which usually include a machine-readable formal grammar (and vocabulary). The act of checking a document against these constraints is called validation, and this is what the *W3C markup validator* does. The focus of the tool is in validating Web documents as an important step which can dramatically help improving and ensuring their quality. Given an URL or a file upload, the tool validates the document and produces a text report. *W3C markup validator* does not perform a fully quality check but includes usability enhancements, improved feedback, and better support for both W3C and nonW3C document types. The *W3C markup validator* source code is available and a step-by-step guide is provided for the installation of the tool on a server.

Due to the reasons explained below we place *W3C markup validator* at *conformance* from the assessment criteria dimension, *online* but also *install on hard drive* from the supporting tool dimension and *evaluation* from the assessment deliverables dimension. Finally, we say that *W3C markup validator's* test scope is *simple and limited*, *W3C markup validator's* human intervention is *medium* and *W3C markup validator's* report style is *text-based*. Note that in spite of *Bobby, TAW, WAVE,* and *Cynthia Says* share the same classification space with *W3C markup validator*, there is a difference among them: while the formers test and monitor for compliance with some accessibility guidelines or standards (WCAG 1.0, 1999; Section 508, 2003), *W3C markup validator* is a tool that evaluates conformance to the technical specification of a Web document written using a markup language.

DISCUSSION

One of the main advantages of having an evaluation framework for classifying accessibility approaches is the feedback that results from comparing them. While working with WAAM we found that this framework is simple to use and allows evaluating any accessibility approach. Even though most of the approaches apply conformance reviews, our framework can also be used to classify those approaches that have developed their own evaluation method. In this sense, approaches that generate an accessible Web page version can be classified as *others* and according with the kind of method they use, that is, an ontology, an heuristic, a markup framework, and so forth. This is the case of *Dante* (Yesilada et al., 2004), since this approach has developed a Web Authoring for Accessibility (WAfA) tool that it is an ontology to enhance the mobility of visually impaired Web travelers. As another case from the supporting tool dimension, our framework considers approaches have an specific tool support but also manual approaches. For example, *Dante* is available to function *within a browser* but also *installed on hard drive* while *Dante within WSDM* (Plessers et al., 2005) is a *manual* approach. This distinction between *Dante* and *Dante within WSDM* can be addressed at the supporting tool dimension. Now, let us to consider a case from the assessment deliverables dimension. In spite of mainly approaches provide *evaluation* and *evaluation & repair* assessment deliverables, our framework also considers approaches that apply *filter & transformation* processes performed by transcoders. By using the former example, *Dante* is classified as *filter & transformation* since the approach transforms a Web page with respect to an annotation process driven by the WAfA ontology.

Tables 2, 3, and 4 show respectively each framework *dimension* (and their associated *factor*) for the fifteen classified approaches. As we can see from Table 2, the *assessment criteria* dimension shows a major concentration of the population for the *conformance* category. This is because accessibility is normally tested based on guidelines like the WCAG (1999) through a conformance testing method (called also standards review). Figure 3 summarizes this situation in a percentage circular graphic.

In Table 3, the *assessment deliverables* dimension shows that most of the approaches correspond to the categories *evaluation* and *evaluation & repair*. This is also related with the fact that accessibility is normally tested based on guidelines and mainly with a tool. Figure 4 summarizes this situation in a percentage circular graphic.

Finally, in Table 4 the *supporting tool* dimension distributes population evenly among the categories. The reason for including this view is because many of the approaches have developed more than one supporting tool. We can see also some prevalence over the *install on hard drive* category followed by the *online* category. Figure 5 summarizes this situation in a percentage circular graphic.

CONCLUSION

In October 1997, the W3C WAI launched the establishment of the International Program Office (IPO)[28]. In the conference press about the launch, Tim Berners-Lee, W3C director, commented (Thatcher, Burks, Heilmann, Henry, Kirpatrick, Lauke et al., 2006):

The power of the Web is in its universality. Access by everyone regardless of disability is an essential aspect. The IPO will ensure the Web can be accessed through different combinations of senses and physical capabilities just as other W3C activities ensure its operation across dif- *ferent hardware and software platforms, media, cultures, and countries.*

Undoubtedly, Web accessibility is one of the main actors upon which the success of a Web site depends. As a natural reaction to this reality, a diversity of approaches from accessibility research communities and organizations has literally bloomed up.

With this in mind, this chapter introduced the Web accessibility Assessment Model (WAAM), a framework for classifying Web accessibility assessment approaches. After applying the framework to classify 15 different approaches, we found out it a useful model for understanding and discussing Web accessibility as it allows the identification and classification of many different concerns involved when analyzing an accessibility approach.

From the assessment criteria dimension, WAAM not only considers approaches applying traditional conformance reviews but also approaches using a specific developed evaluation method. Meanwhile, from the supporting tool dimension, WAAM addresses approaches with tool support but manual approaches too. Finally, from the assessment deliverables dimension, WAAM provides a space for classifying evaluation and evaluation & repair approaches, but in addition for filter & transformation approaches as well.

REFERENCES

Benavídez, C., Fuertes, J., Gutiérrez, E., & Martínez, L. (2006). Semi-automatic evaluation of Web accessibility with HERA 2.0. In K. Miessenberg et al. (Eds.), *10th International Conference on Computers Helping People with Special Needs (ICCHP 2006),* (pp. 199-106). Springer-Verlag, ISBN 3-540-36020-4.

Binghamton University. (2001). State University of New York. *Evaluation, repair, and transformation tools for Web content usability and accessibility.* Retrieved October 17, 2007, from http://usable. binghamton.edu/currenttools.html#Repair

Bohman, P., & Anderson, S. (2005). A conceptual framework for accessibility tools to benefit users with cognitive disabilities. In *Proceedings of the International Cross-Disciplinary Workshop on World Wide Web accessibility (W4A)*, (pp. 85-89). ACM 2005.

Brajnik, G. (2004). Comparing accessibility evaluation tools: A method for tool effectiveness. *Universal Access in the Information Society, 3*(3-4), 252-263. Retrieved October, 17, 2007, from http://www.informatik.uni-trier.de/~ley/db/journals/uais/uais3.html

Brajnik, G. (2006). Web accessibility testing: When the method is the culprit. In K. Miessenberg et al. (Eds.), *10th International Conference on Computers Helping People with Special Needs (ICCHP 2006)*, (pp. 156-163). Springer-Verlag.

Brajnik, G., Cancila, D., Nicoli, D., & Pignatelli, M. (2005). Do text transcoders improve usability for disabled users? In S. Harper et al. (Eds.), *International Cross-Disciplinary Workshop on World Wide Web accessibility (W4A 2006)*, (pp. 9-17). ACM 2006.

Cabinet Office. (2003). Web guidelines for UK government Web sites, from http://www.cabinet-office.gov.uk/e-government/resources/handbook/html/htmlindex.asp

Cechich, A., & Piattini, M. (2002). Issues for assessing component-based systems. *In Proceedings of the VIII Congreso Argentino en Ciencias de la Computación (CACIC 2002)*, (pp. 253-262).

CLF. (2001). Common look and feel for the Internet—accessibility. Retrieved October 17, 2007, from http://www.tbs-sct.gc.ca/clf-nsi/index_e.asp

Colajanni, M., Grieco, R., Malandrino, D., Mazzoni, F., & Scarano, V. (2005). A scalable framework for support of advance edge services. In *Proceedings of the International Conference on High Performance Computing and Communication (HPCC 2005)* (pp. 1033-1042).

European Union. (2002). *Council of the European Union: Accessibility of public Web sites—accessibility for people with disabilities: Council resolution.* Retrieved October 17, 2007, from http://www. legi-internet.ro/index.php?id=149&L=2

Goble, C., Harper, S., & Stevens, R. (2000). The travails of visually impaired Web travelers. *In Proceedings of the Eleventh ACM on Hypertext and Hypermedia*, (pp. 1-10).

Gupta, S., & Kaiser, G. (2005). Extracting content from accessibility Web pages. *International Cross-Disciplinary Workshop on World Wide Web accessibility (W4A)*, (pp 26-30). ACM 2005.

Harper, S., Goble, C., & Stevens, R. (2003). Traversing the Web: Mobility heuristics for visually impaired surfers. In *Proceedings of the Fourth International Conference on Web Information Systems Engineering (WISE'03)*, (pp. 200-208).

HKSAR. (2001). *Hong Kong Special Administrative Region: Digital 21 strategy. Tips for improving accessibility of Web pages.* Retrieved October 17, 2007, from http://www.info.gov.hk/digital21/eng/knowledge/access_main.html

Hori, M., Ono, K., Abe, M., & Koyanagi ,T. (2004). Generating transformational annotation for Web document adaptation: Tool support and empirical evaluation. *International Journal of Web Semantics, 2*(1), 1-18.

HREOC. (2003*). Human rights and equal opportunity commission.* The Guide to Minimum Web site Standards Accessibility. Retrieved October 17, 2007, from http://www.agimo.gov.au/practice/mws/accessibility/

Iaccarino, G., Malandrino, D., & Scarano, V. (2006). Personalizable edge services for Web accessibility. *International Cross-Disciplinary Workshop on World Wide Web accessibility (W4A)*, (pp. 23-32). ACM.

Irwin, M., & Gerke, J. (2004). Web-based information and prospective students with disabilities: A study of liberal arts colleges. *EDUCAUSE Quarterly, 27*(4), 51-59.

ISO/DIS 9241-11. (1994). International Organization for Standardization/Draft International Standard. Ergonomic requirements for office work with visual display terminals (VDTs). Part 11: Guidance on Usability.

ISO/IEC 9126-4. (2005). International Organization for Standardization/International Electrotechnical Commission. Software Engineering—Software product quality. Part 4: Quality in use metrics.

ISO/TS 16071. (2002). International Organization for Standardization/Technical Specification. Ergonomics of human-system interaction—Guidance on accessibility for human-computer interfaces.

Ivory, M., Mankoff, J., & Le, A. (2003). Using automated tools to improve Web site usage by users with diverse abilities. *IT & Society, 1*(3), 195-236.

Leporini, B., & Paternò, F. (2004). Increasing usability when interacting through screen readers. *International Journal Universal Access in Information Society (UAIS), 3*(1), 57-70.

Leporini, B., Paternò, F., & Scorcia, A. (2006). An environment for defining and handling guidelines for the Web. In K. Miessenberg et al. (Eds.), *10th International Conference on Computers Helping People with Special Needs (ICCHP 2006)*, (pp. 176-183). Springer-Verlag.

Loiacono, E. (2004). Cyberaccess: Web accessibility and corporate America. *Communications of the ACM, 47*(12), 82-87.

Martín-Albo, J., Bertoa, M. F., Calero, C., Vallecillo, A., Cechich, A., & Piattini, M. (2003). CQM: A software component metric classification model. *In Proceedings of the 7th ECOOP Workshop on Quantitative Approaches in Ob-ject-Oriented Software Engineering (QAOOSE 2003)*, (pp. 54-60).

Matera M., Rizzo F., & Toffetti Carughi, G. (2006). Web usability: Principles and evaluation methods. In E. Mendes & N. Mosley (Ed.), *Web engineering* (pp. 143-179). Springer-Verlag.

Paciello, M. (Ed.). (2000). *Web accessibility for people with disabilities.* R & D Developer Series, Group West Press.

PAS 78. (2006). *Publicly available specification: A guide to good practice in commissioning accessible Web sites, ICS 35.240.30.* Disability Rights Commission (DRC), 2006. Retrieved October 17, 2007, from http://www.drc.org.uk/library/website_accessibility_guidance/pas_78.aspx

Petrie, H., & Weber, G. (2006). People with disabilities: Automatic and manual evaluation of Web sites (Introduction to Special Thematic Session). In K. Miessenberg et al. (Eds.), *10th International Conference on Computers Helping People with Special Needs (ICCHP 2006)*, (pp. 152-155). Springer-Verlag.

Piattini, M., Calero, C., & Genero, M. (2002). *Information and database quality.* Kluwer Academic Publishers.

Plessers, P., Casteleyn, S., Yesilada, Y., De Troyer, O., Stevens, R., Harper, S., & Goble, C. (2005). Accessibility: A Web engineering approach. In *Proceedings of the 14th International World Wide Web Conference (WWW2005)* (pp. 353-362).

Rafla, T., Robillard, P., & Desmarais, M. (2006). Investigating the impact of usability on software architecture through scenarios: A case study on Web systems. *Journal of Systems and Software (JSS2006), 79*(3), 415-426.

Rangin, H. B. (2006). University of Illinois tools and techniques for functional Web accessibility. In K. Miessenberg et al. (Eds.), *10th International Conference on Computers Helping People with*

Special Needs (ICCHP 2006), (pp. 230-233). Springer-Verlag.

Ruiz, J., Calero, C., & Piattini, M. (2003). A three dimensional Web quality model. *In Proceedings of the International Conference on Web Engineering.* (LNCS 2722, pp. 384-385).

Section 508. (2003). *U.S. Federal Government: A quick reference guide to Section 508 resource documents.* Retrieved October 17, 2007, from http://www.accessibilityforum.org/paper_tool.html

Stanca Law. (2004). *Italian legislation on accessibility: Guidelines containing the technical requirements, the definitions of the different accessibility levels and the technical methodologies for the testing of Web site accessibility.* Retrieved October 17, 2007, from http://www.pubbliaccesso.it/biblioteca/documentazione/guidelines_study/index.htm

Takagi, H., Asakawa, Ch., Fukuda, K., & Maeda, J. (2004). Accessibility designer: Visualizing usability for the blind. In *Proceedings of the International ACM Conference on Assistive Technologies (ASSETS2004),* (pp. 177-184). ACM.

Thatcher, J., Burks, M., Heilmann, C., Henry, S, Kirpatrick, A., Lauke, P., et al. (2006). *Web accessibility—Web standards and regulatory compliance.* FriendSoft Press.

WCAG 1.0. (1999). *Web content accessibility Guidelines 1.0. World Wide Web Consortium (W3C) Recommendations.* Retrieved October 17, 2007, from http://www.w3.org/TR/WAI-WEB-CONTENT/

WebAIM. (2006). Web accessibility in mind articles. *Accessibility evaluation tools, 1999-2006.* Retrieved October 17, 2007, from http://www.webaim.org/articles/tools/

Xiaoping, Z. (2004). Evaluation and enhancement of Web content accessibility for persons with disabilities. Doctoral Dissertation, University of Pittsburgh.

Yesilada, Y., Stevens, R., & Goble, C. (2003). A foundation for tool-based mobility support for visually impaired Web users. In *Proceedings of the 12th International World Wide Web Conference (WWW2003),* (pp. 422-430).

Yesilada, Y., Harper, S., Goble, G., & Stevens, R. (2004). Screen readers cannot see: Ontology-based semantic annotation for visually impaired Web travelers. In *Proceedings of the International Conference on Web Engineering (ICWE2004),* (pp. 445-458).

KEY TERMS

Accessible Barrier: Is any condition that makes it difficult for people to achieve a goal when they are using a Web site through specified assistive technology.

Annotation: "A remark attached to a particular portion of a document, and covers a broad range in literature... Web annotation is crucial for providing not only human-readable remarks, but also machine-understandable descriptions, and has a number of applications such as discovery, qualification, and adaptation of Web documents" (Hori, Ono, Abe, & Koyanagi, 2004, p. 2).

Evaluation and Reporting Language (EARL): A general-purpose language developed by the W3C for expressing test results.

False Positive: An issue detected by a test that after a manual evaluation it is not consider an accessibility barrier.

Issue: "An instance of a potential problem detected by a test" (Brajnik, 2004, p. 257).

Potential Problem: A possible accessibility barrier detected by a test that requires manual evaluation to identify if it is an accessibility barrier or not.

Screen Readers: Special applications that vocalize the onscreen data. Pages are typically read from the top left to the bottom right, line by line, one word at a time.

Transcoder: A Web-server system that produces, on fly, a transformed version of a Web page requested by a user or a browser (Brajnik, 2005).

Travel Objects: The environmental features or elements that travelers use or may need to use to make a successful journey (Yesilada, 2003).

True Problem: An accessibility barrier detected by a test.

ENDNOTES

1   See http://www.w3.org/WAI/

2   See http://www.sidar.org/index.php or http://www.fundacion.sidar.org/index_en.php

3   See http://www.cast.org/.

4   See http://aware.hwg.org/

5   See http://www.webaim.org/

6   See http://www.utoronto.ca/atrc/

7   See http://www.fundacionctic.org/web/contenidos/es

8   See http://www.watchfire.com/.

9   See http://webxact.watchfire.com/.

10   See http://www.usablenet.com/.

11   At http://www.tawdis.net/taw3/cms/es

12   At http://www.sidar.org/index.php#probhera

13   See http://www.w3.org/Style/CSS/

14   See http://www.php.net/

15   See http://cohse.semanticweb.org/

16   See http://www.w3.org/DOM/

17   A complete list of barriers can be found at http://www.dimi.uniud.it/giorgio/publications.html#hcihw05

18   See http://disabilities.temple.edu/

19   See http://www.uiuc.edu/

20   See http://home.worldonline.es/jlgranad/xhtml/xhtml1.htm

21   See http://www.icdri.org/

22   See http://www.cynthiasays.com/

23   See http://services.alphaworks.ibm.com/

24   See http://www.webstore.jsa.or.jp/webstore/Top/indexEn.jsp

25   See http://www-306.ibm.com/able/guidelines/web/accessweb.html

26   See http://www.w3.org/QA/

27   See http://www.w3.org/TR/#Recommendations

28   See http://www.w3.org/WAI/IPO/Activity

Chapter XII
Maximizing Web Accessibility Through User–Centered Interface Design

Soonhwa Seok
The University of Kansas, USA

ABSTRACT

Digital inclusion and Web accessibility are integral parts of modern culture and, as such, have implications for social accountability. The World Wide Web Consortium (W3C) has suggested standards and guidelines regarding the inclusion of people with special needs, with an emphasis on higher accessibility and adaptability as the main goal of Web design. The user interface is the place where users can interact with the information by using their minds. Users with special needs can acquire information by using a human centered user interface. This article highlights the need to investigate the relationship between cognition and user interface.

INTRODUCTION AND BACKGROUND

A highly developed digital society needs to be integrated in order to function to meet each individual's differentiated needs. Inclusion is reflected in the modern special education classroom. This practice of teaching and learning mirrors the changes in society because the classroom is the place where a collaborative, collective and real-time community is built consisting of teachers,

educational executives, administrators, researchers, and parents. The terms inclusion, zero reject, and universal design, characterize a fully inclusive classroom. Zero reject means "students cannot be excluded from educational services based on their disability, severity of disability, contagious conditions, or costs of services" (Wood, 2006, p.9). The term inclusion is used to designate educational services and placement of students with disabilities in the general education classroom, facilitated by classroom-provided supports, adaptation, modification, and accommodation for each individual student (Hunt & Marshall, 2006; Wood, 2006). Finally, universal design for learning refers to a curriculum or educational approach using assistive or educational technology to individualize teaching and learning (Turnbull, Turnbull, & Wehmeyer, 2005). In the inclusive classroom, the learning characteristics of the student with the disability are analyzed, and all characteristics are integrated into a teaching unit that best meets the student's needs.

DIGITAL INCLUSION AND WEB ACCESSIBILITY

Digital inclusion and Web accessibility are leading the change of the digital Web culture. This movement brings about zero reject and differentiated inclusion on the Web by using universally designed content with built-in flexibility. Digital inclusion involves "social inclusion, the ever-developing information and communication technologies," and Web design for "equal accessibility and opportunity" for all the individuals, especially for the individuals with disabilities; Web accessibility is therefore, "social inclusion" (Bradbrook & Fisher, 2004, p. 2; World Wide Web Consortium [W3C], 2005, ¶ 5).

The ultimate goal of Web access is to improve productivity and the quality of communication. Productivity is improved as individual's social function improves as a result of his or her efforts in a social unit. The term *Web accessibility* means that individuals with disabilities are able to function on the Web, including engaging in cognitive and physical activities, such as navigating, comprehending, analyzing, synthesizing, manipulating, producing and evaluating information. They can also communicate with others on the Web for their own purposes, and contribute to the Web culture. In short, Web accessibility results in productive and universal access to information and other individuals (Bowie, Adler, Civille, & Gill, 1996; W3C, 2005).

Web accessibility brings about social accountability for individuals who would otherwise be placed outside the Internet culture because of their physical, sensory, or cognitive limitations, as well as different cultural and linguistic backgrounds. The term disability is often not defined in a Web context, although it is broadly used in Section 508 of the American law, W3C, and other legal documents. This is because some individuals with special needs regard themselves as not having a disability and being very independent, although they may have functional limitations or barriers imposed by society and the environment (Hunt & Marshall, 2006; Thatcher, 2006; W3C, 2005). Multiple social attempts have been made to facilitate and build Web accessibility, including guidelines, standards, and Website evaluation efforts established by the Americans with Disabilities Act, Section 508, the W3C, the Center for Applied Special Technology (CAST), the British Broadcasting Corporation (BBC), IBM, and Microsoft (Thatcher, 2006).

GUIDELINES FOR WEB ACCESSIBILITY

The ADA is a piece of civil rights legislation that protects people with disabilities from discrimination in four major areas: (a) private-sector employment, (b) public services, (c) public accommodations, and (d) telecommunications. When passed in 1990, the ADA sought to reduce obstacles to "equal access to employment, state and local government programs, transportation, public buildings, and communication technology" (Wisdom, White, Goldsmith, Bielavitz, Davis, & Drum, 2006, p. 20). While the ADA attempts to include the Internet and other services, the law itself is not explicitly clear on the Internet access.

Although the accessibility of a Web site is ultimately the responsibility of the designer of the site, federal legislation sets the standard for accessibility. Section 508 was implemented to ensure that

Table 1. Organizations with Web accessibility guidelines and their URLs

Institution	URL
British Broadcasting Corporation (BBC)	http://www.bbc.co.uk/accessibility/
U.S. Department of Justice (ADA)	http://www.usdoj.gov/crt/ada/adahom1.htm
Center for Applied Special Technology (CAST)	http://www.cast.org/
International Business Machines (IBM)	http://www-306.ibm.com/able/laws/index.html
Microsoft Corporation	http://www.microsoft.com/enable/
U.S. Office of Governmentwide Policy (Section 508)	http://www.section508.gov/

government Web sites are accessible; however, the law now extends to include all schools that receive federal and state funds (Carter, 2004). Meant to create high-quality information that is accessible to all viewers, key components of Section 508 state that there should be "a text equivalent for every nontext element; all information conveyed through color must also be conveyed without color; and frames should be titled with text that identifies the frame and facilitates navigation" (Jaeger, 2006, p. 170). By passing laws such as Section 508, the federal government has made it clear that Web accessibility is an important issue and must be provided in the field of education. Table 1 lists the URLs of organizations that have established Web accessibility guidelines.

W3C guidelines developed by Chisholm, Jacobs, and Vanderheiden (2000) identify the following ways to ensure Web content accessibility:

1. Provide equivalent alternatives to auditory and visual content.
2. Don't rely on color alone.
3. Use markup and style sheets and do so properly.
4. Clarify natural language usage.
5. Create tables that transform gracefully.
6. Ensure that pages featuring new technologies transform gracefully.
7. Ensure user control of time-sensitive content changes.
8. Ensure direct accessibility of embedded user interfaces.
9. Design for device-independence.
10. Use interim solutions.
11. Use W3C technologies and guidelines.
12. Provide context and orientation information.
13. Provide clear navigation mechanisms.
14. Ensure that documents are clear and simple. (Chisholm, Jacobs, & Vanderheiden, 2000, ¶ 6).

Furthermore, Section 508-1194.22 provides Web accessibility guidelines related to 16 usability items (Section 508, 2006, § 1194.22):

1. A text equivalent for every nontext element shall be provided (e.g., via "alt," "longdesc," or in element content).
2. Equivalent alternatives for any multimedia presentation shall be synchronized with the presentation.
3. Web pages shall be designed so that all information conveyed with color is also available without color, for example from context or markup.
4. Documents shall be organized so they are readable without requiring an associated style sheet.
5. Redundant text links shall be provided for each active region of a server-side image map.
6. Client-side image maps shall be provided instead of server-side image maps except where the regions cannot be defined with an available geometric shape.

7. Row and column headers shall be identified for data tables.
8. Markup shall be used to associate data cells and header cells for data tables that have two or more logical levels of row or column headers.
9. Frames shall be titled with text that facilitates frame identification and navigation.
10. Pages shall be designed to avoid causing the screen to flicker with a frequency greater than 2 Hz and lower than 55 Hz.
11. A text-only page, with equivalent information or functionality, shall be provided to make a Web site comply with the provisions of this part, when compliance cannot be accomplished in any other way. The content of the text-only page shall be updated whenever the primary page changes
12. When pages utilize scripting languages to display content, or to create interface elements, the information provided by the script shall be identified with functional text that can be read by assistive technology.
13. When a Web page requires that an applet, plug-in or other application be present on the client system to interpret page content, the page must provide a link to a plug-in or applet that complies with §1194.21(a) through (l).
14. When electronic forms are designed to be completed on-line, the form shall allow people using assistive technology to access the information, field elements, and functionality required for completion and submission of the form, including all directions and cues.
15. A method shall be provided that permits users to skip repetitive navigation links.
16. When a timed response is required, the user shall be alerted and given sufficient time to indicate more time is required (¶ 7).

Section 508 (2006, § 1194.24) also mandates specific modes of video and multimedia presen-tation. Three items were developed related to multimedia accessibility:

1. All training and informational video and multimedia productions which support the agency's mission, regardless of format, that contain speech or other audio information necessary for the comprehension of the content, shall be open or closed captioned.
2. All training and informational video and multimedia productions which support the agency's mission, regardless of format, that contain visual information necessary for the comprehension of the content, shall be audio described.
3. Display or presentation of alternate text presentation or audio descriptions shall be user-selectable unless permanent.

The Web-accessibility standards in W3C and Section 508 are designed to increase the usability, accessibility, and adaptability of the Web information system for people with sensory, cognitive, cultural, linguistic, and any other physical impairments, by means of the user - computer interaction, or user interface. The standards address the built-in, flexible technology or its application on the Web. Section 508 and W3C cover the following areas:

- Usability of software applications and operating systems
- Accessibility of Web-based Internet information and application
- Application of built-in telecommunication product
- Flexibility of built-in video or multimedia product
- Assistive technology of self contained, closed products, desktop and potable computers.

The universal goal of a democratic society is to improve the quality of all citizens' lives.

Thus, Web accessibility should benefit all individuals, with or without disabilities. The Internet, especially for individuals with a disability, can provide information to improve the quality of all citizens' lives.

DOMAINS OF INSTRUCTIONAL OBJECTIVES

Bloom, Engelhart, Frust, Hill, & Krathwohl (1956) defined the three domains of instructional objectives as cognitive, affective, and psychomotor domains. The three domains have been employed in instructional design, Web design, software design, and program design (Belanger, & Jordan, 2000; Bloom et al., 1956). Hodell (2000) added a fourth domain, the interpersonal domain. These domains respectively deal with (a) the process of the mind, (b) motor skills or physical movement, (c) individuals' attitudes and feelings, and (d) interactivity between individuals (Belanger & Jordan, 2000; Bloom et al. 1956; Hodell, 2000).

All four domains should be considered when a Web environment is built, including three layers of the Web environment: (a) content, (b) user interface, and (c) infrastructure. These mirror the construct of Web design, the Website's purpose, its usability, and the designer's philosophy and plan.

Harris (1999) argued that each layer creates synergy between the layers, as well as between users and the layers. The content layer provides the user with knowledge, information, simulation, and other resources. The user interface layer called human computer interface or human-computer interaction allows the users to interact with the content (information), the computer itself, and other users. Finally, the infrastructure layer, which includes the inner, hardware, mechanical system and technology of the machine, supports the interface, content, the user, as well as interactions between all of them.

COGNITION AND THE USER INTERFACE

Web accessibility is a construct that reflects digital inclusion, focusing on individuals with special needs and facilitating human-centered interaction and functionality. The user interface is a computer, Web or technology system that enables users to see, hear, and interact with the content, the computer, or other users. Thus, the user interface is a collective representation of cognitive, psychomotor, affective, and interpersonal processes that can be used to enhance the usability of the system. All users, including those with disabilities, need effective ways to access and acquire knowledge. An effective interface allows individuals to use their minds without heavy physical or mental efforts, which especially benefits individuals with various special needs. This highlights the need to investigate the relationship between cognition and user interface. The next section will discuss cognitive processing models.

COGNITIVE PROCESSING MODELS

The cognitive processing models developed by cognitive constructivists emphasize the most effective strategies for building knowledge (Jonassen, Davidson, Collins, Campbell, & Hagg, 1995; Miller & Miller, 1999; Wilson, Teslow, & Osman-Jouchoux, 1995). Thus, the cognitive processing model considers knowledge as reality and an obtainable objective outside of the individual. Therefore, the individual and knowledge are independent of each other, at a distance, in their own structure. Further, within this model, knowledge is objectively measurable so that the individual can "acquire, replicate, and retain an accurate representation" (Jonassen et al., 1995; Miller & Miller, 1999, ¶ 18; Wilson et al., 1995). The model provides directions for acquiring information.

Cognitive constructivists employ three types of memory to acquire correct information: sensory, short-term, and long-term. Sensory memory is used to emphasize the concentration of the mind for a short time, while information is processed. Strategies in this area include psychophysical variation (e.g., change in color, size, pitch) and discrepant activities (e.g., choice of words, images)" (Miller & Miller, 1999, ¶ 21-23). When the strategies of iconic *short term memory* are implemented in designing Website for individuals with disabilities, items can be divided into (a) four to five chunks (Cattell, 1886), and (b) visual or audible partial content or cue representations, instead of whole reports (Averbach & Sperling, 1961). These strategies are generally employed in teaching practices for all students. Finally, strategies employing models of long-term memory include (a) activation of prior knowledge, (b) presenting information within a meaningful context, and (c) hierarchical sequencing and organization that elaborates and connects new with existing knowledge (Miller & Miller, 1999, ¶ 21-23).

Appropriate strategies for acquiring information should be applied to authentic, functional experiences that have a purpose in the context of the individual's life. Strategies should also encourage the individual to pay attention to the information, so the experience can be transferred to sensory store, short-term memory, and long-term memory with little cognitive load. Figure 1 illustrates the information processing system and types of memory (Ally, 2004, p. 9).

The construct of Web accessibility can more precisely and diversely form this structure (Figure 1) than any other application because the Web construct is adaptable and flexible. The needs of the individual user and the function of the individualized Website determine the structure of the display, degree of user control of navigation, and level of interactivity. The essential goal of this cognitive constructivist paradigm for Web accessibility is easy and accurate transmission and reception of functional information. Digital inclusion generates synergy by applying the cognitive processing models to the individual's needs, and builds an authentic digital functional community, which is the nature of the Web environment.

THE HUMAN-COMPUTER INTERFACE

The human-computer interface (HCI) is a crucial element in producing meaningful and determining factors of usability (Kim & Moon, 1998; Nielsen & Norman, 2000; Roy, Dewit, & Aubert, 2001). Specifically, the user interface is a computer system (Ciavarelli, 2003) that connects the contents or infrastructure and Web users. Thus, users can operate, control, and manage the contents and infrastructure through the medium and user interface (Ciavarelli, 2003; Harris, 1999; Laurillard, 1993). Further, the user interface "provides feedback to the user, such as acknowledging inputs, advising the user of processing wait periods, and providing navigational assistance, error alerts, and corresponding recovery methods" (Ciavarelli, 2003, p. 14).

Figure 1. Types of memory

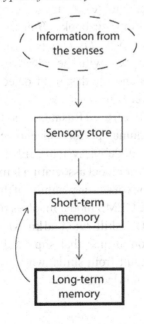

The goal of the interface is to produce higher usability that will increase users' effectiveness and efficiency in using the computer and navigating its contents or texts. It also enhances users' satisfaction and perception of the interaction with the computer (Ciavarelli, 2003; Harris, 1999; Nielson, 1993; Roy et al.). Higher usability is reflected by the following characteristics: (a) requiring minimum efforts to operate, (b) visually agreeable and enjoyable to use, and (c) pursuing few errors and quick recovery from them (Howe, 2005). Therefore, usability is a "cognitive, social," communicational process with an integrated computer technology system (Adler & Winograd, 1992; Berg, 2000, p. 353; Maddix, 1990).

HCI refers to "the design, evaluation, and implementation of interactive computing systems for human use" (Berg, 2000, p. 350; Card, Moran, & Newell, 1983; Ciavarelli, 2003; Head, 1999). Therefore, HCI is the set of knowledge about interaction between the computer systems, users, and productive working environment (Berg, 2000; Carey, 1991; Ciavarelli; Reisner, 1987). Tasks related to theories support interface design, including (a) the perceptual approach (Gibson, 1986); (b) constructivism (Ciavarelli; Duffy & Jonassen, 1992); and (c) the activity theory or information processing approach.

THE GOMS MODEL

Based on the cognitive information processing model, Card, Moran, and Newell (1983) developed a cognitive model of human computer interaction, GOMS. As discussed earlier, the cognitive information processing model has three different memory stages; (a) sensory store, (b) (b) short-term memory, and (c) long-term memory. The sensory store and working memory stages are related to perceptual and motor processing, whereas short-term memory and long-term memory are related to cognitive processing (Card et al., 1983). According to Card et al. (1983), the GOMS model

consists of four components that demonstrate how to process tasks between users and a computer system: (a) goals to be achieved in the process, (b) operators performing the sequencing methods and interacting with the system, (c) methods representing the sequences of the tasks performed by the operators, and (d) selection rules choosing the best strategies and solutions for the best methods to obtain the goals. The GOMS model seeks to "predict the time required to complete the task. In addition, the model can be used to identify and predict the effects of errors on task performance. Error recovery is assumed to involve the same four components as correct actions" (Card, Moran & Newell, 2005. ¶ 2).

ERROR AND COGNITION

Error types mirror the working load of short-term memory. Error occurs when the short-term memory has a heavy workload. There seem to be millions of errors in everyday life. Some research shows that errors have several visible patterns, which can be prevented or reduced by the human centered interface design. James Reason and Donald Norman are two of the most notable psychologists with expertise in error models as illustrated in their books, *Human Error* and *The Design of Everyday Things,* respectively. In addition, they deal with the effective use of the human mind and the design of objects that we encounter everyday.

Reason (1990) used Rasmussen's (1986) classification of human performance to generate his generic error modeling system (GEMS), which is the classic error model associating human errors with the actions or action planning of the working memory. The GEMS model involves three types of action control: skill, rule, and knowledge-based levels. Reason argued that slips and lapse are errors that result from skills, whereas mistakes result from knowledge.

Reason (1990) linked error types to the cognitive steps, planning, storage, and execution, those for which short-term memory is mostly in charge. According to Reason (1990) human error can be categorized into three observable, measurable behaviors: skill, rule, and knowledge:

At the skill-based level, human performance is governed by stored patterns of preprogrammed instructions represented as analogue structures in a time-space domain. Errors at this level are related to the intrinsic variability of force, space or time coordination. (p.43)

Reason asserted that at the rule-based level, "errors are typically associated with the misclassification of situations leading to the application of the wrong rule or with the incorrect recall of procedures" (p. 43). At the knowledge-based level, errors "arise from resource limitations ('bounded rationality') and incomplete or incorrect knowledge" (p. 43). As expertise increases, "the primary focus of control moves from the knowledge-based towards the skill-based levels; but all three levels can co-exist at any one time" (p. 43).

Reason (1990) claimed that the knowledge that is meaningful in a specific context or is not correct, is the main cause of errors. Thus, he argued that most errors are related to the knowledge level, whereas the two skill-level errors are slips and lapses. Based on Reason's error frame, slips are errors caused by over-attention or inattention after an action is completed while intention is forming and the execution or storage of action sequence is failed.

According to Norman, slips are "the performance of an action that was not what was intended" (2002, p. 1). Thus, Norman argued that slips appear as results of the similar, triggering actions or thoughts with inattention. Norman's natural observation resulted in six categories of slips: "capture errors, description errors, date-driven errors, associative activation errors, loss-of-activation errors, and mode errors" (p. 107). He employed an activation-trigger schema system to explain schemata (2002). Rumelhart defined

schemata as "data structures for representing generic concepts stored in memory" (Rumelhart & Ortony, 1977, p. 101); "schemata have variables with constraints and that these variables (or slots) have a limited distribution of possible default values" (Reason, 1990, p. 35; Rumelhart & Ortony, 1977). In Norman's an activation-trigger schema system, errors mostly appear when schema is appropriately chosen and activated but triggered and operated over the longer time frame as a response to activators. This activation-trigger schema system is schematic control model using the working short-term memory; it handles familiar knowledge with speed without heavy workloads (Reason, 1996).

The activation framework has both specific and general activators. The specific activator uses a mental model which is composed of explanations of intended actions and plans (Norman, 2002; Reason, 1996). A less detailed explanation for the planned action is necessary if a collection of intended actions is to be effectively carried at short intervals. General activators support the work of the mind by providing contextual and affective background information, regardless of intentions.

Human-centered interface design analyzes and synthesizes an individual's needs, cultural practice, cognitive ability, and preferences against the measurable goal of functioning in a certain context, using cognitive, psychomotor, and affective constructs (Badre, 2002). Applied to human centered design, the systems increase usability, visibility, and functionality: "They save lives" (Norman, 2002, p. iv) by reducing errors of every day life. The outcome of the human-centered design is "ease of use, ease of learning, memorability, lack of errors, and satisfaction" (Barde, 2002, p.5; Gould & Lewis, 1985; Nielsen, 1993).

When the design that enhances human-computer interaction is considered in the context of Web accessibility, analysis and synthesis of the individual's special needs and the work of the mind, "human perception, memory, and attention," is important so as to ensure the minimal use of their efforts and interaction with technology (Norman, 2002, p. iv). The interdependence and interaction between people, information, and technology exists with a special function and purpose (where there is communication). Thus, analyzing and defining the user's characteristics is the first step to building a Website for individuals with special needs. Their interactions with technology, content, information and other individuals are to be synthesized in the user interface.

Understanding users, their needs, mastery level of technology and their physical and cognitive ability is a prerequisite for designing the human computer interface and evaluating Web accessibility. The goal is to determine the most appropriate interaction modes and reduce the rate of error by providing physical, semantic, cultural and logical constraints (Barde, 2002; Norman, 2002).

Ecology (Web accessibility) should be adapted to meet the needs of individuals in the different categories of disability and the different degrees within a category (severe to mild). Barde (2002) described individual factors that influence Web design. Individual differences may be "grouped into four categories: knowledge, experience, and skill; personality factors; physical and demographic attributes; and user levels" (p. 70). Individuals may differ in "level and type of education as well as in their knowledge, experience, and skill levels" (p. 70). Barde elaborated:

These factors describe the cognitive abilities and styles of projected users as well as their knowledge and experience of the projected Website's domain. Not all factors are necessarily applicable in every Web design situation, but there will be situations in which they all have direct implications for designing the constituents of the interactive environment (p. 70).

HUMAN-CENTERED DESIGN

Design is communication. Human-centered design yields synergy between the content informa-

tion, the user, the designer, and infrastructure, and enhances communication effectiveness. Norman (2002) suggested that human-centered design consists of three elements:

1. Conceptual models which make invisible functions visible by using feedback, as the effect of an interaction, and explanations of its use.
2. Constraints which are a proactive measure to limit the choices of interaction and reduce human errors. Physical, semantic, and cultural constraints are three types of constraints.
3. Affordance is the "perception and actual properties of the thing. It suggests how the device can be possibly operated (p. 9).

The three elements make up a psychology of communicative design. Communication enhances visibility and usability by using the communication medium and human-computer interaction. Usability is defined as "the degree to which users can perform a set of required tasks" (Brinck, Gergle, & Wood, 2002, p. 2). The usability of Web accessibility is measured by the degree of efficiency of the individualized Web design and communication with the technology: functionality given the individual's needs; efficiency of operating time, ease in remembering and learning operations as determined by the individual's physical, cognitive ability and the degree of disability; proactive error-tolerant system; and built-in flexibility of the infrastructure design for the digital inclusion (Brinck, Gergle, & Wood, 2002; Norman, 2002).

DISABILITY CATEGORIES

Most special education textbooks divide disabilities into 12 categories, in accordance with the Individuals with Disabilities Education Act (see Table 2). The potential population of the Web accessibility users reaches over six million, age

6 to 21. Table 2 also illustrates the number of potential Web users in each disability category (Turnbull, 2004).

Section 508 and the W3C do not clearly define Web accessibility users in terms of the individual's age or the degree of disability, only recommending that the Web be made "accessible to people with disabilities" (W3C, ¶ 1). The W3C indicates how the Web may be employed by users with different types of disabilities and "how people with disabilities use the Web." The W3C developed series of scenarios of Web usability by individuals with disabilities: (a) an individual taking online courses with hearing impairment, (b) an accountant with visual impairment, (c) a student with a specific learning disability, and (d) a student with a cognitive disability transitioning from high school. In each case, the assistive technology and the human-computer interface reduced the work-load of short-term memory to enhance the usability of the given Website. The technologies and human-computer interactions are as follows:

1. Keyboard equivalents for mouse-driven commands;
2. Captioned audio portions of multimedia files
3. Appropriate markup of tables, alternative text, abbreviations, and acronyms; synchronization of visual, speech, and Braille display
4. Use of supplemental graphics; freezing animated graphics; multiple search options
5. Magnification; stopping scrolling text; avoiding pop-up windows
6. Clear and simple language; consistent design
7. Consistent navigation options
8. Multiple search options (W3C, ¶ 2)

CONCLUSION AND RECOMMENDATIONS

Web accessibility, especially human-centered, is an ideology because it involves an effort to change the traditional Web culture into digital inclusion, whereby the Web design meets an individual's spe-

Table 2. Categories of disabilities and corresponding numbers and percentages of students ages 6 to 21 served in the 2003-2004 school year

Disability	IDEA, Part B	
	Number	Percentage of total disability population
Special learning disabilities	2,858,260	47.4
Speech or language impairments	1,127,551	18.7
Mental retardation	581,706	9.6
Emotional disturbance	483,850	8.0
Multiple disabilities	132,333	2.2
Hearing impairments	71,903	1.2
Orthopedic impairments	68,188	1.1
Other health impairments	452,045	7.5
Autism	140,920	2.3
Visual impairments	25,814	0.43
Traumatic brain injury	25,534	0.37
Developmental delay	65,921	1.09
Deaf-blindness	1,667	0.03

cial needs considering the user's social, cultural, physical, and cognitive characteristics. Access to the Web translates into access to knowledge and information that enable people to work in a digital society, and therefore, be digitally included. Access to information in turn, translates into access to society and the world. The Web must be accessible to all individuals, regardless of any physical or intellectual disabilities one may have. In order to ensure Web accessibility, guidelines such as the W3C standards and federal legislation such as Section 508 of the Rehabilitation Act have been developed.

It is important to research and design a human-computer interface that will enhance the usability and effectiveness of communication between the users, and between users and technology. Based on the error and cognitive processing models presented here, cognitive, psychomotor, and affective domains should be considered when the user interface is developed. As illustrated, the activities of action planning and storage take place at the knowledge and skill level in the cognitive domain. Execution occurs based on judgment, experience or preference. Execution is related to the affective domain. One of the most effective ways to reduce error is to present conceptual models/frameworks (Nielson, 1993; Jonassen, Strobel, & Gottdenker, 2005), which enable Web users to construct knowledge of how to navigate, determine what can be done, and the sequence of work, with little cognitive demand. Thus, conceptual models help Web users explain and interpret (a) how to access information and technology, (b) how to adapt the context of the interface, and (c) how to communicate with the computer, itself. Jonassen et al. (1995) argued that users can build cognitive strategies to reason, engage, support, and assess information using the qualitative and quantitative model.

Web accessibility must be differentiated and individualized to meet the individual's special needs. Developing effective interfaces for individuals with disabilities involves (a) identifying the user's purpose of digital activity, b) identifying the information and placing it sequentially and, (c) if possible, applying Bloom's five learning objective levels: knowledge, comprehension, analysis, synthesis and evaluation. This classification scheme will improve communication between the information and technology. The relationship between processing and acquiring information is better-linked, and the information is more efficiently retrieved. The levels will provide insight into information processing and individuals with disabilities may interact with the technology simply and easily. In addition, strategies using short-term memory have been adapted from memory strategies for exceptional children and youth, such as (a) chunking information by dividing it into multiple pages, (b) repeating patterned rules to navigate a site, (c) representing meaningful, functional information, and (d) categorizing of information (Hunt & Marshall, p.128). Sound or visual effects, such as feedback or cues at certain intervals, will enhance attention by making hard-to-view items visible.

In a digital age, technology is always present—anywhere, any time. Winner (1980) argued that technology structures the mode of communication, work and consumption in a society. Technology is a pattern of modern culture; it is not just technological device (Borgmann, 1984). Intertwined with cultural, societal and economic factors, the Web is a subculture of modern technology. It is a structure by which we communicate and connect with the external world. In today's digital information society, information is knowledge and can be used as a tool with which people can work (Bowen, Bereiter, & Scardamalia, 1992). The Web is a major source for acquiring information and connecting with the world, especially for the people with physical and intellectual limitations; all without the limitations of time and space. Therefore, all individuals need access to the Web, thus allowing them more opportunities to access and process information independently (Gilbert & Driscoll, 2002).

To meet the needs of our modern technological culture, the number of Web sites continues to increase. With this increase, concerns regarding the quality of Web sites and Web accessibility arise. A major concern is the need for evaluation strategies of Web site effectiveness, and usability, and a system of moral principles or ethics. Other concerns involve (a) the importance of knowing what factors of Web designs maximize Web accessibility, (b) how best to structure content and information for Web delivery and accessibility, and (c) how to evaluate accessibility in a manner that is valid and reliable, while also providing evidence on how to improve the quality of Web information. Given the growth in Web accessibility and the varied circumstances under which it is offered, evaluation instruments and processes are needed to ensure societal, cultural, educational, technical, and economic equity of high-quality Web accessibility.

REFERENCES

Belanger, F., & Jordan, D. (2000). *Evaluating and implementation of distance learning: Technologies, tools, and techniques.* Hershey, PA: Idea Group Publishing.

Bloom, S. B., Engelhart, D. M., Frust, J. E., Hill, H. W., & Krathwohl, R. D. (Eds.). (1956). *Taxonomy of educational objectives; Book 1. Cognitive domain.* New York: Longman, Inc.

Bowie, N., Adler, P., Civille, J., & Gill, J. (1996). *Harvard conference on the Internet & society.* Harvard University.

Bradbrook, G., & Fisher, J. (2004). Digital equality—Reviewing digital inclusion activity and mapping the way forwards. Retrieved October 18, 2007, from http://www.btplc.com/Societyandenvironment/PDF/Digitaldivide2025.pdf

Brinck, T., Gergle, D., & Wood, S. (2002). *Usability for the Web.* Amsterdam: Elsevier.

Card, S. K., Moran, T. P., & Newell, A. (1983). *The psychology of human computer interaction.* Hillsdale, NJ: Lawrence Erlbaum.

Card, S. K., Moran, T. P., & Newell, A. (2005). GOMS model. Retrieved October 18, 2007, from http://tip.psychology.org/card.html

Carey, J. M. (Ed). (1991). *Vision, instruction, and action.* Cambridge, MA: The MIT Press.

Carter, C. (2004). Providing for students with disabilities. An academic library. *Education Libraries, 27*(2), 13-18.

Chisolm, W., Jacobs, I, & Vanderheiden, G. (2000). Techniques for Web content accessibility guidelines 1.0. Retrieved October 18, 2007, from http://www.w3.org/TR/WAI-WEBCONTENT-TECHS/

Duffy, T. M., & Jonassen, D. H. (1992). *Constructivism and the technology of instruction: A conversation.* Hillsdale, NJ: Lawrence Erlbaum Associates.

Gibson, J. J. (1986). *The ecological approach to visual perception.* Hillsdale, NJ: Erlbaum Associates.

Harris, D. (1999). Internet-based learning tools. In D. French, C. Hale, C. Johnson, & G. Farr (Eds.), *Internet based learning* (pp. 165-177). Sterling, VA: Stylus.

Hodell, C. (2000). *ISD from the ground up: A no-nonsense approach to instructional design.* Alexandria, VA: ASTD.

Hunt, N., & Marshall, K. (2006). *Exceptional children and youth.* Wilmington, MA: Houghton Mifflin.

Jaeger, P. (2006). Assessing section 508 compliance on federal e-government Web sites: A multiple-method, user-centered evaluation of accessibility for persons with disabilities. *Government Information Quarterly, 23,* 169-190.

Jonassen, D. H., Davidson, M., Collins, M., Campbell, J., & Hagg, B. (1995). Constructivism and computer-mediated communication in distance education. *American Journal of Distance Education, 9*(2), 7-26.

Jonassen, D. H., Strobel, J., & Gottdenker, J. (2005). Model building for conceptual change. *Interactive Learning Environments, 13*(1-2), 15-37.

Miller, K. L., & Miller, S. M. (1999). Using instructional theory to facilitate communication in Web-based courses. *Educational Technology & Society 2*(3), 1-11. Retrieved October 18, 2007, from http://ifets.ieee.org/periodical/vol_3_99/miller.html

Nielsen, J. (1993). *Usability engineering.* Cambridge, MA: AP Professional.

Norman, D. (2002). *The design of everyday things.* New York: Basic Books.

Rasmussen, J. (1986). *Information processing and human-machine interaction: An approach to cognitive engineering.* Amsterdam: Elsevier Science.

Reason, J. (1990). *Human error.* Cambridge, UK: Cambridge University Press.

Reisner, P. (1987). Discussion: HCI, what is it and what research is needed? In J. M. Carroll (Ed.), *Interfacing thought: Cognitive aspects of human-computer interaction* (pp. 337-341). Cambridge, MA: MIT Press.

Rumelhart, D., & Ortony, A. (1977). The representation of knowledge in memory. In R. C. Atkinson, R. J. Herrnstein, G. Lindzey, & R. D. Luce (Eds.). *Steven's handbook of experimental psychology: Learning and cognition* (pp. 99-135). Hillsdale, NJ: Erlbaum Associates.

Section 508. (2006). Section 508 standards. Retrieved October 18, 2007, from http://www.section508.gov/index.cfm?FuseAction=Content&ID=12#Web

Thatcher, J. (2006). Web accessibility. Retrieved October 18, 2007, from http://www.jimthatcher.com/whatnot.htm

Turnbull, A., Turnbull, H., & Wehmeyer, M. (2005). *Exceptional lives: Special education in today's schools* (5th ed.). Upper Saddle River, NJ: Prentice Hall.

Wilson, B., Teslow, J., & Osman-Jouchoux, R. (1995). The impact of constructivism (and postmodernism) on ID fundamentals. In B. B. Seels (Ed.), *Instructional design fundamentals: A review and reconsideration* (pp.137-157). Englewood Cliffs, NJ: Educational Technology Publications.

Winner. L. (1980). Do artifacts have politics? *Journal of the American Academy of Arts and Sciences, 109*(1).

Wisdom, J., White, N., Goldsmith, K., Bielavitz, S., Davis, C., & Drum, C. (2006). An assessment of Web accessibility knowledge and needs at Oregon community colleges. *Community College Review, 33*(3), 19-37.

Wood, J. (2006). *Teaching students in inclusive settings.* Upper Saddle River, NJ: Pearson.

W3C - World Wide Web Consortium, (2005). Web content accessibility guidelines 1.0. Retrieved October 18, 2007, from http://www.w3.org/WAI/intro/accessibility.php

KEY TERMS

Americans with Disabilities Act (ADA): A civil rights legislation that protects people with disabilities from discrimination against them in four major areas: 1) private-sector employment, 2) public services, 3) public accommodations, and 4) telecommunications.

Cognitive Processing Models: Models developed by cognitive constructivists emphasizing effective strategies for building knowledge.

Domains of Instructional Objectives: Cognitive, psychomotor, affective and interpersonal domains addressing (a) the process of the mind, (b) motor skills or physical movement, (c) individuals' attitudes and feelings, and (d) interactivity between individuals.

GOMS Model: A cognitive model of human computer interaction consisting of four components: (a) Goals to be achieved in the process, (b) Operators performing the sequencing methods and interacting with the system, (c) Methods representing the sequences of the tasks performed by the operators, and (d) Selection rules choosing the best strategies and solutions for the best methods to obtain the goals.

Human-Centered Interface Design: A system used to analyze and synthesize an individual's needs, cultural practice, cognitive ability, and preference with the measurable goal and function in a certain context, using cognitive, psychomotor, and affective constructs.

Section 508: A law implemented to ensure that government Web sites are accessible. The law now extends to include all schools that are provided with federal and state funds

Web Accessibility: Equal accessibility and opportunity to the Web for all the individuals, especially for individuals with disabilities.

Chapter XIII
Usability–Oriented Quality Model Based on Ergonomic Criteria

Francisco Montero
University of Castilla-La Mancha, Spain

María Dolores Lozano
University of Castilla-La Mancha, Spain

Pascual González
University of Castilla-La Mancha, Spain

ABSTRACT

World Wide Web software development is a challenge. The need to provide appealing and attractive user interfaces is combined with the fact that the World Wide Web is not merely an information transfer tool anymore. The capacity to offer additional services plays an important role. The World Wide Web makes these services available to a greater number of individuals who have different characteristics, knowledge and profiles. The World Wide Web demands quick development with high quality level. This chapter makes an important contribution in the field of software product characterization for the World Wide Web, proposing a quality model that focuses on quality in use or usability. Said quality model, which has been partially tested on real users through several experiments, is based on international standards and ergonomic criteria. The model has proved useful for organizing and applying the experience available in the development of user interfaces for Web applications and has improved noticeably its final quality in use.

INTRODUCTION

Information systems quality, from the point of view of the HCI community is centred on what users may personally experience when using a software product as a result of an interaction session with the system through its interface, whether it is a software interface or a hardware one.

Although the HCI community has traditionally used the international standards related with software quality definitions, its main goal is *interaction*, and *interaction* is always performed by means of a User Interface (UI) (Montero et al., 2003a). In this sense, we will start remembering the definition of the term *"User Interface"* just as we are going to use it in this chapter and then we will identify the elements that characterize the UI and how they can affect the interaction and how this interaction affect to the final quality of the product.

According to Bennett (1983) in a UI two models and two languages concur. The models have to do with the user, in the sense that the user has goals to achieve and tasks to perform and he conceives them in a certain way depending on his cognitive level and with the very system which is designed to support some functional requirements. The languages have to do with the way in which the designer allows the users to interact with the system—action language—and with the way in which the system presents the information to the user—presentation language.

All these elements have to be taken into account when considering the quality of the user interface. Reviewing some of the quality models that we can find in the literature (Boehm et al., 1978; McCall, Richards, & Walters, 1977; ISO 9126, etc.) and according to the definitions given for the different factors included in them, we can conclude that most of the elements involved in the UI can be agglutinated in one of these factors: **Usability**. Before the emergence of some of the standards, other authors had defined the concept of Usability by identifying some of these same characteristics that have been finally collected in the standards. For instance, many (Shackel, 1991; Schneiderman, 1992, Nielsen, 1992; Preece, 1994; Constantine & Lockwood, 1999) have characterized usability using different attributes as depicted in Table 11.

Nevertheless, usability refers not only to the User Interface, as the evolution that the term has suffered during its characterization reflects. In the following sections, we will present some tips to show that evolution.

The rest of the chapter is organized as follows: Next section gathers a deep analysis of the term *quality in use* or *Usability* and studies the way in which it can be considered within the software development process, defining some approaches to the Usability Engineering. We will also review some quality models proposed in the literature highlighting its main features and applications. Section 3 presents a proposal for quality assess-

Table 1. Comparison of definitions related with usability

Shackel	Shneiderman	Preece	Nielsen	Constantine & Lockwood
Effectiveness –speed	Performance speed	Productivity	Use Efficiency	Use Efficiency
learning- time	Time to learn	Learnability	Ease to be learned	Ease to be learned
Learning—attention	Remembering Duration	-	Retainability	Ease to be remembered
Effectiveness—errors	Error rate	Productivity	Security / Errors	Use Reliability
Attitude	Satisfaction	Actitude	Satisfaction	Satisfaction

ment, showing the quality model defined and its application in the development process. We finish the chapter with some conclusions and final remarks in section 4. Some key terms and their definitions are listed after the references section.

ANALYSING THE MULTIDIMENSIONAL CONCERNS OF USABILITY

As we can see from the previous considerations, usability is a complex and multidimensional term. Many different aspects converge in its definition. Some of them are objective and can be easily detected and measured but many others have a subjective nature what makes it more difficult to precise.

This section analyses the quality in use from its many different perspective in order to give a more accurate view of the term.

Usability is Presentation

The term *"friendly interface"* has been widely extended within the software development community, and with this term, the important role that the UI of a Software product had was emphasized. This term ceased to be used and at the beginning of the 80' it was replaced by the new term we are now talking about, the *Usability.*

Initially, this property acquired a purely product-dependent connotation, more concretely, regarding its interface. In this sense, we can find some definitions in which usability and ease of use are associated together, considering the ease of use mainly tied to the user interface of the product, that is to say, to its ease to be used, learned or understood. This point of view is the one recorded in the International Standards ISO 9126 or the ISO 14598 devoted to the evaluation of software products.

Traditionally, the Software Engineering discipline has associated the term usability with the UI and more specifically with the ease which a product can be used with, but this is only a partial view of the term (Bevan, 1999). Regarding Usability, different definitions and decompositions into criteria and subcriteria of a lower abstraction level have been proposed. Making a review of the International Standards, we can identify different definitions:

According to the IEEE Std.610.12-1990, *Usability* is the ease with which a user can learn to use, prepare the inputs and interpret the outputs of a system or component. According to ISO/IEC 9126-1 (2001), usability is the capacity of a software product to be understood, learned, used and be made attractive for the user when it is used under certain conditions.

Until now, as we have highlighted, usability is considered as part of the product, and specifically that part that makes it more difficult or easier to use.

Usability is Utilization

Similar to the view previously shown, there exists another conception of usability in which concepts related to the use, without forgetting the usefulness of the very product (Bevan, 1995). According to the ISO 9241-11 (1998), devoted to collect ergonomic requirements, the concept of usability can be defined as *"the level with which a product adapts to the user needs and can be used to achieve the goals with effectiveness, efficiency and satisfaction in a specific context of use."*

In the previous definition, *effectiveness* means that any software system should have clear objectives and these objectives should be reachable. A software system can be more or less effective regarding its goals, be it that they have not been defined explicitly or they are wrongly established or even the very development process has been derived towards some other different goals.

Figure 1. Framework in which usability is considered

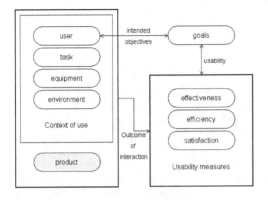

In order to evaluate it, designers should make explicit the goals to be achieved and check if the final users can accomplish them.

Efficiency depends on the users' skills and the software capacities. For this reason, the study of different types of users is needed to analyze this criterion. Efficiency results difficult to measure directly although it is possible to find indirect ratings. Especially, those factors that influence in it by making it increase or going down as for example: the ease to be learned, the ease to be remembered by the user, the feedback level regarding interaction or the control of errors.

Finally, the *satisfaction* level is a subjective state that is reached when the user achieves the goal of his activities and he does it in a satisfactory way.

The framework in which usability is considered is depicted in Figure *1*, where a software product in considered in a context of use, with certain goals, tasks to perform, an equipment and an environment of use. As a result of an interaction among all these elements, the user should achieve the desired goals with effectiveness, efficiency and satisfaction.

ANALYZING AND CONSIDERING THE CONCEPT OF QUALITY IN USE

The conclusions extracted from the previous study are a mixture of concepts dealing with, in some cases, the mere information presentation/visualization, and in other cases with the own application functionality.

The apparent discrepancy of definitions for the same concept has converged in the term *quality in use*. This new term is much closer to the usability concept. As a matter of fact, they are considered equivalents in the International Standard ISO 9126-4. This is the reason why, from now on, usability and quality in use will be considered equivalents and they will be used as such in the rest of this chapter.

The different facets that usability offers has provoked many attempts to achieve it and these attempts have been proposed from different abstraction levels and associated to many of the stages within a software product lifecycle.

It seems obvious that usability has to be considered in any software development and from the very beginning. In this sense, we can make use of the existing experience in different abstraction levels which embrace from general principles to very concrete style guides.

Figure 2. Usability engineering according to (Adapted from Folmer & Bosch, 2004)

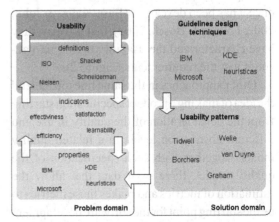

On the other hand, the application of a User-Centred Design (Norman, 1988) demands that before starting a project it is essential to characterize both the users and the more relevant and necessary aspects of the product. Taking into account all these considerations as early as possible we can save time and money, as the subsequent implementation of new concerns or simply new user interfaces implies a huge additional effort.

The main inconvenience of considering the integration of usability criteria within the development process is that this integration cannot be performed in a systematic way (Lozano et al., 2005) in spite of the widely known concept of *Usability Engineering* (Nielsen, 1993) which appeared 20 years ago.

The main reason for not considering the quality in use along the development process is the lack of experience on the elaboration and characterization of quality models and, related to this, the availability of established criteria which can determine the quality of a software product and, therefore, its quality in use. Currently, we have at our disposal factors, criteria and metrics that redound to a better quality in use, and what is missing is the integration of all these elements into the very development process.

There are authors that defend the consideration of the quality in use from the beginning and, besides, they have detected that there are elements at architectural level which determine the subsequent product development and maintenance once it has been developed (Bass, Kates, & John, 2002; Folmer & Bosch, 2004), that is to say, they have characterized the usability taking into account just the requirements (Figure *2*).

Other approaches in the same line too, defend the idea of making a product specification starting from the consideration of the quality in use and different abstraction levels in a related quality model. Together with such specification of the quality model, there exist data that allow the estimation of metrics and makes these metrics to be the starting point for the software development (Seffah & Abecassis, 2001).

Figure 3. Usability engineering according to (Adapted from Seffah & Abecassis, 2001)

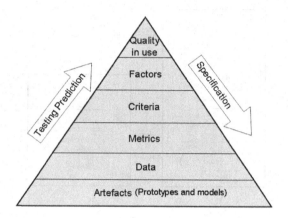

These contributions reflect what is shown in Figure *2*, where the relationship between the needs of a user, when using a software product, and the quality of use and also between the presence of evaluation processes (validation and verification) and the presence of quality internal and external metrics used to carry out said evaluation.

Therefore, we know when to establish usability criteria and which factors and criteria to establish. The latter are those identified in the different international standards observed and, according to those, we have identified metrics to check the performance of some of them, with the use of usability evaluation methods. Nevertheless, an inexperienced engineer in development lacks the expertise to select what and how to develop his/her project. In addition, some of the criteria established in the standards are still high level, which makes them difficult to achieve without the experience needed for the development in any of its stages.

There have been attempts to specify these general studies, which are applicable to interactive systems in general, and characterize them for Web sites which have certain features or a specific nature. From these tasks, we can highlight the QEM (Olsina, 1999) Web proposal, which follows the standard method of other models of describing software quality in terms of quality characteristics like those defined by the ISO/IEC 9126-1 standard. This proposal considers attributes as the properties of an entity that can be measured and it suggests using a quality model to specify them. WebQEM is a quantitative evaluation model used for measuring application and Web site quality. The characteristics of the quality to be measured, suggested by Olsina are: functionality, reliability, efficiency, portability, upkeep capacity and usability. At the same time, usability involves operability, communicativeness, esthetics and style and functionality. Another relevant proposal is Web Tango (Ivory & Hearst, 2001). The Ivory quality model focuses in the development of a methodology which fits into a framework of a completely automatic evaluation model to measure Web site quality. This allows the designers to evaluate the usability of their designs in the early stages of the development with a low resource cost. Ivory has identified and calculated a great number of Web site quantitative measures and has used them to derive statistical models for Web sites having high scores in quality ratings. Therefore, the methodology consists of the computation of a set of 157 metric quantitative measures at a Web page and Web site level, such as: number of fonts, images and words, based on a design recommendation study by known experts and different usability treaties.

Lastly, another outstanding model is the WQM Web site quality model proposed by Mario Piattini and Coral Calero (Ruiz et al., 2003). This is a global Web-quality model which, just like the rest of the models reviewed, is motivated by the need to develop Web applications with quality criteria to avoid poor performance and mistakes. The model came about because it is necessary to classify the metrics and research projects on the World Wide Web, since there are no standards or brainstorming ideas on all the existing initiatives up to now. This model does not exclude other quality models, but rather tries to compile them. It defines three dimensions: Web characteristic,

Figure 4. WQM Quality Model (Adapted from Ruiz et al., 2003)

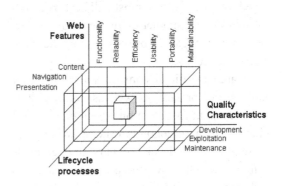

quality characteristic and life cycle process. Notice that Figure *4* is the graphic representation of this model including all three dimensions which compose it and the characteristics of each one.

As seen in the Web-quality models and methodology revision, there is no standard in this field. The only existing agreement in this field is the quality characteristics for software interfaces defined by the organization for international standards ISO 9126 and the widely accepted accessibility guidelines, such as: *Web Accessibility Initiative* (WAI) (WAI99) and Section 508 (Sec508). These are suggested in order to ensure Web quality.

QUALITY ASSESSMENT PROPOSAL

The main problem we face when assessing quality, or any factor it depends on, is that depending on the group the assessor belongs to, be it user, engineer or expert, he or she will associate this concept to his or her best interest. That malleability of the concept of quality makes it inaccurate and conditions its attainment. In IS, the tendency is for software industrialization and the important things are factors such as maintenance simplicity. In HCI, the priority is usability. There is no closed quality model, but there is a first level of quality breakdown, extended and accepted. It is the one associated to standard 9126. From here on, the use of open quality models where everyone considers that which interests him most will be advocated. The solution, as in other fields, depends on how the context is regarded or the domain where the solution is decided.

Because the dimensions offered by the user interface are process as well as product, it is necessary to keep an eye on both. To do so, we believe that the ergonomic criteria are ideal to continue with the development of an open quality model which allows the presence of a series of characteristics to approach the development as well as the evaluation process, and indirectly, its maintenance.

Since ergonomics is the study of work in relation to the environment where it is carried out (the workplace) and with those it is carried out with (the workers), we have relied on ergonomic criteria as defining elements in our quality assessment proposal. With them, it is possible to determine the design or adapting of the workplace to the worker to avoid health problems and increase efficiency. In other words, adapt the job to the worker instead of making the worker adapt himself/herself to the workplace. The criteria which we deem worthy of consideration are Bastien and Scapin's (1993)

ergonomic criteria. They can be integrated with the quality model proposed in standard 9126. With this, we are trying to achieve a quality model based on quality criteria very close to the user and we make reference to those criteria which the user can manage and understand. Said model carries with it experience and, if available, metrics, with which greater action power is obtained.

There are experiments which back up the conclusions observed before. See Figure 5 (Bastien & Scapin, 1996, and Chevalier & Ivory, 2003).

Figure 5 shows the graphical representation of an experiment observed in Bastien, Scapin, and Leulier (1996). We deduce from it that there are criteria, ergonomic criteria, which are not dealt with in the standards, at least not directly, and which enable the identification of a greater number of problems than other more general criteria, which are accepted by the international standards. Notice that these criteria have not been used in the elaboration of quality models. One of

Figure 6. Ergonomic criteria proposed in (Adapted from Bastien & Scapin, 1993)

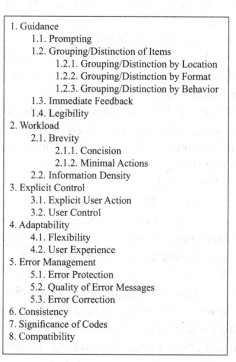

```
1. Guidance
    1.1. Prompting
    1.2. Grouping/Distinction of Items
            1.2.1. Grouping/Distinction by Location
            1.2.2. Grouping/Distinction by Format
            1.2.3. Grouping/Distinction by Behavior
    1.3. Immediate Feedback
    1.4. Legibility
2. Workload
    2.1. Brevity
            2.1.1. Concision
            2.1.2. Minimal Actions
    2.2. Information Density
3. Explicit Control
        3.1. Explicit User Action
        3.2. User Control
4. Adaptability
        4.1. Flexibility
        4.2. User Experience
5. Error Management
        5.1. Error Protection
        5.2. Quality of Error Messages
        5.3. Error Correction
6. Consistency
7. Significance of Codes
8. Compatibility
```

Figure 5. Usability assessment results using ergonomic criteria and international standards (Adapted from Bastien & Scapin, 1996)

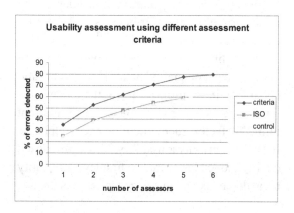

the proposals discussed in this chapter is subject to the consideration of these qualitative criteria for the elaboration of a quality model.

Table 2 shows the original quality model which served as a basis for the elaboration of our proposal (Montero et al., 2003b, 2003c).

The quality model's main characteristics shown in Table 2 are:

- **It is based on international standards**, such as ISO 9126 or ISO 9241 related to quality and others like ISO 13407 and 18529.
- **It is open.** New quality criteria can be incorporated, joining those already identified.
- **It is closed** and can be used to help in the implementation of user interface assessment techniques (Bastien et al., 1999; Chevalier & Ivory, 2003).

- **The use of ergonomic criteria** has proved to be efficient, not only in the undertaking of user interface design meant for the World Wide Web (Scapin et al., 2000), but also for other interfaces: traditional interfaces (Scapin & Bastien, 1997) and virtual environments (Bach & Scapin, 2000).
- **It enables the implementation of design techniques focused on the user** since it is possible to describe quality by using ergonomic criteria. This has been proved empirically with the elaboration of different experiments carried out with real users (Scapin & Bastien, 1997; Chevalier & Ivory, 2003).
- At the same time, ergonomic criteria have proved useful for **style guides organization** tasks related to usability (Scapin &

Table 2. Quality model proposal focusing on usability

Quality	Factor[1]	Criterion[2]	Cont.[3]
Usability	Understandability	compatibility	H
		legibility	M
		prompting	M
		immediate feed-back	H
		significance of codes and behaviour	H
		helpfulness	M
	Learnability	Grouping	H
		minimal actions	H
		conciseness	L
		information density	M
		consistency	H
	Operability	explicit user action	H
		user control	H
		user experience's	H
		flexibility	M
		error protection	H
		quality of error messages	L
		error correction	M
		privacy policies	L
		accessibility	H

Bastien, 2000). This enables us to use them to organize other types of experience.

The previous characteristics justify choosing ergonomic criteria as an element which can be integrated into a quality model proposal focusing on usability, where the aspects related to the conception of the software product beginning from the dimensions it offers as a product and as a process are considered. The ergonomic criteria are shown in Figure 6.

In our proposal, new criteria have been added to the ergonomic criteria, associating them to the quality criteria defined in the standard 9126 and directly linked to usability; that is, to the *understandability, learnability and operability* characteristics. The added criteria take into account aspects related to the helpfulness offered, to the privacy policies which determine the handling of the information obtained by means of the user interface and to the accessibility of the very interface.

The quality model proposed is a principal support element for design quality and experience and depending on that, it can be used in two directions (Montero, 2005): (a) to help in the assessment tasks of the interfaces generated, bearing in mind all the time, quality characteristics very close to the user and to the way in which he/she perceives quality; and (b) metrics can obviously be added to criteria. Our following proposal requires not limiting itself to only this, but using the quality model to organize the available experience, in any of its formats, to deal with user interfaces development tasks.

The advantages of having a quality model available require giving support to designers and developers, especially to inexperienced ones. The model has a lot of experience available in different formats and abstraction levels. One of the most widely used ways to document experience is through the use of style guides. Many style guides are useful to ensure consistency in the development of applications for certain plat-

Figure 7. Quality model and evaluation process

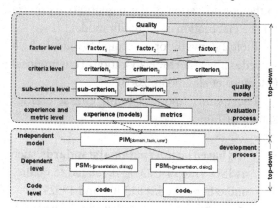

forms, companies (Microsoft, Apple, IBM, etc.) or groups of users. Said consistency is one of the desired quality principles in any software product, but it is also important to take into account many other principles, factors and criteria. One of the crucial decisions is deciding which principles to apply, because different situations and contexts require making different choices.

Here, ergonomic criteria are used for evaluation tasks as well as to tackle experience organization tasks. To be able to tackle both challenges, the criteria are used as quality criteria and subcriteria associated to the quality factors established and proposed in international standards. Ergonomic criteria, which follow a hierarchical breakdown common in quality model proposals, are situated in the levels meant for criteria and subcriteria consideration and would have experience or metrics associated, depending on whether we can find exact ways to measure certain quality parameters.

Criteria Related to *Understandability*

Next, we will describe each of the ergonomic criteria taken from Bastien and Scapin (1993) and those criteria we consider relevant enough to be taken into account for the elaboration of the quality model which came up in the previous section and which are related to how easy an application or software product is to understand (understandability).

The criteria considered in this section are: *compatibility, legibility, prompting, immediate feedback, significance of codes and behavior and helpfulness.*

By *compatibility*, we mean the establishment or search for a proper relationship between the user's characteristics and the organization of inputs, outputs and dialogue too. For example, dialogues should reflect organization or data structure which the user perceives naturally.

By *legibility*, we mean the lexical characteristics of the information presented on the screen, such as labels, titles or cursors.

By *prompting*, we mean the assistance provided to facilitate the carrying out of input operations and, along with those, the necessary assistance to let the user know the alternatives available when several actions are possible. An example of this would be to visualize the measuring units for each value to be provided or indicate to him/her how certain data, which must follow a format, must be provided.

Immediate *feedback* is related to how the system responds to the actions performed by the user. An example of this criterion would be those style guides which recommend that an input from the user get translated into a visible element. If the data introduced were confidential or should be concealed, they must be shown associated to a symbol such as an asterisk, which would prevent it from being seen.

Offering the *significance of codes and behavior* criterion entails the existence of a correspondence for each term and the metaphoric symbol which refers to the same. The codes should be significant and familiar, rather than arbitrary.

Lastly, we have included the *helpfulness* criterion in this section dedicated to relating those criteria, relevant enough, in providing assistance with the comprehension of the software product. The *helpfulness* criterion alludes to the help provided whenever it is regarded adequate to include

a section which offers explicit assistance or additional information about the available task or tasks.

Criteria Related to *Learnability*

In this section, we will show the definitions which correspond to the quality criteria that have to do with the obtaining of additional assistance related to the effort needed to learn how to use a software product (*learnability*).

Out of this group of criteria, we consider it appropriate to bear in mind subcriteria, such as: information and control *grouping*, of any kind (manner or location), *minimal actions, conciseness, information density* and *consistency*. With the *grouping* criterion, we emphasize the need that in order to make the user learn and remember how a software product works, it is necessary to have thought about the organization of the interface elements which make it up, whether they are information or action elements. For this, a clear visual distinction of areas which offer different functions should be provided.

The cut down to *minimal actions* to undertake user's tasks and objectives is essential to learn and remember the tasks that the user can perform using the software product. For example, the cut down of necessary steps to select something from a menu will be a very coveted characteristic.

Conciseness is the criterion through which we consider the use of all recommendations so that the user has the minimum cognitive and perceptive load possible when using a software product. If, for example, a user has to provide information, this information should also be able to be provided by using mnemonics or abbreviations or for certain filling-in values to appear automatically.

Information density is a criterion which, related to the previous one, would have repercussions on the cognitive and perceptive load which a user must exert when using a software product. In this case, the emphasis is on the information as a set, instead of as an individual element. Providing the necessary and useful information to perform an operation and not overloading with unnecessary additional information is a recommendation toward this goal.

Consistency is the criterion through which similar design guidelines are used to tackle design in similar contexts. For example, the fact that the title of the different windows associated to a software product always appear in the same place or that the font formats, screen or access to the functionality are significant examples toward achieving consistency.

Criteria Related to *Operability*

The third coveted group of criteria in a software product is marked by another component which can be associated to usability, according to the definitions available in international standards. This criterion is none other than the easiness to operate the very software product (*operability*).

We have associated the following subcriteria to the operability of a software product: *explicit user action, user control, user experience, flexibility, error protection, quality error messages and error correction, privacy policies* and *accessibility.*

With explicit user action, the relationship between the processing carried out with the device and the actions carried out with the user are emphasized. For example, the need for the user to press the ENTER button to start the processing which leads to updating or changing a context is a recommendation toward this.

User control refers to the fact that users should always be the ones to control the processing carried out with the device. The availability of a CANCEL/BACK button that offers the possibility to erase any change made by the user and restore it to the previous state is an example of achieving these criteria.

Users' experience and flexibility are the criteria that recommendations which redound to the easiness of adaptability and adaptation of a software

product are considered. The first characteristic is inherent to the software product. That is, the product would automatically carry out or suggest the adaptation to the user. On the contrary, the user's experience would depend on the user's ability to modify the device and adapt it to his/her preference or experience.

Error protection, quality of error messages and *error correction* are other criteria which are to the advantage of processing, which the user perceives when using his/her software product.

Lastly, two other criteria, such as privacy policies and helpfulness, which are to the advantage of action and content accessibility, are also considered in the quality model of this section, although they are not included in the ergonomic criteria proposal.

CONCLUSION

Quality has proved to be a confusing concept regarding its description and characterization. Even though there are international standards, they are not complete and remain at a very superficial level. At any rate, the international community realizes the need and resulting advantages of having a universal quality model available (Montero et al., 2003c).

One of the principal limitations of characterizing the quality of a software product is the depth offered by the quality models proposed. A full quality characterization offered by a software product is, probably, neither necessary nor possible (Olsina et al., 2001), besides being subjective and dependent on the specific needs established for each software product developed under the influence of use context and the characteristics of the final users of said product.

In this chapter, there is also a reference to a series of ergonomic criteria (Bastien & Scapin, 1993) which, backed up by a series of experiments described and through which we justify their use for interface assessment tasks and style guide classification, can be used to become part of a quality model proposal focused on usability (Montero et al., 2003b).

That is why this chapter ends with the presentation and proposal of a quality model focused on usability. This model is elaborated by means of first-level of usability breakdown criteria, taken as usability factors, based on international standards, and the use of ergonomic criteria to foster breakdown. The advantage of this second-level breakdown is in the availability of a set of criteria which offers an assessment version and can be used to tackle user interface assessment tasks. This has been tried and tested. The ergonomic criteria used have been integrated in the quality model proposed and are linked to experience and metrics to carry out their assessment. Including experience in the quality model is an important contribution which will enable the guiding of inexperienced designers to obtain quality developments. This quality model has been used, with some modifications, in adaptive agent-based tutoring systems (Lopez-Jaquero et al., 2003) and it has been validated using several experiments (García et al., 2006).

REFERENCES

Bach, C., & Scapin, D. L. (2003, September). *Adaptation of ergonomic criteria to human virtual environment.* In Proceedings of the Ninth IFIP TC13 International Conference on Human-Computer Interaction - INTERACT'03. 2003, Zurich, Switzerland, (pp. 880-883). Amsterdam: IOS Press.

Bass, L., Kates, J., & John, B. E. (2002). *Achieving usability through software architecture.* Retrieved October 18, 2007, from http://www.sei.cmu.edu/publications/documents/01.reports/01tr005.html

Bastien, J. M. C., & Scapin, D. L. (1993). *Ergonomic criteria for the evaluation of human-computer interfaces* (Rep. No. 156). Rocquencourt, France: Institut National de Recherche en Informatique et en Automatique.

Bastien J. M. C., Scapin, D., & Leulier, C. (1999). The ergonomic criteria and the ISO/DIS 9241-10 dialogue principles: A pilot comparison in an evaluation task. *Interacting with Computers 11*(3), 299-322.

Bennett, J. L. (1983). *Building decision support systems.* Reading, MA: Addison-Wesley.

Bevan, N. (1995). Usability is quality of use. In Y. Anzai, K. Ogawa, & H. Mori (Eds.), *Symbiosis of human and artifact: Future computing and design for human-computer interaction* (pp. 349-354).

Bevan, N. (1999). *Quality in use: Meeting user needs for quality.* Journal of System and Software. Research Manager at Serco Usability Services.

Boehm, B.W., Brown, J. R., Lipow, M., MacLeod, G. J., & Merritt, M. J. (1978). *Characteristics of software quality,* North-Holland, N.Y.

Chevalier, A., & Ivory, M. (2003, June 22-27). Can novice designers apply usability criteria and recommendations to make Web sites easier to use? In *Proceedings of the 10th International Conference on Human-Computer Interaction,* Crete, Greece, (Vol. 1, pp. 773-777).

Constantine, L. L., & Lockwood, L. A. D. (1999). *Software for use: A practical guide to the models and methods of usage centered design.* Addison-Wesley.

Folmer, E., & Bosch, J. (2004, January). Architecting for usability. *Journal of Systems and Software, 70*(1), 61-78.

García, F. J., Lozano, M., Montero, F., Gallud, J. A., González, P., & Lorenzo, C. (2006). A controlled experiment for measuring the usability of WebApps using patterns. *Enterprise information systems* Berlin: Springer.

IEEE Std 610.12-1990. (1990). *IEEE standard glossary of software engineering terminology, identi-*

fies terms currently in use in the field of software engineering. Standard definitions for those terms are established. Retrieved October 18, 2007, from http://standards.ieee.org/reading/ieee/std_public/description/se/610.12-1990_desc.html

ISO 9126-1. (2001). *Software engineering - product quality - Part 1: Quality model.*

ISO 9241-11. (1998). *Ergonomic requirements for office work with visual display terminals* (VDTs).

ISO/IEC Standard, ISO-9126. (1991). *Software product evaluation - Quality characteristics and guidelines for their use.*

Ivory, M. Y., & Hearst, M. A. (2001). The state of the art in automating usability evaluation of user interfaces. *ACM Computer Survey 33*(4), 470-516.

López-Jaquero, V., Montero, F., Fernández-Caballero, A., & Lozano, M. (2003, July 22-27). Usability metrics in adaptive agent-based tutoring systems. In *Proceedings of the 10th International Conference on Human - Computer Interaction (HCI, 2003),* Creta, Grecia.

Lozano, M., Montero, F., García, F. J., & Gonzalez, P. (2005). *Calidad en el desarrollo de aplicaciones web: modelos, métodos de evaluación y métricas de calidad.* Ingeniería de la web y patrones de diseño (Capítulo 8). Eds. Paloma Díaz, Susana Montero e Ignacio Aedo. Pearson Prentice Hall.

McCall, J. A., Richards, P. K., & Walters, G. F. (1977). *Factors in software quality,* RADC TR-77-369, US Rome Air Development Center Reports NTIS AD/A-049 014, 015, 055.

Montero, F. (2005). *Integración de calidad y experiencia en el desarrollo de interfaces de usuario dirigido por modelos.* Ph. Thesis. Escuela Politécnica Superior de Albacete. Universidad de Castilla-La Mancha. España.

Montero, F., Lozano, M., & González, P. (2003a). *Calidad en interfaces de usuario.* Calidad en el desarrollo y mantenimiento del software (Capítulo 5). Eds. Mario G. Piattini, Felix O. García. Editorial Ra-Ma.

Montero, F., Lozano, M., López-Jaquero, V., & González, P. (2003b, July 22-27). *A quality model for testing the usability of the Web sites.* In Proceedings of the 10th International Conference on Human - Computer Interaction (HCI, 2003), Creta, Grecia. Human-Computer Interaction: Theory and Practice (part 1). J. Jacko, C. Stephanidis (Eds.). Lawrence Erlbaum Associates. Londrés, Reino Unido.

Montero, F., López-Jaquero, V., Lozano, M., & González, P. (2003c). Usability and Web site evaluation: Quality models and user testing evaluations. *ICEIS*, (1), 525-528.

Nielsen, J. (1992, March). The usability engineering life cycle. *IEEE Computer, 25*(3), 12-22.

Nielsen, J. (1993). *Usability engineering.* Boston, MA: Academic Press.

Norman, D. (1988). *The design of everyday things.* New York: Doubleday.

Olsina, L. (1999). *Metodología cualitativa para la evaluación y comparación de la calidad de sitios Web.* Ph. Thesis. Facultad de Ciencias Exactas. Universidad de la Pampa. Argentina Olsina L., Papa, M. F., Souto, M. E., & Rossi, G. (2001). *Providing Automated Support for the Web Quality Evaluation Methodology,* Proceedings of the Fourth Workshop on Web Engineering, at the 10th International WWW Conference, Hong Kong, pp 1-11.

Preece, J. (1994). *Human-computer interaction.* Reading, MA: Addison-Wesley.

Scapin, D. L., & Bastien, J. M. C. (1997). Ergonomic criteria for evaluating the ergonomic quality of interactive systems. *Behaviour & Information Technology, 16*, 220-231.

Scapin, D. L., Vanderdonckt, J., Farenc, C., Bastide, R., Bastien, C., Leulier, C., et al. (2000). Transferring knowledge of user interfaces guidelines to the Web. In *Proceedings of the International Workshop on Tools for Working with Guidelines*, London: Springer-Verlag.

Schneiderman, B. (1992). *Designing the user interface* (2nd ed.). Reading, MA: Addison-Wesley.

Section 508. (n.d.). Retrieved October 18, 2007, from http://www.section508.gov/

Seffah, A., & Abecassis, W. (2001, May 11-13). Usability patterns as a bridge over the gap between usability practices and software engineering tools. In *Proceedings of the Symposium on Human-Computer Interaction Engineering,* Toronto, Canada.

Shackel, B. (1991). Usability—context, framework, design and evaluation. In B. Shackel & Richardson, (Eds*.), Human factors for informatics usability* (pp. 21-38). Cambridge University Press.

Ruiz, J., Calero, C., & Piattini, M. (2003). A three dimensional Web quality model. In *Proceedings of the Third International Conference on Web Engineering, ICWE 2003*, Asturias, Spain, (pp. 384-385).

W3C Web Accessibility Initiative (WAI). (n.d.). Retrieved October 18, 2007, from http://www.w3.org/WAI/

KEY TERMS

Quality in Use: The capability of the software product to enable specified users to achieve specified goals with effectiveness, productivity, safety and satisfaction in specified contexts of use.

Quality Model: A quality model specifies which properties are important for an artefact (e.g., its usability, its performance, its visibility) and how these properties are to be determined.

Quality: Quality is the totality of characteristics of an entity that bears on its ability to satisfy stated and implied needs.

Usability: Usability is the effectiveness, efficiency and satisfaction with which specified users achieve specified goals in particular environments (process-oriented definition). Usability is the capability of the software product to be understood, learned, used and attractive to the user, when used under specified conditions (product-oriented definition).

User Interface: The user interface (UI) is everything designed into an information device with which a human being may interact and how an application program or a Web site invites interaction and responds to it.

User-Centered Design: User-centered design (UCD) is a highly structured, comprehensive product development methodology driven by: clearly specified, task-oriented business objectives, and recognition of user needs, limitations and preferences.

Web Quality Model: A Web quality model is essentially a set of criteria that are used to determine if a Web site reaches certain levels of quality. Web quality models require also ways to assess if such criteria hold for a Web site.

ENDNOTES

1. At a factors level, the quality model proposed considers those criteria established by the usability standard ISO 9126.
2. At a criteria level, the characteristic considered are (Bastien et al., 1993)'s ergonomic criteria, and other added criteria (privacy policies, accessibility and helpfulness).
3. Refers to the estimated contribution by each criterion to the final usability.

Chapter XIV
The Usability Dimension in the Development of Web Applications

Maristella Matera
Politecnico di Milano, Italy

Francesca Rizzo
Politecnico di Milano, Italy

Rebeca Cortázar
University of Deusto, Spain

Asier Perallos
University of Deusto, Spain

ABSTRACT

Given the emergent need for usability, during last year's traditional development processes have been extended for enabling the fulfillment of usability requirements. Usability Evaluation Methods (UEMs) have been therefore proposed at any stage of the development process, to verify the usability of incremental design artifacts, as well as of the final product. This chapter surveys the most emergent UEMs, to be adopted during the whole lifecycle of Web information systems for promoting usability. For each evaluation method, the main features, as well as the emerging advantages and drawbacks are illustrated. Some future trends, related to the need of evaluating the usability of UEMs are also discussed.

INTRODUCTION

Usability is generally acknowledged as a factor of system quality representing the answer to many frustrating interactions with technology. It describes the quality of products and systems from the point of view of humans who use them.

Different definitions of usability have been so far proposed, which vary according to the models they are based on. Part 11 of the international standard ISO 9241 (*Ergonomic Requirements for Office Work with Visual Display Terminals*) provides guidance on usability, introducing requirements and recommendations to be used during application design and evaluation (ISO, 1997). The standard defines usability as "the extent to which a product can be used by specified users to achieve specified goals with effectiveness, efficiency and satisfaction in a specified context of use." In this definition, *effectiveness* means "the accuracy and completeness with which users achieve specified goals," *efficiency* refers to "the resources expended in relation to the accuracy and completeness with which users achieve goals," and *satisfaction* is described as "the comfort and acceptability of use." Usability problems therefore refer to aspects that make the application ineffective, inefficient, and difficult to learn and to use.

Although the ISO 9241-11 recommendations have become the standard for the usability specialists' community, the usability definition most widely adopted is the one introduced by Nielsen (Nielsen, 1993). It provides a detailed model in terms of usability constituents that are suitable to be objectively and empirically verified through different evaluation methods. According to the Nielsen's definition, usability refers to a number of dimensions:

- **Learnability:** the ease of learning the functionality and the behavior of the system.
- **Efficiency:** the level of attainable productivity, once the user has learned the system.
- **Memorability:** the ease of remembering and recognizing the system functionality, so that the casual user can return to the system after a period of nonuse, without needing to pay attention again on how to use it.
- **Few errors:** the capability of the system to feature a low error rate, to support users making few errors during the use of the system, and in case they make errors, to help them to easy recover.
- **User's satisfaction:** the measure in which the user finds the system pleasant to use.

The previous principles can be further specialized and decomposed into finer-grained criteria that can be verified through different evaluation methods. The resulting advantage is that more precise and measurable criteria contributes toward setting an engineering discipline, where usability is not just argued, but is systematically approached, evaluated and improved (Nielsen, 1993).

When applying usability to Web applications, some refinements need to be operated over the general definitions, to capture the specificity of this application class. Main tasks for the Web include: finding desired information and services by direct searches or discovering new ones by browsing; understanding the information presented; invoking and executing services specific to certain Web applications, such as the ordering and downloading of products. Paraphrasing the ISO definition, Web usability can be therefore considered as the ability of Web applications to support the previous tasks with effectiveness, efficiency and satisfaction. Also, the above mentioned Nielsen's usability principles can be interpreted as follows (Nielsen, 2000):

- **Learnability** must be interpreted as the ease for Web users to identify in the Home Page the contents and services made available through the application, and how to look for specific information using the available links for hypertext browsing. Learnability also means that each page in the hypertext front-end should be composed in a way so as contents are easy to understand and navigational mechanisms are easy to identify.
- **Efficiency** means that users who want to find some contents can reach them quickly through the available links. Also, when users get to a page, they must be able to orient themselves and understand the meaning of the page with respect to their navigation starting point.

- **Memorability** implies that, after a period of nonuse, users are still able to get oriented within the hypertext, for example by means of navigation bars pointing to landmark pages.
- **Few errors** means that in case users have erroneously followed a link, they should be able to return to their previous location, thus recovering easily.
- **Users' satisfaction** finally refers to the situation in which users feel that they are in control with respect to the hypertext, thanks to the comprehension of available contents and navigational commands.

Applying principles for the design of usable Web applications is not sufficient for ensuring the usability of the final product. Even though accurate design techniques are used, it is still necessary to check the intermediate results, and test the final application for verifying if it actually shows the expected features and meets the user requirements. The role of *evaluation*, as a set of methods and tools augmenting the standard development processes, is to help verifying explicitly usability issues.

Defining methods for ensuring the usability of Web applications is one of the current goals of the research in Web Engineering and Human-Computer Interaction. Also, much attention on usability is currently paid by the industry, which is recognizing the importance of adopting usability methods during the development process, for verifying the usability of Web applications before and after their deployment. Some studies have in fact demonstrated how the use of such methods enables cost saving, with a high cost-benefit ratio, since they reduce the need for changes after the application delivery (Nielsen, 1993; Nielsen & Mack, 1994).

This chapter surveys the most relevant usability evaluation methods and tools. For each of them, the main features, as well as the advantages and drawbacks are illustrated. The chapter aims to provide useful concepts and principles that can

support the definition of evaluation plans that best fit the goals to be pursued by a Web application as well as the available resources. The chapter also discusses the always increasing demand for *evaluating the usability of usability evaluation methods,* as it results from the need of: *i)* more effective, efficient and easy to use evaluation methods, and of *ii)* metrics and procedures for evaluating such properties into an evaluation method (Gray & Salzman, 1998; John, 1996; Hartson, Andre, & Williges, 2001).

BACKGROUND

Given the emergent need for usability, during last years traditional development processes have been extended for enabling the fulfillment of usability requirements. usability evaluation methods (UEMs) have been therefore proposed at any stage of the process, to verify the usability of incremental design artifacts, as well as of the final product. This has resulted into the proposal of the so-called *iterative design* (Preece et al., 1994; Conallen, 2002) for promoting usability throughout the whole product lifecycle.

Iterative design is now the most prominent approach for the development of Web applications. The various activities in the development process are repeated and refined until results meet the application requirements. The product lifecycle therefore undergoes several cycles, each producing a prototype or a partial version of the application. At each iteration, the current version of the application is tested and evaluated and then extended or modified to cope with the previously collected requirements, as well as the newly emerged requirements. Such an iterative and incremental lifecycle appears particularly appropriate for the Web context, where applications must be deployed quickly (in "Internet time") and requirements are likely to change during development. Figure 11 illustrates the typical activities in the iterative development of a Web application, as defined in several well-know methodologies for

Figure 1. The iterative design for Web application development (Ceri et al., 2002)

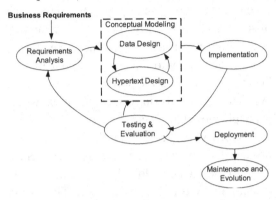

Web application design (Fraternali, 1999; Ceri et al., 2002; Conallen, 2002).

The essence of iterative design is therefore that the only way to be sure about the effectiveness and efficiency of some design decisions is to build prototypes and evaluate them through the use of evaluation methods. The design can be then modified, to correct any false assumption detected during the evaluation activities, or to accommodate new emerged requirements; the cycle of design, evaluation, and redesign, must be repeated as often as necessary.

In this context, evaluation is intended as an extension of testing, carried out through the use of prototypes, with the aim of verifying the application design against usability requirements. Evaluation is central in this model: it is relevant at all the stages in the lifecycle, not only at the end of the product development. All the aspects of the application development are in fact subject to constant evaluation involving both expert evaluators and users. Such need for a constant evaluation also demands for "discount usability engineering," which consists in the adoption of easy to apply, but still efficient, evaluation methods, so as to encourage developers to consider usability issues throughout the whole development cycle (Nielsen, 1993).

The main goals of UEMs are to assess the application functionality, to verify the effect of its interface on the user, and to identify any specific problem with the application, such as functions that show unexpected effects when used in their intended context. Evaluating Web applications in particular consists in verifying whether the application design allows users to easily retrieve and browse contents, and invoke available services and operations. This objective therefore implies not only having appropriate contents and services available into the application, but also making them easily reachable by users through appropriate hypertexts.

Depending on the phase in which evaluation is performed, it is possible to distinguish between *formative* evaluation, which takes place during design, and *summative* evaluation, which takes place after the product has been developed, or even when any prototype version is ready. During the early design stages the goal of the formative evaluation is to check the design team understanding of the users' requirements, and to test design choices quickly and informally, thus providing feedback to the design activities. Later on, the summative evaluation can support the detection of users' difficulties, and the improvement and the upgrading of the product.

Within these two broad categories, there are different UEMs that can be used at different stages of the product development. The UEMs most commonly adopted are *user testing*, where the performance of real users is studied, and *usability inspection*, which is conducted by specialists. Recently, *Web usage analysis* has also emerged as a method for studying Web users' behaviors through the computation of access statistics and the reconstruction of user navigation on the basis of Web access logs. The rest of this section describes in more details these three classes of methods.

User Testing

User testing deals with real behaviors, observed from some representative of real users (Nielsen, 1993). It requires that users perform a set of tasks through physical artifacts, being them prototypes or final systems, while the experimenter observes users behaviors and collects empirical data about the way users execute the assigned tasks. Typical data collected during user testing are user execution time, number of errors, and user satisfaction. After the test completion, the collected data are then interpreted and used to ameliorate the level of the application usability.

Usability testing is explicitly devoted to analyze in details how users interact with the application for accomplishing well-defined tasks. This feature determines the difference between usability testing and beta testing, largely applied in industry. Beta testing is conducted on the final product: after the application release, the end users are contacted and interviewed about their satisfaction. Conversely, usability testing is conducted observing a sample of users that perform specific tasks while interacting with the application. The test is usually video recorded. The list of detected problems is reported together with specific redesign suggestions.

It is recommendable to conduct user testing for studying users while using prototypes. However, this activity is quite expensive. Also, in the development process the feedback has to start coming in at earlier stages, preferably before even the first prototype has been built. The previous reasons have lead to the definition of usability inspection methods, to be used by developers to predict early usability problems that users testing could detect later.

Inspection Methods

Usability inspection refers to a set of evaluation techniques that are an evolution from prior function and code inspection methods used in Software Engineering for debugging and improving code. According to such methods, evaluators examine usability related aspects of an application, trying to detect violations of established usability principles (Nielsen & Mack, 1994), and then provide feedback to designers about possible design improvements. The inspectors can be usability specialists, or also designers and engineers with special expertise (e.g., knowledge of specific domains or standards). In any case, the application of such methods relies on a good understanding of the usability principles, and more specifically of how they apply to the specific application to be analyzed, and on the particular ability of the evaluators in discovering critical situations where principle violations occur.

Usability inspection methods have been proposed when the issue of cost effectiveness started guiding methodological work on usability evaluation (Bias & Mayhew, 1994). The cost of user studies and laboratory experiments became a central issue. Therefore, many proposals were made for usability evaluation techniques based on the involvement of specialists to supplement or even replace direct user testing (Nielsen, 1993; Nielsen & Mack, 1994).

Different methods can be used for inspecting an application (Nielsen & Mack, 1994). Among them, the most commonly used are *Heuristic Evaluation* (Nielsen, 1993), which requires usability specialists to judge whether the application properties conform to established usability principles, and *Cognitive Walkthrough* (Polson et al., 1992), which uses detailed procedures for simulating users' problem-solving processes, trying to see if the functions provided by the application are efficient for users, and lead them to the next correct actions. For more details on inspection methods, the reader is referred to Nielsen and Mack (1994).

Web Usage Analysis

A relatively new direction in the evaluation of Web applications deals with Web usage analysis (Ivory & Hearst, 2001), performed on the record of user accesses to the application pages, collected in a Web server log according to one of the available standard formats. After Web applications are deployed, Web usage analysis can be employed to analyze how users exploit and browse the information provided by the Web site. For instance, it can help discovering those navigation patterns which correspond to high Web usage, or those which correspond to early leaving.

Very often, Web logs are analyzed with the aim of calculating *traffic statistics*. Such a type of analysis can help identify the most accessed pages and contents, and may therefore highlight some user preferences, not detected at design time, that might need to be accommodated by restructuring the hypertext interface. However, traffic analysis is not able to detect users' navigational behavior. To allow deeper insight into users' navigation paths, the research community has been studying techniques to reconstruct user navigation from log files (Cooley, 2003; Eirinaki & Vazirgiannis, 2003; Fraternali et al., 2004). Most of them are based on extensions of Web logging mechanisms, for recording additional semantic information about contents displayed in the accessed pages, to make sense of the observed frequent paths and of pages on these paths (Berendt, Hotho, & Stumme, 2002). Such extensions exploit Semantic Web techniques, such as RDF annotations for mapping URLs into a set of ontological entities. Also, some recent works (Fraternali et al., 2004; Punin, Krishnamoorthy, & Zaki, 2002) have proposed conceptual enrichments of Web logs through the integration of information about the page content and the structure of the hypertext interface, as deriving from the application conceptual specifications. The reconstruction of user navigation can be then incorporated into automatic tools providing designers and evaluators with statistics about the identified navigation paths that can be useful for evaluating and improving the application organization with respect to the actual application usage.

User navigation paths can also be analyzed by means of *Web Usage Mining* techniques, which consist in applying data mining techniques over Web logs, to identify interesting associations among visited pages and contents (Cooley, 2003; Eirinaki & Vazirgiannis, 2003; Facca & Lanzi, 2005). With respect to the simple reconstruction of user navigation, Web Usage Mining can dis-

cover unexpected user behaviors, not foreseen by the application designers, which can be the symptom of design lacks, not necessarily errors. The aim is to identify possible amendments for accommodating such user needs.

Different techniques can be used to mine Web logs. Mining of *association rules* is probably the one most used (Agrawal, Imielinski, & Swami, 1993); it can also be extended to the problem of discovering *sequential patterns* to take into account the temporal characterization of users' accesses (Srivastava et al., 2000).

The discovery of association rules and sequential patterns is interesting from the Web usage perspective, because the results produced can evidence contents or pages that frequently appears in association. If the discovered behavior is not supported by appropriate navigational structures connecting such contents and pages, then it can suggest possible changes for improving the ease of content browsing.

Automatic Evaluation Tools

Even though the cost (in terms of time and effort) of inspection methods and user testing is not particularly high, and their effectiveness has been so far largely proved for augmenting the quality of Web applications, very often it happens that evaluation is not systematically performed at each development step. The reasons can be related to a number of factors (Brajnik, 2004), such as the need of shortening the application release time, the availability of incomplete and vague design specifications, or more simply the lack of resources for conducting evaluation. Also, inspection and user testing are often difficult to manage when a large number of people are involved in the evaluation process. Claims about the number of evaluators needed to detect a sufficient percentage of usability breakdowns, as well as the nature of the qualitative data per se—that does not support systematic verifications and comparisons—are therefore pulling for automatic tools able to efficiently treat the most repetitive evaluation tasks, without requiring much time and skills by human resources.

There are three main categories of Web evaluation tools (Brajnik, 2004), which cover a large set of tests for usability and accessibility:

- **Tools for accessibility analysis**, like webXACT (http://webxact.watchfire.com/), A-Prompt (http://aprompt.snow.utoronto.ca/), LIFT (http://www.usablenet.com), and so forth. The metrics computed correspond to official accessibility criteria (such as those prescribed by W3C), and refer to properties of the HTML page coding, such as browser compatibility, use of safe colors, appropriate color contrast, and so forth.
- **Tools for usability analysis**, such as CWW (Blackmon et al., 2002), WebTango (Ivory, Sinha, & Hearst, 2001), WebCriteria SiteProfile (http://www.coremetrics.com), that analyze site design for verifying usability guidelines. They mostly operate at the presentation layer, with the aim of discovering problems such as the consistency for presentation of contents and navigation commands (e.g., link labels, color consistency, etc.). Very often, they neglect structural and navigation problems. Some recent proposals (see for example (Fraternali et al., 2004)) are now trying to address such issues, by focusing more on the identification of structural lacks in the definition of the hypertext front-end.
- **Tools for Web usage analysis**, which calculate statistics about site activities, and mine data about user behavior. The majority of the commercial tools (e.g., AWSD-WebLog [http://awsd.com/scripts/weblog/index.shtml] and Analog [http://www.analog.cx.]) are traffic analyzers. As also described in Eirinaki and Vazirgiannis (2003), their functionality is limited to producing:
  - **Site traffic reports**, such as total number of visits, average number of hits, average view time, and so forth.
  - **Diagnostic statistics**, such as server errors and pages not found.
  - **Referrer statistics**, such as search engines accessing the application.
  - **User statistics**, such as top geographical regions.
  - **Client statistics**, such as user's Web browsers and operating systems.

Recently, some research works have been also proposed for the analysis of user navigation paths and for Web usage mining (Berendt & Spiliopoulou, 2000; Cooley, 2003; Meo et al., 2004).

Comparison of Methods

User testing provides reliable evaluations, because it involves samples of real users. It allows evaluators to overcome the lack of precision manifested by predictive models when the application domain is not supported by a strong and detailed theory. Such a method, however, has a number of drawbacks:

- It is difficult to *select a proper sample of the user community*: an incorrect sample may lead to wrong perceptions about the user needs and preferences.
- It is difficult, in a limited amount of time, to *train users* to master the most sophisticated and advanced features of a Web application; not well trained users may produce "superficial" conclusions, only related to the most immediate features of the application.
- It is difficult to *reproduce actual situations of usage*, which requires setting up the environment where the application is going to be used, and also the motivations and the goals that users may have in real-life situations (Doubleday et al., 1997). Failure to reproduce such a context may lead to "artificial" conclusions rather than to realistic results.
- User observation gives *little information about the cause of the problem*, because it primarily deals with the symptoms (Doubleday et al., 1997). Not understanding the cause behind a problem has implication for

redesign. In fact, the new design can remove the original symptom, but if the underlying cause remains, a different symptom can be triggered.

Differently from user testing, inspection methods enable the identification of the cause of the problem, because the inspectors exactly report about which part of the design violates usability principles and how. Their main advantage, with respect to user testing, is that they involve fewer experienced people, that is, experts of usability and human factors, who can detect problems and possible future faults of a complex system in a limited amount of time. This is a relevant point, which strongly supports the viability and the acceptability of usability evaluation during the design activities. In fact, it constitutes a low expensive addition to existing practices, so enabling the easy integration of usability goals with the goals of the efficient software design and development (Doubleday et al., 1997). Furthermore, inspection techniques can be used very early in the development process, even when prototypes are not available and evaluation must be conducted over design specifications.

The main disadvantages of inspection methods are, however, the great subjectivity of the evaluation—different inspectors may produce not comparable outcomes—and the heavy dependence upon the inspector skills. Also, experts can misjudge the reactions of real users in two ways, that is, not detecting potential problems, or figuring out problems that will not be significant for users.

According to Brooks (Brooks, 1994), usability inspection methods cannot replace user testing because they are not able to analyze aspects such as trade-offs, or the whole acceptability of the interface, or the accuracy of the mental model of the user. Also, they are not suitable for defining the most usable interface out of several ones, or things that are a matter of preference. On the other hand, usability testing cannot tell whether the interface will "just do the job or delight the user," which is and important information in the competition on the market.

Web usage analysis seems to solve a series of problems in the field of the usability evaluation, since it might reduce the need for usability testing involving samples of real users. Also, with respect to experimental settings, it offers the possibility to analyze the behavior of a high number of users, thus increasing the number of evaluated variables and the reliability of the detected errors. However log files are not without problems. The most severe one is about the meaning of the information collected and how much it describes the real users behavior. In fact, even when they are effective in finding patterns in the users' navigation sessions, such techniques do not solve the problem of how to infer users' goals and expectations, which very often are central for usability evaluation.

Also, Web usage analysis, and in particular Web usage mining, require a substantial amount of pre-processing to clean the logs, extract user navigation sessions containing consistent information, and formatting data in a way suitable for analysis (Cooley, 2003; Srivastava et al., 2000). In particular, user session identification can be very demanding: requests for pages tracked into the Web logs must indeed be grouped in order to identify the navigation paths of single users, but this phase may suffer for problems mainly due to proxy servers, which do not allow the unique identification of users, generally based on IP address. Some solutions to circumvent this problem are illustrated in Cooley, Mobasher, and Srivastava (1999).

While the adoption of automatic tools for Web usage analysis is mandatory, an important observation must be made about tools supporting the analysis of accessibility and usability. Such tools constitute a valuable support for reducing the efforts required to evaluators for analyzing "by hand" the whole application with respect to all the possible usability lacks. However, they are not able to verify exhaustively usability issues. In particular, they cannot assess all those properties that require judgment by human specialists (e.g., usage of natural and concise language). Also, automatic tools cannot provide answers about the nature of a discovered problem and the design revision that can solve it. Automatic tools are therefore very useful when their use complements the activity of human specialists, since they can execute repetitive evaluation tasks to inspect the application and to highlight critical features that are worth to be later inspected by evaluators.

EVALUATING THE USABILITY OF UEMS

In the last decade, the motivation to deliver products that satisfy consumers' demand for usable applications has led to the development of large and expensive usability evaluation frameworks. Despite such an increased focus on usability processes, a substantial amount of software is however still unusable and poorly designed. This is due, in part, to the lack of a sufficiently broad set of cost-effective usability evaluation tools. For example, the traditional lab-based usability evaluation is often too expensive; also, it can be difficult to apply early in the development cycle, when the available running prototypes may lack the functionality to be tested with users (Jeffries et al, 1991; Jeffries & Desurvire, 1992; Kantner & Rosenbaum, 1997). Heuristic Evaluation (Nielsen, 1993) has instead emerged as the most adopted usability evaluation procedure due to its cost-effectiveness if compared with other usability evaluation techniques. Nevertheless, heuristics sometimes are difficult to interpret and apply for different reasons. In particular:

- Heuristic evaluators are not much immersed in using the system as real users are in user testing environments;
- The heuristics are not task-based, that is, they do not suggest procedures to discover problems;
- Very often heuristics lead evaluators to identify a large number of specific, one-time,

and low-priority problems, while neglecting more important issues.

We believe that using "unusable" UEMs can significantly compromise the quality and the integrity of the evaluation, incurring in unnecessary costs and compromising the credibility of the evaluators in front of the rest of the design team. Unfortunately, so far researchers have not devoted sufficient attention and efforts towards the validation of the proposed techniques; therefore different open questions still remain unsolved (John, 1996). For UEMs to provide useful guidance to the design process, comparison studies need to be conducted to allow evaluators to understand the trade-offs of each method (which methods are more effective, in which contexts and for which purposes).

Gray and Salzman (1998) highlighted this problem when documenting specific validity concerns about five UEMs comparison studies. A key concern was related to the identification of general and replicable measures for quantifying and comparing the effectiveness and efficiency of the UEMs. Indeed, although several works concentrate on a comparison-based evaluation of UEMs (Karat, Campbell, & Fiegel, 1992; Nielsen & Phillips, 1993; Desurvire, Kondziela, & Atwood, 1992, Jeffries et al., 1991), such works lack generality, thus it is difficult to identify general procedures and metrics that can be replicated in other circumstances (Gray & Salzman, 1998).

Towards General and Replicable Evaluation Procedures

In order to contribute to the development of metrics for UEMs comparison studies, we are now conducting a series of experiments to test a procedure model we developed in (De Angeli et al., 2003) for measuring the usability of inspection-based UEMs.

We initially moved in this study with the aim to measure the effectiveness of a new UEM, QVAL

(Cortazar, Perallos, & Vazquez, 2002; Perallos & Cortazar, 2006), compared with the Nielsen's Heuristic Evaluation (Nielsen, 1993). With this goal in mind, we first decided to review the literature looking for well-established criteria. We found that very few studies clearly identify the target criteria against which the success of a UEM can be measured (Hartson et al., 2001). Also, the body of literature on UEMs comparison studies does not support accurate or meaningful assessment of UEMs. We therefore decided to re-apply the experimental procedure already adopted in (De Angeli et al., 2003). This action led us to change our initial goal, from the evaluation of a specific usability inspection technique to the definition of a procedure that could be replicated, every time, for the evaluation of UEMs.

The procedure of the initial study aimed to validate a specific inspection technique (Matera, Costabile et al., 2002), whose main characteristic was the introduction of detailed guidelines to guide the inspectors' activity. The experiments wanted to validate whether the systematic approach suggested by this new method was particularly advantageous for naïve evaluators, even with respect to the widely used Nielsen's Heuristic Evaluation.

Two groups of novice inspectors were asked to evaluate a commercial hypermedia CD-ROM applying the newly defined inspection method (Matera et al., 2002) or the traditional Nielsens' Heuristic Evaluation. The performance of the two groups was thus compared.

The validation metrics was defined along three major dimensions: *effectiveness*, *efficiency*, and *user satisfaction*. Such dimensions actually correspond to the principal usability components, as defined by the Standard ISO 9241-11 (ISO, 1997). Therefore, it can be said that the experiment supported the assessment of the usability of the inspection technique (John, 1996).

In the defined metrics, effectiveness was related to the completeness and accuracy with which inspectors performed the evaluation. Efficiency was related to the time spent in relation to the effectiveness of the evaluation. Satisfaction was measured on a number of subjective parameters, such as perceived usefulness, difficulty, acceptability and confidence with respect to the evaluation technique. For each dimension the following measures were defined:

- **Effectiveness Measures**: Effectiveness was decomposed into the *completeness* and the *accuracy* of the evaluators performance, where:
  - **Completeness** corresponds to the percentage of problems detected by a single inspector out of the total number of problems, as resulting from the following formula:

  $$Completeness = \frac{P_i}{n} * 100$$

  where P_i is the number of problems found by the *i-th* inspectors, and n is the total number of problems existing in the application.
  - **Accuracy** was defined by two indices: *precision* and *severity*.
    - **Precision** is given by the percentage of problems detected by a single inspector out of the total number of statements. For a given inspector, precision is computed by the following formula:

    $$Precision_i = \frac{P_i}{s_i} * 100$$

    where P_i is the number of problems found by the *i-th* evaluator, and s_i is the total number of statements the participant reported (including non problems).
    - The **severity** index then refers to the average rating of all the scored statements for each participant.

- **Efficiency Measures:** Efficiency was considered both at the individual and at the group level:

  o **Individual efficiency** refers to the number of problems extracted by a single inspector, in relation to the time spent. It is computed by the following formula:

  $$Ind\_Efficiency_i = \frac{P_i}{t_i}$$

  where P_i is the number of problems detected by the *i-th* inspector, and t_i is the time spent for finding the problems.

  o **Group efficiency** refers to the evaluation results achieved aggregating the performance of several inspectors. At this aim, the Nielsen's cost-benefit curve, relating the proportion of usability problems to the number of evaluators, is computed (Nielsen & Landauer, 1993). This curve derives from a mathematical model, which is based on the prediction formula for the number of usability problems found in a Heuristic Evaluation, as reported in the following:

  $$Found(i) = n(1-(1-\lambda)^i)$$

  where *Found(i)* is the number of problems found by aggregating reports from *i* independent evaluators, *n* is the total number of problems in the application, and λ is the probability of finding the average usability problem when using a single average evaluator.

- **Satisfaction Measures:** A post-experiment questionnaire was used to measure user-satisfaction along three indices: *Evaluator-satisfaction with the application evaluated*, *evaluator-satisfaction with the inspection technique*, and *evaluator-satisfaction with*

the result achieved. The first dimension, apparently out of the scope of the experiment, was meant to verify in which way the used inspection technique influences the inspector severity about the application quality.

Evaluating the QVAL Inspection Method

The above procedure was replicated again to evaluate QVAL (Cortazar et al., 2002; Perallos & Cortazar, 2006).

QVAL is an inspection method addressing several quality factors of Web applications, namely *usability, accessibility, performance, security, functionality, reliability* and *maintenance*. In order to systematically support the evaluation process, the quality factors are decomposed into a set of fine-grained attributes, presented to the evaluators as a set of requirements that a quality application should adhere to. Therefore, the evaluator visiting and inspecting the Web application is systematically guided by a set of very specific requirements, covering several facets of each quality factor. A Web tool also supports the selection by evaluators of the relevant requirements an evaluation session must focus on, the collection of evaluation data, as gathered during the inspection of the selected requirements, and

Figure 2. Visualization of evaluation results in the QVAL tool

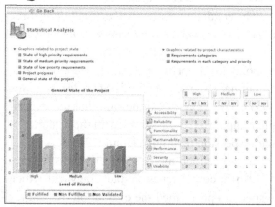

Figure 3. The Nielsen's cost-benefit curve (Nielsen & Landauer, 1993) resulting from the comparison of QVAL with the Heuristic Evaluation

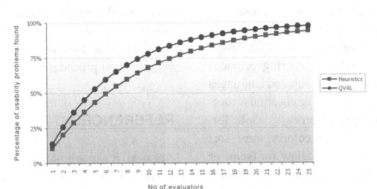

the computation of a set of metrics. As illustrated in Figure 22, finally the tool summarizes visually the results of metrics computation.

The replicated experiment on QVAL involved 36 participants. It confirmed us the general result, already achieved in (De Angeli et al., 2003), of a sharp increasing of the overall quality of inspection when a systematic and structured UEM is used. This advantage clearly emerges from the graph reported in Figure 33, which compares the group efficiency for QVAL and for the Nielsen's Heuristic Evaluation. The QVAL method tends to reach better performance with a lowest number of evaluators. In particular, assuming the 75% threshold of problems found, QVAL can reach it with 9 evaluators, while the Heuristic Evaluation needs instead 12 evaluators.

The advantage of QVAL with respect to the Heuristic Evaluation is also confirmed by the computation of the other indices reported in the previous section. For more details on the experiment procedure and results, the reader is referred to (Matera, Perallos et al., 2006).

As a more general achievement, the results of the experiment also allowed us to formulate a first hypothesis on the validity of the adopted experimental procedure. On one hand, since we have been able to replicate the procedure for a different evaluation method, we believe that the adopted metrics can be considered effective

indicators for the usability of inspection-based UEMs. However, the overall results of our studies also tell us that the external validity of our model procedure may be very context-sensitive, especially in relation to the procedure we adopted for determining the severity of the discovered problems[1] and for normalizing the list of usability problems found by the experimental evaluators[2] (Matera et al., 2006). Also, although some of the identified procedural patterns and the discovered correlations seem stable across the two different studies and settings, a further replication of such studies is necessary to build over time a credible body of empirical knowledge on which to base the generalization of the proposed model procedure and corresponding metrics. We are therefore planning further studies that will help us to further generalize the model of the experimental procedure and the achieved results.

CONCLUSION

The ever-increasing spread of Web information systems, the abundance of their contents and the complexity of their interfaces have determined the current emphasis on usability as a relevant factor for the quality of such systems.

The virtuous process of applying engineering techniques for enhancing the development of Web information systems started a few years ago (Fraternali, 1999; Ceri et al., 2002; Conallen, 2002). The proposal of some conceptual modeling techniques brought many benefits, but even though applying design principles is now widely accepted, the problem of poor application design is still significant. Web Engineering provides designers with a collection of tools and languages for the development of Web applications: tools speed up the development process, while formal specification languages enforce some sort of syntactic correctness and allow for (semi or complete) automatic code generation. However, a quality application is much more than a bug-free piece of code.

Applications that incorporate usability engineering into their development process will be better able to comply with quality requirements. In particular, as reported in (Lowe, 2003), the effort put into evaluation is proportional to the quality of the final applications. In the last decade, several techniques for evaluating the usability of software systems have been therefore proposed. Unfortunately, researchers have not however devoted sufficient efforts towards the validation of such techniques; as such, some open questions persist about them (John, 1996; Matera et al., 2006).

This chapter outlined the major features of the most prominent usability evaluation methods. It also discussed the problem, still under investigation, of identifying some general procedures and metrics for comparing and evaluating UEMs. The described empirical study aims to provide some preliminary answers about the definition of metrics and procedures for measuring the usability of UEMs, thus providing some answers to the questions posed by some researchers and practitioners (Gray & Salzman, 1998; John, 1996; Hartson et al., 2001).

We, however, believe that more replications of the study are needed to further generalize the procedure model. We also believe that the creation of a lab-package would be a very relevant element in making sure that the procedure could be replicated. Whenever possible, the lab-package should contain the materials used in the experiment, such as the satisfaction questionnaire. Raw data from the experiment, as well as the results of their analysis could also be provided, as they could help the researchers while applying the experimental procedure.

REFERENCES

Agrawal, R., Imielinski, T., & Swami, A. (1993, May). Mining association rules between sets of items in large databases. In *Proceedings of the ACM-SIGMOD'93*, Buneman, P., Jajodia, S. (Ed.), *International Conference on Management of Data*, Washington, D.C., (pp. 207-216). New York: ACM.

Berendt, B., Hotho, A., & Stumme, G. (2002, June). Towards Semantic Web mining. In I. Horrocks & J. A. Hendler (Eds.), *The Semantic Web—ISWC 2002: First International Semantic Web Conference,* Sardinia, Italy, (LNCS 2342, pp. 264-278). Berlin: Springer-Verlag.

Berendt, B., & Spiliopoulou, M. (2000). Analysis of navigation behaviour in Web sites integrating multiple information systems. *VLDB Journal, 9*(1), 56-75.

Bias, R.G., & Mayhew, D.J. (1994). *Cost-justifying usability.* Boston: Academic Press.

Blackmon, M. H., Polson, P.G., Kitajima, M., & Lewis, C. (2002, April). Cognitive walkthrough for the Web. In *Proceedings of the CHI'02, International Conference on Human Factors in Computing Systems*, Minneapolis, USA, (pp. 463-470). ACM.

Brajnik, G. (2004, June). Using automatic tools in accessibility and usability assurance. In C. Stephanidis (Ed.), *Proceedings of the ERCIM UI4ALL, 8th International ERCIM Workshop on User Interface for All*, Vienna, (LNCS 3196, pp. 219-234). Berlin: Springer.

Brooks, P. (1994). Adding value to usability testing (pp. 255-271). In (Nielsen & Mack, 1994).

Ceri, S., Fraternali, P., Bongio, A., Brambilla, M., Comai, S., & Matera, M. (2002). *Designing data-intensive Web applications*. Morgan Kauffman.

Conallen, J. (2002). *Building Web applications with UML*. Boston: Addison-Wesley.

Cooley, R. (2003). The use of Web structures and content to identify subjectively interesting Web usage patterns. *ACM TOIT, 3*(2), 93-116.

Cooley, R., Mobasher, B., & Srivastava, J. (1999). Data preparation for mining World Wide Web browsing patterns. *Knowledge and Information Systems, 1*(1), 5-32.

Cortazar, R., Perallos, A., & Vázquez, I. (2002, September). SQ-Met: Internet application quality validation methodology. In *Proceedings of the ICWE'2002, ISSN 1666-1141*, SantaFe, Argentina.

De Angeli, A., Matera, M., Costabile, F., Garzotto, F., & Paolini, P. (2003). On the advantages of a systematic inspection for evaluating hypermedia usability. *International Journal of Human-Computer Interaction, 15(3)*, 315-336.

Desurvire, H. W., Kondziela, J. M., & Atwood, M. E. (1992). What is gained and lost when using evaluation methods other than empirical testing. In *Proceedings of the HCI'92 Conference on People and Computers VII*, New York, (pp. 89-102). ACM.

Doubleday, A., Ryan, M., Springett, M., & Sutcliffe, A. (1997, August). A comparison of usability techniques for evaluating design. In G. C. Van der Veer, A. Henderson, & S. Coles (Eds.), *Proceedings of the ACM DIS'97, Symposium on Designing Interactive Systems: Processes, Practices, Methods and Techniques*, Amsterdam, the Netherlands, (pp. 101-110). New York: ACM.

Eirinaki, M., & Vazirgiannis, M. (2003). Web mining for Web personalization. *ACM TOIT, 3*(1), 1-27.

Facca, F.M., & Lanzi, P.L. (2005). Mining interesting knowledge from Web logs: A survey. *Data & Knowledge Engineering, 53*(3), 225-241.

Fraternali, P. (1999). Tools and approaches for developing data-intensive Web applications: A survey. *ACM Computing Surveys, 31*(3), 227-263.

Fraternali, P., Lanzi, P.L., Matera, M., & Maurino, A. (2004). Model-driven Web usage analysis for the evaluation of Web application quality. *Journal of Web Engineering, 3*(2), 124-152.

Gray, W., & Salzman, M.C. (1998). Demaged merchandise? A review of experiments that compare usability evaluation methods. *Human Computer Interaction, 13*(3), 203-261.

Hartson, H. R., Andre T. S., Williges R. C. (2001). Criteria for evaluating usability evaluation methods. *International Journal on Human Computer Interaction, 13*(4), 373-410.

ISO (International Standard Organization). (1997). ISO 9241: Ergonomics requirements for office work with visual display terminal (VDT)- Parts 1-17.

Ivory, M.Y., & Hearst, M.A. (2001). The state of the art in automating usability evaluation of user interfaces. *ACM Computing Surveys, 33*(4), 470-516.

Ivory, M. Y., Sinha, R. R. & Hearst, M. A. (2001, April). Empirically validated Web page design metrics. In *Proceedings of the ACM CHI'01, International Conference on Human Factors in Computing Systems*, Seattle, USA, (pp. 53-60). New York: ACM.

Jeffries, R., & Desurvire, H.W. (1992). Usability testing vs. heuristic evaluation: Was there a context? *ACM SIGCHI Bulletin, 24*(4), 39-41.

Jeffries, R., Miller, J., Wharton, C., & Uyeda, K.M. (1991). User interface evaluation in the real world: A comparison of four techniques. In *Proceedings of the ACM CHI'91—International Conference on Human Factors in Computing Systems*, New Orleans, USA, (pp. 119-124). New York: ACM.

John, B.E. (1996). Evaluating usability evaluation techniques. *ACM Computing Surveys*, *28*(4es), article no. 139.

Kantner, L., & Rosenbaum, S. (1997). Usability studies of WWW sites: Heuristic evaluation vs. laboratory testing. In *Proceedings of the ACM SIGDOC'97, International Conference on Computer Documentation*, Snowbird, USA, (pp. 153-160). New York: ACM.

Karat, C.M., Campbell, R., & Fiegel, T. (1992). Comparison of empirical testing and walkthrough methods in user interface evaluation. In *Proceedings of the ACM CHI'92 Conference on Human Factors in Computing Systems*, (pp. 397- 404). New York: ACM.

Lowe, D. (2003). Emerging knowledge in Web development. In A. Aurum, R. Jeffery, C. Wohlin, & M. Handzic (Eds.), *Managing software engineering* (pp. 157-175). Berlin: Springer.

Matera, M., Costabile, F., Garzotto, F., & Paolini, P. (2002) The SUE inspection: An effective method for a systematic usability evaluation of hypermedia. *IEEE Transaction on System Man and Cybernetics*, *32(*1), 93-103.

Matera, M., Perallos, A., Rizzo, F., & Cortazar, R. (2006). *On evaluating the usability of UEMs*. DEI-PoliMI Tech. Report.

Meo, R., Lanzi, P.L., Matera, M., Esposito, R. (2004, August). Integrating Web conceptual modeling and Web usage mining. In *Proceedings of the WebKDD'04, International ACM Workshop on Web Mining and Web Usage Analysis* (pp. 135-148). Seattle, USA .

Nielsen, J. (1993). *Usability engineering*. Cambridge, MA: Academic Press.

Nielsen, J. (2000). *Web usability*. New York: New Riders.

Nielsen, J., & Landauer, T.K. (1993, April). A mathematical model of the finding of usability problems. In *Proceedings of the ACM INTER-CHI'93, International Conference on Human Factors in Computing Systems*, Amsterdam, NL, (pp. 296-213). New York: ACM.

Nielsen, J., & Mack, R.L. (1994). *Usability inspection methods*. New York: John Wiley.

Nielsen, J., & Phillips, V. L. (1993). Estimating the relative usability of two interfaces: Heuristic, formal, and empirical methods compared. In *Proceedings of the ACM INTERCHI'93 Conference on Human Factors in Computing Systems*, (pp. 214-221), New York: ACM Press.

Perallos, A., & Cortázar, R. (2006, February). Towards an agile Web quality assessment methodology adaptable to Web site features. In *Proceedings of the EATIS2006*, Santa Marta, Colombia, (pp. 214-223). ISBN 958-8166-38-1.

Polson, P., Lewis, C., Rieman, J., & Wharton, C. (1992). Cognitive walkthrough: A method for theory-based evaluation of user interfaces. *International Journal of Man-Machine Studies*, *36*, 741-773.

Preece, J., Rogers, Y., Sharp, H., Benyon, D., Holland, S., & Carey, T. (1994). *Human-computer interaction*. New York: Addison-Wesley.

Punin, J. R., Krishnamoorthy, M. S., & Zaki, M. J. (2002). Log Markup Language for Web usage mining. In R. Kohavi, B. M. Masand, M. Spiliopoulou, & J. Srivastava (Eds.), *Proceedings of the WebKDD'01- Mining Web Log Data Across All Customers Touch Points*, San Francisco, USA, (Vol. 2356, pp. 88-112). Lecture Notes in Computer Science. Berlin: Springer.

Srivastava, J., Cooley, R., Deshpande, M., & Tan, P.N. (2000). Web usage mining: Discovery and applications of usage patterns from Web data. *SIGKDD Explorations, 1*(2), 12-23.

KEY TERMS

Usability: the extent to which a product can be used by specified users to achieve specified goals with *effectiveness*, *efficiency* and *satisfaction* in a specified context of use.

Usability evaluation methods: techniques that can be applied at any stage of the development process to verify the usability of incremental design artifacts and of the final product.

Iterative design: a design process that cycles through several designs, incrementally improving upon the final product with each pass.

Formative evaluation: evaluation taking place during design.

Summative evaluation: evaluation taking place after the product has been developed, or even when any prototype version is ready.

User testing: an evaluation technique dealing with real behaviors, observed from some representative of real users. It requires that users perform a set of tasks through physical artifacts, being them prototypes or final systems, while the experimenter observes users behaviors and collects empirical data about the way users execute the assigned tasks

Inspection methods: a set of evaluation techniques that are an evolution from prior function and code inspection methods used in software engineering for debugging and improving code. Evaluators examine usability related aspects of an application, trying to detect violations of established usability principles (Nielsen & Mack, 1994), and then provide feedback to designers about possible design improvements.

Web usage analysis: an analysis performed on the record of user accesses to the application pages, collected in a Web server log. After Web applications are deployed, Web usage analysis can be employed to analyze how users exploit and browse the information provided by the Web site. For instance, it can help discovering those navigation patterns which correspond to high Web usage, or those which correspond to early leaving.

ENDNOTES

[1]   Severity was assessed asking a pool of expert evaluators to assign a severity rate to each problem found by experimental evaluators.

[2]   Normalization was performed by experts dropping those findings not corresponding to actual usability problems.

Chapter XV
Handling Usability Aspects for the Construction of Business Process Driven Web Applications[1]

Victoria Torres
Technical University of Valencia, Spain

Joan Fons
Technical University of Valencia, Spain

Vicente Pelechano
Technical University of Valencia, Spain

ABSTRACT

Users consider usability aspects as a key factor when using Web applications. For this reason, in this work we take a special care in this very important issue. In particular, we are centred on usability aspects regarding business process driven Web applications. Therefore, in this work we gather a set of guidelines provided by experts in Web usability and present the solution designed in a particular Web engineering method that follows a model driven development approach. The provided solution bases on the introduction of these guidelines following two different approaches. The former implies handling usability guidelines at the modeling level. The latter implies using them for the definition of the transformation rules that generate the corresponding usable Web applications.

INTRODUCTION

There is a lot of research done in the Web engineering area mainly focused on the automation process of Web application building. Most of this research provides mechanisms to handle some of the aspects that contribute to improve the usability of the generated Web applications. However, there are some works (Ahlstrom & Longo, 2001) that highlight the drawbacks found in existing Web engineering methods. This limitations support the need to endow methods that handle usability aspects along the development process.

Nowadays, the proliferation of Web applications makes usability a key factor to make the difference between them. The usability expertise community has produced both guidelines and standards that face the different usability problems introduced by Web applications. However, in order to ensure that these guidelines are used and applied properly, it is necessary to integrate them during the software development process and provide them with tool support (Abran et. al, 2003, p. 325).

In particular, we are concerned about usability regarding Web applications that support the execution of business processes (BP). In fact, the impact that usability has on productivity makes worth it to take a look carefully on that.

Nowadays, the Web has been adopted as the common platform for application development. As a result we can find in Internet different kind of applications, which range from personal Web sites to e-commerce applications or even corporate intranets.

Web applications have become so complex (mainly due to their size) that users usually do not know what role their work plays in the overall scheme of the applications. As a result, this complexity has a negative effect upon productivity because users get lost on the application trying to find the right place to complete the tasks they are responsible of.

The maturity reached in technology for Web development allows us to find Web sites that provide users not only with information but also with a set of services, behind which we can find business goals that have been previously defined by business processes.

The objectives of this work are (1) to analyze the usability guidelines that ensure the generation of usable Web interfaces and (2) to present how these guidelines can be integrated into a Web engineering method. This integration is performed into a method that follows a model driven approach what implies that these guidelines are going to be introduced either at the modeling level or at the transformation rules that generate the code.

The remainder sections are organized as follows. Section 2 identifies the characteristics of the kind of processes that we are dealing with. In addition, it includes an example for each kind of

process. Section 3 provides an overview over the state of the art developed in the Web engineering area regarding usability aspects. Section 4 presents the mechanisms defined in the OOWS approach to overcome the usability problems that arise when performing BPs. Section 5 presents the solution designed in the OOWS approach to satisfy usability guidelines defined by usability experts. Section 6 provides the implementation strategy. Finally, section 7 concludes the work presented in this paper.

CHARACTERIZING BUSINESS PROCESSES

The term business process (BP) was defined by the Workflow Management Coalition (WFMC) (Workflow Management Coalition, 1999) as "a set of one or more linked procedures or activities which collectively realise a business objective or policy goal, normally within the context of an organisational structure defining functional roles and relationships."

Its usage covers indistinctly abstract, private and collaboration processes. For this reason, depending on the objective for which a process has been defined, we can refer to one of these three usages mentioned previously.

In particular, in this work we contextualize BPs as a mixture between private and collaboration processes (see Figure. 11). In the one hand we define the internal process (private) of the system being built. On the other hand, we also define by means of exchanged messages the interaction (collaboration) that occurs between our system and external organizations.

Regarding the context in which BP are executed we distinguish two kinds of processes, which refer to short-lived and long-lived processes. In order to improve the usability of Web applications that provide support to the execution of different BPs, we have to define properly the mechanisms that the user has to interact with the system (which is by means of user interfaces) according to the context in which these processes are performed.

In the next subsections, we detail the aspects that differentiate these two kinds of processes. Moreover, we introduce for each kind of process a case study that will be used later to exemplify how usability aspects are integrated into the method. The graphical notation used to present these cases is the BPMN notation (Business Process Modeling Notation, 2004).

Finally, before characterizing them, we want to note that we are always referring to processes that in the end are going to be executed by a process engine. Therefore, it is necessary to define for each task included in the process its underlying functionality, which is going to be specified in some of the models included in the method.

Short-Lived Processes

This sort of processes is also called in the literature as "light-weight processes." As the following list shows, its effect has a short period of time and its consequences of a wrong decision are small. Examples of this kind of processes are the "shopping cart" (e-commerce) or a "booking service" (travel agencies) and these processes are characterized by the following features:

- Are completed in a very *short period of time* (intervals can range from seconds to a few hours).
- Involve just *one human participant* (who interacts with the *system/process* to accomplish it) and *one or more "automated" participants.*

Figure 1. Business process definition using the BPMN notation

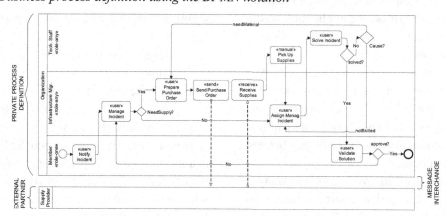

Figure 2. Example of a short-lived process: Checkout Process

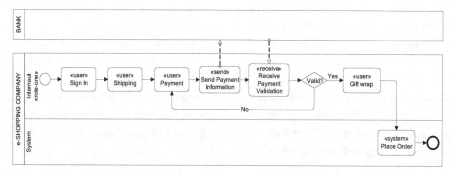

- Are usually *simple and not very large* (big).
- Are *always started by the user (human participant)*.
- The user only participates in one case (instance) of the process at the same time.
- It usually consists in a set of initial tasks oriented to gather data from the user and a final task that performs an operation.

Example: Shopping Cart Business Process

In order to exemplify this kind of processes we present the "shopping cart" BP. This process involves the participation of just one human participant. The process details the steps that are required to accomplish the virtual purchase.

As Figure 22 shows, it is the user who starts the checkout process. Initially, he has to sign in to the system providing her personal information. Then, she is required for information about the shipping details (address, city, country, shipping mode, etc). Then, the user is asked to introduce payment options (credit card, PayPal account, security codes, etc). Once all of this information is gathered, the process starts a payment validation step by using an external validation service provided by a bank entity. If the service validates the sent data then the process concludes creating and placing the order in the system. Otherwise, the user is redirected to the payment step to introduce again the payment data.

Long-Lived Processes

These processes usually define the protocols that have to be followed within an organization in order to achieve certain goals. Examples of this kind of processes could be "Material Purchase Requests" or "Incidence Management Requests." In general, this kind of processes involves not only the coordination of different systems but also the coordination of different people behaving

with different roles. The following list gathers the features observed in this kind of processes:

- Usually take a *long time* for being completed. There are several reasons that justify this prolongation in time such as several human participants, temporal constraints, and so forth.
- Usually involves *more than one human participant* and one or more automated systems.
- Can include *temporal constraints* that provoke that some tasks cannot be started until a specific instant of time.
- Can be *started by any participant* involved in the process. (Therefore, it is advisable that users could find easily the set of pending tasks that she/he is responsible of).
- The user can participate in more than one case (instance) of the process at the same time.

Example: Book Purchase Request Business Process

To exemplify this kind of processes we are going to make use of the "Book Purchase Request" BP.

When a department member needs for a specific book that it is not in the library, she starts a request for a Book Purchase and providing the information about that book. Another user, a Secretary (any of them, «role-any»), must validate the request by creating a pending request or a validated request. If the Secretary denies the purchase request, the system notifies the member (usually by mail). If the purchase request is approved (what is the normal situation), it is sent a book request to an external entity, the University Central Library, which is responsible of the purchase of the requested book. The next step of the process is to wait for the Purchase Notification by the Central Library. When this notification arrives, the system must load the book details into the Department Library and in parallel a Secretary

Figure 3. Example of a long-lived process: Book Purchase Request

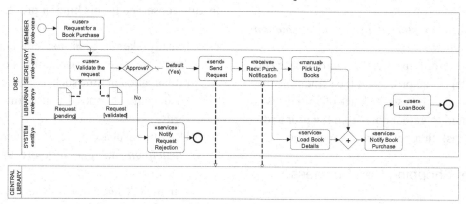

(any of them) must pick up (manual operation) the book from the Central Library. When both actions are fulfilled, the system notifies the invoicing member of the book acquisition and finally one of our Department Librarian must create a book loan to the member.

STATE OF THE ART

The state of the art that has been studied in this work covers the Web engineering area, in particular the most relevant methods developed in the area.

In general, Web engineering methods do not cope with usability issues explicitly in their proposals (WebML (Brambilla et. al, 2006), UWE (Koch et. al, 2004), OO-H (Koch et. al, 2004), OOHDM (Rossi et. al, 2003), WSDM (De Troyer & Casteleyn, 2003)). These proposals only focus on providing the modeling primitives that allow developers to cope with the generation of Web applications. The usability of the generated Web applications is supposed to be high, but there is no hint found during the modeling process that ensures the high grade of usability of the generated artefacts.

These proposals have evolved since their conception providing support, among others, to the generation of business process driven Web

applications. In fact, during the third International Workshop on Web-oriented Software Technologies[2] (IWWOST'03), some of these proposals presented how to cope with the generation of this kind of Web applications by means of their methods. However, all the proposals centred on satisfying the functional requirements (this is providing modeling primitives that allow developers to satisfy business process requirements) leaving behind the usability aspect. As far as we know, there is no previous work that concentrates on the specific usability aspects that arise in this kind of applications.

From the above mentioned proposals, just WebML takes into account the possibility of modeling both short and long running processes. The remainder proposals (UWE, OO-H, OOHDM, and WSDM) just focus on solving the modeling of short running processes.

To cope with some of the problems that arise when executing business process, Schmid et al (Hans & Rossi, 2004) proposed to introduce BP primitives as "first class citizens" into the modeling process. This introduction was performed both in the conceptual and the navigational model. As a result, the design of both models is partitioned into two spaces, one aimed at the modeling of the original primitives defined by each model (entities and navigational nodes, respectively) and another for the modeling of business process aspects (processes and activity nodes, respectively). One of the problems they try to solve with their proposal is to control the situations in which users move from pure navigation to process navigation and vice versa. It is true that these situations can cause inconsistencies regarding the state of the process; however, this kind of issues should not be solved at the modeling level. These problems arise due to the platform in which the application is running. Therefore, we think that if the semantics of the notation used to define business processes is clear, this kind of issues should be solved at the implementation level. Otherwise, we are complicating the modeling process of the navigation.

The lack of attention to usability issues demonstrated by Web engineering methods has been also supported by some of the works found in the automated usability validation area (Atterer et. al, 2006; Cachero et. al, 2006; Marchionono & Crane, 1994; Matera et. al, 2002). They demonstrate that Web engineering solutions currently do not put focus on usability issues of the generated Web sites. Moreover, the research done in this area does not just cover the evaluation of the generated Web applications. It also validates the usability of the modeling process and proposes techniques at the modeling level to help evaluators to evaluate the usability of the generated Web applications.

MECHANISMS FOR HANDLING USABILITY ISSUES

Model driven development (MDD) (Selic, 2003, p. 19) techniques allow the generation of software systems from models. As a result it is possible to obtain the model equivalent representation in terms of a specific technology. During the definition of a development method that follows the MDD approach, we have to specify first the models that are going to be used to represent the system and then the transformation rules that translate these models into the corresponding

system representation. In the one hand, models are built to represent, at a high level of abstraction, a specific aspect (such as its structure, behaviour or presentation) of the system to build. On the other hand, transformation rules can be defined for two purposes, (1) to create/complete a model from another model (moving knowledge between models) or (2) to generate an equivalent representation of the model in terms of an implementation technology.

Therefore, within a Model driven approach, every aspect of the development process should be defined at the modeling level, and this is not an exception for coping with usability issues. We have considered two different mechanisms to handle usability issues, which are defined either at the modeling level or at the transformational level:

- **Considering usability issues at the modeling level**. It implies defining/studying at the modeling level the way to cope with this issues. This mechanism is usually performed through the introduction of new primitives to the corresponding model.
- **Considering usability issues at the transformational level.** This mechanism is transparent to the developer because the usability guidelines that cope with a specific usability problem are directly used in the transformation rules.

Deciding which is the most appropriate mechanism for each aspect depends on the own aspect as we will see in section 5. However, before concluding this section we are going to provide in the following subsection an overview over the OOWS approach (Fons et. al, 2003), the method in which this work has been contextualized.

OOWS: A Method for the Development of Web Applications

This work has been developed in the context of the OOWS (Object Oriented Web Solution)

Figure 4. Models overview

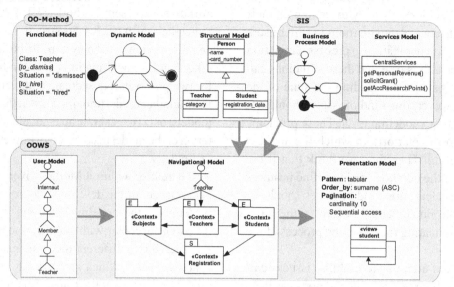

method (Fons et. al, 2003), which is the extension of the object-oriented software production method OO-Method (Pastor et. al, 2001), which introduces the required expressivity to capture the navigational and presentational requirements of Web applications. Figure 4 depicts the models defined by the method as well as the relationships between them. Arrows depicted in Figure 4 show the existing dependences between different models. For instance, the Business Process Model is defined from the functionality defined in both, the Structural Model and the Services Model. Another example is the relationship between the Navigational Model and the SIS models. In this case, the Navigational Model is built as a view over these models, where depending on the kind of user we show or hide some parts of the system. The following paragraphs provide a rough explanation of these models.

The OO-Method (Object Oriented Method for Software Development) models specify the structural and functional requirements of dynamic applications. These models are:

- **the Structural Model**, which defines the system structure (its classes, operations and attributes) and relationships between classes by means of a Class Diagram.

- **the Dynamic Model**, which describes (1) the different valid object-life sequence for each class of the system using State Transitions Diagrams and (2) communication between objects by means of Sequence Diagrams.

- **the Functional Model**, which captures the semantics of the state changes to define service effects using a textual formal specification.

The SIS (Service Interaction Solution) models were introduced to specify the interaction with external partners. These models are:

- **the Services Model**, which brings up external services (functionality provided by external partners) into the modeling level in order to manage them more easily (Torres et. al, 2005).

- **the Business Process Model**, which specify by means of BPMN diagrams a set of processes in which can intervene both functionality provided by the local system as well as functionality provided by external partners. The activities that made up these processes represent functionality defined both in the Structural Model and in the Services Model.

The OOWS (Object Oriented Web Solutions) models were introduced in order to extend conceptual modeling to Web environments. These models are:

- **the User Model**, which defines the kind of users that are going to interact with the Web application. Moreover, it defines inheritance relationships between them.
- **the Navigational Model** allows us defining appropriate system views (in terms of data and functionality) for each kind of user defined in the User Model. This model was extended in a previous work (Torres & Pelechano, 2006) with a set of new primitives in order to integrate business process execution with the Navigation.
- **the Presentation Model** allows us to model presentation requirements (information paging, layout and ordering criteria) of the elements defined in the Navigational Model.

All these models allow us to specify Web applications independently of any implementation technology. Then, by means of the application of a set of transformation rules we can obtain software artefacts for several implementation technologies.

We want to note that the part of the navigational model that provides support for the execution of the modeled BPs is only used to specify the user interfaces that are required for each kind of user to perform each task. It is not necessary to define links between the different user interfaces to specify the order in which users should navigate through them. This is because within the execution of a process the navigation is driven by the process and the user simply has to follow the predefined paths to complete it. In fact, the navi-

gation is implicitly defined in the BP definition, and therefore it is not necessary to move it to the navigational model.

OOWS SUPPORT FOR INTEGRATING USABILITY ISSUES DURING BUSINESS PROCESS EXECUTION

In accordance with the ISO 9241-11 standard, usability refers to "the extent to which a product can be used by specified users to achieve specified goals with effectiveness, efficiency and satisfaction in a specified context of user." In particular, regarding Web applications, usability experts analyze and provide solutions to cope with usability problems that users experience while interacting with the system. As a result of this analysis, experts provide a set of guidelines (Ahlstrom & Longo, 2001; Bailey, 1996; Bailey & Koyani, 2004; Fowler, 1998; van Welie, M.; Mayhew, 1992; Zimmerman et al., 2002) aimed at overcoming the observed usability problems.

If we concentrate just on the problems that can arise when performing a business process in a Web application we find that usability guidelines are oriented to ensure that users understand correctly the data and functionality that is shown to her/him.

Some of these guidelines are easily applied in our method because we start the modeling process by specifying the system domain what implies defining information such as classes, its operations and attributes (including its types).

The following subsections present how the OOWS approach cope with these usability guidelines. Moreover, we take also a look on how other aspects related to process execution (suspending, resuming and cancelling processes, handling multiple tasks at the same time, displaying the task to complete, notifying users when they are expected to complete a task) are handled by the method to improve usability when performing a process. We have organized them in two parts, first we state the usability problem being considered as well as the kind of processes in which this usability problem appears and then we present the solution designed in the OOWS approach to be compliance with the corresponding usability guideline.

Preventing Input Errors

Users are required to input some data (usually by means of a Web form) and they are not provided with enough information regarding the kind of data they are expected to input. As a result, Web forms are sent with data provided in incorrect formats and/or unfilled fields.

This problem refers to usability guidelines gathered in (Bailey, 1996; van Welie, M.; Mayhew, 1992; Zimmerman et al., 2002) and it can appear in both short and long-lived processes. Some of these guidelines are summarized in the following list:

- Provide right field length allowing users to see their entered data (Bailey, 1996).
- Partition long data items to aid users in detecting and reducing entry errors (Mayhew, 1992).
- Minimize user data entry filling input elements providing default values (Zimmerman, et al., 2002).
- Provide examples of input data that help users understanding the information that they are asked to input (Nielsen, 1999; van Welie, M.)
- Do not make mandatory fields those data that it is not required to continue the transaction. (van Welie, M.)
- Use informative error messages.

Solution. These guidelines are handled either at the structural model and the presentation model as follows.

Class attributes and operation's parameter defined in the structural model include among other properties the followings:

- **Data type**: It let us define the type of the attribute.
- **Is mandatory**: It allows specifying weather this attribute is required to execute the operation.
- **Valid value range**: It let us define and control which values can be entered.
- **Default value**: It lets the system suggest a predefined value to the user. The default value is a well-formed formula that is type-compatible with the attribute.

In the presentation model we associate to the attributes included in each navigational class the following properties:

- **Alias**: It allows defining an alternative name to the property being defined in order to present it more clearly to the user. (e.g., An attribute whose name is *tel_number* and its alias is *Phone Number*)
- **Edit mask**: It determines the format that the data shows when the user enters it. This mask is used for several purposes, (1) it is used to show the user an example of the data that she/he is expected to input, (2) it is used to partition long data items following the mask format and (3) it allows to provide a correct length of the input element.
- **Help message**: It allows specifying a text that can be shown to the user to provide some information about the meaning of the data to be entered.
- **Validation message**: is a piece of text that is shown to the user when a validation error occurs on the entered data.

With all this information defined at the modeling level we can generate graphical user interfaces that satisfy the above mentioned usability

Figure 5. Implementation of guidelines for preventing input errors

guidelines and that help the user understanding the data that she/he is asked to introduce.

On the other hand, other usability guidelines (Bailey, 1996; Bailey & Koyani, 2004; Nielsen, 1999; van Welie, M.) are better applied directly in the transformation rules that generate the corresponding code. Examples of guidelines of this type are:

- Using the most appropriate input element (radio buttons, checkbox, list box, etc.) regarding the kind of data being handled (Nielsen, 1999; van Welie, M.).
- Marking mandatory fields clearly (Bailey, 1996; van Welie, M.).
- Check syntactic errors at the client side (avoiding sending incorrect data to the server, what implies lengthening the time dedicated to complete a task) (Bailey & Koyani, 2004).

These three guidelines are introduced in the rules as follows:

- Appropriate widgets for input elements are generated following the guidelines provided by Jackob Nielsen in his Alertbox[3] column in conjunction with the form pattern defined by van Welie, M. These guidelines advice the most appropriate widget depending on the data being represented (number of different options, exclusion, multiple selection, etc.)
- Labels of mandatory input fields are attached with an asterisk.

- Client-side scripting languages (such as JavaScript or VBScript) or Web development techniques (as AJAX) are generated to check syntactic errors at the client side.

Suspending, Resuming and Cancelling Processes

During the execution of a short-lived process, users can stop performing a launched process and move to navigate through the Web site (normally to find some extra information to complete the task that she/he is performing at this moment). However, this movement does not always mean that the user is not interested in the process any more (in fact, in the majority of situations, users will go back to the process in order to complete it).

Then, when the user takes up again the process, she/he can get confused about the current state of the process. The user can think either that (1) the process has been cancelled and the tasks already performed are not valid anymore or the other way round, that (2) the process is still valid and the process is waiting to be finished.

On the contrary, during a long-lived process execution the completion of processes depends on several participants. In this case, the user is just supposed to complete the tasks that she/he has pending to complete. So, the tasks that are not completed will remain in her/his pending list of TO-DO things. In this case, the user has a clear idea about the behaviour of the process, and she/he knows that the already performed tasks will be valid until reaching the end of the process.

Figure 6. Process definition with timer constraint

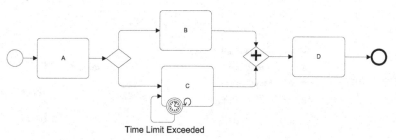

Time Limit Exceeded

Solution. The OOWS approach relies on a process engine which is in charge of handling running instances of processes (for both short and long-lived processes). Therefore, all the process activities that have been already completed will be valid even if the user has left the process for a while. The only case in which this is not valid is when the process definition includes time constraints (defined in the BPM by the use of timer intermediate events, see Figure. 66). In this case, the process definition will guide the user to the corresponding task. However, in order to avoid users leaving processes that have time limitations, we provide users with information regarding the time that they have remaining to complete the process.

As we have mentioned above, the OOWS approach relies on a process engine. Therefore, functionalities such as suspending, resuming and cancelling processes refer to functionality that is usually performed by system administrators. Participants should only cancel started instance processes when the process has been defined with appropriate compensation activities. In the OOWS approach the navigation during the execution of a process is driven by the process engine. Users can move from process execution to simple navigation and then return to complete started instance processes at the proper state.

Moreover, to avoid users leaving the execution of a process in order to get necessary data to complete the task being performed, we introduced in (Torres & Pelechano, 2006) a set of navigational primitives that allow us to define complementary data to the user interfaces used to perform activities. Figure 10 shows an example of use of this primitive in the Navigational Model, which is named Complementary-AIU. Figure 8 and Figure 9 show an implementation of this primitive in the *Purchase Book Request* example.

Handling Multiple Task Instances at the Same Time

Users have to complete *always* one by one each instance activities that they are responsible of. This statement could initially seem quite logic and sound. However, in some cases, this way of proceeding could result tedious for users, worsening as a result their productivity. For instance, consider the case where processes include activities/tasks that consist just in validating some data. In these cases, the user only has to decide if the data is accepted or rejected. If we provide users with a mechanism to handle (completing) multiple instances at the same time we would be improving her productivity and also her mood toward the system.

As this aspect refers to multiple task instances, this usability guideline is only applied to long-lived processes.

Solution. When a logged user checks her list of pending activities (see Figure 7) and after selecting one of them, she will have the opportunity of solving all the activity instances just in one step (see Figure 8).

Figure 7. TO-DO list Web page for the secretary staff

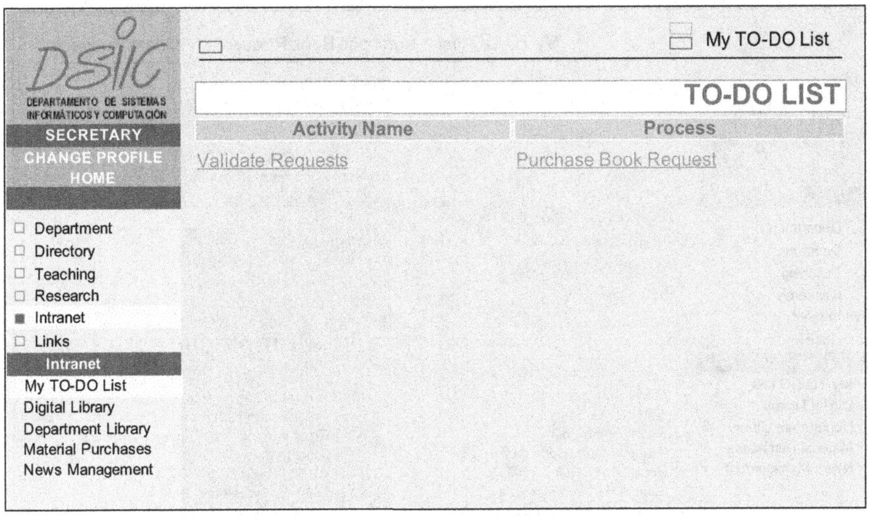

Figure 8 Mechanism for solving multiple task instances at the same time

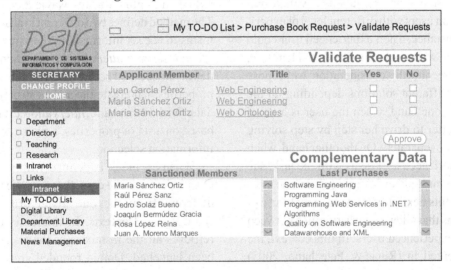

This is only applied to activities whose underlying functionality (operation defined either in the structural model or in the services model) just requires an argument with a controlled value (i.e., enumerations). This occurs with the *Validate Requests* activity defined in the *Purchase Book Request* example where the enumerated values associated to the argument of the operation are *Yes* and *No* (see Figure 8). When the operation requires a large amount of data from the user this approach is not the most appropriate.

When the task requires the introduction (by the user) of a considered amount of information, it is better to solve instance activities one by one in a separate Web form (see Figure 9).

However, this way of handling single instance activities is accessible also when the multiple instance mechanism is active. The way to access to it in this case is by selecting the linked attribute (*Title* from Figure 8).

In addition, we want to note that handling multiple task instances at the same time could not

Figure 9. Mechanism for solving one single task instance

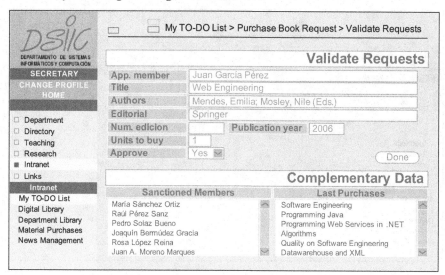

be always the most appropriate way if we take into consideration users with different level of experience. For instance, a non experienced user could get confused with a solution like that. Therefore, taking into account this consideration, we propose to provide different solutions depending on the case. In the one hand, when the user is a novel one, it is better to drive her step by step solving each instance separately. On the other hand, when a more experienced user deals with the task, she could solve multiple task items just in one step. To provide this flexibility we need to make use of mechanisms that allow us to distinguish between novel and experienced users. In this context, the work presented in (Rojas & Pelechano, 2005) defines a process in which users are stereotyped depending on their characteristics.

Information Overflow

The amount of data that is given to the user through the corresponding graphical interface can seem excessive for the task being performed. For some tasks this amount of data can be reduced to just the necessary information.

Solution. The way we cope with this issue in the OOWS method is by the use of indexes

(which are defined in the Navigational Model). The method defines two different kinds of mechanisms to access information; these mechanisms are *indexes* and *filters*. In the one hand, *indexes* define an access structure based on a set of defined properties that create the access structure to the data. On the other hand, *filters* allow establishing, based on a set of properties, a filter constraint or information selection.

When an index is defined within a Process Context[4], as it is the case, the semantic is slightly different from the one given originally for Navigational Contexts. In this case, the index retrieves all the instances of the task that have been launched. Dotted rounded area in Figure 10 shows graphically how indexes are defined in the OOWS approach.

As Figure 10 shows, indexes are defined by three properties, which are:

1. **Name**: Defines the name of the index.
2. **Attributes**: This property indicates the set of attributes that are going to be included when the index gets active.
3. **Link attribute**: This property specifies the attribute (from those included in the MAIN-AIU) that is used to access to each task instance.

Figure 10. Process context that includes an index

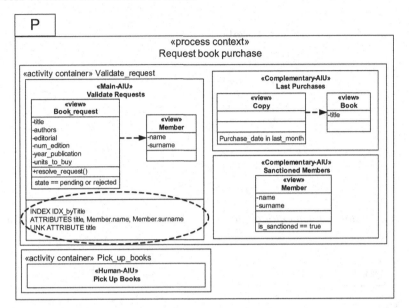

Displaying the Tasks Pending to Complete

When a user starts a short-lived process it is better to display her/him the set of steps/tasks involved in the process. This information can be used by the user to have an idea about the information that she/he has to provide in order to complete the process.

On the contrary, regarding long-lived processes, the user should only be displayed with the *next* pending task and not with the whole list of tasks to complete the process. Moreover, in this case, it is not important to provide the user with information about the steps that she/he has already perform in the process.

Solution. The GUI should include (just for short-lived processes) an area that displays the sequence of tasks/steps that need to be performed in order to finalize a process. Moreover, the current task being performed by the user must be distinguished among the rest of the tasks.

In the OOWS approach we define BPs by means of a Business Process Model (BPM). This model is based on the BPMN notation and allows defin-

ing processes as a set of steps that are assigned to different agents and organized by a flow control. In Torres and Pelechano (2005) authors defined a set of transformation rules that allow obtaining automatically from a BP specification the corresponding Navigational Model (NM) that provides support to the process execution. Then, with these two models (the BPM and the NM) we apply a set of predefined model-to-text transformations that allow us to obtain automatically the Web pages that implement the previously generated NM. In this transformation process we generate the area that displays the sequence of tasks that made up the process and that require user participation.

Figure 11 depicts graphically the models involved in the transformation process to obtain the final Web pages. As this figure shows, only those activities defined in a BP that require interaction with the user are first transformed into *Activity Containers* in the NM, which are later on transformed into the Web pages that will provide support to each of those activities. These generated Web pages include at the top of them a location area emphasizing the current activity within the process.

Figure 11. Strategy to generate the process location area

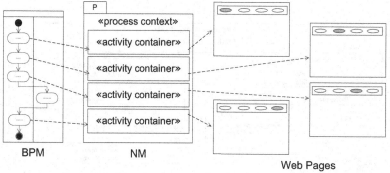

BPM   NM

Web Pages

Figure 12. Shipping action implementation for the checkout process

Figure 13. Original BP definition

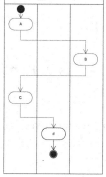

To illustrate this guideline, Figure 12 shows a Web page that corresponds to the implementation of the second activity of the Checkout Process. As this figure shows, the Web page includes an area (at the top) where the user can see the list of activities that constitute the process being executed. Moreover, the current activity is highlighted to help the user identify clearly the current action being performed.

Notify Users when They are Expected to Perform a Task

During the execution of a long-lived process many different participants can take part in it. The completion of an intermediate task implies that new task(s) turns into pending tasks. However, if these new pending tasks require human participation, the people in charge of completing them will not perform their job until they check if there is any pending activity in their TO-DO list what can derive in a longer delay of the process.

Solution. To minimize this problem, we have extended long-lived processes with tasks that notify users when they become responsible of a new activity. These new tasks are added before any activity that requires human participation.

In the one hand, Figure 13 shows an example of a BP definition in which three participants (all defined as users) take part in the process. Following the solution mentioned previously, we generate an extended version of the original BP

Figure 14. Modified BP definition

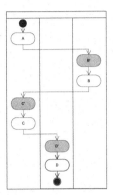

definition as shown in Figure 14. The new grey-coloured added tasks refer to services that send alerts to the involved users in order to make them aware of these new tasks. By default the process sends as alert mechanism via e-mail messages; however, other mechanisms such as Short Message System (SMS) or voice messages could also be considered.

Moreover, in the OOWS approach, similar to the client applications provided by most BPM solutions, when we specify at least one long-lived process, we generate automatically a whole section integrated in the Web application in charge of handling these kinds of processes. In this section users can access to the whole list of pending tasks (TO-DO list) that they are responsible of.

IMPLEMENTATION STRATEGY

As we have mentioned previously, the OOWS approach extends the OO-Method code generation strategy by introducing the Web interface layer and by reusing its business logic and persistence layers. Then, from the conceptual models and by the application of translation patterns we generate the equivalent specification in terms of an implementation language.

In this section, we are going to consider only the primitives that are used within a business

process execution. Then, each Activity Container is transformed into a Web page that contains the areas defined in the original implementation strategy (Navigation area, Location area, information area, User area, Institutional area, Application link area, Input data, Personalization area and access structure area), plus the following areas:

- **Process Navigation area**: This area contains two types of links (1) one that provides access to the user to her/his pending tasks (a TO-DO list) and (2) a second type of link that allows the user to start any of the long-lived processes in which this user, behaving in a specific role, is able to start the process.
- **Input Data area**: This area provides the user with the appropriate Web form to provide the required data to complete a specific task.
- **Complementary Data to perform the task**: In order to improve productivity and avoid users navigating through the Web application to find some data, this area provides the user with complementary information regarding the task being performed.
- **Process Location area**: This area shows the user all the tasks of the process being performed stressing the task in which she/he is within the process at any time (making explicit the progress within the process). This area differs depending on the kind of process being executed.
- **User area**: This area contains information about the user logged into the Web application. This information usually refers to user identifier and user behavioural role.
- **Process Arrangement/Ordering area**: This area provides the user with mechanisms that help her/him to order pending tasks depending on a set of criteria (by date, by priority, by users involved, by deadline, etc.)

In the following table we relate each of the areas defined previously with the two kinds of

Table 1. Summary of type processes and Web pages areas

	Type of Process	
	Short-lived	Long-lived
Process Navigation	×	×
Input Data	✓	✓
Complementary Data	✓	✓
Process Location	✓	×
User	?	☝
Ordering	×	✓

☝ Commendable   ✓ Mandatory   × Not Commendable

✱ It can be several   ? optional

processes distinguished in the chapter.

The following figures show how these different areas are organized within a Web page. Figure 15 shows the organization of the generated Web pages.

Figure 16 depicts possible configurations defined for the information area depicted in Figure 15. In the one hand, left hand image corresponds to the configuration of the TO-DO list Web page. This configuration is only implemented for long-lived processes and provides the user with a list with her/his pending tasks. On the other hand, right hand image corresponds to the configuration displayed to the user to complete a pending task. This configuration is valid for both short and long lived processes.

Figure 16. Information area configuration for long-lived processes

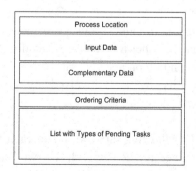

Figure 15. General Web page arrangement

User Info Area	Location Area
Navigational Area	Information Area
Process Navigational Area	

CONCLUSION

In this work we have gathered a set of guidelines that can help improving the usability of Web applications during the execution of a process. We have distinguished two different types of processes depending on the context in which they are executed. The objective of this distinction is to understand better the usability problems that can arise in each case. Then, we have shown how different usability guidelines are introduced in the OOWS Web engineering method to empower the method for the generation of usable process driven Web applications. The mechanisms used to introduce usability guidelines have been defined either at the modeling level or in the transformation rules that generate the corresponding software artefacts.

As further work, we have planned to study how to handle usability guidelines for the generation of Web applications that can be accessed by multiple kinds of devices (telephone mobiles, PDAs, etc.).

REFERENCES

Abran, A., Khelifi, A., Suryn, W., & Seffah, A. (2003, November). Usability meanings and interpretations in ISO standards. *Software Quality*

Journal. Springer Netherlands. ISSN 0963-9314 (Print) 1573-1367 (Online), Computer Science, 11(4), 325-338.

Ahlstrom, V., & Longo, K. (2001). *Human factors design guide update* (Report No. DOT/FAA/CT-96/01) A revision to chapter 8 - computer human interface guidelines. Retrieved October 17, 2007, from http://acb220.tc.faa.gov/technotes/dot_faa_ct-01_08.pdf

Atterer, R., Schmidt, A., & Hußmann, H. (2006, March). Extending Web engineering models and tools for automatic usability validation. Journal of Web engineering, *5*(1), 43-64.

Bailey, R.W. (1996). *Human performance engineering: Designing high quality professional user interfaces for computer products, applications and systems* (3rd ed.). Englewood Cliffs, NJ: Prentice Hall.

Bailey, R.W., & Koyani, S.J. (2004). Searching vs. linking on the Web: A summary of the research. Health and Human Services Technical Report.

Brambilla, M., Ceri, S., Fraternali, P., & Manolescu, I. (2006). Process modeling in Web applications. *ACM Transactions on Software Engineering and Methodology (TOSEM), 15*(4), 1-46.

Business Process Modeling Notation (BPMN, 2004). Version 1.0 - May 3, 2004

Cachero, C., Genero, M., Calero, C., & Meliá, S. (2006). Transformación de Modelos Navegacionales Dirigida por Criterios de Calidad. XV Jornadas de Ingeniería del Software y Bases de Datos. September, 2006.

De Troyer, O., & Casteleyn, S. (2003, July). Modeling complex processes for Web applications using WSDM. In *Proceedings of the Third International Workshop on Web-oriented Software Technologies (IWWOST'03)* (pp. 1-12).

Fons, J, Pelechano, V., Albert, M., & Pastor, O. (2003). Development of Web applications from

Web enhanced conceptual schemas. In *Proceedings of the Workshop on Conceptual Modeling and the Web, ER'03, (Vol. 2813).* Lecture Notes in Computer Science: Springer-Verlag.

Fowler, S. (1998). *GUI design handbook.* New York: McGraw-Hill.

Hans, A. S., & Rossi, G. (2004, January-February). Modeling and designing processes in e-commerce applications. *IEEE Internet Computing, 08*(1), 19-27.

Koch, N., Kraus, A., Cachero, C., & Meliá, S. (2004, May). Integration of business processes in Web application models. *Journal of Web engineering, 3*(1), 022-049.

Marchionini, G., & Crane, G. (1994, January). Evaluating hypermedia and learning: Methods and results from the Perseus project. *ACM Transactions on Information Systems, 12*(1), 5-34.

Matera, M., Costabile, M. F., Garzotto, F., & Paolini, P. (2002). SUE inspection: An effective method for systematic usability evaluation of hypermedia. *IEEE Transactions on Systems, Man, and Cybernetics, Part A, 32*(1), 93-103.

Mayhew, D. (1992). *Principles and guidelines in user interface design.* Englewood Cliffs, NJ: Prentice Hall.

Nielsen, J. (1999, December 20). *Designing Web usability: The practice of simplicity* (1st ed.). Peachpit Press.

Pastor, O., Gomez, J., Insfran, E., & Pelechano, V. (2001). The OO-Method approach for information systems modeling: From object-oriented conceptual modeling to automated programming. *Information Systems, 26,* 507-534.

Rojas, G., & Pelechano, V. (2005, November). A methodological approach for incorporating adaptive navigation techniques into Web applications. In *Proceedings of the International Conference on Web Information Systems Engineering (WISE),* New York, USA, (pp. 203-216).

Rossi , G., Schmid, H., & Lyardet, F. (2003, July). Engineering business processes in Web applications: Modeling and navigation issues. In *Proceedings of the Third International Workshop on Web-oriented Software Technologies (IW-WOST'03)* (pp. 13-21).

Selic, B. (2003, September). The pragmatics of model-driven development. IEEE Software, 20(5), 19-25.

Torres, V., & Pelechano, V. (2006). Building business process driven Web applications. In S. Dustdar, J. L. Fiadeiro, & A. Sheth (Eds.), *Business process management: Proceedings of the 4th International Conference, BPM 2006*, (Vol. 4102, pp. 322-337). Lecture Notes in Computer Science. Berlin/Heidelberg: Springer-Verlag.

Torres, V., Pelechano, V., Ruiz, M., & Valderas, P. (2005). *A model driven approach for the integration of external functionality in Web applications. The Travel Agency System.* MDWE 2005.

van Welie, M. (2007). Retreived October 17, 2007, from http://www.welie.com/patterns/index.html

Workflow Management Coalition. Terminology & Glossary. Document Number WFMC-TC-1011.

Document Status – Issue 3.0. February 1999.

Zimmerman, D. E., Akerelrea, C. A., Buller, D. B., Hau, B., & LeBlanc, M. (2002). Integrating usability testing into the development of a 5-a-day nutrition Web site for at-risk populations in the American Southwest. *Journal of Health Psychology*, 119-134.

ENDNOTES

[1] This work has been developed with the support of MEC under the project SES-AMO TIN2007-62894 and cofinanced by FEDER.

[2] http://www.dsic.upv.es/~west/iwwost03/articles.htm

[3] http://www.useit.com/alertbox/20040927.html

[4] Process context is a primitive defined in the navigational model to specify the way users interact with the system within a process execution by means of graphical user interfaces.

Section III
Metadata, MDE, Metamodels, and Ontologies

Chapter XVI
New Approaches to Portletization of Web Applications

Fernando Bellas
University of A Coruña, Galicia

Iñaki Paz
University of the Basque, Spain

Alberto Pan
University of A Coruña, Galicia

Óscar Díaz
University of the Basque, Spain

ABSTRACT

Portlets are interactive Web mini-applications that can be plugged into a portal. This chapter focuses on "portletizing" existing Web applications, that is, wrapping them as portlets, without requiring any modification. After providing some background on portlet technology, we discuss two kinds of approaches to portletization: automatic and annotation-based. Automatic approaches make use of heuristics to automatically choose the fragments of the Web application pages to be displayed into the space available in the portlet's window. In turn, in annotation-based approaches, it is the portal administrator who annotates each page of the portletized Web application to specify which fragments should be displayed. Annotation-based approaches also allow to supplement the functionality of the original Web application. Each approach is explained by using a sample scenario based on the same Web application. We also pinpoint the advantages and shortcomings of each approach, and outline future trends in portletization.

INTRODUCTION

Moving an application to the Web implies facing its multichannel character. The very same functionality can be offered through a variety of "channels", for example, as a Web application to be accessed from a desktop or a small-screen device (e.g., PDA, smart phone, etc.), or as a portlet available through a portal. Although the functionality remains the same, the characteristics of each channel determine the implementation. The pressure to have a Web presence and the pace at which technology evolves make most organizations support the desktop-oriented Web application first, and at latter stages, care about adapting it for small-screen devices and portals.

Portlets are interactive Web mini-applications, local or remote to the portal, that render markup fragments that the portal can integrate into a page (usually shared by other portlets). Integrating a Web application as a portlet improves the user experience, since the portal can automatically apply user profiles when accessing the Web application. For example, if the application requires authentication, the portal can store authentication parameters to automatically authenticate the user in the application when she or he logs in the portal. Support for smart bookmarks is another example. The portal can allow the user to store bookmarks to specific screens of the application. Each bookmark stores the navigation sequence to reach such a screen (Anupam, Freire, Kumar, & Lieuwen, 2000).

In principle, to integrate a Web application, a specific portlet must be developed. This implies the need to develop a new presentation layer, which is always a time-consuming task. This chapter focuses on "portletizing" existing Web applications, that is, wrapping them as portlets. The wrapping approach allows to expose Web applications as portlets to the portal without requiring any modification to the applications, thus greatly reducing the development time.

The rest of the chapter is organized as follows: First, we provide background on portlet technology and portletization approaches. Then, we exemplify the two main approaches proposed to date by summarizing the portletization techniques which have been the subject of the authors' work. Next, we compare both approaches. Finally, we outline future trends in portletization, as well as present conclusions.

BACKGROUND

Overview of Portlet Technology

The classic approach to integrate a Web application into a remote portal consists in defining a Web service (SOAP/REST) that exposes part of the application's business logic. The problem with this approach is that any portal wishing to integrate such an application must re-implement the user interface. It would be easier if the service was a remote portlet, returning HTML markup fragments rather than plain data. The Web Services for Remote Portlets (WSRP) specification (OASIS Consortium, 2003) standardizes the interfaces of the Web services that a portlet producer (typically, a portal) must implement to allow another application (typically, another portal) to consume its portlets, regardless of the technology which the producer and consumer use (e.g., J2EE, .NET, etc.). Portlet URLs embedded into fragments point to the portal. Whenever the user clicks on a link, the portal receives the HTTP request, invokes an operation on the portlet's producer that returns the markup fragment corresponding to this interaction, and finally composes a page that includes the response of this portlet and those of the remaining portlets in the page.

The Java Portlet Specification (Java Community Process, 2003) standardizes a Java API (JSR 168) for implementing local, WSRP-compatible portlets. Java portlets run in a portlet container, a portal component that provides portlets with a runtime environment. Apart from the portlet container, the typical architecture of a Java portal server (Bellas, 2004) includes other components:

- The WSRP producer component provides an implementation of the WSRP interfaces, so other consumers can access local portlets; and
- The WSRP consumer component is implemented as a local portlet that acts as a generic proxy for any WSRP producer.

The WSRP standard defines portlet modes and window states. Portlet modes refer to the types of functionality that a portlet can perform. In *view* mode, the portlet renders fragments that support its functional purpose (e.g., displaying weather forecasts). In *edit* mode, the portlet lets the user customize the behavior of the portlet (e.g., specifying the default temperature unit). The *help* mode provides help information. Finally, the *preview* mode allows to view the portlet before adding it to a portal page.

Window states act as an indication of the space available in the portlet's window. The *normal* state indicates that the portlet is likely sharing the page with other portlets. When the state is *minimized*, the portlet should not render visible markup. In the *maximized* state, the portlet has more space compared to other portlets in the page. Finally, the *solo* state indicates that the portlet is the only portlet in the page.

The portal decorates the fragments returned by a portlet with buttons to let the user select the portlet mode and window state.

Approaches to Portletization

During the last few years, several approaches have been proposed to address the portletization of Web applications. One way of classifying these applications is according to whether they provide "shallow" or "deep" portletization. These two types of portletization are described below:

- **Shallow portletization** (a.k.a., "Web clipping"): These techniques only allow to portletize a single page (typically, the home page) of the Web application. If the user navigates to a new page (for instance, by clicking on a link in the portletized page), then the rest of the interaction between the user and the application will be outside the scope of the portal system.
- **Deep portletization:** This implies portletizing the whole bulk of pages that comprise

the Web application. In this case, the whole interaction between the user and the Web application occurs inside the portal realm. Díaz and Paz (2005b) describes in detail the issues involved in deep portletization.

The approaches to portletization proposed to date are based on providing a special portlet (hereafter, the "bridge portlet") that navigates automatically to the target Web page (Anupam et al., 2000; Freire, Kumar, & Lieuwen, 2001; Pan, Raposo, Álvarez, Hidalgo, & Viña, 2002), and extracts the desired regions. The techniques proposed to build the bridge portlet can be roughly classified into two different types: *annotation*-based approaches and *automatic* approaches.

In the *annotation*-based approaches, the portal server administrator configures the bridge portlet for a specific Web application by manually identifying the set of regions in which she or he is interested within the target pages. Usually, the process of specifying the desired regions can be entirely performed through a graphical interface that automatically generates a file, sometimes called an *annotation* file (Hori, Ono, Abe, & Koyanagi, 2004). This file specifies the location of those regions (e.g., by using XPath expressions).

Current industrial portal servers (e.g., BEA WebLogic Portal, IBM WebSphere Portal, Oracle Portal, etc.) provide this kind of annotation-based support, but they only allow for shallow portletization. Furthermore, changes in the Web pages (e.g., adding or removing an HTML tag) may easily invalidate the addressing expressions in the generated annotations, which leads to a maintenance nightmare.

In turn, works like Díaz and Paz (2005b) and Paz and Diaz (in press) allow for annotation-based, deep portletization. They also consider the problem of how to generate annotations with resilient addressing expressions, which may keep on working correctly in the presence of certain layout changes in the target pages.

Automatic approaches require minimum human intervention to configure and maintain the bridge portlet for each target Web application. In fact, the portletization of Web applications can be carried out by the end-user. Web pages are displayed according to the space available in the portlet's window (window state), and the system is responsible for automatically (heuristically) obtaining the most "relevant" regions of the target page that fit into the available space. Automatic approaches allow to naturally realize deep portletization.

For instance, in the automatic approach proposed in Bellas, Paz, Pan, Díaz, Carneiro, and Cacheda (in press), when the portlet is in the *solo* state, all the content of the page is displayed. In the *maximized* state, only the body block (all regions except header, footer, and sidebars) is shown. In the *normal* state, the body block is segmented. The bridge portlet is in charge of automatically detecting the main blocks of the page, extracting the body block, and segmenting it.

Annotation-based approaches account for a fine-grained, accurate adaptation of the Web application to the portlet setting, since particular regions of the Web pages can be extracted. However, they need to manually annotate each page in order to specify the regions of interest and how they will be displayed depending on the window state. In consequence, they can only be used by a developer or a portal administrator. Annotations must also be maintained to accommodate the layout changes in the target sources.

In turn, automatic approaches require minimum human intervention, enable end-user portletization, and are more resilient to changes in the target pages. However, since they rely on heuristic-based techniques, they may be less accurate. In addition, they do not allow for fine-grained portletization, that is, when the user is only interested in specific parts of the pages.

The next three sections describe and compare in more detail these two approaches, using a specific case study to further illustrate how they work.

AUTOMATIC PORTLETIZATION

Sample Scenario

This section uses the Yahoo!™ Weather service (*http://weather.yahoo.com*) as a sample scenario to illustrate a possible model of how a Web application can be automatically displayed as a portlet in *view* mode. According to the expected behavior in the standard window states, the bridge portlet automatically adapts Web pages to the space available in the portlet's window. It also tries to keep the original look-and-feel. Figure 1 shows the responses generated by the bridge portlet.

Figure 1(a) shows the first page of the application when the user has selected the *solo* window state. Since the portlet is the only one in the portal page, the bridge portlet decides to show the original content. As the fragment returned by the portlet must be inserted into the portal page, the portlet extracts the markup contained inside the *<body>* tag of the original page, and rewrites the URLs that must be navigable inside the portlet's window.

Figure 1(b) shows the same page when the user selects the *maximized* window state. In this state, the portlet is supposed to have a lot of space in the page, but less than in the *solo* window state. The content of Web pages is often structured in five high-level blocks: header, footer, left sidebar, right side-bar, and body (the content region of the page). From the point of view of the actual content, the body block is the most important one, since the rest of the blocks are usually dedicated to navigational issues and miscellaneous information. In consequence, to save space, the bridge portlet detects the high-level blocks, extracts the body block, and rewrites the URLs that must be navigable inside the portlet's window.

Figure 1(c) shows the same page when the user selects the *normal* window state. Since the portlet is supposed to share the page with other portlets, the bridge portlet must reduce even more the amount of markup it generates. To do so, it

Figure 1. Displaying Yahoo! ™ Weather as a portlet (view mode); to save space, Figures (a) and (b) do not show all the content generated by the bridge portlet.

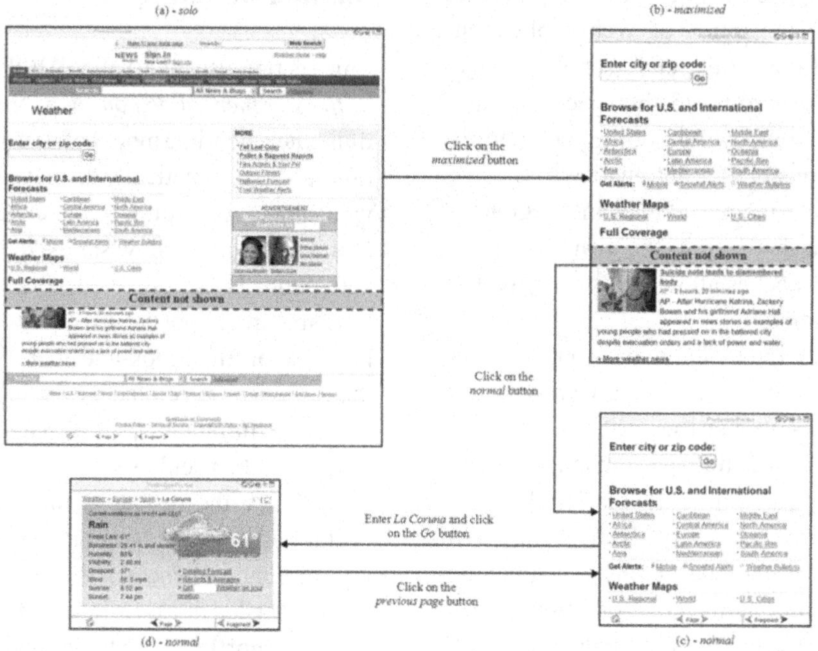

applies the same transformations as in the *maximized* window state and returns a fragment that contains the first part of the body block.

Figure 1(d) illustrates the situation when the user enters *La Coruna* in the form and clicks on the *Go* button. The portlet had rewritten the form's URL previously to point to the portlet itself. In consequence, this interaction causes a request directed to it. The portlet fetches the corresponding page and proceeds as in the previous case.

To keep the application navigable, the bridge portlet includes five *navigability buttons* (enabled or disabled as appropriate) at the bottom of all the generated fragments. Such buttons are links that point to the bridge portlet. The *previous/next fragment* buttons allow the user to navigate through the fragments of a page when the window state is *normal*. The *previous/next page* buttons allow the user to navigate through the pages already visited. For convenience, a *home page* button is also included to let the user go directly to the initial page.

A Case Study

This section provides an overview of the bridge portlet described in Bellas et al. (in press), which allows to automatically display a Web application as a portlet according to the model illustrated previously.

To understand the design of the bridge portlet, it is important to realize that the fragments shown in Figure 1 can be generated by using a chain of transformations that depends on the current window state. For example, when the window state is *maximized*, as in Figure 1(b), the fragment can be generated by: (1) detecting the high-level blocks of the original page and extracting the body block, and (2) including the navigability buttons. When the window state is *normal*, as in Figure 1(c), an additional transformation that splits the body and extracts the appropriate fragment can be applied between the two transformations used in the *maximized* window state.

The above observation gives rise to the framework depicted in Figure 2. *Transformer-ChainManager* allows to obtain a particular chain (*TransformerChain*) of transformation strategies to be applied to a page in a given window state. All transformation strategies implement the *Transformer* interface. The *transform* method in *TransformerChain* allows to execute the chain of transformations on a given page. By default, the framework provides three transformers:

- **BodyExtractor:** It returns the body block by detecting the high-level blocks of the original page and discarding the header, the footer, and the side bars;
- **GeneralSegmenter:** It divides the page into rectangular sections and returns the requested section. The area (in square pixels) of the rectangular sections is specified by a configuration parameter, and represents the approximate size of the portlet's window that the user wishes in the *normal* window state; and
- **PageNavigabilityTransformer:** It inserts the navigability buttons.

The default implementation of the *TransformerChainManager* returns the empty chain when the window state is *solo*, the {*BodyExtrac-tor→PageNavigabilityTransformer*} chain when the window state is *maximized*, and finally, the {*BodyExtractor→GeneralSegmenter→PageNavigabilityTransformer*} chain for the *normal* window state.

Except in the *minimized* window state, when the bridge portlet receives a request for a page, it calls: (1) *getPage* on *PageManager* to retrieve the page; (2) *getTransformerChain* on *Transformer-ChainManager* to obtain the particular chain of transformers to be applied in the current window state; (3) *transform* on *TransformerChain* to generate the fragment by applying the chain of transformations; and finally (4) *postProcessPage* on *PagePostProcessor*. When the window state is *minimized*, the bridge portlet returns an empty fragment (this is the default behavior inherited from *javax.portlet.GenericPortlet*).

The *Page* object returned by *PageManager* provides "getter" methods to access certain information of the page, such as JavaScript code, CSS styles, and the fragment that contains all the tags inside the *<body>* tag. Transformers work with this fragment, since the rest of the tags cannot be included in the portal page. Internally, this fragment is represented as a DOM tree. All transformers work with the standard DOM API. Since some transformers (*BodyExtractor* and *GeneralSegmenter*) need to know the visual informa-

Figure 2. Bridge portlet's framework

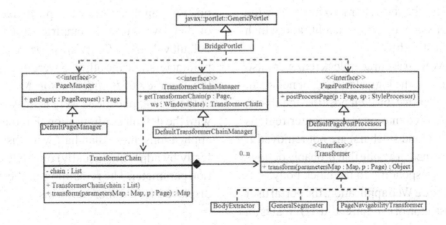

tion of each node, we use a mechanism of DOM Level 3 that allows to attach information to nodes. In particular, each node has an attached object providing visual information of the rectangular region that it defines. This information includes the X and Y coordinates of the left upper corner of the rectangle, and its width and height.

The implementation of *PagePostProcessor* rewrites the URLs that must be navigable inside the portlet's window, includes CSS styles and JavaScript code defined inside the *<head>* tag of the original page, and renames all JavaScript functions/variables and CSS styles to avoid collisions with the rest of the portlets included in the same page and with the portal itself.

The most critical transformer is *BodyExtractor*, since this is currently the only heuristic transformer. Internally, *BodyExtractor* uses four "block removers": *HeaderRemover*, *FooterRemover*, *LeftSideBarRemover*, and *RightSideBarRemover*. The implementation of all block removers is orthogonal. Each remover tries to find a group of nodes that make up a region that visually can be considered as the block that it is trying to remove. A region can be classified as a particular block in function of its shape (width/height ratio) and its position. For example, the header block has a flat shape (high width/height ratio) and is placed at the top of the page. Each remover uses configuration parameters that define the maximum height (for the header and the footer) or width (for the left and right sidebars) of the region, and the minimum (for the header and the footer) or maximum (for the left and right sidebars) width/height ratio which the region must fulfill.

To improve their accuracy, block removers also take into account the logical nesting of nodes. In particular, nodes that, by their position and shape, could be classified into one of the outer regions (header, footer, and sidebars) are not removed if they are contained in a node that probably defines the region corresponding to the block body.

To portletize a Web application, the portal user (and administrator, or even an end-user) creates an instance of the bridge portlet, adds it to a portal page, and selects the *edit* mode. In the *edit* mode, the bridge portlet displays a configuration wizard that allows to specify:

- **The URL of the first page of the application (e.g., http://weather.yahoo.com in the sample scenario):** This is the only field that must be explicitly filled;
- **A set of URL patterns for the URLs that must be navigable inside the portlet's window:** The bridge portlet rewrites the URLs, matching these patterns to point to itself. In the sample scenario, if we wish to keep the search form and the "browse by location" links navigable, we could specify */search/weather2* for the search form, and */regional/** and */forecast/** to browse by location. URL patterns can be specified in "absolute URL" or "absolute path" (as in the example) notation; and
- **The configuration of *BodyExtractor* and *GeneralSegmenter*:** The configuration wizard provides reasonable default values, which have been obtained empirically.

The above information is stored as the portlet's preferences (Java Community Process, 2003), and in consequence, each portlet instance has its own configuration.

Experiments have confirmed the viability of this automatic approach. To this end, 50 Internet Web applications were portletized. Fifteen of them were used to empirically choose good default values for *BodyExtractor*'s configuration parameters, and the other 35 were used to evaluate the accuracy of *BodyExtractor*. More than 70% of the Web applications were displayed perfectly with the default configuration. For the rest of the applications, more than half were displayed perfectly by adjusting (usually) only one configuration parameter. The remaining applications were displayed with minor problems.

ANNOTATION-BASED PORTLETIZATION

Sample Scenario

This section presents a sample scenario, based also on the Yahoo! ™ Weather service, to illustrate an example of the annotation-based approach to portletization. The intention is to build a weather portlet based on the Yahoo! ™ Weather service. Its main functional purpose is to render the weather forecast for a user-provided place.

In this sense, Figure 3 (1) details the decomposition of the Yahoo! ™ Weather service home page depending on the window state.

The Yahoo! ™ Weather home page (see Figure 3(a)) is the first page of the Web application and thus the origin of the fragments. Notice that it has been deliberately decided not to render weather news, which could be used to produce a new portlet. The first fragment viewed in the portlet (see Figure 3(b)) in the *normal* window state shows the form to search for a location. From this fragment, through the use of the bottom links of the fragment ("Locations" and "Maps" links), we can move to a browsed search of a location (see Figure 3(c)) or to a browsed search of a weather map (see Figure 3(d)). From any of them, by maximizing the portlet window, a portlet fragment (see Figure 3(e)) containing all those small fragments is rendered.

Then, searching a location on the form or browsing the locations would end in the presentation of a fragment that contains the forecast for the selected location (See Figure 4).

How the portlet behaves with the use of window states has been described. However, portlets also have modes. Figure 3 (2) shows how the bridge portlet reacts to the use of modes. A form which allows to ask for help on weather terms has been

Figure 3. Yahoo! ™ Weather service decomposition in: (1) Window State fragments for the home page and (2) Portlet Modes in normal window state

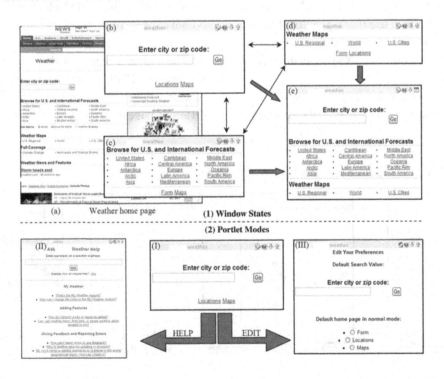

used for the *help* mode, while the *edit* mode allows the user to edit her or his preferences. In this case, the *edit* mode allows to set a default value for the search form or to select a default behavior (one of the three *fragments* extracted from the home page) for the first time the user accesses the portlet (in *normal* window state).

A Case Study

This section introduces the annotation-based bridge portlet framework, described in Paz and Diaz (in press), where the sample previously presented is used to drive the implementation concepts. Annotation refers to the process of increasing the knowledge on a Web application through the use of "notes" that on a later stage can be reused for new means. In this sense, a Web application can be annotated to add semantic meaning to its contents (Paz, Díaz, Baumgartner, & Anzuola, 2006), or as used in this case, to wrap a Web application as a full-featured portlet. Annotations on a Web application can be performed directly on the source pages (HTML), or maintained on a remote repository to be accessed by whoever wants to use them, granting that the Web application is left untouched. Annotations are normally specified as XML documents to ease its reuse.

Among other portletization concepts introduced in previous sections (e.g., URL rewriting,

etc.), it is important to notice that to portletize a Web application, first we should know which parts of the Web application are to be reused, and how they will be reused; the annotations which were produced to be consumed by our bridge portlet framework reflects this fact. These annotations will be stored locally to our framework.

Information extraction patterns can be used to locate a portion on a Web application page. Patterns are "tools" used to locate data on a page. These "tools" range from regular expressions (Atzeni & Mecca, 1997) to complex expression languages (Baumgartner, Flesca, & Gottlob, 2001). Laender, Ribeiro-Neto, Soares da Silva, and Teixeira (2002) presents a good survey on them. However, unlike previous approaches, our aim is not to extract data buried into HTML pages, but chunks of XHTML markup that can become portlet fragments. To characterize these chunks, we resort to a language able to express patterns based on the page structure: XPath. XPath is a standard language to address elements in XML documents. Since HTML documents (Web pages) can be converted to XML through the use of tools, such as JTidy (The JTidy Volunteer Team, 2006), XPath expressions may extract those parts of the page that make up a portion[1].

Thus, given a page, it can be annotated through the use of XPath expressions. Since Web application pages will normally be different, and different pages normally imply distinct content

Figure 4. Yahoo!™ Weather application state machine

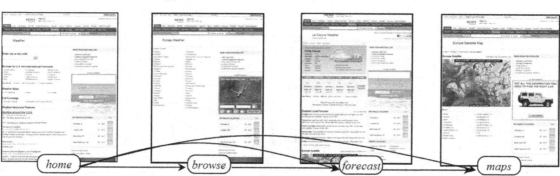

Figure 5. Bridge portlet model

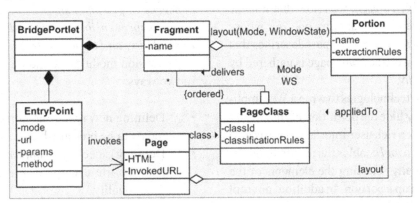

with different structure, an XPath selecting a portion on a page may select nothing at all, or even worse, may select unwanted content on another page. Therefore, pages need to be classified[2]. In this sense, a Web application is seen as a state machine, where the states represent the distinct pages and the arrows represent the user interactions among them (see Figure 4).

The model shown in Figure 5 summarizes these concepts. Basically, a Web application can be seen as a set of pages, while a portlet can be seen as a set of fragments, where both pages and fragments are composed of portions. The model is captured in XML annotation files that are consumed by the bridge portlet.

First of all, notice that a bridge portlet, as a portlet, has portlet modes. However, in a Web application environment, there are no different modes of operation; everything may be intertwined on one page, on different pages, or may not exist at all. Thus, in contrast to the automatic approach, a portlet may have one or more entry points (one per supported mode). For instance, on the sample portlet, the *help* mode fragment comes directly from the Yahoo! ™ Weather help page.

Basically, the process executed by the bridge portlet is as follows:

1. The first page for the current mode of operation is retrieved;
2. The retrieved page is classified among the defined classes;

3. The portions are extracted from the retrieved page; portions denote those semantic units of content on pages (i.e., banners, forms, sections, etc.);
4. A fragment (in the portlet's output) is built using the extracted portions depending on the mode of operation and the window state;
5. The fragment is post-processed to handle URL redirection, CSS, etc.; and
6. Finally, the fragment is submitted to the portal to be rendered, where the user interacts with it and the cycle starts again.

Some examples follow that define the extraction rules of a portion and the classification rules of a page from Yahoo! ™ Weather:

```
<page class="home">
  <classifier>
    <xpath
      select="//div[@class='ulmForm']"/>
  </classifier>
</page>
<portion name="form">
  <extractionRules pageClassRef="home">
    <xpath mode="select">
      //div[@class='ulmForm']
    </xpath>
  </extractionRules>
</portion>
```

The first part specifies what characterizes the *home* page. Given a page, we know that it is the *home* page because it contains one *div* whose class is *ulmForm*. The second part describes that the *form* portion on the *home* page is gathered by selecting that *div*.

Annotation technologies to wrap a Web application normally hide the definition of the extraction patterns on a rich user interface. This is also our case where a *tool* enables the user to build the portlet by visually selecting the elements of the page that make up a portion. In addition, our tool also optimizes the gathered extraction patterns to improve the robustness of the portlet to changes on the Web application through the use of *simulated annealing* (Paz & Diaz, in press). For instance, the XPath expression *//div[@class='ulmForm']* is an optimized version of the absolute XPath expression gathered from the *tool* that selects that *div*. Notice that the XPath expression is based only on an attribute (*class*) that somehow describes its contents.

So far, the focus has been on wrapping the Web application as a portlet so that a Web application can be included as part of the portal. However, the fact of being enacted from a portal has deeper implications. Portals provide diverse commodities to enhance both user experience and seamless application integration.

Some of the implications include integrating the application with the Single Sign-On feature of the portal, perfect CSS harmonization, maintaining a form log with last values typed by the user, personalizing navigation on the Web application through usage mining, and so forth.

Due to the difficulties in foreseeing the specific enhancements that a Web application will need when being portletized, the bridge portlet can be adjusted through the use of *"extensionModules"*. Extension modules are plugin-like packages that extend the portlet with a given functionality using an aspect-like approach. An *aspect* is a unit of modularity that encapsulates crosscutting concerns. As stated in Elrad, Filman, and Bader (2001), *"separating the expressions of multiple concerns ... promises simpler system evolution, more comprehensible systems, adaptability, customizability, and easier reuse"*.

Extension modules extend the bridge portlet in two ways:

- Defining new rendering portions and fragments to be presented; and
- Defining aspects that supplement the bridge portlet's life cycle with the new required functionality.

For instance, enabling the portlet to let the user select which of the fragments is used as a home fragment whenever the portlet is enacted (see Figure 3(III)) implies:

- A new fragment for the *edit* mode that reuses the form;
- A new title portion;
- A new portlet portion that selects the default behavior;
- An aspect that captures the form submission and stores the user's preferences; and
- An aspect which, depending on the user's preferences, modifies the default behavior and selects the user's preferred fragment to be rendered.

```
<fragment name="homeEdit"
            layout="edit.jsp">
    <portion name="newTitle"/>
    <portion name="form"/>
    <portion name="behavior"/>
    <portion name="other"/>
</fragment>
<factory class="org.onekin.TitleFactory">
    <portions><portion name="newTitle"/>
    </portions>
</factory>
<advice class="org.onekin.PrefStoreAdv">
    <pointcut moment="before"
            method="ReadParams"/>
</advice>
```

In this case, the first part specifies a new *fragment* that will be used for the *edit* mode, and which contains the *form*[3] to set a default value, a *newTitle* for the fragment, and several radio buttons to select the default *behavior*. The newly-specified portions (*newTitle* and *behavior*) have to be defined. The *factory* element specifies the implementation class that builds the specified portions. The second part specifies that the *TitleFactory* class creates the *newTitle* portion. Finally, an *advice*, the code that an aspect supplements, needs to be defined. The *PrefStoreAdv advice* will be executed *before* the portlet reads the parameters (*readParams*) from the portlet request in order to capture and set the user's preferences whenever the form has been enacted in the *edit* mode.

This tiny example introduces how a bridge portlet can be extended. However, more complex features can be built through the use of extension modules. Paz et al. (2006) presents how to annotate portlets to be semantically integrated in a portal where data from one portlet feeds other portlets.

DISCUSSION

The sample scenarios included in the two previous sections allow to illustrate the advantages and shortcomings of automatic and annotation-based approaches. One advantage of automatic approaches is that they require minimum human intervention to configure and maintain the bridge portlet, enabling end-user portletization. In the sample scenario illustrated in the automatic portletization section, the user easily configures the bridge portlet by using the *edit* mode to specify the URL of the first page of the application (*http://weather.yahoo.com*) and a set of URL patterns for the URLs that must be navigable inside the portlet's window (*/search/weather2* for the search form, and */regional/** and */forecast/** to browse by location). For some Web applications, it could be necessary to adjust some configuration parameters in either the *BodyExtractor* or

GeneralSegmenter configuration. However, experiments have shown that a high percentage of applications can be displayed perfectly with the default configuration or by adjusting only one configuration parameter.

Another related advantage of automatic approaches is that they are more resilient to changes in the pages of the source Web application, since they do not make use of addressing expressions to extract regions. On the contrary, they use heuristic methods to obtain the most "relevant" page regions depending on the page space available to the portlet.

Finally, another advantage of automatic approaches is that they naturally allow for deep portletization, since it is not necessary to configure or annotate each page of the portletized application.

On the other hand, annotation-based approaches allow for a more precise kind of tuning. For example, in the scenario provided in the annotation-based portletization section, the portal administrator has configured the bridge portlet to display the search form and the two kinds of browsed search in the *maximized* window state (see Figure 3(e)) when the user accesses the first page of the application, and only one of the three components in the *normal* window state (see Figures 3(b), 3(c), and 3(d)). This contrasts with the markup generated by the approach described in the automatic portletization section (see Figures 1(b) and 1(c)), which includes more content in both window states.

However, the level of tuning exhibited by annotation-based approaches requires the use of addressing expressions to extract specific regions, which may break if the markup of the original Web pages changes. Maintenance problems may arise if the number of applications and/or pages to be portletized is high. To alleviate this problem, annotation-based approaches may provide tools to: (1) build the portlet using a rich user interface; and (2) generate change-resilient XPath expressions.

Unlike automatic approaches, annotation-based approaches allow to provide additional modes other than the *view* mode. For instance, in the sample scenario presented in the annotation-based portletization section, the portal administrator has configured the bridge portlet to show the content of the Yahoo! ™ Weather help page when the user selects the *help* mode (see Figure 3(II)). The portlet has also been configured to provide an *edit* mode (see Figure 3(III)) that allows to set a default value for the search form or to select a default behavior the first time the user accesses the portlet. Note that the *edit* mode provided by the bridge portlet in the automatic approach is not specific to the portletized application nor does it supplement its functionality. On the contrary, it provides a mechanism to configure the bridge portlet. Annotation-based approaches also allow the use of extension modules to provide additional functionality which is not provided by the original application.

In conclusion, we can see that the advantages of one approach are the drawbacks of the other, and vice versa. In fact, the two approaches are complementary. When a precise kind of tuning is required, the annotation-based approach is mandatory. Otherwise, the automatic approach is much more maintainable. In consequence, we believe that industrial solutions should provide support for both approaches.

FUTURE TRENDS

As it has been established in previous sections, both annotation-based and automatic approaches to portletization have their own advantages in specific scenarios. Therefore, a complete state-of-the-art package for portletization should support both. For instance, the bridge portlet described in the automatic portletization section could include a new transformer to allow annotation-based portletization, as an alternative to using the *BodyExtractor* transformer. Along these lines,

industrial portal servers should provide similar integrated solutions in the near future if they want to allow portletization in more complex, realistic situations than the ones they currently support.

Another interesting direction that will probably generate further research is that of creating new techniques for identifying and extracting the "relevant" regions in the automatic approach. This can benefit from work in other areas. For instance, a closely-related field is that of automatically adapting content for small-screen mobile devices. One example along these lines is the case study presented in the automatic portletization section. The techniques developed during the last several years for automatically or semi-automatically extracting structured data from Web pages (Arasu & Garcia-Molina, 2003; Laender et al., 2002; Pan et al., 2002) could also be successfully adapted to this new problem. In addition, learning techniques could be employed to exploit the user's past navigation experience on the target Web application to improve the system guesses about what regions are "relevant".

In the case of annotation-based approaches, automatically detecting when addressing expressions breaks is another area where research in Web data extraction could be leveraged. Works such as Raposo, Pan, Álvarez, and Hidalgo (in press) and Lerman, Minton, and Knoblock (2003) addressed the related problem of automatically maintaining Web wrappers.

We predict that portlet composition and inter-operation will be another hot topic. This refers to composing several independently-developed portlets to achieve a common goal. The upcoming versions of current portal standards (Java Community Process, 2003; OASIS Consortium 2003) will soon provide the developer with support to communicate with different portlets. Nevertheless, this does not solve the problem of communicating with portletized Web applications. To make this possible, it is also necessary to correctly interpret the markup generated by the portletized applications. Semantic Web techniques can help overcome these limitations by providing a method to easily specify the structure and semantics of the markup generated by different portlets, as well as for establishing semantic mappings between them. Díaz, Iturrioz, and Irastorza (2005a) describe a pioneer work in this direction.

CONCLUSION

In this chapter, we have studied the problem of "portletizing" existing Web Applications. Portlets are interactive Web mini-applications which run inside a portal server. Each page of the portal is usually shared by several portlets.

Creating a new portlet from an existing Web Application involves issues such as adjusting its content to fit into the available space for the portlet or rewriting the URLs in the navigation links through the pages of the application to be used from inside the portal. Integrating a Web application as a portlet improves the user experience, since they get one-stop access to multiple services and the portal can automatically apply user profiles when accessing them.

We have studied two kinds of approaches for "portletization": annotation-based and automatic. We have exemplified both approaches with the detailed description of two systems from our previous research.

We have also outlined their advantages and shortcomings. We conclude that they serve related but different goals and, therefore, they should be considered complementary to each other. Therefore, it is our opinion that forthcoming industrial solutions should provide integrated support for both approaches in order to allow realistic, successful portletization of existing Web Applications.

We have also argued that more research work is needed in the areas of portlet composition and interoperation and in the use of more sophisticated content extraction techniques for automatic portletization.

ACKNOWLEDGMENT

This work was partially supported by the Spanish Science and Technology Ministry and European Social Funds (FEDER) under projects TSI2005-07730 and TIC2002-01442. Alberto Pan's work was partially supported by the "Ramon y Cajal" program of the Spanish Education and Science Ministry.

REFERENCES

Anupam, V., Freire, J., Kumar, B., & Lieuwen, D. F. (2000). Automating Web navigation with the WebVCR. *Proceedings of the 9th International World Wide Web Conference* (pp. 503–517). ACM Press.

Arasu, A., & Garcia-Molina, H. (2003). Extracting structured data from Web pages. *Proceedings of the International SIGMOD Conference* (pp. 337-348). ACM Press.

Atzeni, P., & Mecca, G. (1997). Cut & paste. *Proceedings of the International Conference in Principles of Database Systems* (pp. 144-153). ACM Press.

Baumgartner, R., Flesca, S., & Gottlob, G. (2001). Visual Web information extraction with Lixto. *Proceedings of the 27ᵗʰ International Conference on Very Large Data Bases (VLDB)* (pp. 119-128). Morgan Kauffmann.

Bellas, F. (2004). Standards for second-generation portals. *IEEE Internet Computing, 8*(2), 54-60.

Bellas, F., Paz, I., Pan, A., Díaz, O., Carneiro, V., & Cacheda, F. (in press). An automatic approach to displaying Web applications as portlets. *Lecture Notes in Computer Science* (issue corresponding to 3rd International Conference on Distributed Computing and Internet Technology, ICDCIT 2006).

Díaz, O., Iturrioz, J., & Irastorza, A. (2005a). Improving portlet interoperability through deep annotation. *Proceedings of the 14th International World Wide Web Conference* (pp. 372-381). ACM Press.

Díaz, O., & Paz, I. (2005b). Turning Web applications into portlets: Raising the issues. *Proceedings of the IEEE/IPSJ International Symposium on Applications and the Internet* (pp. 31–37). IEEE Press.

Elrad, T., Filman, R. E., & Bader, A. (2001). Aspect-oriented programming: Introduction. *Communications of the ACM, 44*(10), 29-32.

Freire, J., Kumar, B., & Lieuwen, D. F. (2001). WebViews: Accessing personalized Web content and services. *Proceedings of the 14th International World Wide Web Conference* (pp. 576-586). ACM Press.

Hori, M., Ono, K., Abe, M., & Koyanagi, T. (2004). Generating transformational annotation for Web document adaptation: Tool support and empirical evaluation. *Journal of Web Semantics, 2*(1), 1–18.

Java Community Process (2003). *Java Portlet Specification - Version 1.0*. Retrieved from http://jcp.org/aboutJava/communityprocess/final/jsr168/index.html

The JTidy Volunteers Team (2006). Jtidy, HTML parser and pretty printer in Java. Retrieved from http://jtidy.sourceforge.net

Laender, A. H. F., Ribeiro-Neto, B. A., Soares da Silva, A., & Teixeira, J. S. (2002). A brief survey of Web data extraction tools. *ACM SIGMOD Record, 31*(2), 84-93.

Lerman, K., Minton, S., & Knoblock, C. (2003) Wrapper maintenance: A machine learning approach. *Journal of Artificial Intelligence Research, 18*, 149-181.

OASIS Consortium (2003). *Web Services for Remote Portlets Specification - Version 1.0*. Retrieved from http://www.oasis-open.org/committees/tc_home.php?wg_abbrev=wsrp

Pan, A., Raposo, J., Álvarez, M., Hidalgo, J., & Viña, A. (2002). Semi-automatic wrapper generation for commercial Web sources. In C. Rolland, S. Brinkkemper, & M. Saeki (Eds.) *Proceedings of IFIP WG8.1 Working Conference on Engineering Information Systems in the Internet Context* (pp. 265-283). Kluwer Academic Publishers.

Paz, I., & Díaz, O. (in press). On portletizing Web applications. *ACM Transactions on the Web (TWeb)*.

Paz, I., Díaz, O., Baumgartner, R., & Anzuola, S. F. (2006). Semantically integrating portlets in portals through annotation. In K. Aberer., Z. Peng, E. A. Rundensteiner, Y. Zhang, & X. Li (Eds.), *LNCS 4255, Proceedings of the 7th I.C. on Web Information Systems Engineering, 2006* (pp. 436-447). Springer.

Raposo, J., Pan, A., Álvarez, M., & Hidalgo, J. (in press). Automatically maintaining wrappers for Web sources. *Data and Knowledge Engineering* (volume and issue still not assigned). Available online through ScienceDirect, http://dx.doi.org/10.1016/j.datak.2006.06.006

KEY TERMS

Annotation approach (for portletization): The approach to *portletization* where the *portal* administrator configures the *bridge portlet* for a specific Web Application by manually identifying in the target pages the set of regions in which she or he is interested. Usually, this process generates a file called an annotation file.

Automatic approach (for portletization): The approach to *portletization* where the configuration of the *bridge portlet* requires none or minimal human intervention, allowing end-users to carry out portletization tasks themselves. These systems use diverse heuristics to automatically obtain the most "relevant" regions of the target pages that fit into the space available in the *portlet*'s window.

Bridge Portlet: A special *portlet* used to wrap an existing Web Application into a *portlet*. When the user interacts with the portletized application, the bridge portlet navigates automatically to the original page in the existing application to extract the desired regions.

Deep Portletization: The kind of *portletization* where the whole bulk of pages comprising the existing Web Application are portletized. In "deep portletization", the whole interaction between the user and the Web application may occur inside the *portal*.

JSR 168: The Java Portlet Specification (JSR 168) standardizes a Java API for implementing local portlets, which can be packaged and deployed in any JSR 168-compliant Java portal. If the Java portal provides WSRP producer functionality, JSR 168 portlets can be remotely accessed by WSRP consumers.

Portal: A portal is a Web application providing their users with integrated Web access to a set of underlying applications providing different services to the user.

Portlet: Portlets are interactive Web mini-applications, local or remote to the portal, that render markup fragments which the portal can integrate into a page (usually shared by other portlets).

Portletization: The term "portletization" refers to wrapping an existing Web application into a *portlet*, thus allowing its integration in a *portal*.

Shallow Portletization: The kind of *portletization* which only allows to portletize a single page (typically the home page) of the existing Web application.

WSRP: The Web services for remote portlets (WSRP) specification standardizes the interfaces of the Web services which a portlet producer (typically a portal) must implement to allow another application (typically another portal) to consume its portlets, regardless of the technology that the producer and consumer use (e.g., J2EE, .NET, etc.).

ENDNOTES

[1]   XSLT is used to extract the portions from the page by solely copying on the output those elements selected by the XPath expressions.

[2]   XPath may also be used to characterize a page based on the existence of a concrete element on the document. Text patterns are used also over URLs to capture navigational characteristics of the corresponding pages.

[3]   This fragment has been assigned to the *edit* mode for the *home* page, which is the entry point to the Web application. Thus the *form* portion has been reused here.

Chapter XVII
Towards the Adaptive Web Using Metadata Evolution

Nicolas Guelfi
University of Luxembourg, Luxembourg

Cédric Pruski
University of Luxembourg, Luxembourg and University of Paris-Sud XI, France

Chantal Reynaud
University of Paris-Sud XI, France

ABSTRACT

The evolution of Web information is of utmost importance in the design of good Web Information Systems applications. New emerging paradigms, like the Semantic Web, use ontologies for describing metadata and are defined, in part, to aid in Web evolution. In this chapter, we survey techniques for ontology evolution. After identifying the different kinds of evolution with which the Web is confronted, we detail the various existing languages and techniques devoted to Web data evolution, with particular attention to Semantic Web concepts, and how these languages and techniques can be adapted to evolving data in order to improve the quality of Web Information Systems applications.

INTRODUCTION

When we consider the evolution of the World Wide Web (WWW) and its development over the last decade, we can see that drastic changes have taken place. Originally, the Web was built on static HTML documents and used as experimental communication means for specific communities in educational institutions and government defence agencies. With its ever-increasing popularity, the WWW is now the largest resource of information in the world. As such, it contains either durable or volatile information that needs to be maintained easily and often with predefined time delays. For example, this is the case for day-to-day news diffusion. The emergence of new paradigms like the Semantic Web (Berners-Lee, Hendler, & Lassila, 2001) has further intensified the evolution of the Web. Since the Semantic Web has the ability to make Web information machines understandable, it correlates to an improvement in the quality of

Web content and Web services, and the result unloads users of tedious search tasks.

These changes are accompanied by the manifestation of new application families such as Web Information System (WIS) applications. WIS applications are developed based on Web content and consequently must adapt to its evolution. Consider, for example, a tourism application for helping users prepare their holidays. If the company introduces a new kind of vacation (e.g., social holidays for elderly people), then the application needs to be maintained in order to cope with the evolution of this domain. The development of WIS applications is not an easy task since it is difficult to clearly catch the semantics of actual Web content, which in turn limits the retrieval of relevant Web information (Guelfi & Pruski, 2006).

Parallel to this development, the use of metadata to drive the advancement of Web-based applications has proven to be a very promising field of research (Suh, 2005) and we believe that the use of metadata can improve the quality of WIS applications. Metadata is useful to describe Web resources in a structured and precise way. It can be used, for instance, to describe the content of tourism resources in our application example. Consequently, languages are needed to define metadata, and techniques are required for the metadata to smoothly follow the evolution of the described resource. To this end, the Semantic Web paradigm can be the key to success. It consists in using ontologies (Gruber, 1993) to define the semantics of a particular domain and then uses the vocabulary contained in these ontologies as metadata to annotate Web content.

In this context, many ontology languages have been intensively studied in the literature (Antoniou & van Harmelen, 2004; Charlet, Laublet, & Reynaud, 2004). Although they provide basic modelling features, they do not offer enough properties to design and maintain ontologies that have the ability to evolve over time. Static ontologies designed with existing languages seem to be unsuitable for today's dynamic Web; what it requires instead are "dynamic" ones, which are built using new kinds of languages and techniques in order to give them the property of being evolvable over time according to the modification of Web content. Since these new languages and techniques will have an important impact on Web-based applications and mainly WIS applications, we need to carefully identify the different kinds of evolution that can affect Web content and to evaluate the current capabilities of existing languages.

In this chapter, we propose to survey state-of-the-art dynamic ontology languages and techniques. This study also contains notes concerning knowledge evolution in other paradigms connected to the WWW, like reactivity (Alferes, Bailey, Berndtsson, Bry, Dietrich, & Kozlenkov, 2004) and Adaptive Hypermedia Systems (AHS) (Brusilovsky, 2001), both of which have elements that should be integrated in the development of advanced WIS applications. Such adaptation techniques can be used, for example, to adapt the presentation of content to users. Imagine our tourism application able to display in bold red font a particular offer, like a fee reduction on a particular service. In order to cope with various kinds of Web content evolution, we will provide some elements regarding the improvement of these languages. Based on our survey and the proposals we make, we believe that it will be easier to understand the impact of languages and technologies on the quality of future WIS applications.

We first discuss existing types of evolution impacting the Web as well as related work in the field of languages and techniques for Web data evolution. Dealing with the evolutionary aspect of Web content, two important research fields stand out: reactivity and AHS. Within the framework of reactivity, several interesting Event-Conditions-Actions (ECA) languages have been proposed to not only make Semantic Web concepts reactive but also classic Web sites. AHS is a young research field that we will talk about in detail since it takes into account knowledge evolution and introduces user adaptation, which is important for future versions of the Web.

Following this, we discuss related work in the field of languages and techniques for ontology evolution of the Semantic Web. Although a set of standards have been established by the World Wide Web Consortium (W3C) and intensively studied in literature, new ones are under investigation. In this section, we will present these emergent languages and techniques. We will briefly introduce standards like Web Ontology Language (OWL) and focus on the description of new languages like dOWL and the presentation of methodologies that have been proposed to deal with ontology evolution. We also propose some perspectives about the extension of the studied languages with respect to ontology evolution.

The next section discusses the impact of the concepts which we have presented on the quality of WIS applications. Based on our remarks, we illustrate what has to be done to increase the quality of WIS applications at each stage of its life cycle, that is, from design to runtime, mainly by taking into account user preferences, experiences, and behaviour. Finally, we wrap up with concluding remarks.

WEB DATA EVOLUTION: PRINCIPLES AND TECHNIQUES

Web Data Evolution

Before addressing the technical aspects of Web data evolution, it is important to understand how evolution occurs on the Web, and to categorize the different kinds of evolution (see Figure 1). Evolution depends mainly on two things: the specificities of data and the domain to which data is related. In order to understand how evolution depends on these two characteristics, several aspects need to be considered.

First, new information can be added or removed from the Web. This is a basic situation that occurs. Web users or developers build a Web site (or Web application) and then publish it on a Web server. The site is then indexed in a Web search engine by a crawler and can be retrieved when searching the Web. The addition to or removal of information from the Web impacts the evolution of content but also Web morphology, an aspect that is often integrated into Web search applications (Page & Brin, 1998).

Second, once published, content often has to be modified according to events that happen in real life. In this instance, we are referring to data update. Depending on the Web site's domain of concern, updating data can be done manually if the changes occur periodically, or semi-automatically if the changes are incessant. We observe that the rates of change are strongly correlated with the domain of the data. Domains can be grouped into two different classes according to their frequency of changes: A domain concerning entertainments where changes are infrequent is called a "hobby Web;" and a business domain is called a "professional Web," where content undergoes incessant evolution. These classes also differ in the specificities of their data. The content of the hobby Web concentrates various formats of data that is directly accessible. In addition to rough text, multimedia files like videos, sound, or images can generally be found. On the contrary, the professional Web contains more room dedicated to textual information, with its content often hidden. This is due to the fact that business companies always have an Information System (IS). Historically developed separate from Web technology (client/server application or mainframes, basic computer networking, etc.), the IS, through its Web publication layer, offers information and services to users connected on the Web. This is the current status for WIS applications, even if some modern companies develop the IS as a WIS application. In this case, information is hidden from non-administrative Web users. Keeping information hidden is also necessary for nonfunctional requirements (security, overloading control, etc.), as well as for functional requirements (human resource management, detailed financial data, etc.). As a result, the published area of the professional Web is dynamically generated via the

Figure 1. An overview of Web evolution

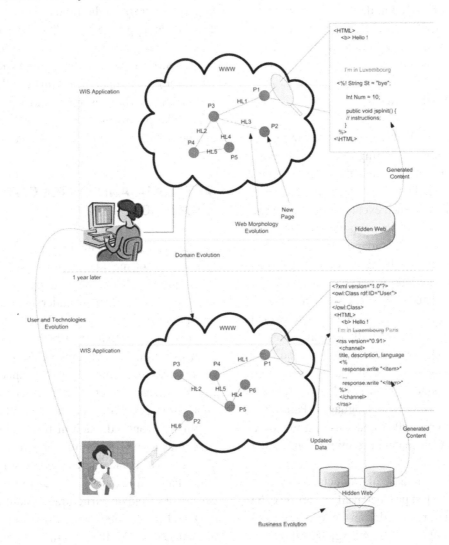

use of scripts that are embedded into the pages source code. In order to cope with the evolution of the data of these WIS applications, developers can use different technologies tailored to the type of content that they want to publish. Among the most promising approaches are:

1. XML-based technologies that allow Web documents to be structured and its extension with metadata allows data exploitation to be optimized (see next section); and
2. Event-Condition-Action (ECA) languages that describe the reactivity of a Web resource

when special events (that reflect IS data evolution) occur.

The third aspect to consider in Web evolution is the presentation of the content. It is orthogonal to the two previous aspects and represents the adaptability of the data presentation to a Web user when data evolves. This implies that the user interface reflects the data evolution. In this case, current implementation uses a metadata-like approach to better present data to the user (see section on Adaptive Hypermedia Systems).

Therefore, to tackle the various kinds of evolution that are presented in this section, new techniques, proposed in the context of young research fields like reactivity and adaptive hypermedia, have been developed.

Reactive Web Sites

Reactivity on the Web is a new emerging paradigm that covers: updating data on the Web, exchanging data about particular events (such as executed updates) between Web sites, and reacting to combinations of such events. Reactivity plays an important role for upcoming Web systems such as online marketplaces, adaptive Semantic Web systems, as well as Web Services and Web Grids. Research on reactivity is particularly studied in the recently-created REWERSE network of excellence. In this context, Web evolution is described as an update or more generally a modification of several individual Web resources. The modifications are the result of events that occur in time and may be triggered by user behaviour. Events are described using ECA languages (Patrânjan, 2005; Schaffert, 2004) and this introduces a new kind of Web content evolution: Conditional Evolution. Consider an e-commerce application that allows the purchase of products. As soon as a user buys the last product available (event), the product must be removed from the set of products offered on the Web site. ECA languages allow the definition of rules for this, which are dynamically interpreted at runtime.

Adaptive Hypermedia Systems

Adaptive hypermedia (Brusilovsky, 2001) is a young research field on the crossroads of hypermedia and user modelling. This emerging technology addresses the evolution of the presentation of the data, but does not directly address the evolution of the data itself. Adaptive hypermedia systems build a model of goals, preferences, and knowledge of each individual user, throughout the interaction with the user, in order to adapt to the needs of that particular user. Studies in adaptive hypermedia rely on the following observations: Traditional hypermedia offers the same Web pages (or more generally speaking, information) to all users whatever their background may be and whatever kind of data evolution has taken place. AHS integrates both user data and behaviour and data evolution to provide the user with an adapted and personalized presentation of data.

METADATA AND ONTOLOGY EVOLUTION

We now need to do an in-depth study of the specificities of metadata and ,in particular, the techniques, methods, and languages that support its definition in order to understand its impact on the development of good WIS applications. Metadata is data that describes other data. The term is common in various fields of computer science; however, metadata is of special interest in information retrieval and Semantic Web applications. Although several definitions were originally proposed, each of them concerned a particular domain of computer science. Generally, a set of metadata describes a single set of data, that is, a resource. There are two distinct classes of metadata: structural (or control) metadata and guide metadata. Structural metadata is used to describe the structure of data such as tables, columns, and indexes in databases. Guide metadata is used to help users with information retrieval tasks; for instance, a date might be useful to eliminate out-of-date data. Metadata may be expressed as a schema of data of a resource or, in its simplest form, as a set of keywords in a structured language whose aim is to better interpret data. Consider the data "L-1359." In its raw form, L-1359 does not have a precise meaning, but if the metadata "zip code" is added (Luxembourg zip code = country's first ISO letter, hyphen, and 4-digit town), the data clearly denotes the city of Luxembourg. Because of metadata, a better interpretation of data is used to:

1. Semantically enhance the capability of retrieving resources. Metadata may be directly visualized by the end-user or may be exploited by automated services and the user unaware of its use. In both cases, metadata allows targeted and more relevant information retrievals;

2. Reduce the complexity of data exploitation through the use of metadata as filters to optimize searching tasks, or via the definition of new compression algorithms for storing purposes, or to automate workflows; and

3. Adapt or personalize data presentation. Metadata is intended to enable variable content presentations. For example, if a picture viewer knows the most important region of an image (e.g., where there is a person in it), it can reduce the image to that region and show the user the most interesting detail on a small screen, such as on a mobile phone. A similar kind of metadata is intended to enable blind people "reading" diagrams and pictures (e.g., by converting them for special output devices or by reading a description using voice synthesis).

A detailed illustration of the usefulness of metadata can be found in the Semantic Web initiative (Berners-Lee, Hendler, & Lassila, 2001). The intent of the Semantic Web is to enhance the usability and usefulness of the Web and its interconnected resources through:

1. Documents "marked up" with semantic information (an extension of the HTML <meta> tags used in today's Web pages for supplying information to Web search engines using Web crawlers). Metadata can focus on a specific part of a document consulted by a user (e.g., a metadata defined to indicate a Web site administrator's email and how many times the page has been visited). Metadata can also be indicators about the location and access mode to a document (e.g., the hyperlink nature of a text that allows access to another Web page or the need for a specific tool to consult displayed information described textually);

2. Metadata with terms extracted from ontologies (Gruber, 1993) that define it and establish mappings with terms from other ontologies. This allows the ability to exploit Web data even if it has been created in a different context (e.g., one user looking for a book on painting may consider the writer as an "author," while another user may consider the writer as an "artist");

3. Software to help end-users of the Web performs tasks using metadata; and

4. Web-based services providing information to software agents or Web services (e.g., an indication of the quality of service: availability, efficiency, security).

Metadata can be distinguished by:

1. **Content:** Metadata can describe the *resource* itself with different focuses like, name and file size, or the *content* of the resource (e.g., "video of artist painting"). The focus can range from the raw level to an abstract one, depending on the functional (or nonfunctional) requirements the metadata must fulfill; and

2. **Evolution:** The metadata definition as well as its value may change during its life cycle (e.g., a file is characterized by its name and location, but later we may need to see the file with its extension code (doc, xls, etc.). Or, we can name and rename a file to reflect the transformation of its updates (Paper_v1, Paper_v2, Paper_v3)).

The Semantic Web aims at giving definition to the Web. However, Web data is constantly evolving and therefore, if metadata from a given ontology describes this changing content, the metadata itself must evolve; otherwise, the semantic of the described data can be erroneous. In most cases, Web data evolution is automatic.

Ideally, the evolution of metadata should occur in the same manner. Moreover, the evolution of the ontology (i.e., the domain) will impact the evolution of metadata. Since concepts can be added to or removed from a given ontology, forming a new vocabulary, metadata that use this "new" ontology has to adapt to these changes. We present, in the next section, the various languages and techniques that have been proposed to support ontology evolution.

TECHNIQUES AND METHODOLOGIES FOR MANAGING CHANGES IN ONTOLOGIES

Changes in ontologies is a topic that has not been intensively studied. However, the existing languages and techniques for ontology engineering introduce two different concepts: ontology evolution and ontology versioning. The former, according to Ljiljana Stojanovic, is "the timely adaptation of an ontology to the arisen changes and the consistent propagation of these changes to dependent artefacts" (Stojanovic, 2004, p. 15). The latter approach is a stronger variant of handling changes to ontologies: Ontology versioning allows access to data through different variants of the ontology. In addition to managing the individual variants of the ontology themselves, it is important to also manage the derivation relations between the variants. These derivation relations then allow definition of the notions of compatibility and mapping relations between versions, as well as transformations of data corresponding to the various versions. Versioning is an approach that can be found mainly in languages for managing changes in ontology. This will be presented in the next section.

In Michel Klein's approach for ontology evolution (Klein, 2004), he proposes a framework (Klein & Noy, 2003) to solve problems relating to ontology evolution. This framework has been developed based on a study of the context of the ontology evolution problem and a comparison with solutions provided by related areas (Klein, 2001; Noy & Klein, 2004). The framework also provides a methodology (Stuckenschmidt & Klein, 2003) described as a change process which is tool-supported (Klein, Fensel, Kiryakov, & Ognyanov, 2002). The proposed process describes the different steps in ontology evolution as well as the different problems that arise from the latter. Klein also focuses on the different kinds of evolution that can interfere in ontology evolution. He points out changes in the conceptualization (the domain can change), changes in the specification (the way for describing a domain can differ), and changes in the languages used to model the domain. An important consideration is how to capture these changes. The proposed framework is based on the ontology of change operations for providing a formal description of the ontology modifications to be applied. However, as there is no limit on the number of composite operations that can be considered, there is no guarantee that the composite operations cover all needs.

On another front, Ljiljana Stojanovic's work focuses on a methodology for ontology evolution (Stojanovic, 2004). The proposed methodology (Stojanovic, Maedche, Motik, & Stojanovic, 2002) can be divided into six different steps occurring in a cyclic loop:

1. **Change capturing:** This consists in the discovery of changes. This task could be done manually by a knowledge engineer or automatically by using any existing change discovery method. Three types of change discovery are defined (Stojanovic, 2004): structure-driven, usage-driven, and data-driven. Whereas structure-driven changes can be deduced from the ontology structure itself, usage-driven changes result from the usage patterns created over a period of time. Data-driven changes are generated by modifications to the underlying dataset, such as text documents or a database representing the knowledge modelled by an ontology;

2. **Change representation:** Before changes are treated, they have to be represented in a suitable format according to the ontology model that is used;

3. **Semantics of change:** Possible problems that might be caused in the ontology by the changes are determined and resolved. For example, we have to decide what to do in the instance of a removed concept. This stage is useful for checking the consistency of the ontology;

4. **Change implementation:** In this step, the knowledge engineer is informed about the consequences of the changes, changes are then applied, and tracking of performed changes are kept;

5. **Change propagation:** To propagate the changes to other related ontologies or software agents; the task of the change propagation phase is to ensure consistency of dependent artefacts after an ontology update has been performed. These artefacts may include dependent ontologies, instances, as well as application programs running against the ontology; and

6. **Change validation:** The validation of the evolution process according to the semantics of changes defined (Step 3); this step can initiate additional new changes that need to be performed. In this case, we start over by applying the change-capturing phase of a new evolution process.

A methodology, H-CHANGE, is also proposed in the context of P2P systems (Castano, Ferrara, & Montanelli, 2006). This methodology has been conceived specifically for the local evolution of peer ontology and for evolving independent ontologies in open contexts, where distributed concept definitions emerge dynamically through interactions of independent peers. The methodology integrates semi-automated change detection techniques based on semantic matchmaking and change assimilation techniques for evolving ontology. Two strategies are applied as techniques for assimilation: assimilation-by-merging or assimilation-by-alignment, according to the level of semantic affinity of the new incoming concept. The choice of the strategy is automated. It is performed according to a threshold-based mechanism.

The complete ontology evolution process is generally not supported by existing tools, but some tools (Haase & Sure, 2004) provide specialized features, like change discovery, keeping track of ontology changes, support for evolution strategies, undo/redo operations, and so forth. These tools aim at helping users perform the changes manually rather than automatically.

Finally, the problem of ontology evolution is considered a special case of a more general problem, *belief change*. Some of the most important concepts of belief change have been revised (Flouris, Plexousakis, & Antoniou, 2006) to apply them to the ontology context evolution. On another side, ontology evolution has also been addressed in different languages. These ones are detailed in the next section.

LANGUAGES FOR DYNAMIC ONTOLOGY

ECA (Event-Condition-Action) Languages for the Semantic Web

Reactivity for the Web is an important component of the vision of the Semantic Web as a closely-intertwined network of autonomous nodes. In contrast to the current Web where many sites only provide information and others simply query them on demand, the Semantic Web will profit from enhanced communication between its nodes, not only for answering queries, but also in its evolution. It is crucial that relevant changes to information used by a Semantic Web agent are consistently and rapidly propagated to all interested parties. In this context, ECA languages like Resource Description Framework Triggering Language (RDFTL) (Papamarkos, Poulovassilis,

& Wood, 2004) have been developed. RDFTL is tailored to Resource Description Framework (RDF) data (resources, properties, and statements organized in graph). It works on RDF graph, and allows nodes or arcs of this graph to be removed, added, or updated on defined events occurring on particular RDF statements.

Simple HTML Ontology Extension (SHOE)

The first initiative concerning the definition of an ontology language tailored for the Web has been Simple HTML Ontology Extensions (SHOE) language (Heflin & Hendler, 2000). SHOE has an XML-based syntax and semantics (Heflin, Hendler, & Luke, 1999) and is a frame-based language built on top of XML that can be easily integrated into HTML documents. It was designed with the aim of integrating machine-readable semantic knowledge in Web documents. One of the main innovations proposed by this language was to use URI to identify concepts, which have been integrated in the definition of DAML+OIL. Another interesting point is that SHOE has the ability to adapt to the evolution of Web data and thus, several primitives have been defined, such as ontology importation (USE-ONTOLOGY tag), local renaming of imported constants (DEF-RE-NAME tag), and ontology versioning (VERSION tag). Despite these interesting points, SHOE suffers from a lack of formalization of the primitives introduced.

Evolution Aspects in W3C Standards

With RDF and RDFS, the W3C has adopted a set of standards devoted to ontology engineering, but it is only since the release of Web Ontology Language (OWL) (McGuinness & van Harmelen, 2004) that changes in ontologies have been tackled. OWL provides a set of six tags for managing ontology versioning. Two of them directly concern the version of the ontology. In fact, owl:versionInfo and owl:priorVersion give information about the current and the previous version of the changing ontology. Two other tags, owl:backwardCompatibleWith and owl:incompatibleWith, contain statements concerning other ontologies that are compatible or incompatible with the current ontology. Lastly, owl:DeprecatedClass and owl:DeprecatedProperty indicate that a particular feature is preserved for backward-compatibility purposes, but these may be phased out in the future. However, despite other OWL constructors, the six tags devoted to ontology versioning do not have any formal semantics expressed in description logics, so reasoning abilities are restricted with these constructors. This confirms that the novelty of the problem related to ontology changes management, combined with the evolution of Web data, requires the Semantic Web community to integrate a better method to express changes in ontologies: Dynamic OWL (dOWL). Through the proposition of dOWL, the authors (Avery & Yearwood, 2003) work to correct what OWL lacks, by enriching the language with new constructors for OWL ontology evolution. It is clear that OWL provides little concerning ontology evolution as it provides no means to express the following: renaming a class or a property; removing a class or a property; redefining the restriction of a class; redefining the domain and the range of a property; redefining a property as being symmetric, transitive, functional, or inverse functional; coalescing many classes or properties into one; or dividing one class or property into many. The dOWL language is an enhanced versioning mechanism for OWL that caters to the evolution of ontology. The dOWL language is defined as an OWL ontology (URL http://www.ballarat.edu.au/javery/2003/4/dowl#) and consists of a set of one or more OWL ontologies, followed by a set of zero or more versions that provide a mapping or translation between the old version(s) and the new version. A version in a dOWL ontology has the same structure as an OWL ontology, except that within the ontology header there are one or more dowl:importsAll or dowl:importsNone elements. The dowl:importsAll element imports all the elements of an ontology just as the owl:imports element, except the elements explicitly mentioned within the dowl:importsAll tag. The dowl:importsNone element imports none of the elements of an ontology except those elements explicitly mentioned within the dowl:importsNone tag. Other tags proposed by the dOWL language are devoted to correct the other features (listed above) that OWL lacks. Although improving some OWL drawbacks, in terms of ontology change management, dOWL does not have a formal semantics, which prevents some advanced reasoning mechanisms.

FUTURE TRENDS

Although Web data is evolving by nature, the Web is also evolving in its philosophy. According to Tim O'Reilly, the Web is moving towards an era of "data lock-in" (O'Reilly, 2004). If one takes a closer look at the WIS applications like Google mail, flickr, or even Amazon, one will observe that their success is the consequence of high storage capacity and their ability to rapidly retrieve, using content managers and metadata-based approaches, the data offered by these applications. For the hobby Web, the consequence is that its data is "locked-in" another company's database. These data and associated services are then used to provide personalized data access or personalized data presentation.

Web 2.0 and future versions of the Web will need to deal with data lock-in and introduce new Web applications in which the user has a priority position, which in turn will give place to new kinds of evolution like "on-demand" evolution where users, not the applications, will be the initiators of the changes, for example, the subscription of users to news diffusion service using RSS stream. Technological improvements that traditionally go with Web evolution provide not only a powerful access to information, but also a smarter access. This means that information is more pertinent with respect to user needs, but also that information is much better presented. These particular aspects will benefit from the acceptance of technologies like AHS. The retrieval of pertinent informa-

tion will be done in large part with "intelligent" software able to reason on Web data thanks to Semantic Web concepts.

Nevertheless, these concepts and languages (mainly) for ontology evolution presented in this chapter will require significant improvement to manage evolution in an appropriate way. Since ontologies are used to model a given domain which is supposed to evolve over time (see Figure 1), the current state-of-the-art on ontology evolution presented in this section provides very little to support this evolution automatically. In fact, the ontology needs a partial (or total) reconstruction each time that a change in the domain occurs. This is particularly annoying for domains that evolve in a cyclic manner. Evolution can also lead to the exclusion of a domain's concept when it is no longer used or, in the contrary, the emergence of a new concept in the domain (like, for instance, the concept *ontology* in the artificial intelligence domain in 1993).

More generally, evolution tends to modify the relations between concepts of a given either to strengthen or to weaken, depending on their usage. Measurements of these modifications are important and should be derivable from the ontology. This is especially important for ontologies used for information retrieval. Actually, if one can select concepts of a given ontology with a short semantic distance, one will be able to build queries that will act as better filters to skim the result of a search.

This is also true if the domain of interest represents user behaviour. Becoming more experienced with the Web and search applications, users modify their habits when searching the Web. Ontologies that support user queries have to reflect these evolutions. Therefore, if the different kinds of domain evolutions are clearly and formally defined, it will be possible to extend the existing languages and OWL in particular with new operators to allow ontologies developed with these languages to evolve automatically (or at least semi-automatically) over time.

Some of the new proposed operators should at least have the following abilities:

1. Allow the definition of the validity duration of an assertion, for instance, how long the assertion "France has the lead of the European Union" is valid. This property would be very important to describe events that occur in a cyclic loop. This is all the more true in the context of the Web. In fact, as illustrated in Figure 1, this may occur in a data update situation. Many Web pages contains the information "last modification" or "last update" with the corresponding date. In consequence, if the author of the Web document is able to give the period for which the document's content is valid, it will, on one hand, enhance the quality regarding data relevance of the Web site information. On the other hand, it will reinforce the popularity of the Web site, which is important for business WIS applications;

2. Allow to specify when a concept has been added to or removed from the ontology. This is important to ensure the compatibility between ontologies, which in turn will preserve basic properties for reasoning purpose, which is one of the main objectives of the Semantic Web vision;

3. Allow the measurement or the specification of the semantic distance between concepts of the ontology. As explained before, this will be helpful for query construction, but it will also enhance the precision of the domain that is represented by the ontology. Moreover, this semantic distance should evolve dynamically over time according to the usage of the concepts or the relations between concepts in the domain. These metrics will therefore improve the quality of the ontology;

4. Introduce "change resistance coefficients" in order to manage the wanted equilibrium between change and stability of the ontology over time. For example, the concept *ontology*

has been identified as a very important concept in the Semantic Web domain. Therefore, it must not be excluded from the ontology (or at least in a long period of time) so this concept should have a strong coefficient that will allow to resist to changes that could try to suppress it. This is important in the context of the Web, since Web site designers publish on their pages many major concepts of a particular domain. Therefore, using the appropriate metadata, designers should be able to specify stable or volatile information; and

5. Allow the definition of degree of freedom that would indicate how concepts will evolve ones compared to the others. This property would be strongly correlated with the usage of the concepts of the ontology and will prevent ambiguity between concepts of the ontology.

Furthermore, the evolution of the ontology should follow some type of dynamic and static "well-formedness" rules that have to be introduced in order to manage coherently the different automatic (or semi-automatic) modification of an ontology. If such rules are integrated in the languages, we believe that it will be much easier for metadata to be maintained over time (mainly) when changes in the domain take place.

METADATA ENABLE WIS IMPROVEMENT

Metadata and Impact on the Quality of WIS Applications

If one considers the key quality aspects for Information Systems applications gathered under the ISO-9126 norm (performance, maintainability, usability, portability, security issues, etc.), the use of metadata as concepts for improving these criteria will be evident. In order to better illustrate the impact of metadata on WIS applications, we will illustrate a basic application example. Consider an online travel agency that sells travel-related products and services to customers on behalf of third-party travel suppliers. First, an important criterion of WIS applications is the capability of integrating several heterogeneous data coming from different Web sources and from IS's own repositories. The information contained in a WIS application can be harvested through the Web by integrating the Semantic Web or metadata embedded in (X)HTML documents (Yahaya, Gin, & Choon, 2005). The WIS application can also be built, for historical needs, upon heterogeneous components. For instance, part of the data can be contained in a traditional relational database and the other part in a database utilizing XML. Therefore, the use of a richer metadata represented in ontology can be used to harmonize the combined use of both databases (Kashyap & Sheth, 1998). From a maintenance point of view, our travel agency will need to keep the information being provided to Web users up-to-date. Should there be changes in fees metadata, reactivity can be used to detect and propagate these changes for users.

If we base the maintainability of WIS applications on metadata, should the metadata become outdated, it will strongly impact the WIS application. As a consequence, we believe that the languages and techniques, if extended as proposed, are good candidates to manage ontology evolution. WIS applications will then benefit from this metadata evolution by having an up-to-date metadata for describing new content.

The availability of the application is also important for success. Our example travel agency could, to prevent failures, duplicate its data in several databases and use metadata to detect the aliveness of the server that hosts the database and react by redirecting requests to available and adequate servers (Di Marzo Serugendo, Fitzgerald, Romanovsky, & Guelfi, 2007).

This small example gives a good illustration of the value of integration of metadata in WIS applications. All that is needed at the time of design is the rigorous definition of specific metadata

that will be used within future WIS applications, according to the application requirements. For instance, if security has to be the most important quality for the WIS application, metadata, like "aliveness of a resource," "availability of a data," and so forth, has to be defined. The use of metadata will improve the quality of the design of WIS applications, and it will help in establishing rules at the time of design for checking the consistency of the WIS application (Stuckenschmidt & van Harmelen, 2004).

Metadata and Adaptation to Users

Adaptation of content to user specificities is the last point that plays an important part in the development of future WIS applications. WIS application developers focus on the presentation of data using AHS technologies (Houben, 2004; Jacquiot, Bourda, Popineau, Delteil, & Reynaud, 2006). We have presented the usefulness of metadata in the adaptation of WIS applications in regard to data evolution. Due to technological improvements that can be hardware- or software-based, users have a growing number of options for consulting WIS content. There are many ways to present data to users according to their own user specificities (experience, background, etc.), and also according to the technologies used to reach WIS content. In the case of our travel agency example, the application should know what kind of device is in use to display the most appropriate information on the user's screen. This feature is all the more important in the case of emerging e-health Web applications. The application adapts to the user's device and to the particular characteristics of the user. If the user is a patient, the application should display only the user information related to his/her own medical treatment, and if the user is allowed to modify special data, the application must control data access. All these described features can be facilitated with the use of control metadata that can be integrated into the WIS application at the time of design. The integration of users in WIS applications will be possible only if the user is modelled in an adequate way. We believe the use of ontology can be of real value to this end. Nevertheless, improvements are needed to precisely model users or categories of users and to make the model adaptable to users and to domain evolution.

CONCLUSION

Although it is unavoidable, the evolution of Web content has not sufficiently been taken into account in the development of Web applications (in general) and in WIS applications (in particular). The emergence of new paradigms, like the forthcoming Web 2.0 and the Semantic Web, confirms that it will be impossible to continue to ignore this evolution, especially regarding WIS applications. Therefore, the use of metadata, though in its beginning stage, seems to be the most promising means in order to manage Web content evolution and improve WIS applications. Even though description of metadata through the use of ontologies has been accomplished, the existing languages and techniques studied in this chapter for ontology evolution provide only an overview of how to cope with Web content evolution. In languages, the notion of ontology versioning has been integrated, but the overwhelming number of concepts (i.e., metadata) for preserving compatibility between several versions of the ontology adds to the complexity and impact on the consistency of these structures. Furthermore, this notion is not dealt with sufficiently in the existing methodologies for ontology evolution. Ideally, ontologies have to evolve smoothly and semi-automatically at the same speed with Web knowledge evolution while remaining compatible with the previous version of the ontology.

Developers of WIS applications must also have in mind another kind of evolution: knowledge of the user for whom the applications are devoted. Many e-commerce applications draw information from the user's profile and behaviour to improve business by proposing products that might be of interest. Companies that base their business on WIS applications need to combine both domain and user evolution. This is why the existing languages and techniques for ontology evolution need to be enriched for optimum outcome.

REFERENCES

Abiteboul, S., Buneman, P., & Suciu, D. (2000). *Data on the Web: From relations to semistructured data and XML*. The Morgan Kaufmann Series in Data Management Systems. Morgan Kaufmann.

Alferes, J. J., Bailey, J., Berndtsson, M., Bry, F., Dietrich, J., Kozlenkov, A., May, W., Patrânjan, P. L., Pinto, A., Schroeder, M., and Wagner, G. (2004). *State-of-the-art on evolution and reactivity*. deliverable I5-D1, Centro de Inteligência Artificial—CENTRIA, Universidade Nova de Lisboa.

Antoniou, G., & van Harmelen, F. (2004). *A Semantic Web primer*. The MIT Press.

Avery, J., & Yearwood, J. (2003). dOWL: A dynamic ontology language. *International Conference WWW/Internet 2003* (pp. 985-988). Algarve, Portugal: IADIS.

Berners-Lee, T., Hendler, J., & Lassila, O. (2001, May). The semantic Web. *Scientific American, 284*(5), 34-43.

Brusilovsky, P. (2001). Adaptive hypermedia. *User Modeling and User-Adapted Interaction, 11*, 87-110.

Castano, S., Ferrara, A., and Montanelli, S. (2006). A matchmaking-based ontology evolution methodology. In *CAiSE INTEROP Workshop on Enterprise Modelling and Ontologies for Interoperability (EMOI—INTEROP 2006)* (pp. 547-558), Luxembourg.

Charlet, J., Laublet, P., & Reynaud, C. (2004). Le Web Sémantique [Special issue]. *Revue d'Information—Interaction—Intelligence (RI3), 4*(2).

Di Marzo Serugendo, G., Fitzgerald, J., Romanovsky, A., & Guelfi, N. (2007). Towards a metadata-based architectural model for dynamically resilient systems. In *Proceedings of the 2007 ACM Symposium on Applied Computing (SAC)* (pp. 566-573), Seoul, Korea.

Flouris, G., Plexousakis, D., & Antoniou, G. (2006). Evolving ontology evolution. In *SOFSEM 2006: Theory and Practice of Computer Science, 32nd Conference on Current Trends in Theory and Practice of Computer Science* (LNCS 3831, pp. 14-29). Merín, Czech Republic.

Gruber, T. R. (1993). A translation approach to portable ontology specifications. *Knowledge Acquisition, 5*(2), 199-220.

Guelfi, N., & Pruski, C. (2006). On the use of ontologies for an optimal representation and exploration of the Web. *Journal of Digital Information Management (JDIM), 4*(3), 158-167.

Haase, P., & Sure, Y. (2004). *State of the art on ontology evolution* (University of Karlsruhe AIFB Rep. No. SEKT-D3.1.1.b). Retrieved December 21, 2005, from http://www.aifb.uni-karlsruhe.de/WBS/ysu/publications/SEKT-D3.1.1.b.pdf

Heflin, J., Hendler, J., & Luke, S. (1999). *SHOE: A knowledge representation language for Internet applications* (Tech. Rep. No. CS-TR-4078). College Park, MD: University of Maryland, Department of Computer Science.

Heflin, J., & Hendler, J. A. (2000). Dynamic ontologies on the Web. *National Conference on Artificial Intelligence (AAAI-2000)* (pp. 443-449).

Houben, G. -J. (2004). Challenges in adaptive Web information systems: Do not forget the link! *Workshops in Connection with 4th International Conference on Web Engineering* (pp. 3-11). Rinton Press.

Jacquiot, C., Bourda, Y., Popineau, F., Delteil, A., & Reynaud, C. (2006). GLAM: A generic layered adaptation model for adaptive hypermedia systems. *Adaptive Hypermedia and Adaptive Web-Based Systems International Conference, AH 2006: Vol. 4018, LNCS* (pp. 131-140).

Kashyap, V., & Sheth, A. (1998). Semantic heterogeneity in global information systems: The role of metadata, context and ontologies. In M. P. Papazoglou & G. Schlageter (Eds.), *Cooperative information systems* (pp. 139-178). Academic Press.

Klein, M. (2001). Combining and relating ontologies: an analysis of problems and solutions. In Gomez-Perez, A., Gruninger, M., Stuckenschmidt, H., and Uschold, M., editors, *Workshop on Ontologies and Information Sharing, IJCAI'01*, (pp. 53-62), Seattle, USA.

Klein, M. (2004). *Change management for distributed ontologies.* Unpublished doctoral dissertation, Vrije Universiteit Amsterdam, The Netherlands.

Klein, M., Fensel, D., Kiryakov, A., & Ognyanov, D. (2002). Ontology versioning and change detection on the Web. *International Conference on Knowledge Engineering and Knowledge Management (EKAW'02): Ontologies and the Semantic Web* (pp. 197-212). Springer-Verlag.

Klein, M., & Noy, N, F. (2003). A component-based framework for ontology evolution. *Workshop on Ontologies and Distributed Systems at IJCAI-03, Acapulco, Mexico.*

McGuinness, D., & van Harmelen, F. (2004*). OWL Web Ontology Language Overview.* W3C Recommendation.

Noy, N. F., & Klein, M. (2004). Ontology evolution: Not the same as schema evolution. *Knowledge and Information Systems, 6*(4), 428-440.

O'Reilly, T. (2004, July). *O'Reilly radar.* Paper presented at the OSCON 2004 Conference.

Page, L. and Brin, S. (1998). The anatomy of a large-scale hypertextual web search engine. In *Proceedings of the Seventh International World-Wide Web Conference*, (pp. 107-117).

Papamarkos, G., Poulovassilis, A., & Wood, P. (2004). RDFTL: An event-condition-action language for RDF. *Web Dynamics Workshop, at WWW'2004.*

Patrânjan, P. -L. (2005). *The language XChange: A declarative approach to reactivity on the Web.* Unpublished doctoral dissertation, Ludwig-Maximilians-Universität München, Germany.

Schaffert, S. (2004). *Xcerpt: A rule-based query and transformation language for the Web.* Unpublished doctoral dissertation, Ludwig-Maximilians-Universität München, Germany

Stojanovic, L. (2004). *Methods and tools for ontology evolution.* Unpublished doctoral dissertation, University of Karlsruhe, Germany.

Stojanovic, L., Maedche, A., Motik, B., & Stojanovic, N. (2002). User-driven ontology evolution management. *European Conference on Knowledge Engineering and Management (EKAW'02),* (pp. 285-300). Springer-Verlag.

Stuckenschmidt, H., & Klein, M. (2003). Integrity and change in modular ontologies. In G. Gottlob & T. Walsh (Eds.), *International Joint Conference on Artificial Intelligence,* (pp. 900-908). Morgan Kaufmann.

Stuckenschmidt, H., & van Harmelen, F. (2004). Generating and managing metadata for Web-based information systems. *Knowledge-Based Systems, 17*(5-6), 201-206.

Suh, W. (Ed.). (2005). *Web engineering: Principles and techniques.* Hershey, PA: Idea Group Publishing.

Yahaya, N. A., Gin, G. P., & Choon, C. W. (2005). Developing innovative Web information systems through the use of Web data extraction technology. *International Conference on Advanced Information Networking and Applications* (pp. 752-757). Washington, DC: IEEE Computer Society.

KEY TERMS

Hidden Web: The hidden Web (or invisible Web or deep Web) is the name given to pages on the World Wide Web that are not indexed by search engines. It consists of pages which are not linked to by other pages, such as dynamic Web pages based on responses to database queries. The deep Web also includes sites that require registration or otherwise limit access to their pages.

Ontology: An ontology is an explicit and formal specification of a conceptualization. In general, an ontology describes formally a domain of discourse. Typically, an ontology consists of a finite list of terms and the relationships between these terms.

Semantic Web: The Semantic Web is an evolving extension of the World Wide Web in which Web content can be expressed not only in natural language, but also in a form that can be understood, interpreted, and used by software agents, thus permitting them to find, share, and integrate information more easily.

Web 2.0: Web 2.0 is a term often applied to a perceived ongoing transition of the World Wide Web from a collection of Web sites to a full-fledged computing platform serving Web applications to end users.

Web resource: A Web resource is any one of the resources that are created during the development of a Web application, for example, Web projects, HTML pages, JSP files, servlets, custom tag libraries, and archive files.

WIS: A Web information system (WIS) is an information system that uses the Web to present data to its users.

Chapter XVIII
Looking for Information in Fuzzy Relational Databases Accessible Via Web

Carmen Martínez-Cruz
University of Jaén, Spain

Ignacio José Blanco
University of Granada, Spain

M. Amparo Vila
University of Granada, Spain

ABSTRACT

The Semantic Web has resulted in a wide range of information (e.g., HML, XML, DOC, PDF documents, ontologies, interfaces, forms, etc.) being made available in semantic queries, and the only requirement is that these are described semantically. Generic Web interfaces for querying databases (such as ISQLPlus ©) are also part of the Semantic Web, but they cannot be semantically described, and they provide access to one or many databases. In this chapter, we will highlight the importance of using ontologies to represent database schemas so that they are easier to access. The representation of the fuzzy data in fuzzy databases management systems (FDBMS) has certain special requirements, and these characteristics must be explicitly defined to enable this kind of information to be accessed. In addition, we will present an ontology which allows the fuzzy structure of a fuzzy database schema to be represented so that fuzzy data from FDBMS can also be available in the Semantic Web.

INTRODUCTION

The Semantic Web is the result of extending the standard Web with languages, information, and resources to enable us to extract information about the meaning of the Web contents automatically (Berners-Lee, Hendler, & Lassila, 2001). This content can be stored in different formats, for example, Web documents, semi-structured schemas, or dynamic data (Hendler, Berners-Lee, & Miller, 2002) as shown in Figure 1. In the Semantic Web, each information source is extended with a structured representation of its semantics (or its meaning). There are several approximations for this (Finin, Mayfield, Joshi, Cost, & Fink, 2005) but one of the most used representations is the ontology concept.

An ontology is a formal description for the discourse domain of a concrete problem, and the intention is for it to be shared between different applications. One of its advantages is that it can be expressed in a language (mostly based on first-order logic) which can be used for reasoning (Gómez-Pérez, Férnandez-López, & Corcho-García, 2003b; Noy, 2004; Staab & Studer, 2004).

A dynamic Web page is a type of Web content which is generated by querying a database (usually using technologies such as JSP, ASP, or PHP). In this case, Web pages cannot be semantically represented since they are front-end for the database. They can, however, be defined by the representation of the database contents which are accessed. Other types of Web pages are even more complex to be defined semantically, for example, generic Web interfaces for querying databases such as ISQLPlus (Oracle ©, n.d.) or WebinTool (Hu, Nicholson, Mungall, Hillyard, & Archibald, 1996) or those developed with database-accessing packages such as LIBSDB (Eriksson, n.d.). These pages allow us to access database information, but they cannot be semantically indexed because their contents depend on the accessed database.

A search in the Semantic Web, however, does not always look for Web documents but data registers. Database schemas allow to access to DB information, but they are also a representation of a particular domain. In this case, such a representation can be very useful in the search retrieval process, and alternative result to classical data. Other alternative results can be references to existing databases (when their schemas are known) or client applications which can enrich the resulting answer. Final users could then choose the answers they need.

Fuzzy databases representing imprecise information (Blanco, Martinez-Cruz, Serrano, & Vila, 2005b; Ma, 2005) are also part of the information which can be shared in the Semantic Web.

This representation allows us to store uncertain and imprecise data together with classical data. However, the difficulty of accessing the database information becomes more complicated when fuzzy information is incorporated into the problem as shown in Blanco et al. (2005b). Agents need to know about the metadata of the fuzzy database in order to search information within it.

Representation and manipulation of fuzzy data in the Semantic Web include certain advantages in the Web search. One such advantage is the capability of including fuzzy information in the answers (including fuzzy database schemas), but the main one might well be the new opportunities that this type of information adds to the data integration process from heterogeneous data, format, or sources.

The use of fuzzy databases in the Semantic Web, however, is closely connected to its formal representation. An ontology representing a fuzzy database can be seen as an interface (Blanco, Martínez-Cruz, Marín, & Vila, 2005a; Calero, Ruiz, Baroni, Abreu, & Piattini, 2005; Perez de Laborda & Conrad, 2005) between the database and the Semantic Web. This interface separates the data representation from its storage and simplifies its definition for accessing it. The resulting ontology represents the metaclasses that define the information structure (the fuzzy database catalog) and the metaclasses containing the stored fuzzy data (the fuzzy database schema). This ontology can be treated homogeneously with all the ontologies in the Web, that is, it can be shared, merged, pruned, or evaluated (Gómez-Pérez et al., 2003b).

The second section of this chapter briefly describes the main topics relating to fuzzy database integration, and describes various concepts about fuzzy databases and the relation between ontologies and relational databases. In the third section, we propose an ontology as an interface for integrating fuzzy databases into the Semantic Web, and also include an example of a fuzzy schema representation. The final section discusses new trends and presents our conclusions.

Figure 1. Comparing documents retrieved from the Web and from the semantic Web

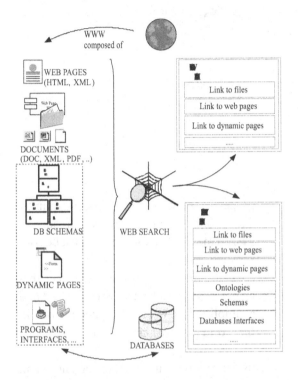

BACKGROUND

While the Web has brought with it new challenges for exchanging, sharing, publishing, and querying information, it is not without its drawbacks; for example, it does not allow semantics to be included in the data retrieved, query results are huge, searches are imprecise, and so forth (for further details, see Lausen and Stollberg's work (2004)). Machine-processable information in the Web requires new technologies (Berners-Lee et al., 2001), and some of these technologies are for structuring Web information contents such as XML or XML-S. However:

- Web content cannot be determined;
- Semantic queries cannot be made because Web pages cannot be interpreted; and
- Intelligent agents cannot obtain significant information.

The Semantic Web was proposed as a solution to these problems, and as many researchers mentioned (Berners-Lee et al., 2001; Goble, 2003), this technology is capable of making the Web information content-understandable and processable by computers and humans.

The Web can be extended to include semantics using one of these two approaches (Sheth, Ramakrishnan, & Thomas, 2005): ontologies or annotations.

The first of these allows the Web content to be represented using the knowledge representation mechanism known as ontologies (see details in the following subsection). This method includes the semantics of the page by attaching the ontology to the page or by including the ontology code in it (Finin et al., 2005). However, McCool (2005) discovered certain problems with this solution, which included:

- complexity of the Semantic Web;
- poor user participation;
- development of very poor applications; and
- restrictive ontology languages.

Figure 2 describes the Semantic Web's common users and the way in which semantic contents are defined in Web pages.

The second solution presents annotations about the Web page content and vocabulary. This solution (McCool, 2006) reduces the complexity of the Semantic Web, retrieves faster query results, and promotes greater participation of Web users and developers. One drawback, however, is that it lacks the rich expressiveness provided by ontologies.

Nevertheless, the Semantic Web remains an alternative to the Classic Web and allows all the information that this contains to be accessed. Web data is represented in many different formats: in the form of documents (e.g., PDF, WORD), as plain text, HTML pages, XML documents, dynamic Web pages (e.g., JSP, ASP, PHP), FLASH contents,

Figure 2. Semantic Web users and different forms of semantic annotation of Web contents

Figure 2. Semantic Web users and different forms of semantic annotation of Web contents

libraries, executables, interfaces or front-end pages, and so forth (see *Figure 1*). We can also find simple data or metadata, access databases, or infer knowledge from them, and we need to define technologies to access all this information in the way and format required for each case.

In this chapter, we will attempt to incorporate the information contained in fuzzy databases into the Semantic Web. This information, like classic information, is stored in different DBMSs (DataBase Management Systems) and is represented using schemas. Schemas representing fuzzy and classic information could be retrieved in the Semantic Web as simple data or tuples, and agents and Web users can then use such schemas to search semantic information in DBMSs using SQL Web interfaces. These schemas are also used for integration with other data structures such as ontologies, XML schemas, or other schemas coming from heterogeneous sources.

Ontologies vs. Databases

Many definitions of the ontology concept have been proposed in recent years (Gómez-Pérez et al., 2003b). Studer, Benjamins, and Fensel (1998) define an ontology as a formal, explicit specification of a shared conceptualization, where:

- *formal* means that it is machine readable;
- *explicit specification* represents the concepts,

properties, relations, functions, constraints, and axioms that are explicitly defined;
- *shared* means that knowledge must be consensual; and
- *conceptualization* represents the fact that an ontology must be an abstract model and a simplified view of some phenomenon in the world that we want to represent.

This definition summarizes the essence of an ontology. Other definitions for ontologies are very similar to the most referenced one which was given by Gruber (1993) or Guarino (1995, 1998).

Ontologies are introduced in the Semantic Web as the main mechanism for describing the content of a Web page (Chandrasekaran, Josephson, & Benjamins, 1999). This description can be made using different languages (Duineveld, Stoter, Weiden, Kenepa, & Benjamins, 2000; Gómez-Pérez, Férnandez-López, & Corcho-García, 2003a; Su & Ilebrekke, 2002). Most of these are based on first-order logic (FOL) (such as OWL (Antoniou & Harmelen, n.d.), RDF (Resource Description Framework (RDF), 1999), KIFF, etc.) and make the definition process very tedious. The most popular are the frame-based languages implemented in ontology management systems (OMS) such as Protégé (Stanford Medical Informatics at the Stanford University School of Medicine, n.d.), WebOde (Arperez, Corcho, Fernandez-López, & Gómez-Pérez, 2001; Ontological Engineering

Figure 3. Basic Ontology Categorization

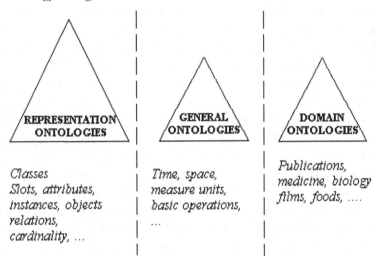

Group (OEG) from the Artificial Intelligence Department of the Computer Science Faculty (FI) from the Technical University of Madrid (Spain), n.d.;), Ontolingua (Stanford University, n.d.), or WebOnto (Open University, n.d.) amongst others. There are, however, drawbacks to all representation methods. FOL-based languages are too complex to be managed, but they are very good at inferring knowledge, and they are independent of the application tool. OMS, meanwhile, represent a very easy ontology development interface, but representations are deeply dependent on the tool. On the other hand, these systems do allow translations to be made into most FOL languages, thereby avoiding syntax mistakes. A detailed classification of ontology representation techniques can be seen in Partners (2004).

Several classifications of ontologies have been given by many authors (Lassila & McGuinness, 2002; Roche, 2003; Steve, Gangemi, & Pisanelli, 1998), and in particular we would like to mention Guarino's (Steve et al., 1998) categorization due to its simplicity, and Lassila and McGuinness's (2002), which has become a reference metric to define what can be considered an ontology or not. In Gómez-Pérez et al. (2003b), there is a brief summary of these classifications, whereby

they are divided into those based on the internal structure or on the subject of conceptualization. This categorization (a brief resume of this is shown in Figure 3) highlights the representation ontologies that define the frame where the remaining ontologies can be defined. General ontologies represent general common knowledge about a certain subject, and domain ontologies allow us to define knowledge about a specific domain.

Ontologies should provide consensual knowledge about a certain domain or area, and theoretically, these should be shared and populated so that this knowledge can be interchanged by the community. Such ontologies would allow common applications to be developed thanks to their compatible formats. Current work, however, demonstrates that each enterprise, project, or study develops its own ontology, uses its own language, and implements its own applications. General purpose ontologies (such as CYC (Lennat, 1995)) failed due to their low acceptance (McCool, 2005; Noy & Hafner, 1997). New trends in ontology representation are leading towards the integration of ontologies using matching and mapping processes (Choi, Song, & Han, 2006).

A large number of database matching algorithms and studies have been revived in order to use similar developments with ontologies (Hai, 2005; Ma, 2005; Mena & Illarramendi, 2001; Staab & Studer, 2004). There is a great deal of debate about whether databases can be considered like ontologies when they represent concrete domain knowledge. Some trends consider database schemas to be lightweight ontologies (Breu & Ding, 2004; Gómez-Pérez et al., 2003b; Noy, 2004) because they lack the axioms which allow inferences to be made. Another considers ontologies and databases to be very similar, but they are not developed to represent the same aspect of the domain (Unchold & Gruninger, 2004). We consider database schemas to represent knowledge as ontologies do, but the resulting hierarchy could be a little flat, and logical axioms could represent different kinds of restrictions (these are database constraints). In general, however, they can be used to share stored information with the other Semantic Web users and agents, and to profit from the new technologies developed around ontologies.

A large number of proposals have been developed to enable database schemas to be accessed using ontologies. Most of these representations focus on populating the DB information in the Semantic Web. These approaches only use relational schemas as a back-end system for retrieving data from databases through ontologies as a query interface (An, Borgida, & Mylopoulos, 2004; Barrasa, Corcho, & Perez, 2003; Bizer, 2003; Dou & LePendu, 2006). The majority of these proposals define a declarative markup language for making the translation. Another uses a traditional closed program that establishes the mapping between the ontology and the database schema (such as Data Genie (Gennari, Nguyen, & Silberfein, n.d.)). Obviously this last choice is deeply dependent on the system and is non-scalable. However, the language-based method is more independent of the system, but programs also carry out the translation.

Another kind of proposal is that which attempts to represent database metadata (the schemas) as ontologies. In Perez de Laborda and Conrad (2005), Perez de Laborda proposes the definition of only a few of the basic relational structures as a meta-ontology in order to communicate peer-to-peer databases. Trinh, Barker, and Alhajj (2006) define most of the relational database structures as an ontology, and this representation includes the DB constraints definition as the semantic restriction of the ontology. Another proposal is Sujatha et al.'s (Upadhyaya & Kumar, 2005) which represents relational database schemas using a tool that translates them into OWL. All these proposals define their ontologies using OWL. Dou, LePendu, Kim, and Qi (2006) develop a process for representing the main relational database structures in the Semantic Web, and this proposal is based on its own declarative language. Calero et al. (2005), on the other hand, described its own ontology using UML (they represented the ANSI Standard SQL 2003 (Information Technology Database Languages SQL, Parts 1 to 4 and 9 to 14, 2003)) and used it in order to represent relational database schemas. Another approach (*Ontobase* (Yabloko, Len, & Next Generation Software, n.d.)) develops a tool that automatically represents database contents as a meta-ontology. *Ontobase* is a *Protégé* plugin that imports database schemas to the protege representation format.

In our proposal, we use Calero et al.'s (2005) ontology for representing the Standard ANSI SQL 2003. In addition, predefined data types are defined in this ontology proposal explicitly, and fuzzy data representation structures are also added to this ontology. This inclusion enables a formal definition to be made of the data structures required for representing fuzzy data in an RDBMS (relational database management system). The following section describes the extension of an RDBMS, before presenting the solutions adopted to make this information accessible in the Semantic Web.

Fuzzy Databases: FIRST Proposal

Many extensions to the relational model have been proposed since Zadeh (1965) introduced the concept of fuzzy sets for representing fuzzy data, and a summary of these extensions can be found in Ma, 2005, 2006; Petry, 1996; Chen, 1999; Medina, Pons, and Vila, 1994; and Galindo, Urrutia, and Piattini, 2006). One of the extensions mentioned consists in adding a membership degree in a tuple as proposed by Baldwin and Zhou (1984) and Raju and Majumdar (1988). Buckles and Petri (1982) and Shenoi and Melton (1989) replace the equivalence between domain values by measures of nearness such as similarity and proximity relationships, respectively. Prade and Testemale (1984) use possibility distributions for attribute values, and Umano and Fukami (1994) add the concepts of non-applicable information. Zemankova and Kaendel use the possibilistic model and a language to represent certainty and similarity relationships. Kacprzyk and Zadrozny (2001) and Rodríguez (2000) propose a language for fuzzy querying. Rundensteiner, Hawkes, and Bandeler (1989) and Chen, Vandenbulcke, and Kerre (1992) use possibility distributions and resemblance relations in the relational databases simultaneously. This representation is also used in Ma (2005) and in Medina et al. (1994), where the possibility value of each tuple in a fuzzy relation is exactly 1. In this last work, Medina et al. (1994) summarize most of the characteristics of the extensions listed above.

In Medina et al. (1994), Medina introduces GEFRED (a fuzzy data representation model) and FIRST (an architecture definition in a real RDBMS in (Medina, Vila, Cubero, & Pons, 1995)). This architecture defines new fuzzy data types and operations enabling the system to make fuzzy queries to the database using an extension of SQL called FSQL (Carrasco, Vila, & Galindo, 2003). An implementation for all relations in the system catalog and an example of how structures can be stored in the database are described in detail in Medina et al. (1995).

In order to represent all the values in a generalized fuzzy domain, various authors entered the following three new data types into a classic RDMBS (Medina et al., 1995):

1. *Fuzzy Data Type 1*, or *CRISP* data type, which represents those attributes storing classical data which can be fuzzy queried;
2. *Fuzzy Data Type 2*, or *POSSIBILISTIC* data type, which represents those attributes storing fuzzy data represented using trapezoid possibility distributions (among others) defined on a numerical domain; and
3. *Fuzzy Data Type 3*, or *SCALAR* data type, which allows attributes storing fuzzy data to be represented using resemblance relations defined on a non-numerical domain.

The aim of this extension is to provide a new set of capabilities to a classical RDBMS. This may be achieved when all accesses to relations in the data catalog are intercepted so the new types and relations can be processed. Some new data catalog relations involved in this processing have therefore been defined, and this new set has been named the fuzzy meta-knowledge base (FMB). Each FMB relation is described below:

1. *FUZZY COL LIST* relation, storing information about attributes of relations that can contain fuzzy data or can be fuzzy queried;
2. *FUZZY OBJECT LIST* relation, storing common information about all the fuzzy concepts stored in the database such as labels;
3. *FUZZY LABEL DEF* relation, storing the possibility distribution related to every fuzzy label defined in the database;
4. *FUZZY APPROX MUCH* relation, storing information for designing possibility distributions on predefined fuzzy concepts in the database such as greater than, much greater than;

5. *FUZZY NEARNESS DEF* relation, storing information about similarity relations between every pair of values of a fuzzy data type 3 attribute; and

6. *FUZZY QUALIFIERS DEF* relation, storing the minimum threshold that is assigned to every qualifier and is defined on a linguistic label.

A fuzzy database schema, however, only uses two of these sets of relations in its definition: FUZZY COL LIST relation (used whenever a fuzzy attribute is defined in the system) and FUZZY APPROX MUCH relation (used when a *Fuzzy Data Type 2* is defined in order to establish restrictions on its domain). The remaining relations are defined to store concrete information, that is, labels and discrete values used in the tuples definition (but this representation is not in the scope of this chapter).

Integration of Information

A great number of systems have already been developed to enable a wide variety of data from many different sources to be integrated. Ontology integration (Choi et al., 2006; Hameed, Preece, & Sleeman, 2004; Noy, 2004) is one of the main goals because of the increasing number of these representations today. Yet it is not the only application area since the Semantic Web has facilitated access to many different kinds of information represented in different formats and even in different languages. Some examples of these different schema types are: relational schemas (represented with SQL), XML (using document type definition and XML schema definition), document schemas, and ontologies (using OWL or RDF) (Hai, 2005).

The integration of information is not, therefore, a simple problem. George (2005) summarizes several kinds of schema heterogeneity and dimensions of integration, and establishes three dimensions:

1. *System Integration,* representing the heterogeneity in the platform where the information is represented;

2. *Schema integration,* representing the heterogeneity between schemas. He identifies five tasks in this process: (a) pre-integration: schema translation into common data model form; (b) comparison: process of semantic conflict identification; (c) conformance: making conflicts compatible for merging by similar representation; (d) merging: integrating schemas; and (e) restructuring: refining schema; and

3. *Semantic Integration,* resolving differences in conceptual data representation by determining equivalence between schema constructs.

Although most approaches for integrating information are based on schema integration techniques from database disciplines, there are certain differences between ontologies and databases, as outlined by Kalfoglou and Schorlemmer (2003), and the two approximations in the process for integrating schemas are: *local as view,* and *global as view* (Goguen, 2005). *Global as view* deals with establishing a generic domain representation (a global schema) where local schemas map to the global schema; this technique is widely used (Aparcio, Farias, & dos Santos, 2005). Meanwhile, *local as view* implies to establish direct correspondences among different local schemas.

There are various proposals for schemas and ontology matching. For example, MAPONTO (An et al., 2004) is a tool that uses logic to establish mappings between ontologies and relational databases. COMA++ (Aumueller, Do, Massmann, & Rahm, 2005) is a tool that solves matching problems between schemas and ontologies written in different languages such as SQL, W3C XSD, and OWL. GLUE (Doan, Madhavan, Domingos, & Halevy, 2002) or Ontomap (Gal, Modica, Jamil, & Eyal, 2005) are other examples of tools used for automated schema matching.

In this work, we attempt to establish a frame in order to develop a tool for integrating fuzzy database schemas with the remaining structures found in the Semantic Web, and we have therefore identified two dimensions in this frame:

1. *System integration* requires the integration of schemas from different RDBMSs such as Oracle ©, MySQL© , PostgreSQL© , DB2© , and so forth. Each system has its own characteristics that must be analyzed in order for this integration to be carried out.
2. *Schema integration* allows heterogeneous schemas to be integrated. These schemas can be represented using different languages such as SQL, XML or OWL. This task requires conflicts to be solved such as: data type conflicts, data scaling conflicts, or missing data conflicts) (Hai, 2005; Ma, 2005).

Due to the specific characteristics of the final dimension, semantic integration, it will be studied once the previous two dimensions have been developed. The global as view approximation, however, will be used to establish correspondences between different schemas.

A fuzzy DB schema representation would then set up a flexible global schema where local schemas map to it. An ontology for representing a fuzzy database representation is presented in the following section.

USING AN ONTOLOGY TO REPRESENT FUZZY DATABASES IN THE SEMANTIC WEB

Fuzzy DBs add semantics to the information in the database, making it more interesting and valuable, and enabling it to be queried and stored more flexibly. For this, the structure that represents the fuzzy information (metadata) should be published and formally defined, so users or intelligent agents can therefore access and exploit it automatically. The Semantic Web is enriched by integrating this kind of information into its query results.

Fuzzy extensions to the relational database model, however, are not a new problem. The definition process of fuzzy information on the system is not as direct as the definition of the classic one, and good knowledge about how the catalog has been extended so as to define fuzzy data is a basic user requirement. The problem is accentuated when new data types, structures, or representations are included in the fuzzy system, making the catalog hard to manage. This is the case studied in Blanco, Martinez-Cruz, et al. (2005b) where fuzzy RDBMS are extended in order to manage logical rules for making deductions with fuzzy data, to make deductions, and to represent data mining operations using fuzzy data.

As we mentioned before, the catalog structures required for representing fuzzy datatypes need to be explicitly defined in the RDBMS. Moreover, the defined schemas of the fuzzy databases need to store information in the catalog so that the system can manage the database properly. The description of this extra fuzzy information prevents the use of already-developed tools for interchanging information between RDBMS. These problems make processes like sharing, merging, recycling, comparing, sending, or exploiting schemas or information more difficult than we could wish for.

Figure 4 represents the problem of integrating fuzzy DB schemas with other representation models or technologies. Section A represents how an FDB schema must establish individual mappings in order to share its contents. The solution to this problem is shown in Section B. This consists in defining an interface that keeps the knowledge representation (logical model) of the fuzzy schema aside from its storage place (DBMS). The mapping must then be defined once from the ontology to the destination resources.

This interface uses an ontology that formalizes the SQL standard including the fuzzy data types

309

defined in the GEFRED model (Medina et al., 1994). In addition, this proposal extends the SQL standard for defining fuzzy tables and columns. Instances of the proposed ontology store the definition of the database schemas, the domains of the attributes, and their default values. These schema representations are therefore independent of any concrete RDBMS representation.

The ontology representing the extended Fuzzy RDBMSs (FRDBMS) also uses OWL (Ontology Web Language) (Antoniou & Harmelen, n.d.) so that it is accessible on the Web and understandable by most agents and currently-developed applications.

Ontology Description

The ontology that defines the extension of the SQL 2003 standard for representing fuzzy data can be divided into the following two sub-ontologies: fuzzy data type ontology, and fuzzy schema ontology.

Fuzzy Data Type Ontology

The SQL standard (in particular, the SQL:2003) defines three kinds of data types: predefined types

Figure 4. Solution to the fuzzy data representation problem

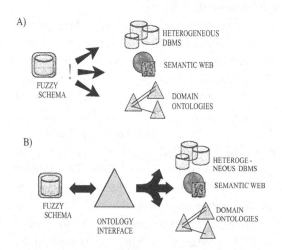

(also known as "built-in data types"), constructed data types, and user-defined data types (more details can be found in ANSI/ISO/IEC International Standard (IS) Database Language SQL Part 2: Foundation (SQL/Foundation), 1999; Calero et al., 2005; Information Technology Database languages SQL. Parts 1 to 4 and 9 to 14, 2003), and these data types have already been represented using different knowledge representation methods. While one of these is based on the use of an ontology to model all the SQL:2003 data types using UML notation (Calero et al., 2005), this representation lacks an explicit representation of the predefined data types that can be found in Pardede and Wenny Rahayu (n.d.) and in *Figure 5,* section A. Fuzzy data type representation, however, is not included in any of these.

Rather than modifying the SQL standard data types, the proposed ontology extends them and in *Figure 5*, section A, they are represented by a dashed line. The extended hierarchy of the ontology is shown in *Figure 5*, section B, where both the standard data types (those which are on the first level of the Pardede hierarchy) and also the fuzzy data types defined in the FIRST architecture are represented. Fuzzy data types and the relations established with the predefined datatype hierarchy are given in further detail.

There is a direct correspondence between the predefined SQL data types and data types represented with OWL, as shown in Table 1.

Fuzzy Schema Ontology

A sub-ontology represents the SQL standard schema that allows any relational database schema to be maintained independently of its DBMS implementation. Once the schema has been loaded into the ontology as a set of instances, it can be imported or exported to another DBMS. It can even be exported into the Web so that its knowledge representation can be shared.

Calero et al.'s (2005) representation models the SQL:2003 standard schemata as an ontology

Figure 5. Taxonomy of predefined SQL data types with an extension with fuzzy data types in dashed line, and fuzzy data type ontology (Pardede & Wenny Rahayu, n.d.)

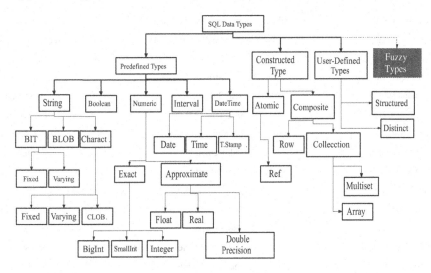

A) (Pardede & Wenny Rahayu, n.d.) taxonomy of predefined SQL data types and an extension with fuzzy data types in dashed line.

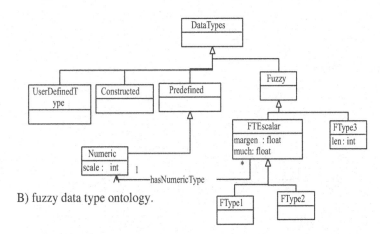

B) fuzzy data type ontology.

using UML notation, and an OCL language to define the constraints. The ontology is therefore translated into the OWL language once it has been adapted to represent fuzzy database structures. The class Column is classified into two subclasses: Base Column and Fuzzy Column (as mentioned in *Figure 6*), where the first represents classic columns and the second represents all the fuzzy attributes. Fuzzy attributes do not relate to any constraint class because they cannot be a foreign key or primary key in the schema. The original

Calero ontology, on the other hand, is pruned, and the resulting ontology lacks representation of the SQL objects since these are not necessary to reach our goals.

A brief sample of the resulting ontology (represented in the OWL language) is shown in *Figure 7* and *Figure 8*. *Figure 7* shows the code for describing the Fuzzy Column Class, its attributes, relations, and constraints.

In this ontology tables and column classes are defined as metaclases (both are sub-classes of owl:

Table 1. Correspondence between SQL data types and XML data types

SQL Data Type	XML Data Type	Facet
String, Bit, Fixed	xsd:hexBinary or xsd:base64Binary	*no facet*
String, Bit, Varying	xsd:hexBinary or xsd:base64Binary	xsd:maxLength
String, Character, Fixed	xsd:String	xsd:length
String, Character, Varying	xsd:String	xsd:maxLength
String, Character, Clob	xsd:String	xsd:maxLength
Boolean	xsd:boolean	no facet
Interval	xsd:duration	xsd:pattern
Numeric, Exact, Numeric	xsd:decimal	xsd:precision, xsd:scale
Numeric, Exact, Decimal	xsd:decimal	xsd:precision, xsd:scale
Numeric, Integer	xsd:integer	xsd:maxInclusive, xsd:minInclusive
Numeric, SmallInt	xsd:integer	xsd:maxInclusive, xsd:minInclusive
Numeric, BigInt	xsd:integer	xsd:maxInclusive, xsd:minInclusive
Numeric, Approx, Real	xsd:float, xsd:double	no facet
Numeric, Approx, Double Precision	xsd:float, xsd:double	no facet
Numeric, Approx, Float	xsd:float, xsd:double	no facet
DateTime, Date	xsd:date	xsd:pattern
DateTime, Date	xsd:time	xsd:pattern
DateTime, T.Stamp	xsd:dateTime	xsd:pattern

Figure 6. Fuzzy schema ontology

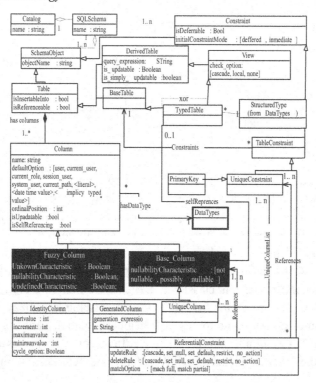

Figure 7. Fuzzy column class represented in OWL

```
<!-- Definition of    FuzzyColumn   Class --><!-- Class Definition -->

<owl:Class   rdf :ID=" FuzzyColumn   ">
 < rdfs :subClassOf  >
  <owl:Class   rdf :resource="#Column"/>
 </ rdfs :subClassOf  >
</owl:Class>

<!-- DataType   Definitions -->
<owl: DatatypeProperty   rdf :ID=" NullabilityCharacteristic   ">
 < rdfs :domain rdf :resource="#  FuzzyColumn   "/>
 < rdfs :range rdf :resource="http://   www.w3.org   /2001/ XMLSchema  #boolean"/>
</owl: DatatypeProperty  >

<!-- The same for    UndefinedCharacteristic   , UnknownCharacteristic   ,
is Updatable , isSelfReferencing   . And using in   rdfs :range .. XMLSchema   #String
<owl: DatatypeProperty    rdf :ID=" DefaultOption   ">
 < rdfs :range>
  <owl: DataRange  >
  <owl: oneOf  >
   < rdf :List>
    < rdf :first rdf :datatype ="& xsd ;String">user</  rdf :first>
    < rdf :rest>
     < rdf :List>
     < rdf :first rdf :datatype ="& xsd ;integer">current_user</   rdf :first>
     ....
     </ rdf :List>
    </ rdf :rest>
   </ rdf :List>
  </owl: oneOf  >
  </owl: DataRange  >
 </ rdfs :range>
</owl: DatatypeProperty  >

<!-- Objects Properties Definitions -->
 <owl: ObjectProperty    rdf :ID=" hasDataType   ">
 < rdfs :range rdf :resource="#  FuzzyColumn   "/>
 < rdfs :domain rdf :resource="#  DataType "/>
 </owl: ObjectProperty  >

<!-- Restrictions Definition -->
<owl:Class   rdf :about="#  FuzzyColumn   ">
 < rdfs :subClassOf  >
  <owl:Restriction>
   <owl:cardinality   rdf :datatype ="http://  www.w3.org  /2001/ XMLSchema  #int "
   >1</owl:cardinality>
   <owl: onProperty  >
    <owl: DatatypeProperty    rdf :about="#  NullabilityCharacteristic  "/>
   </owl: onProperty  >
  </owl:Restriction>
 </ rdfs :subClassOf  >
```

Figure 8. Table class represented in OWL

```
<!-- Definition of Table Class -->
<!-- Class Definition -->

<owl:Class   rdf :ID="#Table">
 < rdfs :subClassOf  >
  <owl:Class   rdf :resource="#   SchemaObject   "/>
 </ rdfs :subClassOf  >
 < rdfs :subClassOf   rdf :resource=
"http:// www.w3.org  /2002/07/owl#Class"/>
 </owl:Class>

<!-- DataType   Properties Definitions -->

<owl: DatatypeProperty   rdf :ID=" isReferenceable   ">
 < rdfs :range rdf :resource=
"http:// www.w3.org  /2001/ XMLSchema  #boolean"/>
 < rdfs :domain rdf :resource="#Table"/>
 </owl: DatatypeProperty  >

 <!-- The same for is      Insertable   into -->

<!-- Objects Properties Definitions -->
 <owl: ObjectProperty   rdf :ID=" hasColumns   ">
 < rdfs :range rdf :resource="#Column"/>
 < rdfs :domain rdf :resource="#Table"/>
 </owl: ObjectProperty  >

<!-- Restrictions Definition -->
 <owl:Class   rdf :about="#Table">
 < rdfs :subClassOf  >
  <owl:Restriction>
   <owl: onProperty  >
    <owl: DatatypeProperty    rdf :about="# isReferenceable   "/>
   </owl: onProperty  >
   <owl:cardinality    rdf :datatype =
"http:// www.w3.org  /2001/ XMLSchema  #int "
   >1</owl:cardinality>
  </owl:Restriction>
 </ rdfs :subClassOf  >

<!-- the same for    isInsertableInto   -->
 < rdfs :subClassOf  >
  <owl:Restriction>
   <owl: onProperty  >
    <owl: ObjectProperty   rdf :ID=" hasColumns   "/>
   </owl: onProperty  >
   <owl: minCardinality   rdf :datatype =
"http:// www.w3.org  /2001/ XMLSchema  #int "
   >1</owl: minCardinality  >
  </owl:Restriction>
 </ rdfs :subClassOf  >
</owl:Class>
```

class). These metaclasses allows us to define all the tables and attributes described in the schema as classes. *Figure 8* describes the class Table and shows the definition of this characteristic.

Both sub-ontologies are connected by means of a specific property that joins the classes Datatypes and Columns as in Calero et al. (2005). The relation *hasDataType* establishes the connection between datatypes and columns. This connection is represented in *Figure 6*.

The translation process of this ontology from UML representation into OWL is direct. The following matching rules are shown:

- UML classes as ontology classes;
- UML attributes as datatype properties;
- UML relations as object properties;
- UML cardinality relations as cardinality restrictions;
- UML closed values as owl:oneof restriction;

Figure 9. Example of fuzzy database schema

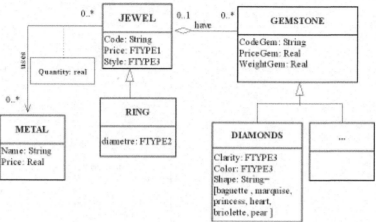

- UML logical restrictions as Boolean restrictions (e.g. owl:unionOf)

More detailed correspondences between OWL and UML are explained in Falkovych, Sabou, and Stuckenschmidt (2003); and Brockmans, Volz, Eberhart, and Loffler (2004).

Example

In this section, we will show an example of a database schema that includes fuzzy attributes in its definition. The selected example is a jewelry database *(*Figure 9*)* which represents the gemstones contained in their jewelry. We present a semi-completed schema (since the classes of all existing gemstones are not represented). Only

some of the most significant elements will be described in this example for reasons of space.

Surprisingly, diamonds have always had fuzzy attributes among their features. Some of their characteristics are normally represented with linguistic labels, for example, clarity and color attributes. *Table 3* and *Table 4* shows these labels, respectively.

As we can see, a fuzzy representation would allow these labels to be inferred, giving a membership degree when a precise value is not known. Even more generic labels can be generated in order to facilitate valuation by using a degree. For example, if we say that a diamond has the color Yellow with a degree of 0.5, then we can infer that it is type W.

Table 3. Labels for representing diamond clarity

Label	Description
FL	Flawless
IF	Internally Flawless
VVS(VVS1,VVS2)	Very very small internal inclusions
VS (VS1, VS2)	Very small internal inclusions
SI (SI1, SI2, SI3)	Small inclusion
P	Piqué
I (I1,I2,I3)	Imperfect

Table 4. Labels for representing diamond color

Label	Description
D, E, F	Colorless
G, H, I, J	Nearly colorless
K, L, M	Faint Yellow
N, O, P, Q, R	Very Light Yellow
S, T, U, V, W, X, Y, Z	Light Yellow

Figure 10. Instantiation of class table in OWL code and class columns

```
<!-- Definition of Jewel -->
<!-- the prefix " fdtscho " is used to represent the Ontology
for Fuzzy Databases Schema Representation -->

<!-- Ring Class Instances Definition -->

< fdtscho :BaseTable  rdf :ID="Ring">
  < fdtscho :hasColumns   rdf :resource="#Code">
  < fdtscho :hasColumns   rdf :resource="#Price">
  < fdtscho :hasColumns   rdf :resource="#Style">
  < fdtscho :hasColumns   rdf :resource="# CodeGem ">
  < fdtscho :hasColumns   rdf :resource="#Diameter">
</ fdtscho :BaseTable  >

<!-- Diamonds Class Definition -->

< fdtscho :BaseTable  rdf :ID="Diamonds">
  < fdtscho :hasColumns   rdf :resource="# CodeGem ">
  < fdtscho :hasColumns   rdf :resource="# PriceGem ">
  < fdtscho :hasColumns   rdf :resource="# WeightGem ">
  < fdtscho :hasColumns   rdf :resource="#Clarity">
  < fdtscho :hasColumns   rdf :resource="#Color">
  < fdtscho :hasColumns   rdf :resource="#Shape">
</ fdtscho :BaseTable  >

<!-- Definition of Attributes by means the        Instantiation  of
Fuzzy or Base Column Classes -->

  < fdtscho :UniqueColumn    rdf :ID="Code">
  < rdfs :comment  rdf:datatype =
"http:// www.w3.org  /2001/ XMLSchema  #string"
    >Code Identifier</   rdfs :comment>
  < fdtscho :hasDataType   rdf :resource="#Code_DT"/>
  < fdtscho :nameCol  rdf :datatype =
"http:// www.w3.org  /2001/ XMLSchema  #string"
    >Code</   fdtscho :nameCol >
  </ fdtscho :UniqueColumn  >

<!-- Similar definition similar for       CodeGem  , PriceGem ,
WeightGem  , Shape resource -->

  < fdtscho :FuzzyColumn    rdf :ID="Price">
  < fdtscho :hasDataType   rdf :resource="#Price_  FDT "/>
  < fdtscho :nameCol  rdf :datatype =
"http:// www.w3.org  /2001/ XMLSchema  #string"
   >Price</   fdtscho :nameCol >
  </ fdtscho :FuzzyColumn  >

<!-- Definition similar for Style, Diameter, Clarity, Color
(they are subclass of Fuzzy Column)-->
```

Figure 11. Instantiation of class datatypes in OWL code

```
<!-- Definition of Jewel -->
<!-- the prefix " fdtscho " is used to represent the Ontology for
Fuzzy Databases Schema Representation -->

<!-- Instantiation  of DataType  Classes -->

  < fdtscho :FType1  rdf :ID="Price_  FDT ">
  < fdtscho :much rdf :datatype =
"http:// www.w3.org  /2001/ XMLSchema  #float"
   >1.0</ fdtscho :much>
  < fdtscho :margin rdf :datatype =
"http:// www.w3.org  /2001/ XMLSchema  #float"
   >200.0</ fdtscho :margin>
  < fdtscho :hasNumericType   rdf :resource="#Price_DT"/>
  </ fdtscho :FType1  >

  <!-- Similar definition similar for Diameter -->

  < fdtscho :FType3  rdf :ID="Style_  FDT ">
  < fdtscho :len rdf :datatype =
"http:// www.w3.org  /2001/ XMLSchema  #int"
   >3</ fdtscho :len>
  </ fdtscho :FType3  >

<!-- Similar definition for  Clarity and Color-->

  < fdtscho :Float rdf :ID="Price_DT">
  < fdtscho :precision rdf :datatype =
"http:// www.w3.org  /2001/ XMLSchema  #int"
   >2</ fdtscho :precision>
  </ fdtscho :Float>

  <!-- Similar definition for      PriceGem , WeightGem  -->

< fdtscho :Varying  rdf :ID=" CatName _DT">
  < fdtscho :lenghtStr rdf :datatype =
"http:// www.w3.org  /2001/ XMLSchema  #int"
   >50</ fdtscho :lenghtStr >
  </ fdtscho :Varying>

<!-- Similar definition for Code,       CodeGem  -->
```

Although the diameter of a ring has a numeric value, a ring size can also be defined using linguistic labels in order to establish generic sizes (e.g., S, M, L, XL, XXL), which is why this is a Fuzzy Type 2 attribute.

Fuzzy Type 1 is defined when we want to fuzzily query on this attribute, but its values cannot be fuzzily stored. This situation could occur in the price attribute in the jewelry database, for example, if we want to know which rings are considered "cheap".

The resulting ontology of the jewelry schema consists of a set of instances of the previously

These attributes can therefore be defined as Fuzzy Data Type 3, that is, using discrete values with a similarity relation between them.

defined ontology. Various parts of the OWL code show how this schema is represented below. *Figure 10* and *Figure 11* represent instances of the classes Table, Columns, and Datatypes, respectively.

Applications

Developing fuzzy schemas as ontologies is an attempt to facilitate the integration information process between fuzzy databases and other representations. As described in the previous sections, fuzzy databases have their own representation and languages, which further complicates the use of developed schema mapping tools.

In this work, various operations relating to fuzzy database integration have emerged (as shown in *Figure 12*), and these basically consist of:

- Exporting a schema to several heterogeneous DBMS (as shown in *Figure 12*, section A);
- Interchanging data between different homogeneous schemas or DBMS DBMS (as shown in *Figure 12*, section B); and
- Integrating different schemas from heterogeneous sources into a single merged schema DBMS (as shown in *Figure 12*, section C).

This last one is the most complex problem to resolve, and many approaches have been proposed for this. The main difficulty in resolving this problem is due to the enormous variety of schema (as mentioned in the previous section). Nevertheless, fuzzy database schema integration could not increase the complexity of this problem due to the flexibility of the data represented in them.

DISCUSSION

Although there are a large number of approaches for representing fuzzy data in database management systems, this information has not transcended from the database discipline. Current knowledge

Figure 12. Schema exportation to several DBMS

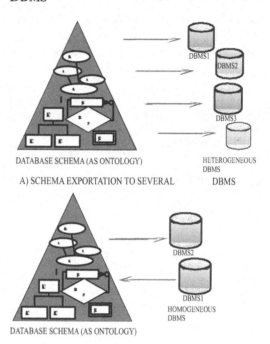

DATABASE SCHEMA (AS ONTOLOGY)
HETEROGENEOUS DBMS
A) SCHEMA EXPORTATION TO SEVERAL DBMS

DATABASE SCHEMA (AS ONTOLOGY)
DBMS2
DBMS1
HOMOGENEOUS DBMS

B) INTERCHANGE OF INFORMATION BETWEEN HOMOGENEOUS DATABASES

DATABASE SCHEMA (AS ONTOLOGY)
HETEROGENEOUS DBMS

C) DATA FUSION OR SCHEMA INTEGRATION

representation mechanisms, such as ontologies, represent relational database schemas in many formats, but they all store classical information, and it is extremely difficult to find the fuzzy data representation structures in the fuzzy database environment. In this chapter, we have proposed an ontology for such schemas and this definition helps fuzzy database users access its information using new data management techniques such as the Semantic Web.

Our following task is to develop a framework that will allow us to represent the domain ontology defined by the instances of this ontology. These instances that represent a FDB schema would be transformed into a new domain ontology, and this ontology should have classes, properties, and restrictions represented as a hierarchy. This representation is obviously closely related to a relational database structure although its instances are directly related to the tuples in the represented database. On the other hand, special structure definitions are required in order to store fuzzy values in the ontology. For example, distribution functions should be able to be defined as the varying string structure is.

The defined ontology can be considered as a general ontology (or perhaps a meta-ontology) due to the metaclasses that it contains. This is the case of the classes Table and Columns. When these classes are instantiated, new classes should be generated in order to allow the tuples relating to them to be defined.

More applications can be found using the representation of fuzzy schemas as ontologies. These schemas are more flexible in the integration process due to the flexibility of their elements. Uncertain or imprecise data are not very restrictive when a matching rule attempts to map one representation to another, and so sometimes a membership degree is the only requisite. Fuzzy database schemas also enrich the heterogeneity of the Semantic Web. New database content can be reached and processed computationally if required.

Public descriptions of databases (with fuzzy or classical data) are necessary in the Semantic Web, and allow access to database information that is not available as an HTML Web page. This happens because database owners do not always want to develop a back-end interface for Web access although their databases are available to the public. New opportunities for developing applications (or services) enabling automatic access to public database content will emerge.

Fuzzy schemas have been represented as an ontology using the OWL language because it is independent of a tool or a concrete representation structure. It has also been defined as standard by the W3C, and most tools representing ontologies can read and handle this format. OWL, however, is a complex language with extremely lengthy definitions. Hand-written OWL code is a very tedious process and it is very easy to make mistakes when writing it. Most OWL ontologies are developed by using an ontology management tool and then translating them. Another option is to develop an OWL editor.

Although there are several tools for working with OWL ontologies, we choose JENA (Programme., n.d.) because it provides a well-documented API for managing OWL elements. There are libraries such as OWL API (Bechhofer, n.d.) or SESAME (Kampman & Broekstra, n.d.) but these are less intuitive than JENA. Another alternative is to develop a plugin in an existing ontology management system, but this has not been done as all these tools use their own local representation structures.

This work only attempts to extend the contents of the Semantic Web rather than to analyze the poor success of the Semantic Web to date. There have been many developments in the framework of ontology definition and knowledge representations, but as McCool (2005) analyzed in his work, not enough applications or services have been developed so far. This proposal is therefore expected to be used by a large number of Semantic Web clients in the near future.

CONCLUSION

Although integration techniques and tools for reconciling schemas from heterogeneous sources (included DB) have often been proposed, there is no information about how to represent the fuzzy data stored in fuzzy database management systems in order to make it accessible in the Semantic

Web. This work proposes a frame for representing fuzzy schema structures as ontologies.

This work also represents new advantages in the information retrieval process in the Semantic Web, since they enable an ontology to be used to retrieve schemas from all types of databases. This information is used to access public databases by means of client interfaces which are available online. This access can be made by the end users or automatically by agents.

By treating the schemas represented with this proposal as ontology data, users can then exploit them with all of the developed technologies for managing ontologies, and some of the operations that can be performed with ontologies are: comparing, pruning, importing, exporting, evaluating, integrating, mapping, merging, alignment, reasoning, and so forth.

REFERENCES

An, Y., Borgida, A., & Mylopoulos, J. (2004). Refining mappings from relational tables to ontologies. *Proceedings of the VLDB Workshop on the Semantic Web and Databases (SWDB '04)* (pp. 57-62).

ANSI/ISO/IEC International Standard (IS) Database Language SQL, Part 2: Foundation (SQL/Foundation) (1999). *ISO/IEC 9075-2:1999 (E)*.

Antoniou, G., & van Harmelen, F. (n.d.). Web ontology language: OWL. In S. Staab & R. Studer (Eds.), *Handbook on ontologies* (pp. 67-93). Springer-Verlag.

Aparcio, A. S., Farias, O. L. M., & dos Santos, N. (2005). Applying ontologies in the integration of heterogeneous relational databases. *Proceedings of the 2005 Australasian Ontology Workshop (AOW '05)* (pp. 11–16). Darlinghurst, Australia: Australian Computer Society, Inc.

Arperez, J. C., Corcho, O., Fernandez-Lopez, M., & Gómez-Pérez, A. (2001). WebOde: A scalable workbench for ontological engineering. *Proceedings of the 1st International Conference on Knowledge Capture (K-CAP '01)* (pp. 6-13). New York: ACM Press.

Aumueller, D., Do, H. -H., Massmann, S., & Rahm, E. (2005). Schema and ontology matching with COMA++. *Proceedings of the 2005 ACM SIGMOD International Conference on Management of Data (SIGMOD '05)* (pp. 906–908). New York: ACM Press.

Baldwin, J. F., & Zhou, S. Q. (1984). A fuzzy relational inference language. *Fuzzy Sets and Systems* (14), 155-174.

Barrasa, J., Corcho, O., & Perez, A. G. (2003). Fund finder: A case study of database to ontology mapping. *International Semantic Web Conference, Lecture Notes in Computer Science, 2870* (pp. 17–22). Springer-Verlag.

Bechhofer, S. (2007). *API for OWL ontologies*. Retrieved from http://owl.man.ac.uk/api/readme.html

Berners-Lee, T., Hendler, J., & Lassila, O. (2001). The semantic Web. *Scientific American, 284*(5), 28-37.

Bizer, C. (2003). D2R map—A database to RDF mapping language. *Proceedings of the 12th International World Wide Web Conference* (pp. 17–22).

Blanco, I., Martínez-Cruz, C., Marín, N., & Vila, M. A. (2005a). About the use of ontologies for fuzzy knowledge representation. *Proceedings of the International Conference in Fuzzy Logic and Technology, EUSFLAT 2005* (pp. 106-111).

Blanco, I., Martínez-Cruz, C., Serrano, J., & Vila, M. (2005b). A first approach to multipurpose relational database server. *Mathware and Soft Computing, 12*(2-3), 129-153.

Breu, M., & Ding, Y. (2004). Modelling the world: Databases and ontologies. *Whitepaper by IFI, Institute of Computer Science, University of Innsbruck*.

Brockmans, S., Volz, R., Eberhart, A., & Loffler, P. (2004). Visual modeling of OWL DL ontologies using UML. *The Semantic Web, ISWC 2004, Lecture Notes in Computer Science, 3298* (pp. 198-213). Berlin: Springer-Verlag.

Buckles, B. P., & Petry, F. E. (1982). A fuzzy representation of data for relational databases. *Fuzzy Sets and Systems* (7), 213-226.

Calero, C., Ruiz, F., Baroni, A., Brito e Abreu, F., & Piattini, M. (2005). An ontological approach to describe the SQL:2003 object-relational features. *Computer Standards and Interfaces Journal, 28*(6), 695-713.

Carrasco, R. A., Vila, M. A., & Galindo, J. (2003). FSQL: A flexible query language for data mining. *Enterprise Information Systems 4*, 68-74.

Chandrasekaran, B., Josephson, J., & Benjamins, V. (1999). What are ontologies, and why do we need them? *IEEE Intelligent Systems, 14*(1), 20-26.

Chen, G. Q. (Ed.) (1999). *Fuzzy logic in data modeling; Semantics, constraints, and database design*. Kluwer Academic Publisher.

Chen, G. Q., Vandenbulcke, J., & Kerre, E. E. (1992). A general treatment of data redundancy in a fuzzy relational data model. *Journal of the American Society of Information Sciences* (3), 304-311.

Choi, N., Song, I. -Y., & Han, H. (2006). A survey on ontology mapping. *SIGMOD Record, 35*(3), 34–41.

Doan, A., Madhavan, J., Domingos, P., & Halevy, A. (2002). Learning to map between ontologies on the semantic Web. *Proceedings of the Eleventh International WWW Conference* (pp. 662-673). *Hawaii*.

Dou, D., & LePendu, P. (2006). Ontology-based integration for relational databases. *Proceedings of the 2006 ACM Symposium on Applied Computing (SAC '06)* (pp. 461–466). New York: ACM Press.

Dou, D., LePendu, P., Kim, S., & Qi, P. (2006). Integrating databases into the semantic Web through an ontology-based framework. *Proceedings of the 22nd International Conference on Data Engineering Workshops (ICDEW'06)* (p. 54). Washington, DC: IEEE Computer Society.

Duineveld, A. J., Stoter, R., Weiden, M. R., Kenepa, B., & Benjamins, V. R. (2000, June). Wonder-tools? A comparative study of ontological engineering tools. *International Journal of Human-Computer Studies, 52*(6), 1111-1133.

Eriksson, U. (n.d.). LIBSBD: Database library for supporting multiple database management. Retrieved from http://siag.nu/libsdb/

Falkovych, K., Sabou, M., & Stuckenschmidt, H. (2003). UML for the semantic Web: Transformation-based approaches. *Knowledge Transformation for the Semantic Web*, 92–106.

Finin, T., Mayfield, J., Joshi, A., Cost, R. S., & Fink, C. (2005). Information retrieval and the semantic Web. *Proceedings of the 38th Annual Hawaii International Conference on System Sciences (HICSS '05)- Track 4* (p. 113.1). Washington, DC: IEEE Computer Society.

Gal, A., Modica, G., Jamil, H., & Eyal, A. (2005). Automatic ontology matching using application semantics. *AI Magazine, 26*(1), 21–31.

Galindo, J., Urrutia, A., & Piattini, M. (Eds.). (2006). *Fuzzy databases modeling, design, and implementa- tion*. Hershey, PA: Idea Group Publishing.

Gennari, J., Nguyen, M., & Silberfein, A. (n.d.). *Datagenie*. Retrieved from http://protege.cim3. net/cgi-bin/wiki.pl?DataGenie

George, D. (2005). Understanding structural and semantic heterogeneity in the context of database schema integration. *Journal of the Department of Computing* (pp. 29-44). UCLan: IEEE Computer Society.

Goble, C. (2003). Guest editorial: The semantic Web: An evolution for a revolution. *Computer Networks, 42* (5), 551-556.

Goguen, J. A. (2005). Data, schema, ontology, and logic integration. *Logic Journal of the IGPL, 13*(6), 685–715.

Gómez-P´erez, A., F´ernandez-Lopez, M., & Corcho-Garc´ıa, O. (2003a). Methodologies, tools, and languages for building ontologies. Where is their meeting point? *Data and Knowledge Engineering* (46), 41-64.

Gómez-Pérez, A., Férnandez-Lopez, M., & Corcho-García, O. (2003b). *Ontological engineering.* New York: Springer-Verlag, Inc.

Gruber, T. R. (1993). *Toward principles for the design of ontologies used for knowledge sharing* (Tech. Rep. KSL 93-04). Stanford, CA: Knowledge Systems Laboratory, Stanford University.

Guarino, N. (1995). Formal ontology, concept analysis and knowledge representation. *International Journal of Human and Computer Studies, 43*(5/6), 625-640.

Guarino, N. (1998). Formal ontologies and information systems. *Proceedings of FOIS '98* (pp. 3-15).

Hai, D. H. (2005). *Schema matching and mapping-based data integration.* Unpublished doctoral dissertation, Interdisciplinary Center for Bioinformatics and Department of Computer Science, University of Leipzig. Germany.

Hameed, A. Preece, A. & Sleeman, D. (2004). Ontology Reconcilitation. In S. Staab & R. Studer (Eds) *Handbook on ontologies* (pp. 231-250). Springer

Hendler, J., Berners-Lee, T., & Miller, E. (2002). Integrating applications on the semantic Web. *Journal of the Institute of Electrical Engineers of Japan, 122*(10), 676-680.

Hu, J., Nicholson, D., Mungall, C., Hillyard, A. L., & Archibald, A. L. (1996). WebinTool: A generic Web to database interface building tool. *Proceedings of the 7th International Workshop on Database and Expert Systems Applications (DEXA '96)* (p. 285). Washington, DC: IEEE Computer Society.

Information Technology Database Languages SQL, Parts 1 to 4 and 9 to 14 (2003). *9075-1:2003 to 9075-14:2003 International Standards.*

Kacprzyk, J., & Zadrozny, S. (2001). SQLF and fQuery for access. *Proceedings of the Joint 9th IFSA World Congress and 20th NAFIPS International Conference: Vol. 4* (pp. 2464-2469).

Kalfoglou, Y., & Schorlemmer, M. (2003). Ontology mapping: The state of the art. *The Knowledge Engineering Review, 18*(1), 1-31.

Kampman, A., & Broekstra, J. (n.d.). Sesame. Retrieved from http://www.openrdf.org/

Lassila, O., & McGuinness, D. (2002). *The role of frame-based representation on the semantic Web, KSL-01-02* (Tech. Rep.). Stanford, CA: Knowledge Systems Laboratory, Stanford University.

Lausen, H., & Stolberg, M. (2004, April). *Semantic Web portals—State of the art survey* (Tech. Rep. 2004-04-03). DERI, Digital Enterprise Research Institute.

Lennat, D. (1995). CYC: A large-scale investment in knowledge infrastructure. *Communications of the ACM, 33*(8), 33-38.

Ma, Z. (2005). *Fuzzy database modeling with XML.* Springer.

Ma, Z. (2006). *Fuzzy database modeling of imprecise and uncertain engineering information.* Springer.

McCool, R. (2005). Rethinking the semantic Web, part I. *IEEE Internet Computing,* 86-88.

McCool, R. (2006). Rethinking the semantic Web, part II. *IEEE Internet Computing,* 93-96.

Medina, J. M., Pons, O., & Vila, M. A. (1994). GEFRED: A generalized model of fuzzy relational databases. *Information Sciences, 76*(1-2), 87-109.

Medina, J. M., Vila, M. A., Cubero, J. C., & Pons, O. (1995). Towards the implementation of a generalized fuzzy relational database model. *Fuzzy Sets and Systems, 75*, 273-289.

Mena, E., & Illarramendi, A. (2001). *Ontology-based query processing for global information systems*. Norwell, MA: Kluwer Academic Publishers.

Noy, N. F. (2004). Semantic integration: A survey of ontology-based approaches. *SIGMOD Record, 33*(4), 65-70.

Noy, N. F., & Hafner, C. D. (1997). The state of the art in ontology design. A survey and comparative review. *The American Association for Artificial Intelligence*, (18), 53-74.

Ontological Engineering Group (OEG) from the Artificial Intelligence Department of the Computer Science Faculty (FI) from the Technical University of Madrid (Spain). (n.d.). *WebOde Ontology Engineering Platform*. Retrieved from http://webode.dia.fi.upm.es/WebODEWeb/index.html

Network of Excellence INTEROP, (2004, November). Ontology-based integration of Enterprise Modelling and Architecture & Platforms, Deliverable D8.1, *State of the Art and State of Practice Including Initial Possible Research Orientations*, Version 1.2, p. 12. Retrieved from www.interop-noe.org

Open University (n.d.). *WebOnto*. Retrieved from http://webonto.open.ac.uk/

Oracle (n.d.). *ISQLplus Web environment*. Retrieved from http://150.214.108.124/isqlplus

Pardede, E., & Wenny Rahayu, J. (n.d.). Impact of new SQL standard to database modeling. Retrieved from http://homepage.cs.latrobe.edu.au/ekpardede/paper/ENCYCLOPEDIA05-1.pdf

P′erez de Laborda, C., & Conrad, S. (2005). Relational.OWL: A data and schema representation format based on OWL. *Proceedings of the 2nd Asia-Pacific Conference on Conceptual Modelling (CRPIT '43)* (pp. 89–96). Darlinghurst, Australia: Australian Computer Society, Inc.

Petry, F. E. (1996). *Fuzzy databases: Principles and applications*. Kluwer Academic Publishers.

Prade, H., & Testemale, C. (1984). Generalizing database relational algebra for the treatment of incomplete/uncertain information and vague queries. *Information Sciences* (34), 113-143.

Programme, H. L. S. W. (n.d.). *Jena: A semantic Web framework for Java*.

Raju, K. V. S. V. N., & Majumdar, A. K. (1988). Fuzzy functional dependencies and lossless join decomposition of fuzzy relational database systems. *ACM Transactions on Database Systems, 13*(2), 129-166.

Resource Description Framework (RDF) (1999). Retrieved from http://www.w3.org/RDF/

Roche, C. (2003). Ontology: A survey. *Proceedings of the 8th Symposium on Automated Systems Based on Human Skill and Knowledge (IFAC 2003), Goteborg, Sweden*.

Rodríguez, L. J. T. (2000). Extending RDBMS for allowing fuzzy quantified queries. *Proceedings of DEXA 2000, LNCS 1873* (pp. 407-416). Springer-Verlag.

Rundensteiner, E. A., Hawkes, L. W., & Bandler, W. (1989). On nearness measures in fuzzy relational data models. *International Journal Approximate Reasoning* (3), 267-298.

Shenoi, S., & Melton, A. (1989). Proximity relations in the fuzzy relational databases. *Fuzzy Sets and Systems, 31*(3), 285-296.

Sheth, A., Ramakrishnan, C., & Thomas, C. (2005). Semantics for the semantic Web: The implicit, the formal, and the powerful. *Journal on Semantic Web and Information Systems*, *1*(1), 1-18.

Staab, S., & Studer, R. (Ed.) (2004). *Handbook on ontologies*. Springer.

Stanford Medical Informatics at the Stanford University School of Medicine. (n.d.). *Protégé*. Retrieved from http://protege.stanford.edu/

Stanford University. (n.d.). *Ontolingua*. Retrieved from http://www.ksl.stanford.edu/software/ontolingua/

Steve, G., Gangemi, A., & Pisanelli, D. (1998). Ontology integration: Experiences with medical ontologies. In N. Guarino (Ed.) *Formal ontology in information systems*, (pp. 163-178). IOS Press.

Studer, R., Benjamins, V., & Fensel, D. (1998). Knowledge engineering: Principles and methods. *IEEE Transactions on Data and Knowledge Engineering*, *25*(1-2), 161-197.

Su, X., & Ilebrekke, L. (2002). A comparative study of ontology languages and tools. *Proceedings of CAiSE 2002* (pp. 761-765).

Trinh, Q., Barker, K., & Alhajj, R. (2006). RDB2ONT: A tool for generating OWL ontologies from relational database systems. *Proceedings of AICT/ICIW* (p. 170). IEEE Computer Society.

Umano, M., & Fukami, S. (1994). Fuzzy relational algebra for possibility-distribution-fuzzy-relational model of fuzzy data. *Journal of Intelligent Information Systems*, *3*, 7-28.

Unchold, M., & Gruninger, M. (2004). Ontologies and semantics for seamless connectivity. *SIGMOD Record*, *33*(4), 58-64.

Upadhyaya, S. R., & Kumar, P. S. (2005). ERONTO: A tool for extracting ontologies from extended E/R diagrams. *Proceedings of the 2005 ACM Symposium on Applied Computing (SAC '05)* (pp. 666–670). New York: ACM Press.

Yabloko, Len, & Next Generation Software. (n.d.). *OntoBase plug-in for Protégé*. Retrieved from http://www.ontospace.net/pages/3/index.htm

Zadeh, L. A. (1965). Fuzzy sets. *Information and Control*, *83*, 338-353.

KEY TERMS

Ontologies: An ontology is a data model that represents a domain and is used to reason about the objects in that domain and the relations between them.

Database schemas: Database schema is a description of the structure of a database or a directory (file systems); these can be: (a) conceptual schema, a map of concepts, and their relationships; (b) logical schema, a map of entities, and their attributes and relations; and (c) physical schema, a particular implementation of a logical schema.

SQL: SQL is the most popular computer language used to create, modify, retrieve, and manipulate data from relational database management systems.

Semantic Web: The Semantic Web is a project that intends to create a universal medium for information exchange by putting documents with computer-processable meaning (semantics) on the World Wide Web.

Data base catalog: The database catalog of a database instance consists of metadata in which definitions of database objects such as basis tables, view tables, synonyms, value ranges, indexes, users, and user groups are stored.

OWL: Language Markup language for publishing and sharing data using ontologies on the Internet. OWL is a vocabulary extension of the Resource description framework (RDF) and is derived from the DAML+OIL Web Ontology Language (see also DAML and OIL). Together with RDF and other components, these tools make up the Semantic Web project.

Data mapping is the process of creating data element mappings between two distinct data models. Data mapping is the first step in creating a data transformation between a data source and a destination.

Schema integration: It is a process that takes two schemas as input and produces a mapping between the elements that correspond to each other semantically.

Fuzzy database management system: It is a system or software designed to manage a relational database, and run operations on the data requested by numerous clients. This system is extended in order to include the management of fuzzy data on it.

Heterogeneous data integration tools provide translation and integration for data sources over schemas of different species.

Chapter XIX
A Web Metadata Based–Model for Information Quality Prediction

Ricardo Barros
COPPE—Federal University of Rio de Janeiro, Brazil

Geraldo Xexéo
COPPE—Federal University of Rio de Janeiro, Brazil

Wallace A. Pinheiro
COPPE—Federal University of Rio de Janeiro, Brazil

Jano de Souza
COPPE—Federal University of Rio de Janeiro, Brazil

ABSTRACT

Currently, in the Web environment, users have to deal with an enormous amount of information. In a Web search, they often receive useless, replicated, outdated, or false data, which, at first, they have no means to assess. Web search engines provide good examples of these problems: As reply from these mechanisms, users usually find links to replicated or conflicting information. Further, in these cases, information is spread out among heterogeneous and unrelated data sources, that normally present different information quality approaches. This chapter addresses those issues by proposing a Web Metadata-Based Model to evaluate and recommend Web pages based on their information quality, as predicted by their metadata. We adopt a fuzzy theory approach to obtain the values of quality dimensions from metadata values and to evaluate the quality of information, taking advantage of fuzzy logic's ability to capture humans' imprecise knowledge and deal with different concepts.

INTRODUCTION

Recently, the volume of information[1] available to the users has increased enormously. At the Web, it is possible to search for information on an unlimited number of contexts and categories across a wide range of information environments, such as databases, application systems, electronic library systems, corporate intranets and the Internet as well. This information presents different levels of quality, with original sources ranging from multi-national corporations to individuals with limited knowledge. With so much information available, quality has become an important discriminator when deciding which information to use and which to discard (Burgess, Gray, & Fiddian, 2004).

In this sense, the difficulties to identify, separate, and assess the quality of information have caused financial losses and compromised decision-making processes (Eckerson, 2002; English, 1999; Redman, 1998).

In spite of extensive discussion in literature, there is no consensus on an appropriate approach to improve the quality of information, as for the effectiveness of proposals and the expected benefits. However, there is a common sense that the effort to reach a good information quality standard must be high priority (Eckerson, 2002; Redman, 1998).

This chapter describes a model to explore the benefits of using Web metadata for information quality prediction. In our approach, we start from separated evaluations for each quality dimension and aggregate them regarding to several rules and context characteristics to obtain aggregated evaluations. We apply a fuzzy theory approach to obtain the values of quality dimensions from metadata values and to evaluate the quality of information, taking advantage of fuzzy logic's ability to capture humans' imprecise knowledge and deal with different concepts.

We also apply the fuzzy theory approach to identify user expectations about information quality (Xexéo, Belchior, & da Rocha, 1996; Yager, 1991; Zadeh, 1988).

We adopted an ontology represented by a UML[2] model to formalize, keep, and share the concepts and its instances used in all steps of the evaluation process[3] to predict information quality.

There is a real example to illustrate how it has been used, taking the metadata *update date, query time, update time, forward links, back-*

wards links, hubs, and authorities and applying them as basis to evaluate quality dimensions *timeliness, completeness,* and *reputation* in an *economy* context.

The remainder of this chapter is organized as follows. In the next section we present a background. Afterwards we demonstrate our proposal and show the architecture and some technical details as well. Finally, we delineate the expected results by an example, and we point out some future trends and conclude the chapter.

BACKGROUND

Brief Introduction to Fuzzy Logic

Fuzzy logic is also another extension realized in Boolean logic that may be considered a generalization of multi-valued logic. By modeling the uncertainties of natural language through concepts of partial truth – truth-values falling somewhere between completely true and completely false (Kantrowitz, Horstkotte, & Joslyn, 1997) – fuzzy logic deals with such values through fuzzy sets in the interval [0,1]. These characteristics allow fuzzy logic to manipulate real-world objects that possess imprecise limits. Utilizing fuzzy predicates (old, new, high, etc.), fuzzy quantifiers (many, few, almost all, etc.), fuzzy truth-values (completely true, more or less true) (Dubois & Prade, 1991) and generalizing the meaning of connectors and logical operators, fuzzy logic is seen as a means of approximate reasoning (Grauel, 1999).

It was introduced by Dr. Lotfi Zadeh of UC/ Berkeley in the 1960's as a way to model the uncertainty of natural language. Zadeh (1965) says that rather than regarding fuzzy theory as a single theory, we should regard the process of "fuzzification" as a methodology to generalize any specific theory from a crisp (discrete) to a continuous (fuzzy) form. Thus, recently researchers have also introduced "fuzzy calculus", "fuzzy differential equations", "fuzzy systems", "fuzzy logic with engineering applications", and so on (Cox, 1994; Kantrowitz et al., 1997; Klir & Yuan, 1995).

Just as there is a strong relationship between Boolean logic and the concept of a subset, there is a similar strong relationship between fuzzy logic and fuzzy set theory.

In classical set theory, a subset A of a set X can be defined as a mapping from the elements of A to the elements of the set $\{0,1\}$, $A:X \rightarrow \{0,1\}$.

This mapping may be represented as a set of ordered pairs, with exactly one ordered pair present for each element of X. The first element of the ordered pair is an element of the set X, and the second element is an element of the set $\{0,1\}$. The value "zero" is used to represent non-membership, and the value "one" is used to represent membership. The truth or falsity of the statement x is in A is determined by finding the ordered pair whose first element is x. The statement is true if the second element of the ordered pair is 1, and the statement is false if it is 0.

Similarly, a fuzzy subset A of a set X can be defined as a set of ordered pairs, each with the first element from X, and the second element from the interval $[0,1]$, with exactly one ordered pair present for each element of X. This defines a mapping between elements of the set X and values in the interval $[0,1]$. In extreme cases, the degree of membership is 0, in which case the element is not a member of the set, or the degree of membership is 1, if the element is a 100% member of the set. The set X is referred to as the universe of discourse for the fuzzy subset A.

The membership of an element within a certain set becomes a question of degree, substituting the actual dichotomist process imposed by *crisp* sets, when this treatment is not suitable (Turksen, 1991; Zimmermann, 1991).

Frequently, the mapping is described as a function, the membership function of A. The degree to which the statement x is in A is true is determined by finding the ordered pair whose first element is x. The degree of truth of the statement is the second element of the ordered pair. In practice, the terms "membership function" and "fuzzy set" get used interchangeably.

Summarizing, a fuzzy set is characterized by a membership function, which maps the elements of a domain, space, or discourse universe, X for a real number in $[0, 1]$. Formally, $\tilde{A}:X \rightarrow [0,1]$. Thus, a fuzzy set is presented as a set of ordered pairs in which the first element is $x \in X$, and the second, $\mu_{\tilde{A}}(x)$, is the degree of membership or the membership function of x into $\tilde{A}$, which maps x in the interval $[0,1]$, or, $\tilde{A} = \{(x, \mu_{\tilde{A}}(x))| \ x \in X\}$ (Klir & Yuan, 1995; Zadeh, 1965).

Therefore, here is an example. Let us talk about people and "age". In this case, the set $X = \{5, 10, 20, 30\ 40, 50, 60, 70, 80\}$ (the universe of discourse) is the set of "ages".

Let us define fuzzy subsets "child", "young", "adult", and "old", which will answer the question "to what membership degree is person x "child", "young", "adult", and "old"?" Zadeh (1965) describes "age" as a linguistic variable, which represents our cognitive category "age group". To each person in the universe of discourse, we have to assign a degree of membership in the fuzzy subsets. The easiest way to do this is with a membership function based on the person's age. The fuzzy set $\tilde{A}$, "young", could be described as:

$$\tilde{A} = \{(5,1)(10,1)(20,\ 0.8)(30,0.5)(40.02)(50,0.1)(60,0)(70,0)(80.0)\}$$

Then, a fuzzy set emerges from the "enlargement" of a *crisp* set that begins to incorporate aspects of uncertainty. This process is called fuzzification.

Nevertheless, the literature already contains families of parameterized membership functions such as triangular, exponential, Gauss functions, and so forth. Each one of these functions is characterized by a fuzzy number that is a convex and normalized fuzzy set defined in the set of the real numbers R, such that its membership function has the form $[250,750]$: $\mu_{\tilde{A}} : R \rightarrow [0,1]$ (Klir & Yuan, 1995; Zimmermann, 1991).

Defuzzification is the inverse process, that is, it is the conversion of a fuzzy set into a *crisp* value (or a vector of values) (Zimmermann, 1991). Theoretically, any function in the form of $\tilde{A} : X \to [0,1]$ can be associated with a fuzzy set, depending on the concepts and properties that need to be represented, along with the context in which the set is inserted.

There are many defuzzification methods (at least 30), such as centroid (centroid of area), bisector (bisector of area), MOM (mean value of maximum), SOM (smallest absolute value of maximum), LOM (largest absolute value of maximum), and others. The more common techniques are the centroid and maximum methods. In the centroid method, the crisp value of the output variable is computed by finding the variable value of the center of gravity of the membership function for the fuzzy value. In the maximum method, one of the variable values at which the fuzzy subset has its maximum truth value is chosen as the crisp value

for the output variable (Cox, 1994; Kantrowitz et al., 1997; Klir & Yuan, 1995).

The main concepts of our proposal and how these concepts have been extended by fuzzy set and fuzzy logic theory will be shown later.

Quality and Information Quality

In spite of the existence of different efforts to create a definition of quality, "no single definition or standard of quality exists" (Smart, 2002, p. 130).

Previous initiatives, exemplified in Table 1, tried to define, organize, and prioritize the required information, improving its quality to the end user.

Quality and information quality has attracted the interest of many researchers in a great number of disciplines, including computer science, library science, information science, and management of information systems. Certainly, a strong commer-

Table 1. Examples of quality evaluation approaches

Initiatives	Approaches
(Strong, Wang, & Guarascio, 1994)	Presents a framework that captures the aspects of data quality that are important to Data Consumers
(Wand & Wang, 1996)	Suggests rigorous definition of data quality dimensions by anchoring them in ontological foundations, and shows how such dimensions can provide guidance to systems designers on data quality issues
(Redman, 1998)	Categorizes every question related to low data quality impact on the three levels of the organizations: operational, tactical, and strategic
(English, 1999)	Proposes a method for reducing costs and increasing profits, improving the Data Warehouse and business information quality
(Twidale & Marty, 1999)	Outlines a new collaborative approach to data quality management
(Lee, 2004)	Finds that experienced practitioners solve data quality problems by reflecting on and explicating knowledge about contexts embedded in, or missing from, data
(Loshin, 2001)	Analyzes data quality under knowledge management point of view; it defines data quality as "adequacy for the use" and stands out that quality evaluation is dependent of the user' context.
(Pipino, Lee, & Wang, 2002)	Describes the subjective and objective assessments of data quality, and presents three functional forms for developing objective data quality metrics
(Burgess et al., 2004)	Proposes a hierarchical generic model of quality that can be used by the information consumer to assist in information searching, by focusing the returned result set based on personal quality preferences
(Peralta, Ruggia, Kedad, & Mokrane, 2004)	Addresses the problem, in the context of data integration systems, using cost graphic models, which enable the definition of evaluation methods and demonstration of propositions in terms of graph properties
(Kim, Kishore, & Sanders, 2005)	Applies the concepts of data quality in the context of e-business systems

cial interest in this last area exists, with emphasis in the costs and the impact for the organizations in consequence of low data quality. These impacts can influence directly some competitive differential paradigms in most enterprises (Redman, 1998).

Metadata

The most common definition of *metadata* is the literal translation: "Metadata is data about data", and *Web metadata* "is machine-understandable description of things on (and about) the Web"[4].

In some approaches presented previously, different metadata can be associated with data, including metadata to improve or restrict quality, according to some set of dimensions. Rothenberg (1996) outlines a range of metadata fields that can be used in this way. These metadata must be provided by a database to support data quality evaluation and improve the effective longevity of digital data, by ensuring their future accessibility and readability. We only focus on a subpart of his wider analysis, which references the data-value level metadata, such as source information (source, derivation, time of generation/entry, etc.).

These initiatives, however, did not explore the benefits of using Web metadata. In this case, there are some several alternatives to be considered to capture metadata. For example, search engine APIs[5], third-party services, using protocols like W3C PICS (Platform for Internet Content Selection)[6] and also the metadata provided by the original data source, such as the proposed Dublin Core[7]. Table 2 illustrates metadata captured by each one of these sources.

In our approach, we developed a crawler to retrieve Web Documents and adopt the JUNG - Java Universal Network/Graph Framework[8] to obtain derived metadata, such as *hubs* and *authorities* (Kleinberg, 1998).

Kleinberg (1998) states that the Internet is annotated with "precisely the type of human judgment we need to identify authority" (p. 670). Based on this, he developed a set of algorithms, called *HITS (hyperlink induced topic search)*, for extracting information from the hyperlink structures of those environments. He states that the annotation on the Internet "almost says something about the way the Web has evolved". He thinks "it's about the way people link information in general, not just on the Web." (pp. 670-671)

Table 2. Sources to capture metadata

Google	PICS	Meta-Tags of Dublin Core
Query parameters	**Attributes of Service**	
Key: **q**: query terms, start, maxresults, filter, restricts, safesearch, **lr**: language restrict, **ie**: input encoding, **oe**: output encoding	category, default, description, extension, icon, name, PICS-version, rating-service, and rating-system	
Query special Operators	Attributes of Categories	
Special Query Capability, Include Query Term, Exclude Query Term, Phrase Search, Boolean OR Search, Site Restricted Search, Date Restricted Search Title Search (term), Title Search (all), URL Search (term), URL Search (all) Text Only Search (all), Links Only, Search (all), File Type Filtering, File Type Exclusion, Web Document Info, Back Links, Related Links, Cached Results Page		Title, Creator, Subject, Description, Publisher, Contributor, Date, Type, Format, Identifier, Source, Language, Relation, Coverage, Rights, and so forth
Returned Results	description, extension, icon, integer, label, label-only, max, min, multivalue, name, transmit-as, and unordered	
<summary>, <URL>, <snippet>, <title> , <cachedSize>, <directoryTitle>, <hostName>, <relatedInformationPresent>, <directoryCategory>		
Categories of Directories		
<fullViewableName>, <specialEncoding>		

The goal of *HITS* is to rank pages on the Web, through the discovery of related authoritative information sources. *HITS* introduces two concepts: *Authorities* and *Hubs*. *Authorities* are sites that other Web pages link to frequently on a particular topic. *Hubs* are sites that cite many of these *authorities*. Kleinberg (1998) observes that there is a certain natural type of equilibrium between *hubs* and *authorities* in the graph defined by the network structure of a hyperlinked environment, and he exploits this to develop a set of algorithms that identifies both types of pages simultaneously. Kleinberg's method says that the best *authorities* will be those that point to the best *hubs*, and the best *hubs* will be the ones that point to the best *authorities*. This calculation is repeated several times. Each time the program increases the *authority* weight to sites that link to sites with more *hub* weight, and it increases *hub* weight to sites that link to sites with more *authority* weight. He says that ten repetitions are enough to return surprisingly focused lists of *authorities* and *hubs*. In practice, convergence is achieved after only 10-20 iterations. *HITS* operates on *focused sub graphs* of the Web that are constructed from the output of a text-based Web search engine, like Google, Alta Vista, and so forth. From there on, text is ignored, and the application only looks at the way that pages in the expanded set are linked to one another.

Quality Dimensions

Despite the habitual use of some terms to indicate data quality, there is not a rigorously-defined or standardized set of data quality dimensions. Table 3 shows a subset of data quality dimensions able to represent users' quality expectations defined by Pipino et al. (2002).

To carry out information quality evaluation, we need initially to identify the set of quality dimensions. The most appropriate set depends on the user application, the selection of metrics, and the implementation of the evaluation algorithms that measure or estimate such quality dimension (Peralta et al., 2004). Wand and Wang (1996) states that the choice of these dimensions is primarily based on intuitive understanding, industrial experience, or literature review.

Table 3. Data Quality Dimensions (Pipino et al., 2002)

Dimensions	Definitions (The extent to which...)
Accessibility	data is available, or easily and quickly retrievable
Appropriate Amount of Data	the volume of data is appropriate for the task at hand
Believability	data is regarded as true and credible
Completeness	data is not missing and is of sufficient breadth and depth for the task at hand
Concise Representation	data is compactly represented
Consistent Representation	data is presented in the same format
Easy of Manipulation	data is easy to manipulate and apply to different tasks
Free-of-Error	data is correct and reliable
Interpretability	data is in appropriate languages, symbols, and units, and the definitions are clear
Objectivity	data is unbiased, unprejudiced, and impartial
Relevancy	data is applicable and helpful for the task at hand
Reputation	data is highly regarded in terms of its source or content
Security	access to data is restricted appropriately to maintain its security
Timeliness	data is sufficiently up to date for the task at hand
Understandability	data is easily comprehended
Value-Added	data is beneficial and provides advantages from its use

Tillman (2003) emphasizes that we need to have in mind the current state of the Internet, to adopt generic criteria for information quality prediction. This understanding is very important to determine the best set of quality dimensions, due to constant changes in the Web.

There is an example provided later to illustrate our approach, where we work with *Completeness*, *Reputation* and *Timeliness*.

Context

Dey (2001) states that "context is any information that can be used to characterize the situation of an entity. An entity is a person, place, or object that is considered relevant to the interaction between a user and an application, including the user and applications themselves". "This definition makes it easier for an application developer to enumerate the context for a given application scenario. If a piece of information can be used to characterize the situation of a participant in an interaction, then that information is context" (pp. 3-4).

The context specifies a scope or a boundary for a knowledge domain. In practice, contexts have been implicit in information quality management, yet they have been a critical part of resolving information quality problems (Dey, 2001; Lee, 2004; Pinheiro & Moura, 2004). Google[9] and similar Web sites have organized hierarchical structures by topics into categories, such as *Math*, *Economics*, *Social Sciences*, and *Technology*.

Pipino et al. (2002) classifies the objective assessments into task-independent or task-dependent metrics. Task-independent metrics reflect states of the data without the contextual knowledge of the application, and can be applied to any data set, regardless of the tasks at hand. In contrast, task-dependent metrics are developed in specific application contexts, which include the organization's business rules, company and government regulations, and constraints provided by the database administrator. We present an approach that combines the subjective and objective assessments of data quality, and illustrates how it has been used in practice.

Moreover, we focus the task-dependent metrics classification, considering that our approach proposal involves semantic contextualization.

A WEB METADATA-BASED MODEL FOR INFORMATION QUALITY PREDICTION

Figure 1 shows an UML diagram that would be seen as a taxonomy to define terms and relationships among these terms and, additionally, a set of transformation and membership functions, responsible for keeping some real semantic

Figure 1. Web metadata-based model for information quality prediction ontology

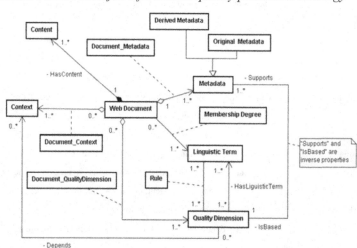

constraints. Hence, according to this ontology, searched Web documents are evaluated, taking into account their metadata and the semantic contextualization.

Web Document Class

This class defines the set of retrieved Web documents to be evaluated.

Definition 1: The Web Document is a set:

$$WebDoc = \{webdoc_1, webdoc_2, ... webdoc_n\}$$

Where each $webdoc_i$, $1 \leq i \leq n$, is an instance of document.

Metadata Class

This class defines the set of Web metadata used as a base for the information quality evaluation. Original metadata are retrieved "as-is" with the information, while derived metadata are obtained by transformation functions.

Definition 2: A metadata of a document (*Document_Metadata Association Class*) is some information about the document and the document data, that is, its contents. The Metadata Class represents a set:

$$M = \{m_1, m_2, ...m_n\}$$

Where each m_i, $1 \leq i \leq n$, is an instance of the identified metadata.

Definition 3: An original metadata is a metadata that can be directly retrieved from a document or from a third-party engine using a document as a key. The Original Metadata Class represents a set:

$$OM = \{om_1, om_2, ...om_n\}$$

Where each om_i, $1 \leq i \leq n$, is an instance of the original metadata. A simple example of original metadata is its *query date*.

Definition 4: A derived metadata is metadata that cannot be directly retrieved from a document or a third-party engine, but rather must be derived from metadata through some computable function. We use *m* to represent metadata, *om* to represent original metadata and *dm* to represent derived metadata, indexed when necessary. To represent a function that calculates the value of a specific derived metadata dm_i we use the notation fd_i. The derived metadata class represents a set:

$$DM = \{dm_1, dm_2, ...dm_n\}$$

Table 4. Original and the derived metadata

Original Metadata	Functions to obtain Derived Metadata (*fd*)
ud_i—update date of a Web document i	**(1)** *(UT) Update Time* $= ut_i = tq_i - ud_i$
qt_i—query date of a Web document i	**(2)** *Authority* $= a_i = \Sigma h_j$, where: $j \in BL_i$
BL_i—number of links which points to the Web document i on a context	**(3)** *Hub* $= h_i = \Sigma a_j$, where: $j \in E_i$
FL_i—number of links going out of the Web document i on a context	The calculation of *Authorities* and *hubs* considers a set S of documents on a context. It is an iterative process where all of the weights initialize on 1. Afterwards, *hub* and *authority* weights are calculated, and the results are normalized. This process is repeated until the convergence of values a and h of all documents. We adopt JUNG to obtain the values of *hubs* and *authorities*.

Where each dm_i, $1 \leq i \leq n$, is an instance of the derived metadata. A simple example of derived metadata is its *update time*.

We also define: $M = OM \cup OM$ and $OM \cap DM = \phi$

Table 4 gives four examples of original metadata and three examples of derived metadata. The first example, *Update Time*, derives from the original metadata: *Update Date* and *Query Date*. The second and third ones adopt the concepts of *Authorities* and *Hubs* (Kleinberg, 1998) as denoted later.

Quality Dimension and Linguistic Term Classes

The quality dimensions class defines the set of quality dimensions. It represents the adopted information quality evaluation criteria and factors. The operation of *fuzzification* to transform the derived metadata to quality dimensions instances is a membership function of fuzzy sets. The Linguistic Term Class defines a set of adjectives or adverbs related to the linguistic variables.

Definition 5: A quality dimension is defined as some user perspective about document quality. The Quality Dimension Class represents a set:

$$QD = \{qd_1, qd_2, ...qd_n\}$$

Where each qd_i, $1 \leq i \leq n$, is an instance of the quality dimension. A simple example of quality dimension is *completeness*.

At this point, we should clarify one important point of the model. While metadata describe documents and are created with the possible information that one can, directly or indirectly, obtain about a document or its contents, quality dimensions describe the user perspective about the expected quality of a document (*Document_QualityDimensions Association Class*),

regardless of the possibility to calculate it. In this model, we presume that it is possible to make a direct relationship between one quality dimension and another specific metadata. Therefore, the relationships "*Supports*" and "*IsBased*" indicate that a quality dimension can be represented, with some degree of uncertainty, from a metadata value. This relationship represents this association as an inverse property.

Definition 6: A quality dimension qd_i, is represented as a linguistic variable (*HasLinguisticTerm relationship*) that can assume, possibly simultaneously, the values of its applicable fuzzy linguistic term (*Linguistic Term Class*): lt_{ij}.

Where j is a specific linguistic term and i is a specific variable linguistic.

When evaluating a document according to a quality dimension, the model provides a linguist interpretation of the respective metadata value for that document (*Membership Degree Association Class*). This is illustrated by the three following examples:

- Let R be the referential set for all possible values for the quality dimension *reputation*. *Reputation* assumes the corresponding metadata *authority* as the base data for the linguistic variable. For a given document, based on the *authority* to the document i on a context (its *reputation*), the model should provide its membership value for all sets defined by the linguistic variables.
- Let C be the referential set for all possible values for the quality dimension *completeness*. *Completeness* assumes the corresponding metadata *hub* as the base data for the linguistic variable. For a given document, based on the *hub* to the document i on a context (its *completeness*), the model should provide its membership value for all defined sets defined by the linguistic variables.

332

- Let T be the referential set for all possible values for the quality dimension *timeliness*. *Timeliness* assumes the corresponding metadata *update time* as the base data for the linguistic variable. For a given document, based on how many hours ago the document was updated (its *update time*), the model should provide its membership value for all sets defined by the linguistic variables.

The number of linguistic terms for subjective evaluation can be established in accordance with the project convenience, possible application domain peculiarities, or determination of the managing team of quality. We know that at least five or seven linguistic terms are more indicated to obtain a better classification. For the sake of simplification, here we only define three linguistic terms to describe *timeliness, reputation,* and *completeness* as linguistic variables. The linguistic terms are classified as: *bad, regular,* and *good,* involving every possibility of fuzzy subsets of T, denoted by $\widetilde{N}(T)$.

To exemplify the definitions above, Figure 2 illustrates the linguistic variable *timeliness* and its possible values, the linguistic terms *Bad, Regular,* and *Good* denoted as $\widetilde{B}$, $\widetilde{R}$, and $\widetilde{G}$:

$$\widetilde{B} = \{(tu_i, \mu_{\widetilde{B}}(tu_i)) | tu_i \in TU\};$$

$$\widetilde{R} = \{(tu_i, \mu_{\widetilde{R}}(tu_i)) | tu_i \in TU\};$$

$$\widetilde{G} = \{(tu_i, \mu_{\widetilde{G}}(tu_i)) | tu_i \in TU\};$$

Where $\mu_{\widetilde{B}}(tu_i):TU \rightarrow [0,1]$, $\mu_{\widetilde{R}}(tu_i):TU \rightarrow [0,1]$, $\mu_{\widetilde{G}}(tu_i) \rightarrow [0,1]$ represent fuzzy membership functions that map the element ut_i (*update time* of a Web document) into $\widetilde{B}$, $\widetilde{R}$, and $\widetilde{G}$, respectively.

Content Class

This class defines the set of values representing data, metadata, and context of a Web document (*HasContent relationship*). This is defined as the intrinsic aspects of data representation. For example, all stored data, metadata attributes, context, user categories, and their values, for which the results are interesting to some user.

Definition 7: The Content Class represents a set:

$$T = \{Content_1, Content_2, ...Content_n\}$$

Figure 2. Linguistic variable "Timeliness" (Adapted from: Klir & Yuan, 1995)

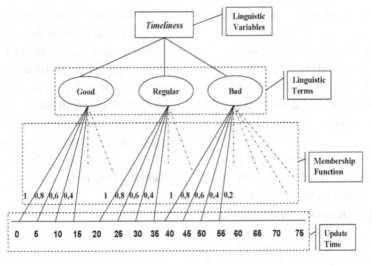

Table 5. Fuzzy rule base to economy context

Input Variables *(SIQP)*		Timeliness		
Completeness	**Reputation**	Bad	Regular	Good
Bad	Bad	*Bad*	*Bad*	*Regular*
Bad	Regular	*Bad*	*Regular*	*Regular*
Bad	Good	*Regular*	*Regular*	*Regular*
Regular	Bad	*Bad*	*Regular*	*Regular*
Regular	Regular	*Regular*	*Regular*	*Regular*
Regular	Good	*Regular*	*Regular*	*Good*
Good	Bad	*Regular*	*Regular*	*Regular*
Good	Regular	*Regular*	*Regular*	*Good*
Good	Good	*Regular*	*Good*	*Good*
		Output Variables (GIQP)		

Where each *Content$_i$*, $1 \leq i \leq n$, is a content instance.

Context Class

This class defines the set of contexts. They are retrieved together with the information, as with the metadata (*Document_Context Association Class*).

Definition 8: The Context Class represents a set:

$$C = \{c_1, c_2, ...c_n\}$$

Where each c_i, $1 \leq i \leq n$, is the instance of the context. A simple example of context is *economy*.

So far, we have obtained the evaluation results, separately, by content and by each considered linguistic terms defined by each linguist variable (quality dimension). In this work, we name these evaluations as *SIQP – Single Information Quality Prediction*.

For example, there are three *SIQP* ($\mu_{\tilde{B}}(tu_i)$, $\mu_{\tilde{R}}(tu_i)$ and $\mu_{\tilde{G}}(tu_i)$) to each Web document, that take into account the linguistic terms *Bad, Regular,* and *Good* and the linguistic variable *Timeliness*.

From these *SIQP*, we obtain the *GIQP—Global Information Quality Prediction*—by application of rules (*Rule Association Class*). There is a semantic contextualization regarding the rules definition (*Depends relationship*).

Table 5 exemplifies a set of rules to the context *economy*. It provides 27 different rules, the fuzzy propositions, that express relationships between linguistic variables and fuzzy sets. In this table the input variables *(SIQP)*: *Completeness, Reputation,* and *Timeliness* implicate an output variable *GIQP*. Among these several fuzzy propositions, we can cite, as an example: "if the input variables *Completeness* is *Regular* and *Reputation* is *Good* and *Timeliness* is *Good* then the output variable *GIQP* is *Good*".

In this work, the membership functions related to the linguistic variables (input variables) of each page are analyzed by **fuzzy inference implication**. The resultant membership functions (output variables) of each page are analyzed by the **fuzzy inference aggregation**.

During the inference procedure some mappings are executed that establish an input/output behavior (Cox, 1994; Góis & Tania, 2005). These mappings are based on:

- **Implication:** combination of input fuzzy sets that activate a specific rule. Normally, the implication by minimum has been used. In other words, the output set has a membership degree equal to the minimum membership degree, among the membership degrees from input sets. For example, if $\mu_{\bar{B}}(h_i) = 0,3$ and $\mu_{\bar{R}}(a_i) = 0,5$ and $\mu_{\bar{G}}(tu_i) = 0,7$ then $\mu_{\bar{R}}(giqp_i) = 0,3$; and
- **Aggregation:** combination of output fuzzy sets generated from activated rules. Normally, the aggregation by maximum has been used. In other words, the maximum membership degree is selected among membership degrees from each output set separately. For example, if $\mu_{\bar{B}}(giqp_i) = 0,2$ and $\mu_{\bar{R}}(giqp_i) = 0,4$ and $\mu_{\bar{G}}(giqp_i) = 0,3$ then $\mu_{\bar{R}}(giqp_i) = 0,4$.

The next definition describes the *defuzzification*. This is very important in our approach, in order to rank the Web documents set by information quality evaluation.

Definition 9: The *defuzzification* process is a function that associates to each fuzzy set an ele-

ment of crisp set. There are many ways to execute the *defuzzification*, such as: centroid (centroid of area), bisector (bisector of area), MOM (mean value of maximum), SOM (smallest absolute value of maximum), and LOM (largest absolute value of maximum) (Cox, 1994). This is executed after the **fuzzy inference aggregation**.

SYSTEM ARCHITECTURE AND TECHNICAL DETAILS

Figure 3 shows the system architecture. Its components are described as follows:

- **Information Quality Prediction Layer:** This layer is responsible to control and mediate the processing and flow of information among the other components;
- **Crawler:** This component was developed in Java to retrieve the Web document and the original metadata in a breadth-first strategy (Baeza-Yates, Castillo, & Marin, & Rodriguez, 2005). It also generates the graphs (vertices and arcs) from Web documents to *JUNG* component, in the *Pajek* format[10];

Figure 3. Web metadata-based model for information quality prediction architecture

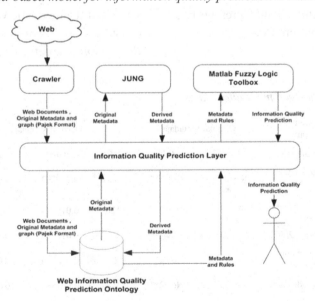

- **JUNG:** This is a software library that provides a common and extendible language for modeling, analysis, and visualization of data that can be represented as a graph or network. We adopt *JUNG* to calculate the *hubs* and *authorities* of the Web Documents using *Pajek* format. It is written in Java, which allows JUNG-based applications to make use of the extensive built-in capabilities of the Java API, as well as those of other existing third-party Java libraries[11];

- **Matlab Fuzzy Logic Toolbox:** This is a collection of functions built on the *MATLAB* numeric computing environment[12]. It provides tools to create and edit fuzzy inference systems within the framework of *MATLAB*; and

- **Web Information Quality Prediction Ontology:** This ontology was already described previously.

EXPECTED RESULTS

To illustrate our approach, we elaborate a real example using *Timeliness*, *Reputation,* and *Completeness* as specific quality dimensions. We consider one specific scenario to *economy* context. This process has three steps. Table 6 presents five obtained results from our crawler.

The first step defines the metadata sets *OM* e *DM* according to Table 6:

$$OMi = \{ud_i, qt_i\}$$

$$DM_i = fd(OM_i) = \{ut_i, a_i, h_i\}$$

The second step defines the fuzzy membership sets for *timeliness, reputation,* and *completeness*, respectively. Figures 4a and 4b show the mapping of membership functions for the fuzzy set *bad, regular,* and *good*. The triangular numbers, which compose each set, have the same base width. The triangular number related to the regular set is in the middle of the metadata numeric interval.

Based on Figures 4a and 4b, it is possible to accomplish the *fuzzification* mapping from the metadata values presented in Table 6, and to obtain the membership degrees of the linguistic variables (quality dimensions) to each fuzzy set (*Bad, Regular,* and *Good*). The results of this operation are shown in Table 7.

The third step defines the *defuzzification* process. The LOM (largest absolute value of maximum) was used to obtain the final value shown by Table 8.

In the *Economy* context, it is possible to observe that the linguistic variable *Timeliness* was considered as important as *Completeness* and *Reputation*. The defined set of rules is responsible

Table 6. Original and derived metadata values

Query Context: economy	Original Metadata		Derived Metadata		
Web Sites	**UD**	**QT**	**UT**	**Authority**	**Hub**
Economist. com Surveys[13]	Nov 25th	Nov 28th	72	0.019793	0.026939
Economist Conferences[14]	Nov 23rd	Nov 28th	120	0.018074	0.022909
The World In 2007[15]	Nov 21st	Nov 28th	168	0.017019	0.017008
Economist.com Opinion[16]	Nov 28th	Nov 28th	12	0.012019	0.053238
Scottrade[17]	Nov 22nd	Nov 28th	144	0.007503	0.007331

Figure 4a. Graph of fuzzy membership functions to reputation and completeness

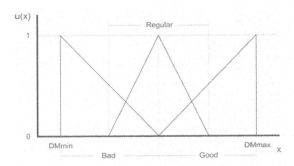

Figure 4b. Graph of fuzzy membership functions to timelines

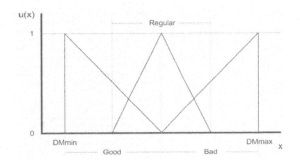

Table 7. Fuzzification results

Query Context: economy	Fuzzification Results		
Web Sites	*Timeliness*	*Reputation*	*Completeness*
Economist.com Surveys	$\mu_{\tilde{B}}(tu_l)=0.25$ $\mu_{\tilde{R}}(tu_l)=0.55$ $\mu_{\tilde{G}}(tu_l)=0$	$\mu_{\tilde{B}}(a_l)=0$ $\mu_{\tilde{R}}(a_l)=0$ $\mu_{\tilde{G}}(a_l)=1$	$\mu_{\tilde{B}}(h_l)=0.167110$ $\mu_{\tilde{R}}(h_l)=0.7157852$ $\mu_{\tilde{G}}(h_l)=0$
Economist Conferences	$\mu_{\tilde{B}}(tu_l)=0$ $\mu_{\tilde{R}}(tu_l)=0.25$ $\mu_{\tilde{G}}(tu_l)=0.4$	$\mu_{\tilde{B}}(a_l)=0$ $\mu_{\tilde{R}}(a_l)=0$ $\mu_{\tilde{G}}(a_l)=0.727254$	$\mu_{\tilde{B}}(h_l)=0.33829$ $\mu_{\tilde{R}}(h_l)=0.3734191$ $\mu_{\tilde{G}}(h_l)=0$
The World In 2007	$\mu_{\tilde{B}}(tu_l)=0$ $\mu_{\tilde{R}}(tu_l)=0$ $\mu_{\tilde{G}}(tu_l)=1$	$\mu_{\tilde{B}}(a_l)=0$ $\mu_{\tilde{R}}(a_l)=0$ $\mu_{\tilde{G}}(a_l)=0.559862$	$\mu_{\tilde{B}}(h_l)=0.58895$ $\mu_{\tilde{R}}(h_l)=0$ $\mu_{\tilde{G}}(h_l)=0$
Economist.com Opinion	$\mu_{\tilde{B}}(tu_l)=1$ $\mu_{\tilde{R}}(tu_l)=0$ $\mu_{\tilde{G}}(tu_l)=0$	$\mu_{\tilde{B}}(a_l)=0.283470$ $\mu_{\tilde{R}}(a_l)=0.4830675$ $\mu_{\tilde{G}}(a_l)=0$	$\mu_{\tilde{B}}(h_l)=0$ $\mu_{\tilde{R}}(h_l)=0$ $\mu_{\tilde{G}}(h_l)=1$
Scottrade	$\mu_{\tilde{B}}(tu_l)=0$ $\mu_{\tilde{R}}(tu_l)=0$ $\mu_{\tilde{G}}(tu_l)=0.7$	$\mu_{\tilde{B}}(a_l)=1$ $\mu_{\tilde{R}}(a_l)=0$ $\mu_{\tilde{G}}(a_l)=0$	$\mu_{\tilde{B}}(h_l)=1$ $\mu_{\tilde{R}}(h_l)=0$ $\mu_{\tilde{G}}(h_l)=0$

Table 8. Results to GIQP

Query Context: Economy	Derived Metadata			GIQP
Web Sites	UT	Authority	Hub	*Defuzzification* by LOM
Economist.com Surveys	72	0.019793	0.026939	0.61
Economist Conferences	120	0.018074	0.022909	0.66
The World In 2007	168	0.017019	0.017008	0.61
Economist.com Opinion	12	0.012019	0.053238	1
Scottrade	144	0.007503	0.007331	0.16

Figure 5. Fuzzification and defuzzification process

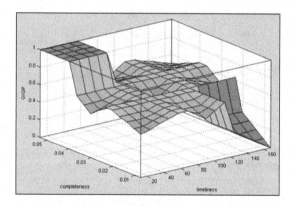

Figure 6a. GIQP from completeness and timelines

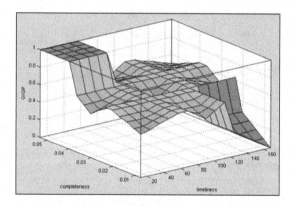

Figure 6b. GIQP from reputation and timelines

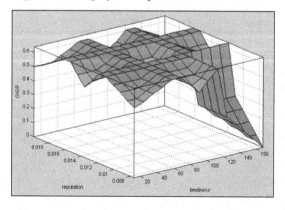

Figure 6c. GIQP from reputation and completeness

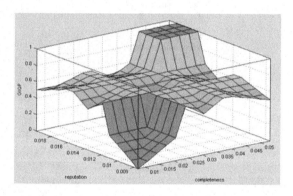

by this occurrence. If we consider the values of *Authority* and *Hubs* separately, it provides a different raking of the Web document.

Figure 5 shows the process of *fuzzification* and *defuzzification* to the Web document "http://www.economist.com/surveys/". The values of metadata are presented at the top as well the value of *GIQP* obtained by *defuzzification*. This identified the 27 rules previously defined, and the activated rules are highlighted. Moreover, the *GIQP* resultant sets obtained from the implication procedure are shown. To obtain the value of *GIQP*, these sets are aggregated by maximum values, then the resultant sets go through to the *defuzzification* process.

Figures 6a, 6b, and 6c show the surfaces obtained from the rules to *Timeliness, Reputation, Completeness,* and *GIQP.* Each Figure shows the association between two linguistic variables. The final result corresponds to the *GIQP.* From these Figures, it is possible to analyze the contribution of each linguistic variable to the *GIQP* and, if necessary, the rules can be adjusted considering the context (*Economy*).

FUTURE TRENDS

As we have seen previously, with the continuous growth of the available information volume in the Web, users can have difficulties in finding relevant information, although the information retrieval area has been carrying out a fundamental role in this direction, providing techniques that make possible more efficient searches (Baeza-Yates et al., 1999).

This fact occurs due to the volume of data to be processed, the heterogeneity and distribution of the information sources, the lack of a metadata standard to describe the data semantics in the Web pages, and the difficulty of the users to express their information needs through a search that adopts key words (Lawrence, 2000; Mizzaro, 1997; Moura, 2003).

The possibility to evaluate and recommend Web documents based on their quality criteria leads to new opportunities and more efficient strategies for deciding which information to use and which to discard, in view of so much information available (Burgess et al., 2004).

Recommender-systems are one of the proposals to deal with this problem. These systems are personalized services developed to help people with the diversity and the information overload, since the systems make it possible for people to share their opinions and experiences. The main approach of this solution is to find interesting items for users, rather than to eliminate irrelevant items.

Another aspect to be considered is the fact that the search systems do not store information on the user, nor on the context in which the search is requested (Lawrence, 2000). In this sense, the information filtering area deals with the information overload problem, considering the use of filters to eliminate irrelevant information (Belkin & Croft, 1992). Filtering generally uses user profiles to represent the user information needs, and uses intelligent agents to handle tasks for eliminating items of the information flow (Maes, 1994).

Our investigation addresses those issues by proposing a Web Metadata-Based Model.

The current version of the implemented prototype already adopts the fuzzy theory approach to obtain the graphs and the fuzzy membership sets (Cox, 1994; Klir & Yuan, 1995), in order to identify users' information quality level expectations on their retrieved Web documents.

This would carry forward to extra research tasks, such as detailed fuzzy membership sets, implication, aggregation mappings, and the defuzzification process, to work with five or seven linguistic terms, in order to obtain a better classification of the Web documents. Consequently, the membership function and the rules should be refining.

In addition, it should expand the model and the prototype, including in the evaluation process other quality dimensions and metadata, in order to improve the quality evaluation results as a whole.

As another venue for future research, we also intend to propose a methodology that adopts user- and context-aware quality filters based on Web metadata retrieval. This methodology starts from an initial evaluation and adjusts this evaluation to consider context characteristics and user perspectives to obtain aggregated evaluations values. This aims to provide the theory to implement a pos-query or browse support mechanisms.

Furthermore, this can be embodied as a final step of a Web information retrieval engine or as a recommender system running in collaboration with a browser. We believe that this is a fertile area for research, and one that has not been totally explored yet.

CONCLUSION

Due to the amount of available information being so large, being of varying levels of quality, and being comparatively easy to access, it is becoming increasingly difficult to find precisely what is required, particularly if the user does not have precise knowledge of their information needs (Burgess et al., 2004).

The problems regarding information quality involve many different users' profiles. Beyond Internet users, these problems occur, similarly, in complex corporative environments that keep their proper Web as one or more intranets. The awareness of problems inherent in low information quality is the first obstacle to be overcome in looking for alternative solutions. The impacts which are more tangible, such as the dissatisfaction of the users and the organizations, the increase of costs, the inefficient decision-making processes, and the reduction of the ability to execute the strategy, are already bad enough. Other minor impacts can make these problems worse. It does not have to be this way, however; the mechanisms to improve data quality are available and have been effectively applied in some projects.

As stated in our chapter, it addresses those issues by proposing a strategy to deal with the growing amount of low-quality information available to users on the Web. This work is related to some study areas such as: information, data quality, and metadata; processes of quality evaluation; fuzzy logic; and fuzzy sets for quality evaluation, contexts, and ontologies. It aims the investigation and aggregated application of the advantages inherent in each of these areas to acquire solutions to identified problems. In this sense, we hope to contribute to the generation of new alternative answers that lead to innovative results.

Then, we build a general model to explore the benefits of using Web metadata for information quality prediction, and recommend (or not) the Web documents based on their information quality.

In the given example to the context *economy*, users can identify their expectations about information quality, and a set of 27 different rules (fuzzy propositions) were created that express relationships between linguistic variables and fuzzy sets.

There is a formalization of the different components involved in the quality evaluation process; it is certain that future studies are necessary to explore its computational and social consequences, as well as the effective costs of this quality improvement. The main and most immediate costs are related to the adaptation of environments and systems to adopt this methodology.

Our proposed solution aims to provide better and novel attainments to improve the information quality evaluation results and to increase the trustworthiness in information retrieval processes as a whole.

REFERENCES

Baeza-Yates, R., Castillo, C., & Marin, M. and Rodriguez, A. (2005). Crawling a country: Better strategies than breadth-first for Web page ordering. *Proceedings of the Industrial and Practical Experience Track of the 14th Conference on World Wide Web, Chiba, Japan* (pp. 864–872). ACM Press.

Belkin, N. J., & Croft, W. B. (1992). Information filtering and information retrieval: Two sides of the same coin? *Communications of the ACM, 35*, 29-38.

Burgess, M. S. E., Gray, W. A., & Fiddian, N. J. (2004). Quality measures and the information consumer (Research in Progress). *Proceedings of the Ninth International Conference on Informa-*

tion Quality (ICIQ-04) (pp. 373-388). Retrieved June 25, 2006, from http://www.iqconference.org/ICIQ/iqpapers.aspx?iciqyear=2004.

Cox, E. (1994). *The fuzzy systems handbook: A practitioner's guide to building, using, and maintaining fuzzy systems*. London: Academic Press.

Dey, A. K. (2001). Understanding and using context. *Personal and Ubiquitous Computing Journal, 5*, 4-7.

Dubois, D., & Prade, H. (1991). Fuzzy sets in approximate reasoning. Part 1: Inference with possibility distributions. *Fuzzy Sets and Systems, IFSA, Special Memorial Volume: 25 Years of Fuzzy Sets*. Amsterdam, NY: North-Holland Publishing.

Eckerson, W. (2002). Data quality and the bottom line: Achieving business success through a commitment to high quality data. *The Data Warehousing Institute Report Series, 1*, 1-32.

English, L. P. (1999). *Improving data warehouse and business information quality-methods for reducing costs and increasing profits*. Wiley.

Góis, J. A., & Tania, M. C. (2005). Integração fuzzy de imagens e dados heterogêneos no auxílio à avaliação de impacto ambiental. *Anais XII Simpósio Brasileiro de Sensoriamento Remoto, Goiânia, Brasil, INPE* (pp. 3037-3044).

Grauel, A. (1999). Analytical and structural considerations in fuzzy modeling. *Fuzzy Sets and Systems, 101*, 205-206.

Kantrowitz, M., Horstkotte, E., & Joslyn, C. (1997). Answers to questions about fuzzy logic and fuzzy expert systems. Retrieved June 25, 2006, from http://www-cgi.cs.cmu.edu/afs/cs/project/ai-repository/ai/areas/fuzzy/faq/fuzzy.faq

Kim, Y. J., Kishore, R., & Sanders, R. L. (2005). DQ to EQ: Understanding data quality in the context of e-business systems. *Communications of the ACM, 48*, 75-81.

Kleinberg, J. M. (1998). Authoritative sources in a hyperlinked environment. *Proceedings of the 9th ACM-SIAM Symposium on Discrete Algorithms* (pp. 668-677). Retrieved June 25, 2006, from http://www.cs.cornell.edu/home/kleinber/auth.pdf.

Klir, G. J., & Yuan, B. (Ed.). (1995). *Fuzzy sets and fuzzy logic: Theory and applications*. New Jersey: Prentice Hall.

Lawrence, S. (2000). Context in Web search. *IEEE Data Engineering Bulletin, 23*, 25-32.

Lee, Y. W. (2004). Crafting rules: Context-reflective data quality problem solving. *Journal of Management Information Systems, 20*(Winter, 2003-2004), 93-119.

Loshin, D. (2001). *Enterprise knowledge management - The data quality approach*. Morgan Kaufman.

Maes, P. (1994). Social interface agents: Acquiring competence by learning from users and other agents. *Working Notes of the AAAI Spring Symposium on Software Agents, Stanford, CA* (pp. 71-78).

Mizzaro, S. (1997). Relevance: The whole history. *Journal of American Society for Information Science, 48*(9), 810-832.

Moura, A. M. (2003). The semantic Web: Fundamentals, technologies, trends. *Proceedings of XVII Brazilian Symposium of Databases, Gramado, Brazil*.

Peralta, V., Ruggia, R., Kedad, Z., & Mokrane, B. (2004). A framework for data quality evaluation in a data integration system. *Proceedings of Brazilian Symposium of Database* (pp. 134-147).

Pinheiro, W. A., & Moura, A. M. C. (2004). An ontology-based approach for semantic search in portals. *Database and Expert Systems Applications (DEXA), IEEE Computer Society, 15*, 127-131.

Pipino, L. L., Lee, Y. W., & Wang, R. Y. (2002). Data quality assessment. *Communications of the ACM, 45*, 211-218.

Redman, T. C. (1998). The impact of poor data quality on the typical enterprise. *Communications of the ACM, 41*, 79-81.

Rothenberg, J. (1996). Metadata to support data quality and longevity. *Proceedings of the 1st IEEE Metadata Conference* (pp. 16-18).

Smart, K. L. (2002). Assessing quality documents. *ACM Journal of Computer Documentation, 26*(3), 130-140.

Strong, D., Wang, R. Y., & Guarascio, M. L. (1994). Beyond accuracy: What data quality means to data consumers: TDQM research program, USA. *Journal of Management Information Systems, Spring 1996, 12*(4), 5-33.

Tillman, H. N. (2003). Evaluating quality on the Net. Director of Libraries, v. © Copyright 1995, 1996, 1997, 1998, 1999, 2000, 2001, 2003, Babson College, Babson Park, Massachusetts. Retrieved June 25, 2006, from http://www.hopetillman.com/findqual.html

Turksen, I. B. (1991). Measurement of membership functions and their acquisition. *Fuzzy Sets and Systems, IFSA; Special Memorial Volume: 25 Years of Fuzzy Sets.* Amsterdam, NY: North-Holland Publishing.

Twidale, M. B., & Marty, P. F. (1999). An investigation of data quality and collaboration (Tech. Rep. UIUCLIS—1999/9+CSCW). University of Illinois at Urbana-Champaign.

Wand, Y., & Wang, R. (1996). Anchoring data quality dimensions in ontological foundations. *Communications of the ACM, 39*, 86-95.

Xexéo, G., Belchior, A., & da Rocha, A. R. C. (1996). Aplicação da Teoria Fuzzy em Requisitos de Qualidade de Software. Memorias-I, XXII CLEI, Santafé de Bogotá, Colombia, Junio (pp. 3-7).

Yager, R. R. (1991). Connectives and quantifiers in fuzzy sets. *Fuzzy Sets and Systems, IFSA; Special Memorial Volume: 25 Years of Fuzzy Sets.* Amsterdam, NY: North-Holland Publishing.

Zadeh, L. A. (1965). Fuzzy sets. *Information and Control, 8*, 338-353.

Zadeh, L. A. (1988). Fuzzy logic. *IEEE Transaction Computing, 35*, 83-92.

Zimmermann, H. J. (1991). *Fuzzy set theory and its applications, 2nd rev. ed.* Boston: Kluwer.

KEY TERMS

Context and Contextualization specify a scope or a boundary for a knowledge domain (Lee, 2004).

Fuzzy sets are an extension of classical set theory and are used in fuzzy logic. In classical set theory, the membership of elements in relation to a set is assessed in binary terms according to a crisp condition: An element either belongs or does not belong to the set. By contrast, fuzzy set theory permits the gradual assessment of the membership of elements in relation to a set (Klir & Yuan, 1995).

Fuzzy logic is derived from fuzzy set theory dealing with reasoning that is approximate rather than precisely deduced from classical predicate logic. It can be thought of as the application side of fuzzy set theory dealing with well-thought-out real-world expert values for a complex problem (Klir & Yuan, 1995).

Information quality is a multidimensional concept, since users must deal with both subjective perceptions of the individuals involved with the data, and objective measurements based on the dataset under evaluation (Pipino et al., 2002).

Metadata is data about data, and **Web metadata** "is machine-understandable description of things on (and about) the Web"[18].

PICS™ specification enables labels (metadata) to be associated with Internet content. It was originally designed to help parents and teachers control what children access on the Internet, but it also facilitates other uses for labels, including code signing and privacy. The PICS platform is one on which other rating services and filtering software have been built.

Quality dimensions represent the adopted information quality evaluation criteria and factors able to represent users' quality expectations (Pipino et al., 2002).

ENDNOTES

[1] The reader must be aware of the subtle difference between *data* and *information*. In this chapter, we consider that data is the representation (notation) and information is the meaning (denotation), and we use these terms indistinctly.

[2] http://www.uml.org/

[3] http://www.w3.org/2004/OWL/

[4] http://www.w3.org/Metadata/.

[5] http://www.google.com/apis/

[6] http://www.w3.org/PICS/#RDF)

[7] http://dublincore.org/

[8] http://jung.sourceforge.net/

[9] http://www.google.com/dirhp

[10] http://vlado.fmf.uni-lj.si/pub/networks/pajek/

[11] http://jung.sourceforge.net/

[12] http://www.mathworks.com/

[13] http://www.economist.com/surveys/

[14] http://www.economistconferences.com/

[15] http://www.theworldin.com/

[16] http://www.economist.com/opinion

[17] http://www.scottrade.com/index.asp?supbid=68597

[18] http://www.w3.org/Metadata/

Chapter XX
Towards Quality Web Information Systems Through Precise Model–Driven Development

Fernando Molina
University of Murcia, Spain

Francisco J. Lucas
University of Murcia, Spain

Ambrosio Toval Alvarez
University of Murcia, Spain

Juan M. Vara
Rey Juan Carlos University—Madrid, Spain

Paloma Cáceres
Rey Juan Carlos University—Madrid, Spain

Esperanza Marcos
Rey Juan Carlos University—Madrid, Spain

ABSTRACT

Recent years have seen the arrival of the Internet as the platform that supports most areas within organizations, a fact which has led to the appearance of specific methodologies and tools for the construction of Web information systems (WIS). However, an absence of functionalities for the verification and validation (V&V) has been detected in the methodologies and tools of the models which have been built. This chapter presents one of these methodologies for WIS development (MIDAS) and shows how it has been completed with the definition of a strategy for the formal specification of its models with V&V objectives. This will contribute to increasing the quality of the models used in WIS development. The plug-in architecture which integrates this formal approach within CASE tools for WIS development is also shown.

INTRODUCTION

In the last decade, the Web has become the principal medium available to all kinds of organizations for supporting and spreading information. Initially, the Web was considered merely as an element that permits organizations to be present in the Internet. However, nowadays the Web is the fundamental platform that supports most organizations' areas. Recently, the Web Information Systems (WIS) has undergone an exponential increase. Two reasons for this growth are that the potential Web audience is greater than any other medium and that the Web has demonstrated that it is a good medium to access information for nontechnical users. Although we might think that WIS development is carried out in the same way as traditional information system (IS) development, there are critical factors that distinguish this development (Ginige & Murugesan, 2001). Moreover, studies like Epner (2000) show that the traditional methodologies can be successful in the development of simple WIS but they are not appropriate for the development of complex systems, and that a very high percentage of WIS development projects do not satisfy the needs for which they were developed.

These facts have motivated intensive research in the scope of WIS modelling and have led to the appearance of a new discipline, Web engineering, whose objective is to facilitate systematic and semiautomatic WIS development, adapting the well-known practices of Software Engineering to Web development. To achieve this, numerous methodologies, languages, tools, and design patterns specifically adapted to the WIS scope have been developed. Some of the most relevant proposals are HDM, RMM, OOHDM, OO-H, UWE, and so forth. Another of the methodologies used for WIS development is MIDAS (Cáceres, Marcos, & Vela, 2003), a methodological framework for WIS development, which proposes an architecture based on the model driven architecture (MDA) (Miller & Mukerji, 2001) from the Object Man-

agement Group (OMG). Moreover, in order to support the whole methodology, an MDA tool (M2DAT—MIDAS MDA Tool) is being developed, which integrates all the techniques proposed in MIDAS for the semiautomatic generation of WIS and whose early functionalities have already been presented in previous papers (Vara, De Castro, & Marcos, 2005). MIDAS will be explained in more depth in the next sections.

In spite of the proliferation of methodologies and tools for WIS development, we have detected that most of them do not include activities or features related to V&V for the analysis of the models built or, if they exist, they are rather weak. V&V of models can be used to detect errors and inconsistencies in the early stages of WIS development and can help to increase the quality of the models built as well as the code generated from them. These activities are especially important in proposals aligned with MDA (like MIDAS), because it proposes that models should be used as a mechanism to carry out the whole software development process.

With this objective in mind, a proposal using an approach based on term rewriting (which is close to theorem-proving strategies) has been carried out to make a formal V&V of the models used in WIS development (allowing the demonstration of properties on them) (Lucas, Molina, Toval, de Castro, Cáceres, & Marcos, 2006). The strategy proposed is based on the algebraic specification of the metamodels used during the development process and the implementation of the necessary properties on them. Maude programming language (Clavel, Durán, Eker, Lincoln, Martí-Oliet, Meseguer, & Talcote, 2005), which has been used in numerous study cases (Martí-Oliet & Meseguer, 2002), is also used here.

Maude is an algebraic specification language based on equational and rewriting logic. The use of formal methods adds rigour and precision to the V&V models activities. Moreover, the need to specify the metamodels of the diagrams used in WIS development precisely has helped to detect inconsistencies and ambiguities in their definition. This strategy helps modellers to build models with fewer errors and provides the basis for demonstrating, in a formal way, fulfilment (or not) of properties considered interesting in this scope. Meyer (1997) justified the use of formal methods in the development of systems with specific requirements such as reusability. WIS can be included in this group, due to the potential audience of these systems and the wide reuse of the Web Services produced during the development process.

It is important to emphasize that all the aspects related to the underlying formal techniques (like Maude, algebraic specifications, etc.) are completely transparent to WIS development CASE tool users. This feature is achieved by means of a plug-in for formal V&V and property demonstration. This plug-in is integrated in M2DAT, but it could be integrated in any other MDA tool for WIS development. Thus, a precise and powerful formal verifier and properties demonstrator for the MDA tools used for WIS development will be provided but, at the same time, it has a useful and simple interface that hides the more complicated details of the strategy from modellers.

In this chapter, we present part of the formal specification of the Hypertext Modelling Method of MIDAS (HM³). By applying the HM³ method, the navigation model of a WIS is obtained starting from the conceptual data model and the user requirements in the use case model. In order to achieve a precise specification of the WIS modelling, we have to formalize the metamodels of the models involved in the modelling process. We have already completed the formalization of the Extended Navigation model, the output model generated in HM³. This formalization serves as a case study of the need and utility of formal specifications in software development, and supplies us with the guidelines to complete the formalization process of the whole method.

The rest of the chapter is structured as follows. First, an overview of MIDAS methodology will

be shown, focusing on the Hypertext Modelling Method (HM³) of MIDAS and the tool that gives support to the whole proposal (M2DAT). Next, the strategy for V&V models in WIS development will be explained in depth along with the architecture of the plug-in that automatizes this strategy and the way it is connected to MIDAS and M2DAT. Finally, the chapter highlights the main contributions and the open issues of this proposal.

STATE OF THE ART

The evolution of Web technologies has involved Web software products in a continuous improving process. At the early stages of the Web, just a few organizations used a set of very simple Web pages to publish their information, while nowadays the vast majority of public and private organizations all over the world use the Web as the main communication channel, whether they want to get in touch with their customers, with other organizations, or even with the other components of the same organization. Moreover, these organizations have found on the Web a place to offer new services, thus expanding their business capacity and resulting in a new kind of market: the e-business or e-commerce, a market where the interaction between the customer and the company mainly (or even exclusively) takes place over the Web.

With the development of more and more Web applications and Web Information Systems (WIS), a need for well-defined Web development processes has arisen and is dealt with in a new working and research area, called Web engineering (Ginige & Murugesan, 2001). The first methodological proposals on this topic were, in general, adaptations from classical methodologies for specific kinds of development. Thus, some works appeared in the hypermedia and multimedia fields, like: HDM (Garzotto, Paolini, & Schwabe, 1993), RMM/ERMM (Isakowitz, Stohr, & Balasubramanian, 1995), OO-HDM

(Schwabe, Esmeraldo, Rossi, & Lyardet, 2001), Ariadne (Díaz, Aedo, & Montero, 2001), UWE (Hennicker & Koch, 2000) and W2000 (Baresi, Garzotto, & Paolini, 2003); other proposals came directly from approaches for Database development, like the ones from Fraternali (1999), Araneus (Atzeni, Merialdo, & Mecca, 2001), and WebML (Ceri, Fraternali, & Bongio, 2000). Methods like WSDM (De Troyer & Casteleyn, 2003) began to design Web sites in a user-oriented manner, and others extended development methodologies for general purposes (Conallen, 2000; Gómez, Cachero, & Pastor, 2000). Nevertheless, in recent years, the new technological proposals for the Web, such as XML, Web Services Business Process automatization, Semantic Web, and so forth, as well as the impact of the Model-Driven Architecture (MDA) (Kleppe, Warmer, & Bast, 2003; Miller & Mukerji, 2001) as a framework for Information Systems development have contributed to the evolution of the techniques and methodologies for WIS development. HM³, the proposal that is formalized in this chapter, comes also from the Web engineering field, so it has a few similarities with some of the most relevant studies in this area. On the other hand, the most important contributions of HM³ come from its user-oriented approach, with its focus on the services provided by the system and the development process proposed to carry out the hypertext development. The HM³ process for hypertext development focuses on the sequence of steps that the user must complete in order to obtain a given service from the system; that sequence of activities is represented by an Activity Diagram for each service provided by the system.

However, as we commented above, the activities related to V&V do not receive the attention that they deserve in these methodologies and tools. This fact, along with the importance of managing quality models in model-driven approaches, justified the need to include explicit V&V activities in these WIS methodologies and tools. This chapter shows how these activities can be included in a WIS development process.

THE HYPERTEXT MODELLING METHOD OF MIDAS

The Hypertext Modelling Method of MIDAS (HM³) defines a process, new models to elaborate, and the mappings between them. In this section, we present the HM³ process and describe the specific tasks associated with the generation of each proposed model. Before describing the process, we present a brief description of MIDAS, the framework in which this method has been designed.

MIDAS Framework

MIDAS can be thought of as a methodological approach composed of simple methodologies, each focused on solving a specific problem in the context of WIS development, like developing the WIS Database (Marcos, Vela, & Cavero, 2003), collecting the WIS behavior (De Castro, Marcos, & Lopez Sanz, in press), or modelling the WIS hypertext (Caceres, De Castro, & Marcos, 2004). Here we focus on the MIDAS method to model the hypertext aspect of the WIS (HM³), whose final output is the *Extended Navigation Model*.

MIDAS is a methodological framework for the agile development of WIS which proposes a Model-Driven Architecture (Cáceres et al., 2003) based on the MDA proposed by the Object Management Group (Kleppe et al., 2003; Miller & Mukerji, 2001). It proposes modelling the WIS according to two orthogonal dimensions (see Figure 1): On the one hand, it takes into account the platform-dependence degree (based on the MDA approach) and specifies the whole system by Computation-Independent Models (CIMs), Platform-Independent Models (PIMs), and Platform-Specific Models (PSMs) and, on the other hand, it proposes modelling the system according to three basic aspects: hypertext, content, and behavior. From now on, we will focus on the proposal for hypertext development framed in MIDAS.

Figure 1. MIDAS architecture and HM³

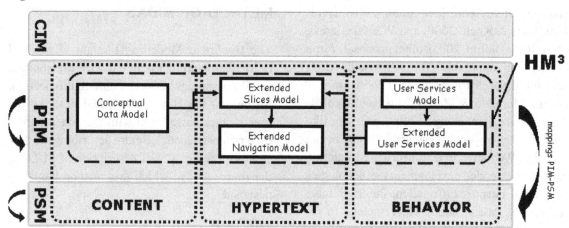

HM³ Process

HM³ proposes a model-driven process to obtain the navigation model, which takes into account the conceptual user services. The HM³ process is an iterative and incremental process that takes as input artefacts the set of user requirements, collected in the *User Services Model,* and the conceptual data model, and gives as output artefact the *Extended Navigation Model.* Figure 2 summarizes the HM³ process.

The user requirements are collected in the *User Services Model* in which the main *actors* of the system as well as the *user services* related to each actor are identified (i.e., the *Conceptual User Services*).

Next, each *conceptual user service* is shredded into one or more *user services,* whether they are *composite* or *basic* (*structural* or *functional*) *services,* thus obtaining the *Extended Use Cases Model.* This task is accomplished iteratively until no more *composite services* are detected. Equally,

Figure 2. The HM³ process

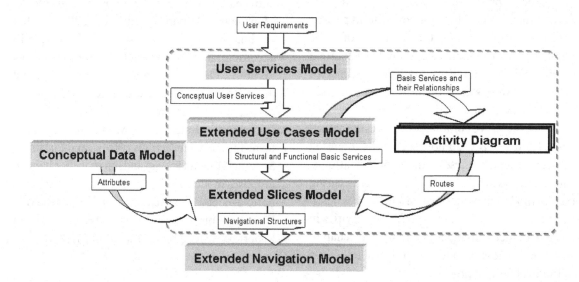

the possible *extend* and *include* relations between the different *basic services* are identified. Moreover, one activity diagram is generated for each *conceptual user service* to define the sequence of *basic services* that composes the *conceptual user service*, the so-called *service route*.

Each of the *structural* and *functional basic services* identified in the *Extended Use Cases Model* is mapped into a *structural* or *functional slice* in the *Extended Slices Model*. The attributes for these slices are obtained from the respective classes included in the *Conceptual Data Model*. A route name is allocated to each activity diagram in order to identify each service route, and the slices comprised in the service route are linked by directed associations according to the activity diagram. Possible forks should be also identified. Thus, if the service route "X" includes the subroute "Y", it will be stereotyped as "X.Y".

Finally, the *Extended Navigation Model* is obtained merely by adding the navigational structures, such as *indexes* or *menus,* to the *Extended Slices Model.*

The HM³ Profile

A UML profile is a package that contains modelling elements that have been customized for a specific purpose or domain, using extension mechanisms such as stereotypes, tagged definitions, and constraints (OMG, 2006). Since HM³ defines a new group of elements to model the hypertext of a WIS from a user-services-oriented approach, the UML metamodel has to be extended

by means of a new profile comprising these new modelling elements. This extension is defined on structural and behavioural elements of UML 2.0 (OMG, 2006). Like this, the newly-defined profile, the HM³ profile, depends on those UML elements, as shown in Figure 3(a).

The HM³ profile proposed is structured in two packages, as shown below in Figure 3(b): the *User Services* and the *Navigation* packages. The user service package contains the modelling elements for behavioural aspects of the WIS, including both the user services and extended-use cases metamodels. The navigation package comprises the modelling elements related to the hypertext aspects of the WIS, including the *Extended Slices* and *Extended Navigation* metamodels.

Likewise, the HM³ gathers all the new concepts presented and defined as part of the method. Table 1 collects the stereotypes defined for the presentation of those concepts, along with the UML metaclass that each one extends, as well as the model in which it is used.

Metamodels

Each metamodel included in the HM³ profile extends the UML metamodel to support the representation of the syntax and the semantics of the new concepts. Moreover, we have specified the restrictions associated with each metamodel using the Object Constraint Language (OCL) (OMG, 2006), as well as the mapping of these restrictions at model level. For an in-depth explanation on the semantics associated to any one of the new ele-

Figure 3. HM³ profile: a) Relationships with UML packages; b) Package structure of HM³ package

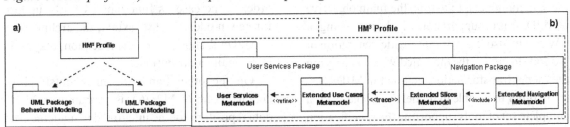

Table 1. Stereotyped elements of UML for the HM³ profile

Models of HM³	Stereotypes	Description	UML Meta-Class
User Services Model	**<<*CUS*>>**	Conceptual User Service	
Extended Use Cases Model	<<CS>>	Composite Service	Use Case
	<<SBS>>	Structural Basic Service	
	<<FBS>>	Functional Basic Service	
Extended Slices Model and *Extended Navigation Model*	<<SS>>	Structural Slice	Class
	<<FS>>	Functional Slice	
	<<route>>	Route	Association

ments included in the different metamodels, the reader is referred to Caceres et al. (2004).

Model Transformation Rules

In relation to the way that mappings should be defined, the MDA Guide (Miller & Mukerji, 2003, pp. 3-6) states that *"the mapping description may be in natural language, an algorithm in an action language, or a model in a mapping language"*. In this case, and as a first approach to modelling transformations on HM³, we decided to describe the transformation rules in natural language and later express them as graph transformation rules (Rozenberg, 1997) in the work presented in Caceres, De Castro, Vara, & Marcos (2006).

M2DAT: MIDAS MDA Tool

M2DAT (MIDAS MDA Tool) is an MDA tool for WIS development that supports the MIDAS framework (Vara et al., 2005). It aims to provide a way to put the proposals of MIDAS to use, that is, the metamodels and the mappings between those metamodels. Like this, the main objective of M2DAT is to support not only the modelling of a WIS, but also the semi-automatic generation of the code to deploy the modelled WIS by applying the model transformations defined in MIDAS.

In order to be able to model the whole WIS, a complete set of tools supporting the specification

of each one of the models that are considered in MIDAS framework should be provided. Moreover, to obtain the final code that implements the WIS, that is, to complete the proposed MDA development process, a tool supporting the complete cycle of model transformations described in MIDAS should also be developed. We have collected all these tools in M2DAT. Hence, it can be thought of as a tool composed of different tools to work with the different models proposed in MIDAS.

Focusing now on HM³, M2DAT has to support the elaboration and management of the four new models considered in the development process depicted in Figure 2, as well as the Conceptual Data Model and the Activity Diagrams. In addition, M2DAT should be able to support the different model transformations included in Figure 2; for example, it should be able to obtain the Extended-Use Cases Model from the Uses Services Model.

As MIDAS is a continuously-evolving methodology that periodically incorporates new aspects in the development process, M2DAT, its supporting tool, should be highly scaleable in order to increase its functionality with support for new models. To this extent, the architecture of M2DAT, shown in the next section, may well be its main contribution.

On the other hand, the most outstanding characteristic of M2DAT is probably its XML data repository for the integrated management of models. The M2DAT repository has been built over an Oracle XML database. Thus, M2DAT takes advantage of the well-known properties of databases to improve the storage and management of models.

M2DAT Architecture

M2DAT follows the architecture depicted in Figure 4. On the one hand, it is a three-tier architecture that comprises the graphic user interface tier, the application logic tier, and the persistence tier (i.e., GUI, Objects, Database). However, when focusing just on the vertical layers depicted in the picture, the architecture can be thought of as a set of modules or subsystems, one for each different model considered in MIDAS. Defined in this way, the architecture of M2DAT is highly scaleable: To support a new metamodel, a new subsystem will be developed and easily integrated with the rest; the development process for the new subsystem will be clearly stated since it will be similar to the process which was followed to develop the previous subsystems. Therefore, the experiences in developing them will serve to improve the

development process for each new subsystem. In Figure 4, three different subsystems are included in the M2DAT architecture: From left to right, we can find the User Services subsystem, the Extended Use Cases subsystem and finally, an *Others* subsystem is depicted, showing how new subsystems could be added and integrated in M2DAT to extend its capabilities.

It should be considered that each M2DAT subsystem should give support to a different UML metamodel. This is the idea that guides the definition of M2DAT architecture. Each subsystem allows the specification and edition of an extended UML model. Moreover, the tool should provide some kind of model persistence in order to store and recover a UML model. To accomplish this task, the XML technical space was chosen in M2DAT: A set of XML Schemas is used to specify the metamodels for each different model considered in MIDAS (W3C, 2001). These XML Schemas also serve to describe the structure of the XML documents in which each different model is stored. Like this, a given model is not valid if the XML document that represents such model does not conform to the respective XML Schema.

Figure 4. M2DAT architecture

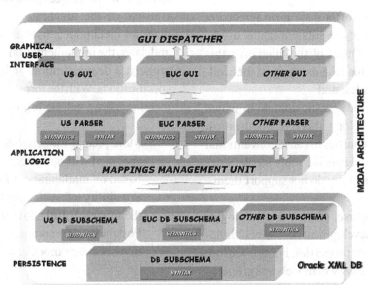

PRECISE WIS DEVELOPMENT

V&V and Demonstration Properties Proposal

In the previous section, the architecture of M2DAT was shown. This architecture includes a validation module in the application logic layer whose function is to inform users about the completeness and correctness of the models being used. This module receives as input the XML document that contains the semantics of the model and parses it against its XML Schema, which defines the diagram metamodel, that is, it analyzes the XML file and checks that it has the structure of the XML Schema used in its definition. Thus, it is possible to verify that a model is correct from its static semantics point of view, that is, how the constructors defined in the diagram metamodel must be used and interrelated. However, it is necessary to emphasize that a syntactically-correct model can still contain errors and ambiguities from the dynamic semantics point of view of the models, with regard to the well-formedness rules of their metamodels or with regard to specific properties related to the specific domain to which the model belongs. Briefly, all these properties can be related to:

- Static semantics of the diagram in agreement with the rules of the notation that is used;
- Dynamic semantics of the diagrams; this semantics defines the meaning of the well-formedness rules; and
- Semantics of the specific domain to which the diagrams belong; this is one of the most interesting properties because conventional CASE tools and specific tools for WIS development generally do not support them.

As mentioned above, current methodologies and tools for WIS development do not include activities to verify these properties. For this reason, a strategy for precise V&V of models and property demonstrations on them has been proposed. The inclusion of this strategy in a WIS development methodology will permit modellers to detect the errors and to demonstrate the properties previously commented. This strategy is based on the algebraic specification of the diagram metamodels involved in the WIS development process and, moreover, in the implementation of proofs and property demonstrations on them. The language used for this algebraic specification is Maude, which will be explained in the next section. The benefits obtained thanks to this strategy are more precise models (with less errors, ambiguities, or inconsistencies) and detection of errors in the early phases of WIS development; in summary, the strategy contributes to increasing the quality of the WIS being built and the productivity of its development process. Moreover, a plug-in for WIS CASE tools is being developed with the idea that modellers can use this proposal and obtain its benefits in an easy way. In the next sections, the strategy and the plug-in architecture will be explained in detail.

V&V Strategy

As we commented previously, a formal strategy using the formal language Maude is proposed to carry out these V&V activities. This strategy consists of the algebraic specification of the diagram metamodels used in WIS development and, later, the implementation of V&V proofs and properties demonstrations using these algebraic specifications. With the formalization of a diagram metamodel, we get the following advantages:

- More precise models, because they must be specified without ambiguities in languages based on mathematical formalisms;
- Possibility of verifying formally whether the models fullfil some properties;
- Possibility of making precise transformations between models; and

- Validation of our models through simulation, since Maude allows us to create prototypes automatically because the metamodel specification is directly executable. The use of this feature in WIS will be undertaken in a future work.

In this chapter, some of these advantages will be shown through the navigation models used in MIDAS methodology.

Extended Navigation Model

We illustrate our strategy with the navigation model. This model is used in MIDAS and in other methodologies for WIS development to model the possible routes that users can follow during their interaction with the WIS. We will show how the inclusion of V&V techniques in these models contributes to increasing the quality of the system being developed.

The extended navigation model is based on the extended slices model (Cáceres et al., 2004). In this last model, a system is decomposed into significant parts, named *slices*, and hyperlinks that join these slices. There are two kinds of slices: *structural slices*, which show a piece of information that will be shown in groups; and *functional slices*, which show another kind of

information or functionalities that allow us to represent the interaction between the WIS and its users. Figure 5 shows a simplified version of this diagram metamodel.

The slices are linked to directed relations which indicate the possible routes that could be followed from here on. Each route is represented by a stereotyped association with <<*route*>> and a tagged value *RouteName*. An extended navigation model example that models a web of flight shopping is shown in Figure 6.

The validation module in M2DAT can check that these navigation models are syntactically correct. However, there are other interesting properties of these models that could be verified. Most are related to *routes*. For example, these properties could be related to reachability objectives, that is, to check that a user of the WIS could reach a service from a start point or, in a general form, that WIS users can use all the services provided by the system from the initial page. Moreover, it could be possible to verify that cycles do not exist in the routes defined in the model, nor unconnected routes, as well as verifying that all the routes (or subroutes) that appear in a menu are available from it or that all valid ends reachable from a menu correspond to the ends indicated in the menu where the route starts.

Figure 5. Simplified version of metamodel of the extended navigation model

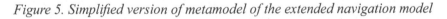

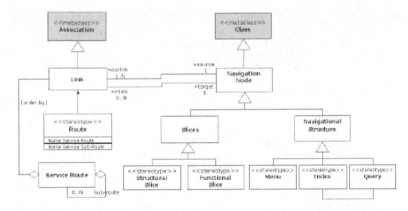

Figure 6. Example of an Extended Navigation Model

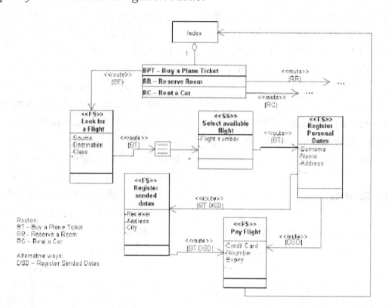

Extended Navigation Model Formalization

In the last section, the main elements that compose the *Extended Navigation Model* have been shown. Below, we show how these elements have been formalized in Maude language.

HM[3] proposes defining one route for each conceptual *user service*. A route represents the sequence of steps that a user must follow to complete the service. In the formalization of a route, there are two elements involved (see Figure 5): *ServiceRoutes* and *Routes*. In the formalization

developed, a *ServiceRoutes* list is used as a route identifier. Furthermore, this list also represents the hierarchy that can exist between routes, that is, a route can have subroutes. This hierarchy has been formalized by a *ServiceRoute* list, which allows subroutes of any length to exist.

Now, we will see how a route has been formalized. A *Route* contains, on the one hand, a *ServiceRouteList* which indicates the route or subroute that it represents, and, on the other hand, information about whether it can finish. Figure 7 shows the *route* and *route list* formalization.

Figure 7. Route and route list formalization

```
(fmod ROUTE is sort Route .
    pr SERVICEROUTELIST .
    pr ROUTEEND .
    op route : ServiceRouteList RouteEnd -> Route [ ctor ] .
    op getSRL : Route -> ServiceRouteList .
    ...
endfm)

(fmod ROUTELIST is ...
    *** Returns true, if the route is included in the route list.
    op isIn : Route RouteList -> Bool .
    ...
endfm)
```

Figure 8. Navigation node formalization

```
(fmod NAVIGATIONNODE is sort NavigationNode .
    pr NAVIGATIONNODENAME .
    pr ROUTELIST .
    op navigationNode : NavigationNodeName RouteList -> NavigationNode [ ctor ] .
    ...
    *** Returns true, if the node is a valid end for the route.
    op isValidEnd : NavigationNode Route -> Bool .
    ...
endfm)
```

Figure 9. Link formalization

```
(fmod LINK is sort Link .
    pr LINKEND . pr LINKNAME . pr ROUTELIST .
    op link : LinkName LinkEnd LinkEnd RouteList -> Link [ ctor ] .
    op getLinkName : Link -> LinkName .
    op getLinkEndSource : Link -> LinkEnd .
    ...
endfm)
```

Figure 10. Extended navigation model formalization

```
(fmod NAVIGATIONDIAG is sort NavigationDiag .
    pr NAVIGATIONNODELIST . pr LINKLIST .
    op navigationDiag : NavigationNodeList LinkList
        -> NavigationDiag [ ctor ] .
    op getNavigationNodeList : NavigationDiag -> NavigationNodeList .
    op getLinkList : NavigationDiag -> LinkList .
    ...
endfm)
```

Navigation Nodes

In the metamodel of this diagram, the *navigation nodes* represent significant units, named slices, mentioned in previous sections. These elements are made up by a *name* and a *route list*. The *route list* indicates which routes can finish at this node. The formalization of this element appears in Figure 8.

Links

A *Link* is used to connect two slices. A link is also made up by a route list that indicates which routes can cross through the link. Furthermore,

a link also informs us if a route can finish at its destination node. Figure 9 shows part of the *Link* formalization.

Extended Navigation Model

Once we have formalized these elements, the complete navigation model can be formalized. Its constructor receives as input a *NavigationNodes* list and a *Links* list. Figure 10 shows the module that formalizes this model.

With this formalization, it is already possible to represent any navigational model that we develop.

Properties Formalization

Now we have seen the extended navigation model formalization, we show an example of a property specification. Some auxiliary operations that will make the information management and the property specification easier have been created (for example, *'nextLinks'* that returns the *Links* which have a certain *NavigationNode* as source; or *'getTargetNodes'* that returns the source nodes of each *Link* of a *Links list*). As we commented previously, some of the most interesting properties that can be defined in this model are related to routes and possible inconsistencies and ambiguities among them. The next section shows an example of a property that can be verified among these models and how it has been formalized.

Example: Analysis of Valid Routes

The statement of this property would be: *"All the routes that appear in a navigational model must be valid"*. This is one of the basic properties which this kind of model must fulfil. A route is a succession of links that starts in a menu and finishes at a valid end. Two conditions must occur in order to fulfil the property:

- All the routes must have a valid end; and
- If for a given route there is a link tagged R1 and it arrives at a given node, the route must be able to continue through another link also tagged R1, unless the node is a valid end for this route.

This property can be guaranteed if the second condition is fulfilled for all the link-nodes that made up the route, starting at the initial node and arriving at a valid end. Hence, the property has been specified in this way. Figure 11 shows the Maude module that specifies the operations and equations that verify the property.

The schema used in this property is identical to the definition and verification of other domain properties. Firstly, the property statement is enunciated in understandable terms for the WIS developers (for example, in natural language). Then, the algorithm that verifies the property is defined informally. And, finally, the property is implemented formally using *Maude*.

In order to illustrate how this property is verified, an error has been included in the model shown in Figure 6. The error introduced is the following: When a route tagged *BT* arrives at the node named *"Look for a Flight"*, there is no link

Figure 11. Module that verifies that the routes of a model are valid

```
(fmod VERIFICATIONS is
  pr UTILSDNAV . pr STRING .
  op testValidRoute : NavigationDiag NavigationNodeList ServiceRouteList -> String .

  var NN : NavigationNode . var NNL : NavigationNodeList .
  var R : ServiceRouteList . var ND : NavigationDiag .
  *** This route finishes in a valid final node. So, this partial route
  *** does not have errors
  eq testValidRoute (ND, nullNavigationNodeList, R) = "" .
  eq testValidRoute (ND, NN NNL, R) =
  if selectLinks(nextLinks(ND, NN), route(R,noRouteEnd))
  == nullLinkList
  and not(isValidEnd(NN, route(R,noRouteEnd))) then
      "ERROR, the route " + ... + " which is not a valid final node."
  else testValidRoute(ND,
     getTargetNodes(ND, selectLinks(nextLinks(ND, NN),
  route(R,noRouteEnd))) NNL, R)
     fi .
endfm)
```

Figure 12. Property reduction in Maude

```
reduce in exampleNavigD :
    testValidRoute(reserveND,index,'BT)
    result String :
    "ERROR, the route BT finishes in the slice lookForFlight which is
    not a valid final node. "
```

tagged *BT* leaving the node, and this node is not a valid end for this route. In Figure 12, we can see the output of *Maude* when the property is verified using the operation *testValidRoute*.

It is important to emphasize that all those aspects related to the underlying formal techniques (like Maude, algebraic specifications, etc.) are completely transparent to users of the WIS development tool.

Precise V&V Plug-in Architecture

The V&V models and properties demonstration strategy shown previously can be included in a CASE tool used for WIS development. Thanks to this integration, the CASE tool users could use all the functionalities shown in an easy and comfortable way. The integration will be carried out using a plug-in that hides all the details of the underlying proposal. This section shows the software architecture that will be developed to support the strategy. Figure 13 shows an overview of the *plug-in* architecture.

Figure 13. General plug-in architecture

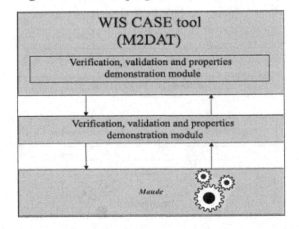

On the one hand, there will exist a module (client module) integrated in the CASE tool. Thus, the use of Maude and the communication with it will be completely transparent for the users of the tool. On the other hand, there will exist another module (server module) that executes Maude and maintains the communication with the client module. The communication between client and server modules can be carried out by the Internet, thus obtaining independence between the CASE tool and the modules that interact with Maude. Figure 14 shows in more detail the elements that make up this V&V plug-in. It is important to emphasize that this proposal is illustrated using MIDAS and M2DAT, but both the strategy and the plug-in which supports it could be integrated in any other methodology or CASE tool for WIS development.

Below, the architecture of the plug-in and the description of each one of its components are shown. Figure 14 shows this detailed architecture. The modules that make up the architecture are:

- **CASE tool for WIS development:** This is the tool that supports the development process of Web Information Systems, in this case, M2DAT. This tool should provide a mechanism that permits access to the different elements that make up the models (as classes, attributes, and methods of each class, links between classes, etc.);
- **Verification, validation, and properties demonstration module (from now on, client module):** This is the module that will be integrated in the CASE tool and will enable the request of services for precise V&V of the models used in the tool or demonstration of

properties on them. This module comprises the following components:

○ **Graphic User Interface (GUI):** The users of the CASE tool interact with this graphic interface. Users can select the properties to check (all the properties or only some of them) and the validation tests to make on the models built in the tool. Moreover, this GUI will allow requests to be sent to the server module;

○ **Translator from models to Maude specifications:** This module translates the model built in the CASE tool into its equivalent formal term. The model translated will be the model loaded in the GUI at each moment (step 1 in Figure 14). In order to complete its task, the module uses the functions provided by M2DAT to access model elements. This translation process is carried out automatically. Thus, the users do not need to know the details of the underlying formal specification;

○ **Request sending and results reception module:** This module will receive the Maude specifications obtained from the translation process (step 2 in Figure 14) and a description of the properties to check as well as the validation test to carry out. First, this module sends this information to the server module, which maintains communication with Maude. Afterwards, this module receives the results of this process of formal V&V sent from the server module (step 6) and shows these results to CASE tool users in an understandable format for them (for example, a textual description in natural language); and

○ **Inverse translator:** This module will be included in the future, when the functionalities related to precise

transformations between models will be added. The module will receive as input a Maude term that represents a new model obtained by transformation from the original model (step 7 in Figure 14) and will produce the representation of this new model in the format used by the WIS development tool. This module is being developed.

• **Verification, validation, and properties demonstration module (from now on, server module):** This module is executed in a remote server and keeps communication with the client module and Maude. This module includes the following components:

○ **Request reception module:** This module receives requests sent from the client module that contains the

Figure 14. Plug-in architecture modules

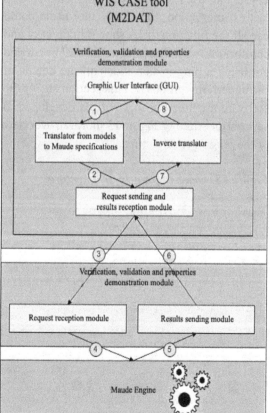

Maude specifications corresponding to the models and a description about the properties to verify among them (step 3). It separates this information and sends it to Maude engine in an adequate form (step 4); and

o **Results sending module:** The execution in Maude of each of the request produces an answer, that is, a result. The module receives these results (step 5) and, when the request management finishes, sends it to the client module (step 6).

• **Maude:** The Maude environment is where the activities of verification of properties and validation of models will be made.

FUTURE TRENDS

At present, we are working on the integration of this approach with the rest of the models proposed by MIDAS and the inclusion of business process modelling in the MIDAS Framework. The formal specification of the different models considered in the MIDAS proposal (e.g., models for Web services definition, extended-use cases models, etc.) is being carried out. Moreover, we are working on the identification of new interesting properties to verify and validation proofs to carry out on each of these models and their formalization in Maude. Thus, we will offer formal support for V&V of the rest of the models involved in the WIS development, and we will offer a more powerful verifier with larger V&V models capabilities to users of WIS development CASE tools. Furthermore, the V&V of the transformations that are carried out between the different models of the MIDAS methodology are being tackled to check the correctness of these transformations and the semantics equivalence between the source and target models. We are also working on the integration of the plug-in for V&V in M2DAT and on the inclusion of all the new capabilities developed in this plug-in.

One of the main benefits of this proposed approach will undoubtedly be the maximizing of the automation of the WIS development process. Thus, in future works we are going to implement the proposed models and mappings in a CASE tool that allows MIDAS to generate the WIS semi-automatically.

CONCLUSION

The Internet boom has led to the arising of a new generation of Information Systems, the so-called Web Information Systems. Consequently, numerous methodologies to develop WIS have been proposed. All those proposals for WIS development are quite young, so they have only focused on completing their proposals, and overlook the verification and validation of the models being considered.

This chapter shows, on the one hand, an overview of the MIDAS methodology and the architecture of M2DAT, the tool which gives support to their models and, on the other, the viability and advantages of formal V&V techniques in this scope and how these techniques can be put to use, automatized, and combined with existing methodologies for WIS development, and their respective supporting tools, through a plug-in.

The added plug-in provides a powerful formal verifier based on the Maude formal language that helps to improve the quality of the models (i.e., the software) generated by M2DAT, thus producing models which contain less errors or inconsistencies thanks to this process. Moreover, the action of this formal verifier is completely transparent to the final user of M2DAT, thanks to the integration of the proposal. Finally, the task of formalizing the metamodels in the MAUDE language has served to detect inconsistencies and ambiguities in the metamodels themselves, leading to a more refined version of the metamodels.

REFERENCES

Atzeni, P., Merialdo, P., & Mecca, G. (2001). Data-intensive Web sites: Design and maintenance. *World Wide Web, 4*(1-2), 21-47.

Baresi, L., Garzotto, F., & Paolini, P. (2000). From Web sites to Web applications: New issues for conceptual modeling. *Proceedings of 2° International Workshop on the World Wide Web and Conceptual Modeling (WCM2000)* (pp. 89-100).

Caceres, P., De Castro, V., & Marcos, E. (2004). Navigation modeling from a user services oriented approach. In T. Yakhno (Ed.), *Proceedings of the Third Biennial International Conference in Advanced in Information Systems (ADVIS 2004)* (pp. 150-160). Springer-Verlag.

Caceres, P., De Castro, V., Vara, J. M., & Marcos, E. (2006). Model transformations for hypertext modeling on Web information systems. *Proceedings of the 2006 ACM Symposium on Applied Computing (SAC 2006)* (pp. 1232-1239).

Cáceres, P., Marcos, E., & Vela, B. (2003). A MDA-based approach for Web information system development. *Workshop in Software Model Engineering (WiSME) in UML '2003*. Retrieved December 21, 2007 from http://www.metamodel.com/wisme-2003/

Ceri, S., Fraternali, P., & Bongio, A. (2000). Web modeling language (WebML): A modeling language for designing Web sites. *Computer Networks, 33*(1-6), 137-157.

Clavel, M., Durán, F., Eker, S., Lincoln, P., Martí-Oliet, N., Meseguer, J., & Talcote, C. (2005). *Maude Manual (Versión 2.2.)*. Retrieved from http://maude.csl.sri.com

Conallen, J. (2000). *Building Web applications with UML*. Addison Wesley.

De Castro, V., Marcos, E., & Lopez Sanz, M. (2006). Service composition modeling: A case of study. *International Journal of Web Engineering and Technology*, 335-353.

De Troyer, O., & Casteleyn, S. (2003). Modeling complex processes for Web applications using WSDM. *Proceeding of the Third International Workshop on Web Oriented Software Technology, Oviedo* (pp. 1-12).

Díaz, P., Aedo, I., & Montero, S. (2001). Ariadne, a development method for hypermedia. *Proceedings of DEXA 2001* (pp. 764-774).

Epner, M. (2000). *Poor project management number-one problem of outsourced e-projects* (Research Briefs). Cutter Consortium.

Fraternali, P. (1999). Tools and approaches for developing data-intensive Web applications: A survey. *ACM Computing Surveys, 31*(3), 227-263.

Garzotto, F., Paolini, P., & Schwabe, D. (1993, January). HDM - A model-based approach to hypertext application design. *ACM TODS, 11*(1), 1-26.

Ginige, A., & Murugesan, S. (2001). Web engineering: An introduction. *IEEE MultiMedia, 8*(1), 14-18.

Gómez, J., Cachero, C., & Pastor, O. (2000). Extending a conceptual modeling approach to Web application design. *Proceedings of the Conference on Advanced Information Systems Engineering (CAiSE'00)* (pp. 79-93). Springer-Verlag.

Hennicker, R., & Koch, N. (2000). A UML-based methodology for hypermedia design. *Proceedings of UML' 2000* (pp. 410-424).

Isakowitz, T., Stohr, E.A.S., & Balasubramanian, P. (1995). RMM: A methodology for structured hypermedia design. *Communications of the ACM, 58*(8), 34-43.

Kleppe, A., Warmer, J., & Bast, W. (2003). *MDA explained, the model driven architecture: Practice and promise*. Addison Wesley.

Lucas, F. J., Molina, F., Toval, A., de Castro, M. V., Cáceres, P., & Marcos, E. (2006). Precise WIS development. *ACM Proceedings, The Sixth International Conference on Web Engineering (ICWE'06)* (pp. 71-76), *Palo Alto, California.*

Marcos, E., Vela, B., & Cavero, J. M. (2003). Methodological approach for object-relational database design using UML. *Journal on Software and Systems Modeling (SoSyM), 2,* 59-72.

Martí-Oliet, N., & Meseguer, J. (2002). Rewriting logic: Roadmap and bibliography. *Theoretical Computer Science, 285*(2), 121-154.

Meyer, B. (1997). The next software breakthrough. *IEEE Publication, 30,* 113-114.

Miller, J., & Mukerji, J. (2003). *MDA Guide V1.0.1, OMG Document - omg/03-06-01.* Retrieved from http://www.omg.org/cgi-bin/doc?omg/03-06-01

OMG (2006). *Object Management Group.* Retrieved from http://www.omg.org/

Rozenberg, G. (Ed.). (1997). *Handbook of graph grammars and computing by graph transformation.* Singapore: World Scientific.

Schwabe, D., Esmeraldo, L., Rossi, G., & Lyardet, F. (2001). Engineering Web applications for reuse. *IEEE MultiMedia, 8*(1), 20-31.

Vara, J. M., De Castro, V., & Marcos, E. (2005). WSDL automatic generation from UML models in a MDA framework. *International Journal of Web Services Practices, 1,* 1-12.

W3C XML Schema Working Group (2003). *XML Schema Parts 0-2: Primer, Structures, Datatypes.* W3C Recommendation. Retrieved October, 2003, from http://www.w3.org/TR/xmlschema-0/, http://www.w3.org/TR/xmlschema-1/, and http://www.w3.org/TR/xmlschema-2/, 2001

KEYWORDS AND DEFINITIONS

Formal specification: Description of a model in a comprehensive and consistent way; a model can be given, for example, for an application domain, for a requirement or a set of requirements, for a software architecture, or for a program organization. It is expressed in a formal language. A formal language specifies at meta-level a syntax, a semantics, and a proof system.

Maude: Maude is a high-performance reflective language and system supporting both equational and rewriting logic specification and programming for a wide range of applications. Maude is an extensible and powerful language that allows many advanced metaprogramming and metalanguage applications. Some of the most interesting applications of Maude are metalanguage applications, in which Maude is used to create executable environments for different logics, theorem provers, languages, and models of computation.

Model / Metamodel: A model is a set of statements about some system under study. Here, *statement* means some expression about the SUS that can be considered true or false (although no truth value has necessarily to be assigned at any particular point in time). We can use a model to describe an SUS. In this case, we consider the model correct if all its statements are true for the SUS. A *metamodel* is a specification model for a class of SUS, where each SUS in the class is itself a valid model expressed in a certain modelling language. That is, a metamodel makes statements about what can be expressed in the valid models of a certain modelling language.

Model-Driven development: Its defining characteristic is that software development's primary focus and products are models rather than computer programs. The main advantage of this is that we express models using concepts that are much less bound to the underlying implementation technology and are much closer to the problem domain relative to most popular programming languages. This makes the models easier to specify, understand, and maintain; in some cases, it might even be possible for domain experts, rather than computing technology specialists, to produce systems. It also makes models less sensitive to the chosen computing technology and to evolutionary changes to that technology (the concept of platform-independent models is often closely connected to MDD).

User-Services-Oriented: A way to address the construction of the navigation model of Web Information System; the method is based on identifying conceptual user services, that is, specific services required by the user. Like this, the navigation model is focused on identifying the services required by the user and one specific route for each one of those user services that guides the navigation of the user through the WIS.

Verification: Verification tries to show that a system is being built correctly. Usually, it involves satisfying specific properties of the diagram metamodels or properties related to the system domain. This verification can be made using formal or informal methods. Checklists and algorithms, which analyze a model looking for errors or abnormal situations, are informal verification techniques. Theorem proving and model checking are formal verification techniques.

Validation: Validation analyzes whether the observable behaviour of a system is in agreement with the requirements. With regard to validation techniques, one of the most used is the scenarios and use-case simulation. This technique analyzes the system behaviour in order to ensure that it is the same as the functionality expected of the system. Simulation languages (as ASL) or tools (as Statemate) can be used.

Web engineering: This is a relatively new branch of software engineering, which addresses the specific issues related to design and development of large-scale Web applications. In particular, it focuses on the methodologies, techniques, and tools that are the foundation of complex Web application development and which support their design, development, evolution, and evaluation.

Chapter XXI
The Use of Metamodels in Web Requirements to Assure the Consistence

M.J. Escalona
University of Seville, Spain

G. Aragón
Everis, Spain

ABSTRACT

The increasing complexity and the many different aspects that should be treated at the same time require flexible but powerful methodologies to support the development process. Every day, the requirements treatment in Web environments is becoming a more critical phase because developers need suitable methods to capture, define, and validate requirements. However, it is very important that these methods assure the quality of these requirements. The model-driven engineering is opening a new way to define methodological approaches that allow control and relate concepts that have to be treated. This chapter presents a Web methodological approach to deal with requirements, NDT (navigational development techniques) based on model-driven engineering. As it is presented, NDT proposes a set of procedures, techniques, and models to assure the quality of results in the Web requirements treatment.

INTRODUCTION

Since *The Net of Nets* was born in the 1970's, as a net to spread research material, an amazing change in the use of the Internet has taken place (Cazorla & Carrasco, 2001). In the last years, the Internet and hypermedia developments have become a popular tool, and the number of users who work with it every day has grown crazily. For companies and organisations, the Internet is a suitable way to promote their businesses, as well as a powerful way to contact with their clients and employees all over the world.

Since the development of hypermedia systems in the Internet appeared, the research community has detected the need to propose new methodologies, techniques, and models in order to offer a suitable reference environment for the new and special characteristics of the Internet. That is why, in the last few years, a new research line in the software engineering has been developed: Web engineering. Web engineering *is the systematic, structured, and quantifiable application of methodological proposals to the development, evaluation, and maintenance of Web applica-*

tions (Desphande, Marugesan, Ginige, Hanse, Schawabe, Gaedke, & White, 2002).

At first, the development of Web systems was an ad hoc process. Applications were developed without following any structured process to guarantee the quality of the results. When the Web engineering appeared as a new research line, several new methodological approaches were proposed, and some surveys and comparative studies agreed that it was necessary to offer new methodological environments to deal with the special characteristics of the Web (Barry & Lang, 2001; Koch, 2001; Lang, 2002; Retschitzegger & Schwinger, 2000).

Nowadays, all over the world, the research community accepts the idea that Web projects have special characteristics (critical navigation, hypermedia, customisation, etc.) which must be carefully dealt in the life cycle and which need their own models and techniques (Deshpande et al., 2002).

In the first approaches, the most treated phase was the design phase. However, in the last few years, the research community has detected the importance of requirements. Approaches for Web requirements have to offer suitable environments to define, capture, and validate requirements. But they also have to offer appropriated ways to

assure the quality of results. In order to get these aims, the research community is proposing the use of model-driven engineering (MDE) (Schmidt, 2006). This chapter starts with a short survey of Web methodologies, and it analyses the importance of requirements. In the third section, an approach based on model-driven engineering NDT (navigational development techniques) (Escalona, 2004) is presented, and practical advantages in the use of model-driven Web engineering are analysed. In the fourth section, some related works that are offering model-driven applications in the Web engineering environment are presented. And, finally, the chapter ends with some conclusions and future works.

WEB METHODOLOGIES

In the last few years, the growing interest in the Internet has led to the generation of a high number of proposals which offers a frame of reference for the Web environment. Figure 1 shows the most representative ones in chronological order.

In the picture, the continuous lines indicate that the most recent methodologies are based on, or receive the ideas from, the previous ones. The dashed lines link the methodologies which have a same author.

Figure 1. Web methodologies

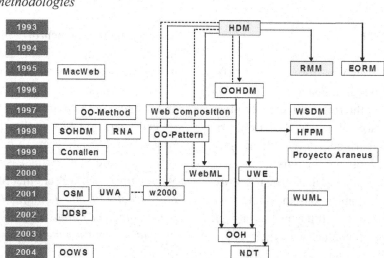

However, if these approaches are analysed, some aspects left can be concluded.

The first aspect is their life cycles. These methodologies mainly centred their works on the last phases of the life cycle. Only OOWS (Fons, Pelechano, Albert, & Pastor, 2003) and UWA (2001) offer specific treatment of Web requirements, and only some of them like RNA (Bieber, Galnares, & Lu, 1998) or UWE (Koch, 2001) cover the phase of requirements in their life cycle but without specific techniques.

The Web engineering is a very young concept, and presents a relative lack of maturity and a high ambiguity in the definition of the covering of life cycle, the performing of activities and tasks, the using of models and techniques, and the dealt aspects (Cachero, 2003). But, as it is concluded in comparative studies (Barry & Lang, 2001; Koch, 2001; Lang, 2002; Retschitzegger & Schwinger, 2000), the work is focussed on the design part. However, this trend is changing. In the last few years, research groups have detected the need to enrich their proposals with specific models for the requirements processing in the Web. Thus, proposals like OOHDM (Schwabe & Rossi, 1998), which did not consider the requirements phase in its first versions, now include a concrete phase which proposes to take into account the use cases and an own technique named UIDs (Vilain, Schwabe, & Sieckenius, 2002) to represent Web requirements.

The empirical experience shows that, because of the growing complexity of Web systems, each day it is becoming more and more important to capture the needed requirements to model specific characteristic of the Web environment. However, empirical results also conclude that sometimes it is very difficult to translate users' necessities into Web analysis models.

The keeping of the consistence between models in different phases of the life cycle, is a very important aspect to assure the quality of the results. This aspect acquires a critical character in the requirements phase. Frequently, require-ments are defined using nonformal models, and the translation into analysis models depends on the analyst's experience.

An actual research trend to keep the consistence is the use of model-driven approaches (Schmidt, 2006). In model-driven Web engineering, concepts are the most important, independent of the way to represent them. MDWE proposes to represent concepts using metamodels. The development process is supported with a set of transformations and relations between concepts that make the development more agile and assure the consistence between models.

The power of MDWE is provoking so much interest that classical approaches are evolving to this new paradigm. For instance, in Moreno, Fraternali, and Vallecillo (2006) and Schauerhuber, Wimmer, and Kapsammer (2006), metamodels for WebML (Ceri, Fraternali, & Bongio. 2000) are presented, or in Baresi, Garzoto, and Maritati (2002), a metamodel for W2000 (Baresi, Garzotto, & Paolini, 2001) is offered. Even some initial model-driven approaches, like UWE (Koch, 2001), are evolving to the new standard defined by the OMG like the use of QVT (OMG, 2004) for defining transformations (Koch, 2006).

Another important issue in Web engineering is the need of using standard aspects. There are too many methods, techniques, and terminologies defining the same concept. As it is presented in the next section, MDWE also solves this aspect. In MDWE, the way to represent aspects is not the important fact. MDWE works with concepts independently of the artefact to represent it.

In conclusion, in the last few years an important increase of Web methodologies can be detected. However, two important aspects have to be considered in them:

1. Requirements phase is a very important phase for the Web methodologies real application. The incorporation of final users and clients to define systems necessities is fundamental in Web development to assure the quality of results.

2. The necessity of offering suitable procedures to assure the consistence between phases is the way to get suitable results in the Web development. These procedures have to be as mechanical as possible in order to be useful for companies in the enterprise environment.

NDT (NAVIGATIONAL DEVELOPMENT TECHNIQUES)

NDT is a methodological approach to deal with requirements in Web Environments. NDT was proposed in order to support the requirements engineering and the analysis phase of Web Systems, and it is based on the model-driven engineering paradigm.

As it was introduced in the previous section, several comparative studies have proved that one of the less-treated phases in Web engineering is the requirements phase (Barry & Lang, 2001; Koch, 2001; Lang, 2002; Retschitzegger & Schwinger,, 2000). Most approaches in Web engineering are focused on analysis and design phases. They usually propose to use classical requirements techniques, like use cases, in order to capture and define requirements in Web environments.

Although the technique of use cases is suitable to deal with requirements and it is usually very easily understood by the user, they are frequently very ambiguous (Insfran, Pastor, & Wieringa, 2001; Vilain et al., 2002). For this reason, in the last few years, several research groups are working in specific requirements treatments for the Web environment. For instance, OOHDM has proposed the UID (User Interaction Diagrams) (Vilain et al., 2002), a specific technique to deal with interaction requirements.

Another conclusion from comparatives studies is that, in Web engineering, different aspects of software are treated in different ways. This idea is supported in the analysis and design phases for several approaches. OOHDM, WSDM (De Troyer

& Leune, 1998), WebML, or OOH (Cachero, 2003), where conceptual, navigational, interaction, and so forth, aspects are modelled with different models, are only some examples. This idea of concept separation can be advantageous to the requirements phase. UWE deals separately with information requirements, functional requirements, and so forth; W2000 defines different use cases for functional and navigational requirements.

Finally, another important fact detected by the comparative studies is that sometimes requirements are defined in a very ambiguous way, and it is very difficult for the analysis to translate the knowledge from the requirements definition to the analysis models.

Using these ideas, NDT was developed; it proposes a MDE approach in order to offer a suitable environment to capture, define, analyze, and validate Web requirements. In the next section, NDT will be presented, followed by a brief view of its life cycle and its structure. Immediately following this, a metamodel for NDT is offered.

NDT is not only a theoretical approach; it is being applied in several real projects in companies in Andalusia. Later in the chapter, the advantages of using an approach based on MDE in our real projects are analyzed.

Introduction to NDT

NDT was born from some exhaustive comparative studies between Web proposals. NDT proposes a complete and detailed requirements phase to systematically acquire the analysis models of Web systems. It is an approach to specify and analyze Web information systems.

NDT development process can be defined as a bottom-up process. The development process is focussed on a very detailed requirements definition guided by objectives, which covers three sub-phases: *requirements capture, requirements definition,* and *requirements validation.* NDT only covers the first phases in the life cycle. It is a bottom-up process where models are independent. Also, it is necessary to emphasize that workflows in NDT going from requirements to analysis are systematic. These workflows are defined using the MDE paradigm, as it will be presented. The necessity of offering systematic process to develop Web design models has been detected by several research groups. These workflows can even automatic be if the development team uses its associated tool of NDT, NDT-Tool (Escalona, Mejías, & Torres, 2003).

The process starts by defining objectives. Using a described procedure, requirements are captured and defined. Requirements are classified and dealt with depending on whether they are: *information storage requirements, actors' requirements, functional requirements, interaction requirements,* or *nonfunctional requirements*. In this sense, NDT follows the idea of concept separation used by other approaches.

These requirements are described in NDT using some special defined patterns. A pattern is a template with specific fields which must be completed by the developer. When requirements are validated, the NDT process continues defining three models:

- *the conceptual model*, which is a class diagram; it expresses the static view of the system;
- *the navigational model*, which shows how users can navigate in the system; and
- *the abstract interface model*, which shows the abstract interface of the system.

One of the main contributions of the NDT process is that it offers a systematic way to get analysis models from requirements, which makes each model independent. It is systematic because NDT offers transformations which indicate how each model has to be obtained from the requirements definition. In NDT, the different models are related between them because each of them represents a different aspect of the same system. However, they are independent because each of them can be obtained independently from the requirements. When the development team applies these transformations, they obtain the

Figure 2. NDT development process

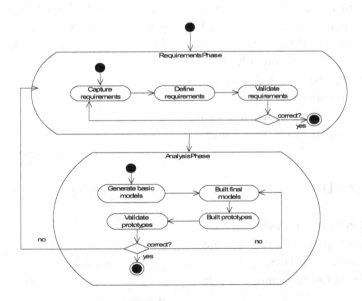

basic models: *the conceptual basic model, the navigational basic model, and the basic abstract interface model.*

These basic models can be modified in order to obtain models more suitable to the system. In this way, they obtain *the final conceptual model, the final navigational model, and the final abstract interface model.* The step from basic models to final models is not automatic because it requires analysts' experience to be applied. However, NDT offers some guides and heuristics to get them.

The navigation and the conceptual models are class diagrams. However, the abstract interface model is a set of evaluated prototypes. Users and customers can evaluate these prototypes. This section is the last one in the NDT life cycle. Starting with developed models and making sure that they are correct, the development team can apply other Web methodologies like UWE or OOHDM to deal with other following phases like design and implementation.

The main objective of NDT is to offer systematic processes to build models which other Web methodologies use as the starting point of their development process and to guarantee the quality of these models. Thus, we can conclude that NDT is not a complete Web methodological proposal. It is a methodological procedure to get a conceptual, a navigational, and an abstract interface model from the users' requirements. This methodological procedure is based on the MDE paradigm. It allows to assure the consistence between requirements and concepts in the analysis phase.

To conclude with this short presentation, an activity diagram describes the NDT development process in Figure 2.

A Metamodel for NDT

As it was presented in the previous section, NDT offers systematic ways to go from the requirements model to the analysis models. These systematic ways are possible for the use of the model-driven paradigm.

Following the architecture defined by MDA (model-driven architecture) (OMG, 2003), the requirements artefacts of NDT are defined using a CIM metamodel. In the analysis phase, a group of PIM metamodels are also defined. With a group of formal transformations, the group of metamodels in the PIM level can be systematically derived from the CIM metamodel. In Figure 3, this idea is presented.

In classical Web engineering, ideas detected in the requirements phase must be translated into concepts by analysts in the analysis models. Analysts' experience was essential and critical in this step. In the MDWE paradigm, the definition of the process is different. In each phase of the life cycle, concepts are studied, detected, and defined using a metamodel. Concepts in each metamodel are studied and related with other concepts in other metamodels. For instance, in the requirements phase of NDT the concept storage information requirement is defined, and in the analysis phase the concept conceptual class is detected. A storage information requirement defined by the user will be present in a conceptual class in the analysis conceptual model. These rules and relations define the set of systematic transformations.

But transformations not only make easier the translation of concepts; they also assure the consistence between phases in the life cycle. Thus, using the same example, each storage in-

Figure 3. NDT model-driven approach

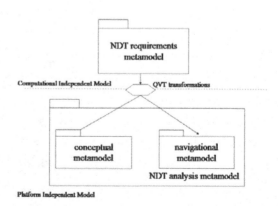

formation requirement has to be translated into a class in the analysis. If a storage information requirement is not represented by a class in the analysis conceptual model, a requirement is lost in the development process.

In its first version, NDT metamodels were not MOF metamodels, and transformations were not based in any formal language for transformations. However, nowadays, NDT metamodels are defined using a UML profile, and transformations are being defined using QVT.

The proposed metamodel for NDT in the requirements phase is presented in Figure 4. This requirements metamodel follows the structure of WebRe (Escalona & Koch, 2006b). WebRe is an approach of metamodel for requirements in Web engineering that groups concepts of different approaches: NDT, W2000, UWE, and UIDs of OOHDM.

However, in this case, this metamodel has been extended in order to support all the aspect of NDT requirements phase. The metamodel is divided into two packages: the *Behaviour* and the *Structure*. In the first package, concepts related with the behaviour of the system are presented.

In this package, classes represent conduct aspects. With the *WebUser*, class represents any actor in the system. As it was presented, the study of actor requirements is a very complex phase of NDT. Not only does it detect different users in the systems, but it also studies their relations. For this reason, in the metamodel, the relation of *incompatible* was included. Two actors are incompatible when their role cannot be *play* at the same time for the same person.

Another class in the behaviour package is the *WebUseCase* Class. This class represents the group of functional requirements of the systems. When a functional requirement includes any transactional activity, this functional requirement is an instance of *WebTransactionalUseCase*.

Finally, in the behaviour package a group of classes that represent activities is included. These are *Browse*, *Phase,* and *Transaction. Browse* represents navigation activities in the system without any transaction activity. *Phase* is a kind of activity that defines queries and search activities. And finally, *Transaction* represents activities where transactions are executed.

Figure 4. NDT requirements metamodel

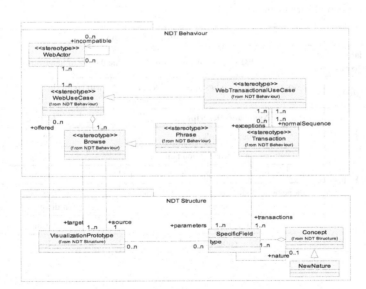

369

Figure 5. NDT requirements profile

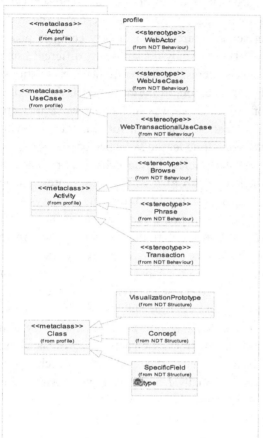

In the structure package, *Concept* class represents any information storage by the system. Each Concept is composed of a group of *SpecificField*. Each SpecificField defines each piece of information stored by the Concept.

NDT defines a special concept named *NewNature*. NewNature is a kind of Concept that represents global data structures in the company, not for the system. For instance, the definition of personal data of users must be stored in the same way in each system in the company. Thus the structure of this information is a new nature.

This metamodel is based on UML artefacts. For this reason, a profile for it can be defined. In Figure 5, this profile is presented.

Although these concepts could be represented with UML artefacts, in NDT the selected technique to define requirements are patterns. As it was presented, patterns are tables with specific fields to collect any piece of information specific for each concept.

In NDT, the structured way to define requirements that is offered by the patterns is very important. In Table 1, an example of pattern is presented. This pattern represents the definition of a storage information requirement taken from

Table 1. A storage requirements pattern

RA-01	Patient's Basic Data	
Associated Objectives	OBJ-01: to manage automatically the degree of handicap	
Description	The storage information has to be confidential, and it will controlled by a high security system.	
Specific Fields	**Name and Description**	**Nature**
	Name: patient's name	String
	DNI: patient's identification number	String
	Birth data: the data when the patient was born	String
	Phone number: the contact patient's phone number	Number Cardinality: 1..n
	E-mail: patient's email	String
	Weight: patient's weight	Real

a real project defined completely in Villadiego, Escalona, Torres, and Mejías (2004). It represents the necessity of storing information about patients in a medical system.

In this pattern, we find special fields necessary to define storage requirements. The first one is the identifier of the requirements, RA-01, and its name. The Associated Objectives field stores the objectives of the system that will be gotten (or partially gotten) by the implementation of the requirement. Finally, in the field of specific fields, the specific piece of data storage for each patient is presented. Similar patterns are defined for each kind of requirements in the project.

Patterns are essential in all the life cycle of NDT. They offer a very structured definition of requirements, very useful for analysts in the analysis phase. But they also offer a suitable definition for users. Patterns are completely defined using the user's language. Thus, they can be easily valuated by them.

Patterns also offer a suitable way to represent each concept and relation in the metamodel. Thus, storage information requirements are instances of the Concept class. With the field *SpecificField*, the relation between each Concept and Specific Field is represented.

In the next phase of NDT, the analysis phase, some metamodels are used. However, as it was noted, most approaches of Web engineering offer models and techniques for the analysis phase. For this reason, NDT does not offer new models. After some comparative studies (Escalona & Koch, 2004; Escalona et al., 2006), NDT assumes UWE metamodel for the analysis phase. Thus, NDT uses Conceptual and Navigational metamodel of UWE (Kraus & Koch, 2003) in the analysis phase.

The election of UWE is based in the use of UML. UWE metamodels are completely based on UML, and they have a suitable defined profile.

In conclusion, NDT is a Web approach focused on the first phases of the life cycle. It offers a model-driven development process in order to assure the consistence of the model and to make

easier the development of each model in each phase. It is completely oriented to the interaction between the development team and the final user with the use of pattern, and its development process is supported by a tool named NDT-Tool. In this sense, NDT seeks to cover a gap in the Web engineering, offering a detailed requirements approach that is compatible with other accepted approaches, mainly UWE.

Practical Conclusions

As stated previously, NDT is being used in several real projects. In Escalona et al. (2006), a complete evolution of the approach and its applications can be found. Nowadays, NDT has been used as a requirement approach by the Culture Government in Andalusia (www.juntadeandalucia.es/cultura/) and by the Andalusian Health Service (Servicio Andaluz de Salud, http://www.juntadeandalucia.es/servicioandaluzdesalud). Besides these, some private companies, like Everis, have included NDT in their projects.

For this reason, NDT model-driven approach has been tested by real development teams, and it was applied in real development environments. These experiences were a good feedback for our research results. In this section, some advantages detected in the use of metamodels are presented.

Advantages of Metamodels for Tools

Although NDT has an associated tool, NDT-Tool, it is, in fact, not prepared for very big projects. In a special collaboration with the Andalusian Health Service, NDT was selected as the requirements methodology. This project, named Diraya, is a very ambitious project to manage any information in any hospital in Andalusia. It will be implanted in 34 hospitals in Andalusia, and it will be used by more than 62,000 final users composed of doctors, nurses, and so forth. It is being developed by six companies, and the number of people in the development team is more than 34.

In order to find a suitable tool for this project, we made a comparative study of commercial tools. Nowadays, several commercial tools are offering the possibility of including metamodels and transformation rules. Enterprise Architecture, Rational Rose, or IRqA are only some examples. Although for Diraya the final selection was Enterprise Architecture, in fact, other possibilities were available for the project.

The evolution of the tools to MDE and the definition of approaches using metamodel and standard transformation languages open a high number of possibilities for companies. They can select the most suitable tool for them according to their preferences, their licences, their internal elections, and so forth.

For us, the fact of having metamodels to define NDT was an important advantage in practical collaboration in order to offer an extensive tool catalogue.

Advantages of Metamodels for Fusing Approaches

In the Diraya project, there was an important requirement defined by the health environment: They need to use HL7. HL7 is a standard for the communication of health information systems. HL7 is defined by a set of metamodels. It has four metamodels: for *use cases and interaction*, for the *information model*, for the *message design,* and for *data type and vocabulary*. In the Diraya project, NDT was used for the requirements and the analysis phase. However, HL7 had to be used in the design phase. Using metamodels, we developed a set of transformation rules that were used in the translation between NDT analysis models and HL7 metamodels.

In the Culture Government, a similar situation appeared. They have some standard metamodels to deal with bibliography and documental artefacts in historical archives.

This experience proved that metamodels were very useful to fuse different approaches. These advantages can also be used to make compatible different approaches that work with the same concepts, although they use different artefacts for representing them, like it was presented in Escalona et al. (2006).

Advantages of Metamodels for Assuring the Consistence

The use of metamodels is also very interesting in assuring the consistence. When a group of analysts interview a group of users to define systems requirements, they capture the definition of users, their problems, and their expectations. However, analysts are thinking in their languages: computer models. When analysts are capturing requirements, they are mentally creating the analysis models for the systems. This prevision of the model is necessary to get the best requirements from the users, but sometimes the preview hides or conditions the analyst perception.

In the Diraya project, a very interesting conclusion was obtained. Analysts defined requirements using patterns according to users' requirements. When the basic analysis models were systematically defined from the requirements, they discovered that their mental models were not the same that the models defined by the users. Thus, they detected the inconsistence, and they had to review requirements and models in order to get the best one.

MDWE lets derive the analysis models described in the requirements necessities, and it offers an important measure of the consistence and, obviously, an improvement of the final quality.

Important Weak Points

In the enterprise environment, however, we also find some important weak points in the use of metamodels. The most important one is the lack of experience in the use of metamodels. Development teams and final users are not in the habit of working with concepts and transformations. The idea of metamodels and abstract concepts are not clear for them, and, in our experience we had to work very hard in this line.

Besides this, although transformations help them to keep the consistence and to reduce the development time, the idea of transforming one model to another model is not very extended in the enterprise environment.

However, when the development team knows and understands this new idea for working, they face the advantages. Obviously, the application of model-driven approaches requires an initial inversion in the project to train the development team. In our experiences, the use of pattern was very positive for explaining how the metamodel concepts were used in practice because, as previously mentioned, they are very clear for the user and they represent the metamodel in a very simple way.

RELATED WORK

MDWE is being used more every day in the Web engineering environment. As it was shown, it offers important benefits for the development, the consistence, and the definition of concepts. This tendency is also being followed in the requirements phase.

One of the most recent works is Valderas, Pelechano, and Pastor (2006). This paper presents an approach to transform a Web requirements model to a set of prototypes. They propose a requirements treatment based on the task metaphor. Valderas et al. offer an extension of this approach to deal with the specific characteristics of Web requirements. After that, they present a way to derive the navigational model of OOWS (Fons et al., 2003). Firstly, they propose to define requirements like tasks; these tasks are translated into an AGG Graph. Using Graphs transformations, analysis models are obtained. The approach is supported with a tool that is available. This work is very interesting because they offer a suitable

solution for transformation supported by a tool. However, its transformations are not based in OMG tendencies. This shows that they are not compatible with other similar approaches.

In Escalona and Koch (2006b), the power of metamodels is presented. In comparative studies about Web approaches, a general conclusion is that similar concepts are used or represented with a different number of models, techniques, or artefacts. Thus, for instance, navigational classes are presented with different elements in UWE, OOHDM, or WebML. In their study, Escalona and Koch show how a metamodel can represent a concept independently of its representation or notation; only concepts are important. They present a metamodel for Web requirements, named WebRe, which represents requirements models of W2000, NDT, OOHDM, and UWE. In Koch, Zhang, and Escalona (2006), they continue their works using QVT to get analysis models from this metamodel. These works are interesting because they are completely based on UML (OMG, 2005) and QVT, with standards defined by OMG. However, the study results are too theoretical.

Fernández and Mozón (2000) present the possibilities of working with metamodels and tools. They present how a requirements metamodel can be easily defined in IRqA (Integral Requisite Analyzer). IRqA is a commercial tool that lets define metamodels for requirements. In this sense, their study presents the power of tools that support metamodels because they are suitable for any approach which is defined using metamodels. Their work is very practical, in fact, but it is not an approach for Web environments. They do not offer specific artefacts to deal with Web environments; they only offer an approach for classical requirements treatment.

However, although these works are specific for requirements, other classical approaches are working in the MDE environment. For instance in Moreno, Fraternali, and Vallecillo (2006) and Schauerhuber, Wimmer, and Kapsammer (2006), some metamodels for WebML can be found. They present how metamodels can represent classical concepts independent of the artefact used to represent them.

In their study, Meliá and Gómez (2005) present an approach, WebSA (Web Software Architecture). WebSA provides the designer with a set of architectural models and transformation models to specify a Web application. Although they work in the design phase, their approach is very interesting because they follow MDA and QVT in a very exhaustive way.

To conclude, MDA and, in a more general way, the use of metamodels and the model-driven engineering is a field of the software engineering that is being more accepted every day in the Web engineering environment.

CONCLUSION AND FUTURE WORKS

This chapter has presented an approach based on model-driven engineering named NDT. NDT is a methodology based on the requirements and analysis phases that uses the power of metamodels to assure the consistence between phases and to make easier the development process. The chapter presents NDT as an example of Web approach, and it offers the practical experience in the application of MDWE in the enterprise environment.

The use of model-driven paradigm in Web engineering is being proposed by several research groups, as it was presented in this chapter, and it is opening a new important research line that tries to solve some classical problems in Web engineering:

1. To make the development process more agile with the use of derivation processes;
2. To assure the consistence between phases with the use of metamodels; and
3. To get a common language in different approaches, using the definition of concepts in metamodels.

As upcoming future work, we have three important lines. The first one is oriented to the practical use of model-driven Web engineering. As we mentioned in the chapter, we collaborate with several companies in the applications of these research results. Thus, nowadays, we collaborate as a quality consultancy in the Diraya project and in other important projects with the Andalusian Government, like Mosaico. In these collaborations, we make certain that the application of NDT and its model-driven procedure are being applied correctly. In doing this, we get important feedback for our research results.

Another important future work is the research in tools. As shown, the use of UML profiles is very useful for adapting commercial tools, like Enterprise Architecture, to our approach. However, these commercial tools usually offer their own transformation languages, and they are not based on standard. For this reason, we are looking for tools that allow to define QVT transformations. Nowadays, we are analysing SmartQVT (Schmidt, 2006) and Moment (Queralt, Hoyos, Boronat, Carsí, & Ramos, 2006). Both of them support QVT, although we have just started to value them.

Finally, we have another important open line in the fusion of approaches. As it was mentioned previously, comparative studies conclude that there are too many approaches, techniques, or processes in the Web engineering. However, as it is analysed in Escalona et al. (2006), concepts are the same in different approaches. For us, it is very important to analyse other approaches' metamodels and compare them with the NDT metamodel. These comparisons allow us to analyse common and different ideas in each approach, as well as the advantages and disadvantages of each one. The use of metamodel to compare or make compatible Web engineering approaches is easier when they are MOF metamodels or when an UML profile is defined. In this sense, the classical problem of multiple terminologies for the same concept or the same terminology for different concepts detected in surveys or comparative studies is lost. The use of metamodels allows us to focus the work only on the most important aspect, the concepts.

REFERENCES

Baresi, L., Garzoto, F., & Maritati, M. (2002). W2000 as a MOF metamodel. *Proceedings of the 6th World Multiconference on Systemics, Cybernetics, Informatics—Web engineering track.* Vol 1.

Baresi L., Garzotto, F., & Paolini, P. (2001). Extending UML for modeling Web applications. *Proceedings of the Annual Hawaii International Conference on System Sciences, Miami, FL* (pp. 1285-1294).

Barry, C., & Lang, M. (2001). A survey of multimedia and Web development techniques and methodology usage. *IEEE Multimedia*, (April-July), 52-56.

Bieber, M., Galnares, R., & Lu, Q. (1998). Web engineering and flexible hypermedia. *Proceedings of the 2nd Workshop on Adaptative Hypertext and Hypermedia* (pp. 75-78).

Cachero, C. (2003). *An extension to the OO methods for the modelling and automatic generation of hypermedial interfaces.* Doctoral thesis, University of Alicante.

Cazorla, A., & Carrasco, J. (2001). Internet evolution. *Telefónica communication I+D.*

Ceri, S., Fraternali, P., & Bongio, A. (2000). Web modelling language (WebML): A modelling language for designing Web sites. *Proceedings of the Conference WWW9/Computer Networks: Vol. 33*(1-6) (pp. 137-157).

Deshpande, Y., Marugesan, S., Ginige, A., Hanse, S., Schawabe, D., Gaedke, M., & White, B. (2002). Web engineering. *Journal of Web engineering, 1*(1), 3-17.

De Troyer, O., & Leune, C. (1998). WSDM: A user-centered design method for Web sites. Computer networks and ISDN systems. *Proceedings of the 7th International World Wide Web Conference* (pp. 85- 94). Elsevier.

Escalona, M. J. (2004). *Modelos y técnicas para la especificación y el análisis de la navegación en sistemas software.* Doctoral thesis, University of Seville, Spain.

Escalona, M. J., Gutierrez, J. J., Villadiego, D., León, A., & Torres, A. H. (2006a). Practical experience in Web engineering. *Proceedings of the 15th Interantional Conference on Information System Development (ISD 2006)* (pp. 421-434). *Budapest, Czeck Republic.*

Escalona, M. J., & Koch, N. (2004). Requirements engineering for Web applications: A comparative study. *Journal on Web engineering, 2*(3), 193-212.

Escalona, M. J., & Koch, N. (2006b). Metamodelling the requirements of Web systems. *Proceedings of the 2nd International Conference on Web Information Systems and Technologies (WebIST 2006), Setúbal, Portugal* (pp. 310-317).

Escalona, M. J, Mejías, M., & Torres, J. (2003). NDT-Tool: A tool case to deal with requirements in Web information systems. *Proceedings of IV International Conferences on Web engineering* (pp. 212-213). Springer Verlag.

Fernández, J. L., & Monzón, A. (2000). A metamodel and a tool for software requirements management. *Reliable Software Technologies.* Ada-Europe, Germany.

Fons, J., Pelechano, V., Albert, M., & Pastor, O. (2003). Development of Web applications from Web enhanced conceptual schemas. *Proceedings of the 22nd IS International Conference on Conceptual Modeling (ER), Chicago, Illinois (EE. UU.)* (pp. 232-245). Springer Verlag.

Insfrán, E., Pastor, O., & Wieringa, R. (2002). Requirements engineering-based conceptual modelling. *Requirements Engineering Journal, 7*(1), 61-72.

HL7. (2007). Retrieved from http://www.hl7. org/

Koch, N. (1999). *A comparative study of methods for hypermedia development* (Tech. Rep. 9905). Munich, Germany: Ludwig-Maximilian-University.

Koch, N. (2001). Software engineering for adaptive hypermedia applications. Doctoral thesis, *FAST Reihe Softwaretechnik Vol. 12*. Munich, Germany: Uni-Druck Publishing Company.

Koch, N. (2006). Transformations techniques in the model-driven development process of UWE. *Proceedings of the 2nd Model-Driven Web engineering Workshop (MDWE 2006)* (Vol. 155). Palo Alto, CA: ACM.

Koch, N., Zhang, G., & Escalona, M. J. (2006). Model transformations from requirements to Web system design. *ACM International Conference Proceeding Series: Proceedings of the 6th International Conference on Web engineering (ICWE 2006), Palo Alto, CA* (pp. 281-288). ACM.

Kraus, A., & Koch, N. (2003). *A metamodel for UWE* (Tech. Rep. 0301). Ludwig-Maximilians-Universität München.

Lang, M. (2002). Hypermedia system development. Do we really need new methods? Site-where parallels intersect. *Informing Science*, 883-891.

Meliá, S., & Gómez, J. (2005). Applying transformations to model driven development of Web applications. *Proceedings of ER Workshops, 2005* (pp. 63-73)

Moreno, N., Fraternali, P., & Vallecillo, A. (2006). A UML 2.0 profile for WebML modelling. *Proceedings of the II International Workshop on Model-Driven Web engineering* (vol 155.). *Palo Alto, CA.*

OMG (2003). *MDA Guide, Version 1.0.1*. Retrieved from http://www.omg.org/docs/omg/03-06-01.pdf

OMG (2005). *Unified Modeling Language: Superstructure, version 2.0. Specification, Object Management Group*. Retrieved from http://www.omg.org/cgi-bin/doc?formal/05-07-04

Queralt, P., Hoyos, L., Boronat, A., Carsí, J. A., & Ramos, I. (2006). Un motor de transformación de modelos con soporte para el lenguaje QVT relations. *III Taller sobre Desarrollo de Software Dirigido por Modelos*. MDA y Aplicaciones (DSDM'06). España.

Query QVT-Merge Group (2004). Revised submission for MOF 2.0 query/views/ transformations RFP. *Object Management Group*. Retrieved from http://www.omg.org/cgi-bin/apps/doc?ad/04-04-01.pdf.

Retschitzegger, W., & Schwinger, W. (2000). Towards modelling of data Web applications - A requirements perspective. *Proceedings of the American Conference on Information Systems, AMCIS 2000: Vol. 1* (pp. 149-155).

Schauerhuber, A., Wimmer, M., & Kapsammer, E. (2006). Bridging existing Web modeling languages to model-driven engineering: A metamodel for WebML. *Proceedings of the II International Workshop on Model-Driven Web engineering* (vol. 155). *Palo Alto, CA.*

Schmidt, D. C. (2006, February). Model-driven engineering. *IEEE Computer*, 25-31.

Schwabe, D., & Rossi, G. (1998). *An object oriented approach to Web-based application design, theory, and practice of object systems 4(4)*. New York: Wiley and Sons.

SmartQVT. Retrieved from http://sourceforge. net/projects/smartqvt

UWA (2001). *UWA Requirements Elicitation: Model, Notation, and Tool Architecture*. Retrieved from www.uwaproject.org

Valderas, P., Pelechano, V., & Pastor, O. (2006). A transformational approach to produce Web application prototypes from a Web requirements model. *International Journal of Web engineering and Technology (IJWET)*, 1476-1289.

Vilain, P., Schwabe, D., & Sieckenius, C. (2002). *A diagrammatic tool for representing user interaction in UML. (UML '2000)* (LNCS, pp. 133-147). York, England.

Villadiego, D., Escalona, M. J., Torres, J., & Mejías, M. (2004). *Application of NDT to the system for the recognition, declaration, and qualification of the handicap grade* (Int. Rep. LSI-2004-02). University of Seville.

KEY TERMS

Software engineering: Techniques, models, and processes to develop quality software

Model-driven engineering: Paradigm of software engineering where the development of software is directed using models and transformations

Requirements: Set of necessities defined by users or experts in a software system.

Requirements treatment: Set of techniques, models, and processes to elicit, define, and validate requirements in Web development

Software quality assurance: Group of techniques and methods to assure that the developed software is according to system requirements

Chapter XXII
A Quality–Aware Engineering Process for Web Applications

Cristina Cachero Castro
Universidad de Alicante, Spain

Coral Calero
University of Castilla-La Mancha, Spain

Yolanda Marhuenda García
Universidad Miguel Hernández de Elche, Spain

ABSTRACT

This chapter introduces the necessity to consider quality management activities as part of the Web engineering (WE) process to improve the final quality of Web applications with respect to creative practices. We explore principles and achievements that, uncovered in different Web quality lines of research, provide insights into how to deal with quality in each of the different workflows that a typical WE process defines, from requirements to implementation. Also, in order to preserve the semiautomatic nature of WE processes, we propose the definition of measurable concepts, measures, and decision criteria in a machine-readable way that facilitate the automation of the quality evaluation process, thus preserving the model-driven engineering (MDE) nature of WE processes. In this way, we are providing the user of a WE methodology with the advantages associated with managing quality from the early stages of development with little extra development costs.

INTRODUCTION

It is an avowed fact that WE practices, understood as the application of systematic, disciplined, and quantifiable approaches to the cost-effective development and evolution of high-quality applications in the World Wide Web (Heuser, 2004), lack an impact on industry (Lang & Fitzgerald,

2005). We can name at least two possible reasons for this behaviour:

- From the point of view of Web developers, it is too hazardous to decide on the use of a methodology that systematizes the Web application construction, due to the small amount of reliable information available on methodologies, technologies, and tools. In fact, just around 5% of the claims of the WE field about improved time-to-market and reduced development costs are based on actual facts, even if it is well-known that conventional wisdom, intuition, conjecture, and proofs of concepts are known not to be reliable sources of credible knowledge (Mendes, 2005); and
- From the point of view of the final user of the application, the use by the Web developers of a WE methodology does not guarantee any kind of improvement on the quality in use of the deployed applications. In fact, it has been empirically assessed that, while Web stakeholders' interest is focused, besides cost and time-to-market, on usability and visual appearance (Calero, Ruiz, & Piatinni, 2005), these concerns are just tangentially tackled in Web methodologies.

We believe that this situation is a clear symptom of the immatureness of the field. There is a lack of reliable data that empirically supports all the WE claims (reduced costs, time-to-market, and better quality in use of the developed applications). Although the existence of WE tools is already permitting to gather project data that are corroborating the WE claims regarding costs and time-to-market, we are still far from being able to assure that, merely by following a given WE methodology, the developed application is going to comply with a set of predefined quality requirements. In fact, WE development processes do not even consider specific support for this type of requirements. As far as we know, only

WebSA (Meliá & Gómez, 2006), which tackles architectural issues that may influence some aspects related to the final quality in use of the application, is an exception in this sense.

We do believe that this situation should be reversed if we aim at increasing the confidence of industry on our methodologies. Unfortunately, the WE community is not yet familiar with systematic quality evaluation issues, and therefore tools and guidelines to ease this shift are necessary. Concretely, a general framework is needed in WE to guide the way in which WE methodologies are able to:

- Assure the quality of the different WE development processes (i.e., process quality), and empirically prove the advantages that they provide to analysts, designers, developers, and maintainers compared to creative approaches. Given the fact that WE processes are commonly based on the MDE paradigm (Kent, 2002), this process quality involves assessing the quality of the semi-automated transformations defined as part of any WE methodology;
- Assure the quality of the WE intermediate artifacts (i.e., internal product quality). These artifacts correspond with the intermediate models generated as part of the process, and it should be empirically proven how they help (indeed) to manage the complexity of Web development;
- Assure the quality of the application that is delivered using such methodologies under testing conditions (i.e., external product quality), and how it relates to the internal product quality; and
- Assure the quality of the application that is delivered using such methodologies under real conditions of use (i.e., quality in use), and how it relates to the external and internal product quality.

For these assurances to stop being a utopia, the first step consists in defining how quality evaluation issues can be incorporated at the different levels of abstraction defined by WE methodologies. As an additional requirement, this incorporation should take place without hampering the cost and/or time to market of the delivered application.

In order to cover this objective, we present in this chapter how quality requirements can be expressed as software artifacts. In our approach, such artifacts are called measurement models, and they are based on underlying quality models that are particular to each level of abstraction. Additionally, we illustrate how specific quality evaluation activities that take as input such measurement models can be included in a typical WE process to assess the internal quality of the traditional WE artifacts (requirements, domain, navigation, presentation, and implementation models). We justify why such internal quality assessment can be used as a predictor of the quality in use of the resulting Web application. The inclusion of measurement models and quality assessment activities, together with the justification of the relationship between internal quality and quality in use, clearly improves the capability of WE methodologies to provide Web applications that are of better quality than those developed with creative practices.

In order to frame our proposal, in the next section we present an overview of existing work on quality models, with special emphasis on usability models, Web quality models, conceptual model quality evaluation, and quality assurance processes. The third section presents our proposal for the enrichment of a typical WE process with quality assessment activities. In the first subsection, we present how it is possible to operationalize WE quality models as WE measurement models which are instantiations of an ontology-based measurement metamodel. This ontology support contributes to avoid terminology inconsistencies, while the use of a metamodel assures the syntactic correctness of the WE measurement model (including completeness restrictions and focus on specific stakeholders and specific WE artifacts). The second subsection integrates the different WE quality models and their corresponding WE measurement models into a WE quality evaluation process that can be seamlessly integrated with a generic WE development process. It also presents how such WE quality evaluation process is compliant with the ISO 14598. The third subsection briefly explains how the use of WE measurement models and standard QVT-based transformation rules permit the definition of both evaluation and evolution actions over WE models. Also, they make possible that the resulting WE quality-aware development process still preserves the semiautomatic nature of the WE traditional processes. Finally, in the fourth section, conclusions and further lines of research are presented.

QUALITY FRAMEWORKS

Quality Concepts

All along the years, many different definitions of quality have been proposed. Garvin (1984) proposes five different perspectives of quality: transcendental view, user view, manufacturing view, product view, and value-based view. Two of them are especially relevant from the point of view of Software Engineering (SE) in general and WE in particular:

- **Conformance to specification (manufacturing view)**: Quality is defined as a matter of products whose measurable characteristics satisfy a fixed-beforehand defined specification. Its importance lies in the fact that this perspective can be assessed early in the application development cycle; and
- **Meeting customer needs (user view)**: Quality is defined, independent of any measurable characteristic, as the product capability to

meet customer expectations, whether these are explicit or not. Its importance lies in the fact that this perspective reflects the final objective of any software development.

Both quality understood as *conformance to specification* and as *meeting customer needs* have been a continuous concern for Web developers, due to the necessity for most of these applications to keep the audience coming back to the site (Fraternali & Paolini, 2000). Talking in terms of the OMG Standard Metapyramid (ISO/IEC 10027, 1990) (see Figure 1), the Web quality evaluation effort has been traditionally centred on the M1-Implementation level (measures over the application code, without running it, such as fonts, colours, position of menus) and M0-test level of abstraction (code running under testing conditions, such as the use of network resources, page load time, etc.) (Calero et al., 2005). These two levels are reflected in the myriad of design guidelines (Nielsen, 2000) and automated measures (Ivory, 2004) that have been gathered in literature as relevant for Web development. While guidelines are, for the most part, ambiguous and hard to follow (Ivory & Megraw, 2005), Web measures over the implementation level have showed themselves as a systematic and accurate way of

evaluating products. In fact, quality assessment of Web interfaces, with the help of measures, matches in some cases up to 80% of the results based on expert evaluation of the same Web pages (Ivory & Hearst, 2001).

The definition and application of measures over the deployed application comply with a *meeting customer needs* perspective. However, performing improvements at such a late stage of development is avowed to have a negative impact on the final product cost and quality (Briand, Morasca, & Basili, 1999). In fact, the cost associated with removing a defect during design is, on average, 3.5 times greater than during requirements; at implementation stage, the effort associated with removing the same defect can be up to 50 times greater, and up to 170 times greater after delivery (Bohem, 1981). Other empirical studies have shown that moving quality evaluation effort up to the early phases of development can be 33 times more cost-effective than testing done at the end of the development (Moody, 2005).

Our concern therefore is how to combine such traditional *meeting customer needs* perspective with an early evaluation of the main internal product characteristics (that implies a *conformance to specification* perspective) so that it is possible to minimize the financial and temporal costs

Figure 1. The OMG Standard Metapyramid with additional WE subdivisions to distinguish among different levels of abstraction at M1 level (adapted from ISO 10027)

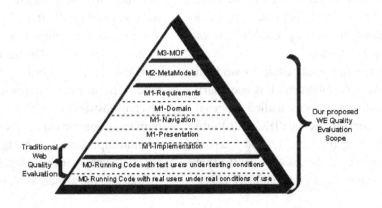

associated with quality evaluation. Fortunately, the ISO set of quality standards establishes an interesting relationship between these two quality perspectives. It sets that the *conformance to specifications* degree of a given software product (which includes not only the code, but also the intermediate artifacts generated as part of a WE process), which can be evaluated through an internal/external quality/model, may be a valid predictor of the ability of the product to meeting user needs (quality in use), even if the exact accuracy of such prediction is an open issue that depends on variables such as type of application or context of use. Otherwise stated, improving the internal/external quality of a Web application through the use of an internal/external product quality model may positively influence the quality in use of such product. This (indirect) relationship between software structural properties (which can be assessed through internal measures taken from models that emerge at the software design stage) and quality in use properties has been repeatedly demonstrated (Briand & Wüst, 2002). Reasons why structural properties have an impact on quality in use have been suggested by Briand et al. (1999). According to them, software that is big (i.e., having many components) and has a complex structure (i.e., showing many relationships between the software's components) results in a high cognitive complexity, which is defined as the mental burden of the people that perform tasks on the software. This high cognitive complexity causes the software to display undesirable properties such as high effort to be used or maintained, simply because it is more difficult to understand, develop, modify, test, or interact with such software.

In order to put this relationship to work in the context of Web development, it is necessary to translate customers' needs (called external quality requirements in the ISO/IEC 9126) into a set of suitable specifications (called internal quality requirements in the ISO/IEC 9126) that the analysts/designers can systematically check

during the development process. Let us illustrate how to deal with this translation with an example. A Web application with, let us say, six navigation steps from the home page to a given target page has not necessarily a low level of quality in use *per se*, but it turns into a low-quality-in-use application if it causes the user to be less effective, efficient, or even to feel less comfortable with the application. The user would not probably be able to identify the exact nature of the problem. All he/she would be able to say would be that he/she is not comfortable using the system or, at most, that the way to achieve the goals is too cumbersome. However, actions should be taken to fix the problem. While the developer may infer that the problem lies in the definition of navigation paths that are too long and therefore could work on shortening the path that caused the problem at implementation level, it would have been preferable if someone had translated the customer need (navigate fast and accurately) into a *conformance to specification* quality requirement such as: "The maximum depth of any navigational map should be limited to three levels". Even more interesting would it have been if such a requirement had been handed in to the developer while he was designing the navigation model of the application, so that the error would have been prevented rather than detected.

Again in terms of the OMG Standard Metapyramid, with the set of models and metamodels provided by WE, the set of measures at M1 level of abstraction can be broadened to include new measures on requirements models (Si-Said, Akoka, & Comyn-Wattiau, 2006), domain models (Genero, 2002), navigational models (Abrahao, Condory-Fernández, Olsina, & Pastor, 2003; Baresi, Morasca, & Paolini, 2003) and presentation models. Some examples of measures at these new levels of abstraction are cohesion of requirements, number of domain classes, complexity of domain relationships, number of navigational classes, density of the navigational map, number of widgets included in the presentation model, coherence in the use of widgets, colours, and fonts, and so on. Also, measures on implementation models and at M0 levels of abstraction are still valid. Going one level of abstraction further, we could even define measures at M2 level, for example, number of metamodel concepts involved in the M1 models that support the M0 running Web application.

All these possibilities are, however, hampered by the aforementioned fact that Web development is still commonly based on creative approaches, where early artifacts are scarce and lack the necessary rigor to perform measurements on them. Therefore we claim that, in order to manage Web quality from the early stages of development, WE methodologies must increase their presence in industry. Only with WE practices is it possible to build up the characteristics that make up the quality in use of the Web application during the whole Web development process, and not only once the deployment phase has been attained.

However, a broader use of WE methodologies that provide a suitable set of early artifacts is not enough. For WE to be able to guarantee a certain level of quality in the applications developed, WE methodologies need to be extended to include explicit quality artifacts and quality assessment activities at every stage of development. Conscious of this fact, in this chapter we propose an enriched WE process that includes such elements. In order to perform such inclusion in a sensible and consistent way, we have based our proposal on principles and achievements that, uncovered in different quality lines of research, provide insights into how to deal with quality in each of the different workflows that a typical WE process defines, from requirements to implementation. Next, we briefly present our main findings.

Related Work

In order to evaluate the quality in use of a Web application from the early stages of development, we need an evaluation instrument. One possibility is to use a certain quality model. A quality model is defined in ISO as the set of characteristics and the relationships between them which provide the basis for specifying quality requirements and evaluating quality. According to the ISO/IEC 9126 (2001) and ISO/IEC 14598 (1999), the overall objective of any quality evaluation process should be meeting customer needs. Provided that we narrow the term "customer" to that of "end-user", this concept of quality from the end-users' perspective is what the ISO/IEC 9126 standard defines as quality in use, that is, the efficiency, productivity, security, and satisfaction with which users use the application to satisfy specific goals under specific conditions. From this definition, it is possible to extract the four characteristics (efficiency, productivity, security, and satisfaction) that, according to the ISO/IEC 9126, make up a quality in use product quality model. On the other hand, the Web application, as any other software product, presents certain characteristics that can be evaluated before it has been deployed, namely (again according to ISO/IEC 9126) usability, functionality, reliability, and efficiency[1]. All these characteristics, together with the elements (measures, decision criteria, and so on) that permit to evaluate them, make up the ISO/IEC 9126 internal/external product quality model.

Quality models aiming at classifying the set of relevant attributes for a software product are far from scarce. Roughly speaking, the inception of all these models can be defined according to two dimensions:

- Whether the proposals are based on intuitive approaches, on theoretical grounds (ontologies, semiotic theory, etc.), or on empirical approaches (collecting data from software consumers to identify quality attributes); and
- Whether the proposals are developed from scratch or tailored to any other previous work.

In addition to this inception axis, we can classify quality models according to their purpose. Some of them aim at covering every quality characteristic of the software product (general quality models). Others focus on specific aspects such as maintainability, portability, usability, and so on. From those specific aspects, usability has been proven to be a milestone for the success of Web applications, which is reflected in the fact that 81% of the myriad of design guidelines and automated measures that have been gathered in literature as relevant for Web development are related to the usability concept (Calero et al, 2005). For this reason, in this chapter we will pay special attention to usability models and their implications for Web development.

Another important distinction is whether they aim at being applicable to any type of system or to a specific application type. From the point of view of our research, those that focus on the quality assessment of Web interfaces are especially relevant.

Last, if we want to systematize and increase the level of abstraction at which usability is measured in Web applications, it is important to take into account recent research in conceptual modeling quality evaluation.

In the next subsections, we review all these families of quality models.

General Quality Models

Well-known pioneer models that specifically consider usability include McCall, Richards, and Walters (1977); Boehm (1981); Dromey (1995); and ISO/IEC 9126 (2001).

The General Electrics Model of McCall is the (to our knowledge extent) first attempt to bridge the gap between users and developers. He already distinguishes among three major perspectives for defining the quality of a software product, which correspond with different stakeholders working at different levels of abstraction in the development life cycle. Among them, the prod-

uct operations perspective refers to the end user perspective during the usage of the application, and it includes a usability quality factor, regarded as a behavioural characteristic. For this usability factor, McCall defines three criteria (measurable attributes on the product): operability, training, and communicativeness, and for each criterion he defines a set of measures to control them.

Boehm's quality model is an attempt to qualitatively define software quality by a given set of attributes and measures. Again, this model defines three perspectives, from which "as-is-utility" refers to the end-user perception of the software during its usage (at execution time). Boehm divides this "as-is-utility" into reliability, efficiency, and human engineering, and considers that these three components make up the usability concept. He further relates these concepts with the measurable software attributes of self-containedness, accuracy, completeness, robustness/integrity, consistency, accountability, device efficiency, accessibility, and communicativeness.

Dromey's quality model presents a product-based quality model that recognizes that quality evaluation differs for each product, and that a more dynamic idea for modeling the process is needed to be wide enough to apply for different systems. Similar to the previous models, Dromey centres on the implementation of the software product on the one hand, and on the quality characteristics on the other hand, and tries to establish relationships among both dimensions. He defines "descriptive" as a product attribute, and connects such attribute with the quality characteristic "usability". Another important addition of Dromey's quality model is that he defines a process that involves five steps, from choosing the quality characteristics relevant for the evaluation to evaluating the product and identifying weaknesses.

Last, the ISO family of standards includes a general framework with characteristics, sub-characteristics, and measures that can be used to evaluate a software product (ISO/IEC 9126, 2001; ISO/IEC 9241, 1998). The ISO/IEC 9126 provides a software product quality model that is intended to be used as a general-purpose standard. It defines usability as an internal (that is, measurable on intermediate products) quality characteristic, and subdivides it into understandability, learnability, operability, attractiveness, and compliance to standards. The ISO/IEC 9241-11 regards usability as an external quality characteristic (equivalent to what the ISO/IEC 9126 calls quality in use) and decomposes it in effectiveness, efficiency, and satisfaction, all concepts aimed at being measured once the application has been deployed. Due to the widespread use of the ISO family of standards, many proposals have aimed at tailoring/refining/improving ISO models. For example, QUINT2 (Van Zeist, Hendriks, Paulussen, & Trienekens, 1996) and SquaRE (Suryn, Abran, & April, 2003) are examples of quality models that regard the ISO/IEC 9126 and/or ISO/IEC 9241-11 as valid but incomplete quality models, and therefore try to complete them with additional features.

Usability Models

Usability models defined from scratch include the proposals of Bajaj and Krishnan (1999); Dix, Finlay, Abowd, and Beale (2004); Nielsen (2000); Shneiderman and Plaisant (2005); Ivory (2004); and Seffah, Donyaee, Kline, and Padda (2006). All of them are based on intuition.

Bajaj and Krishnan specifically deal with usability of Web applications, and distinguish between readability (coherence and cognitive overhead), information grouping quality (coupling, cohesion), flexibility (learnability, efficiency of use, memorability), and download time.

The model proposed by Dix et al. includes three main characteristics: learnability, flexibility, and robustness, each one being subdivided into sub-characteristics.

Nielsen proposes a model that is divided into social and practical acceptability (inside of which he positions usability). Usability for Nielsen is further subdivided into easy to learn, efficient to use,

easy to remember, fewer errors, and subjectively pleasing, the first four factors being objective characteristics of the software product.

Shneiderman and Plaisant propose a similar subdivision and define usability as a set of five measurable human factors: speed of performance, time to learn, retention over time, rate of errors by users, and subjective satisfaction.

Ivory gathers 157 page and site measures that provide some support for assessing 56 of the 62 features (90%) identified as impacting usability in the Web design literature, and classifies them as attending to their level of abstraction (element, element formatting, page formatting, page performance, and site architecture).

Finally, an interesting unification of usability models into a single consolidated, hierarchical model called QUIM is presented in Seffah et al. (2006). This model uses ISO/IEC 9241-11 as a baseline. It comprises 10 factors, each of which corresponds to a specific facet of usability that is identified in an existing standard or model. These 10 factors are decomposed into 26 sub-factors that are further decomposed into 127 specific metrics. Furthermore, this is the only model (to our knowledge extent) that includes user and environment characteristics (defined in the ISO/IEC 9241-11) as explicit parts of the model. In this model, internal and external factors affecting usability are not distinguished.

Web Quality Models

Regarding Web quality models, in the last few years some interesting proposals have appeared (Abrahao & Insfran, 2006; Calero et al., 2005; Moraga, Calero, & Piattini, 2006; Olsina & Rossi, 2002).

In Web quality model (WQM) (Calero et al., 2005), the QUINT2 model is evaluated as the most suitable for Web applications and therefore it is used as the basis for their proposal. WQM completes the QUINT2 model with new measurable concepts and with Web measures that are used to quantify each measurable concept. However, neither the stakeholder nor the particular Web artifact on which measures can be performed are considered as relevant in the three-dimensional cube that defines the quality model.

WebQEM (Olsina & Rossi, 2002) is also a quantitative approach especially devoted to the assessment of Web quality (including usability). It includes a process, a set of measures, and a tool to automate the measuring process.

The usability model presented in Abrahao and Insfran (2006) is more WE-oriented in the sense that it specifically takes into account specific WE artifacts (domain, navigation, presentation, implementation), although it still disregards the fact that different stakeholders may be interested in different measurable concepts, as well as that not every measurable concept can be assessed at every level of abstraction.

Last, the usability model centred on portlets (Web mini-applications) presented in Moraga et al. (2006) focuses on implementation portlet properties. This usability model is in-between ISO and a proprietary model, follows the software measurement ontology (SMO) for its definition, and is the only one that, to our knowledge extent, includes specific decision criteria associated to the indicators for each of the information needs, although no empirical proof of their validity is provided.

Conceptual Modeling Quality

While the quality models presented above were in its majority conceived with the deployed application in mind, conceptual modeling quality provides insight into how the assessment of quality can be performed at higher levels of abstraction. The first structured approach to the conceptual modeling quality evaluation dates back to the contribution of Von Halle (1991), where he defines features of data models which maximize value to the organization. Batini, Ceri, and Navathe (1992) is another well-known approach to data

model quality that defines completeness, correctness, minimality, expressiveness, readability, self-explanation, extensibility, and normality as relevant quality criteria to Entity Relationship (ER) schema evaluation. Levitin and Redman (1995) define quality dimensions, reinforcements, and trade-offs. Lindland, Sindre, and Solvberg (1994) propose to evaluate the quality of schemas along three dimensions: syntax, semantics, and pragmatics. Inside each one of these concepts, there are two sub-concepts: completeness and validity. Krogstie, Lindland, and Sindre (1995) extend the Lindland framework with agreement goal and social construction theory. In Misic and Zhao (2000), the Lindland et al. framework is adapted and extended to the comparison of reference models. Nelson, Monarchi, and Nelson (2001) also complete the Lindland et al. framework with three new dimensions: perceptual, descriptive, and inferential. In Poels, Nelson, Genero, and Piattini (2002), this type of quality dimension is completed with two additional dimensions: object of study (the model, the process, or the process facilitators) and research goal (understanding, measuring, evaluating, assuring, or improving quality). Kesh (1995) distinguishes between ontological features (those related to the model) and behavioural features (something that the software exhibits when it is executed). For him, usability is a synonym of end-user quality and refers to a behavioural feature that is influenced by ontological features such as completeness or conciseness. In Assenova and Johannensson (1996), a different set of criteria are proposed for the evaluation of ER schemas: homogeneity, explicitness, rule simplicity, rule uniformity, query simplicity, and stability, together with a set of transformations aimed at improving the quality of schemas.

Of special relevance for the aim of this chapter is the quality management framework proposed in Moody and Shanks (2003). This framework is the first, to our knowledge extent, to include: (1) a quality model that takes into account stakeholders; (2) a research methodology to validate the quality model; and (3) an empirical validation process that makes the framework suitable for process quality management and not merely for product quality assessment. The quality model includes six empirically-validated quality factors: completeness, integrity, flexibility, understand-ability, correctness, simplicity, integration, and implementability.

WE Evaluation Process

Whatever quality model is chosen, for it to be of real use it must be accompanied with a quality evaluation process. This process indicates, among other things, where and how to apply the quality model and its accompanying measures.

In this sense, as we have stated above, traditional Web quality assessment has been traditionally performed as a monolitic activity once the application was deployed. Such Web assessment is mostly based on mass inspection (Moody & Shanks, 2003), most of the time with the aid of automated measures and tools, but with little concern for systematization. One of the best-known attempts to improve this way of assessing Web application quality is WebQEM (Olsina & Rossi, 2002). WebQEM introduces a systematic evaluation process that is made up of four phases: quality requirements definition and specification, elementary evaluation, global evaluation, and conclusions. However, the tailorable quality requirement tree and the measures that it includes suggest that the authors still bear in mind that this process is applied only once the Web application has been deployed, and disregards the list of intermediate outgoing artifacts that are produced by a standard WE process.

Moody and Shanks (2003) promote the use of problems detected in products (noticed through product quality assessment methods) to reengineer the process that drives the construction of such products (achieving a process quality assessment framework). However, their framework says little about how to obtain high quality products in the first place.

Research Issues

The revision of the myriad of different quality models and quality evaluation processes that have been presented above leads to several theoretical and practical issues that must be handled (Moody, 2005; Seffah et al. (2006):

- **P1: Terminology inconsistencies:** Most approaches (with the exception of those based on theoretical grounds) lack a definition for quality concepts that is precise and concise. For instance, while in the ISO/IEC 9241-11 usability refers to the end-user perception as a whole (and therefore encompasses efficiency, effectiveness, and satisfaction), in the ISO/IEC 9126 end-user perception is referred to as quality in use, and usability is only one of the internal characteristics that may affect such quality in use;

- **P2: Incomplete definition:** Most quality models are outlined but not fully developed. All of them define measurable concepts, some of them also define attributes, few of them include (most often partial) measures, and scarcely any define decision criteria or indicators. Therefore, intensive work is necessary by the people using them to get them operational. An example of a quality model suffering from this problem is the ISO/IEC 9126 itself.

- **P3: Lack of focus:** Most quality models provide an extensive (and mostly tangled) coverage of stakeholders and levels of abstraction. An example of such assertion is the QUIM model (Seffah et al., 2006), which aims at being a consolidated usability model that integrates all possible perspectives. As another example, WQM (Calero et al., 2005) covers 10 factors, 26 sub-factors, and 127 measures that may be related to any WE artifact, from analysis to implementation.

- **P4: Lack of simplification and validation:** Quality models that include measures usually pay little attention to the theoretical/empirical validation of the included measures. Furthermore, although empirical research has shown that a few measures (three in Moody & Shanks, 2003) most times suffice to obtain significant gains in quality, quality models usually include an extensive, even redundant, set of measures. Such verboseness unnecessarily increases the complexity and therefore hampers the potential usefulness of the quality models.

- **P5: Interdependencies and measure interpretations not clear:** In most quality models (again the notable exception are those models based on theory), the degree of influence of individual internal quality factors on the quality in use of the application, as well as their interdependencies, are not well established. For example, the role of learnability versus understandability in the usability model presented in Abrahao and Insfran (2006) is an open issue. Also, little information is provided on how to interpret measurement results.

- **P6: Lack of integration with current practices:** Quality models and quality assessment processes are usually defined in isolation, with no link with the particular application characteristics and/or the application development process.

- **P7: Disregard for standard process quality frameworks:** Most quality models define criteria and, in some cases, measures for evaluating products (error detection), but not how to develop products in a way that assures a certain level of quality (error prevention).

- **P8: Lack of guidelines for improvements:** Even in the case of being able to evaluate a certain quality characteristic, to our knowledge extent, no quality model provides a clue about how (by means of which changes in the artifacts) such evaluation could be improved, let alone to which extent such changes may affect the evaluation of other characteristics included in the quality model.

- **P9: Lack of tool support:** Tool support for the definition of quality models and, even more important, for the automation of the measurement process on a given application is scarce.

For our proposal, in order to keep these problems to the minimum, we have defined certain requirements that should be preserved when defining WE quality models and integrating them with traditional WE development processes:

- **R1:** WE quality models should be expressed using a set of concepts with clear semantics and relationships, in order to ease their understanding and assure a structural coherence. This palliates problems P1, P2, and P3.

- **R2:** WE quality models should be defined taking into account a specific stakeholder and a specific software artifact. This palliates problem P3.

- **R3:** WE quality models should be empirically validated before being included in the WE process. This palliates problems P4 and P5.

- **R4:** WE quality models should be accompanied by a WE quality evaluation process. Such a process must be defined and seamlessly integrated with the WE development process. This means following an MDE approach. This contributes to overcome problems P6 and P7.

- **R5:** For the definition of the WE quality evaluation process, standards should be followed when possible. This alleviates problem P7.

- **R6:** Guidelines should be provided when possible to improve WE artifacts according to the WE quality artifact under consideration. Such guidelines should also, if possible, preserve the semiautomatic nature of the WE process. This contributes to solving problem P8.

- **R7:** The integration of WE quality models in the WE process should always be accompanied by tool support. Basing such integration on standards (for which tool support is provided by third parties) simplifies the task of finding such tool support, therefore contributing to alleviating problem P9.

Next, we present how we have integrated these requirements in a sound proposal that enriches the traditional WE development process with: (1) a set of quality models as evaluation instruments of the different software artifacts; (2) a set of quality measurement models that operationalize and tailor each quality model to face the particular needs of the application under development; and (3) concrete quality activities that must be carried out in conjunction with every process workflow, from requirements to implementation.

A QUALITY-AWARE WEB ENGINEERING DEVELOPMENT PROCESS

Quality models include, as we have presented before, quality needs in the form of characteristics and sub-characteristics with which a given application should be compliant. However, the traditional and informal way of expressing such quality models pose many problems, as we have recollected in the Research Issues section. For this reason, we propose a definition of WE quality models that is based on an underlying ontology, as we illustrate next.

A WE Software Measurement Metamodel (SMM)

As we presented in the Research Issues section, one of the problems that existing quality models face is terminology inconsistencies (P1). In order to overcome this problem, we need a common vocabulary both to express WE concepts and to express quality concepts. Such common vocabulary usually comes in ontology form.

Ontologies, defined as explicit, formal, and shared specifications of a conceptualization, have been widely used in Software Engineering (SE) (Ruiz & Hilera, 2006). Ontologies are descriptive in nature. They try to identify all the elements that are relevant in a given domain, and provide an exact definition of each of them. Ontologies also identify the relationships among the elements and what these relationships mean.

The use of an ontology not only avoids vocabulary conflicts and inconsistencies, but also establishes the adequate level of detail for the definition of each concept. While the definition of a WE ontology is in its first stages of development and remains out of the scope of this chapter, the greater maturity of the measurement field causes a proposal for a software measurement ontology (SMO) to be already available.

The SMO was first presented in García, Bertoa, Calero, Vallecillo, Ruiz, Piattini, and Genero (2005) and has since then been used to define some quality models (Moraga et al., 2006). Our reason for choosing this ontology has been twofold. The first reason is that this ontology comes together with a software measurement metamodel (SMM) (Ferreira, García, Bertoa, Calero, Vallecillo, Ruiz, Piattini, & Braga, 2006). Metamodels, unlike ontologies, are prescriptive in nature, and aim at identifying how a given domain must be built, explaining the kind of entities and how they are interconnected in a given context. The SMO provides to the SMM the degree of completeness and shareness of concept that common metamodels, defined in the context of a particular organization, lack. This shareness of concept simplifies and homogenizes the way in which such a metamodel is instantiated to define machine-readable measurement models. The second reason for choosing the SMO is that it is, to our knowledge extent, the most complete one that explicitly characterizes the relationships between abstract quality concepts on one side and concrete software measurement strategies on the other.

Figure 2. WE measurement metamodel

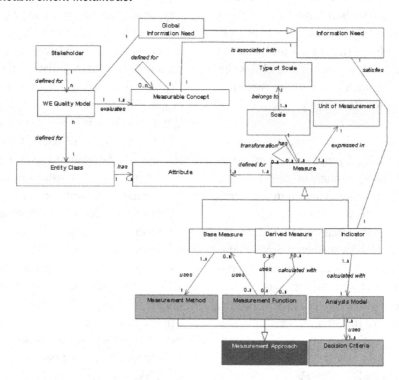

The SMM presented in Ferreira et al. (2006) is a mirror of the underlying SMO, and may be instantiated to define, in a systematic and non-ambiguous way, a measurement model that includes all the necessary concepts for the operationalization of a given quality model. The main advantage of using metamodels instead of ontologies in the context of a software development process stems in their prescriptive rather than descriptive nature, what permits the designer to make assumptions on the measurement models that are not possible with ontologies. Also, metamodels can be tailored for specific contexts. Due to space reasons, interested readers are referred to García et al. (2005) for a whole description of the different elements that make up the SMM and their relationships.

Although the SMM does not guide the selection of the concrete measurable concepts and attributes that must be included in a certain measurement model (this needs to be done by extensive research on existing models, theories, experience, and/or empirically-proven assumptions, whose result is a given quality model), it provides (by means of the underlying ontology) a clear definition of such concepts. A brief summary of such concepts is presented in Table 1.

Given the fact that we aim at simplifying as much as possible the definition of WE measurement models, we have adapted the SMM to make their instantiation more intuitive for Web designers. The construction of this WE-SMM, presented in Figure 2, has implied the following actions over the original SMM:

- We have limited the risk for inconsistencies in the measurement model by eliminating SMM redundant relationships: the relationship *measurable concept-attribute* and the relationship *analysis model-measure*;
- We have limited the set of valid *entity classes* to the outgoing artifacts of the WE development process. Additionally, for each *quality model* only one *entity class* is permitted. In this way, *measurable concepts* that are to

Table 1. SMM terms definition

Term	Definition
Measurement Approach	Sequence of operations aimed at determining the value of a measurement result (A measurement approach is either a measurement method, a measurement function, or an analysis model)
Measurement	A set of operations having the object of determining the value of a measurement result, for a given attribute of an entity, using a measurement approach
Measurement Result	The number or category assigned to an attribute of an entity by making a measurement
Information Need	Insight necessary to manage objectives, goals, risks, and problems
Measurable Concept	Abstract relationship between attributes of entities and information needs
Entity	Object that is to be characterized by measuring its attributes
Entity Class	The collection of all entities that satisfy a given predicate
Attribute	A measurable physical or abstract property of an entity, that is shared by all the entities of an entity class
Quality Model	The set of measurable concepts and the relationships between them which provide the basis for specifying quality requirements and evaluating the quality of the entities of a given entity class
Measure	The defined measurement approach and the measurement scale (A measurement approach is either a measurement method, a measurement function, or an analysis model)
Scale	A set of values with defined properties
Type of Scale	The nature of the relationship between values on the scale
Unit of Measurement	Particular quantity, defined and adopted by convention, with which other quantities of the same kind are compared in order to express their magnitude relative to that quantity
Base Measure	A measure of an attribute that does not depend upon any other measure, and whose measurement approach is a measurement method
Derived Measure	A measure that is derived from other base or derived measures, using a measurement function as measurement approach
Indicator	A measure that is derived from other measures using an analysis model as measurement approach
Measurement Method	Logical sequence of operations, described generically, used in quantifying an attribute with respect to a specified scale (A measurement method is the measurement approach that defines a base measure)
Measurement Function	An algorithm or calculation performed to combine two or more base or derived measures (A measurement function is the measurement approach that defines a derived measure)
Analysis Model	Algorithm or calculation combining one or more measures with associated decision criteria (An analysis model is the measurement approach that defines an indicator)
Decision Criteria	Thresholds, targets, or patterns used to determine the need for action or further investigation, or to describe the level of confidence in a given result

be measured on different WE artifacts are forced to belong to different quality models;

- We have introduced a *global information need* that is connected with the WE quality model as a whole to justify its definition. For the structure of this *global information need,* we propose to use the Goal Question Method template for goal definition (Bohem, 1981);

- In order to keep the quality model simple, we have limited the connection of each *measurable concept* to a single *information need*;
- For the same reason, we have established that each *information need* should be satisfied by a single *indicator*, implying that the *measurable concept* connected with the *information need* is also associated with that *indicator*;
- In order to assure that every *attribute* is measurable, every *attribute* defined in a WE quality model should be associated with at least one *measure* that is devoted to measuring such *attribute*. This restriction makes sure that the evaluation model is operationally defined by means of *measures*, that is, not reliant on subjective interpretations of concepts (Moody, 2005);
- In order to establish a single way of calculating *indicators*, we propose that every *measure* is associated with a single *analysis model*;
- In order to further contextualize the WE quality model and help to keep the focus, we have added a *stakeholder* element to the original SMM; and
- Finally, we have omitted from the WE-SMM the *measurement package*, due to the fact that their elements do not contribute to the definition of quality models, but rather to the results of their operationalization.

Additionally, and although not directly reflected in the WE-SMM, in order to control the quality model complexity, we recommend the limitation of the hierarchy depth of *measurable concepts* to two levels of detail. Also, following the ISO/IEC 9126 example, these two levels should be characterized by familiar labels and concise definitions. Similarly, *attributes* associated with *entity classes* should also be familiar and provide concise definitions. Finally, in order to facilitate a hypothetical merging of measurement models at different levels of abstraction into a general, well-structured WE global measurement model, we recommend that attributes for the different models have unique names in the context of the WE field.

From these refinements, the inclusion of stakeholders is, from our point of view, especially relevant. Stakeholders are usually not explicitly identified in existing quality models. However, as stated in Calero et al. (2005), they are important in any quality model, as different Stakeholders will generally be interested in different Measurable Concepts. Moody (2005) define four stakeholders for ER models: Business User, External Analyst, Information Architect, and Database Designer. The fact that we are interested in assessing the quality of the final Web application (and not of a model *per se*), together with the characteristics of the WE process, has driven the definition of a different set of stakeholders, which make up the set of allowed instantiations for the Stakeholder metamodel concept, namely:

- **Analysts/Designers:** They are the link between customers and developers and are focused on the intermediate products, that is, the WE artifacts (models). According to Si-Said et al. (2006), their concern is the specification and usage perspectives of the WE models. Analyst/Designers have a compliance to specifications perspective of quality.
- **Developers/Maintainers:** They are in charge of implementing/maintaining the system (implementation and code level). Therefore, they are also focused on intermediate artifacts (models), namely on artifacts that convey the Implementation perspective (Si-Said et al., 2006). They share with designers a "compliance to specifications" perspective of quality.
- **Customers:** They have a meet customer needs perspective of quality. According to the ISO/IEC SQuaRE (Suryn et al., 2003), they can be divided in two subgroups:

Figure 3. Simplified version of WE process

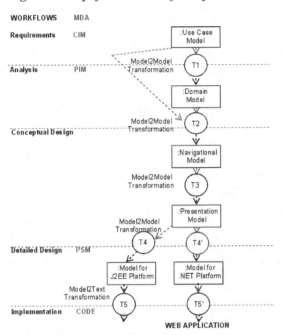

1. **Acquirers:** They are interested in cost, time, and functionality. If we consider that models (intermediate products in the WE development process) may be used as communication artifacts, then according to Si-Said et al. (2006) the completeness and understandability of the models may influence the acquirer's perception of quality in use. Also, ac-

quirers may be interested, regarding the final Web application, in the efficiency, effectiveness, and security of such an application, as long as all these factors have an impact on productivity, and therefore on cost and time gains.

2. **End users:** They are the ones that will eventually interact with the application. For them, efficiency, effectiveness, security, and satisfaction (that is, quality in use) of the deployed application are the only factors that matter.

This classification is slightly different from the perspective presented in Olsina and Rossi (2002) where visitors, developers, and managers are distinguished. It also differs from that of Dromey (1995) in that it adds the analyst/designer perspective of quality.

The concepts and relationships included in this metamodel force a certain structure similarity to any quality model defined based on them. In the case of WE, this similarity not only facilitates the understanding and discussion of new WE quality models for practitioners familiar with other WE quality models, but it also helps in the merging process of all these models in a global WE measurement model.

Figure 4. Quality in the WE lifecycle (adapted from ISO/IEC 9126)

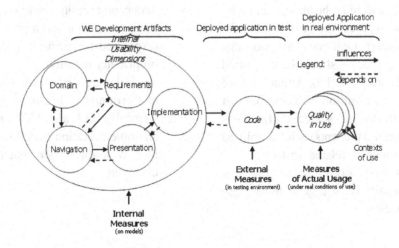

Figure 5. Quality-aware WE development process

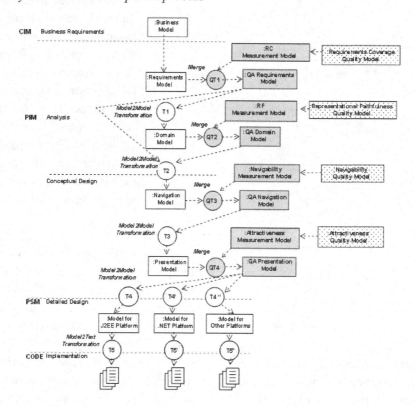

Integration of a WE Quality Evaluation Process with the WE Development Process

As we presented above, a quality model (and thus also any of the measurement models that may operationalize it) must be accompanied by a quality evaluation process to be of real use for practitioners. In order to facilitate its adoption, this quality evaluation process should be integrated with current WE practices (P6). Although there is no agreement on a common Web development process, most methodologies share a set of artifacts and activities. Figure 3 presents such a simplified version, together with its related artifacts.

This process, based on the MDE paradigm (Kent, 2002), departs from a general business model and includes:

1. a manually-performed functional requirements workflow, whose outgoing artifact is a use case model;

2. an analysis workflow, whose output is a domain model (usually an ER diagram or a UML class diagram);

3. a conceptual design workflow, whose outputs are a navigation and a presentation model (expressed by means of UML profiles or proprietary notations);

4. a detailed design workflow that introduces platform and technology specific features (typically J2EE and .NET); and

5. an implementation workflow, which results in a Web application that is ready to be deployed.

Variants of this process model exist, usually to include additional Platform-Independent Models (PIMs) and/or Platform-Specific Models (PSMs) (architectural models, business process models, different languages and/or platforms, etc.) that further enrich the application specification. Additionally, WE methodologies promote the use of automatic and/or semiautomatic transformations among most of these artifacts (represented as stereotyped activities in Figure 3) that, based on the underlying metamodels, streamline the process and guarantee traceability among and between concepts.

The use of a WE process with semiautomatic transformations prevents some development problems such as inconsistencies among models, lack of traceability, lack of technical soundness, and so forth. However, this semiautomatic nature of the WE process also may cause the propagation of quality flaws through levels of abstraction. Otherwise stated, quality problems that are now only detected at implementation time may have been introduced not during the implementation phase but at any previous stage of development. As an example, a low cohesion of the Web application requirements (Si-Said et al., 2006) may cause, during the construction of the Navigation Model, that the interface structure is defined in an improper manner. The reason is that the Requirements Model (usually a UML Use Case Diagram) is used in most WE approaches to decide how to perform such division (Cachero, Koch, Gómez, & Pastor, 2002). Even more evident, missing requirements will cause dismissed quality because the user perceives a lack of functionality.

This notwithstanding, the fact that during the construction of every WE artifact the system is enriched and refined with respect to previous levels of abstraction, causes that the end-user perceived level of quality may be also hampered by the introduction of new quality flaws during such enrichment. As an example, even if the requirements model presents a high quality level, the new information introduced at the domain level may introduce new kinds of quality problems. Imagine, for example, that certain domain relationships (which are present in the end-user's mind) are not included in the domain model. This domain model (see Figure 3) is the basis on which the navigation model, which is in charge of defining the user paths through the application, is constructed. Therefore, missing relationships in the domain model will be propagated to the navigation model and cause missing relationships among concepts in the final application interface. If the user looks for these relationships while interacting with the application, this omission is likely to diminish his/her perceived degree of quality.

Going one step further, the refinements performed at navigation level may cause new kinds of quality problems to appear. For instance, even in the face of high quality requirements and conceptual models, we may design a set of tangled navigation paths that mislead the user in his/her goals pursuit, and therefore diminish the end-user perceived level of quality. Additionally, a poorly-designed presentation model (e.g., a model that does not include position signals, where widgets are poorly chosen, and so on) may also induce other kinds of quality problems for the end-user, who may feel that the interface appearance does not fit his/her needs. Last but not least, usability problems can be introduced on the running code itself by means of implementation decisions that hamper load times, performance, security, and so on.

The six WE models (Use Cases, Domain, Navigation, Presentation, Implementation, and Executable Code) presented in Figure 3 imply, therefore, six different purposes of evaluation that must be taken into account when defining the quality models and its related operationalizations (measurement models), namely:

- Use Case Model → Requirements Coverage,
- Domain Model → Representational Faithfulness,

- Navigation Model → Navigability,
- Presentation Model → Attractiveness,
- Implementation Model → Implementation Decision Quality, and
- Executable Code → Quality as Tested under conditions that emulate as closely as possible the expected conditions of use.

From these six types of WE products, the first five can be regarded as internal products in the sense that they are models of the application, and not the application itself, while the deployable Web application is an external product (the product that actually reaches the market). A graphical representation of the products and their hypothetical quality interrelationships is presented in Figure 4. Such relationships are based on the ISO/IEC assumption that quality at one level of abstraction may be used to predict quality and lower levels of abstraction and the already-mentioned underlying traceability of concepts among the different WE models.

Namely, in Figure 4 we can graphically observe how the internal quality dimensions may affect an external quality dimension, that is, the quality of the final application (code) as perceived under testing conditions. Finally, such external quality may influence the actual quality of the application in real contexts of use.

As we mentioned above, our proposal includes the encapsulation of each pair purpose of evaluation-product type in an independent WE quality model that is translated into one or more WE measurement models (each one reflecting one possible tailoring of the quality model). Additionally recall that, in order to preserve the MDE paradigm implicit in the WE process that we presented in Figure 3, machine-readable measurement models (greyed in Figure 5) must be derived from underlying WE quality models (dotted in Figure 5). Last, it is important to note that, in order to assure the reusability of our framework, for the definition of WE quality models it would be necessary to reach a consensus and identify a set of common attributes

Figure 6. Evaluation process (adapted from ISO 14598-1)

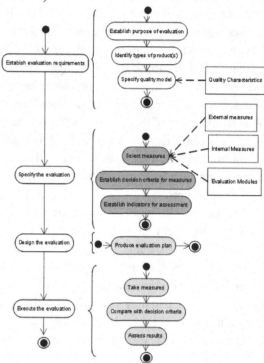

that characterize any of the WE models proposed by any of the best-known WE methodologies, and centre WE quality models on such common concepts. We do claim that such a common set of concepts exists at each level of abstraction, as the recent MDWEnet initiative[2] backs. Only such attributes, together with a general definition of measures, independent from particular notations, should be included in WE quality models in order to make them reusable among WE methodologies. How such reuse can be achieved is presented in Cachero, Meliá, Genero, Poels, and Calero (2006b) and is briefly revisited in an upcoming section, named Automation of the Evaluation Process and Design Guidelines.

One question that may have arisen in the mind of the reader at this point is why we have not simply proposed to use the ISO/IEC 14598 (1999) to define the Web quality evaluation process. Even if it is true that the ISO set of standards accompanies the definition of quality models (ISO/IEC 9126, 2001) with a software evaluation process (defined in the ISO/IEC 14598), it is a well-known fact that both standards are not sufficient to direct the practitioner in the quality evaluation process (Suryn et al., 2003). One reason for this fact may be that ISO/IEC 14598 was finished before the last version of the ISO/IEC 9126, and while it provides generic linkages between the high-level concepts of the ISO/IEC 9126 quality instruments (characteristics, sub-characteristics, and measures), the evaluation process is not yet specified in the format of specific prescriptive quality engineering practices. In particular, the current versions of these ISO/IEC standards do not provide a clear mapping between the quality engineering instruments already developed and the various phases of the WE development process (Suryn et al., 2003).

The first benefit of using the steps defined in Figure 5 to perform a Web quality evaluation process is that it covers such mapping because it relates, through the instantiation of the WE-SMM, specific quality models to specific WE artifacts, and provides an automated way to perform the measurement process on each of the artifacts. Additionally, this merging process guarantees that each problem is detected and solved as soon as possible in the development life cycle, which, as we have already outlined, diminishes costs and time to market of high-quality Web applications.

However, while performing such mapping we are interested in fulfilling the ISO/IEC 14598 requirements, as they reflect an agreement between researchers and practitioners. ISO/IEC 14598 poses two main requirements for compliance. On one hand, the quality evaluation must be based on a quality model. On the other hand, ISO/IEC 14598 demands that the evaluation process should follow the steps presented in Figure 6. Next we will justify why our proposal covers both demands.

As we saw in the previous section, the WE field restricts both the purposes of evaluation (according to stakeholders) and the set of artifacts which are involved (according to the workflow in which we are involved). By choosing the WE quality model that is going to serve as a basis to instantiate a given WE measurement model, the designer is in fact already covering some of the ISO 14598 activities (namely, *establish purpose of evaluation and identify types of products* in Figure 6). The evaluation purpose when operationalizating quality models and applying them to each one of the intermediate WE artifacts is twofold:

1. deciding on the completion of the process and when to send products to the next process (when the internal evaluation is satisfactory); and

2. using that internal evaluation to predict or estimate end-product quality.

Nonetheless, the purpose of the evaluation once the Web application has already been implemented is also twofold:

1. deciding on the acceptance of the product; and

2. deciding when to release the product. The type of product is the one that was associated to the chosen quality model.

The construction of the measurement model that operationalizes the quality model covers the specification of quality requirements in terms of quality characteristics and sub-characteristics (measurable concepts in terms of the WE-SMM), as suggested in ISO/IEC 14598. The correctness of the resulting measurement model is assured by the WE-SMM and the underlying validated general quality model. The completeness of the measurement model is also influenced (although not guaranteed) by these two elements.

During the measurement model instantiation, the activities *measure selection, decision criteria establishment,* and *indicator assessment* in Figure 6 must be performed. Due to the fact that we depart from independent quality models for each level of abstraction again facilitates the execution of these activities. Ideally, all measures contained in a WE quality model should be reflected in any measurement model derived from such a quality model, and applicable to any Web application. Only decision criteria and indicators are likely to need to be fine-tuned according to the particular type of application. The reason is that quality requirements are not the same for different domains (e.g., e-commerce applications and educational applications) and, even inside a given domain, requirements could vary (e.g., requirements are not the same for dealing with an educational application for children as with one for computer science professionals).

The *evaluation plan production* activity (Figure 6) is also implicit in the WE process presented in Figure 5. Briefly speaking, our proposed schedule is to evaluate each artifact as soon as it is produced in the development process. On the other hand, the evaluation method is expressed during the measurement model construction.

Finally, we propose to execute the evaluation in an automatic way, by means of transformation rules that interact with the WE-SMM and with the particular WE artifact metamodel in order to get measured results, calculate indicators, compare indicators with decision criteria and, if feasible, evolve the models to improve the indicator value. All these activities are briefly described in the next section.

Automation of the Evaluation Process and Design Guidelines

As we presented in Figure 5, our proposal includes the execution of the WE quality evaluation process in an automatic way, following the MDE paradigm, thus alleviating P9. This is achieved by means of QVT-based transformation rules that interact with the WE-SMM and with the particular WE artifact metamodel provided by WE methodolo-

gies. During this interaction, the transformation rule permits to: (1) calculate measures/indicators results; (2) compare indicators with decision criteria; (3) annotate the models with the evaluation results; and (4) if feasible, evolve the models to improve the measure value. To achieve these goals, each transformation rule contains in its *when* clause a translation of the selected measure/indicator and its related threshold values in terms of OCL expressions over the chosen WE artifact metamodel. A detailed description and a proof of concept of how this automation of the evaluation process works can be found in Cachero et al. (2006b). Here we will limit ourselves to just briefly outlining some open issues regarding such automated execution.

First, and given the fact that the ISO/IEC 14598 does not establish what to do if the result of executing an evaluation rule (a rule that contains the codification of the measure) does not meet the criteria, in the context of our proposed quality-aware WE process, two actions are possible:

1. Annotate the model to warn the designer, who would be in charge of manually performing the changes which are needed; or
2. Automatically trigger a chain of subordinated evolution rules that evolve the model to improve the measure until the value is consistent with the quality requirements.

Whichever action takes place, the result of applying such transformation rules on the original models is a quality-assessed WE model, as we can observe in Figure 5. Interested readers can find examples of both types of rules in Cachero, Genero, Calero, and Meliá (2006a) and Cachero et al., (2006b), respectively.

Although the automated nature of the WE process would suggest the second types of actions, it is not always possible to automatically decide which changes to make on the models. Therefore, extensive research needs to be done in order to come up with model evolutions that truly improve the quality of the final application.

Also we would like to note how measures, indicators, and decision criteria defined for a certain application remain coded in such transformation rules, which need to be defined only once for each WE methodology. From them, indicators should be validated as predictors of the actual product quality (measured on the deployed code under real conditions of use), and the result of such validation also stored in some kind of project repository. The shape of the project repository, which ideally should be defined by consensus in order to be able to merge results gathered with different WE methodologies and refine the predictive power of indicators, also remains an open line of research.

CONCLUSION AND FURTHER WORK

In this chapter, we have proposed an approach to evaluate Web quality that provides all the elements that, according to the ISO/IEC 14598, are essential parts of a software quality evaluation, namely: (1) a quality model, (2) a method of evaluation, (3) a software measurement process, and (4) supporting tools.

We have integrated all these elements following the claim that, *to develop good software* (and thus good Web-based software), *quality requirements should be specified, the software quality assurance process should be planned, implemented and controlled, and both intermediate products and final products should be evaluated. Also, to achieve objective software quality evaluations, the quality attributes of the software should be measured using validated metrics* (ISO/IEC 14598, 1999).

How all these elements contribute to alleviate each of the problems detected in the Research Issues section is discussed in the section named A Quality-Aware Web engineering Development Process and can be summarized as follows:

- **P1:** Use of a SMO (section name: A WE software measurement metamodel (SMM));
- **P2 and P3:** Operationalization of quality models by means of a WE-SMM instantiation that takes into account a specific stakeholder and a specific WE artifact (section name: A WE software measurement metamodel (SMM));
- **P4 and P5:** Empirical validation of quality models (not tackled in this chapter);
- P6 and P7: Definition of a quality assurance process that is ISO compliant and that is integrated with the WE development process (section name: Integration of a WE Quality Evaluation Process with the WE Development Process); and
- **P8 and P9:** Automation of the quality assessment process by means of transformation rules that have tool support and that may simply evaluate or evaluate and evolve the WE models according to certain quality criteria (section name: Automation of the Evaluation Process and Design Guidelines).

The main purpose of our approach is to ease the shift of the WE community towards addressing quality during the systematic development of Web applications. In order to systematize such quality concerns in a seamless way, our framework operationalizes quality models by means of measurement models that are integrated by means of transformation rules with the traditional WE development process, therefore preserving the semiautomated nature of such processes.

The definition of such measurement models as instances of a WE-SMM has several advantages:

- The WE-SMM provides a table of contents which makes visible what information is necessary to include in the measurement model and how this information is related;
- The WE-SMM supports the manipulation of the measurement model in an automatic way, since information will show an homogeneous structure;

- The WE-SMM supports the reuse of measurement models since it facilitates the establishment and maintenance of libraries of measurement models;
- The WE-SMM supports standardization of measurement models since the format is compliant with an accepted SMO; and
- The WE-SMM covers all the information defined in ISO/IEC 14598-6 as necessary parts of an evaluation module documentation.

Nonetheless, the definition of a quality evaluation process that is based on the MDE paradigm also provides several advantages:

- Automation of the quality assurance process.
- Leverage of costs and time frames, and
- Standard tool support.

Finally, the integration of the MDE-based quality assurance process with the MDE-based WE process means that the use of a WE process to develop a Web application implicitly assumes a planned, synchronized quality assurance of both intermediate and final products, easing the adoption of quality practices in the WE field.

The modified WE process presented in this chapter constitutes a step towards the Total Quality Management (Zultner, 1992). We agree with Legris, Ingham, and Collerette (2003) in that the empirical evidence of output quality of WE methodologies, as well as result demonstrability, would influence its perceived usefulness, which in turn explains up to 40% of technology adoption. As a conclusion, we may say that our approach implies, to a certain extent, a shift in the centre of gravity of WE from creating technology-centred solutions towards satisfying the stakeholders (Suryn et al., 2003).

However, the use of our proposal also poses some risks that must be taken into account and that constitute future lines of research:

- We provide a fixed quality evaluation process planning, which depends on the main WE process planning. This fact could not be feasible and/or advisable in certain circumstances;
- The agreement on common quality models for each level of abstraction is far from trivial and may depend on the background of the researchers/practitioners involved in reaching the agreement;
- The quality model tailoring process necessary to construct a measurement model that meets specific application quality requirements is not a trivial task. First, a previous task of transforming quality requirements into specification requirements at each level of abstraction is needed. Also, decision criteria associated with each specification requirement are not easy to establish;
- The usefulness of assuring quality must be counterbalanced with the extra complexity added to the WE process due to its merging with the quality evaluation process. However, we think that the automation of the measurement process alleviates this problem;
- Quality-assured models are of little use if transformation rules themselves are not also quality-assured. The process followed to transform each model into another should be evaluated to assure not only efficiency but also to preserve the level of quality assured in previous levels of abstraction;
- Extensive work must be done to define each measure in terms of transformation rules for each WE approach. Keeping the number of measures included in the models low and reaching an agreement on a common WE metamodel may leverage such risk; and
- Similarly, differences in semantics associated to each level of abstraction among WE methodologies may hamper the task of defining a common quality model that includes measures and that serves as a basis to define

measurement models. Again, reaching an agreement on a common WE metamodel may leverage this risk.

We have left out of the scope of this chapter related fields of research, such as the quality of the models *per se,* or the quality of the process as it improves the cost of building applications. However, we believe that some of the concepts presented in this chapter may be reused to study the impact of using a WE methodology on such fields of research.

Last, we are aware that research knowledge is not intrinsically valuable: It only becomes valuable if it is used in practice (Moody, 2005). Successful WE technology practice depends on two-way knowledge transfers between research and practice, rather than ideas flowing in only one direction. Therefore, there is a need for collaboration between researchers and practitioners if we are to convert our new ideas (inventions) in real innovations, adopted by the Web community.

ACKNOWLEDGMENT

This chapter has been supported by the Spanish Ministry of Science and Technology (Grant PR2006-0374 for University Teaching Staff Stages at foreign universities, projects MEC-FEDER (TIN2004-03145), ESFINGE (TIN2006-15175-C05-05), METASIGN (TIN2004-00779) and DSDM (TIN2005-25866-E)). Also, this research is part of the DADASMECA project (GV05/220), financed by the Valencia Government and the DADS (PBC-05-012-2) and the DIMENSIONS (PBC-05-012-1) projects, financed by the Regional Science and Technology Ministry of Castilla-La Mancha (Spain).

REFERENCES

Abrahao, S., Condory-Fernández, N., Olsina, L., & Pastor, O. (2003). Defining and validating metrics for navigation models. *Proceedings of the Ninth IEEE International Software Metrics Symposium* (pp. 200-210). Chichester, UK: IEEE Press, Wiley.

Abrahao, S., & Insfran, E. (2006). Early usability evaluation in model-driven architecture environments. *Proceedings of the Sixth IEEE International Conference on Quality Software.* Chichester, UK: IEEE Press, Wiley.

Assenova, P., & Johannesson, P. (1996). Improving quality in conceptual modelling by the use of schema transformations. *Proceedings of ER 1996* (pp. 277-291).

Bajaj, A., & Krishnan, R. (1999). CMU-WEB: A conceptual model for designing usable Web applications. *Journal of Database Management, 10*(4), 33-43.

Baresi, L., Morasca, S., & Paolini, P. (2003). Estimating the design effort of Web applications. *IEEE Metrics,* 62-72.

Batini, C., Ceri, S., & Navathe, S. B. (1992). *Conceptual database design: An entity relationship approach.* Redwood City, CA: Benjamin-Cummings Publishing Company.

Bohem, B. W. (1981). *Software engineering economics.* Englewood Cliffs, NJ: Prentice Hall Inc.

Briand, L. L., Morasca, S., & Basili, V. (1999). Defining and validating measures for object-based high-level design. *IEEE Transactions on Software Engineering, 25*(5), 722-743.

Briand, L. L., & Wüst, J. (2002). Empirical studies of quality models in object-oriented systems. *Advances in Computers, 59,* 97-166.

Cachero, C., Genero, M., Calero, C., & Meliá, M. (2006a). Quality-driven automatic transformations of object-oriented navigational models. *Proceedings of ER 2006 (Workshops)* (pp. 329-338). Heidelberg, Germany: Springer Verlag.

Cachero, C., Koch, N., Gómez, J., & Pastor, O. (2002). Conceptual navigation analysis: A device and platform independent navigation specification. *Proceedings of the 2nd International Workshop on Web Oriented Software Technology, Málaga, Spain.*

Cachero, C., Meliá, M., Genero, G., Poels, G., & Calero, C. (2006b). *Towards improving the navigability of Web applications: A model-driven approach* (Working Paper D/2006/7012/64). Retrieved from www.feb.ugent.be/Fac/Research/WP/Papers/wp_06_419.pdf

Calero, C., Ruiz, J., & Piatinni, M. (2005). Classifying Web metrics using the Web quality model. *Online Information Review Journal OIR, 29*(3).

Dix, A., Finlay, J., Abowd, G., & Beale, R. (2004). *Human computer interaction, 3rd ed.* Prentice Hall.

Dromey, R. G. (1995). A model for software product quality. *IEEE Transactions on Software Engineering, 21*(2), 146-162.

Ferreira, M., García, F., Bertoa, M., Calero, C., Vallecillo, A., Ruiz, F., Piattini, M., & Braga, J. L. (2006). Medición del Software: Ontología y Metamodelo (Tech. Rep.). University of Castilla-La Mancha.

Fraternali, P., & Paolini, P. (2000). Model-driven development of Web applications: The autoweb system. *ACM Transactions on Information Systems (TOIS), 18*(4), 323–382.

García, F., Bertoa, M., Calero, C., Vallecillo, A., Ruiz, F., Piattini, M., & Genero, M. (2005). Towards a consistent terminology for software measurement. *Information and Software Technology, 48*(8), 631-644.

Garvin, D. (1984). What does "product quality" really mean? *Sloan Management Review*, (Fall), 25-45.

Genero, M. (2002). *Defining and validating metrics for conceptual models.* Doctoral thesis, University of Castilla-La Mancha.

Heuser, L. (2004). The real world or Web engineering? *Proceedings of the Fourth International Conference on Web engineering* (pp. 1-5) Heidelberg, Germany: Springer-Verlag.

ISO/IEC 9126 (2001). *Software engineering – Product quality – Part 1: Quality model.* Geneva, Switzerland: International Organization for Standardization.

ISO/IEC 9241 (1998). *Ergonomic requirements for office work with visual display terminals (VDTs) – Part 11: Guidance on usability.* Geneva, Switzerland: International Organization for Standardization.

ISO/IEC 10027 (1990). *Information technology – Information resource framework.* Geneva, Switzerland: International Organization for Standardization.,

ISO/IEC 14598 (1999). *Information technology— Software product evaluation.* Geneva, Switzerland: International Organization for Standardization.

Ivory, M. Y. (2004). *Automated Web site evaluation.* Norwell, MA: Kluwer Academic Publishers.

Ivory, M. Y., & Hearst, M. A. (2001). The state of the art in automating usability evaluation in user interfaces. *ACM Computing Surveys, 33*(44), 470-516.

Ivory, M. Y., & Megraw, R. (2005). Evolution of Web site design patterns. *ACM Transactions on Information Systems, 23*(4), 463-497.

Kent, S. (2002). Model-driven engineering. *Proceedings of the Third International Conference on Integrated Formal Methods* (pp. 286-298). Heidelberg, Germany: Springer-Verlag.

Kesh, S. (1995). Evaluating the quality of entity relationship models. *Information and Software Technology, 37*(12), 681-689.

Krogstie, J., Lindland, O. I., & Sindre, G. (1995). Defining quality aspects for conceptual models. *Proceedings of ISCO 1995* (pp. 216-231).

Lang, M., & Fitzgerald, B. (2005). Hypermedia systems development practices: A survey. *IEEE Software, 22*(2), 68-75.

Legris, P., Ingham, J., & Collerette, P. (2003). Why do people use information technology? A critical review of the technology acceptance model. *Information and Management, 40*(3), 191.

Levitin, A., & Redman, T. (1995). Quality dimensions of a conceptual view. *Information Processing and Management: An International Journal, 31*(1), 81-88.

Lindland, O. I., Sindre, G., & Solvberg, A. (1994). Understanding quality in conceptual modeling. *IEEE Software, 11*(2), 42-49.

McCall, J. A., Richards, P. K., & Walters, G. F. (1977). *Factors in software quality, Vol. 1, 2, and 3.* National Technical Information Service.

Meliá, S., & Gómez, J. (2006). The WebSA approach: Applying model-driven engineering to Web applications. *Journal of Web engineering, 5*(2), 121-149.

Mendes, E. (2005). A systematic review of Web engineering research. *Proceedings of the 2005 International Symposium on Empirical Software Engineering* (pp. 10-18).

Misic, V. B., & Zhao, J. L. (2000). Evaluating the quality of reference models. *Proceedings of the 19ᵗʰ Conference on Conceptual Modeling, ER 2000* (pp. 484-498).

Moody, D. L. (2005). Theoretical and practical issues in evaluating the quality of conceptual models: Current state and future directions. *Data & Knowledge Engineering, 55*, 243-276.

Moody, D. L., & Shanks, G. G. (2003). Improving the quality of data models: Empirical validation of a quality management framework. *Information Systems, 28*, 619-650.

Moraga, M., Calero, C., & Piattini, M. (2006). Ontology driven definition of a usability model for second generation portals. *Proceedings of the 1st International Workshop on Methods, Architectures, & Technologies for E-Service Engineering (MATeS 2006)* (p. 155). ACM Press..

Nelson, H. J., Monarchi, D. E., & Nelson, K. M. (2001). Ensuring the "goodness" of a conceptual representation. *Proceedings of the 4th European Conference on Software Measurement and ICT Control (FESMA 2001), Heidelberg, Germany.*

Nielsen, J. (2000). *Designing Web usability: The practice of simplicity.* Berkeley, CA: New Riders.

Olsina, L., & Rossi, G. (2002). Measuring Web application quality with WebQEM. *IEEE Multimedia Magazine, 9*(4), 20-29.

Poels, G., Nelson, J., Genero, M., & Piattini, M. (2002). Quality in conceptual modeling - New research directions. *Proceedings of the International Workshop on Conceptual Modeling Quality at ER 2002* (pp. 243-248). Springer.

Ruiz, F., & Hilera, J. R. (2006). Using ontologies in software engineering and technology. In C. Calero, F. Ruiz, & M. Piattini (Eds.), *Ontologies for software engineering and software technology.* Berlin/Heidelberg, Germany: Springer.

Seffah, A., Donyaee, M., Kline, R. B., & Padda, H. K. (2006). Usability measurement and metrics: A consolidated model. *Software Quality Journal, 14*, 159-178.

Shneiderman, B., & Plaisant, C. (2005). *Designing the user interface: Strategies for effective human-computer interaction, 4th ed.* Addison-Wesley.

Si-Said, S., Akoka, J., & Comyn-Wattiau, I. (2006). Use case modeling and refinement: A quality-based approach. *Proceedings of ER 2006* (pp. 84-97).

Suryn, W., Abran, A., & April, A. (2003). ISO/IEC SQuaRE. The second generation of standards for software product quality. *Proceedings of the 7th*

IASTED International Conference on Software Engineering.

Van Zeist, B., Hendriks, P., Paulussen, R., & Trienekens, J. (1996). *Kwaliteit van softwareprodukten—Praktijkervaringen met een kwaliteitsmodel,* Kluwer Bedrijfswetenschappen. (in Dutch).

Von Halle, B. (1991). Data: Asset or liability? *Database Programming Design, 4*(7), 21-24.

Zultner, R. E. (1992). The Deming way: Total quality management for software. *Proceedings of Total Quality Management for Software Conference,* Washington, DC, April.

KEY TERMS

Web quality model: The set of characteristics and the relationships between them which provide the basis for specifying quality requirements and evaluating quality for Web applications

Web engineering practices: The application of systematic, disciplined, and quantifiable approaches to the cost-effective development and evolution of high-quality applications in the World Wide Web

Model-driven engineering (MDE): This is a software development approach whose primary focus is on models, as opposed to source code. Models are built representing different views on a software system. They can be refined, evolved into a new version, and can be used to generate executable code. The ultimate goal is to raise the level of abstraction, and to develop and evolve complex software systems by manipulating models only.

Web application: An application delivered to users from a Web server over a network such as the World Wide Web or an intranet

Measurable concept: Abstract relationship between attributes of entitites and information needs

Software engineering management: The application of management activities - planning, coordinating, measuring, monitoring, controlling, and reporting - to ensure that the development of software is systematic, disciplined, and measured

ENDNOTES

[1] We have intentionally left out of this list the ISO/IEC 9126 characteristics of maintainability and portability, which we consider relevant for stakeholders different from the final user (analysts, designers, developers, maintainers, and so on.)

[2] Interested readers can follow the lines of work and the state of evolution of this project by contacting the MDWEnet project members (http://www.pst.informatik.uni-muenchen.de/~zhangg/cgi-bin/mdwenet/wiki.cg)

Chapter XXIII
Restrictive Methods and Meta Methods for Thematically Focused Web Exploration

Sergej Sizov
University of Koblenz-Landau, Germany

Stefan Siersdorfer
University of Sheffield, UK

ABSTRACT

This chapter addresses the problem of automatically organizing heterogeneous collections of Web documents for the generation of thematically-focused expert search engines and portals. As a possible application scenario for our techniques, we consider a focused Web crawler that aims to populate topics of interest by automatically categorizing newly-fetched documents. A higher accuracy of the underlying supervised (classification) and unsupervised (clustering) methods is achieved by leaving out uncertain documents rather than assigning them to inappropriate topics or clusters with low confidence. We introduce a formal probabilistic model for ensemble-based meta methods and explain how it can be used for constructing estimators and for quality-oriented tuning. Furthermore, we provide a comprehensive experimental study of the proposed meta methodology and realistic use-case examples.

INTRODUCTION

The novel Web exploration paradigm of *focused crawling* or *topical crawling* can be viewed as an attempt to automate intellectual preprocessing and post-processing of Web information (Chakrabarti, 2003; Sizov, Biwer, Graupmann, Siersdorfer, Theobald, Weikum, & Zimmer, 2003; Sizov, Siersdorfer, Theobald, & Weikum, 2002). In contrast to a search engine's generic crawler (which serves to build and maintain the engine's index), a focused crawler is interested only in a specific, typically small, set of topics. Each of the visited documents is classified into the crawler's hierarchy of topics to test whether it is of interest at all and where it belongs within a user-specific taxonomy. This step is automated using classification techniques from machine learning such as Naive Bayes, Maximum Entropy, Support Vector Machines (SVM), or other supervised learning methods. The outcome of the focused crawl can be viewed as the index of a personalized information service or a thematically-specialized search engine. The crawler, along with its document repository, resides on the user's local computer and does not require any centralized services, making the approach robust, objective, and privacy-preserving.

An important aspect of thematically-focused Web exploration applications is the recognition and elimination of thematically-irrelevant documents. Common IR methods usually address „closed" scenarios with a limited number of predefined categories. This is a very significant difference to the „open" Web scenario for which comprehensive learning of all existing topics and themes is clearly impossible. Ideally, a quality-oriented Web IR method should automatically recognize (and reject) documents that do not belong to the desired topics of interest. Another example of a post-processing task is the filtering of the data repository. As a result of the crawl evaluation, the user may decide to remove from the repository relevant but "uncertain" documents with low classification confidence. The reduced repository is expected to contain smaller but much more concise collections of highly-relevant documents.

In this chapter, we discuss meta methods based on ensembles of classification or clustering methods for quality-oriented organization of document collections. Our main focus lies on *restrictive* solutions: organizing only a subset of the data, but doing so with much higher accuracy. Our goal is to allow the user managing the crawl results in a robust way and with minimized human efforts by:

- elimination of thematically-irrelevant "junk" documents;
- robust and tunable categorization of crawl inputs;
- restrictive filtering of crawl results; and
- collaborative organization and filtering of relevant topics.

More generally, this chapter introduces widely-applicable techniques for improving the quality of Web systems. The methodology addressed here can be used for the largely-automated generation of thematically-focused portals and Web taxonomies, "needle-in-a-haystack" expert Web search, design of quality-oriented intelligent user interfaces, and other related applications.

RELATED WORK

There is a plethora of work on text document classification using a variety of probabilistic and discriminative models (Chakrabarti, 2002). The emphasis of this body of work has been on the mathematical and algorithmic aspects, and the engineering aspects of how to cope with trade-offs and how to tune a classifier with regard to properties of the training data.

The machine-learning literature has studied a variety of ensemble-based meta methods such as bagging, stacking, or boosting (Breiman, 1996; Freund, 1999; Kuncheva, 2004; Littlestone & Warmuth, 1989; Wolpert, 1992) and also combinations of heterogeneous learners (e.g., Yu, Chang, & Han, 2002). For bagging, an ensemble consists of classifiers built on bootstrap replicates of the training set. The classifiers outputs are combined by the plurality vote. For stacking, multiple classifiers are trained on parts of the training set and evaluated on the remaining training documents. The outputs of the classifiers are used as feature values for training a new classifier (stacked generalization). Boosting can be viewed as a model averaging method. Here a succession of models is built, each one trained on a data set in which the points misclassified by the previous model are given more weight.

The approach of intentionally splitting training sets for meta learning has been investigated by Chan (1996). The solution proposed in Schein, Popescul, Ungar, and Pennock (2002) studied the accuracy-loss trade-off in a ROC curve model (for a recommender system).

For SVM classifiers, some isolated tuning issues have been considered in the literature. The popular SVM Light software package (Joachims, 1998) provides various kinds of thresholds and variations of SVM training (e.g., SVM regression, transductive SVMs, etc.). Brank, Grobelnik, Milic-Frayling, and Mladenic (2003) have proposed to introduce a bias for the separating hyperplane towards negative training samples, and advocated that this is beneficial when the number of positive training samples is very low.

There is recent work on combining multiple clustering methods in an ensemble learning manner, using consensus functions for clustering based on information theoretic measures (Strehl & Gosh, 2002), constructing a co-association matrix and performing hierarchical clustering on this matrix (Fred & Jain, 2002), combining clusterings pairwise and iteratively (Dimitriadou, Weingessel, & Hornik, 2002), using graph-partitioning methods (Fern & Brodley, 2004), or combining clusterings on different subspaces of a given feature space (Topchy, Jain, & Punch, 2003).

Algorithms for distributed clustering are described in Kargupta, Huang, Sivakumar, and Johnson (2001) and Li, Zhu, and Ogihara (2003). The distributed execution of k-means was discussed in Dhillon and Modha (2000). Privacy-preserving distributed classification and clustering were also addressed in the prior literature: In Vaidya and Clifton (2004), a distributed Naive Bayes classifier is computed; in Merugu and Ghosh (2003), the parameters of local generative models are transmitted to a central site and combined.

TECHNICAL BASICS

Document Representation

All methods discussed in this chapter represent documents as multidimensional feature vectors. In the prevalent bag-of-words model, the features are derived from word occurrence frequencies (Baeza-Yates & Ribeiro-Neto, 1999; Manning & Schuetze, 1999) (e.g., capturing tf or $tf \cdot idf$ weights of terms). In addition, feature selection algorithms (Madison, Yang, & Pedersen, 1997) can be applied to reduce the dimensionality of the feature space and eliminate "noisy", non-characteristic features, based on term frequencies or advanced information-theoretic measures for feature ordering (e.g., mutual information (MI), information gain (Madison et al., 1997), or conditional MI (Wang & Lochovsky, 2004)).

Text Categorization

Classifying text documents into thematic categories usually follows a supervised learning paradigm and is based on training documents that need to be provided for each topic.

Feature vectors of topic-labeled text documents are used to train a classification model for each topic, using probabilistic models (e.g., Naive Bayes) or discriminative models (e.g., SVM). Linear support vector machines (SVMs) construct a hyperplane $\vec{w} \cdot \vec{x} + b = 0$ that separates the set of positive training examples from a set of negative examples with maximum margin. This training requires solving a quadratic optimization problem whose empirical performance is somewhere between quadratic and cubic in the number of training documents (Burges, 1998). For a new, previously unseen, document $\vec{d}$ the SVM merely needs to test whether the document lies on the "positive" side or the "negative" side of the separating hyperplane. The decision simply requires computing a scalar product of the vectors $\vec{w}$ and $\vec{d}$. SVMs have been shown to perform very well for text classification (see, e.g., Dumais & Chen, 2000; Joachims, 1998).

Unsupervised Partitioning of Document Collections

Clustering algorithms partition a set of objects, text documents in our case, into groups called *clusters*. They can be roughly divided into the following groups (Ester, Kriegel, & Sander,

2001): partitioning methods, hierarchical methods, density-based methods, grid-based methods, and model-based methods. In this chapter, we consider partitioning methods: The dataset is divided into disjoint partitions. The number k of clusters is a tuning parameter for this family of clustering algorithms (Han & Kamber, 2001).

A simple, very popular member of the family of partitioning clustering methods is *k-Means* (Hartigan & Wong, 1979): k initial centers (points) are chosen, every document vector is assigned to the nearest center (according to some distance or similarity metric), and new centers are obtained by computing the means (centroids) of the sets of vectors in each cluster. After a number of iterations (according to a stopping criterion), one obtains the final centers, and one can cluster the documents accordingly. A similar algorithm, which can be considered as a "smoothed" form of k-Means is *EM clustering* (Han & Kamber, 2001; Manning & Schuetze, 1999): in every iteration, the probabilities of the objects for being contained in the different clusters are updated using the expectation-maximization technique.

RESTRICTIVE META CLASSIFICATION AND CLUSTERING

Making Simple Classifiers Restrictive

In many quality-oriented Web retrieval applications, the user can tolerate the loss of some (potentially relevant) results in order to substantially improve the quality of the remaining subset. The idea of restrictive classification is to avoid making a decision about a test document at all if that decision can be made only with relatively low confidence. So, out of a given set of unlabeled data U, the restrictive method chooses a subset S of documents that are either accepted or rejected for the given topic label, and abstains on

the documents in $U - S$. Quality measures such as precision, recall, F1, accuracy, and error are computed on the subset S, and we call the ratio $|U - S| / |U|$ the document *loss*.

We can use confidence measures to make simple methods restrictive. For SVMs, a natural confidence measure is the distance of a test document vector from the separating hyperplane. We can tune these methods by requiring accepted or rejected documents to having a distance above some threshold, and abstain otherwise. The threshold is our tuning parameter.

Given an application-acceptable loss of L percent, we can make a classifier restrictive by dismissing the L percent of the test documents with the lowest confidence values.

Restrictive Meta Classifiers

For restrictive meta classification (Sizov, Siersdorfer, & Weikum, 2004), we combine the evidence of multiple distinct classification methods to improve the trade-off between classification quality and loss. More formally, we are given a set $V = \{v_1, ..., v_k\}$ of k binary classifiers with results $R(v_i, d)$ in $\{+1, -1\}$ for a document d, namely, +1 if d is accepted for the given topic by v_i, and -1 if d is rejected. We can combine these results into a meta result: $Meta(d) = Meta(R(v_1, d), ..., R(v_k, d))$ in $\{+1, -1, 0\}$ where 0 means abstention. A family of such meta methods is the linear classifier combination with thresholds (Siersdorfer & Sizov, 2003). Given thresholds t_1 and t_2, with $t_1 > t_2$, and weights $w(v_i)$ for the k underlying classifiers, we compute $Meta(d)$ as follows:

$$Meta(d) = \begin{cases} +1 & \text{if } \sum_{i=1}^{n} R(v_i, d) \cdot w(v_i) > t_1 \, (1) \\ -1 & \text{if } \sum_{i=1}^{n} R(v_i, d) \cdot w(v_i) < t_2 \, (2) \, (1) \\ 0 & \text{otherwise} \end{cases}$$

This meta classifier family has some important special cases, depending on the choice of the weights and thresholds:

1. voting (Breiman, 1996): Meta returns the result of the majority of the classifiers;
2. unanimous decision: If all classifiers give us the same result (either +1 or -1), Meta returns this result, 0 otherwise; and
3. weighted averaging (Wang, Fan, Yu, & Han, 2003): Meta weighs the classifiers by using some predetermined quality estimator, for example, a leave-one-out estimator (Han & Kamber, 2001) for each v_i.

The restrictive and tunable behaviour is achieved by the choice of the thresholds: We dismiss the documents where the linear result combination lies between t_1 and t_2. In the rest of the chapter, we will consider only the unanimous-decision meta classifier as the simplest of the above cases in order to demonstrate the feasibility of our approach. The approach itself carries over to more sophisticated instantiations of the meta classifier framework.

Using Restrictive Meta Classification for Junk Elimination

In classical application scenarios for machine learning, it is assumed that all underlying classifiers had sufficient training data: both positive and negative samples of every thematic that might occur among the test documents. In this section, we drop this assumption and make a major step forward to cope with corpora that are not necessarily "in tune" with the thematic classes that were defined a priori. This is a very significant case with "open" corpora like the Web with a huge amount of topics and documents for which comprehensive training is absolutely impossible (Siersdorfer et al., 2004). From the user perspective, the ability of the information system to "filter out" irrelevant contents (junk) substantially improves both result quality and subjective acceptance.

Figure 1. Contingency table for restrictive classification with junk reduction

		classification result		
		+	-	0
real class	pos	P+	P-	P0
	neg	N+	N-	N0
	junk	J+	J-	J0

Trade-Offs for Restrictive Classification in the Junk Elimination Scenario

In this section, we describe the trade-offs that occur in restrictive classification if the test set contains junk documents (besides documents of interest). Consider a training set T consisting of documents from two classes *pos* and *neg*, and a set of unlabeled documents U containing documents from *pos* and *neg*, and *junk* documents that are not in these classes. The scenario can be easily generalized to a set of l classes $C = \{c_1, ..., c_l\}$ instead of two classes. Given a document $d \in U$, a restrictive classifier gives us the result +1 if it classifies the document into *pos*, -1 if it classifies the document into *neg*, 0 if the classifier abstains. The possible combinations between the real classes and the possible results of a classifier are shown in the contingency table in Figure 1.

An appropriate restrictive classifier should optimize the following quality measures:

1. Maximize ***junk reduction*** (fraction of junk documents dismissed by the classifier):

$$junkRed := \frac{|J0|}{|J+| + |J-| + |J0|} \quad (2)$$

2. Minimize ***loss*** (fraction of dismissed documents from the classes of interest pos and neg) (See Box 1.)

Box 1.

$$loss := \frac{|P0| + |N0|}{|P+| + |P-| + |N+| + |N-| + |P0| + |N0|} \qquad (3)$$

Box 2.

$$error := \frac{|P-| + |N+| + |J+| + |J-|}{|P+| + |P-| + |N+| + |N-| + |J+| + |J-|} \qquad (4)$$

3. Minimize *error* (fraction of non-dismissed documents classified into the wrong class) (See Box 2)

As *document reduction* (not to confuse with the loss), we define the fraction of documents in U, where the classifier abstains:

$$docRed := \frac{|P0| + |N0| + |J0|}{|U|} \qquad (5)$$

The document reduction can be observed directly from the classifier output without knowing the real class labels of the documents in U. The document reduction has an implicit influence on *junkRed*, *loss*, and *error*. In practice, we observe a trade-off between the loss, on the one hand, and junk reduction and error, on the other hand. We can use restrictive methods and meta methods to make simple methods restrictive,

as described in the Making Simple Classifiers Restrictive section and the Restrictive Meta Classifiers section.

A Probabilistic Model for Restrictive Meta Methods in a Reduction Scenario

In this section, we present a probabilistic model for the case that test documents may contain junk documents, and we provide approximations for *loss*, *error*, and *junkRed*. This leads to a better understanding of why restrictive meta methods (restrictive classification, restrictive clustering) can be used for junk elimination.

Consider the unanimous-decision meta method. We associate a Bernoulli random variable X_i with each classification method v_i, where $X_i = 1$ if v_i classifies a document into class *pos* and $X_i = 0$ if v_i classifies a document into class *neg*. We want to compute the probability

Box 3.

$$P(X_1 = 1 \wedge X_2 = 1 | Junk) =$$
$$cov(X_1, X_2 | Junk) + P(X_1 = 1 | Junk) \cdot P(X_2 = 1 | Junk) \qquad (6)$$
where
$$cov(X_1, X_2 | Junk) = \frac{1}{n-1} \sum_j (x_1 - \overline{x_1})(x_2 - \overline{x_2}) \qquad (7)$$
is the covariance for the data points (x_1, x_2) of the joint distribution of (X_1, X_2) on the set of junk documents.

Box 4.

$$P(X_1 = x_1, ..., X_k = x_k \mid Junk) = \tag{8}$$
$$P(X_{root} = 1 \mid Junk) \prod_{(i,j) \in E'} \frac{P(X_i = x_i, X_j = x_j \mid Junk)}{P(X_i = x_j \mid Junk)}$$

where X_{root} is the root node of the tree G' and $x_i \in \{0,1\}$.

Box 5.

$$P(X_1 = 1, ..., X_k = 1 \mid Junk) =$$
$$P(X_1 = 1 \mid Junk) \prod_{i=1}^{k-1} P(X_{i+1} = 1 \mid X_i = 1 \mid Junk) = \tag{9}$$
$$P(X_1 = 1 \mid Junk) \prod_{i=1}^{k-1} \frac{P(X_i = 1, X_{i+1} = 1 \mid Junk)}{P(X_i = 1 \mid Junk)}$$

Box 6.

$$P(X_1 = 1, ..., X_k = 1 \mid Junk) = \tag{10}$$
$$P(X_1 = 1 \mid Junk) \prod_{i=1}^{k-1} \frac{P(X_i = 1 \mid Junk) P(X_{i+1} = 1 \mid Junk) + cov}{P(X_i = 1 \mid Junk)}$$

$P(X_1 = ... = X_k \mid Junk)$ that the classifiers v_i provide a unanimous decision if they are presented a junk document. From basic probability theory, it follows that (See Box 3).

To model the most important correlations among $l > 2$ classification methods, we use a tree dependence model, which is a well-known approximation method in probabilistic IR (Van Rijsbergen, 1977):

We define a *Dependence Graph* $G = (V, E)$ where V consists of the Bernoulli variables X_i and which contains for all X_i, X_j $(i \neq j)$ an undirected edge $e(X_i, X_j)$ with weight $w(e(X_i, X_j))) = cov(X_i, X_j)$. We approximate the Dependence Graph by a maximum spanning tree $G' = (V, E')$ which maximizes the sum of the edge weights. The nodes in G' with no edges in between are considered as independent. So we obtain: (See Box 4.)

Now we introduce the following special case: For any two classification methods v_i, v_j the covariance has approximately the same value cov. With $w(e(X_i, X_j)) = cov$ we can (without loss of generality) choose X_1 as the root node and the edges (X_i, X_{i+1}) as tree edges. Now we have: (See Box 5.)

By considering equation 8 and the above assumption about the covariance we obtain: (See Box 6.)

Analogously we obtain $P(X_1 = 0, ..., X_k = 0 \mid Junk)$.

If we assume that for *junk* documents the classes *pos* and *neg* are equally likely, we can substitute in the above formulas:

Box 7.

$$junkRed = 1 - P(X_1 = ... = X_k \mid Junk) = \tag{12}$$
$$1 - (P(X_1 = 0, ..., X_k = 0 \mid Junk) + P(X_1 = 1, ..., X_k = 1 \mid Junk))$$

Box 8.

$$P(X_1 = 1, ..., X_k = 1 \mid C) = \tag{13}$$
$$P(X_1 = 1 \mid C) \prod_{i=1}^{k-1} \frac{P(X_i = 1 \mid C)P(X_{i+1} = 1 \mid C) + cov'}{P(X_i = 1 \mid C)}$$

where cov' is the covariance on the documents in C. Analogously we obtain $P(X_1 = 0, ..., X_k = 0 \mid C)$.

Box 9.

$$junkRed = 1 - (P(X_1 = 1, ..., X_k = 1 \mid Junk) + P(X_1 = 0, ..., X_k = 0 \mid Junk)) \tag{14}$$

$$loss = 1 - (P(X_1 = 1, ..., X_k = 1 \mid C) + P(X_1 = 0, ..., X_k = 0 \mid C)) \tag{15}$$

$$error = \frac{P(C)P(X_1 = 0, ..., X_k = 0 \mid C) + P(Junk)P(X_1 = ... = X_k \mid Junk)}{1 - junkRed \cdot P(Junk) - loss \cdot P(C)} \tag{16}$$

$$docRed = junkRed \cdot P(Junk) + loss \cdot P(C) \tag{17}$$

$$P(X_i = 1 \mid Junk) = P(X_i = 0 \mid Junk) = \frac{1}{2} \tag{11}$$

For the junk reduction we substitute the above formulas into: (See Box 7.)

To compute the probabilities that all classifiers v_i classify a document into the same class, if the document belongs to one of the classes in $C = \{pos, neg\}$, we associate a Bernoulli variable X_i with each classification method v_i, where $X_i = 1$ if v_i classifies a document correctly, 0 otherwise. We want to compute the probabilities $P(X_1 = 1, ..., X_k = 1 \mid C)$ and $P(X_1 = 0, ..., X_k = 0 \mid C)$ that all classifiers classify a document correctly / incorrectly if the document belongs to one of the classes in C.

With analogous arguments as above we obtain the following approximation: (See Box 8.)

Let $P(C)$ be the probability that a document belongs to a class in C and $P(Junk)$ be the probability that a document is a junk document. Then we obtain approximations for *junkRed*, *loss*, *error*, and *docRed* by inserting the above expressions into: (See Box 9.)

As an illustrative example, we consider the case that the $k > 2$ classification methods have the same probability $p < 0.5$ to misassign a document from C (i.e., the classification methods perform better than random), that in the case of a junk document the assignment of the classes *pos* or *neg* are equally likely, that we have in all cases a covariance $c < p(1 - p)$ (i.e., the classification methods are not perfectly correlated), and that our document corpus contains 50% junk documents. In this case, we would obtain for *junkRed*, *loss*, and *error*: (See Box 10.)

Box 10.

$$junkRed = 1 - \left(\frac{c+1/4}{1/2}\right)^{k-1} \tag{18}$$

$$loss = 1 - \left((1-p)\left(\frac{c+(1-p)^2}{1-p}\right)^{k-1} + p\left(\frac{c+p^2}{p}\right)^{k-1}\right) \tag{19}$$

$$error = \frac{p\left(\frac{c+p^2}{p}\right)^{k-1} + \left(\frac{c+1/4}{1/2}\right)^{k-1}}{\left(\frac{c+1/4}{1/2}\right)^{k-1} + (1-p)\left(\frac{c+(1-p)^2}{1-p}\right)^{k-1} + p\left(\frac{c+p^2}{p}\right)^{k-1}} \tag{20}$$

It is easy to show that for $k \to \infty$ the loss converges monotonically to 1, and the error to 0 (i.e., with more classification methods, we can obtain a lower error but pay the price of a higher loss). Furthermore also *junkRed* converges to 1 and the salient invariant *loss > junkRed* holds. Even $\frac{1-loss}{1-junkRed}$ converges to ∞; this means, that with increasing k we dismiss much more junk documents than documents of interest. The covariance plays the role of a "smoothing constant": with higher correlated classification methods, the convergence of both loss and error is slowed down.

Restrictive Meta Clustering

Making Simple Methods Restrictive

Analogously to the idea of restrictive classification, the idea of restrictive clustering (Sizov & Siersdorfer, 2004) is to avoid making a decision about a document at all, if that decision can be made only with low confidence. So out of a given set of unlabeled data U, our method chooses a subset S of documents that are assigned to clusters, and abstains on the documents in $U - S$. We call the ratio $|U - S| / |U|$ of dismissed documents the document *loss*.

We can use confidence measures to make simple methods restrictive. For the different variants of the k-means method, a natural confidence measure is the inverse distance of a document vector from the nearest centroid (or some other similarity measure).

Restrictive Meta Methods

For meta clustering we are given a set $C = \{c_1, ..., c_l\}$ of different clustering methods. A document d is assigned to one of k clusters with labels $\{1, ..., k\}$: $c_i(d) \in \{1, ..., k\}$. The idea of meta clustering is to combine the different clustering results in an appropriate way.

Meta Mapping

To combine the $c_i(d)$ into a meta result, the first problem is to determine which cluster labels of different methods c_i correspond to each other. Note that cluster label 2 of method c_i does not necessarily correspond to the same cluster label 2 of method c_j, but could correspond to, say, cluster label 5. With perfect clustering methods, the solution would be trivial: The documents labeled by c_i as a would be exactly the documents labeled by c_j as b, and we could easily test this with one representative per cluster. This assumption is, of course, unrealistic; rather, clustering results exhibit certain fuzziness so that some documents end up in clusters other than their perfectly-suitable cluster. Informally, for different clustering methods, we would like to associate the clusters with other clusters which are "most correlated".

Box 11.

$$overlap(A_1, ..., A_x) := \frac{|A_1 \cap ... \cap A_x|}{|A_1| + ... + |A_x| - |A_1 \cap ... \cap A_x|} \quad (22)$$

Formally, for every method c_i we want to determine a bijective function $map_i : \{1, ..., k\} \rightarrow \{1, ..., k\}$ which assigns each label $a \in \{1, ..., k\}$ assigned by c_i to a meta label $map_i(a)$. By this mapping, the clustering labels of the different methods are associated with each other, and we can define the clustering result for document d using method c_i as:

$$res_i(d) := map_i(c_i(d)) \quad (21)$$

We now describe different ways to obtain the map_i functions.

Correlation-based approach: We want to maximize the correlation between the cluster labels. For sets $A_1, ..., A_x$, we can define their *overlap* as (See Box 11.)

Now using

$$A_{ij} := \{d \in U \mid res_i(d) = j\} \quad (23)$$

we can define the *average overlap* for a document set U and the set of clustering methods C as

$$\frac{1}{k} \sum_{j=1}^{k} \frac{1}{\binom{l}{2}} \sum_{(i,m) \in \{1,...,k\}^2, i<m} overlap(A_{ij}, A_{mj}) \quad (24)$$

We are interested in the meta mappings map_i which maximizes the average overlap. This problem can be transformed into a multidimensional assignment problem (MAP) (Pierskalla, 1968) which has been shown to be NP-complete; thus this approach is only viable for small values of k and l. A greedy simplification is to maximize the overlap between pairs of clustering methods,

for example, c_1 and c_2, c_2 and c_3, ..., c_{l-1} and c_l, and to use transitivity to compute an overall mapping.

In Sizov and Siersdorfer (2004), we additionally describe alternative mapping approaches, using variances between cluster overlaps (coined *purity-based mapping*) or association rule mining.

Meta Functions

After having computed the mapping, we are given a set $C = \{c_1, ..., c_l\}$ of l clustering methods with results $res_i(d)$. For simplicity we consider here the case of $k = 2$ clusters and choose $res_i(d) \in \{+1, -1\}$ for a document d, namely, +1 if d is assigned to cluster 1, and -1 if d is assigned to cluster 2. We can combine these results into a meta result: $Meta(d) = Meta(res_1(d), ..., res_l(d))$ in $\{+1, -1, 0\}$ where 0 means abstention. This is analogous to the combination of the results in meta classification, as described in the Restrictive Meta Classifiers section.

Restrictive Methods and Meta Methods in Peer-to-Peer Systems

In this section, we apply the meta classification and clustering approach, described above, in the context of peer-to-peer (P2P) systems. Our approach is to combine models from multiple peers and to construct an advanced decision model (collaborative classification, collaborative clustering) that takes the knowledge of multiple P2P users into account.

In our framework, we are given a set of k peers $P = \{p_1, ..., p_k\}$. Each peer p_i maintains its collection of documents D_i. The idea is to build concise individual models on each peer and then combine the models into a metamodel. More formally, in the first step each peer p_i builds a model $m_i(D_i)$ using its own document set D_i. In the second step, the models m_i are propagated among the k peers over the network. To avoid high network load, it is crucial for this step that the models m_i are a very compressed representation of the document sets D_i. In the next step, each peer p_i uses the set of received models $M = \{m_1,...,m_k\}$ to construct a metamodel $Meta_i(m_1,...,m_k)$. From now on, p_i can use the new metamodel $Meta_i$ (instead of the "local" model m_i) to analyze its own data D_i.

For classification, instead of transferring the whole training sets T_i, only the models m_i need to be exchanged among the peers. For instance, linear support vector machines (SVMs), as described in the Technical Basics section, can be represented in a very compressed way: as tuples $(\vec{w}, \vec{l}, b)$ of the normal vector $\vec{w}$ and bias b of the hyperplane and $\vec{l}$, a vector consisting of the encodings of the terms (e.g., some hashcode) corresponding to the dimensions of $\vec{w}$, $\vec{l}$ provides us with synchronization between the feature spaces of the different peers. Similar space-saving representations are possible for other learning methods (e.g., Bayesian Learners). In addition, building the classifiers this way is much more efficient than building one "global" classifier based on $T = \cup T_i$ because the computation is distributed among the peers, and for classifiers with highly nonlinear training time (e.g., SVM), the splitting can save a lot of time (see Sizov et al., 2003).

Analogous representations can be obtained for distributed clustering models. For the k-means clustering algorithm (see the Technical Basics section), the clustering model can be represented as $(z_1,...,z_l, \vec{l})$, where the z_i are vector representations of the computed centroids, and $\vec{l}$ contains encodings of the feature dimensions, and provides us with a synchronization of the feature spaces, as described above for classification.

We can then exchange clustering and classification models, and combine them using meta methods as described in the Restrictive Meta Classifiers section and the Restrictive Meta Clustering section.

Estimators and Tuning

The main ingredients of the estimation and tuning process are:

1. estimators for base classifiers (based on cross-validation between training subsets T_i);
2. estimators for the pair-wise correlations between the base classifiers $\{m_1,...,m_k\}$; and
3. probabilistic estimators for loss and error based on 1. and 2.

For the cross-validation, at least two peers from the P2P overlay network, p_i and p_j, must cooperate: p_i sends a tuple $(m_i, IDs(T_i))$, consisting of its classifier m_i and a list of IDs (not contents!) of its training documents, to p_j. The peer p_j uses the list of submitted IDs to identify duplicates in both collections and performs cross-validation by m_i on $T_j - T_i$. In the Web context, the IDs of T_i can be easily obtained by computing content-based "fingerprints" or "message digests" (e.g., MD5 (Rivest, 1992)). The resulting error estimator (a simple numerical value) for m_i can be forwarded from p_j back to p_i or to other peers.

For the computation of pair-wise covariance, at least three peers, p_i, p_j and p_m, must cooperate: p_i and p_j send their classifiers and document IDs to p_m and p_m cross-validates in parallel both classifiers on $T_m - T_i - T_j$. By this procedure we get also accuracy estimators.

Finally, the estimators for *covariance* and *accuracy* (numerical values) can be distributed among the peers, and estimators for the overall meta classifier can be built. When the estimated quality of the resulting meta classifier does not meet the application-specific peer requirements (e.g., the expected accuracy is still below the specified threshold), the initiating peer may decide to invoke additional nodes for better meta classification. Note that for meta clustering, estimators *cannot* be built in the same easy way, because for the unsupervised case we cannot evaluate base methods by cross-validation.

EVALUATION

Testbed

To simulate different quality-oriented Web retrieval scenarios (focused Web crawling, sending queries to "Deep Web" portals, analyzing recent newsgroup discussions or publications in electronic journals) we performed multiple series of experiments with real-life data from the newsgroups collection (newsgroups). This collection contains 17,847 postings collected from 20 Usenet newsgroups. Particular topics ("rec.autos", "sci.space", etc.) contain between 600 and 1,000 documents.

Junk Elimination

For junk elimination experiments, we "spoiled" the test set for each pair of evaluated topics by increasing this set by 50%, by adding randomly-chosen "junk documents" from different topics.

As an application example, we tested junk reduction for a Web crawl. We obtained our training set from a bookmark file containing 79 documents of the categories "Movies" and "Computer Science" and started the crawl on the portals shown in Figure 2. By this Web crawl, we obtained an overall number of 1,061 documents consisting of 400 documents about computer science, 348 documents about movies, and 313 junk documents.

In our experiments, we considered the following base methods:

Figure 2. Starting points for the Web crawl

Computer Science:
http://www.developer.com/
http://www.techweb.com
http://directory.google.com/Top/Computers/ComputerScience/
http://library.albany.edu/subject/csci.htm
http://dir.yahoo.com/Science/Computer

Movies:
http://www.allmovieportal.com/
http://www.galatta.com/
http://adutopia.subportal.com/cgi-bin/apollo/apollo.cgi
http://dir.yahoo.com/Entertainment/MoviesAndFilm/Genres/
http://www.badmovies.org

- **base1:** Feature selection by Mutual Information (top 200 terms); learning by linear SVM;
- **base2:** Feature selection by Information Gain (top 200 terms); learning by linear SVM; and
- **base3:** Feature selection by Chi Squared Statistics (top 200 terms); learning by linear SVM.

There are many alternative ways to build the base classifiers, for example, using Naive Bayes, Decision Trees, and so forth. Here we chose linear SVM because it has been shown to often outperform other methods in text classification tasks (see, e.g., Dumais, Platt, Heckerman, & Sahami, 1998).

In the first experimental serial, we compared the meta results with the results of the underlying base methods and the restrictive base methods (inducing the same document reduction as the meta method). Figures 3 and 4 summarize results of this evaluation for the newsgroups collection and the Web crawl dataset.

In the second experimental serial, we compared each base method for different degrees of restrictivity (inducing different document reductions). Figure 5 summarizes results of evaluation for restrictive classification.

Figure 3. Error of meta classification

# Train Docs	Meta		restrictive Base			Base			Data-set
			base1	base2	base3	base1	base2	base3	
	avg docRed	avg error	avg error	avg error	avg error	avg error	avg error	avg error	
25	0.165	0.344	0.358	0.358	0.358	0.419	0.416	0.417	News-groups
50	0.166	0.316	0.327	0.328	0.329	0.398	0.396	0.397	
100	0.143	0.31	0.318	0.315	0.315	0.385	0.381	0.381	Web
79	0.074	0.301	0.282	0.319	0.327	0.323	0.348	0.351	

Figure 4. Loss and junk reduction of meta classification

# Train Docs	Meta			restrictive Base			Base			Data-set
				base1	base2	base3	base1	base2	base3	
	avg docRed	avg loss	avg jRed	avg loss	avg loss	avg loss	avg jRed	avg jRed	avg jRed	
25	0.165	0.109	0.276	0.118	0.122	0.12	0.259	0.251	0.254	News-groups
50	0.166	0.098	0.301	0.103	0.108	0.108	0.29	0.281	0.282	
100	0.143	0.077	0.275	0.078	0.079	0.078	0.272	0.271	0.273	Web
79	0.074	0.044	0.144	0.032	0.055	0.06	0.173	0.118	0.143	

The main observations are:

- The junk reduction is (for restrictive base methods as well as for meta methods) always significantly higher than the loss (i.e. we dismiss a higher percentage of junk than of documents of interest).
- We can clearly observe the trade-offs between *loss*, on the one hand, and *error* and *junkRed*, on the other hand, described in the *trade-offs for restrictive classification in the junk elimination scenario* section and analyzed in the *probabilistic model for restrictive meta methods in a reduction scenario* section.

Clustering

For clustering experiments, we randomly chose 50 *k*-tuples of topics (with *k=3* and *k=5*) from the newsgroups collection. Finally, we computed macro-averaged results for these topic tuples.

Our quality measure describes the correlation between the actual topics of our datasets and the clusters found by the algorithm. Consider that the cluster labels can be permuted: Given two classes $class_1$ and $class_2$, it does not matter, for example, whether a clustering algorithm assigns label *a* to all documents contained to $class_1$ and label *b* contained in $class_2$, or vice versa; the documents belonging together are correctly put together, the quality should reach its maximum value (i.e., 1), and the error should be equal to 0.

Let k be the number of classes and clusters, N_i the total number of clustered documents in $class_i$, N_{ij} the number of documents contained in $class_i$ and having cluster label *j*. We define:

417

Figure 5. Error, loss, and junk reduction of restrictive base methods

doc Red	base1 avg error	base2 avg error	base3 avg error	base1 avg loss	base2 avg loss	base3 avg loss	base1 avg jRed	base2 avg jRed	base3 avg jRed	Data-set
0.0	0.42	0.417	0.417	0	0	0	0	0	0	News-groups
0.1	0.386	0.384	0.383	0.073	0.075	0.074	0.154	0.15	0.153	
0.2	0.348	0.346	0.345	0.145	0.147	0.146	0.31	0.307	0.309	
0.3	0.307	0.305	0.304	0.218	0.22	0.219	0.463	0.461	0.462	
0.4	0.261	0.259	0.26	0.297	0.298	0.298	0.605	0.605	0.604	
0.5	0.216	0.215	0.216	0.385	0.387	0.387	0.729	0.727	0.726	
0.6	0.176	0.172	0.173	0.488	0.487	0.487	0.825	0.827	0.825	
0.7	0.139	0.135	0.137	0.602	0.6	0.601	0.897	0.899	0.897	
0.8	0.108	0.102	0.105	0.727	0.725	0.726	0.947	0.95	0.948	
0.9	0.081	0.076	0.078	0.86	0.859	0.859	0.98	0.982	0.981	
0.0	0.323	0.348	0.351	0	0	0	0	0	0	Web
0.1	0.266	0.311	0.316	0.041	0.074	0.079	0.24	0.163	0.15	
0.2	0.214	0.265	0.284	0.095	0.143	0.164	0.45	0.335	0.284	
0.3	0.168	0.215	0.229	0.166	0.214	0.225	0.62	0.505	0.479	
0.4	0.152	0.198	0.206	0.27	0.31	0.317	0.709	0.613	0.597	
0.5	0.134	0.162	0.177	0.377	0.4	0.409	0.792	0.738	0.716	
0.6	0.127	0.146	0.167	0.497	0.509	0.521	0.843	0.815	0.786	
0.7	0.116	0.119	0.15	0.62	0.62	0.634	0.888	0.888	0.856	
0.8	0.113	0.117	0.122	0.745	0.746	0.747	0.93	0.927	0.923	
0.9	0.131	0.056	0.093	0.873	0.862	0.868	0.962	0.987	0.974	

$$accuracy = \max_{(j_1,...,j_k) \in perm((1,...,k))} \frac{\sum_{i=1}^{k} N_{i,j_i}}{\sum_{i=1}^{k} N_i} \quad (25)$$

and

$$error = 1 - accuracy \quad (26)$$

As *loss* we simply define the fraction of documents dismissed over the whole document set. We use the macro-average of loss and error as an aggregation measure for a larger number of experiments.

In our experiments, we considered the following base methods:

- **base1:** k-Means, no feature selection, pre-clustering with $k \cdot 20$ documents;
- **base2:** iterative feature selection applied on k-Means, pre-clustering with $k \cdot 20$ documents on a pre-selected feature space (df), after each iteration: feature selection (step 1: top-2000 according to df, step 2: top-500 according to MI), number of iterations: 5; and
- **base3:** transforming feature vectors using SVD (SVD rank = 2), application of k-Means on the transformed vectors. We found that a higher SVD rank results in a lower clustering accuracy in consistence with observations made by Hasan and Matsumoto (1999).

Figure 6. Restrictive base methods for k=3 and k=5

loss	k = 3			k = 5			Data-set
	base1	base2	base3	**base1**	**base2**	**base3**	
	avg err	**avg err**	**avg err**	**avg err**	**avg err**	**avg err**	
0.0	0.346	0.332	0.317	0.430	0.403	0.572	
0.1	0.337	0.321	0.303	0.416	0.390	0.551	
0.2	0.325	0.311	0.293	0.403	0.380	0.521	
0.3	0.315	0.302	0.282	0.386	0.369	0.486	
0.4	0.302	0.294	0.272	0.371	0.363	0.451	News-groups
0.5	0.286	0.289	0.260	0.351	0.356	0.413	
0.6	0.266	0.278	0.229	0.328	0.347	0.365	
0.7	0.251	0.270	0.186	0.302	0.327	0.303	
0.8	0.237	0.259	0.142	0.270	0.294	0.234	
0.9	0.209	0.341	0.088	0.224	0.233	0.156	

Figure 7. Meta clustering results for k=3 and k=5

k = 3									
Map	Meta		Restrictive Base			Base			Data-set
	avg loss	avg err	base1	base2	**base3**	base1	**base2**	base3	
			avg err	avg err	avg err	avg err	avg err	avg err	
MapA	0.420	0.242	0.269	0.304	0.255				
MapB	0.479	0.199	0.255	0.291	0.242	0.341	0.326	0.317	News-groups
MapC	0.413	0.240	0.268	0.300	0.257				
k = 5									
Map	Meta		Restrictive Base			Base			Data-set
	avg loss	avg err	base1	base2	base3	base1	base2	base3	
			avg err	avg err	**avg err**	avg err	avg err	avg err	
MapA	0.622	0.320	0.316	0.330	0.348				
MapB	0.758	0.264	0.286	0.281	0.264	0.439	0.403	0.578	News-groups
MapC	0.567	0.341	0.329	0.339	0.378				

Of course, the introduced meta approach can be used with any other clustering methods as well.

Figure 6 shows the loss-error trade-off for the base methods for $k = 3$ and $k = 5$: By inducing a loss, we can obtain a significant reduction of the error.

With the three base methods, we built a restrictive meta clustering algorithm based on the "unanimous decision" function and the three different meta-mappings, namely:

1. **MapA:** correlation-based mapping,
2. **MapB:** purity-based mapping, and
3. **MapC:** mapping using association rules.

We compared the meta results with the results of the underlying base methods and the restrictive base methods (inducing the same loss as the meta method in each experiment). The results are shown in Figure 7. They clearly show that the meta approach provides a lower error than its underlying base methods at the cost of moderate

Figure 8. Results of restrictive meta classification and clustering

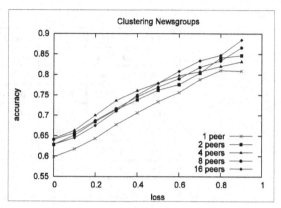

loss. More important, the meta method performs typically better than the restrictive version of each base method for the same loss.

Collaborative Scenarios

Experiments with Supervised Learning Methods (Collaborative Classification)

For each topic pair, we randomly chose 200 training documents per class and kept a distinct and randomly-chosen set of documents for testing the classifiers.

In each experiment, the training data was distributed over 16 peers (data collections in sizes suitable for larger network experiments are hard to get for our scenarios) using equal-sized subsets with approximately 15% overlap (corresponding to peers that contain non-disjoint training data). Among these peers, we randomly chose 1, 2, 4, 8, and all 16 peers to simulate various P2P classification scenarios. The configuration with one peer corresponds to the "local" classification that does not involve sharing of classifiers. Analogously to previous experiments, our quality measure is the fraction of correctly-classified documents (accuracy) among the documents not dismissed by the restrictive algorithm. The *loss* is the fraction of dismissed documents.

Finally, we computed micro-averaged results for all groups of topic pairs. Figure 8 shows the observed dependencies between the numbers of cooperating peers, the induced loss, and the resulting accuracy. It can be observed that the meta classification and restrictive meta classification by multiple cooperating peers clearly outperforms the single-peer solution for all settings of the user-defined *loss*, including the non-restrictive meta classification with *loss* = 0. The quality of the meta algorithm clearly increases with the number of participating peers. In general, the difference between the one-peer solution and the meta solution is statistically significant for four and more participating peers and all values of the induced loss.

Experiments with Unsupervised Learning Methods (Collaborative Clustering)

The topics from classification experiments were also used to evaluate distributed meta clustering. All documents from randomly-combined selections of three or five topics were considered as unlabeled data and distributed among peers analogously to classification experiments from the previous section, with approximately 15% overlap. The goal of the clustering algorithm was to reproduce the partitioning into topics on each peer with possibly high accuracy. Our quality measure describes the correlation between the actual topics of our datasets and the clusters found by the algorithm. For this purpose, we used clustering quality metrics introduced above for non-distributed clustering evaluation, and the computed macro-averaged results among all peers of each experiment.

For all peers, k-means was used as the underlying base method. We compared the one-peer clustering (i.e., clustering that can be executed by one peer on its local dataset without cooperation with others) with meta clustering, exchanging centroids from cooperating peers, and correlation-based mapping of the final clusters. Analogously to classification experiments, we also considered restrictive meta clustering, dismissing exactly the same number of documents with the worst clustering confidence on each peer.

The results are shown in Figure 8. The main observations are similar to the ones discussed for the supervised case.

CONCLUSION AND FUTURE WORK

In this chapter, we proposed the methodology of restrictive methods and meta methods for quality-oriented Web IR applications such as thematically-focused search.

In a P2P environment, different peers might organize their documents into distinct topic taxonomies. In this case, we aim to solve the "topic mapping" problem in the presence of multiple label sets, which would enable us to build meta classification models. This goal can be achieved by estimating the similarity between peer document collections or the similarity of classifiers built locally on distinct peers and validated on collections of other peers. As a side effect, we could generate richer and more fine-grained taxonomies from multiple smaller taxonomies of many peers, and obtain a grouping of peers into "cliques" sharing the same interests.

There is a need for space-efficient encodings of machine learning models and efficient and scalable algorithms for the propagation of these models in a P2P environment (using e.g., Epidemic Protocols or P2P architectures such as Chord). Here the dynamic aspects of the P2P environment, allowing peers to get connected or disconnected in the network, must be taken into account, too.

In a large P2P environment, there may be corrupt users that aim to pollute the statistical learning models by intentionally introducing incorrectly-labeled data. The automatic detection of these peers, on the one hand, and the automatic recognition of "networks of trust" that do not pursue contradicting interests, on the other hand, are important. A key element of this approach could be the mutual evaluation of the peers in the environment and the mapping of the results into a graph-based representation. A similar approach could be applied for detecting qualitative differences of the data among the peers that could allow us the construction of enhanced weighting schemes for metamodels.

REFERENCES

The 20 Newsgroups Data Set. Retrieved from http://www.ai.mit.edu/~ jrennie/20Newsgroups/

Baeza-Yates, R., & Ribeiro-Neto, B. (1999). *Modern information retrieval*. Addison Wesley.

Brank, J., Grobelnik, M., Milic-Frayling, N., & Mladenic, D. (2003). *Training text classifiers with SVM on very few positive examples* (Tech. Rep. MSR-TR-2003-34). Microsoft Corporation.

Breiman, L. (1996). Bagging predictors. *Machine Learning, 24*(2), 123–140.

Burges, C. (1998). A tutorial on support vector machines for pattern recognition. *Data Mining and Knowledge Discovery, 2*(2), 121–167.

Chakrabarti, S. (2002). *Mining the Web: Discovering knowledge from hypertext data*. Morgan Kaufman.

Chakrabarti, S. (2003). *Mining the Web: Discovering knowledge from Web data*. Morgan Kaufmann.

Chan, P. (1996). *An extensible meta-learning approach for scalable and accurate inductive learning.* Doctoral thesis, Department of Computer Science, Columbia University, New York.

Dhillon, I., & Modha, D. (2000). A data-clustering algorithm on distributed memory multiprocessors. *Large-Scale Parallel Data Mining, Lecture Notes in Artificial Intelligence,* 245–260.

Dimitriadou, E., Weingessel, A., & Hornik, K. (2002). A combination scheme for fuzzy clustering. *Proceedings of the 2002 AFSS International Conference on Fuzzy Systems, Calcutta, India* (pp. 332–338). Springer-Verlag.

Dumais, S., & Chen, H. (2000). Hierarchical classification of Web content. *Proceedings of the 23rd ACM International Conference on Research and Development in Information Retrieval (SIGIR), Athens, Greece* (pp. 256–263).

Dumais, S., Platt, J., Heckerman, D., & Sahami, M. (1998). Inductive learning algorithms and representations for text categorization. *Proceedings of the Seventh International Conference on Information and Knowledge Management* (CIKM '98), Bethesda, MD (pp. 148–155). ACM Press.

Ester, M., Kriegel, H. -P., & Sander, J. (2001). *Knowledge discovery in databases.* Springer.

Fern, X. Z., & Brodley, C. E. (2004). Solving cluster ensemble problems by bipartite graph partitioning. *Proceedings of the Twenty-First International Conference on Machine Learning (ICML '04), Banff, Alberta, Canada* (p. 36). ACM Press.

Fred, A. L. N., & Jain, A. K. (2002). Data clustering using evidence accumulation. *Proceedings of the International Conference on Pattern Recognition ICPR, Quebec, Canada: Vol. 4* (pp. 276–280). IEEE Computer Society.

Freund, Y. (1999). An adaptive version of the boost by majority algorithm. *Proceedings of the Workshop on Computational Learning Theory (COLT), Santa Cruz, CA* (pp. 102–113).

Han, J., & Kamber, M. (2001). *Data mining: Concepts and techniques.* Morgan Kaufmann.

Hartigan, J., & Wong, M. (1979). A k-means clustering algorithm. *Applied Statistics, 28,* 100-108.

Hasan, M., & Matsumoto, Y. (1999). *Document clustering: Before and after the singular value decomposition* (Tech. Rep. No. 134). Information Processing Society of Japan, Natural Language Technical Reports.

Joachims, T. (1998). Text categorization with support vector machines: Learning with many relevant features. *ECML.*

Kargupta, H., Huang, W., Sivakumar, K., & Johnson, E. (2001). Distributed clustering using collective principal component analysis. *Knowledge and Information Systems, 3*(4), 422–448.

Kuncheva, L. (2004). *Combining pattern classifiers: Methods and algorithms.* Wiley-Interscience.

Li, T., Zhu, S., & Ogihara, M. (2003). Algorithms for clustering high dimensional and distributed data. *Intelligent Data Analysis, 7*(4), 305–326.

Littlestone, N., & Warmuth, M. (1989). The weighted majority algorithm. *FOCS.*

Madison, W., Yang, Y., & Pedersen, J. (1997). A comparative study on feature selection in text categorization. *ICML.*

Manning, C., & Schuetze, H. (1999). *Foundations of statistical natural language processing.* MIT Press.

Merugu, S., & Ghosh, J. (2003). Privacy-preserving distributed clustering using generative models. *Proceedings of the International Conference on Data Mining (ICDM), Melbourne, FL* (pp. 211–218).

Pierskalla, W. (1968). The multi-dimensional assignment problem. *Operations Research, 16,* 422–431.

Rivest, R. (1992). *RFC 1321: The MD5 Message Digest Algorithm.* Retrieved from http://www.ietf.org/rfc/rfc1321.txt

Schein, A., Popescul, A., Ungar, L., & Pennock, D. (2002). Methods and metrics for cold-start recommendations. *Proceedings of the ACM Conference on Research and Development in Information Retrieval.*

Siersdorfer, S., & Sizov, S. (2003). Construction of feature spaces and meta methods for classification of Web documents. *Proceedings of the 10th Conference Datenbanksysteme fuer Business, Technologie und Web (BTW), Leipzig, Germany* (pp. 197–206).

Siersdorfer, S., & Weikum, G. (2005). Using restrictive classification and meta classification for junk elimination. In D. Losada & J. M. F. Luna (Eds.), *Proceedings of the 27th European Conference on Information Retrieval (ECIR '05), Santiago de Compostela, Spain: Vol. 3408. Lecture Notes in Computer Science* (pp. 287–299). Information Retrieval Specialist Group of the British Computer Society (BCS-IRSG), Springer.

Sizov, S., Biwer, M., Graupmann, J., Siersdorfer, S., Theobald, M., Weikum, G., & Zimmer, P. (2003). The BINGO! System for information portal generation and expert Web search. *Proceedings of the 1st Conference on Innovative Systems Research (CIDR), Asilomar, CA.*

Sizov, S., & Siersdorfer, S. (2004). Restrictive clustering and metaclustering for self-organizing document collections. *Proceedings of the 27th International Conference on Research and Development in Information Retrieval (SIGIR), Sheffield, UK* (pp. 226–233).

Sizov, S., Siersdorfer, S., Theobald, M., & Weikum, G. (2002). BINGO!: Bookmark-induced gathering of information. *Proceedings of the 3rd International Conference on Web Information Systems Engineering (WISE), Singapore* (pp. 323–332).

Sizov, S., Siersdorfer, S., & Weikum, G. (2004). Goal-oriented methods and meta methods for document classification and their parameter tuning. *Proceedings of the ACM Conference on Information and Knowledge Management (CIKM), Washington, DC* (pp. 59–68).

Strehl, A., & Gosh, J. (2002). Cluster ensembles - A knowledge reuse framework for combining multiple partitions. *Journal of Machine Learning Research, 3,* 583–617.

Topchy, A., Jain, A. K., & Punch, W. (2003). Combining multiple weak clusterings. *Proceedings of the Third IEEE International Conference on Data Mining (ICDM '03), Melbourne, FL* (p. 331). IEEE Computer Society.

Vaidya, J., & Clifton, C. (2004). Privacy preserving Naive Bayes classifier for vertically partitioned data. *Proceedings of the SIAM International Conference on Data Mining, Orlando, FL.*

Van Rijsbergen, C. (1977). A theoretical basis for the use of co-occurence data in information retrieval. *Journal of Documentation, 33*(2), 106–119.

Wang, G., & Lochovsky, F. (2004). Feature selection with conditional mutual information maxi-min in text categorization. *Proceedings of the 13th ACM Conference on Information and Knowledge Management (CIKM), Washington DC* (pp. 342–349).

Wang, H., Fan, W., Yu, P., & Han, J. (2003). Mining concept-drifting data streams using ensemble classifiers. *Proceedings of the 9th ACM International Conference on Knowledge Discovery and Data Mining (SIGKDD), Washington, DC* (pp. 226–235).

Wolpert, D. (1992). Stacked generalization. *Neural Networks, 5,* 241–259.

Yu, H., Chang, K., & Han, J. (2002). Heterogeneous learner for Web page classification. *Proceedings of the IEEE International Conference on Data Mining (ICDM), Maebashi, Japan* (pp. 538–545).

Chapter XXIV
WSRP–O:
An Ontology to Model WSRP Compliant Portlets

Mª Ángeles Moraga
University of Castilla-La Mancha, Spain

Ignacio García-Rodríguez de Guzmán
University of Castilla-La Mancha, Spain

Coral Calero
University of Castilla-La Mancha, Spain

Mario Piattini
University of Castilla-La Mancha, Spain

ABSTRACT

The use of Web portals continues to rise, showing their importance in the current information society. Specifically, this chapter focuses on portlet-based portals. Portlets are Web components, and they can be thought of as COTS but in a Web setting. Recently, the Web service for remote portlets (WSRP) standard has come into existence. Its aim is to provide a common interface in order to allow the communication between portal and portlets. Bearing all that in mind, in this chapter we propose an ontology for this standard. This ontology offers an understandable summary of the standard. Thus, the ontology leads both portlet and portal developers to focus their effort on developing the portlet domain logic instead of implementing its communication.

INTRODUCTION

A portal is a Web presence that consolidates a variety of information and services, for example, searching, news, e-mail, discussion groups, and e-commerce (Ma, Bacon, Petridis, & Windall, 2006). The aim of many Web portals is to select, organize, and distribute content (information, or other services and products) in order to satisfy its users/customers (Domingues, Soares, & Jorge, 2006). Therefore a Web portal is an entry door for users.

Today, portlet is the basic component of a portal, which represents an interactive Web mini-application and is deployed on a portal server (Java Community Process, 2003). Portlets are used by portals as pluggable user interface components that provide a presentation layer to Information Systems, that is, they are the individual components displayed in the portal that provide content for it. (Java Community Process, 2003)

Therefore, a portlet is a producer-hosted component that generates content design for aggregating and processing interactions generated from that content (OASIS, 2003). It can be thought as a Web component that comprises a full-fledged Web application to be delivered through a Web portal.

When portlets came into existence, their main problem was the lack of interoperability between the portlet and the portal in which it was aggregated. Portlets had to be custom-developed for each portal server because the API was different for each server (Linwood & Minter, 2004). However, this problem was eliminated when the Web services for remote portlets (WSRP) standard appeared. This standard allows portal developers to aggregate portlets developed by third parties without modifying the code.

Despite the existence of the WSRP standard, there are different companies which offer portlets that do not adhere to this standard (see http://www.jahia.net/jahia/571). These portlets present several problems between them; the following ones can be highlighted:

1. Nonexistence of interoperability between portlets and portal; and
2. Impossibility of offering these portlets to different portal developers.

Currently it is possible to find portlet repositories where portal developers can acquire a portlet which satisfies their needs (i.e., they do not have to develop the portlet, they only have to use it) (Montejava, 2006). Indeed, the Open Source Portlet Repository Project has been recently launched (Blattman et al. 2006) to foster the free and open exchange of portlets. A Portlet Repository can be defined as "a library of ready-to-run applications that you can download and deploy directly into your portal with, in most cases, no additional setups or configurations". Other similar portlet-sharing sites include Portlet Swap (jboss.org) and Portlet Exchange (portletexchange.com).

The majority of portlets, which are offered in repositories, adhere to the WSRP standard. This standard defines four different interfaces for accessing and interacting with portlets, but the specification is not easily understood and there is a lack of a methodological base for the development of portlets.

On the other hand, a new software development paradigm has emerged, the model-driven architecture (MDA). MDA allows developers to not focus on the design, because they can use abstract languages or metamodels which lead to the development of artefacts (OMG, 2003). In particular, the OMG's model-driven architecture is a new software development method which enables heterogeneous interaction and integration, and improves software portability (OMG, 2001).

Bearing all that in mind, it is possible to conclude that the use of MDA to make easier the development of new portlets which adhere to WSRP, as well as the adaptation of existing portlets that do not adhere to WSRP, would be useful. Therefore, one effective way to develop or adapt portlets which adhere to WSRP standard is to create an ontology which supports the portlet development.

Ontologies reduce the problems associated with terminological ambiguity, and allow us to share knowledge and facilitate the communication between people and/or systems, even those having differing necessities and viewpoints (Ruiz & Hilera, 2006). By using an ontology, both portlet and portal developers can focus their effort on developing the portlet domain logic instead of understanding the standard. For all these reasons, we have created a specific ontology, namely WSRP-O, for the WSRP standard.

This chapter is structured as follows. The second section gives a brief view of portlets and standards for portlets. In the third section, the ontology for WSRP is shown. Finally, in the fourth section, conclusions are drawn, and areas of future research are discussed.

STATE OF THE ART

This section is divided into three subsections. The first subsection presents a brief overview of Web portals; the second subsection summarizes the main concepts about portlets and the standards related to them. Finally, the last subsection presents a related literature review on ontologies.

Web Portals

Portals provide a way of access to a local or remote network, for example, to a company in the case of a corporate portal, or to general-interest topics and services in the case of a public portal. In general, portals provide (Marshak & Seybold, 2003) us with:

- A custom framework for presenting pages and components within each page and organizing information for specific communities;
- Personalization capabilities for individual users;
- A set of "portlets" (components that integrate data, applications, content, and resources, and present information to the portal user);
- A single sign-on to the set of applications accessed via the portal; and
- Other features, such as search and collaboration.

According to Marshak and Seybold (2003), portals can be divided into generations:

- **First generation:** *Access Portal:* They were used to provide a set of links to other information and resources;
- **Second generation:** *Aggregation Portals*: They bring information back to the portal

so that the user does not need to seek their information elsewhere; and

- **Other generations:** *Workspace Portals* (where the portal becomes the users' work environment, including all the appropriate information, tools, and resources) and *Adaptive Portals* (where the portal experience itself is dynamically dependent on the user's context and the ongoing process).

Bellas (2004) also divides portal into generations. He affirms that first generation portals tended to present a monolithic software architecture that compromised portal development and management, but second-generation portals let users create one or more personal pages composed of personalizable portlets: interactive Web mini-applications, local or remote to the portal, that render markup fragments (news, weather, sports, and so on) that the portal can aggregate into a page.

In the next subsection, a brief overview on portlets is given.

Portlets and Standards for Portlets

A portlet is a multi-step, user-facing application to be delivered through a Web application (e.g., a portal). Therefore, a portlet includes both logic conforming to some specification of the producer's environment and a particular configuration of any settings or properties that the portlet exposes (OASIS, 2003).

When portlets came into existence, each portal independent development environment (IDE) vendor had a different application program interface (API) for developing portlets; therefore, portlets presented a lack of interoperability. However, the delivery of the Web Services for Remote Portlets (WSRP) specification overcomes this problem.

The goal of the WSRP standard is to enable an application designer or administrator to pick from a rich choice of compliant remote content and application providers (portlets), and integrate them with just a few mouse clicks and no programming effort (OASIS, 2003). To do this, WSRP defines four interfaces:

- **Service Description Interface:** a required interface that allows consumers to find out the capabilities of the producer and about the portlets it hosts, including the metadata necessary for a consumer to interact with each portlet properly;
- **Markup Interface:** a required interface, used to request the generation of markup and the processing of interactions with that markup;
- **Registration Interface:** an optional interface, used to establish a relationship between a producer and a consumer; and
- **Portlet Management Interface:** an optional interface, used to allow consumers to manage the persistent state and life cycle of portlets explicitly.

For each interface, the standard defines different operations for carrying out the specified functionality. It may be worth emphasizing that the WSRP standard is independent of the programming language. Therefore, it is not specific for any platform.

In order to develop a portlet using a specific programming language, other standards have appeared. For example, JSR 168 (Java standarization request) Standard is specific for portlets which are developed by using Java. The standard includes the full specifications of classes, interfaces, and method signatures (Java Community Process, 2003).

However, the use of a standard is not a trivial task; the vocabulary is complex and is generally hard to understand. In view of this situation, a tool which simplifies the standard, such as an ontology, would be necessary.

ONTOLOGIES

First of all, we should provide a definition of ontology: "An ontology defines the basic terms and relations comprising the vocabulary of a topic area as well as the rules for combining terms and relations to define extensions to the vocabulary (Neches, Fikes, Finin, Gruber, Senator, & Swartout, 1991, p.40)".

In addition, different definitions about ontologies can be found in the literature. The majority of them provide a set of common elements. According to Corcho, Fernández-López, and Gómez-Pérez (2006), these elements are:

- **Classes:** represent concepts which are taken in a broad sense; for example, in our case I_Markup is a class which represents the interface *markup* of the standard;
- **Relations:** represent a type of association between concepts of the domain; for example, in WSRP-O, a relationship is used to set up the union between an operation and the data type of their inputs and output;
- **Formal axioms:** serve to model sentences that are always true. They are normally used to represent knowledge that can not be formally defined by the other components. In our case, formal axioms are represented using constraints that represent a formal axiom using a constraint. In order to develop a constraint, OCL (*Object Constraint Language*) well-formedness rules are defined (these well-formedness rules are shown in the third section); and
- **Instances:** are used to represent elements or individuals in an ontology.

According to Calero, Ruiz, Baroni, Brito, Abreu, and Piattini (2006) the ontology representation language should have rich and formal abstractions. Taking into account all these, a language, namely OWL, for the representation of ontologies has appeared. However, it is also possible to represent ontologies using semiformal languages such as UML. Some examples of ontologies that use UML can be found in Calero, Ruiz, and Piattini (2005); Ruiz, Vizcaíno, Piattini, and García (2004); Wang & Chan, 2001). UML-based ontologies have the obvious advantage of being more widely understandable (especially by the portal developers which are more familiarized with UML than with the ontological languages) and of being aligned with the Model-Driven Engineering (MDE) movement (PlanetMDE, 2005).

Nowadays, and depending of the point of view, it is possible to find many classifications for the concept of ontology. Paying attention to the generality level of the concepts that ontologies represent, it is possible to identify the classification exposed in Guarino (1998). In this study, the following "levels" are identified:

- **High-level ontologies:** describe general concepts, not focusing in a particular problem, and trying to unify criteria between different communities;
- **Domain ontologies:** describe the concepts involved in a generic domain;
- **Task ontologies:** the described vocabulary is related with task or activities; and
- **Application ontologies:** the described concepts belong to domain and task levels, specializing the concepts from these ontologies.

In this study, all the concepts included in the domain and task ontologies are specialized from high-level ontologies.

On the other hand, exploring the generality level, it is possible to find other interesting classifications, such as Fonsel (2004), where it is possible to find the following levels:

- **Generic or common-sense ontologies:** try to capture and represent general knowledge of the world, taking into account concepts such as space, time, and so on;
- **Representational ontologies:** represent concepts not linked to a particular domain,

and thus, represent concepts expressed in an object of framework-oriented approach;

- **Domain ontologies:** represent knowledge valid for a particular sort of domain; and
- **Method and task ontologies:** represent concepts to deal with method and tasks definition.

Nonetheless, independently of the level, ontologies are specially useful for (Ruiz & Hilera, 2006): *clarifying the knowledge structure* (concepts and relationships among them must be identified during the ontological analysis); *reducing conceptual and terminological ambiguity* (an ontology constitutes a shared knowledge and points of view); and *allowing the sharing of knowledge* (the adequate representation of the concepts and relationships of a specific domain can be shared with anyone with similar needs for the same domain). Meanwhile, for Pisanelli, Gangemi, and Steve (2002), the most important characteristics are: (1) an explicit semantic and taxonomy; (2) a clear link between concepts, their relationships, and generic theories; (3) context modularization; minimal axiomatization to pinpoint differences between similar concepts; (4) a good politic of name choice; and (5) a rich documentation.

Because ontologies are not restricted to Software Engineering, but any domain, Ruiz & Hilera (2006) proposes a particular taxonomy to classify ontologies in the Software Engineering and Technology (or *SET*, as authors abbreviate) realm. This ontology is composed by two simple categories:

- **Ontologies of domain:** that describes knowledge of the SET domain, and
- **Ontologies as software artefacts:** used as different kinds of artefacts in some software process.

These categories are hierarchically divided according to the division of Table 1.

Table 1. Categories and subcategories in the Ruiz & Hilera (2006) SET ontology taxonomy

Domain	Software Engineering	Generic (all-domain)
		Specific (sub-domain)
	Software Technology	Software
		Data
		Information Technology and Systems
Software Artefacts	At Development Time	For Engineering Processes
		For Other Processes
	At Run Time	As Architectural Artefacts
		As Information Resources

AN ONTOLOGY FOR WSRP STANDARD: WSRP-O

The main objective of this study is to develop an ontology for the WSRP standard. For this reason, in order to describe the ontology proposed in this study, UML class diagrams are used. In addition, the proposed ontology gives support to develop new portlets as well as to adapt existing portlets to the standard. As we have already mentioned, the UML diagrams are accompanied by some constraint defined by using OCL.

According to the taxonomy for Software Engineering and Technology proposed by Ruiz & Hilera (2006) and mentioned in the previous section, WSRP-O can be classified as a *Domain ontology* (because it describes the knowledge of a particular knowledge in technology). Inside

of the *domain* category (see Table 1), WSRP-O can be subclassified as a *Software Engineering ontology*, and specifically as a *Specific ontology*, because WSRP-O has been mainly developed to support portlet construction.

In Figure 1, a global overview of the ontology is shown.

As we can see, the ServiceDescription and Markup interfaces are compulsory, whereas Registration and PortletManagement interfaces are optional. This fact is represented using cardinalities: "1" for the compulsory class, and "0..1" for the optional class. In particular, the aim of each interface is (OASIS, 2003):

- **Self Description:** allows Consumers to find out about the capabilities of the Producer and about the Portlets that it hosts, including the metadata necessary for a Consumer to properly interact with each Portlet;
- **Markup:** used to request and interact with markup fragments;
- **Registration:** used to establish a relationship between a Producer and a Consumer; and
- **Portlet Management:** grants access to the life cycle of the hosted Portlets.

All these interfaces contain different operations. These operations have two common concepts: *fault* and *result*. For this reason, we have created a base class (named Operation) representing these common concepts (Figure 2).

The *Fault* class represents the possible error message that can arise as a result of the opera-

Figure 1. A global overview of the ontology

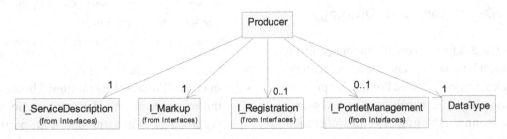

Figure 2. *"Basic portlet operation" as a base class for all the operations of the ontology*

tion, whereas the response represents the result of the operation when any error has occurred. The error messages, as well as the data type of the response, depend on the operation. For this reason, a constraint for each operation will be created to specify the possible faults and results of an operation. The constraint indicates the kind of allowed error messages, along with the allowed data type of the response, for each operation. Finally, it may be worth emphasizing that an operation has to return a fault or a response, but it is not possible to return both of them. In order to represent this restriction, the following constraint has been defined.

```
context Operation
    inv:
        ((result <> null) xor (fault <> null))
```

Moreover, a class, namely *DataType* (see Figure 2), for the allowed data type in the WSRP standard has been included in the ontology. The aim of this class is to describe the different data types proposed in the standard.

The ontology is broken down according to interface decomposition into sub-ontologies. In each sub-ontology, the different operations which are allowed are represented. In addition, in order to represent the allowed data types, another sub-ontology for data types has been included. Next, the different sub-ontologies are presented.

ServiceDescription Sub-Ontology

This interface defines an operation for acquiring the Producer's metadata. The operation, namely ServiceDescription, allows a Producer to provide information about its capabilities in a context-sensitive manner. The header of this operation is the following:

```
ServiceDescription = getServiceDescription
(RegistrationContext, desiredLocales)
```

In Figure 3 the sub-ontology for this interface is shown.

The well-formedness rules that complement the *ServiceDescription* sub-ontology are the following:

```
context getServiceDescription
    inv allowedFaults:
        (self.fault.name="InvalidRegistration"
or
    self.fault.name="OperationFailed))

context getServiceDescription
    inv resultKind:
        self.result.isKindOf(ServiceDescription)
```

The first rule represents the possible values for the error messages, whereas the second rule specifies the possible return value data type of the result.

Markup Sub-Ontology

Markup interface has operations to generate markup and process interactions with that markup. Figure 4 shows markup sub-ontology.

This sub-ontology is composed of four different operations:

- **getMarkup:** This operation renders the current state of a portlet; therefore, using it, we can obtain a portlet's markup. The header of the operation is:

  ```
  MarkupResponse = getMarkup (Registration-
  Context, PortletContext, RuntimeContext,
  UserContext, MarkupParams)
  ```

- **performBlockingInteraction:** The aim of this operation is to send user interactions to the producer. During this operation, portlets can process user interactions while letting the producer affect their state; however, any

Figure 3. Service description sub-ontology

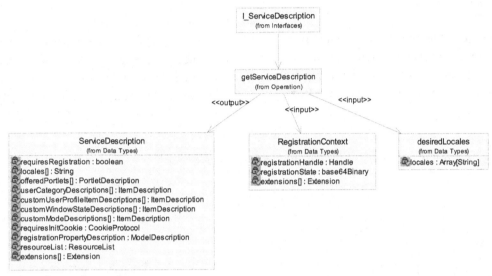

Figure 4. Markup sub-ontology

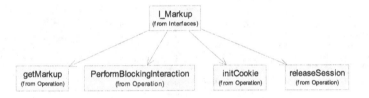

or all of the following may happen: (a) Consumers can use the *performBlockingInteraction* operation to send user interactions to the Producer. During this operation, portlets can process user interactions while letting the Producer affect their state. Note that the scope of the *getMarkup* operation is limited to generating *markup* for a portlet without affecting the current state of the portlet; (b) when a user interacts with a portlet (e.g., by submitting a form), the Consumer uses the *performBlockingInteraction* to send the submitted data to the Producer. During the course of this operation, any or all of the following may happen; (c) portlets can access and process the request data during a *performBlockingInteraction* request; (d) portlets can change their navigational state; (e) portlets can make persistent changes to the state of the portlet; (f) portlets can ask the Consumer to redirect the user to arbitrary URLs; (g) portlets can change their current mode and/or window state; and (h) the Producer can choose to generate and return the portlet's markup as an optimization (OASIS, 2005). Its header is:

```
BlockingInteractionResponse = perform-
BlockingInteraction (RegistrationCon-
text, PortletContext, RuntimeContext,
UserContext, MarkupParams, Interaction-
Params)
```

- **initCookie:** The objective of this operation is to provide assistance to initialize the cookies. The header is:

```
ReturnAny = initCookie (RegistrationCon-
text)
```

- **releaseSession:** The consumer informs the producer that it will no longer be using a set of sessions. The header of the operation is:

```
ReturnAny = release Sessions (Registra-
tionContext, session IDs)
```

In Figure 5, Figure 6, Figure 7, and Figure 8, the operations are shown in more detail.

The well-formedness rules that complement the *Markup* sub-ontology are shown in Box 1.

Registration Sub-Ontology

The registration interface provides the necessary operations to allow a consumer to register with a producer. Registration allows the producer to associate portlets and any portlet customization data with the consumer that is interacting with it (OASIS, 2005).

Figure 5. Get markup operation (it is part of markup sub-ontology)

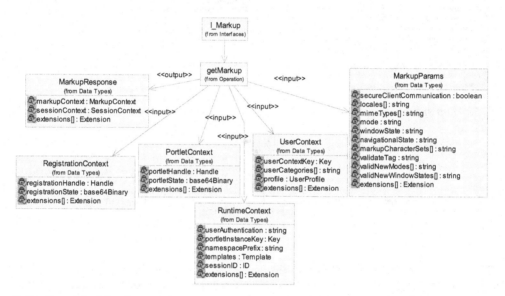

Figure 6. Perform blocking interaction operation (it is part of markup sub-ontology)

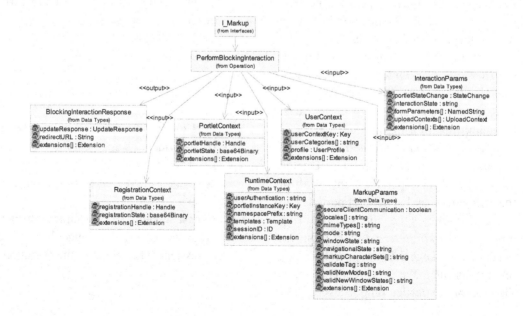

Figure 7. Init cookie operation (it is part of markup sub-ontology)

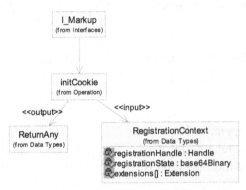

Figure 8. Release session operation (it is part of markup sub-ontology)

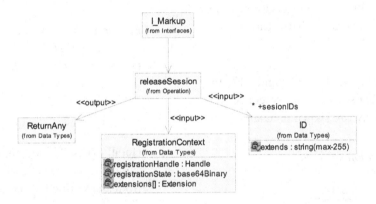

Box 1.

```
context getMarkup
    inv allowedFauls:
        (self.fault.name="AccessDenied) or
        self.fault.name="InconsistentParameters")) or
    self.fault.name="InvalidRegistration" or
    self.fault.name="MissingParameters" or
    self.fault.name="OperationFailed" or
    self.fault.name="InvalidUserCategory" or
    self.fault.name="InvalidHandle" or
    self.fault.name="InvalidCookie" or
    self.fault.name="InvalidSession" or
    self.fault.name="UnsupportedMode" or
    self.fault.name="UnsupportedWindowState" or
    self.fault.name="UnsupportedLocale" or
    self.fault.name="UnsupportedMimeType")

context getMarkup
    inv resultKind
        self.result.isKindOf(MarkupResponse)

context performBlockingInteraction
    inv allowedFauls:
        (self.fault.name="AccessDenied" or
        self.fault.name="InconsistentParameters" or
        self.fault.name="InvalidRegistration" or
        self.fault.name="MissingParameters" or
        self.fault.name="OperationFailed" or
        self.fault.name="InvalidUserCategory" or
        self.fault.name="InvalidHandle" or
        self.fault.name="InvalidCookie" or
        self.fault.name="InvalidSession" or
```

Box 1. continued

```
        self.fault.name="UnsupportedMode" or
        self.fault.name="UnsupportedWindowState" or
        self.fault.name="UnsupportedLocale" or
        self.fault.name="UnsupportedMimeType" or
        self.fault.name="PortletStateChangeRequired")

context performBlockingInteraction
    inv resultKind:
    self.result.isKindOf(BlockingInteractionResponse)

context initCookie
    inv allowedFauls:
        (self.fault.name="AccessDenied" or
    self.fault.name="InvalidRegistration" or
    self.fault.name="OperationFailed")

context initCookie
    inv resultKind:
        self.result.isKindOf(ReturnAny)

context releaseSession
    inv allowedFauls:
        (self.fault.name="AccessDenied" or
        self.fault.name="InvalidRegistration" or
        self.fault.name="MissingParameters" or
        self.fault.name="OperationFailed")

context releaseSession
    inv resultKind:
        self.result.isKindOf(ReturnAny)
```

As we can see in the sub-ontology (Figure 9), the operations for the Registration interface are:

- **register:** This operation lets a consumer register with a producer. Its header is:
  ```
  RegistrationContext = register (Regis-
  trationData)
  ```
- **modifyregister:** This operation lets a consumer modify an existing relationship with a producer. The header of this operation is:
  ```
  RegistrationState = modifyRegistration
  (RegistrationContext, RegistrationData)
  ```
- **deregister:** This operation lets a consumer terminate a registration. The header is:
  ```
  ReturnAny = deregister (RegistrationCon-
  text)
  ```

In Figure 10, Figure 11, and Figure 12, the register, modifyRegistration, and deregister operations respectively. are shown in detail.

Figure 9. Registration sub-ontology

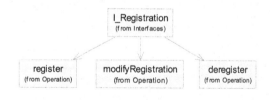

The well-formedness rules that complement the Registration sub-ontology are shown in Box 2.

portletManagement Sub-Ontology

The purpose of the portletManagement interface is to let consumers manage the persistent state and life cycle of portlets explicitly (OASIS, 2005). In Figure 13, the sub-ontology for this interface is shown.

The portletManagement interface provides the following operations (OASIS, 2003):

- **getPortletDescription:** This operation allows a producer to provide information about the portlet that it offers in a context-sensitive manner. The header is:
  ```
  PortletDescriptionResponse = get-
  PortletDescription (RegistrationContext,
  PortletContext, UserContext, desiredLo-
  cales)
  ```
- **clonePortlet:** This operation allows the consumer to request the creation of a new portlet from an existing portlet. Its header is:
  ```
  PortletContext = clonePortlet (Registra-
  tionContext, PortletContext, UserCon-
  text)
  ```
- **DestroyPortlets:** This operation lets a consumer inform the producer that a con-

Figure 10. Register operation (it is part of registration sub-ontology)

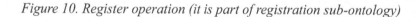

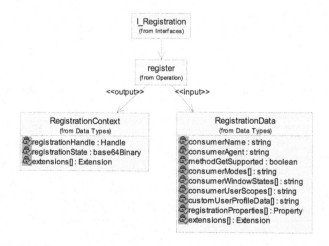

Figure 11. Modify registration operation (it is part of registration sub-ontology)

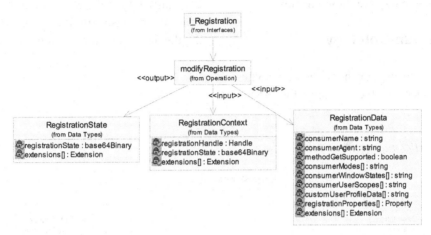

Figure 12. Deregister operation (it is part of registration sub-ontology)

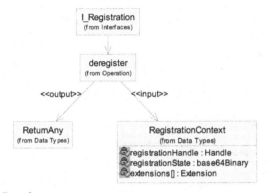

Box 2.

```
context register
    inv allowedFauls:
     (self.fault.name="MissingParameters" or
     self.fault.name="OperationFailed")

context register
    inv resultKind:
        self.result.isKindOf(RegistrationContext)

context modifyRegistration
    inv allowedFauls:
        (self.fault.name="InvalidRegistration" or
        self.fault.name="MissingParameters" or
        self.fault.name="OperationFailed")

context modifyRegistration
    inv resultKind:
        self.result.isKindOf(RegistrationState)

context deRegister
    inv allowedFauls:
        (self.fault.name="InvalidRegistration" or
        self.fault.name="OperationFailed")

context deregister
    inv resultKind:
        self.result.isKindOf(ReturnAny)
```

sumer-configured portlet will no longer be used. The header is:

```
DestroyPortletsResponse = destroyPortlets
(RegistrationContext, portletHandles)
```

- **setPortletProperties:** This operation lets a consumer modify the properties of consumer-configured portlets. The header is:

```
portletContext = setPortletProperties
(RegistrationContext, PortletContext,
UserContext, PropertyList)
```

- **getPortletProperties:** This operation provides the means for the consumer to fetch the current values of the published portlet's properties. The header is:

```
PropertyList = getPortletProperties
(RegistrationContext, PortletContext,
UserContext, names)
```

- **getPortletPropertyDescription:** This operation allows the consumer to discover the published properties of a portlet and information that could be useful in generating a user interface for editing the portlet's configuration. The header of this operation is:

```
PortletPropertyDescriptionResponse =
getPortletPropertyDescription (Registra-
tionContext, PortletContext, UserContext,
desiredLocales)
```

In Figure 14, Figure 15, Figure 16, Figure 17, Figure 18, and Figure 19, the different operations included in this sub-ontology are shown in detail.

The well-formedness rules for the *PortletManagement* sub-ontology are shown in Box 3:

dataTypes Sub-Ontology

A sub-ontology focused on the allowed data types has been included in the ontology for WSRP.

The objective of this sub-ontology is to provide constraint for the different data types which can be used, and to specify their structure. In Figure 20, the datatypes sub-ontology is presented.

Figure 13. Portlet management sub-ontology

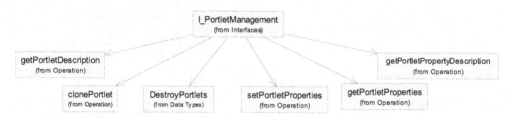

Figure 14. Get portlet description operation (it is part of portlet management sub-ontology)

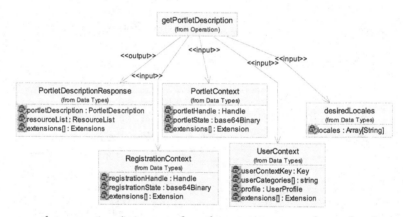

Figure 15. Clone portlet operation (it is part of portlet management sub-ontology)

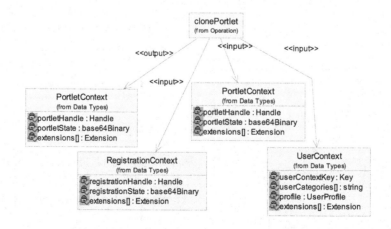

Figure 16. Destroy portlets operation (it is part of portlet management sub-ontology)

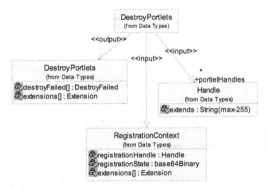

Figure 17. Set portlet properties operation (it is part of portlet management sub-ontology)

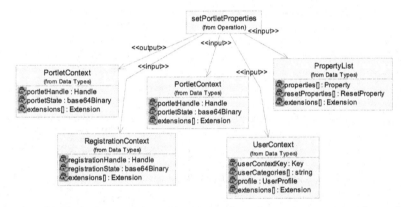

Figure 18. Get portlet properties operation (it is part of portlet management sub-ontology)

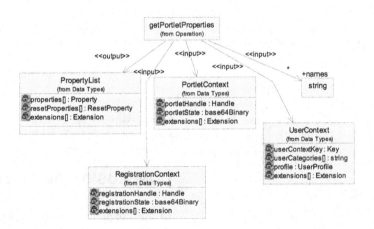

Figure 19. Get portlet property description operation (it is part of portlet management sub-ontology)

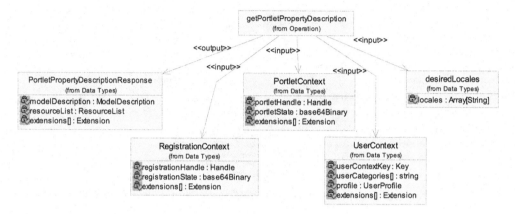

Box 3.

```
context getPortletDescription
    inv allowedFauls:
        (self.fault.name="AccessDenied" or
        self.fault.name="InconsistentParameters" or
        self.fault.name="InvalidRegistration" or
        self.fault.name="MissingParameters" or
        self.fault.name="OperationFailed" or
        self.fault.name="InvalidUserCategory" or
        self.fault.name="InvalidHandle")

context getPortletDescription
    inv resultKind:
        self.result.isKindOf(PortletDescriptionRespon
se)
context clonePortlet
    inv allowedFauls:
        (self.fault.name="AccessDenied" or
        self.fault.name="InconsistentParameters" or
        self.fault.name="InvalidRegistration" or
        self.fault.name="MissingParameters" or
        self.fault.name="OperationFailed" or
        self.fault.name="InvalidUserCategory" or
        self.fault.name="InvalidHandle" or
        self.fault.name="InvalidCookie")

context clonePortlet
    inv resultKind:
        self.result.isKindOf(PortletContext)

context setPortletProperties
    inv allowedFauls:
        (self.fault.name="AccessDenied" or
        self.fault.name="InconsistentParameters" or
        self.fault.name="InvalidRegistration" or
        self.fault.name="MissingParameters" or
        self.fault.name="OperationFailed" or
        self.fault.name="InvalidUserCategory" or
        self.fault.name="InvalidHandle")

context setPortletProperties
    inv resultKind:
        self.result.isKindOf(PortletContext)

context destroyPortlet
    inv allowedFauls:
        (self.fault.name="InconsistentParameters" or
        self.fault.name="InvalidRegistration" or
        self.fault.name="MissingParameters" or
        self.fault.name="OperationFailed")
```

Box 3. continued

```
context destroyPortlet
    inv resultKind:
        self.result.isKindOf(DestroyPortlets)

context getPortletProperties
    inv allowedFauls:
        (self.fault.name="AccessDenied" or
        self.fault.name="InconsistentParameters" or
        self.fault.name="InvalidRegistration" or
        self.fault.name="MissingParameters" or
        self.fault.name="OperationFailed" or
        self.fault.name="InvalidUserCategory" or
        self.fault.name="InvalidHandle")

context getPortletProperties
    inv resultKind:
        self.result.isKindOf(PropertyList)

context getPortletPropertyDescription
    inv allowedFauls:
        (self.fault.name="AccessDenied" or
        self.fault.name="InconsistentParameters" or
        self.fault.name="InvalidRegistration" or
        self.fault.name="MissingParameters" or
        self.fault.name="OperationFailed" or
        self.fault.name="InvalidUserCategory" or
        self.fault.name="InvalidHandle")

context getPortletPropertyDescription
    inv resultKind:
        self.result.isKindOf
        (PortletPropertyDescriptionResponse)
```

CONCLUSION AND FUTURE WORK

In this chapter, an ontology for the WSRP standard, namely WSRP-O, has been proposed. The main objective of the presented ontology is to help portlet developers to adapt or develop a portlet according to the WSRP standard. Using the ontology, the portlet developer can easily establish the specific elements for portlets which have to be included. Thereby, the necessary time to develop a

Figure 20. Data types sub-ontology

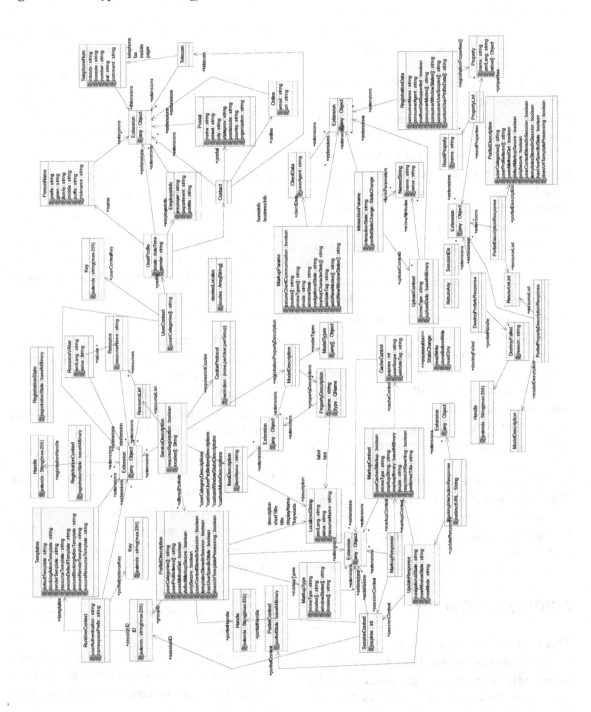

portlet will be reduced since the portlet developer will not need to read and understand the WSRP standard. Moreover, as a consequence of the time savings, it will also be possible to reduce the cost of developing the portlet.

On the other hand, if the portlet developer uses the ontology, their efforts can be focused on the logic domain rather than on the portlet characteristics.

It must be emphasized that the WSRP standard is generic, that is, it is not specific of any programming language. Hence, an example about how a person can develop a portlet using the ontology has not been included. All portlets must be conformed to the WSRP standard (independently of its programming language); therefore, the WSRP-O ontology (which is independent of the programming language) can be used to ensure this fact. For this reason, different ontologies are under development. Each one of these ontologies will be specific for a given programming language.

As a result, we will have the ontology of the WSRP standard, which will be generic. Using this ontology, the portlet developer can establish the necessary generic elements. Next, taking into account the programming language in which the portlet has to be developed, the ontology specific for this programming language must be used. This last ontology helps the portlet developer to establish the necessary elements of a portlet, taking into account the programming language of the portlet.

ACKNOWLEDGMENT

This work is part of the DIMENSIONS (PBC-05-012-1) and ENIGMAS (PBI-05-058) projects supported by Junta de Comunidades de Castilla-La Mancha, the FAMOSO (2007: FIT-340000-2007-71) project supported by Ministerio de Industria, Turismo y Comercio, and ESFINGE (TIM2006-15175-C05-05) supported by Ministerio de Educación y Ciencia.

REFERENCES

Bellas, F. (2004). Standards for second-generation portals. *IEEE Internet Computing. 8*(2), 54-60.

Blattman, J., Krishnan, N., Polla, D., & Sum, M. (2006). *Open-source portal initiative at Sun, part 2: portlet repository.* Retrieved July, 2007, from http://developers.sun.com/prodtech/portalserver/reference/techart/portlet-repository.html#2.

Calero, C., Ruiz, J., & Piattini, M. (2005). Classifying Web metrics using the Web quality model. *Online Information Review, 29*(3), 227-248.

Calero, C., Ruiz, F., Baroni, A., Brito, F., Abreu, E., & Piattini, M. (2006). An ontological approach to describe the SQL:2003 object-relational features. *Computer Standards and Interfaces, 28*(6), 695-713.

Corcho, O., Fernández-López, M., & Gómez-Pérez, A. (2006). Chap. 1: Ontological engineering: Principles, methods, tools, and languages. In C. Calero, F. Ruiz, & M. Piattini (Eds.), *Ontologies for software engineering and software technology* (pp. 9-61). New York: Springer-Verlag.

Domingues, M. A., Soares, C., & Jorge, A. M. (2006). A Web-based system to monitor the quality of meta-data in Web portals. *Proceedings of the IEEE/WIC/ACM International Conference on Web Intelligence and Intelligent Agent Technology (WI-IAT 2006 Workshops)(WI-IATW'06)* (pp. 188-191).

Fonsel, D. (2004). *Ontologies: A silver bullet for knowledge management and electronic commerce.* Berlin

Guarino, N. (1998). Formal ontology and information systems. *Proceedings of FOIS'98* (pp. 3-15). *Trento (Italy).* Amsterdam, The Netherlands: IOS Press.

Java Community Process (2003). *JSR 168 Portlet Specification.* Retrieved from http://www.jcp.org/en/jsr/detail?id=168

Linwood, J., & Minter, D. (2004). *Building portals with the Java portlet API.* New York: Apress Apress

Ma, C., Bacon, L., Petridis, M., & Windall, G. (2006). Towards the design of a portal framework for Web services integration. *Proceedings of the Advanced International Conference on Telecommunications and International Conference on Internet and Web Applications and Services (AICT-ICIW'06)* (pp. 163-170).

Marshak, D. S., & Seybold, P. B. (2003). What customer-centric executives need to know about portals. *An Executive's Guide to Portals*, 1-4.

Montejava (2006). *Los Portales Empresariales sacan el máximo partido a las aplicaciones de negocio.* Retrieved from http://www.montejava.es/articulo3.asp

Neches, R., Fikes, R. E., Finin, T., Gruber, T. R., Senator, R., & Swartout, W. R. (1991). Enabling technology for knowledge sharing. *AI Magazine, 12*(3), 87-127.

OASIS (2003). *Web Service for Remote Portlets (WSRP), Version 1.0.* Retrieved from http://www.oasis-open.org/commitees/wsrp/

OASIS (2005). *Web Services for Remote Portlets, 1.0 Primer.* Retrieved from http://www.oasis-open.org/committees/wsrp

OMG (2001). *Model driven architecture (MDA)* (Doc. No. ORMSC/2001-07-01).

OMG (2003). *MDA Guide Version 1.0.1, Object Management Group* (Doc. No. OMG/2003-06-01), 62..

Pisanelli, D. M., Gangemi, A., & Steve, G. (2002). Ontologies and information systems: The marriage of the century? *Proceedings of LYEE Workshop, Paris.*

PlanetMDE (2005). MDE (Model Driven Engineering). *Community Portal.* Retrieved from http://www.planetmde.org

Ruiz, F., Vizcaíno, A., Piattini, M., & García, F. (2004). An ontology for the management of software maintenance projects. *International Journal of Software Engineering and Knowledge Engineering, 14*(3), 323-349.

Ruiz, F., & Hilera, J. R. (2006). Chap. 2: Using ontologies in software engineering and technology. In C. Calero, F. Ruiz, & M. Piattini (Eds.), *Ontologies for software engineering and software technology* (49-102). New York: Springer Verlag.

Wang, X., & Chan, C. W. (2001). Ontology modeling using UML. *Proceedings of the 7th International Conference on Object Oriented Information Systems Conference (OOIS'2001), Calgary, Canada* (pp. 59-68).

KEY TERMS

Web portals: Internet-based applications that enable access to different sources (providers) through a single interface which provides personalization, single sign-on, and content aggregation from different sources, and which hosts the presentation layer of information systems.

Quality model: Set of dimensions and the relationships between them relevant to a context, which can be split up into sub-dimensions; these sub-dimensions are composed of attributes whose objective is to assess the quality. For each attribute, one or more metrics can be defined in order to assess its value.

Portal quality: Degree to which the portal facilitates services and provides relevant information to the customer.

Ontology: Defines the basic terms and relations comprising the vocabulary of a topic area, as well as the rules for combining terms and relations to define extensions to the vocabulary.

Portlet: A basic component of a portal, used by portals as pluggable user-interface components, which represents an interactive Web mini-application and is deployed on a portal server.

WSRP: Web services for remote portlets, a standard whose aim is to allow the development of standard portlets.

JSR 168: Java standarization request, a standard that is specific for portlets which are developed by using Java.

Chapter XXV
Philosophy of Architecture Design in Web Information Systems

Tony C. Shan
Bank of America, USA

Winnie W. Hua
CTS Inc., USA

ABSTRACT

This article defines a comprehensive set of guiding principles, called philosophy of architecture design (PAD), as a means of coping with the architecture design complexity and managing the architectural assets of Web information systems in a service-oriented paradigm. This coherent model comprises a multidimensional collection of key guiding principles and criteria in system analysis, modeling, design, development, testing, deployment, operations, management, and governance. The systematic framework provides a multidisciplinary view of the design tenets, idioms, principles, and styles (TIPS) in the IT architecting practices for engineering process and quality assurance. There are 26 constituent elements defined in the scheme, the names of which form an array of A-Z using the first letter. The characteristics and applicability of all 26 dimensions in the PAD model are articulated in detail. Recommendations and future trends are also presented in the context. This overarching model has been extensively leveraged in one format or another to design a wide range of Web-based systems in various industry sectors.

INTRODUCTION

In today's fast-paced global business landscape, Information Technology (IT) is facing an unprecedented challenge to do more with less. IT must keep creating and adding values to the business, while managing to lower the total cost of ownership (TCO) without sacrificing the quality and level of services. To satisfy the increasing and constantly-changing business demands, IT must build more flexible, complex, scalable, extensible, innovative, and forward-thinking technical solutions.

The enterprise computing environment in large organizations has grown exponentially in the past few years, with hundreds, if not thousands, of information systems applications developed, purchased, or acquired to provide electronic services to both external customers and internal employees. It is not uncommon nowadays that heterogeneous architectures and technologies are all over the place, in order to meet diverse functional and non-functional requirements from different lines of business. The financial service industry, for example, is no exception. The banking business process is normally composed of various business sectors in consumer, commercial, wealth management, corporate investment, and capital markets. Services can be accessed by means of a broad range of delivery channels such as branches, Automated Teller Machines (ATMs), Web browsers, interactive voice response, call centers, emails, mobile devices, instant messaging, snail mails, and so on. To effectively manage the architecture assets and optimize the design practices in such a diverse paradigm, a multidisciplinary design approach is critical to abstract concerns, separate duties, mitigate risks, and encapsulate complexity.

BACKGROUND

Extensive investigations have been conducted in the past two decades to establish practical approaches to dealing with the issue of architecture complexity that has grown drastically as the computing space has evolved from a monolithic to a service-oriented paradigm. A logical structure was designed in the Zachman Framework (Zachman, 1987) as a piece of pioneer work to classify and organize the descriptive representations of an enterprise IT environment that are significant to the management and the development of information systems in an organization. In the form of a two-dimensional matrix mainly used as a planning or problem-solving tool, the framework has successfully achieved a level of penetration in the domain of business and information systems architecture and modeling. Due to historical reasons, however, it tends to implicitly align with the data-driven approach and process-decomposition methods, and it operates above and across the individual project level. Similar to the Zachman Framework, Extended Enterprise Architecture Framework (E2AF) (IEAD, 2004) also uses a 2-D matrix covering business, information, system, and infrastructure, but it is designed in a more technology-oriented fashion. The Open Group Architectural Framework (TOGAF) (The Open Group, 2007) describes a detailed framework with a set of supporting tools for developing enterprise architecture to meet the business and information technology needs of an organization. Architecture Development Method (ADM), Enterprise Architecture Continuum, and TOGAF Resource Base constitute the core parts of TOGAF. The scope of TOGAF includes Business Process Architecture, Applications Architecture, Data Architecture, and Technology Architecture. Instead of focusing on the level of individual application architecture, TOGAF is targeted towards the enterprise architecture level.

All these three approaches are heavyweight methodologies, which imply a fairly steep learning curve to get over the hump, so that they are unlikely to become a good fit for small and medium-size organizations. Contrary to the heavyweight methods, Model-Driven Architecture (MDA) (OMG, 2007) takes an agile approach. MDA aims to separate business logic or application logic from the underlying platform technology. The core of MDA is the Computation-Independent Model (CIM), Platform-Independent Model (PIM), and Platform-Specific Model (PSM), which provide greater portability and interoperability as well as enhanced productivity and maintenance. MDA is primarily for the software modeling portion in the development life cycle process.

Rational Unified Process (RUP) (Kruchten, 2003) was intended to overcome the shortcomings in previous methods by applying the standard Unified Modeling Language (UML) in a use-case-driven, object-oriented, and component-based approach. The overall system structure is interpreted through 4+1 views from multiple perspectives. RUP is more process-oriented, and originated as a waterfall approach, though it can be used iteratively through the life cycle of an individual project. The physical infrastructure and development/testing tools are hardly addressed in RUP, with virtually no coverage on software maintenance and operations. Recent expansion of RUP includes Enterprise Unified Process (EUP) and open source Unified Process (OpenUP).

Other related work on IT architecture frameworks is largely tailored to particular domains, though the fundamental principles and general purposes remain the same. These serve as useful references for a team to construct their own models for their organization. The C4ISR Architecture Framework (DoD C4ISR Architecture Working Group, 1997) provides comprehensive architectural guidance for the various Commands, Services, and Agencies within the United States Department of Defense, so that the interoperability and cost-effectiveness are guaranteed in

the military systems. The Treasury Enterprise Architecture Framework (TEAF) (Treasury Department CIO Council, 2000) is to guide the planning and development of enterprise architectures in all bureaus and offices of the Treasury Department. The Federal Enterprise Architecture (FEA) framework (Federal Office of Management and Budget, 2007) gives U.S. federal agencies the direction and guidance for structuring enterprise architecture. The Purdue Enterprise Reference Architecture (PERA) (Purdue University, 1989) is aligned to computer-integrated manufacturing. ISO/IEC 14252 (a.k.a., IEEE Standard 1003.0) defines an architectural framework built on POSIX open systems standards. The ISO Reference Model for Open Distributed Processing (RM-ODP) (Putman, 2001) is a coordinating framework for the standardization of Open Distributed Processing in heterogeneous environments. It defines an architecture that integrates the support of distribution, interworking, and portability, using five "viewpoints" and eight "transparencies". Solution Architecting Mechanism (Shan & Hua, 2006) proposed a holistic approach for IT-solution modeling and design.

In spite of the evolutionary growth for quite a few years, a large portion of today's information system development practices are still ad hoc, manual, and error-prone, which inevitably leads to chaotic outcomes and failures in the execution. A recent Standish Group report (The Standish Group, 2007) revealed that 46% of IT projects were behind schedule, over budget, or did not meet all the requirements in 2006, whereas close to one-fifth of projects were forced to be canceled before completion or were unsuccessfully deployed by the end users. A lack of a systematic model describing the key guiding principles is directly attributed to this unfortunate situation.

A new model is proposed in the next section, with more detailed descriptions of the key characteristics and features of the elements covered in the section that follows. The subsequent two sections present the best-practice recommendations and future trends, followed by the conclusions section.

CONCEPTUAL MODEL

As discussed in the preceding section, virtually all prior investigations revealed the architecture guiding principles, to some extent, from single or limited perspectives. The necessity of a comprehensive scheme to describe the IT architecture design philosophy becomes evidently obvious, demanding a systematic, disciplined approach. A highly structured framework is thus designed in this article to meet this ever-growing need. This overarching model presents a comprehensive and holistic view of key architecture guiding tenets, idioms principles, and styles (TIPS).

The PAD model is a holistic metric to help analyze and optimize the strategies, thought processes, methods, trade-offs, decision-making, technology justification, risk mitigation, and patterns in the Web information systems design. PAD comprises 26 dimensions. The first letters of these dimension names form a chain of A-Z. Figure 1 shows a graphical representation of the scheme.

CONSTITUENT ELEMENTS IN PAD

In the next few subsections, we will discuss the detailed characteristics of each element in the PAD model, and where these elements may be appropriately applied in the architecture design.

A-PIE

Abstraction, Polymorphism, Inheritance and Encapsulation (A-PIE) are the key attributes of object-oriented analysis, design, and programming (OOA/D/P). "Class" is used in Abstraction to represent real-world entities in an object-oriented

fashion. Instead of being predetermined at design time, the behaviors of class instances become dynamic via Polymorphism at runtime. Inheritance maximizes the class- and interface-level. The implementation details from the external callers are hidden in Encapsulation, to promote loose coupling and implementation independency. A-PIE is the foundation of object-oriented design approach, which is further extended to support component-based and service-oriented designs.

Binding

The traditional binding in information systems is static at the API level, which is predetermined at the design time. Most RPC calls are also static in terms of the callee's location, as the IP of a remote provider is preconfigured at the deployment time, though a virtual IP or DNS name may be used. A distributed object model offers dynamic binding at runtime, as seen in CORBA, RMI, and EJB. In this approach, a service consumer sends a lookup request to a service registry to locate the endpoint of a service provider, and then bind to the provider to invoke a service call. This mechanism provides location transparency, which is also exploited in the Web services query through a UDDI registry.

Container

Creating objects in the traditional object-oriented programming is via the instantiation of classes, and the developer is responsible for managing the life cycle of objects. The de-allocation of objects that are no longer used on the heap is an often-forgotten task in coding, which consequently leads to a memory leak in the runtime environment. The latest programming languages like Java and C# overcome this daunting problem by bundling a garbage collector in the runtime engine (JVM or CLR), which automatically collects all unused objects and recycles the heap space on a periodical basis.

Figure 1. Philosophy of architecture design

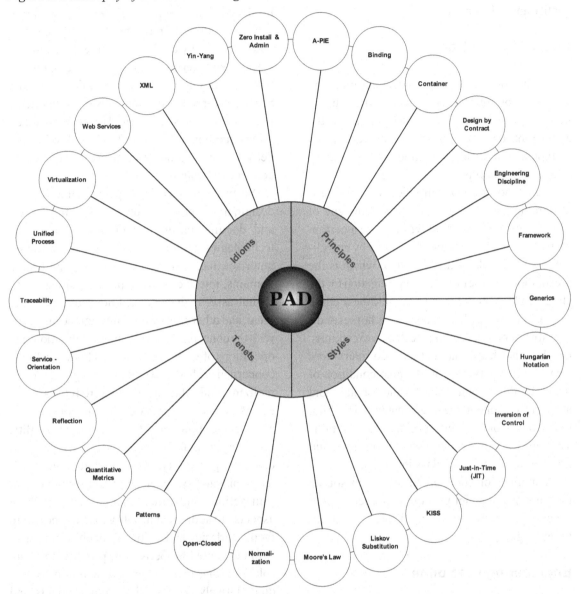

Further, the component model takes advantage of a component container to centrally manage the lifetime of a component instance. This mechanism frees the developers from worrying about the plumbing-level initialization, activation, passivation, deletion, and multi-threading concurrency of component instances. For example, the Servlet container in the JEE platform hosts custom-built Servlets and manages their life cycles. What a developer needs to do is simply to override the doGet() or doPost() methods to implement the business processing logic, and leave the remaining component management to the Servlet container. Similarly, the Web container and EJB container follow the exact same design approach. These kinds of programming models dramatically increase the development productivity and minimize possible error points in the program code, resulting in much better overall application quality and robustness.

Design by Contract

Design by contract is a prescriptive design idiom that checkable interface specifications for application components must be precisely defined by the application designers, based on the conceptual metaphor of a business contract and the theory of abstract data types.

A method of a class in object-oriented programming usually represents a certain type of functionality. The method will impose a certain obligation that is guaranteed on entry by any client module invoking this function, which is the precondition for the method—an obligation for the client, and a benefit for the supplier (the method itself). Those cases that are outside of the precondition are not handled, or are treated as exceptions. On the other hand, the method also guarantees a certain property on exit: the post-condition of the method—an obligation for the supplier, and apparently a benefit (the main benefit of invoking the method) for the client. The method maintains a certain set of properties, assumed on entry, and guaranteed on exit: the class invariants.

A number of commercial and open source tools are available for pre- or post-processing to support design by contract in different programming languages.

Engineering Discipline

To effectively design and develop large-scale Web information systems, engineering disciplines are mandatory to ensure a delivery of quality solutions. Engineering in general is defined as the application of mathematics and science to produce solutions that are useful to the end users. As an interdisciplinary approach, systems engineering is a means to design, realize, and deploy successful systems solutions. It is a discipline to apply the engineering techniques to engineer the development of information systems in a

methodical fashion. Tangible artifacts are usually produced in traditional engineering disciplines, such as integrated circuits by electrical engineers and buildings by civil engineering. What makes system engineering unique, on the contrary, is that systems engineering actually does not build products directly. Instead, systems engineers focus on abstract systems, and make use of disciplines in other engineering fields to develop and deliver tangible products as the realization of the conceptual designs.

Software engineering copes with the analysis, design, development, deployment, maintenance, and documentation of software by applying technologies, practices, and disciplines from computer science, systems engineering, application domains, interface design, project management, digital asset management, knowledge management, and other areas. Software engineering deals with the conception, development, validation, and operations of a software system. This discipline is concerned with identifying, defining, designing, realizing, and validating the required characteristics of the resultant software. The major software aspects are functionality, security, scalability, reliability, availability, composability, testability, usability, portability, maintainability, auditability, deployability, extensibility, customizability, transaction, and other characteristics. These aspects are addressed in software engineering to facilitate design and technical specifications that, if implemented properly, will produce software solutions that can be verified qualitatively and quantitatively to meet these requirements and conform to the standards and policies.

Systems engineering and software engineering tend to be integrated more seamlessly as the IT solutions become more software-intensive, and software-as-a-service (SaaS) is gaining momentum.

Framework

A framework is a semi-complete cohesive structure upon which concrete IT solutions can be organized and developed. A framework includes a skeleton structure, support programs, code libraries, a scripting capability, common services, interfaces, component packages, and other software packages/utilities to help design and glue together different components of a application solution. The prominent types of frameworks are Process, Hardware, Software, Network, Infrastructure, Testing, and Audit and Control Framework.

A software framework is a reusable design platform and building blocks for a software system and/or subsystems. The primary software frameworks include Domain, Conceptual, Platform, Service, Application, Component, Development, and Aspect Framework. Further, the Application Framework group consists of Monolithic Application, Thick-Client Application, Web Application, Pervasive Application, and Ubiquitous Application Framework. The Web Application Framework category comprises Request-Based, Component-Based, Hybrid, Meta, Container, and RIA-Based Framework.

Selecting one of these frameworks is dependent on the overall architectural decisions as well as the specific functionality of the application. Frameworks are not always required but can significantly reduce the time and effort needed to develop an application from scratch. Other architectural considerations may drive the use of specific frameworks or the migration from an old/obsolete framework to a mainstream framework in the design process.

Generics

Generics in C++, Java and C# are a computer-programming technique that allows one value to take different data types in a type-safe manner, while keeping certain contracts such as subtypes and signature. Nested generic types are allowed in most programming languages.

Unlike templates in C++, just one compiled version of a generic class is generated in generic Java code, which does not take primitive data types as the type parameters—only object types are permitted. The type suitability in Java generics is validated at compile time. A subsequent process, called type erasure, removes the generic type information in the generic classes, only retaining the information for the superclasses. This nature of design inherently prevents Java from creating an array of a generic type, because the component type of the array cannot be predetermined.

On the contrary, generics are implemented as a first-class citizen at runtime in .NET generics, which have no type erasure applied. This design choice leads to additional capabilities of alleviating some of the limitations of type erasure, for example, the inability to create generic arrays, and allowing reflection with preservation of generic types. The consequence is that the performance hit from the overheads of runtime casts and expensive boxing conversions are eliminated. Additionally, the primitive and value types have specialized implementations, when used as generic arguments, resulting in more effective generic collections and methods.

Hungarian Notation

In computer programming, the Hungarian notation is a naming convention, in which an object is named in such a way that the name reflects the object's type or intended use. In the basic combined programming language (BCPL), the machine word is the only data type, so that a developer has to memorize the variable types in implementing the logic. To remedy this problem, the Hungarian notation provides a means to explicitly indicate the data types of variables in the variable names. Although BCPL was its first major use, the notation was actually designed to be language-independent.

The Hungarian notation prescribes that a variable name is formed with two parts: the first part being one or more lower-case letters that are mnemonics for the data type or purpose of that variable, and the second part being the given name—whatever the name the developer has chosen. The first character of the given name is usually a capital letter to distinguish it from the type indicators. Otherwise, the case of this character denotes scope.

The Hungarian notation has two types: Systems Hungarian notation and Applications Hungarian notation. The most common form is the Systems Hungarian notation, in which the actual data type of a variable is encoded in the prefix. In contrast, the verbose Applications Hungarian notation gives a hint as to what the variable's purpose is, or what it represents—the semantic type of the variable rather than the structural type.

Inversion of Control

Inversion of control (IoC) is an important principle in object-oriented programming, which decouples the application logic and reduces the direct dependency. Since the dependencies of an object are "injected" into the approach, IoC is also known as the Dependency Injection Principle. Numerous frameworks take advantage of this unique capability. It has been implemented via different high-level programming languages such as Smalltalk, C++, Java, Visual Basic .Net, and C#.

Inversion of control is with respect to how an object obtains references to its dependencies. This is typically via a lookup mechanism in many environments. The drawback of this approach is that a lookup method inevitably brings forth an explicit dependency on a particular environment. To overcome this shortcoming, the control is inversed; in place of a lookup, the object's dependencies are passed via the arguments to a constructor or via the setter methods after construction, which leads to the name "inversion of control".

The key benefit of inversion of control is the elimination of the coupling with specific lookup mechanisms and implementations of the classes, which consequently provides extra flexibility in application testing and runtime operations. More specifically, dependency between the application code and a particular deployment environment is eliminated, so that the functionality can be tested independently in a simple standalone environment. As a result, testing becomes faster and easier for better quality assurance in the end products. The loose-coupling feature of IoC also enables a true plug-and-play capability in a production environment.

A popular Web application framework, Spring, uses the IoC with an IoC container built in for both Java and .Net languages.

Just-in-Time

Just-in-time (JIT) compilation is also known as dynamic translation, which is a technique in computing to dynamically translate bytecode into native machine code, and improve the performance of bytecode-compiled applications. JIT is based on two types of runtime execution styles: dynamic compilation and bytecode compilation.

Compilation occurs on the fly during execution in a dynamic compilation environment. The Common Lisp programming language, as an example, has a compile function that can compile new functions created during the execution. The old Visual Basic language used the same interpretation mechanism. Although it is useful in interactive debugging, dynamic compilation is disadvantageous due to the translation overheads and unnecessary repetitive compilation of the same code logic in a hands-off deployed system.

Alternatively, source code is transformed to an intermediate representation state called bytecode in a bytecode-compiled system. Bytecode is not the machine code for any particular computer, so it is platform-independent and portable to any computer architecture as long as the platform has a virtual machine to interpret the bytecode in execution. This mechanism is used in both Java (JVM) and .Net (CLR).

A JIT environment transforms source code to a portable and optimized bytecode as the first step. The bytecode is then packaged and subsequently deployed to the runtime environment. During execution, the bytecode is loaded into memory and translated into native machine code on the production systems. Not every class in a package is loaded and translated. Rather, only the functions or files needed are compiled at the time when they are about to be executed—just in time.

JIT aims to take advantage of the benefits of both native and bytecode compilation. The syntax validation, error checking, profiling, debugging, and basic optimization are performed at compile time. The deployable bytecode package is portable to different architecture platforms. The bytecode-to-machine code compilation is significantly faster than straight-from-source code. Compilers from bytecode to machine code follow the virtual machine standards, and can be developed independently for portability and superior performance, as seen in products like JRockit.

Better execution performance is observed as the compiled code is cached in memory during execution, avoiding subsequent recompilation of the same bytecode. A slight slowdown, however, may be encountered during the initialization of a program, when certain optimization is processed for the target CPU and operating system prior to the bytecode compilation. Nevertheless, the portability and performance enhancement of the JIT compilation is beneficial in most use cases.

The JIT concept has been expanded to the solution design area, resulting in agile and lightweight modeling and design approaches.

KISS

The KISS (Keep It Simple and Straightforward) principle is a tenet emphasizing simplicity as a key goal and asset in a process and design. A variety of expansions of the acronym "KISS" have been used over the years, and uncertainty exists about which of them, if any, was the original one.

As the IT context grows and the IT portfolio expands progressively, IT solutions tend to become more complex, resulting in solutions that are far more burdensome than the problem. In some cases,

seemingly "clever" solutions are developed simply for the sake of using cutting-edge technology without clear alignment with business values and drivers, which leads toward overkills or overcomplicated solutions that do not deal with unusual cases within the targeted problem domain. There is a tendency, sometimes, towards complicating a simple problem by overengineering solutions in order to achieve reusability, extensibility, and openness in the design.

The KISS principle is a suggestion to prevent this complication from happening. KISS advocates using the simplest and most straightforward method whenever applicable. The KISS principle today is often used in IT system development: The solution should be designed to be as simple and straightforward as possible, avoiding creeping featurism.

Liskov Substitution

In object-oriented programming, the Liskov substitution principle is a particular definition of subtype. Let f(x) be a property provable about objects x of type N. Then f(y) should be true for objects y of type M where M is a subtype of N.

Hence Liskov's notion of "subtype" is rooted in the notion of substitutability. In other words, if M is a subtype of N, then objects of type N in a program is replaceable with objects of type M without altering any of the desirable behaviors of that logic.

The Liskov substitution principle is closely related to the design by contract methodology, leading to some restrictions on how contracts can interact with inheritance:

- Preconditions cannot be strengthened in a subclass. This means that a subclass cannot have stronger preconditions than its superclass;
- Post-conditions cannot be weakened in a subclass. This means that a subclass cannot have weaker post-conditions than its superclass; and

- No new exceptions should be thrown by methods of the subclass, except where those exceptions are themselves subtypes of exceptions thrown by the methods of the superclass.

Moore's Law

Gordon Moore, cofounder of Intel, made an interesting observation in 1965 that the number of transistors per square inch on integrated circuits had doubled every year since the invention of the integrated circuit. Based on the historical statistics, Moore's prediction was that this trend would continue on for the foreseeable future. Even though the pace in subsequent years has slightly decelerated, the density has still doubled in a cycle of approximately 18 months, which becomes the current definition of Moore's Law. A majority of experts expect Moore's Law to hold for at least another 20 years.

Normalization

In relational database modeling, normalization is a process of rationalizing the logical data model of a database to remove redundancy, rearrange data elements, eliminate repeating data, and lessen the potential for anomalies during data operations. Normalizing data also improves data integrity and consistency, while simplifying the data model extension in the future. The formal classifications used to define the level of normalization in a relational database are called Normal Forms (NF).

There are six types of normal forms. The general requirements of 1NF are that a primary key is used to uniquely identify each row in a table. 2NF requires that the data subsets that apply to multiple rows in a table are removed and placed in separate tables. In 3NF, columns that are not wholly dependent on the primary key are eliminated. In fact, most applications in 3NF are fully normalized. Nonetheless, potential update anomalies in 3NF databases have been discovered.

Boyce-Codd Normal Form (BCNF) further refines 3NF to remove the anomalies. The representation of many-to-many and one-to-many relationships are handled in 4NF and 5NF. 6NF is merely applicable to temporal databases.

The use of normalization has been extended to other areas, such as canonical forms for products and services.

Open-Closed

In object-oriented programming, the Open-Closed principle advises that a class must be both open and closed, where open equals extensibility and closed means that extension is the only way to modify the behaviors of the class. In other words, once a class has gone through the development cycle, including design, coding, review, testing, and configuration management, it is discouraged to change the class rather than extend the class.

The Open-Closed Principle has been used in two ways, both of which use inheritance to resolve the obvious dilemma, but the goals, techniques, and results are different. The first approach is implementation inheritance. Implementation can be reused through inheritance, but interface specifications need not be. The existing implementation is closed to modifications, and new implementations do not need to implement the existing interface. The other approach is virtual inheritance. Interface specifications can be reused through inheritance, but implementation need not be. The existing interface is closed to modifications, and new implementations must, at a minimum, implement that interface.

Patterns

In software engineering, a design pattern is a general, repeatable, and proven solution to a commonly-occurring problem in solution design. A design pattern is usually a half-baked design that cannot be directly transformed into code. It is intended to describe how to solve a problem and the consequence in many different situations. Object-oriented design patterns address the design concerns in OOA/D/P space, typically prescribing the relationships and interactions between classes or objects. Algorithms are out of the scope of design patterns, since they are targeted to the level of computational problems rather than design problems.

Design patterns provide tested, proven development practices, leading to accelerated development process. In software design, a set of issues that can cause major problems may not emerge until the late stage of the development life cycle. But these issues must be addressed and contemplated as early as possible to minimize the risk of failure. Design patterns help to bring up subtle issues that may be easily overlooked, and improve communications and code readability for those familiar with the patterns based on common terminologies.

On the other hand, anti-patterns are a catalog of pitfalls, which are classes of commonly-reinvented bad solutions to problems. They are lessons to be learned to help the development team to be aware of and avoid these practices in the future work. When non-working systems are investigated, the instances of known anti-patterns may be recognized, or new anti-patterns can be created.

Quantitative Metrics

Metrics are a system of parameters or ways of assessing an activity that is to be measured quantitatively and periodically, along with the routines to perform such measurement and the process to interpret the assessment in the light of previous or comparable results. Metrics are usually specialized by the subject area, in which case they are no longer valid outside a certain domain.

The measurements or metrics used in business operation models can track trends, productivity, resource usages, financial impacts, and cost benefits. The metrics to be tracked are usually key performance indicators (KPI). Quantitative metrics are used in IT service management, such as ITIL, which measures the effectiveness of the various

IT processes at delivering information services to external customers and internal clients.

Data from different organizations can be gathered together, against an agreed set of metrics, to form a benchmark, which allows companies to evaluate their performance against industry peers, in order to objectively assess how well they are performing. Industry sector metrics can also be benchmarked for apple-to-apple comparisons. The Transaction Performance Council (TPC), for example, defines a set of vendor-independent benchmark metrics for transaction processing and database.

Reflection

Reflection in computer science is defined as a capability of a computer program to alter its own structure and behavior by observing the execution environment and adjusting as needed. It is a process by which a computer program of a certain type can be modified during the execution process, depending on abstract features of the code and the runtime behavior. Static reflection at compile time is rarely supported in a handful of programming languages, and the majority of usages are dynamic reflection at runtime. Reflection is more commonly used in high-level virtual machine-programming languages like Java than in lower-level programming languages like C.

The programming style using reflection is called reflective programming. Reflection can be used for self-optimizing or self-modifying an application. A reflective sub-component in an application monitors the execution of a process, and optimizes or modifies itself in relation to the function that the application is performing by modifying the application's own memory area, where the program is loaded.

Reflection can be used to dynamically adapt a given application to different situations as well. For example, if a program, which was designed to use a class A to communicate with a service X, now needs to interact with a different service Y via a different class B, which has different method names, the program would need a rewrite if the method names were hard-coded in the application. Reflection can avoid the code change. Using reflection, the application logic has knowledge about the methods in class A, and class A is designed to provide information regarding which method should be invoked for what functionality. The application selects the required method at runtime and invokes it, depending on what it has to perform. When a different service Y needs to be called, via class B, the application searches the methods in the new class to find the required methods and invoke them. Not a single line of code needs to be modified. To make this even more dynamically configurable, the class names will not be hard-coded in the code. Instead, a property file is used to store the names of classes, which are correctly searched-for and loaded during execution. This technique is very useful in the design of frameworks, with a "hot-swap" capability to accommodate additional custom classes developed in individual projects. However, be aware that this type of reflection does incur overheads in runtime execution.

Service-Orientation

Service-Oriented Architecture and Development (SOA/D) are the modernized approaches to designing and developing enterprise computing solutions. A service-oriented architecture (SOA) is an architectural style facilitating service interactions. A service in this context is regarded as a unit of work performed on behalf of a computing entity such as a computer application or a human user. A service can be an atomic or composite function. SOA specifies to a mechanism how to enable a computing entity to carry out a unit of work in response to a request from another entity. Service interfaces are specified via a standard description language, which is used to validate the request payload. The interactions are self-contained and loosely-coupled, and each interaction is stateless by nature, although stateful transactional communications can be implemented to correlate a series of interactions to form a conversational session.

In some respects, SOA is an evolution in architecture maturity, rather than a revolution. It is another level of architecting practice that leverages a great many capabilities, tenets, doctrines, and patterns in the prior approaches. Nevertheless, SOA brings forth unprecedented benefits and advantages with respect to the flexibility, interoperability, openness, agility, transparency, platform-independency, and alignment with business processes.

Traceability

Traceability is the ability to chronologically correlate the distinctively-individual entities in a way that matters. In IT development, the term traceability refers to the ability to link the solution artifacts from end to end: business vision, goals, business requirements, rationales, process design, service modeling, implementation, code, test cases, deployment executables, and operation environment. The systems engineering practices trace various activities in the development life cycle, for example, portfolio management, dependency analysis, impact assessment, compliance verification, design validation, risk evaluation, inventory rationalization, and trade-off justification.

Traceability in distributed transaction processing refers to the use of a unique piece of data (e.g., a sequential number or timestamp-based unique ID) that can be traced through the entire transaction flow of all participating systems. Data contents and semantics at any point in the chain can be monitored to validate accuracy and completeness—transaction footprint, via the traceability key, to audit the specific activity.

A matrix is the common form to create several tracing streams on different aspects, but standards are yet to be developed in this regard. Maintenance of the trace matrix is a difficult task, as the data captured is a snapshot at a certain time. Automated end-to-end tracing and reporting in real-time is a challenge in the IT industry.

Unified Process

The Unified System Development Process or Unified Process is a well-known process framework for iterative and incremental system development. The Unified Process covers more than a simple process, as an extensible framework that is customizable to be tailored to specific firms and/or initiatives.

The Rational Unified Process (RUP) is the most popular and well-documented refinement of the Unified Process. RUP is an iterative software development process, which can be customized for particular projects as well. RUP is a comprehensive process framework from multiple perspectives. This heavyweight model can be streamlined and adapted by the development organizations and software project teams that will choose relevant artifacts in the process for their individual needs.

The Enterprise Unified Process (EUP) is an extension of the Rational Unified Process. In addition to the four phases defined in RUP, EUP adds two more phases: Production and Retirement. EUP also includes one additional project discipline and seven extra enterprise disciplines.

The Open Unified Process (OpenUP) is a part of an open-source process framework developed by the Eclipse open-source organization, called the Eclipse Process Framework (EPF). It provides best practices from a variety of software development thought-leaders and the broader software development community that covers a diverse set of perspectives and development needs. OpenUP preserves the essential characteristics of RUP and Unified Process, including iterative development, use-cases- and scenarios-driven development, risk management, and architecture-centric approach.

Virtualization

Virtualization in the IT world is a term that refers to the abstraction and allocation of resources in different aspects of computing. It is a technique to encapsulate the physical characteristics of computing resources, which become transparent to the systems, applications, or end users interacting with the resources. For example, a single physical resource (such as a server, an operating system, a memory space, a program, a cache, or a storage repository) can function as several logical resources, or multiple physical resources (such as CPU pools, server clusters, or storage networks) can serve as a single logical resource.

Generally speaking, there are two types of virtualization: execution virtualization and resource virtualization. The execution virtualization uses a virtual machine as a runtime environment, sometimes referred to as server virtualization, which has several approaches: emulation (full virtualization with dynamic recompilation), native virtualization (full virtualization), para-virtualization (a special API that requires OS modifications), OS virtualization (operating system level), and application virtualization (a layer between an application and the operating system).

The resource virtualization aggregates, spans, and concatenates all combined multiple resources into larger resources or resource pools, such as RAID, channel bonding, clustering, and grid computing. Partitioning is the splitting of a single large resource (such as disk space, network bandwidth, or server) into a number of smaller cells that can be more easily utilized as self-independent virtual units. This is sometimes also called "zoning" in storage networks and "farm/hotel" in a server environment.

Web Services

Web Services define a platform-independent standard based on XML to communicate with distributed systems. It is designed to support interoperable interactions between computing entities over a network, typically using SOAP, WSDL, and UDDI. The common implementation styles of Web services are RPC, SOAP, and REST.

Quality of services is a big challenge in the Web services realization. A plethora of WS-* standards, recommendations, specifications, and proposals have been released, which are mainly managed by three organizations: W3C, OASIS, and WS-I. The maturity of these specifications varies drastically. For example, two interoperable constructs in the WS-Addressing specification, endpoint references and message information headers, convey information that is traditionally transmitted at the messaging or transport protocol level. The underlying information is standardized in these constructs into a uniform format that can be processed independently of application or transport method. In the security area, WS-Security, WS-Policy, WS-Trust, WS-Federation, WS-SecureConversation, and WS-I BSP form a set of enabling technologies and governance for authenticity, confidentiality, integrity, non-repudiation, and interoperability in Web service interactions.

XML

Extensible Markup Language (XML) specifies a simple and flexible text-based format derived from SGML, ISO Standard 8879. XML was originally developed for large-scale electronic publishing, but it is now playing a significant role in the data exchange and transmission on the Internet. XML uses a tree-based structure to describe and organize data contents in text, which are manifested with markup tags. In essence, an XML document is composed of a declaration, elements, attributes, symbolic entities, and comments.

An XML document must be well-formed, following a standard set of rules, and valid, conforming to a particular set of user-defined content rules, specified in XML schemas. Individual parts of an XML document can be referenced

via XPath. Similar to SQL for database access, XQuery can access, manipulate, and retrieve XML data. To resolve the naming conflict issue, XML namespaces associate prefixes identified by URI references with XML elements and attribute names taken from different vocabularies, so that no naming collisions would occur.

Thanks to its flexibility, extensibility, platform-independency, and self-documenting structure, XML has been widely used as the de facto standard to specify the data format and conduct content validation for data exchange and application integration.

Yin-Yang

The Yin and Yang represent two primal opposing but complementary forces that one finds in all things in the universe. The concepts originate in ancient Chinese philosophy and metaphysics. Yang symbolizes the principles of maleness: the Sun, Heaven, conception, light, heat, dominance, and so on, whereas Yin characterizes the principles of femaleness: the Moon, the Earth, materialization, darkness, coldness, submission, and the like.

These two opposite forces are interrelated and reliant on each other in existence. The Heaven at the Yang side conceptualizes the ideas of things, while the Earth at the Yin side produces their material forms. Creation occurs under the force of Yang, while the completion of the created thing occurs under Yin. In some sense, each of the opposite sides generates the other. This production of Yin from Yang and Yang from Yin is in inherently iterative cycles, and no one force rules or determines the other eternally. There are a variety of counters in the universe: health and sickness, power and submission, strategy and tactics, and wealth and poverty. These are explained in reference to the temporary dominance of one force over the other. As no one force would prevail forever, all conditions are subject to change into their opposites, regardless of the circumstances.

Zero Install and Admin

Zero Install and Admin is a method to distribute and manage software products. The traditional deployment is a process which may be arduous to reverse in a series of installation steps before the application can be used: purchase/download a software package, extract the application, and install a group of files. A package distributed using Zero Install only needs to run, and it usually comes as a single file. The first time that an application is accessed, it is downloaded from the Internet and is cached. The package may be persisted on a local machine in some scenarios if permission is authorized. Most of these applications run inside a Web browser using their full URI, and the user's machine acts like a virtual runtime platform.

Zero Admin implies that the software package is in a self-service mode, meaning that it typically checks with a central server to validate the version and patch level when it is launched. If an update has been released, the software will prompt the user to allow automatic download of the updates to upgrade the package to the latest version. In some cases, the model caches the application binary with auto-versioning, and only retrieves the delta, if any, from the server and then launches the application. One example of this type of design is Java Web Start.

APPLYING PAD IN DESIGN WORK

The 26 elements in the PAD model are summarized in Table 1, with descriptions on the key characteristics and where they may be leveraged. These guiding principles can be applied in different areas of the architecture design, validation, standardization, certification, management, process, and governance.

From a methodology and process perspective, the Unified Process principle helps build a foundation for the IT life cycle management. Applying the Yin-Yang principle can balance the conflict-ing factors and interests as well as contradictory priorities/timelines among the stakeholders in the trade-off analysis to reach a compromised agreement in support of both long-term and tactical needs. The engineering disciplines are mandatory to formalize the design practices in a standardized process.

From a portfolio perspective, SOA is a viable approach to alleviate the integration chaos in large firms. The KISS principle helps to enforce just-enough designs and to simplify the IT infrastructure to be rational and flexible. Quantitative metrics provide objectively-quantifiable assessments on the key performance indicators, which, coupled with the qualitative results, lead to better decision-making in real-time.

From a project architecture perspective, Moore's Law gives an empirical projection of the computing power in the foreseeable future, assisting capacity planning and benchmarking in the project architecture. Traceability of requirements and functionality implementations is important to manage the project architecture end-to-end in the system development life cycle. Frameworks can dramatically expedite the project architecture design by leveraging the proven reference models and matured domain technologies/solutions.

From a system integration perspective, design by contract must be followed to ensure that the interacting client and provider are loosely-coupled, and that the internal implementation changes at one side have no impact on the other side; the dependency is only at the interface level. Web services are the de facto standard implementation style for enterprise integration in synchronous and asynchronous manners. Dynamic binding enables location transparency of a service provider via a lookup mechanism at runtime, providing seamless scalability and high availability.

From a software component perspective, a container model provides an execution environment to manage the component life cycle outside the application code. This improves the development productivity dramatically, and also simplifies the implementation of the nonfunctional requirements such as transactions and security in a declarative way. Inversion of control injects the dependency through annotations or aspects, resulting in a much cleaner and concise code. Reflection enables the instantiation of objects and components dynamically in real-time.

From an object design perspective, A-PIE establishes a baseline for object-oriented analysis and design. Generics provide a flexible template model to design data structures and algorithms that are not tied with a specific data type. Design patterns catalog a rich set of proven solutions to common design challenges and concerns.

From a coding implementation perspective, the Liskov substitution and Open-Closed principles are the fundamentals of the inheritance and over-riding capabilities in the object-oriented design. The Hungarian notation enforces an effective naming convention in the code, which is useful with the coding styles in structural analysis and inspection of source codes.

From a service design perspective, XML is the base of the formal Web services description language (WSDL), which is used to define the service attributes and validate the service request/response data contents. Similar to data

Table 1. Constituent elements in PAD model

Principle	Key Characteristics	Where to Apply/Use
A-PIE	Abstraction, Polymorphism, Inheritance, and Encapsulation in the object-oriented method	Key capabilities in OO analysis, design, and programming; used in class design in OOP
Binding	Dynamic binding in real-time to discover services via lookups	Distributed object computing mechanism, such as CORBA, RMI, and EJB; also used in Web services lookups through a UDDI registry
Container	Host services and manage the life cycle of components in the component-based model	Servlet container, EJB container, Web container; container classes are used in OOP
Design by Contract	Every invocation has preconditions and post-conditions as well as exceptions. The contract is formed between the caller and the provider.	Interface design; method signature definitions; separate concerns; encapsulating implementation details
Engineering Discipline	Holistic systematic approach to designing and developing large-scale distributed applications	End-to-end development life cycle; design methodology and process
Framework	A well-defined reusable structural and behavioral model in which applications can be organized and developed	High-level project analysis and design; infrastructure, architecture, system, application, module, and component levels
Generics	A technique that allows one value to take different data types as long as certain contracts such as subtypes and signature are kept	Flexible data structure designs
Hungarian notation	A naming convention, in which an object is named in such a way that the name reflects the object's type or intended use	Module design and code implementation
Inversion of Control	High-level modules should not depend upon low-level modules. Abstractions should not depend upon details. Details should depend upon abstractions. Dependency of an object is injected.	AKA IoC; IoC containers like Hivemind, Spring, PicoContainer, Seasar, and Apache Excalibur
Just-in-time (JIT)	Optimized on-the-fly compilation by the virtual machine during the program execution; lazy instantiation of objects and pre-caching	JIT creation of singleton service objects in the Hivemind framework
KISS	Keep it simple and straightforward; simplification on portfolio and assets	Adoption of new technologies; architectural options, justification, and tradeoffs; risk mitigations
Liskov substitution	References to base types in a module must be replaceable by the references to derived types without changing the behaviors of the module.	Decoupling and interface-based design

Continued. on following page

Table 1. continued

Principle	Key Characteristics	Where to Apply/Use
Moore's Law	The number of transistors per square inch on integrated circuits is doubled every 18 months.	Computing power grows exponentially.
Normalization	The process of restructuring the logical data model of a database to remove redundancy, rearrange data elements, eliminate repeating data, and reduce the potential for anomalies during data operations	A need to improve data consistency and simplify future extension of the logical data model; data normalization and denormalization; XML canonicalization
Open-Closed	Software entities should be open for extension, but closed for modification.	Module, component, and class designs
Patterns	Proven common solutions to common problems	Analysis, architecture, design, integration, security, deployment, service, persistence, and business patterns
Quantitative Metrics	KPIs; scorecards; dashboards; quantifiable approach; quantitative combined with qualitative	Use benchmarks and quantitative scorecards for design decisioning and validation.
Reflection	Dynamic instantiation of class instances for loose-coupling flexibility.	Overheads in execution
Service-orientation	Service-oriented computing paradigm	Service-oriented design methods: top-down, bottom-up, and middle-out; service engineering
Traceability	End-to-end tracing of correlated entities from requirement to deployment	Artifacts in system development life cycle
Unified Process	RUP is expanded to Enterprise UP, part of which is open sourced as OpenUP	System design/development methodology; model-driven design with standardized and interoperable notations
Virtualization	Service level—registry services (UDDI and ebXML); programming model level—JVM and CLR; OS level—VMWare and Xen; hardware level—partitioning; resource level—grid computing; network level—VLAN; storage level—SAN	Vertically-decoupled and horizontally-integrated; on-demand provisioning with optimized use of resources
Web Services	WS-* standards, recommendations, specifications, and proposals	Integration of heterogeneous systems; interoperability
XML	Extensible self-describing markup language	Data exchanges in message or object formats
Yin-Yang	A pair of primal opposing but complementary forces found in all things in the universe; balancing and interdependency	SWOT-like analysis and justifications that combines art, engineering, and scientific approaches
Zero Install and Admin	A means of developing, distributing, and managing software	Thin client model; automation in thick client deployment

normalization in database schema design, service normalization is an important step in the late stage of the service analysis design phase to refine service granularity, group/regroup service candidates, and rationalize the service relationships. XML canonicalization is an application of normalization on XML data.

From a runtime environment perspective, server virtualization lets applications share the resources to cut the cost of investment on hardware and software for individual projects in a silo mode. Grid computing, coupled with a workload manager, provides on-demand resource allocations dynamically to meet the computing needs of systems. Zero Install and Admin make the software upgrade and patch maintenance much easier from the user and administrator standpoints. Just-in-Time design and compilation enhance the portability and execution optimization. The same principle can be applied to design an efficient data caching strategy in the overall architecture design.

FUTURE TRENDS

As new technologies, products, platforms, and frameworks emerge at an unprecedented pace, the complexity of Web information systems grows exponentially. The old ad hoc manual approaches are no longer valid to build and deliver large-scale information systems in a cost-effective manner. Rather, the architecture design must transit to a systematic discipline following a set of best-practice principles and tenets. The architecture development, management, governance, and standardization tend to leverage the cross-disciplinary doctrine of science, engineering, and arts. A rationalized combination of principles applied to different design and validation areas pragmatically will help separate concerns, simplify complexity, improve quality, accelerate solution delivery, reduce cost, mitigate risks, empower practitioners, and rationalize the process, which ultimately makes IT more nimble and adaptive to align with the business operations model more closely.

CONCLUSION

A comprehensive set of guiding principles, named Philosophy of Architecture Design (PAD), is defined in this work to effectively cope with the architecture design complexity and manage the architectural assets of Web information systems applications in a service-oriented paradigm. This comprehensive model comprises multi-dimensional metrics of key design criteria and decision points in system engineering design, development, and management. The holistic framework provides a multidisciplinary view of the design tenets, idioms, principles, and styles (TIPS) in the IT architecting practices for quality assurance and service robustness. There are 26 constituent elements defined in the scheme, the names of which form an array of A-Z using the first letter. The characteristics and applicability of all 26

dimensions in the PAD model are articulated in detail. Recommendations and future trends are also presented in the context.

The Philosophy of Architecture Design (PAD) framework is presented in this article as a disciplined solution. This overarching scheme can be customized or subsetized to form the best-of-breed variants to guide Web information systems development of real-world project work in a systematic fashion.

REFERENCES

DoD C4ISR Architecture Working Group (1997). *C4ISR Architecture Framework, Version 2*. Retrieved May 18, 2007, from http://www.fas.org/irp/program/core/fw.pdf

Federal Office of Management and Budget (2007). *Federal Enterprise Architecture Framework*. Retrieved May 18, 2007, from http://www.whitehouse.gov/omb/egov/a-2-EAModelsNEW2.html

IEAD (Institute for Enterprise Architecture Developments) (2004). *Extended Enterprise Architecture Framework*. Retrieved May 18, 2007, from http://www.enterprise-architecture.info

Kruchten, P. (2003). *The rational unified process: An introduction, 3rd ed*. MA: Addison Wesley.

OMG (Object Management Group) (2007). *Model Driven Architecture*. Retrieved May 18, 2007, from http://www.omg.org/mda

Purdue University (1989). *The Purdue Enterprise Reference Architecture*. Retrieved May 18, 2007, from http://pera.net

Putman, J. R. (2001). *Architecting with RM-ODP*. NJ: Prentice Hall PTR.

Shan, T. C., & Hua, W. W. (2006). Solution architecting mechanism. *Proceedings of 10th IEEE Enterprise Distributed Object Computing Conference* (pp. 23-32). CA: IEEE Computer Society.

The Open Group (2007). *The Open Group Architecture Framework*. Retrieved May 18, 2007, from http://www.opengroup.org/togaf

The Standish Group (2007). *The Standish Group Chaos Report 2006*. Retrieved May 18, 2007, from http://www.standishgroup.com

Treasury Department CIO Council (2000). *Treasury Enterprise Architecture Framework, Version 1*. Retrieved May 18, 2007, from http://www.eaframeworks.com/TEAF/teaf.doc

Zachman, J. A. (1987). A framework for information systems architecture. *IBM Systems Journal, 26*(3), 276-295.

KEY TERMS

A-PIE: Abstraction, polymorphism, inheritance, and encapsulation in the object-oriented method

Design by contract: Every method/service invocation has preconditions and post-conditions, as well as exceptions defined between the caller and the provider

Framework: A well-defined reusable structural and behavioral model in which applications can be organized and developed

Hungarian notation: A naming convention in computer programming, in which an object is named in such a way that the name reflects the object's type or intended use

Inversion of control: High-level modules should not depend upon low-level modules. Details should depend upon abstractions, but not the other way around. The dependency of an object is injected in this approach.

Just-in-time: Optimized on-the-fly compilation by the virtual machine during the program execution

Liskov substitution: References to base types in a module must be replaceable by the references to derived types without changing the behaviors of the module.

Normalization: The process of restructuring the logical data model of a database to remove redundancy, rearrange data elements, eliminate repeating data, and reduce the potential for anomalies during data operations

Reflection: Dynamic instantiation of class instances for loose-coupling flexibility

Yin-Yang: A pair of primal opposing but complementary forces found in all things in the universe, with respect to balancing, interdependency, and transformation

Section IV
Search Engine and Information

Chapter XXVI
Improving the Quality of Web Search

Mohamed Salah Hamdi
University of Qatar, Qatar

ABSTRACT

Conventional Web search engines return long lists of ranked documents that users are forced to sift through to find relevant documents. The notoriously-low precision of Web search engines coupled with the ranked list presentation make it hard for users to find the information they seek. Developing retrieval techniques that will yield high recall and high precision is desirable. Unfortunately, such techniques would impose additional resource demands on the search engines which are already under severe resource constraints. A more productive approach, however, seems to enhance post-processing of the retrieved set. If such value-adding processes allow the user to easily identify relevant documents from a large retrieved set, queries that produce low precision/high recall results will become more acceptable. We propose improving the quality of Web search by combining meta-search and self-organizing maps. This can help users both in locating interesting documents more easily and in getting an overview of the retrieved document set.

INTRODUCTION

Historically, more information has almost always been a good thing. However, as the ability to collect information grew, the ability to process that information did not keep up. Today, we have large amounts of available information and a high rate of new information being added, but contradictions in the available information, a low signal-to-noise ratio (proportion of useful information found to all information found), and inefficient methods for comparing and processing different kinds of information characterize the situation. The result is the "information overload" of the user, that is, users have too much information to make a decision or remain informed about a topic.

Information overload on the World Wide Web is a well-recognized problem. Research to subdue this problem and extract maximum benefit from the Internet is still in its infancy. Managing information overload on the Web is a challenge, and the need for more precise techniques for assisting the user in finding the most relevant and most useful information is obvious. With largely unstructured pages authored by a massive range of people on a diverse range of topics, simple browsing has given way to filtering as the practical way to manage Web-based information. Today's online resources are therefore mainly accessible via a panoply of primitive but popular information services such as search engines.

Search engines are very effective at filtering pages that match explicit queries. Search engines, however, require massive memory resources (to store an index of the Web) and tremendous network bandwidth (to create and continually refresh the index). These systems receive millions of queries per day, and as a result, the CPU cycles devoted to satisfying each individual query are sharply curtailed. There is no time for intelligence which is mandatory for offering ways to combat information overload.

Search engines rank the retrieved documents in descending order of relevance to the user's information needs according to certain predetermined criteria. The usual outcome of the ranking process applied by a search engine is a long list of document titles. The main drawback of such an approach is that the user is still required to browse through this long list to select those that are actually considered to be of interest. Another shortcoming is that the resultant list of documents from a search engine does not make distinctions between the different concepts that may be present in the query, as the list inevitably has to be ranked sequentially. The problem lies mainly in the presentation of the list of document titles. These documents are usually listed serially, irrespective of the similarity or dissimilarity in their contents, that is, it does not make distinctions between the different concepts. Thus, two documents appearing next to each other in the list may not necessarily be of a similar nature and vice versa. As the list of documents grows longer, the amount of time and effort needed to browse through the list to look for relevant documents increases.

What is needed are systems, often referred to as information customization systems (Hamdi, 2005, 2006a, 2006b, 2006c, in press), that act on the user's behalf and that can rely on exist-

ing information services like search engines that do the resource-intensive part of the work. These systems will be sufficiently lightweight to run on an average PC and serve as personal assistants. Since such an assistant has relatively modest resource requirements, it can reside on an individual user's machine. If the assistant resides on the user's machine, there is no need to turn down intelligence. The system can have substantial local intelligence.

In an attempt to circumvent the problems of search engines discussed above and contribute to resolving the problem of information overload over the Web, we propose improving the quality of Web search (from the user's perspective) by combining meta-search (University of California, Berkeley, 2006) and unsupervised learning (Deco & Obradovic, 1996; Ripley, 1996; Sarle, 1994).

A meta-search engine simultaneously searches multiple search engines and returns a single list of results. The results retrieved by this engine can be highly relevant, since it is usually retrieving the first items from the relevancy-ranked list of hits returned by the individual search engines. The Kohonen feature map (Kohonen, 1989, 1995) is then used to construct a self-organizing semantic map such that documents of similar contents are placed close to one another.

The goal is to conceptualize an information retrieval approach which uses traditional search engines as information filters and the semantic map as a browsing aid to support ordering, linking, and browsing information gathered by the filters.

In the remaining part of this chapter, we first present background information about the Web, search engines, and the problem of the imprecision of user queries. We then introduce two approaches for dealing with this problem, namely, guided search and meta-search. We then focus on enhancing post-processing of search results and discuss clustering as a solution to the problems related to the presentation of the list of retrieved documents. After that, the adopted self-organizing semantic map approach is described in detail. The information customization system SOMSE that combines meta-search and self-organizing semantic maps, issues related to the implementation and evaluation of SOMSE, and future trends are discussed respectively in each of the next sections. The final section presents a short summary of the chapter.

BACKGROUND

Since its advent in the early 1990's, the World Wide Web has grown to billions of pages today. This huge number of pages is estimated to be several times larger than the number of pages of all the books ever printed since the invention of the printing press over 500 years ago. In fact, the Web is now clearly the most widely-used communication medium, the largest source of data and information available anywhere, and the quickest, easiest, and cheapest means of access to valuable content.

The ubiquity of the Internet and the Web caused the emergence of a great deal of search engines, and search became the second most popular activity on the Web. In recent years, always more and more innovative and sophisticated search engines have started appearing. These systems index Web sites, images, Usenet news groups, content-based directories, and news sources, and allow sophisticated searches, with required and forbidden words, and the ability to restrict results based on a particular language or encoding.

Google, for example, supports a rich query syntax that allows the user to access additional capabilities of the search engine. If, for example, a common word is essential to getting the results the user wants, it can be included by putting a "+" sign in front of it. The user can exclude a word from the search results by putting a minus sign ("-") immediately in front of it. It is possible to search for complete phrases by enclosing them in quotation marks or connecting them with hyphens.

Words marked in this way will appear together in all results exactly as entered. Boolean OR search is possible. To retrieve pages that include either word A or word B, an uppercase OR between terms is used. Site restricted search, date restricted search, title search, and plenty of other options are possible (see Google, 2006, for details).

Unfortunately, only a small number of Web users actually know how to utilize the true power of these engines. Most average Web users make searches based on imprecise query keywords or sentences, which return unnecessary, or worse, inaccurate results. The need to accept these queries while overcoming the limitations of their imprecision has given rise to research into ways of improving the retrieval results based on this assumption. A number of research studies on automatic keyword and phrase extraction for query expansion and on using user feedback has been reported (e.g., Narita & Ogawa, 2000; Salton & Buckley, 1990; Xu & Croft, 1996). Recently, however, motivated by the introduction of Web Services of search engines, which allow developers to query the server directly from their application, another class of systems, aimed at dealing with these problems and producing search results that are most relevant to user queries, have started to emerge. These systems usually adopt *"guided search"* or *"meta-search"*, or combinations of the two.

DEALING WITH THE IMPRECISION OF USER QUERIES

Guided Search

In guided search, the system helps guide the user's searching sessions and serves as an advanced interface to a given search engine. One example is GuideBeam (http://www.guidebeam.com). GuideBeam has a simple start page, with just a box to type in a keyword or phrase. Clicking the search button results in a list of categories based on the keywords. The user can keep picking categories to target his search. GuideBeam works based on "rational monotonicity". This principle prescribes how the user's current query can be expanded in a way which is consistent with the user's preferences for information. Users can intuitively navigate to the desired query in a context-sensitive manner. This is known as "Query by Navigation". The goal is to elicit a more precise query from the user, which will translate into more relevant documents being returned from the associated search engine (Bruza & van Linder, 1998).

Another example is Google API Proximity Search (GAPS) (http://www.staggernation.com/cgi-bin/gaps.cgi). GAPS is a Perl script that uses the Google API (Google, 2006) to search Google for two search terms that appear within a certain distance from each other on a page. It does this by using a seldom-discussed Google feature: within a quoted phrase, * can be used as a wildcard meaning "any word". So to search for *coppola* within 2 words of *nepotism*, in either order, 6 queries are needed: "coppola nepotism", "coppola * nepotism", "coppola * * nepotism", "nepotism coppola", "nepotism * coppola", and "nepotism * * coppola". The GAPS script simply constructs these queries, gets the first page of Google results for each query, compiles all the results, and presents them in a specified sort order (Staggernation, 2006). Guided Google (Hoong & Buyya, 2004) is a similar system that performs simple manipulation and automation of existing Google functions. It supports search based on hosts and is also able to generate all combinations of the keywords that appear in the query and search for them.

Meta-Search

In meta-search, the user submits keywords in the search box of the system, and the system transmits the search simultaneously to several individual search engines, Web directories, and (sometimes) to the so-called Deep Web (Bergman, 2001), a collection of online information not indexed by traditional search engines such as content that resides in searchable databases (dynamically-generated sites) and that can only be discovered by a direct query. After collecting the results, the meta-search engine usually removes the duplicate links and, according to its algorithm, combines or ranks the results into a single merged list. Meta-search engines do not own a database of Web pages; they send the search terms to the databases maintained by search engine companies.

The meta-search engine Dogpile (www.dogpile.com), for example, searches Google, Yahoo, LookSmart, Ask.com, MSN Search, and others. Sites that have purchased ranking and inclusion are blended in ("Sponsored by..." link below search result). Dogpile accepts Boolean logic, especially in advanced search modes. It also allows the user to see each search engine's results separately in a useful list for comparison. There is also a "domain filter" for filtering generic domain extensions like .com, .gov, and .edu, and a "search filter" for filtering potentially-explicit content from search results.

SurfWax (www.surfwax.com) is another example of a meta-search engine that searches a better-than-average set of search engines including WiseNut, AllTheWeb, CNN, and LookSmart. It accepts quotes " " and +/- to include and exclude words. Default is AND between words. The results can be sorted by source, relevance, or alphabetically. SurfWax's SiteSnaps (quick summaries of individual results that capture relevant information) and other features help the user dig deeply into results. Clicking on a source link allows viewing complete search results. Clicking on the snap button to the left of a source link allows viewing helpful SiteSnaps extracted from that site in a frame on the right. There are many additional features for probing within a site.

There are plenty of other examples of meta-search engines with different features. See, for example, Cohen (2006) to learn more about many of them.

Meta-search engines usually return only a limited number of the documents available to be retrieved from the individual engines that they have searched. The cut-off may be determined by the number of documents that are retrieved, or by the amount of time that the meta-search engine spends at the other sites. Some systems give the user a certain degree of control over these factors.

Meta-search engines save searchers a considerable amount of time by sparing them the trouble of running a query in each search engine. Using a meta-search engine can also increase the likelihood of finding relevant information. Results retrieved by meta-search engines can be highly relevant, since they are usually retrieving the first items from the relevancy-ranked list of hits returned by the individual search engines.

As already mentioned, it is estimated that the Web consists of billions of Web pages, and the number is steadily increasing. Each single search tool such as Google, Yahoo, and so forth, indexes only a small part of the Web. Moreover, all have different programs that use different criteria to build their databases with the intention to balance the number of returns against precision. Every search engine will therefore index different Web pages. As a result, if a user uses only one search engine, he will miss relevant results that can be found in other search engines. Meta-search engines help to fill in the gaps by searching many search engines simultaneously.

Meta-search has also intrinsic advantages that are based on voting. You might be surprised to find that, on average, only very few of the top ten search engine results are the same. Search engine overlap is not as great as many would think! Spink, Jansen, Blakely, and Koshman (2006) is just one of the many reports on how little overlap occurs among the top results of regular engines like AltaVista, Google, Yahoo, and so forth. The overlapping search results are presumably better than the unique hits found by a single engine. When a single search engine is used, these unique

hits compete for space and user attention with the consensus-best results, which the user is unable to distinguish from the unique hits.

Meta-search can also be seen to improve on search engines by canceling noise. Search engines adopt several different sources of evidence to rank Web pages matching a user query, such as textual content, title of Web pages, anchor text information, or the link structure of the Web. The use of the latter measure, for example, usually relies on the assumption that a link to a page represents a vote from a user that sustains the quality of that page. However, relying on this assumption may lead to wrong conclusions, especially when the links are intentionally created to artificially boost the rank of some given set of pages. These spam pages (Wu & Davison, 2005), "pay for placement" pages, as well as pages ranked high because of noisy links on the Web that are created in a non-intentional way (da Costa Carvalho, Chirita, de Moura, Calado, & Nejdl, 2006), are considered as Web noise that negatively affects the results of individual search engines.

Valdes-Perez (2005) holds a viewpoint favoring meta-searching by saying "more heads are better than one" (p. 1) and compares improving the search results using meta-search to performing averaging of noisy signals in electrical engineering, which cancels out random noise and reveals the original noise-free signal. Since Web noise affects regular search engines in different ways, meta-search filters noise by averaging the votes of the underlying engines, revealing the consensus best results.

ENHANCING POST-PROCESSING OF SEARCH RESULTS

Clustering of Search Results

Despite the many advantages of meta-search engines, these systems still suffer from the problems related to the presentation of the list of retrieved documents mentioned earlier. A possible solution to this problem is to (online) cluster search results into different groups, and to enable users to determine at a glance whether the contents of a cluster are of interest. Document clustering has long been proven to be an aid to searchers. If the clustering is done well, it saves the searcher time and effort in assessing the variety of possible meanings and aspects of a very long list, and provides quick identification of the clusters that best match interests. Document clustering is especially helpful to people who are new to a subject area and do not know the key terms. Additionally, document clustering can disambiguate words that have multiple meanings, depending on the context. Jaguar is a classic example. Is that the cat (panthera onca), the car, the club, or the football team?

Clustering works from the premise that closely-associated documents tend to be relevant to the same requests (van Rijsbergen, 1999). Close association is determined by analyzing the text for similarity among the documents in words and phrases being used. Each cluster can be labeled by a short phrase description derived from the co-occurrence of significant words.

Clustering methods do not require predefined categories as in classification methods. Thus, they are more adaptive for various queries. Nevertheless, clustering methods are more challenging than classification methods because they are conducted in a fully unsupervised way.

Most clustering algorithms use the vector space model of information retrieval (Salton & McGill, 1983), in which text documents are represented as a set of points (or term vectors) in a high-dimensional vector space. Each direction of the vector space corresponds to a unique term in the document collection, and the component of a document vector along a given direction corresponds to the importance of that term to the document. Similarity between two texts is traditionally measured by the cosine of the angle between their vectors, though Cartesian distance is also used. Documents judged to be similar by this measure are grouped together by the clustering algorithm.

Automatic document clustering is an active and challenging field of research. Recently, researchers have begun to investigate to what extent the pattern recognition power of neural networks can be exploited for this purpose. Deogun, Bhatia, and Raghavan (1991); Lin, Soergel, and Marchionini (1991); MacLeod and Robertson (1991); Wermter (1991); Kohonen (1997); and Merkl (1997) are just some examples.

In general, using these algorithms to cluster a collection of documents represented using term vectors is computationally expensive. This is because of the high dimensionality resulting from the large number of terms in the collection. As the size of the document collection increases, the number of unique words (or terms) also increases. The set of terms in a document increasingly occupies only a small fraction of all the terms in the collection. In other words, the term vector for each document becomes increasingly sparse. There are a number of ways of reducing the high dimensionality of the term vector without necessarily losing its discriminative value. Khan and Khor (2004), for example, used principal component analysis (PCA) (Jolliffe, 1986) to capture the underlying correlation of the terms before using an Adaptive Resonance Theory (ART) neural network (Carpenter & Grossberg, 1988) to build the clusters of documents.

In the case of a meta-search engine, however, the high dimensionality problem does not seem to be a severe issue because the system is usually retrieving only the first few items from the relevancy-ranked list of hits returned by the individual search engines. Hence, the resulting total number of documents returned will be relatively small. The meta-search engine SOMSE described in this chapter, for example, returns a maximum of 60 documents. Additionally, as there is no time to download the original documents from the Web, the system will take short snippets returned by the individual search engines as input for clustering. The resulting vocabulary will therefore be relatively small. Additional operations applied on the vocabulary terms such as stemming, stop word removal, and removal of high- and low-frequency words will make the vocabulary and hence the dimensionality still smaller. Thus, we can afford more complex processing, which can possibly let us achieve better results.

We have adopted the Kohonen's self-organizing feature map (Kohonen, 1989, 1995) for the purpose of clustering the Web search results returned by the meta-searcher. Emphasis on frequencies and distributions of underlying input data, understanding of the computer's role in producing an associative map similar to the feature map in the brain, and projection of a high-dimensional space to a two-dimensional map are the most distinguishing characteristics of Kohonen's feature map.

Kohonen's self-organizing feature map is very well known as a clustering and dimension reduction tool. Clustering can be used for categorization of input vectors. Dimension reduction can be used for visualization and for reducing information in order to ease search, storage, or processing of another kind. The self-organizing feature map algorithm has been widely used in many different engineering and scientific applications such as image recognition, signal processing, and connectionist natural language processing. In addition, it is also widely used in visualization as a dimension (feature) reduction tool. The robustness of the algorithm, with its appealing visualization effects, has also made it a prime candidate in several large-scale information categorization and visualization projects (e.g., Chen, Schuffels, & Orwig, 1996; Honkela, Kaski, Lagus, & Kohonen, 1996; Orwig, Chen, & Nunamaker, 1997).

Self-Organizing Semantic Maps

Kohonen's feature map is one of the major unsupervised learning methods in the family of artificial neural networks. Kohonen based his neural network on the associative neural properties of the brain (Kohonen, 1989). The topology of the Kohonen self-organizing network is shown in Figure 1.

This network contains two layers of nodes, an input layer and an output (mapping) layer, in the shape of a two-dimensional grid. The input layer acts as a distribution layer. The network is fully connected in that every output node is connected to every input node. The number N of nodes in the input layer is equal to the number of features or attributes associated with the input (N-dimensional vector). Each node of the output layer also has the same number of features as there are input nodes (N-dimensional weight vector).

Kohonen's feature map algorithm takes a set of input objects, each represented by a N-dimensional vector, and maps them onto nodes of the two-dimensional grid. Initially, the components of the weight vectors assigned to nodes of the two-dimensional grid are small random values. They are adjusted through the following learning process:

Figure 1. Architecture of Kohonen's feature map

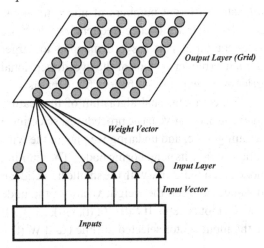

1. Select an input vector randomly from the set of all input vectors;
2. Find the winning node of the grid, that is, the node whose weights are closest to the input vector in the N-dimensional space; and
3. Adjust the weights of the winning node and the weights of its neighboring nodes in the grid, so that they become still closer to the input vector in the N-dimensional space.

This process goes through many iterations (usually hundreds or thousands of repeated presentations; each input vector is presented many times) until it converges, that is, the adjustments all approach zero. Each input vector is then mapped to a grid node closest to it in the N-dimensional space.

The process corresponds to a projection of the input space onto the two-dimensional grid. The result, called a feature map, should be a spatial organization of the input data organized into clusters of similar (neighboring) regions. Two main properties of such a feature map are (Ritter & Kohonen, 1989): (i) The feature map preserves the distance relationships between the input data as faithfully as possible; while some distortion is unavoidable, the mapping preserves the most important neighborhood relationships between the input data, and makes such relationships geographically explicit; and (ii) the feature map allocates different numbers of nodes to inputs based on their occurrence frequencies. The more frequent input patterns are mapped to larger domains (bigger regions of the two-dimensional grid) at the expense of the less frequent ones.

The computational algorithm of the feature map consists of two basic procedures, selecting a winning node, and updating weights of the winning node and its neighboring nodes. The winning node is defined as that with the smallest Euclidean distance between the weight vector of the node and the input vector. If $X(t) = (x_1(t), x_2(t), ..., x_N(t))$ is the input vector selected at time t and $W^k(t) =$

$(w^k_1(t), w^k_2(t), ..., w^k_N(t))$ is the weight vector for node k at time t, the winning node s is the node that produces the smallest distance d_s:

$$d_s = \|X(t) - W^s(t)\| = \min_k \|X(t) - W^k(t)\| \quad (1)$$

After the winning node s is selected, the weights of s and the weights of the nodes in a defined neighborhood (e.g., all nodes within a square, a diamond, or a circle around the winning node) are adjusted to become more similar to the input vector. In this way, similar input patterns are more likely to select this node again in the future. The adjustment of the weight vectors is achieved as follows:

$$W^k(t+1) = W^k(t) + \eta(t) * [X(t) - W^k(t)] \quad (2)$$

where $\eta(t)$ is an error-adjusting (learning) coefficient ($0 < \eta(t) < 1$) that decreases over time and converges to 0. Intuitively, this formula says that: If a component of the input vector is greater than the corresponding weight, increase the weight by a small amount; if the input component is smaller than the weight, decrease the weight by a small amount; the larger the difference between the input component and the weight component, the larger the increment (decrement).

Note that the update procedure does not require any external "teaching" signals, so the algorithm is an unsupervised, self-organizing algorithm. To guarantee that the self-organizing algorithm functions properly, two control mechanisms are imposed. The first is to shrink the neighborhood of a node gradually over time. A large neighborhood will achieve ordering, and a small neighborhood will help to achieve a stable convergence of the map (Kohonen, 1989). By beginning with a large neighborhood and then gradually reducing it to a very small neighborhood, the feature map achieves both ordering and convergence properties. The second mechanism is the error-adjusting coefficient $\eta(t)$. Since $\eta(t)$ is a slowly decreasing function that converges to 0, the updating will eventually stop and the map converges (mathematical proof of the convergence of the algorithm as well as additional algorithmic details of neighborhood selection and adjustment can be found in Kohonen (1989) and Lippmann (1987)).

Kohonen initially defined the coefficient $\eta(t)$ over geographic neighborhoods: at time t, $\eta(t)$ is a small constant within a given neighborhood, and 0 elsewhere. A more recent version of the feature map adapts the Gaussian function to describe the neighborhood and $\eta(t)$. One of the successful stories of current neural network approaches is to apply nonlinear, continuous functions such as the sigmoid function and the Gaussian function to the learning process. The Gaussian function is supposed to describe a more natural mapping so as to help the algorithm converge in a more stable manner. In this chapter, we adopt a Gaussian function for $\eta(t)$ similar to that used in Lin et al. (1991):

$$\eta(t,k,s)=A1*exp(-t/A2)*exp(-t*d(k,s)/A3) \quad (3)$$

where d(k,s) is the Euclidian distance between the node k and the winning node s in the two-dimensional grid. A1, A2, and A3 are three parameters. In the formula, the first Gaussian function controls the weight update speed, and the second Gaussian function defines the neighborhood shrinkage. Thus, $\eta(t,k,s)$ unifies the learning coefficient and the neighborhood definition. Note that $\eta(t,k,s)$ depends on the time t and on the distance of the node k from the winning node s.

It has been demonstrated that the feature map learning algorithm can perform relatively well in noise (Lippmann, 1987). Hence, as already mentioned, its application potential is enormous. Here, in the area of search result clustering, we are faced with a tremendous amount of "noise" in the input data resulting from the indexing of free-form documents. Document snippets returned by search engines are usually very short and noisy, so we can get broken sentences or useless symbols, numbers, or dates on the input.

The three steps of learning process are repeated many times for each document and thus account for most of the processing time required. Steps Two (compute distance to all nodes) and Three (update weights) require iterations through all coordinates in the input vector. The processing time T for the algorithm is proportional to the number of document presentation cycles and the vector size:

$$T = O(NC) \quad (4)$$

where N is the input vector size and C is the number of document presentation cycles. For textual categorization, input vector size can be as large as the total number of unique terms in the entire collection. The number of unique terms in a collection is typically proportional to the size of a collection (Grefenstette, 1994). Representing the size of a collection as S, we can define N in terms of S as $N = O(S)$. Similarly, because each document is presented multiple times, C can be represented by S as $C = O(S)$. Thus, the total processing time T could be estimated as:

$$T = O(NC) = O(S^2) \quad (5)$$

Given the fact that the size of text collections (i.e., the number of search results or more specifically, the number of snippets) returned by a meta-search engine, as already discussed, is relatively small, the algorithm's time complexity of "square of the size of collection" is still scaleable.

THE SELF-ORGANIZING META-SEARCH ENGINE (SOMSE)

SOMSE works according to the following general algorithm:

- Get the user query;
- Get the collection of search results from the underlying individual search engines;

- Build an inverted index for this collection (from the snippets);
- Determine the vocabulary (set of unique terms in the collection);
- Represent the documents (snippets) in the collection as N-dimensional vectors, and use them as input for the self-organizing feature map;
- Train the self-organizing feature map; and
- Draw the map and make it useful for browsing.

SOMSE queries the three most popular search engines: Google, Yahoo, and MSN. By default, SOMSE is configured to return the first 20 results from Google (first two pages), the first 20 results from Yahoo, and the first 20 results from MSN. It is possible that there may be fewer than 60 results returned by the search. This can also happen when SOMSE automatically removes identical results from the list. This choice for the number of results from each search engine is justified, since users do not usually search through more than the first few pages, because most users consider these pages (beyond the first few) as irrelevant to their search.

There are two possible modes of clustering Web search results. The system can either respond in seconds by clustering the snippets returned by the underlying search engines, or it can download the original documents from the Web and cluster them, requiring more time, as downloading the documents can be quite slow. On the other hand, the clustering quality of the latter mode is higher since more information is present. However, the degradation in the quality of the clusters is usually moderate when snippets are used instead of the original documents (Zamir & Etzioni, 1998). Additionally, most search engines are well designed to facilitate users' relevance judgment only by the snippet. We can therefore assume that the snippet contents are informative enough. SOMSE therefore performs the clustering on the returned snippets, allowing fast interaction with the user.

First, an inverted index of the returned collection of search results is produced. During indexing, stop words are omitted and some basic stemming rules are applied (Porter, 1980). Additionally, the most frequently-occurring words (those appearing h times or more, h is a parameter that is computed as follows: $h = max\_frequency + 1 - r$, where max_frequency is the frequency of the most frequent term in the collection and $r = 0, 1, 2, \ldots$ specifies the number of frequencies that should be excluded beginning from the highest frequency) and the least frequently occurring words (those appearing no more than one time, l is a parameter) are excluded. High-frequency words usually occur in most of the documents and have therefore no discriminative value. Rare words are omitted on the argument that they will produce very small clusters. The remaining unique terms (stems) are retained and used as the set of indexing words (vocabulary) for the collection of search results.

These words and the documents of the collection form a matrix of documents versus indexing words, where each column is a N-dimensional document vector, and each row corresponds to a word (stem) of the vocabulary. A document vector contains "1" in a given row if the corresponding word occurs in the document snippet and "0" otherwise.

The document vectors are used as input to train a feature map of N features and a two-dimensional grid of M output nodes (say, a 10-by-14 map of 140 nodes). Following the Kohonen's algorithm:

- Each feature corresponds to a selected word;
- Each document is an input vector;
- Each node on the map is associated with a vector of weights which are assigned small random values at the beginning of the training;
- During the training process, a document is randomly selected, the node closest to it in N-dimensional vector space according to

the Euclidian distance is chosen; the weight of the node and weights of its neighboring nodes are adjusted accordingly;

- The training process proceeds iteratively for a certain number of training cycles; it stops when the map converges; and
- When the training process is completed, submit each document as input to the trained network again and assign it to a particular grid node (concept) in the map.

A semantic map of documents that contains very rich information is then constructed. The map displays on each node a number that indicates the number of documents mapped to that node. These numbers collectively reveal the distribution of the documents on the map. Clicking on a node will cause the corresponding document list to be shown to the user and the user can browse through that cluster.

As mentioned earlier, it is not enough for a clustering system to create coherent clusters, but the system must also convey the contents of the clusters to the users concisely and accurately. The system is most useful when the user can decide at a glance whether the contents of a cluster are of interest.

The map is divided into concept areas (more precisely, word areas) or regions. The areas to which a node belongs is determined as follows: compare the node to every unit vector (containing only a single word), and assign to the node the unit vector (or the word) that it represents. The same effect can also be achieved as follows: assign a word to each node by choosing the one corresponding to the largest weight in the weight vector of the node (winning term).

Neighboring nodes which contain the same winning terms belong to the same concept/topic region (group, area). The resulting map thus represents regions of important terms/concepts with the documents assigned to them. Because of the cooperative feature of the neighboring nodes in the map, the areas are assured of conti-

nuity. Therefore, concept regions that are similar (conceptually) appear in the same neighborhood. Similar documents are assigned into the same or similar concepts.

The areas are also labeled as follows: compare each unit vector to every node and label the winning node with the word corresponding to the unit vector. When two words fall into the same area, the two words are merged and used as the label for that area. This usually happens when the two words often co-occur. In this way, areas could get longer labels. For some deeper discussion on the automatic labeling of self-organizing maps, we refer to Rauber and Merkl (1999).

The size of the areas corresponds to the frequencies of occurrence of the words. Usually, the word that appears most often in the collection will have the largest area. The word that appears second-most-frequently in the collection will have the second largest area. However, as the mapping is a nonlinear one, the sizes and the frequencies do not have a linear relationship. In fact, there is a tendency to make "the rich richer, and the poor poorer", that is, the large ones look even larger, and the small ones sometimes simply disappear.

Not only the frequencies of occurrence of the words but also the frequencies of word co-occurrence influence the map. Words that more often co-occur than others will be assigned to neighbor areas. Frequency of word co-occurrence visualized on the map by the neighborhood property of areas may compensate for inconsistency and incompleteness in the indexing of documents (see Belew, 1986; Lin et al., 1991; Mozer, 1984). This is especially helpful because of the problem that originates in the fact that snippets contain little to no redundancy in terms of the information presented in the snippets as well as in the choice of words. Due to their limited length and condensed structure, word repetition and clarification of the most important aspects within the text usually are not present, resulting in less specific vector representations of the documents. Thus using only the snippets provides a somewhat more challenging task than using the complete documents. As there is no time to download the original documents from the Web, the system should produce high-quality clusters even when it only has access to the snippets returned by the search engines. This is assured by the above property of the self-organizing map. Additionally, using words representing the areas and neighbor areas on the map, the user can look for possible combinations of words to form terms relevant to his request. This allows flexibility and encourages the user to search for terms that best describe his request.

The labels themselves aid in identifying the most important features within every node and thus help to understand the information represented by a particular node. In spite of the little redundancy present in snippets, the labels turn out to be informative in so far as they help the user to understand the map and the set of search results as such. Especially in cases where little to no knowledge on the set of search results itself is available (e.g., when the user is new to a subject area and doesn't know the key terms), the resulting representation can lead to tremendous benefits in understanding the characteristics of the collection of search results.

In summary, the Kohonen's feature map is a practical algorithm based on a profound mathematical analysis. The self-organizing map reveals the frequencies and distributions of underlying data. The self-organizing map achieves this through the spatial arrangement of nodes on the map. The distance between documents, the nearest neighbors of each word, and the size of each area, are all determined by, and therefore reflect, the internal structure of input data. Additionally, the self-organizing map allows much flexibility. It does not assign links between words, specifically. Instead, it shows the tendency of adjacency of words or documents, and therefore leaves much space for human recognition and imagination.

SOMSE exploits the obvious advantage of the two-dimensional map, namely, the fact that it can be displayed on a screen and uses it as an interface that replaces long lists of ranked documents. Since the map makes underlying structures of the document space visible, the semantic map interface will likely allow more efficient browsing and selection of documents from the document space.

IMPLEMENTATION AND EVALUATION

SOMSE, the tool presented here, is currently only a research prototype developed to serve as a proof-of-concept.

The evaluation of a clustering interface is notoriously difficult, particularly in the context of Web search engines, which are used by a heterogeneous user population for a wide variety of tasks: from finding a specific Web document that the user has seen before and can easily describe, to obtaining an overview of an unfamiliar topic, to exhaustively examining a large set of documents on a topic, and more. A clustering system will prove useful only in a subset of these cases.

In a first study, we asked three human evaluators to cluster and label the search results returned by SOMSE as ranked lists (before clustering) for 30 queries. We specially selected three types of queries: ambiguous queries, entity names, and general terms, since these queries are more likely to contain multiple sub-topics and will benefit more from clustering search results. All the 30 queries are listed in Table 1. Each evaluator was assigned a different type of queries.

Table 1. The thirty queries used in the preliminary study

Type	Queries
Ambiguous queries	jaguar, apple, saturn, jobs, jordan, tiger, trec, ups, quotes, matrix
Entity names	susan dumais, clinton, iraq, dell, disney, world war 2, ford
General terms	health, yellow pages, maps, flower, music, chat, games, radio, jokes, graphic design, resume, time zones, travel

The idea was to consider maps generated by people and compare them to the maps generated by SOMSE. An experiment has been designed to let the three evaluators generate semantic maps. Each evaluator is given the same documents (snippets) that are used to train the self-organizing semantic map in SOMSE and a large grid (A1 paper) for each query. Each evaluator is given the task to produce semantic maps for each query of one of the above types of queries. Each snippet is printed on a small card which can be placed in a node on the grid. The task given to evaluators is to put the cards on the grid based on their perceived document similarities. It is emphasized that snippets can be put on any locations of the grid, and that relative distances among documents are more important than the locations. Evaluators are told that the purpose of such a map is to make browsing and selection of documents from the map easier.

From the results of this experiment, it was clear that there are both similarities and differences between the maps generated by SOMSE and the maps generated by the evaluators. There were also some similarities between the processes of map generation.

Other preliminary experimental results demonstrate that we can generate correct clusters with meaningful short (and, hopefully, more readable) names, that could improve users' browsing efficiency through the search result. Also, the time for building the self-organizing is acceptable (a few seconds).

FUTURE TRENDS

To what extent SOMSE produces coherent clusters, and if it actually outperforms, in this respect, other clustering algorithms in the Web search domain is being currently investigated.

We need to make further experiments to gain more insights into the nature of clustering using SOMSE. It may be necessary to develop a model of the user's use of the clustering results and to create relevance judgments for search results. We believe that through a series of investigations, we should better understand the construction and the properties of the self-organizing semantic map, by which we can produce an interface to make underlying information visible to the user.

When the system is tested thoroughly, a Web-based version of the search tool may be adopted. Many projects have been exploring this path and have made their tools freely available and accessible online.

Another improvement that could be tempted is to speed up the process of building the self-organizing map. This could be reached by reducing the dimensionality of input vectors before doing clustering, using, for example, principal component analysis (PCA) to capture the underlying correlation of the terms as adopted by Khan and Khor (2004). Another possible solution is to use a scaleable self-organizing map (SSOM) algorithm, that is, a data structure and an algorithm that take advantage of the sparsity of coordinates in the document input vectors in order to reduce the self-organizing map computational complexity. Ideas similar to those of Roussinov and Chen (1998) could be adopted.

Another point is related to the fact that the current clustering is still a flat clustering method. We believe a hierarchical structure of search results, that is, learning a hierarchy of classes that may be present in the input, is necessary for more efficient browsing. For this, we should build hierarchical Kohonen's maps. We produce a hierarchical taxonomy of the clustered documents as well as the concepts discovered in them. We could do it similarly to the way it has been described in Chen, Schuffels, and Orwig (1996). Documents belonging to the same categories are recursively used to produce smaller maps corresponding to a deeper level in the resulting hierarchy (zoom function). It is easy to see that the concepts are ordered from more general concepts (top) to more narrow ones (bottom).

CONCLUSION

The problems of information overload and vo-cabulary differences have become more pressing with the emergence of the increasingly more popular Internet services. The main information retrieval mechanisms provided by the prevailing Internet Web software are based on either key-word search (e.g., Google and Yahoo) or hypertext browsing (e.g., Internet Explorer and Netscape). This research has aimed to provide an alternative concept-based categorization and search capabil-ity based on a combination of meta-search and self-organizing maps. Kohonen's self-organizing map is very well known as a clustering and di-mension-reduction tool. Clustering can be used for categorization of input vectors. Dimension reduction can be used for visualization and for reducing information in order to ease search, storage, or processing of another kind.

SOMSE allows the user to have a different perspective of searching. It gives a lateral way of looking at the results. With the search results obtained and the way that they are presented, the users will hopefully get a better idea of what they are searching for, and hence learn to issue more accurate queries.

REFERENCES

Belew, R. K. (1986). *Adaptive information re-trieval: Machine learning in associative networks.* Doctoral thesis, University of Michigan, Computer Science Department, Ann Arbor, MI.

Bergman, M. K. (2001). The deep Web: Surfac-ing hidden value. *The Journal of Electronic Publishing, 7*(1). Retrieved November 17, 2006, from http://www.press.umich.edu/jep/07-01/berg-man.html

Bruza, P. D., & van Linder, B. (1998). Preferential models of query by navigation. In F. Crestani, M. Lalmas, & C. J. van Rijsbergen (Eds.), *Informa-tion retrieval: Uncertainty and logics, Vol. 4, of the Kluwer international series on information retrieval* (pp. 73-96). Norwell, MA: Kluwer Academic Publishers.

Carpenter, G. A., & Grossberg, S. (1988). The ART of adaptive pattern recognition by a self-organizing neural network. *IEEE Computer, 21*(3), 77–88.

Chen, H., Schuffels, C., & Orwig, R. (1996). Inter-net categorization and search: A machine learning approach. *Journal of Visual Communications and Image Representation, 7*(1), 88-102.

Cohen, L. (2006). Internet tutorials. *Web Support Librarian, University at Albany, SUNY.* Retrieved November 11, 2006, from http://www.internet-tutorials.net/

da Costa Carvalho, A. L., Chirita, P., de Moura, E. S., Calado, P., & Nejdl, W. (2006). Site level noise removal for search engines. *Proceedings of the 15th International Conference on World Wide Web (WWW '06), Edinburgh, Scotland* (pp. 73-82). New York: ACM Press.

Deco, G., & Obradovic, D. (1996). *An informa-tion-theoretic approach to neural computing.* New York: Springer-Verlag.

Deogun, J. S., Bhatia, S. K., & Raghavan, V. V. (1991). Automatic cluster assignment for docu-ments. *Proceedings of the 7th IEEE Conference on Artificial Intelligence Applications, Miami Beach, FL* (pp. 25-27).

Google (2006). *Google SOAP Search API Refer-ence.* Retrieved November 4, 2006, from http://www.google.com/apis/reference.html

Grefenstette, G. (1994). *Explorations in automatic thesaurus discovery.* Boston, MA: Kluwer Aca-demic Publishers.

Hamdi, M. S. (2005). Extracting and customizing information using multiagents. In A. Scime (Ed.), *Web mining: Applications and techniques* (pp. 228-252). Hershey, PA: Idea Group Publishing.

Hamdi, M. S. (2006a). MASACAD: A multi-agent system for academic advising. *International Journal of Intelligent Information Technologies, 2*(1), 1-19

Hamdi, M. S. (2006b). MASACAD: A multiagent-based approach to information customization. *IEEE Intelligent Systems, 21*(1), 60-67.

Hamdi, M. S. (2006c). Information overload and information customization. *IEEE Potentials, 25*(5), 9-12.

Hamdi, M. S. (in press). MASACAD: A multi-agent approach to information customization for the purpose of academic advising of students. *Elsevier Applied Soft Computing Journal.*

Honkela, T., Kaski, S., Lagus, K., & Kohonen, T. (1996, January). *Newsgroup exploration with WEBSOM method and browsing interface* (Rep. No. A32). Helsinki, Finland: University of Technology.

Hoong, D., & Buyya, R. (2004). Guided Google: A meta search engine and its implementation using the Google distributed Web services. *International Journal of Computers and Applications, 26*(1), 181-187.

Jolliffe, I. T. (1986). *Principal component analysis.* New York: Springer-Verlag.

Khan, S. M., & Khor, S. W. (2004). Web document clustering using a hybrid neural network. *Applied Soft Computing Journal, 4*(2004), 423-432.

Kohonen, T. (1989). *Self-organization and associative memory, 3rd ed.* Berlin: Springer-Verlag.

Kohonen, T. (1995). *Self-organization maps.* Berlin, Heidelberg: Springer-Verlag.

Kohonen, T. (1997). Exploration of very large databases by self-organizing maps. *Proceedings of the IEEE International Conference on Neural Networks: Vol. 1* (pp. 1-6).

Lin, S., Soergel, D., & Marchionini, G. (1991). A self-organizing map for information retrieval. *Proceedings of the 14th Annual ACM SIGIR International Conference on Research and Development in Information Retrieval, Chicago, Illinois* (pp. 262-269).

Lippmann, R. P. (1987). An introduction to computing with neural networks. *IEEE Acoustics Speech and Signal Processing Magazine, 4*(2), 4-22.

MacLeod, K. J., & Robertson, W. (1991). A neural algorithm for document clustering. *Information Processing and Management, 27*(4), 337-346.

Merkl, D. (1997). Exploration of text collections with hierarchical feature maps. *Proceedings of the 20th International ACM SIGIR Conference on Research and Development in Information Retrieval (SIGIR'97)* (pp. 186-195).

Mozer, M. C. (1984, June). *Inductive information retrieval using parallel distributed computation* (Res. Rep.). San Diego, CA: University of California at San Diego.

Narita, M., & Ogawa, Y. (2000). The use of phrases from query texts in information retrieval. *Proceedings of the 23rd Annual International ACM SIGIR Conference on Research and Development in Information Retrieval (SIGIR 2000), Athens, Greece* (pp. 318-320).

Orwig, R., Chen, H., & Nunamaker, J. F. (1997). A graphical, self-organizing approach to classifying electronic meeting output. *Journal of the American Society for Information Science, 48*(2), 157-170.

Porter, M. F. (1980). An algorithm for suffix stripping. *Program, 14*(3), 130-137.

Rauber, A., & Merkl, D. (1999). Automatic labeling of self-organizing maps: Making a treasure-map reveal its secrets. *Proceedings of the Pacific-Asia Conference on Knowledge Discovery and Data Mining (PAKDD'99), Beijing, China* (pp. 228-237).

Ripley, B. D. (1996). *Pattern recognition and neural networks*. Cambridge, UK: Cambridge University Press.

Ritter, H. and Kohonen, T. (1989). Self-organizing semantic maps. *Biological Cybernetics, 61*, 241-254.

Roussinov, D., & Chen, H. (1998). A scalable self-organizing map algorithm for textual classification: A neural network approach to thesaurus generation. *Communication and Cognition, 15*(1-2), 81-112.

Salton, G., & Buckley, C. (1990). Improving retrieval performance by relevance feedback. *Journal of the American Society for Information Sciences, 41*(4), 288–297.

Salton, G., & McGill, M. J. (1983). *Introduction to modern information retrieval*. New York: McGraw-Hill.

Sarle, W. S. (1994). Neural networks and statistical models. *Proceedings of the Nineteenth Annual SAS Users Group International Conference* (pp. 1538-1550). Cary, NC: SAS Institute Inc. Retrieved April 7, 2007, from ftp://ftp.sas.com/pub/neural/neural1.ps

Spink, A., Jansen, B. J., Blakely, C., & Koshman, S. (2006). A study of results overlap and uniqueness among major Web search engines. *Information Processing & Management, 42*(5), 1379-1391.

Staggernation (2006). *Google API Proximity Search (GAPS)*. Retrieved November 4, 2006, from http://www.staggernation.com/gaps/readme.php

University of California, Berkeley (2006). Metasearch engines. *UC Berkeley - Teaching Library Internet Workshops*. Retrieved April 7, 2007, from http://www.lib.berkeley.edu/TeachingLib/Guides/Internet/MetaSearch.html

Valdes-Perez, R. (2005). Meta-search: More heads better than one? *ZDNet News*. Retrieved November 24, 2006, from http://news.zdnet.com/2100-9588_22-5647280.html

van Rijsbergen, C. J. (1999). *Information retrieval, 2nd ed.*. Retrieved November 28, 2006, from http://www.dcs.gla.ac.uk/~iain/keith/index.htm

Wermter, S. (1991). Learning to classify natural language titles in a recurrent connectionist model. *Proceedings of the 1991 International Conference on Artificial Neural Networks, Espoo, Finland: Vol. 2* (pp. 1715-1718).

Wu, B., & Davison, B. (2005). Identifying link farm spam pages. *Proceedings of the 14th World Wide Web Conference, Industrial Track, Chiba, Japan* (pp. 820-829).

Xu, J., & Croft, W. B. (1996). Query expansion using local and global document analysis. *Proceedings of the 19th Annual International ACM SIGIR Conference on Research and Development in Information Retrieval (SIGIR '96), Zurich, Switzerland* (pp. 4–11). New York: ACM Press.

Zamir, O., & Etzioni, O. (1998). Web document clustering: A feasibility demonstration. *Proceedings of the 21st International ACM SIGIR Conference on Research and Development in Information Retrieval (SIGIR '98), Melbourne, Australia* (pp. 46-54).

KEY TERMS

Information overload: Historically, more information has almost always been a good thing. However, as the ability to collect information grew, the ability to process that information did not keep up. Today, we have large amounts of available information and a high rate of new information being added, but contradictions in the available information, a low signal-to-noise ratio (proportion of useful information found to all information found), and inefficient methods for comparing and processing different kinds of information characterize the situation. The result is the "information overload" of the user, that is, users have too much information to make a decision or remain informed about a topic.

Information customization (IC) systems: IC systems are systems that customize information to the needs and interests of the user. They function proactively (take the initiative), continuously scan appropriate resources, analyze and compare content, select relevant information, and present it as visualizations or in a pruned format. Building software that can interact with the range and diversity of the online resources is a challenge, and the promise of IC systems is becoming highly attractive. Instead of users investing significant effort to find the right information, the right information should find the users. IC systems attempt to accomplish this by automating many functions of today's information retrieval systems and providing features to optimally use information.

Recall and precision: Recall and precision are two retrieval evaluation measures for information retrieval systems. Precision describes the ability of the system to retrieve top-ranked documents that are mostly relevant. Recall describes the ability of the system to find all of the relevant items in the corpus. If I is an example information request (from a test reference collection), R is the set of relevant documents for I (provided by specialists), A is the document answer set for I generated by the system being evaluated, and $Ra = R \cap A$ is the set of relevant documents in the answer set, then recall = $|Ra|/|R|$ and precision = $|Ra|/|A|$.

Search result ranking: Ranking, in general, is the process of positioning items such as individuals, groups, or businesses on an ordinal scale in relation to others. A list arranged in this way is said to be in rank order. Search engines rank Web pages depending on their relevance to a user's query. Each major search engine is unique in how it determines page rank. There is a growing business in trying to trick search engines

into giving a higher page rank to particular Web pages as a marketing tool. The makers of search engines, of course, strive to make sure that such tricks are ineffective. One way that they do this is by keeping their algorithmic details confidential. They also may play the spy versus spy game of watching for the use of such tricks and refining their ranking algorithms to circumvent the tricks. At the same time, some search companies try to play double agent by selling improved page rank (positioning in search results).

Inverted index: An inverted index is an index into a set of documents of the words in the documents. The index is accessed by some search method. Each index entry gives the word and a list of documents, possibly with locations within the documents, where the word occurs. The inverted index data structure is a central component of a typical search engine indexing algorithm. A goal of a search engine implementation is to optimize the speed of the query: find the documents where word X occurs. Once a forward index is developed, which stores lists of words per document, it is next inverted to develop an inverted index. Querying the forward index would require sequential iteration through each document and to each word to verify a matching document. The time, memory, and processing resources to perform such a query are not always technically realistic. Instead of listing the words per document in the forward index, the inverted index data structure is developed, which lists the documents per word. With the inverted index created, the query can now be resolved by jumping to the word ID (via random access) in the inverted index. Random access is generally regarded as being faster than sequential access.

Browsing: The definition of browsing is to inspect, in a leisurely and casual way, a body of information, usually on the World Wide Web, based on the organization of the collections, without clearly-defined intentions. Hypertext is an appropriate conceptual model for organization.

Usually, hypertext systems encourage browsing by stimulating the user to follow links. Today, most hypertext systems employ the point-and-click paradigm for user interaction; information is just one click (of the mouse button) away.

Unsupervised learning: Consider a system which receives some sequence of inputs $x1$, $x2$, $x3$, ..., where xt is the sensory input at time t. This input, called the data, could correspond to an image on the retina, the pixels in a camera, or a sound waveform. It could also correspond to less-obviously sensory data, for example, the words in a news story, or the list of items in a supermarket shopping basket. In unsupervised learning, the system simply receives inputs $x1$, $x2$, ..., but obtains neither supervised target outputs, nor rewards from its environment. It may seem somewhat mysterious to imagine what the system could possibly learn, given that it does not get any feedback from its environment. However, it is possible to develop a formal framework for unsupervised learning based on the notion that the system's goal is to build representations of the input that can be used for decision-making, predicting future inputs, efficiently communicating the inputs to another system, and so forth. In a sense, unsupervised learning can be thought of as finding patterns in the data above and beyond what would be considered pure, unstructured noise. Two very simple classic examples of unsupervised learning are clustering and dimensionality reduction.

Quality of Web search: Seen from a user's perspective, this term is related to the notion of "user satisfaction". The more satisfied that a user is with the search results and the different aspects of searching, the higher is the rating of the search system. Assessing the quality of a Web search system and the results that it produces is notoriously difficult. For search results, criteria for determining the good, the bad, and the ugly include: scope and depth of coverage, authority, currency, accuracy and reliability, motive and purpose, ease of use and design issues, and so forth. Web search systems are used by a heterogeneous user population for a wide variety of tasks: from finding a specific Web document that the user has seen before and can easily describe, to obtaining an overview of an unfamiliar topic, to exhaustively examining a large set of documents on a topic, and more. A search system will prove useful only in a subset of these cases.

Chapter XXVII
The Perspectives of Improving Web Search Engine Quality

Jengchung V. Chen
National Cheng Kung University, Taiwan

Wen-Hsiang Lu
National Cheng Kung University, Taiwan

Kuan-Yu He
National Cheng Kung University, Taiwan

Yao-Sheng Chang
National Cheng Kung University, Taiwan

ABSTRACT

With the fast growth of the Web, users often suffer from the problem of information overload, since many existing search engines respond to queries with many nonrelevant documents containing query terms based on the conventional search mechanism of keyword matching. In fact, both users and search engine developers had anticipated that this mechanism would reduce information overload by understanding user goals clearly. In this chapter, we will introduce some past research in Web search, and current trends focusing on how to improve the search quality in different perspectives of "what", "how", "where", "when", and "why". Additionally, we will also briefly introduce some effective search quality improvements using link-structure-based search algorithms, such as PageRank and HITS. At the end of this chapter, we will introduce the idea of our proposed approach to improving search quality, which employs syntactic structures (verb-object pairs) to automatically identify potential user goals from search-result snippets. We also believe that understanding user goals more clearly and reducing information overload will become one of the major developments in commercial search engines in the future, since the amounts of information and resources continue to increase rapidly, and user needs will become more and more diverse.

INTRODUCTION

More and more information and resources can be obtained from the Internet. Because of this, people rely on the Web to obtain abundant information and resources. Nowadays, whether looking for data, tools, or software, finding a restaurant or ordering a plane ticket, or even participating in an Internet group and sharing resources with users around the world can be accomplished in the environment of the Web. Thus, search engines that could help users easily find information and resources become more and more important. The search quality of search engines is an important issue for us.

Search engines deliver a large number of results after a user submits a query, causing trouble to the user due to the extra effort required to locate the information that they need. The intent of search engines is to assist users in finding the information they need, but conventional search engines use the mechanism of keyword matching when considering the documents containing relevant query terms. Sometimes, there are a large number of returned documents, and many of these are nonrelevant documents. Hence, in order to improve the keyword-matching mechanism effectively, several different mechanisms have recently been developed, such as link-structure-based search algorithms and identification of user behaviors or user goals. In this chapter, we will introduce some past research in Web search; we will explain, in some detail, current trends which focus on how to improve Web search quality in five perspectives, including "what", "how", "where", "when", and "why"; and we will also refer to the link-structure-based algorithms that can effectively improve search quality. At the end of this chapter, we will briefly introduce the major idea of our new method, which employs syntactic structures (verb-object pairs) to automatically identify potential user goals from search-result snippets. Hence, we are investigating two interesting and important issues:

1. Can we effectively identify possible user goals by utilizing search results?
2. Based on the identified user goals, can high-quality search be provided to users by filtering out lots of nonrelevant search results?

IMPROVING WEB SEARCH QUALITY BASED ON FOUR PESPECTIVES

With the fast growth of the Web, users can obtain abundant information easily using search engines. Many conventional search engines use keyword matching with the submitted query and all the Web pages around the world to provide users with a list of relevant Uniform Resource Locators (URLs). At present, search engines can improve the search quality by analyzing the information about user behavior. We can use What, How, When, and Where (3W1H) to describe some views of the research so far.

"What" Perspective: Keyword Matching

What do users want to search? Conventional search engines use *keyword matching* as the mechanism. That is, if the document shares common terms with the submitted query, then the document is considered to be relevant. However, this mechanism causes the search engines to find many documents considered as relevant, which in turn causes the user to suffer from the problem of information overload. In reality, any document which contains the query terms is not necessarily relevant, since these query terms may also be mentioned in some nonrelevant documents. Cui, Wen, Nie, and Ma (2002) and Silverstein, Henzinger, Marais, and Moricz (1999) indicated that the length of users' submitted queries is generally short, and the meaning of a query can be ambiguous. The query "apple", for example, is hard to understand semantically by a search engine. Does it mean "Apple Computer Company", or "apple fruit", even or "Apple Daily in Taiwan"? Therefore, in the situation that a user submits this kind of query, the search results, based on the mechanism of keyword matching, must contain many nonrelevant (or non-user-needed) documents. Hence, understanding what users need is a very important issue.

"How" Perspective: Click-Through Data

In order to understand what users want to search, some researchers focus on analyzing *click-through data*. Click-through data is the user's behavior ranging from submitting a query, to clicking on a series of Web pages, and finally finding the target Web page. Hence, this kind of research is under the "how" issue – How do users find the information they want? The links on result pages do not lead directly to the suggested document, but point to a proxy server. These links encode the query and the URL of the suggested document. Therefore, the proxy server can receive the user's submitted query and the clicked URL. Click-through data is recorded by the above-mentioned mechanism. Each record in the query log in the proxy server is composed of a query, and some clicked URL, or some other information such as a user's Internet Protocol (IP) address. After observing the records in the query log, we can find that click-through data can reveal the interaction between each user and the search engine, and thus understand which Web page is favored by users and which Web page is interesting to users. Thus, by click-through data, we can analyze user behavior effectively and further increase the precision of search results. Many existing search engines such as Yahoo have considered the click-through data because of its importance in understanding user behavior. Some researchers have analyzed click-through data in the past. Fox, Karnawat, Mydland, Dumais, and White (2005) considered click-through data as a

very important factor to a Web search engine, and the research of Joachims (2002) also proposed an automatic-learning ranking function with support vector machine (SVM) by utilizing click-through data, which can effectively improve the quality of search results.

Click-through data is not absolutely reliable, because not every user is an expert. The clicked Web page may be not relevant to the submitted query if the user randomly or even maliciously clicks the search results. Therefore, there is some noise in click-through data. Some researchers focused on how to interpret click-through data accurately and analyzed the behavior of clicking result pages. They indicated that users decide which page to click on according to the snippets, and this clicking behavior reflects the relevance of documents. The clicked document is considered more relevant to the query than those which are not clicked. But the researchers also indicated that there are two biases in user behavior. The first is "trust bias": Users prefer to click on the document with higher ranking, whether these documents are relevant or not. That is, the click frequency of high-rank documents is higher than that of low-rank documents. The second is "quality bias": A user will click a result page depending on not only the relevance of its search-result snippet, but also the quality of other search-result snippets. Therefore, a user will choose and click one result page while other result pages are not chosen, based on their search-result snippets; however, the clicked page may or may not be relevant to the user. Hence, they drew a conclusion that click-through data can only evaluate the relative relevance, but not absolute relevance, of one result page with the submitted query. We can observe that click-through data has limited value in analyzing user behavior. We still need to consider other sophisticated methods to analyze user behavior more accurately.

"When" and "Where" Perspectives: Temporal and Regional Variations

Other researchers propose that *time* (when) (Beitzel, Jensen, Chowdhury, Grossman, & Frieder, 2004; Chien & Immorlica, 2005; Zhao, Hoi, Liu, Bhowmick, Lyu, & Ma, 2006) and *location* (where) (Buyukkokten, Cho, Garcia-Molina, Gravano, & Shivakumar, 1999; Ding, Gravano, & Shivakumar, 2000; Gravano, Hatzivassiloglou, & Lichtenstein, 2003) are important factors to consider (Balfe & Smyth, 2004; Chien & Immorlica, 2005; Zhao et al., 2006). Different cultures in different regions/countries have their specific meanings for the same vocabulary or words. For example, the color white has opposite meanings for Japanese and Chinese people. The color red is widely perceived as good luck among Chinese people, while the color white is used to represent sadness, for example, a funeral. By contrast, white in Japan represents purity and best wishes. Thus if a query word "white envelope" is keyed in, the search results could be considered totally meaningless to a searcher in a different society. Similarly, the same query word from the same user could imply different intentions at different times. For example, "weather forecast" keyed in by an Internet searcher during daytime or nighttime could have different connotations However, current research on time and location factors (i.e., WHEN and WHERE) has mainly been based on click-through analysis.

Buyukkokten et al. (1999) discussed how to map a site to its geographic location. Also, they designed an interface to help a user to search a certain URL; this interface can display other sites connected to the queried site in different locations. We will discuss Web resource and user query respectively, with respect to global and local views.

Web Resource

Ding et al. (2000) proposed two complementary methods to classify the geographical scope of a Web resource: (1) context-based: use the distribution of geographically-related words in Web pages; if there are no geographical words or these words are not sufficient to analyze, then it is not an effective way to classify the Web page; and (2) link-structure-based: evaluate the scope of the Web resource by using the distribution of links that lead to different geographical locations. However, a person using this method may find that the links are few. Based on the above problems, these two methods should be viewed as complementary. If geographically-related words are not sufficient, we can utilize the link-structure-based method to classify the Web resource. On the other hand, if the quantity of links is small, we can use the context-based method to process the classification. By these two complementary methods, the process of classification is more accurate.

User Query:

If search engines do not analyze the geographical information about the user and the query and, additionally, the query is ambiguous, the obtained search results are usually not optimal.

Gravano et al. (2003) considered that global queries usually contain no geographical words, but local ones do. Also, the first letter of the geographical word is usually a capital letter. They proposed a step using a part-of-speech (POS) tagger, and combined the evaluation method of different geographical words such as logistic regression, SVMs, or something to classify queries. However, they did not consider the technique of natural language processing (NLP). The meaning of China, for example, can be interpreted as "the country of China" or "porcelain china". Gravano regarded all words with the tag "geographical noun" as a geographical noun and neglected the ambiguity of queries, which resulted in low classification accuracy.

User Query \ Web Resource	Local	Global
Local	Good	Bad
Global	Bad	Good

We use Figure 1 to illustrate the content which we have discussed above. Figure 1 shows that it is better to mainly utilize local Web resources as the result of local user queries. Conversely, it is better to mainly utilize global Web resources as the result of global user queries.

Beitzel et al. (2004) considered the viewpoint of time to discuss queries. They made a statistical analysis regarding one hour as a unit. They indicated that the flow of queries during different time units may be different. Zhao et al. (2006) further indicated that it is not suitable to use the conventional mechanism, accumulating query frequency, to evaluate the similarity of queries, because there are some relations between queries and time. We can observe that the difference between each value in an interval-based method is not obvious. However, if we view the value in incremented time intervals, there are some particular meanings of the value. The key difference between the interval-based method and the incremented method is that the former individually considers the similarity of queries per unit time interval, but the latter considers the average similarity in the period of the accumulated time intervals. Chien & Immorlica (2005) utilized the temporal correlation to find the similarity between queries. Click-through data plays a more and more important role in existing commercial search engines, and it can improve search engines to provide more accurate search results. Zhao et al. (2006) utilized the history data and click-through data, to analyze the semantic relation between queries during different time units. They also indicated that queries will affect the occurrence of events or patterns according to different time dimensions.

CURRENT TRENDS

"Why" Perspective: User Goals

As mentioned above, the query submitted by the average user is short, with a length of about two words. If the user searches "apple", we cannot easily understand if the user want to "find the Apple Computer company", or "understand the nutrition of apples", or even "watch the Apple Daily". As the above examples show, determining the user's real goal from such a short query becomes a very important issue. We understand that the user's goal in submitting a query is important to them; to understand user goals, we need to resolve the problem of query ambiguity.

Rose and Levinson (2004) and Lee, Liu, and Cho (2005) defined categories of *user goals*. Rose and Levinson (2004) classified user goals into not only two categories, Informational and Navigational, but also into a Resource category which had not been previously defined. They also classified these three categories into more detailed categories. They indicated that the user goal of an informational query, "black hole", is to obtain the information related to the topic of the query, and that there is no specific site in the user's mind. When a user submits a navigational query such as "Yahoo!", they usually want to find the specific site already in their mind, which might have been browsed previously or might be assumed as existing in the Web. When there is a suitable Web page, the user will click on it. If a user submits a query like "MSN Messenger", classified in the Resource category, they most likely want to download software or obtain some entertainment resources.

In the research of Lee et al. (2005), they analyze whether user goals can be predicted, that is, whether some queries can be easily classified into the Informational or the Navigational category. For example, most users who submit this query, "Best Buy", usually want to browse the official site of the company, Best Buy. But there are still some queries which are difficult to identify as to which category they belong. In other words, these kinds of queries are unpredictable. When users submit the kind of person-name query, "Michael Jackson", they may want to browse Michael Jackson's official site, or they may want to browse information about his news or lyrics. Hence, they utilize two features, user-click behavior and anchor-link distribution, to automatically analyze the property of queries. The result of analysis indicated that 23 of the 50 selected queries from among the most popular queries in the authors' department were difficult to identify as to which one category they belonged. In other words, these queries could not be judged as belonging to either the Informational category or the Navigational category. From the research of Rose et al. (2004) and Lee et al. (2005), we find that it is indiscriminate to classify queries into predefined categories. We believe that these predefined categories cannot satisfy all users around the world, and that the real user goals are not restricted by the use of search engines in some specific categories.

Furthermore, some researches (Agichtein, Brill, Dumais, & Ragno, 2006b) are utilizing implicit relevance feedback to effectively interpret user preference, where the implicit relevance feedback is obtained by the interaction between millions of people and search engines. The authors utilized three different features, query-text, browsing, and click-through data, to represent user behaviors. Additionally, they trained a classifier to generate an optimal weighting value into the user behavior feature and further derived a predictive model of user behavior. Finally, they utilized a learned user behavior model to evaluate the level of user preference of each result with respect to a query. Overall, we can observe that this research cannot identify user goals clearly

and definitely, but may judge which results are more relevant and preferred by users according to the interaction between users and search engines. Agichtein, Brill, and Dumais (2006a) utilized the user behavior data to improve the ranking of search results, but they did not identify concrete user goals to re-rank the search results.

Other Methods: Link-Structure-Based Ranking Algorithms

To effectively correct the mistakes of displaying unrelated outputs that contain the same keyword, scholars came up with a new idea known as the "link-structure-based" and "ranking algorithm" such as PageRank (Page, Brin, Motwani, & Windograd, 1998) and HITS (Kleinberg, 1998). PageRank prioritizes the Web sites by using Web sites that contain the most In-Link. HITS separates the Out-Link and In-Link into Authority and Hub. Authority denotes Web sites that contain the most In-Links, and Hub is similar to a Yahoo! Portal, containing many Out-Links that can connect to Web sites with Authority. Therefore, using PageRank or HITS can greatly improve the results of searching by keyword.

However, because users' habits and needs are so diverse, link-structure-based algorithm might not be able to effectively operate in the near future. Users do not always look for what is popular -- they want what they need. At that point, user goal identification becomes important for determining users' goals and satisfying their diverse needs.

OUR APPROACH: AUTOMATIC USER GOAL IDENTIFICATION

Problem Description and Ideas

In most instances, users enter a very short keyword, and often the results are not entirely relevant. For example, if the user searches the

Figure 2. A search-result snippet with the query "Michael Jackson"

Michael Jackson – mp3, download mp3, music download free music
Michael Jackson feature on ARTISTdirect. Includes free downloads music videos, bio, discography and merchandise information.
www.artistdirect.com/music/ artist/card/0,,448122,00.html   - 65k - Cached - Similar pages

keyword "Michael Jackson", a variety of Michael Jackson's information pops up, ranging from personal information to information on his most recent album, but what the user really wants to know is where to download Michael Jackson's music. In this case, the search engine uses the keyword method, resulting in the generation of too many useless results. The use of user goal identification can greatly increase the relevance of the results; because the keyword search range would be greatly reduced, more accurate results could be shown to the user.

The goals of the user are identified so that the computer knows "why" the user uses a certain word or phrase to do the search (Lee et al., 2005; Rose & Levinson, 2004). Refers to user goals are limited to two or three patterns, but we hope to go one step further, by understanding the motives of the different patterns. We want to do this because we believe that understanding the motives of the patterns would be more useful than just understanding the patterns alone.

By reviewing the query log and click distribution (Lee et al., 2005), we can determine a pattern of the user's habit; by learning through the logs, we can finally understand the users' goals. This information is highly confidential, and cannot be easily obtained.

Using the Michael Jackson case, if the user wants to know "where to download Michael Jackson's music", the search engine needs to know exactly what he/she wants. The search should be separated into many parts, such as: "I" – Who?, "Download" - Action?, and "Michael Jackson" - What? Clearly defining the search will allow the search engine to give the user a more satisfying result.

Figure 2 illustrates the snippet retrieved with the query "Michael Jackson" from the Google Search Engine (2006). The snippet is sorted at about the 100th rank, so it would take quite a lot of time to browse through the search-result snippets one by one, and finally find this relevant snippet.

As described in the "how" perspective section, click-through data research is effective for improving the ranking of search results, and is popularly utilized by the existing search engines. Therefore, we can assume that certain snippets in the retrieved search results will contain terms which are related to or the same as the user goals. Figure 2 shows that a snippet includes a few potential terms related to user goals, whose combined pairs, such as "download music", demonstrate some different user goals.

We intend to utilize Web search results to discover a variety of user goals. To this end, we further propose a novel probabilistic inference model which effectively employs syntactic structure.

Method

We will attempt to analyze user goals in the viewpoint of natural language processing (NLP). We will begin with the assumption that a user's goal may be expressed in the form of a sentence in his/her mind. In general, a typical sentence includes a subject (S), a verb (V), and an object (O). For example, the SVO structure is the most common structure in English/Chinese sentences. Also, we assume that the subject of the hidden sentence in the user's mind is the user himself/herself, and the combined pair of the verb and the object, called the VO-pair in this chapter, can represent a potential user goal.

To understand which verbs and objects (nouns) are more suitable for use in determining user goals, we made some preliminary analysis by randomly selecting 100 queries from the top 1,000 popular queries from Dreamer (Taiwanese Search Engine, 1998), after removing the pornographic queries. First, we used a POS tagger to acquire the different verbs and nouns that are most-commonly used, and then manually judged the verbs and nouns suitable for user goals. Table 1 shows the percentage of verbs with the verb tags Va (active intransitive verb), Vc (active transitive verb), and Ve (active transitive verb with sentential object), which has the largest percentage of verbs with tags. Table 2 shows that the percentage of objects with noun tags Na (common noun) and Nc (location noun) are more than those of objects with other noun tags. Thus, in this initial work, we consider only six main types of VO-pairs: "Va+Na", "Va+Nc", "Vc+Na", "Vc+Nc", "Ve+Na", and "Ve+Nc".

We are proposing an effective model for identifying user goals from search-result snippets, based on the above six types of VO-pairs. It is expected that our new method could provide users with high-quality search results by understanding user goals more clearly.

CONCLUSION

In this chapter, we first introduced some past research about solving the Web search problems of information overload and short query search in four perspectives, which are "What", "How", "When", and "Where" (3W1H), respectively. Also introduced in this chapter was a new research trend toward an additional perspective, "Why", which mainly focuses on identifying a variety of user goals or understanding user behavior and user preference. We hope that these brief discussions can help readers to understand the current developments and future trends in the research

Table 1. Statistic of verb classes

Verb class	Percentage	Possible user goals
VA (active intransitive verb)	13.4%	tour, shop, teach
VB (semi-transitive verb)	0.5%	file, make room reservation
VC (active transitive verb)	60.0%	download, sell, listen
VD (ditransitive verb)	1.2%	peddle, send, provide
VE (active transitive verb with sentential object)	18.7%	discuss, introduce, report
VF (active verb with vp object)	0.5%	plan, apply, contrive
VG (classificatory verb)	0.6%	become, compound
VH (stative intransitive verb)	0.8%	love, commerce, upgrade
VJ (stative transitive verb)	3.5%	share, enjoy, connect
VK (stative verb with sentential object)	0.5%	display, accelerate, notice
VL (stative verb with vp object)	0.3%	start, keep

Table 2. Statistic of object (noun) classes

Object (noun) class	Percentage	Possible user goals
Na (common noun)	87.8%	book, music, game
Nb (proper noun)	5.0%	university, Yahoo, Melody
Nc (location noun)	7.0%	website, lodge, New York
Nd (time noun)	0.2%	Christmas, spring, future

of Web search. We have also briefly introduced our proposed approach, which employs syntactic structures (verb-object pairs) to automatically identify potential user goals from search-result snippets. We believe that understanding user goals more clearly and reducing information overload will become one of the major developments in commercial search engines in the future, because the amounts of information and resources continue to grow and user needs will become more and more diverse.

REFERENCES

Agichtein, E., Brill, E., & Dumais, S. (2006a). Improving Web search ranking by incorporating user behavior. *Proceedings of the ACM Conference on Research and Development on Information Retrieval (SIGIR)*.

Agichtein, E., Brill, E., Dumais, S., & Ragno, R. (2006b). Learning user interaction models for predicting Web search result preferences. *Proceedings of the ACM Conference on Research and Development on Information Retrieval (SIGIR)*.

Balfe, E., & Smyth, B. (2004). Query mining for community based Web search. *Proceedings of the International Conference on Web Mining (WI'04)*.

Beitzel, S. M., Jensen, E. C., Chowdhury, A., Grossman, D., & Frieder, O. (2004). Hourly analysis of a very large topically categorized Web query log. *Proceedings of the ACM Conference on Research and Development on Information Retrieval (SIGIR)*.

Buyukkokten, O., Cho, J., Garcia-Molina, H., Gravano, L., & Shivakumar, N. (1999, June). Exploiting geographical location information of Web pages. *Proceedings of the ACM SIGMOD Workshop on the Web and Databases (WebDB'99)*.

Chien, S., & Immorlica, N. (2005). Semantic similarity between search engine queries using temporal correlation. *Proceedings of the International Conference on the World Wide Web* (pp. 2-11).

Cui, H., Wen, J.-R., Nie, J.-Y., & Ma, W.-Y. (2002). Probabilistic query expansion using query logs. *Proceedings of the 11th International Conference on the World Wide Web* (pp. 325–332).

Ding, J., Gravano, L., & Shivakumar, N. (2000). Computing geographical scopes of Web resources. *Proceedings of the 26th Very Large Database Conference (VLDB)* (pp. 545–556).

Fox, S., Karnawat, K., Mydland, M., Dumais, S. T., & White, T. (2005). Evaluating implicit measures to improve the search experience. *ACM Transactions on Information Systems*.

Google Search Engine (2006). Retrieved from http://www.google.com

Gravano, L., Hatzivassiloglou, V., & Lichtenstein, R. (2003). Categorizing Web queries according to geographical locality. *Proceedings of the 12th CIKM Conference* (pp. 325-333).

Joachims, T. (2002). Optimizing search engines using click-through data. *Proceedings of the ACM Conference on Knowledge Discovery and Datamining (SIGKDD)*.

Joachims, T., Granka, L., Pang, B., Hembrooke, H., & Gay, G. (2005). Accurately interpreting click-through data as implicit feedback. *Proceedings of the ACM Conference on Research and Development on Information Retrieval (SIGIR)*.

Kleinberg, J. M. (1998). Authoritative sources in a hyperlinked environment. *Proceedings of ACM-SIAM Symposium on Discrete Algorithms*.

Lee, U., Liu, Z., & Cho, J. (2005). Automatic identification of user goals in Web search. *Proceedings of the 14th International Conference on the World Wide Web* (pp. 391–400).

Page, L., Brin, S., Motwani, R., & Windograd, T. (1998). *The pagerank citation ranking: Bring order to the Web*. Stanford Digital Library Technologies Project.

Rose, D. E., & Levinson, D. (2004). Understanding user goals in Web search. *Proceedings of the 13th International Conference on the World Wide Web* (pp. 13–19).

Silverstein, C., Henzinger, M., Marais, H., & Moricz, M. (1999). Analysis of a very large Web search engine query log. *SIGIR Forum, 33*(3) (Originally published as DEC Systems Research Center Technical Note, 1998).

Zhao, Q., Hoi, C. -H., Liu, T. -Y, Bhowmick, S. S., Lyu, M. R., & Ma, W. -Y (2006). Time-dependent semantic similarity measure of queries using historical click-through data. *Proceedings of the International Conference on the World Wide Web.*

KEY TERMS

Search quality: A nature of providing users with useful search results

User behavior: Users' interaction with the search engine

Keyword matching: A search mechanism which considers a document relevant if it shares common terms with the query

Click-through data: The information which can reveal the behavior of users from submitting a query to finally finding the target Web pages

User goal identification: To identify what the user wants to do when submitting a query

Information retrieval: To retrieve information useful or relevant to the query

Natural language processing: A field of studying the problems of automated generation and understanding of natural human languages

Chapter XXVIII
Web Search Engine Architectures and their Performance Analysis

Xiannong Meng
Bucknell University, USA

ABSTRACT

This chapter surveys various technologies involved in a Web search engine with an emphasis on performance analysis issues. The aspects of a general-purpose search engine covered in this survey include system architectures, information retrieval theories as the basis of Web search, indexing and ranking of Web documents, relevance feedback and machine learning, personalization, and performance measurements. The objectives of the chapter are to review the theories and technologies pertaining to Web search, and help us understand how Web search engines work and how to use the search engines more effectively and efficiently.

INTRODUCTION

Web search engines have become an integral part of the daily lives of common people. Every day ordinary folks search through popular search engines for information ranging from a travel arrangement, food, movies, health tips, education, to topics in pure academic research. In this chapter, we survey various aspects of Web search engines. They include system architectures, information retrieval theories, indexing and ranking of documents, relevance feedback, personalization, machine learning, and perfor-

mance measurements. The discussion will review the basic ideas and theories pertaining to each of the areas, followed by practical examples used in search engines where possible. These examples are gathered either from published literatures or from the author's personal experiences and observations. The chapter will end with performance measurements of a set of popular search engines. The objectives of this chapter are to review the theories and technologies pertaining to Web search, and help us understand how Web search engines work and how to use the search engines more effectively and efficiently.

The chapter is divided into multiple sections. General architectures of a search engine will be reviewed in the second section. The topics include system architectures, sample hardware configurations, and important software components. The third section gives an overview of information retrieval theory, which is the theoretical foundation of any search systems, of which Web search engine is an example. Various aspects of a search engine are examined in detail in subsequent sections. Link analysis and ranking of Web documents are studied in the fourth section. Issues of indexing are discussed in the fifth section, followed by the presentations of relevance feedback and personalization in the sixth and seventh sections. The subject of Web information system performance is dealt with in the eighth section. The ninth section lists some important issues that are not surveyed in this chapter, followed by some conclusions in the last section.

In general, search engine companies are very reluctant to share any of the inner workings of the search engines for commercial and competitive reasons. Google, as an exception, actually published a few papers about their architectures and their file systems (Barroso, Dean, & Holzle, 2003; Brin & Page, 1998). AltaVista, one of the oldest search engines around, also documented its architecture in an internal technical report in the early days of search engines (Sites, 1996). The main theoretical aspect of any search engine lies in the theory of information retrieval. The classic texts such as Salton (1989) and van Rijsbergen (1975), as well as more recent texts such as Baeza-Yates and Ribeiro-Neto (1999) give solid background information on this front. We will review the relevant aspects of information retrieval that are widely used in today's search engines. With millions of pages relevant to a particular query, ranking of the relevant documents becomes extremely important to the success of a search engine. None other than the algorithm of PageRank is more important to the core of the ranking algorithms of search engines. Since the introduction of the algorithm in 1998 (Page, Brin,

Motwani, & Winograd, 1998), many revisions and new ideas based on the PageRank algorithm have been proposed. This chapter reviews some of the most important ones. The chapter will then discuss the issues of relevance feedback and its applications to Web searches. Relevance feedback allows the user of a search engine to interactively refine the search queries such that the more relevant results would come to the top of the search results (Chen, Meng, Fowler, & Zhu, 2001; Rocchio, 1971). Personalization and machine learning are some of the examples of refinement techniques aimed at increasing search accuracy and relevancy. Though not yet widely used in public search engines, these techniques show important improvement in search results (Meng & Chen, 2001; Mobasher, Dai, Luo, Nakagawa, Sun, & Wiltshire, 2002). The final technical aspect discussed in this chapter is the performance measurement. How can we evaluate the performance of a Web search engine? What do we mean when we say that one search engine is "better" than another? The chapter will visit some historical papers on this issue and discuss some modern-day measures that can be effectively used in gauging the performance of a Web search engine. The performance can be seen from two different perspectives: that of a user's information needs, that is, whether or not the search engine found what the user wanted; and that of a system response, that is, how fast a search engine can respond to a search query. We will examine both issues (Meng & Chen, 2004, Meng, Xing, & Clark, 2005).

The chapter serves as an overview of a variety of technologies used in Web search engines and their relevant theoretical background.

GENERAL ARCHITECTURES OF SEARCH ENGINES

Architectures of search engines can vary a great deal, yet they all share some fundamental components. This is very similar to the situation of automobiles where the basic concepts for core components of an automobile are the same across different types of cars, but each maker and model can have their own special design and manufacturing for the component. From the hardware point of view, a search engine uses a collection of computers running as a networked server. These computers are, most likely, just ordinary computers off the shelf. To increase the processing and storage capacity of a search engine, the owner of the search engine may decide to interconnect a large number of these computers to make the server a cluster of computers.

General System Architecture of a Search Engine

Search engines consist of many parts that work together. From a system architecture point of view, however, a number of basic components are required to make a search engine work. Figure 1 is an overview of basic system architecture.

Huge amounts of data exist on the Web. They are in the form of static or dynamic textual Web pages, static images, video and audio files, among others. Indexing images, video, and audio data presents a different set of challenge than for that of textual data. For the work of a search engine, the logic is very similar among different types of data. For the purpose of this chapter, we concen-

trate on textual data only. A search engine has to use some form of Web crawlers (also known as spiders and robots) to visit the Web, collecting data from Web pages. A typical search engine would send numerous crawlers visiting various parts of the Web in parallel. As pages are being collected, the crawlers send the data to an indexer (see Indexing section for a detailed discussion of indexers) for processing. The job of an indexer is to parse each Web page into a collection of tokens and to build an indexing system out of the collected Web pages. The major portion of the indexed data should remain on a secondary storage device because of the huge volume, while the frequently-accessed data should be in the main memory of the search engine computer(s). The indexing system typically is an inverted system which has two major components, a sorted term list and a posting list for each of the terms. When the indexing system has been built, the search engine is ready to serve users' search queries. When a search query is issued, the parser separates the query into a sequence of words (terms). The term list of the indexing system is searched to find the documents related to the query terms. These documents are then ranked according to some ranking algorithms and presented to the user as the search results. See the Web Information Retrieval and Link Analysis section for detailed discussion of ranking algorithms.

A Basic Architecture of the Google Search Engine

While the exact structure of a search engine would most likely be a tightly-kept trade secret, Google, the search engine industry leader, did publish some of its architecture (Barroso et al., 2003; Brin & Page, 1998) and file systems (Ghemawat, Gobioff, & Leung, 2003) in some conference and magazine papers. Here we describe Google's system architecture based on published information (Barroso et al., 2003; Brin & Page, 1998). According to the data published in Barroso et al. (2003), Google

Figure 1. Overview of search engine architectures

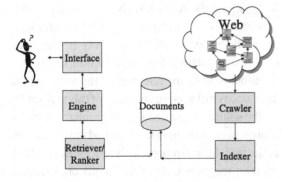

(at the time) used about 15,000 off-the-shelf PCs across its sites worldwide. These PCs range from single-processor 533-MHz Celeron to dual-processor 1.4 GHz PIII, each of which has one or more 80G IDE drives as a local storage. The PCs are mounted on racks. Google's racks consist of 40 to 80 - x86-based servers mounted on either side of a custom-made rack. Each side of the rack contains 20 - 2-u, or 40 - 1-u servers. Several generations of CPU are in active use so the upgrade of the hardware can be done incrementally. Google typically keeps their hardware for about two to three years of life cycle. The servers on the racks are connected by 100 Mbps Ethernet switches. Each rack has one or two gigabit uplinks to connect to the rest of the racks. According to a recent *New York Times* estimate, Google now has 450,000 servers across 25 locations (Markoff & Hansell, 2006).

Major components of the Google search engine, according to their paper (Brin & Page, 1998), include: a collection of distributed Web crawlers that visit Web pages and collect data from the Web; a URL server that sends lists of URLs harvested from the visited Web pages by the indexer to the crawlers to crawl more Web pages; a Storeserver which compresses and stores the fetched pages; and an indexer that converts each document into a set of word occurrences called *hits* and builds the indexing system for search. The hits record the word, its position in the document, the font size, and capitalization information. The indexer distributes these hits into a set of lexical-ordered "barrels", creating a partially-sorted forward index. The indexer also parses out all the links in every Web page and stores important information about them (points to and from, text of the link) in an anchor file.

When a user queries Google, the query execution is divided into two phases. In the first phase, the index servers first consult an inverted index that map each query word to a hit list. Multiple index servers may be involved at this point if the query contains multiple words. The index servers then determine a set of relevant documents by intersecting the hit lists of each query word. A relevance score is computed for each document in the hit list collection. The result of this phase is an ordered list of document IDs, not the actual URLs with snips. In the second phase of the query execution, the document servers take the document IDs generated from the first phase and compute the actual title and URL for each, along with a summary (snips). Now the results are ready to be sent back to the user. Documents are randomly distributed into smaller shards (small portions of Google indices). Multiple server replicas are responsible for handling each shard. The original user queries are routed through a load balancer to different index and document servers.

According to Barroso et al. (2003), each of the Google document servers must have access to an online, low-latency copy of the entire Web that can be accessed quickly by the search engine. Google stores dozens of copies of the Web across its clusters. Other supporting services of a Google Web server (GWS), besides document servers and index servers, include spell-check service and advertising service (if any).

INFORMATION RETRIEVAL THEORY AS A BASIS OF WEB SEARCH

The theory and practices of information retrieval (IR) has its long history. For example, one of the popular models of IR is the vector model, which dates back to the 1960's (Salton, 1971; Salton & Lesk, 1968). A typical IR task contains two aspects: Given a corpus of textual natural-language documents and a user query in the form of a textual string, find a collection of ranked documents that are relevant to the user query. The successful accomplishment of this task relies on the solutions to a number of problems: how to represent each of the document and the document collection; how to represent the query; how to find the relevant documents in the document collection for the given query; what exactly *relevant* means, among others. The following discussions attempt to address these issues.

Vector Space Model

Documents and queries can be represented in many different forms. One of the popular and effective models is the *vector space model*. Assume a document collection is represented by $D = \{d_i, i = 1,...,m\}$, the total vocabulary in the document collection is represented by $T = \{t_i, i = 1, ..., n\}$, that is, there are n different terms in the document collection. Then each document in the collection D can be represented as a vector of terms:

$$d_i = (w_{i1}, w_{i2}, ..., w_{in}) \text{ for } i = 1, ..., m \quad (1)$$

where each entry w_{ij} is the weight of the term j in document i, or term j's contribution to document i. If term t does not appear in document i, then $w_{it} = 0$. There can be different means to determine the value of the weight. For the purpose of illustration, a *term-frequency-inverted-document-frequency* or *tf-idf* definition is used here. To define *tf-idf*, some other notions are needed. Term frequency, or tf_{ij} is defined as the number of times the term i appears in document j, normalized by the maximum term frequency in this document. Assume the collection of document contains a total of N documents. The document frequency, or df_i, of term i is defined as the number of documents in the collection containing the term. Inversed document frequency of term i, or idf_i is defined as:

$$idf_i = \log(\frac{N}{df_i})$$

Then the contribution of term i to document j can be represented as

$$w_{ij} = tf_{ij} * idf_i = tf_{ij} * \log(\frac{N}{df_i}) \quad (2)$$

Thus in the vector space model, the collection of documents can be represented as a set of vectors, each of which is represented by the term weights that make up a document.

Relevance between a Query and the Documents in the Collection

Now that a document is represented by a term weight vector, we can discuss what it means for a document or a collection of documents to be relevant to a given query. In the vector space model, a query is also represented by term weights, as if it were a regular document in the collection. The key difference is that a typical query consists of only a few words, while a document could contain thousands or tens of thousands of different words. According to Spink, Wolfram, Jansen, and Saracevic (2001), a typical Web user search query contains two to three words only. Consequently, the vector representing the query is very sparse, but nonetheless it is a vector. The relevance between the query and the documents then is typically measured by the cosine similarity, the angle between the query vector and the document vector. The similarity can be written as

$$sim(Q, D_i) = \frac{\vec{Q} \bullet \vec{D_i}}{|\vec{Q}| * |\vec{D_i}|} = \frac{\sum_{k=1}^{n} q_k * w_k}{\sqrt{\sum_{k=1}^{n} q_k^2} \sqrt{\sum_{k=1}^{n} w_k^2}}$$

$$(3)$$

where n is the size of the vocabulary and q_k are the *tf-idf* term weights for the query vector Q. This value is between 0 and 1, inclusive. If the two vectors (documents) have no common terms, the similarity value is 0. If the two vectors are identical, completely overlapping each other, the similarity value is 1. If a document is similar to the query, the value would be closer to 1. Among all documents that are relevant to the query, they can be ranked by this cosine similarity value. The larger the value, the more relevant will the document be to the query.

WEB INFORMATION RETRIEVAL AND LINK ANALYSIS

Traditional IR works on a collection of documents consisting of free texts. The Web information retrieval (or Web search) has a distinct feature that the Web documents typically have hypertext links (Nelson, 1965) (or simply *links*) pointing to each other. Thus, the Web is a *graph* of document nodes in which documents are connected to each other by the hyperlinks that the documents use to point to other documents on the Web. Because of this hyperlink nature of the Web, link analysis of various kinds played an important role in understanding the Web structure and helping to build algorithms and data structures that are effective for Web searches. The research in link analysis helped by providing effective ranking algorithms to rank the Web pages based on various criteria. Two pieces of work were especially notable, the *PageRank* algorithm by Page and Brin (Page et al., 1998) and the link analysis and its results in identifying *authorities* and *hubs* by Kleinberg (1999). Xi and others were trying to unify the work of various link analyses into *link fusion*, a link analysis framework for multi-type interrelated data objects (Xi, Zhang, Zheng, Lu, Yan, & Ma, 2004).

While the basic ranking mechanism in IR and Web search is based on the notion of cosine similarity defined in (3), real search engines use additional information to facilitate the ranking such as the location of the term in a document (if a term is close to the beginning of the document, or close to the title or abstract, it may be more important than if it appears in other parts of the document, say in the appendix), the font color and font size of the term (the larger the font is, the more likely it is important), proximity to other search terms, among others (Brin & Page, 1998). One of the most important ranking algorithms in Web search is called *PageRank* algorithm (Page et al., 1998).

The *PageRank* Algorithm

The PageRank algorithm (Page et al., 1998) is based on the notion that if a page is pointed at by many other pages, it is likely that this page is important. That a Web page p is *pointed at* by a Web page q means that inside the text of Web page q there is at least one hypertext (HTML) link that references Web page p. For example, if the URL for Web page p is http://www.some. domain/pageP.html
then page q points to page p if this URL appears inside the text of q. The *PageRank* of a Web page is the summation of the contributions from all the Web pages that point to this Web. Specifically the *PageRank* is defined as follows.

$$R(p) = \sum_{q:q \to p} \frac{R(q)}{N_q} + E(p) \qquad (4)$$

$R(p)$ is the page rank of p and N_q is the outgoing degree of Web page q which is a count of how many other Web pages to which this page is referencing. The idea is that one's page rank contribution to another Web page should be distributed among all the Web pages to which this page is referencing. $E(p)$ is a small replenishing constant so that if a collection of pages point only to themselves without contribution to the rest of the Web, they do not become a sink of all the page ranks. The basic *PageRank* algorithm is as follows.

Brin and Page (1998) show that the algorithm converges relatively fast. On a collection of 320 million Web pages, the algorithm converges in about 52 rounds of iterations. The algorithm can be applied off-line after the crawlers have collected all the Web pages that they can visit in a given period of time. Once page ranks are built

Figure 2. The PageRank algorithm

Let S be the total set of pages.
Let $\forall p \in S$: $E(p) = \alpha/|S|$ (for some $0 < \alpha < 1$, e.g. 0.15)
Initialize $\forall p \in S$: $R(p) = 1/|S|$
Until ranks do not change (much) (*convergence*)
For each $p \in S$:

$$R'(p) = \sum_{q:q \to p} \frac{R(q)}{N_q} + E(p)$$

$$c = 1 / \sum_{p \in S} R'(p)$$

For each $p \in S$: $R(p) = cR'(p)$ (*normalize*)

for all the Web pages that have been crawled, one does not need to recompute the page ranks until another round of crawling is needed. Page ranks are the core of Google's ranking algorithm (Brin & Page, 1998), although we do not know the exact algorithm(s) that Google uses to rank the Web pages today.

Hubs and Authorities

While Google's *PageRank* algorithm works on a global collection of Web pages, a group of researchers at Cornell University proposed a similar idea that works on a set of Web pages that are relevant to a query. According to Kleinberg (1999), *authorities* are pages that are recognized as providing significant, trustworthy, and useful information on a topic. *Hubs* are index pages that provide many useful links to relevant content pages (topic authorities). The relation between authorities and hubs of a subject is that good authorities are pointed at by good hubs and good hubs point to good authorities. This relation can be formulated as follows: Assume h_i are values of hubs and a_i are values of authorities for a given search topic, then

$$h_p = \sum_{q:p \to q} a_q \quad a_p = \sum_{q:q \to p} h_q$$

Figure 3. The HITS algorithm

Initialize for all $p \in S$: $a_p = h_p = 1$
For $i = 1$ to k:
For all $p \in S$: $a_p = \sum_{q:q \to p} h_q$ (*update auth. scores*)

$h_p = \sum_{q:p \to q} a_q$ (*update hub scores*)

For all $p \in S$: $a_p = a_p/c$, $h_p = h_p/c$

$\sum_{p \in S} (a_p / c) = 1$ (*normalize* **a**)

$\sum_{p \in S} (h_p / c) = 1$ (*normalize* **h**)

Based on this idea, Kleinberg (1999) proposed the HITS (Hypertext Induced Topical Search) algorithm to compute the authorities and hubs of a search topic. The first part of the algorithm is to construct a base set of Web pages for a given query by the following steps:

- For a specific query Q, let the set of documents returned by a standard search engine be the *root* set R;
- Initialize the page collection S to R;
- Add to S all pages pointed to by any page in R; and
- Add to S all pages that point to any page in R.

S is the base set for the topic searched by the query Q. Now apply the iterative algorithm HITS to obtain the authorities and hubs for this topic.

When the HITS algorithm converges, the pages with higher values of a_is are the authority pages, and the ones with higher values of h_is are the hub pages for the given subject, respectively.

INDEXING

When crawlers pass Web documents (Web pages) to it, the indexer parses each document into a collection of terms or tokens. The indexer builds an inverted indexing system out of this collection of indexing terms and their related documents. The indexing system usually maintains a sorted list of terms. Each of these terms would own a list of documents in which this term appears. Because one can locate these documents through the indexing term, the system is called an *inverted index system*. After an indexing system is built, the system can serve user queries by looking through the term list and retrieving the documents by the indexing term(s). Typically an indexer would go through the following steps to build an indexing system for search:

1. Lexical analysis: Parse each document into a sequence of tokens;

2. Stop words removal: Remove words that do not provide significant benefit when searching. Words such as "of", "the", "and" are common stop words;

3. Stemming if needed: Stemming a word is to find the root of a word. The indexing system thus may store the root of a word only, avoiding words of a common root. An example would be "comput" for computing, computation, computer, and others;

4. Selecting terms for indexing: Even after stop words removal, the terms to be indexed are still large in numbers. An indexing system may decide to weed out more words that are considered less significant for the purpose of search; and

5. Updating the index system.

Figure 4 illustrates the concept of an inverted indexing system.

The term list is a sorted list of term nodes, each of which may contain the term ID, the document frequency of the term, and other information. Each term node points to a posting list which is a sorted data structure such as a tri or a hash table. Each document that contains the term in the term list corresponds to one node in the posting list. The node may include information such as document ID, and the location, fonts, and other information as how the term appears in this document.

When a search query is issued, the user interface part of the search engine passes the query to the retriever (see Figure 1 for illustration). The retriever searches through the term list and retrieves all documents that appear in the posting list of the term(s) from the query. The ranking component of the search engine applies certain ranking algorithms to sort the retrieved documents before presenting them to the user as the search result.

Maintaining and Updating Index

Maintaining and updating index for large-scale Web information is a difficult and challenging task. Over the years, researchers have proposed various ways of dealing with the issue. Incremental update of the index seems to be most reasonable and effective. In the work of Tomasic, Garcia-

Figure 4. Illustration of a typical indexing system

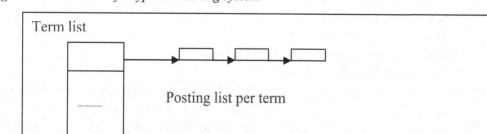

Molina, and Shoens (1994), a dual-structure index is proposed, where the frequently-accessed indices are stored in *long* posting lists, and infrequently-accessed indices are stored in *short* posting lists. The idea is to amortize the cost of writing an infrequently-accessed index to disk file(s). In a more recent piece of work, Lim and colleagues (Lim, Wang, Padmanabhan, Vitter, & Agarwal, 2003) use the idea of *landmark* and the *diff* algorithm to incrementally update the inverted index for the documents that have been analyzed and indexed.

Relevance Feedback

Once an IR system such as a search engine presents the search results to the user, if the system allows the user to refine the search query based on the initial search results that have been presented, the IR system is said to employee some *relevance feedback* mechanisms. The concept of relevance feedback dates back to the 1960's and 1970's. For example, Rocchio (1971) is one of the best-known sources of the discussion of the subject. The basic idea of relevance feedback is to use a linear additive method to expand (refine) the user query so the search engines (or any IR systems) can refine the search based on updated information contained in the refined query. The outline of the relevance feedback algorithm is presented in Figure 5.

One particular and well-known example of relevance feedback is Rocchio's similarity-based relevance feedback (Rocchio, 1971). Depending on how updating factors are used in improving

Figure 5. A basic relevance feedback algorithm

Start with an initial query vector $\mathbf{q}_0$.
At any step $k \geq 0$, improve the k-th query vector $\mathbf{q}_k$ to

$$\mathbf{q}_{k+1} = \mathbf{q}_k + \alpha_1 \mathbf{d}_1 + \ldots + \alpha_s \mathbf{d}_s,$$

where $\mathbf{d}_1, \ldots, \mathbf{d}_s$ are the documents judged by the user at this step, and the updating factors $\alpha_i \in R$ for $i = 1, \ldots s$.

the k-th query vector as in the basic algorithm, a variety of relevance feedback algorithms have been designed (Salton, 1989). A similarity-based relevance feedback algorithm is essentially an adaptive, supervised-learning algorithm from examples (Chen & Zhu, 2000; Salton & Buckley, 1990). The goal of the algorithm is to learn some unknown classifier that is determined by a user's information needs to classify documents as relevant or irrelevant. The learning is performed by means of modifying or updating the query vector that serves as the hypothetical representation of the collection of all relevant documents. The technique for updating the query vector is linear addition of the vectors of documents judged by the user. This type of linear additive query-updating technique is similar to what is used by the Perceptron algorithm (Rosenblatt, 1958), a historical machine-learning algorithm. The linear additive query-updating technique has a disadvantage: Its *converging rate* to the unknown target classifier is *slow* (Chen & Zhu, 2000; Kivinen, Warmuth, & Auer, 1997). In the real world of Web search, a huge number of terms (usually keywords) are used to index Web documents. To make the things even worse, no users will have the patience to try, say, more than 10 iterations of relevance feedback in order to gain some significant search precision increase. This implies that the traditional linear additive query-updating method may be too slow to be applicable to Web search, and this leads to the design and testing of a new and *faster* query-updating method for user preference retrieval. This new algorithm is called MA, for Multiplicative Adaptive (Chen & Meng, 2002). The key idea in the MA algorithm is listed in Figure 6.

Meng and Chen (2005) implemented the MA algorithm in their experimental MARS search engine. The experiment data show that the algorithm is very effective in refining search results. See Meng and Chen (2005) for more details.

The theory and practice both prove that relevance feedback is a powerful mechanism to increase the quality of search. In industry prac-

Figure 6. The multiplicative adaptive query expansion algorithm

Algorithm $MA(q_0, f, \theta)$:
(i) Inputs:

$\mathbf{q}_0$: the non-negative initial query vector
$f(x)$: $[0,1] \rightarrow R^+$, the updating function
$\theta \geq 0$, the classification threshold

(ii) Set $k = 0$.
(iii) Classify and rank documents with the linear classifier $(\mathbf{q}_k, \theta)$.
(iv) While (the user judged the relevance of a document **d**) {

for (i = 1, …, n) {
$/^*$ $\mathbf{q}_k = (q_{1,k}, \ldots, q_{n,k})$, $\mathbf{d} = (d_1, \ldots, d_n)$ $^*/$
if $(d_i \neq 0)$ {
$/^*$ adjustment $^*/$
if $(q_{i,k} \neq 0)$ set $q_{i,k+1} = q_{i,k}$ else set $q_{i,k+1} = 1$

if (**d** is relevant) $/^*$ promotion $^*/$
set $q_{i,k+1} = (1 + f(d_i))\, q_{i,k+1}$
else $/^*$ demotion $^*/$
set $q_{i,k+1} = q_{i,k+1} / (1 + f(d_i))$
else $/^*$ $d_i == 0$ $^*/$
set $q_{i,k+1} = q_{i,k}$
} $/^*$ end of for $^*/$
} $/^*$ end of while $^*/$

(v) If the user has not judged any document in the k-th step, then stop. Otherwise, let $k = k + 1$ and go to step (iv).

tice, we see very little, if any, work of relevance feedback employed by any search engine. This is mostly due to the fact that any relevance feedback implementations on the search engine side would require a considerable amount of resources. Even if it were implemented, it is not clear how or if users would have the patience to use relevance feedback to improve search quality.

PERSONALIZATION

Information on the World Wide Web is abundant. Finding accurate information on the Web in a reasonable amount of time is very difficult. General-purpose search engines such as Google help users to find what they want faster than it used to be. But with the exponential growth in the size of the Web, the coverage of the Web by general-purpose search engines has been decreasing, with no search engine able to index more than about 16% of the estimated size of the publicly indexable Web (Lawrence & Giles, 1999). In response to

this difficulty, three general approaches have been taken over the years. One is the development of *meta-search engines* that forward user queries to multiple search engines at the same time in order to increase the coverage and hope to *include* in a short list of top-ranked results what the user wants. Examples of such meta-search engine include MetaCrawler and Dogpile. Another approach is the development of *topic-specific* search engines that are specialized in particular topics. These topics range from vacation guides to kids' health. The third approach is to use some group or personal profiles to personalize the Web search. Examples for such efforts include Outride (Pitkow, Schütze, Cass, Cooley, Turnbull, Edmonds, Adar, & Breuel, 2002), GroupLens (Konstan, Miller, Maltz, Herlocker, Gordon, & Riedl, 1997) and PHOAKS (Terveen, Hill, Amento, McDonald, & Creter, 1997), among others. General-purpose search engines cover large amounts of information, even though the percentage of coverage is decreasing. But users have a hard time to efficiently locate what they want. The first generation of meta-search engines addresses the problem of decreasing coverage by simultaneously querying multiple general-purpose engines. These meta-search engines suffer, to a certain extent, the inherited problem of *information overflow* so that it is difficult for users to pin down specific information for which they are searching. Specialized search engines typically contain much more accurate and narrowly-focused information. However, it is not easy for a novice user to know where and which specialized engine to use. Most personalized search projects reported so far involve collecting user behaviors at a centralized server or a proxy server. While it is effective for the purpose of e-commerce where vendors can collectively learn consumer behaviors, this approach does present the privacy problem. Users of the search engines would have to submit their search habits to some type of server, though most likely the information collected is anonymous.

Meng (2001) reported the project PAWS, Personalized Adaptive Web Search, a project to ease the Web search task without sacrificing privacy. In PAWS, two tasks were accomplished, *personalization* and *adaptive learning*. When a search process starts, a user's search query is sent to one or more general-purpose search engines. When the results are returned, the user has the choice of personalizing the returned contents. The personalizing component compares the returned documents with the user's profile. A similarity score is computed between the query and each of the documents. The documents, listed from the most similar to the least similar, will then be returned to the user. The user will have the opportunity to mark which documents are relevant and which ones are not. This selection is sent to the PAWS as feedback. The learning component of the PAWS promotes the relevant documents and demotes the irrelevant ones, using the MA algorithm described in the Relevance Feedback section (Chen & Meng, 2002). This interaction can continue until the user finds what she wants from the document collection. The experiment results show that the personalization of the search results was very effective. See Meng (2001) for detailed results.

Performance Evaluation

While user perception is important in measuring the retrieval performance of search engines, quantitative analyses provide more "scientific evidence" that one particular search engine is "better" than another. Traditional measures of *recall* and *precision* (Baeza-Yates & Ribeiro-Neto, 1999) work well for laboratory studies of information retrieval systems. However, they do not capture the performance essence of today's Web information systems for three basic reasons. One reason for this problem lies in the importance of the ranking of retrieved documents in Web search systems. A user of Web search engines would not go through the list of hundreds and thousands of results. A user typically goes through a few pages of ten results. The *recall* and precision *measures* do not explicitly present the ranks of retrieved documents. A relevant document could be listed as the first or the last in the collection. They mean the same as far as recall and precision are concerned at a given recall value. The second reason that recall and precision measures do not work well is that Web search systems cannot practically identify and retrieve all the documents that are relevant to a search query in the whole collection of documents. This is required by the *recall/precision* measure. The third reason is that these *recall/precision* measures are a pair of numbers. It is not easy to read and interpret quickly what the measure means for ordinary users. Researchers (see a summary in Korfhage, 1997) have proposed many *single-value* measures such as estimated search length *ESL* (Cooper, 1968), averaged search length *ASL* (Losee, 1998), *F harmonic mean*, *E-measure*, and others to tackle the third problem.

Meng (2006) compares, through a set of real-life Web search data, the effectiveness of various single-value measures. The use and the results of *ASL*, *ESL*, average precision, F-measure, E-measure, and the *RankPower*, applied against a set of Web search results. The experiment data was collected by sending 72 randomly-chosen queries to *AltaVista* and *MARS* (Chen & Meng, 2002; Meng & Chen, 2005).

The classic measures of user-oriented performance of an IR system are *precision* and *recall*, which can be traced back to the time frame of the 1960's (Cleverdon, Mills, & Keen, 1966; Treu, 1967). Assume a collection of N documents, of which N_r are relevant to the search query. When a query is issued, the IR system returns a list of L results where $L <= N$, of which L_r are relevant to the query. Precision P and recall R are defined as follows:

$$P = \frac{L_r}{L} \text{ and } R = \frac{L_r}{N_r}$$

Note that $0 <= P <= 1$ and $0 <= R <= 1$. Essentially, the *precision* measures the portion of the retrieved results that are relevant to the query, and *recall* measures the percentage of relevant results that are retrieved out of the total number of relevant results in the document set. A typical way of measuring precision and recall is to compute the precision at each recall level. A common method is to set the recall level to be of 10 intervals with 11 points ranging from 0.0 to 1.0. The precision is calculated for each of the recall levels. The goal is to have a high precision rate, as well as a high recall rate. Several other measures are related to the measure of precision and recall. *Average precision and recall* (Korfhage, 1997) computes the average of recall and precision over a set of queries. The *average precision at seen relevant documents* (Baeza-Yates & Ribeiro-Neto, 1999) takes the average of precision values after each new relevant document is observed. The *R-precision* (Baeza-Yates & Ribeiro-Neto, 1999) measure assumes the knowledge of the total number of relevant documents R in the document collection. It computes the precision at R-th retrieved documents. The *E measure* $E = 1 - \dfrac{1+\beta^2}{\dfrac{\beta^2}{R} + \dfrac{1}{P}}$

which was proposed in Van Rijsbergen (1974) can vary the weight of precision and recall by adjusting the parameter β between 0 and 1. In the extreme cases when β is 0, $E = 1 - P$, where recall has the least effect, and when β is 1, $E = 1 - \dfrac{2}{\dfrac{1}{R} + \dfrac{1}{P}}$

where recall has the most effect. The *harmonic F measure* (Shaw, 1986) is essentially a complement of the *E measure*, $F = \dfrac{2}{\dfrac{1}{R} + \dfrac{1}{P}}$.

The precision-recall measure and its variants are effective measures of the performance of information retrieval systems in the environment where the total document collection is known, and the subset of documents that are relevant to a given query is also known.

The drawbacks of the precision-recall-based measures are multifold. Most noticeably, as Cooper pointed in his seminal paper (Cooper, 1968): It does not provide a single measure; it assumes a binary relevant or irrelevant set of documents, failing to provide some gradual order of relevance; it does not have built-in capability for comparison of system performance with purely random retrieval; and it does not take into account a crucial variable, the amount of material relevant to the query which the user actually needs. The *expected search length (ESL)* (Cooper, 1968; Korfhage, 1997) is a proposed measure to counter these problems. ESL is the average number of irrelevant documents that must be examined to retrieve a given number i of relevant documents. The weighted average of the individual expected search lengths can then be defined as follows:

$$ESL = \frac{\sum_{i=1}^{N} i * e_i}{\sum_{i=1}^{N} i} \qquad (5)$$

where N is the maximum number of relevant documents, and e_i is the expected search length for i relevant documents.

The *average search length (ASL)* (Losee, 1998, 1999, 2000) is the expected position of a relevant document in the ordered list of all documents. For a binary judgment system (i.e., the document is either relevant or irrelevant), the average search length is represented by the following relation:

$$ASL = N[QA + (1-Q)(1-A)] \qquad (6)$$

where N is the total number of documents, Q is the probability that ranking is optimal, and A is the expected proportion of documents examined in an optimal ranking, if one examines all the documents up to the document in the average position of a relevant document. The key idea of *ASL* is that one can *compute* the quality of an IR system without actually measuring it, if certain parameters can be learned in advance. On the other hand, if one examines the retrieved documents, the value *A* can be determined experimentally, taking the total number of retrieved relevant documents divided by the total number of retrieved documents; thus the quality indicator *Q* can be computed.

Except the basic *precision* and *recall* measures, the rest of the aforementioned measures are single-value measures. They have the advantage of representing the system performance in a single value; thus it is easier to understand and compare the performance of different systems. However, these single-value measures share a weakness in one of the two areas. Either they do not consider explicitly the positions of the relevant documents, or they do not explicitly consider the count of relevant documents. This makes the measures nonintuitive and difficult for users of interactive IR systems such as Web search engines to capture the meanings of the measures.

To alleviate the problems using other single-value measures for Web search, Meng and Chen proposed a single-value measure called *Rank-Power* (Meng & Chen, 2004) that combines the precision and the placements of the returned relevant documents. The measure is based on the concept of *average ranks* and the *count* of returned relevant documents. A closed-form expression of the optimal *RankPower* can be found such that comparisons of different Web information retrieval systems can be easily made. The *Rank-Power* measure reaches its optimal value when all returned documents are relevant.

RankPower is defined as follows.

$$RankPower(N) = \frac{R_{avg}(N)}{n} = \frac{\sum_{i=1}^{n} S_i}{n^2} \quad (7)$$

where N is the total number of documents retrieved, n is the number of relevant documents among N, and S_i is the place (or the position) of the ith relevant document.

While the physical meaning of *RankPower* as defined above is clear -- average rank divided by the count of relevant documents -- the domain in which its values can reach is difficult to interpret. The optimal value (the minimum) is 0.5 when all returned documents are relevant. It is not clear how to interpret this value in an intuitive way, that is, why 0.5. The other issue is that *RankPower* is not bounded above. A single relevant document listed as the last in a list of m documents assures a *RankPower* value of m. If the list size increases, this value increases. In their recent work, Tang, Chen, Fu, and Cheung (2006) proposed a revised *RankPower* measure defined as follows:

$$RankPower(N) = \frac{\frac{n(n+1)}{2}}{\sum_{i=1}^{n} S_i} = \frac{n(n+1)}{2\sum_{i=1}^{n} S_i} \quad (8)$$

where N is the total number of documents retrieved, n is the number of relevant documents among the retrieved ones, and S_i is the rank of each of the retrieved, relevant document. The beauty of this revision is that it now constrains the values of the *RankPower* to be between 0 and 1, with 1 being the most favorite and 0 being the least favorite. A minor drawback of this definition is that it loses the intuition of the original definition, which is the average rank divided by the count of relevant documents.

The experiment and data analysis reported in Meng (2006) compared *RankPower* measure with a number of other measures. The results show that the *RankPower* measure was effective and easy to interpret. A similar approach to that was discussed in Korfhage (1997) was used in the study. A set of 72 randomly-chosen queries are sent to the chosen search engines. The first 200

Table 1. Average recall and precision at the first 20 returned results

Recall	0.00	0.10	0.20	0.30	0.40	0.50	0.60	0.70	0.80	0.90	1.00	sum	Avg
0.00	4	0	0	0	0	0	0	0	0	0	0	**4**	**0.00**
0.10	0	2	1	1	3	0	0	1	1	1	1	**11**	**0.48**
0.20	0	6	4	1	1	4	2	5	0	3	4	**30**	**0.52**
0.30	0	0	1	2	8	4	1	1	0	0	0	**17**	**0.43**
0.40	0	1	0	0	2	1	0	0	1	1	0	**6**	**0.52**
0.50	0	0	0	0	0	0	1	0	0	0	0	**1**	**0.60**
0.60	0	0	0	0	0	0	0	0	0	0	0	**0**	**0.00**
0.70	0	1	0	1	0	0	0	0	0	0	0	**2**	**0.20**
0.80	0	0	0	0	0	0	0	0	0	0	0	**0**	**0.00**
0.90	0	0	0	0	0	0	0	0	0	0	0	**0**	**0.00**
1.00	0	1	0	0	0	0	0	0	0	0	0	**1**	**0.10**
sum	**4**	**11**	**6**	**5**	14	9	4	7	2	5	5	72	
avg	0.00	0.32	0.20	0.32	0.26	0.27	0.30	0.20	0.25	0.22	0.18		Precision

returned documents for each query are used as the document set. Each of the 200 documents for each of the queries is examined to determine the collection of relevant document sets. This process continues for all 72 queries. The average recall and precision are computed at each of the recall intervals. The results are listed in Table 1.

Shown in Table 2 are the numerical values of the various single-value measures collected from the same data set. Following Cooper (1968)'s discussion, five different types of ESL measures were studied. These five types are listed as follows:

- **Type-1:** A user may just want the answer to a very specific factual question or a single statistic. Only one relevant document is needed to satisfy the search request;
- **Type-2:** A user may actually want only a fixed number (for example, *six*) of relevant documents to a query;
- **Type-3:** A user may wish to see *all* documents relevant to the topic;
- **Type-4:** A user may want to sample a subject area as in Type-2, but wish to specify the ideal size for the sample as some proportion, say *one-tenth*, of the relevant documents; and

- **Type-5:** A user may wish to read *all* relevant documents in case there should be less than five, and exactly *five* in case there exist more than five.

Notice that various ESL measures are the number of irrelevant documents that must be examined in order to find a fixed number of relevant documents; ASL, on the other hand, is the average position of the relevant documents; and *RankPower* is a measure of average rank divided by the number of relevant documents with a lower bound of 0.5. In all cases, the smaller the values are, the better the performance is. Revised *RankPower* has values between 0 and 1 with 0 being the least favorite and 1 being the most favorite.

We can draw the following observations from the data shown in Table 2. Note that these observations demonstrate the effectiveness of single-value measures, especially the *RankPower*. The focus was not on the comparison of the actual search engines since the experimental data is a few years old:

1. In ESL Type-1 comparison, AltaVista has a value of 3.78 which means, on the average,

Table 2. Various single-value measures applied to the experiment data

		AV	MARS
ESL	Type 1	3.78	0.014
	Type 2	32.7	25.7
	Type 3	124	113
	Type 4	7.56	0.708
	Type 5	25.7	17.3
ASL	Measured	82.2	77.6
	Estimate	29.8	29.8
RankPower		3.29	2.53
Revised Rank Power		0.34	0.36

one needs to go through 3.78 irrelevant documents before finding a relevant document. In contrast, ESL Type-1 value for MARS is only 0.014, which means a relevant document can almost always be found at the beginning of the list. MARS performs much better in this comparison because of its relevance feedback feature.

2. ESL Type-2 counts the number of irrelevant documents that a user has to go through if he/she wants to find *six* relevant documents. AltaVista has a value of 32.7 while MARS has a value of 25.7. Again because of the relevance feedback feature of MARS, it performs better than AltaVista.

3. It is very interesting to analyze the results for ESL Type-3 request. ESL Type-3 request measures the number of irrelevant documents that a user has to go through if he/she wants to find all relevant documents in a fixed document set. In our experiments, the document set is the 200 returned documents for a given query, and the result is averaged over the 72 queries used in the study. Although the average *number* of relevant documents is the same between AltaVista and MARS (see the values of estimated ASL), because of the way MARS works, the positions of these relevant documents are different. This

results in different values of ESL Type-3. In order to find all relevant documents in the return set in which the average value is 29.8 documents, AltaVista would have to examine a total of 124 irrelevant documents while MARS would have to examine 113 irrelevant documents, because MARS would have arranged more relevant documents to the beginning of the set.

4. ESL Type-4 requests indicate that the user wants to examine one-tenth of all relevant documents and how many irrelevant documents the user has to examine in order to achieve this goal. In this case, all relevant documents in the returned set of 200 have to be identified before the 10% can be counted. On average, AltaVista would have to examine about eight irrelevant documents before reaching the goal, while for MARS it takes less than one irrelevant document.

5. ESL Type-5 requests examine up to a certain number of relevant documents. The example quoted in Cooper's (1968) paper was five. For AltaVista, it takes about 26 irrelevant documents to find five relevant documents, while MARS requires only about 17.

Some Other Important Issues

There are a number of other important issues closely related to search engines. These include, but are not limited to, crawling the Web (Diligenti, Coetzee, Lawrence, Giles, & Gori, 2000), document clustering (Mandhani, Joshi, & Kummamuru, 2003), multi-language support of the indexing and search of Web data (Sigurbjornsson, Kamps, & de Rijke, 2005), user interface design (Marcus & Gould, 2000), and social networks (Yu & Singh, 2003). Due to limited space, we could not inclusively present them all in this chapter.

CONCLUSION

We surveyed various aspects of Web search engines in this chapter. We discussed systems architectures, information retrieval theories on which Web search is based, indexing and ranking of retrieved documents for a given query, relevance feedback to update search results, personalization, and performance measurement of IR systems, including the ones suitable for Web search engines. Web search engines are complex computing systems that employ techniques from many different disciplines of computer science and information science including hardware, software, data structures and algorithms, and information retrieval theories, among others. The chapter serves as an overview of a variety of technologies used in Web search engines and their related theoretical background. The intended conclusions that the readers should take away from reading this chapter are as follows:

1. Search engines are enormously-complex computing systems that encompass many different segments of sciences and technologies such as computer science (algorithms, data structures, databases, distributed computing, human-computer interfaces), information science (information retrieval, information management), and electrical and computer engineering where the hardware systems can be interconnected and used effectively. The success of search engines depends on even more diverse fields such as social sciences. This is an exciting field of study, and we are still exploring the tip of the iceberg.

2. Although the search engine technologies have been going through many changes, the fundamentals have not. Search engines collect, analyze, and disseminate information to satisfy the user needs. There are many challenging issues ahead of the researchers to improve many aspects of a search engine. They include, but are not limited to, large-scale data collection, analysis, and maintenance, user interfaces, efficient and effective retrieval of information, and social aspects of information engineering, among others.

3. This chapter reviews general technologies of a search engine, with an emphasis on the evaluation of search engine performances. As the chapter indicates, the proposed measure *RankPower* can capture the essence of a user's information needs by taking both the ranks and the number of relevant search results into accounts.

REFERENCES

Aggarwal, C. C., Al-Garawi, F., & Yu, P. S. (2001). Intelligent crawling on the World Wide Web with arbitrary predicates. *Proceedings of the 10th Conference on World Wide Web* (pp. 96-105). ACM.

Baeza-Yates, R., & Ribeiro-Neto, B. (1999). *Modern information retrieval.* Addison Wesley.

Barroso, L. A., Dean, J., & Holzle, U. (2003). Web search for a planet: The Google cluster architecture. *IEEE Micro, 23*(2), 22-28.

Brin, S., & Page, L. (1998). The anatomy of a large-scale hypertextual Web search engine. *Proceedings of the Seventh Conference on World Wide Web.* ACM.

Chen, Z., & Meng, X. (2002). MARS: Applying multiplicative adaptive user preference retrieval to Web search. *Proceedings of the 2002 International Conference on Internet Computing, Las Vegas, Nevada, June 24-27, 2002* (pp. 643-648). CSREA Press.

Chen, Z., Meng, X., Fowler, R. H., & Zhu, B. (2001). Features: Real-time adaptive feature learning and document learning. *Journal of the American Society for Information Science, 52*(8), 655-665.

Chen, Z., & Zhu, B. (2000). Some formal analysis of the Rocchio's similarity-based relevance feedback algorithm. *Proceedings of the Eleventh International Symposium on Algorithms and Computation* (also in *Lecture Notes in Computer Science 1969*) (pp. 108-119).

Cleverdon, C. W., Mills, J., & Keen, E. M. (1966). *Factors determining the performance of indexing systems: Vol. 1 – Design.* Cranfield, England: Aslib Cranfield Research Project.

Cooper, W. S. (1968). Expected search length: A single measure of retrieval effectiveness based on weak ordering action of retrieval systems. *Journal of the American Society for Information Science, 19*(1), 30-41.

Diligenti, M., Coetzee, F. M., Lawrence, S., Giles, C. L., & Gori, M. (2000). Focused crawling using context graphs. *Proceedings of the 26th VLDB Conference, Cairo, Egypt* (pp. 527-534).

Ghemawat, S., Gobioff, H., & Leung, S. T. (2003). The Google file system. *Proceedings of SOSP'03* (pp. 29-43).

Kivinen, J., Warmuth, M. K., & Auer, P. (1997). The perceptron algorithm vs. winnow: Linear vs. logarithmic mistake bounds when few input variables are relevant. *Artificial Intelligence, 97*(1-2), 325-343.

Kleinberg, J. M. (1999). Authoritative sources in a hyperlinked environment. *Journal of the ACM, 46*(5), 604-632.

Konstan, J. A., Miller, B. N., Maltz, D., Herlocker, J. L., Gordon, L. R., & Riedl, J. (1997). GroupLens: Applying collaborative filtering to usenet news. *Communications of the ACM, 40*(3), 77-87.

Korfhage, R. R. (1997). *Information storage and retrieval.* John Wiley & Sons.

Lawrence, S., & Giles, C. L. (1999). Accessibility of information on the we. *Nature, 400*, 107-109.

Lim, P., Wang, M., Padmanabhan, S., Vitter, J. S., & Agarwal, R. (2003). Dynamic maintenance of Web indexes using landmarks. *Proceedings of the 2003 World Wide Web Conference, Budapest, Hungary* (pp. 102-111).

Losee, R. M. (1998). *Text retrieval and filtering: Analytic models of performance.* Boston: Kluwer Publisher.

Losee, R. M. (1999). Measuring search engine quality and query difficulty: Ranking with target and freestyle. *Journal of the American Society for Information Science, 50*(10), 882-889.

Losee, R. M. (2000). When information retrieval measures agree about the relative quality of document rankings. *Journal of the American Society for Information Science, 51*(9), 834-840.

Mandhani, B., Joshi, S., & Kummamuru, K. (2003). A matrix density based algorithm to hierarchically co-cluster documents and words. *Proceedings of the 2003 World Wide Web Conference, Budapest, Hungary.* Retrieved December 19, 2007, from http://www2003.org/cdrom/papers/refereed/p704/index.html

Marcus, A., & Gould, E. W. (2000). Crosscurrents: Cultural dimensions and global Web user-interface design. *Interactions, 7*(4), 32-46.

Markoff, J., & Hansell, S. (2006). Hiding in plain sight, Google seeks more power. New York Times. Retrieved November 10, 2006, from http://www.nytimes.com/2006/06/14/technology/14search.html?pagewanted=2&ei=5088\&en=c96a72bbc5f90a47&ex=1307937600&partner=rssnyt&emc=rss

Meng, X. (2006). A comparative study of performance measures for information retrieval systems (poster presentation). *Proceedings of the Third International Conference on Information Technology: New Generations, Las Vegas, NV, April 10-12, 2006* (pp. 578-579).

Meng, X., & Chen, Z. (2001). PAWS: Personalized adaptive Web search. *Abstract Proceedings of WebNet 2001, AACE, Norfolk, VA* (full paper in CD version of conference proceedings) *October 23-27, 2001* (p. 40).

Meng, X., & Chen, Z. (2004). On user-oriented measurements of effectiveness of Web information retrieval systems. *Proceedings of the 2004 International Conference on Internet Computing* (pp. 527-533), *Las Vegas, NV.*

Meng, X., & Chen, Z. (2005). MARS: Multiplicative adaptive refinement Web search. In A. Scime (Ed.), *Web mining: Applications and techniques* (pp. 99-118). Hershey, PA: Ideas Group Publishing.

Meng, X., Xing, S., & Clark, T. (2005). An empirical performance measurement of Microsoft's search engine. *Proceedings of the 2005 International Conference on Data Mining* (pp. 30-36).

Mobasher, B., Dai, H., Luo, T., Nakagawa, M., Sun, Y., & Wiltshire, J. (2002). Discovery of aggregate usage profiles for Web personalization. *Data Mining and Knowledge Discovery, 6*(1), 61-82.

Nelson, T. (1965). A file structure for the complex, the changing, and the indeterminate. *Proceedings of the 20th National Conference* (pp. 84-100). Association for Computing Machinery.

Page, L., Brin, S., Motwani, R., & Winograd, T. (1998). *The PageRank citation ranking: Bringing order to the Web.* Stanford Digital Library Technologies Project. Retrieved from http://www-db.stanford.edu/~backrub/pageranksub.ps

Pitkow, J. E., Schütze, H., Cass, T. A., Cooley, R., Turnbull, D., Edmonds, A., Adar, E., & Breuel, T. M. (2002). Personalized search. *Communications of the ACM, 45*(9), 50-55.

Rocchio, Jr., J. J. (1971). Relevance feedback in information retrieval. In G. Salton (Ed.), *The smart retrieval system - Experiments in automatic document processing* (pp. 313-323). Englewood Cliffs, NJ: Prentice Hall.

Rosenblatt, F. (1958). The perceptron: A probabilistic model for information storage and organization in the brain. *Psychological Review, 65*(6), 386-407.

Salton, G. (1971). *The SMART retrieval system - Experiments in automatic document processing.* Englewood Cliffs, NJ: Prentice Hall, Inc.

Salton, G. (1989). Automatic text processing. Reading, MA: Addison-Wesley Publishing.

Salton, G., & Buckley, C. (1990). Improving retrieval performance by relevance feedback. Journal of the American Society for Information Science, 41(4), 288-297.

Salton, G., & Lesk, M. E. (1968). Computer evaluation of indexing and text processing. Journal of the ACM, 15(1), 8-36.

Shaw, Jr., W. M. (1986). On the foundation of evaluation. Journal of the American Society for Information Science, 37(5), 346-348.

Sigurbjornsson, B., Kamps, J., & de Rijke, M. (2005). Blueprint of a cross-lingual Web retrieval collection. Journal of Digital Information Management, 3(1), 9-13.

Sites, R. (1996). Retrieved from http://gatekeeper.dec.com/pub/DEC/SRC/publications/sites/talk/AltaVista_Technical.pdf

Spink, A., Wolfram, D., Jansen, B. J., & Saracevic, T. (2001). Searching the Web: The public and their queries. Journal of the American Society for Information Science and Technology, 52(3), 226-234.

Tang, J., Chen, Z., Fu, A. W., & Cheung, D. W. (2007). Capabilities of outlier detection schemes in large databases: Framework and methodologies. *Knowledge and Information Systems, 11*(1), 45-84.

Terveen, L., Hill, W., Amento, B., McDonald, D., & Creter, J. (1997). PHOAKS: A system for sharing recommendations. *Communications of the ACM, 40*(3), 59-62.

Tomasic, A., Garcia-Molina, H., & Shoens, K. (1994). Incremental updates of inverted lists for text document retrieval. *Proceedings of 1994 SIGMOD Conference, Minneapolis, MN* (pp. 289-300).

Treu, S. (1967). Testing and evaluation -- Literature review. In A. Kent, O. E. Taulbee, J. Belzer, & G. D. Goldstein (Eds.), *Electronic handling of information: Testing and evaluation* (pp. 71-88). Washington, DC: Thompson Book Co.

Van Rijsbergen, C. (1974). Foundation of evaluation. *Journal of Documentation, 30*(4), 365-373.

Van Rijsbergen, C. (1975). *Information retrieval.* Retrieved July, 2006, from http://www.dcs.gla.ac.uk/Keith/Preface.html

Xi, W., Zhang, B., Zheng, C., Lu, Y., Yan, S., & Ma, W. Y. (2004). Link fusion: A unified link analysis framework for multi-type interrelated data objects. *Proceedings of the 2004 World Wide Web Conference, May 17-24, 2004, New York* (pp. 203-211).

Yu, B., & Singh, M. P. (2003). Searching social networks. *Proceedings of the 2nd International Joint Conference on Autonomous Agents and Multi-Agent Systems (AAMAS)* (pp. 65-72). ACM Press.

KEY TERMS

Information retrieval: A branch of science that deals with the representation, storage, organization of, and access to information with the prime aim of retrieval information for a given set of queries

Vector space model: A model in which all documents are represented as a vector of weights contributed by each of the terms found in these documents

Inverted index: An indexing system in which the terms point to documents to which the terms belong

Relevance feedback: A mechanism through which an IR system generates a set of results for a given query; the user is allowed to send feedback of some form to the IR system to improve search accuracy

Rank: The order with which the retrieved documents are presented; the closer to the beginning of the list, the more favored the document is

Cosine similarity: A measure used to evaluate the relevance between a query and a document in vector space model; this measure is based on the cosine of the angle between the two vectors, the query, and the document

Term frequency: The number of times that a term appears in a document

Document frequency: The number of documents containing a particular term

Estimated search length (ESL): The average number of irrelevant documents that one has to examine in order to retrieve a given number of relevant documents

Averaged search length (ASL): The expected position of a relevant document in the ordered list of all documents

Chapter XXIX
Towards a Model for Evaluating Web Retrieval Systems in Non–English Queries

Fotis Lazarinis
University of Sunderland, UK

ABSTRACT

As the Web population continues to grow, more non-English users will be amassed online. The purpose of this chapter is to describe the methods and the criteria used for evaluating search engines and to propose a model for evaluating the searching effectiveness of Web retrieval systems in non-English queries. The qualities and weaknesses related to the handling of Greek and Italian queries are evaluated based on this method. The fundamental purpose of the methodology is to establish quality measurements on search engine utilization from the perspective of end users. Application of the proposed evaluation methodology aids users to select the most effective search engine and developers to identify some of the modules of their software that need improvements.

INTRODUCTION

Since its conception in 1992 (Berners Lee, Caillau, Groff, & Pollermann, 1992), the World Wide Web (WWW or Web) has rapidly become one of the most widely-used services of the Internet along with e-mail. Its friendly interface and its hypermedia features attract a significant number of users around the globe. As a result, the Web has become a pool of various types of data, dispensed in a measureless number of locations. Finding information that satisfies specific criteria is a regular daily activity of almost every Web user. Web search engines provide searching services through their uncomplicated interfaces.

Some recent statistical estimations claim that 64.2% of the online population are non-English speakers (Global Reach, 2004). This makes the Web a multicultural and multilingual information space. Therefore, the preferences and requests of non-English-speaking users should undoubtedly be taken into account in the design of any Web information system and especially in Web retrieval systems, since they are utilized on a daily basis by virtually every Web surfer.

Even though several Web search engines exist, most of their features and virtues are catered for the English language only. For example, the query "Book Agatha Christie" in Google retrieves pages mentioning the word "books" as well. This is easily understood as the matching terms are emboldened. In contrast, the queries "Livre Agatha Christie" in French, "Libro Agatha Christie" in Italian and Spanish and "Βιβλίο Αγκάθα Κρίστι" in Greek, retrieve only pages which include exactly the query terms as they are typed in the query. This query could be more problematic in the case of German where the word Book changes from "Buch" in singular to "Bücher" in plural. Both diacritics and endings change in this case. In general, in natural languages with conjugations and intonation like Greek and in languages with non-Latin alphabets, like Greek, Russian, Arabic, Asian, and African languages, searching the Web imposes additional difficulties which should be taken into account so as to design search systems of high quality and effectiveness. In addition to Web search engines, several e-shops maintain local search systems to facilitate their customers searching their catalogs. In these systems, it is imperative to comprehend and assimilate the characteristics of the local natural languages.

The majority of the search engine evaluation studies focus on precision (relevance) of the top-ranked pages returned in specific queries. However, since Web retrieval systems are utilized by several people with medium or low technical expertise, and since the natural language of the queries affect the process, other factors should additionally influence their development and evaluation.

In this chapter, we focus on creating and testing a generalized evaluation methodology which combines interface issues, for example, adaptation to the local language, with searching effectiveness, for example, case insensitivity or effect of the removal of common words (stopwords). The model is presented and analyzed, and it is then applied to evaluating the capabilities of Greek-

and Italian-supporting Web search engines. This framework can serve as the basis for evaluating the effectiveness of Web retrieval systems and of local e-shop search engines in non-English text retrieval. The fundamental purposes of the methodology are:

- To establish quality measurements at every stage of search engine utilization from the perspective of end users;
- To help non-English users in selecting the most effective and user-friendly search engine; and
- To aid developers of search engines in identifying some of the modules of their software that need improvements, so as to satisfy the needs of searchers of various ethnicities.

Search Engine Evaluation

Evaluation is an important aspect in an information retrieval (IR) system (Cleverdon, Mills, & Keen, 1966; Robertson, 1969). Cleverdon et al. (1966) listed six criteria that could be used to evaluate IR systems: (i) coverage, (ii) time lag, (iii) recall, (iv) precision, (v) presentation, and (vi) user effort. Of these criteria, recall and precision have most frequently been applied in assessments of IR software tools. Information retrieval on the Web is fairly different from retrieval in traditional indexed databases. This difference arises from the high degree of dynamism of the Web, its hyperlinked character, the absence of a controlled indexing vocabulary, the heterogeneity of document types and authoring styles, and the easy access that different types of users may have to it (Gwizdka & Chignell, 1999). Therefore, the six evaluation criteria proposed reshaped to fit in this environment. Chu and Rosenthal (1996) evaluated the capabilities of AltaVista, Excite, and Lycos, and proposed a methodology for evaluating search engines in terms of five aspects:

- **Composition of Web indexes (coverage):** Collection update frequencies and size can have an effect on retrieval performance;
- **Search capability:** They suggest that search engines should include "fundamental" search facilities such as Boolean logic and scope limiting abilities;
- **Retrieval performance (precision, recall, time lag):** such as precision, recall, and response time;
- **Output option (presentation):** This aspect can be assessed in terms of the number of output options that are available and the actual content of those options; and
- **User effort:** how difficult and effortful it is to use the search engine by typical users.

Most search engine evaluation attempts focus on the third criterion. For example, eight search engines were reviewed, and their effectiveness was calculated based on the traditional IR measures of recall and precision at varying numbers of retrieved documents (Gordon & Pathak, 1999). Dunlop (1997) used the expected search length to construct graphical evaluation methods to measure retrieval performance from AltaVista. These graphs were introduced as supplementary to precision-recall graphs. AltaVista, Infoseek, Lycos, and Open Text were used in another evaluation study (Su, Chen, & Dong, 1998). The authors employed the measured precision and partial precision for the first 20 hits returned by the search engines. They also defined an evaluative measure that compared ratings of relevance on a five-point scale. Similar approaches used in more recent studies (Hsieh-Yee, 1998; Oppenheim, Morris, & McKnight, 2000). Other research papers focus additionally on issues such as the search interface and the response pace of search engines (Courtois, Baer, & Stark, 1995).

Non-English Web Searching

The studies reviewed in the previous section provide frameworks and models for evaluating the capabilities of search engines, but they usually focus on precision and recall, neglecting other factors such as user effort, for instance. More importantly, they focus only on English queries. It has been argued that existing search engines may not serve the needs of many non-English-speaking Internet users (Chung, Zhang, Huang, Wang, Ong, & Chen, 2004). The latter observation indicates that the multiculturalism and multilingualism dimensions of the Web may have not been efficiently confronted in search engines. That is why a few recent studies assessed Web retrieval systems in light of the spoken language of the users and focused on non-English and non-Latin queries.

Polish-supporting search engines were examined in Sroka (2000). Polish versions of English-language search engines and homegrown-Polish search engines were assessed. The searching capability and retrieval performance were considered. Main emphasis was given to the precision criterion, which was based on relevance judgments for the first 10 matches from each search engine. Of the five search engines evaluated, Polski Infoseek and Onet.pl had the best precision scores, and Polski Infoseek turned out to be the fastest Web search engine.

The performances of general and Arabic search engines were compared based on their ability to retrieve morphologically-related Arabic terms. The findings highlight the importance of making users aware of what they miss by using the general engines, underscoring the need to modify these engines to better handle Arabic queries (Moukdad, 2004).

Experimentation with Russian, French, Hungarian, and Hebrew queries revealed some of the inefficiencies of worldwide search engines related to issues such as capitalization, and singular and plural forms of query terms (Bar-Ilan

& Gutman, 2005). Their results indicate that in the examined cases, the general search engines ignore the special characteristics of non-English languages, and sometimes they do not even handle diacritics well.

Another research article explored the characteristics of the Chinese language and how queries in this language are handled by different search engines (Moukdad & Cui, 2005). Queries were entered in two major search engines (Google and AlltheWeb) and two search engines developed for Chinese (Sohu and Baidu). Criteria such as handling word segmentation, number of retrieved documents, and correct display and identification of Chinese characters were used to examine how the search engines handled the queries. The results showed that the performance of the two major search engines was not on a par with that of the search engines developed for Chinese.

The capabilities of the local Greek search engines of e-commerce sites were reviewed in Lazarinis (2007a). This study focused mainly on the existence of search engines and on interface issues. Yet a few inefficiencies of the local search engines of the e-shops related to the attributes of the Greek language were revealed. For instance, most of the search engines are case-sensitive and let stopwords negatively influence the retrieval of products. In Lazarinis (2005), an initial evaluation of the capabilities of Web search engines revealed some of the deficiencies of international and domestic search engines in Greek queries.

All these studies try to understand and identify the inefficiencies of search engines with respect to non-English and non-Latin languages. They also aim at understanding the regional differences and trends in Web searching (Jansen & Spink, 2005). On this direction, CLEF experiments aim at testing, tuning, and evaluating IR systems operating on European languages in both monolingual and cross-language contexts (CLEF, 2006).

The previous research papers and experiments reveal a lot of the qualities and inefficiencies of stand-alone information retrieval systems and search engines in non-English queries. However, each study assesses Web searching information systems from a different perspective, although some criteria are common.

ISO 9126 software evaluation standard (ISO 9126, 2001) defines functionality, usability, and efficiency as some of the attributes which determine software quality. Restating and simplifying these requirements, we believe that the triptych which should characterize a search engine is *simple to use, fast,* and *effective.* Convenient and localized versions for accessing a retrieval system would allow users of various nationalities and cultural backgrounds to try it. Fast and effective searching mechanisms would lead people to "stick with it".

Evaluation Model

Utilization of a searching system from non-English-speaking users presupposes support for non-English queries. Easy access to the offered services is translated to localized versions of the existing searching options. Fast and effective mechanisms need a large document base to be indexed by the search engine, intelligent mining algorithms, and advanced techniques which effectively aid users in their information hunting and even compensate for minor errors (e.g., spelling errors).

Based on these observations and the studies discussed in the previous sections, we have identified a set of criteria to populate our model. These criteria are clustered into two classes:

1. Searching options,
2. Effectiveness.

These sets of attributes are analyzed further, as shown in Figure 1. The aggregation of these criteria aims at constructing a compact yet efficient model for measuring the "understanding" of international and local search engines to a specific natural language. The primary goal of the model is to provide an internationalization test for Web

Figure 1. Criteria of the evaluation model

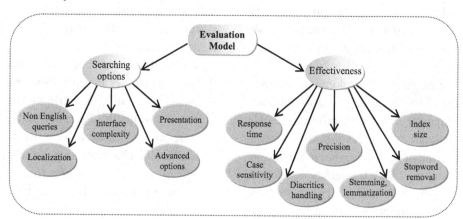

searching systems and, eventually, to be able to suggest improvements in search engines, so as to increase their searching effectiveness and reduce the required user effort in monolingual non-English queries. This test will eventually help users to realize which search engine is better and more effectively satisfies their "information needs".

Semantics of the Model

In this section, the attributes of the evaluation model and the assessing method of each criterion are presented. Some of the criteria presented below are quantitative and could be noted as supported or not supported, and some are qualitative and can be evaluated with the aid of users. In any case, the purpose of our user-centric model is to identify some of the limitations of search engines and not to rank search engines in a numeric scale.

Searching Options

Under the heading "searching options", we classify the attributes which fall within the easy access goal of search engines from non-English-speaking users:

- Support for non-English queries is obviously an essential attribute. Some search engines

may not handle non-Latin queries, and some may not effectively handle terms with diacritics in natural languages which are based on the Latin alphabet. This attribute is noted as supported or not supported. The evaluator needs to be prudent in this case, as searching support may be influenced by the Web browser in case it does not support a specific character set.

- Localization is an indicator referring to the ability of a search engine to adapt its interface to a local natural language. Localization of software and Web interfaces is an important operation which needs to address several social and cultural factors in addition to technical demands (Del Galdo & Nielsen, 1996; Hofstede, 1991). Here we restrict our study of the localization support to the interface and the offered services of search engines. A search engine may be noted as not localized, partially localized, or fully localized. The first value means that a search engine does not adapt at all to a specific language, the second type refers to the adaptation of certain interface parts and services only, and the last indicates that all the provided services and interface components are localized.

- Interface complexity refers to the complexity of the information presented in the initial Web page. A number of search engines act as Web portals as well. This approach leads to increased downloading time, which can be irritating when the speed of the Internet connection is low. Additionally, it may cause confusion and disorientation to users, as the textbox where the query is typed and the procedure's initiation button are not easily viewable. Interface complexity can be assessed by users themselves, as our opinion would be subjective due to our expertise in utilizing search engines. Complex interfaces may cause localization problems as well, as some of the text presented in the search engine's homepage may not be properly adapted, or it may be localized in such a way that could cause confusion and even insult specific user populations (Hofstede, 1991).

- Advanced options, such as those offered by Google and Yahoo, is an attribute which is important to English and non-English-speaking users (e.g., Google scholar, Yahoo video). Many nationwide search engines, although they have straightforward interfaces which local users can effortlessly utilize, they offer only basic searching facilities. Services such as book search and image or video search are not supported. Inevitably, these systems will become obsolete as users become more competent in search engine utilization. The existence of advanced retrieval options will eventually "magnetize" Web surfers, as it is an important quality feature.

- Presentation is an attribute used in assessing standard retrieval systems and Web search engines. In our work, this feature is related to the presentation of the potentially-relevant documents. This attribute is qualitative and not quantitative, and is used to assemble the observations and problems raised by users. For example, condensed presentation forms

and short or no summaries of the results could be the grounds of additional difficulties in surfing within the relevant documents.

Effectiveness

"Effectiveness" groups all these attributes which aid or prevent users from retrieving relevant documents within acceptable time limits. For example, response time is a measure of effectiveness which could distinguish national and international search engines, informing users about which are faster, and thus their utilization would increase their productivity. Other factors, such as the size of the documents searched by the search engine (index size) and the precision, affect the number of retrieved relevant documents. Efficient handling of diacritics and case sensitivity of query terms are important in natural languages with complex conjugations and intonation. Stemming, lemmatization, and stopword removal increase the retrieval effectiveness, and they are supported in English Web retrieval:

- Response time is a quantitative measure and can be analyzed into two sub-categories: the time to load the initial search engine's Web page, and the time required for retrieving the relevant set of documents. This attribute can be mechanically measured using the same Internet connection and by running a number of queries so as to measure the average retrieval time.

- Precision (relevance) is a standard measure used in information retrieval systems (Baeza-Yates & Ribeiro-Neto, 1999; Robertson, 1969). Here precision can be measured at specific recall points. In other words, as in previous studies (Chu & Rosenthal, 1996), precision can be measured in the top-ranked documents. For example, it can be calculated in the first 10 or 20 results which ones hold the highest possibility to be viewed by users (Silverstein, Henzinger, Marais, & Moricz, 1998).

- Index size refers to the number of Web documents which a search engine has in its database. These pages will be searched when a user submits a query. The more documents that are indexed, the more possibly-relevant documents will be retrieved. This element cannot be conclusively measured unless the search engine has revealed its actual index size. But even then it would have to divide this number according to the language codes of the pages contained in the index. Since this is not possible, the only way to get a rough idea is by running some sample queries in different search engines. The recalled set of documents will then provide an estimate of the index size of each search engine.

- Case sensitivity is a feature that does not affect English Web searching. For example, the queries "Ancient Athens" and "ANCIENT ATHENS" produce exactly the same results in Google. However, the results differ between the Greek queries "Αρχαία Αθήνα" and "ΑΡΧΑΙΑ ΑΘΗΝΑ" (Ancient Athens). These queries are equivalent in meaning (content), but differ in their forms (context). Web users should be aware of this difference so as to achieve higher precision. Assessment of this attribute is objective, as it can be noted as supported or not supported.

- Diacritics handling concerns the intonation marks and other accent marks, such as umlaut, which many spoken languages support. For example, the term "European" is written in Greek as "Ευρωπαϊκή". Both intonation and umlaut are used. Other languages, like French or Serbian, contain more accent marks. Search engines should be able to handle diacritics to efficiently support user requests. Effective handling of diacritics is clearly important as, in several occasions, users do not type the diacritics (Lazarinis, 2007b). Search engines should compensate for this difference, and it should not be treated as user negligence whatsoever. If search engines do not act accordingly, several relevant documents will be eventually missed. For example, when the query "Poverta" (Poverty) is submitted in Yahoo.it, then documents containing the proper form of the word "Povertà" are also retrieved. On the contrary, the Greek query "Ευρωπαικη" (no umlaut used) retrieves no relevant documents in Yahoo.com, at least in the first 10 pages. In Google.com (or .gr), the query "Ευρωπαικη" retrieves the same documents as "Ευρωπαϊκή", though.

- Stemming is the process of reducing a word to its stem or root form. This procedure equalizes the morphological variants of words that have similar semantic interpretations. Lemmatization involves the reduction of words to their respective headwords (i.e., lemmas). In the linguistic dictionaries, every entry corresponds to a lemma that defines a set of words with the same lexical root. Lemmatization is closely related to stemming. The difference is that a stemmer finds the stem of a word while a lemmatizer tries to find the lemma for a given word. Google supports a mixture of these techniques, which is closer to lemmatization rather than stemming. For example, the query "evaluating Web sites" retrieves documents which contain the terms "evaluate Web sites" or the terms "evaluation Web sites" as it can be concluded from the highlighted matching terms of the relevant documents. In Web retrieval, stemming may lead to recall of countless Web documents and thus may be an inapplicable technique. However, Greek and other languages exhibit notable morphological variance in terms while the content remains the same. This is due to tense, noun, and adjective declensions, plural and singular forms, and composite words. For example, all three queries "Εθνική πινακοθήκη Αθηνών", "Εθνική πινακοθήκη Αθήνας" and "Εθνική πινακοθήκη Αθήνα" mean "National art gallery of Athens", but they are expressed in different inclinations (nominative, genitive, etc.). Nevertheless, they express exactly the same information need. Light stemming like suffix removal (e.g., removal of the final sigma in Greek) or lemmatization would probably improve recall and precision of search engines, at least in the highly-ranked results.

- Stopword removal is supported by Google and other international search engines in English queries. Stopwords are the terms which appear too frequently in documents, and thus their discriminatory value is low (Salton & McGill, 1983; van Rijsbergen, 1979). For instance, users are informed that the word "of" is an ordinary term and is not used in the query "National Art Gallery of Athens". Additionally, the queries "I won the Nobel" and "won the Nobel" produce the same rank of pages. Removal of stopwords (Baeza-Yates & Ribeiro-Neto, 1999) is an essential part of typical IR systems. Although significant relevant work has been performed in English and suitable stopword lists have been constructed, such lists have not been constructed for most of the European, Asian, and African languages. Thus the effect of stopwords in retrieval has not been thoroughly studied in these languages. A possible way to study the influence of stopwords in Web retrieval is by running composite queries containing both significant terms and stopwords and then running the same query without the stopwords. This way one could get an initial estimate of the positive or negative influence of nonsignificant words in Web retrieval and discern whether an international search engine values all the attributes of a language.

APPLYING THE EVALUATION MODEL: GREEK AND ITALIAN SEARCHING

To value the importance of the model and to measure the understanding of search engines to non-English queries, we applied the methodology in Greek- and Italian-supporting search engines. For conducting our assessment, we used some of the most predominantly-known worldwide .com search engines: Google, Yahoo, AlltheWeb, MSN, AOL, and Ask. The .com search engines were selected based on their popularity (Sullivan, 2005). Where it was possible, we used the local versions of search engines, for example, Yahoo.it and Google.gr. Also, for comparison reasons, some native Greek and Italian search engines were evaluated: In.gr, Anazitisis.gr, Virgilio.it, and Libero.it. Table 1 presents the exact URLs of the search engines used in our experiments.

Searching Options

For assessing the searching options and some of the issues related to the searching effectiveness, we asked six users to help us. All the subjects of

Table 1. URLs of the search engines used in the evaluation experiments

International	Greek	Italian
www.google.gr www.google.it	www.in.gr	www.virgilio.it
www.yahoo.com www.yahoo.it	www.anazitisis.gr	www.libero.it
www.alltheWeb.com		
www.msn.com - it.msn. com		
search.aol.com		
www.ask.com - it.ask. com		

the experiments were Greek speakers, and two of them were additionally fluent in Italian. Participants were also asked to construct a number of sample queries for the subsequent experiments. Users had varying degrees of computer usage expertise. The trial searches were conducted on the same day at the end of September, 2006. They were carried on in a computer lab sharing the same Internet connection. Each session lasted two didactic hours.

Searching Support

To test the ability of international search engines to support Greek and Italian users in their search, we asked the users to run two-one-word Greek and two-one-word Italian queries in international search engines. National search engines were not considered in this phase as they undoubtedly support queries in their native natural language. The localized versions (e.g., Google.gr or Yahoo.it) of search engines were tested, but as expected they do support queries in Greek and Italian.

As far as it concerns Greek, all international search engines but Ask.com were capable of running the queries and retrieving possibly-relevant documents. Ask.com did not retrieve any results at all, meaning that indexing of Greek documents is not supported. Ask.com was included in the subsequent tests only for comparison purposes, even though none of the users would actually end up using it since it retrieves no results. The Italian queries were normally run in every search engine.

This short experiment revealed that there are some search engines which still do not support some non-Latin languages, although they hold a share in the user preference pie chart (Sullivan, 2005).

Localization

Localization is the process of adapting an interface to a specific language. Our participants rated this feature as highly important as many users have basic or no knowledge of English. Although search engines have uncomplicated and minimalist interfaces, their adaptation to the local language is essential as users could easily comprehend the available options.

From the international search engines, only Google automatically detects local settings and adapts to Greek. Nevertheless, none of the reviewed international Web retrieval systems qualifies for the *fully localized* title. Google merely adapts to Greek its basic searching services. For instance, Froogle, Book search, Scholar, and Video search are services of Google offered in English only. Non-English Web searchers may not even be aware of these services. Indeed, all of our participants were not aware of these features and clearly could not be benefited by them.

In Italian, the situation is different, however. Four out of the six international search engines are fully localized to the Italian language. However, again a significant proportion (1/3, or 33.33%) of the major international search engines do not offer localized interfaces to Italian users, and thus they cannot efficiently communicate their searching qualities to them. Additionally, it.ask.com and it.msn.com use non-intuitive URLs (i.e., of the form www.searchegnine.it) and, although search engines detect automatically the local settings and adapt accordingly, this may be a problem when an individual wants to force the usage of the Italian version of Ask.com and MSN.com.

Interface Complexity

Yahoo, MSN, AOL, In.gr, Virgilio.it, and Libero. it act as Web portals containing categorized links, news, photos, and animated gifs. These features cause an increase in the downloading time (see Table 2) which is a problematic situation, especially when the Internet connection is slow. Also, presenting a wealthy of features in the same page is a practice that may cause confusion and disorientation to users. The most important problems brought up by our assistants were "slow downloading", "in which textbox to type the query" and "which button to click to initiate searching". These difficulties may obstruct some users from completing their searching tasks.

Advanced Options

All the international search engines presented in Table 1, and especially Google and Yahoo, are well known for their advanced searching options. Unfortunately, none of the native Greek searching systems offers image or video or other advanced services. Both the Italian search engines offer these options to their users. However, it should be noted that, as it states, Libero.it is powered either by Google or by Virgilio.it and, therefore, it should be considered as a localized version of Google or equivalent to Virgilio.it. In any case, this is not important to users who are interested only in "getting their job done", and surely Libero. it aids them although it is another search engine's wrapping.

Presentation

AlltheWeb, In.gr, and Libero.it present the rank in a condensed form, without leaving adequate space between results, and present the findings with smaller letters with a brief or no summary. Participants were dissatisfied with the condensed presentation output, because it was more difficult to distinguish between the resulting URLs. Also, short summaries increase human effort, as they

have to first visit the Web page and then decide if it is relevant. Summarization is a quite difficult task in IR, and most systems provide inadequate summaries (Amitay & Paris, 2000). This task is even harder when the document collection is enormous and of varying natural languages as in the Web.

Searching Effectiveness

For a search engine to be effective, it needs to be fast and accurate. Accuracy is interpreted as retrieval of relevant documents. To put it simply, the more relevant documents that a searching system locates, the more accurate it is. The searching effectiveness class focuses on assessing some of the factors which influence the discovering of relevant documents in acceptable time limits.

Response Time

The time to load the initial page and the time spent so as to retrieve the potentially-relevant Web pages to a user query are clearly important. Table 2 presents the time needed to load the homepage of the search engines of our study and the average searching time. Time to load usually depends directly on the size of the page; thus, search engines which operate additionally as Web portals need more time. Average searching time was calculated by using three queries consisting of one, two, and three words, respectively. These two elements were calculated using Opera's Web browser built-in capabilities on a 128K Internet

Table 2. Time (seconds) needed to load search engines and average searching time

Search engine	Load time	Avg. search time	Searchengine	Load time	Avg. search time
google.com	1	1	ask.com	4	3.3
yahoo.com	10	3.6	in.gr	9	5.67
alltheWeb.com	3	3.3	anazitisis.gr	3	8.33
msn.com	11	2.6	virgilio.it	8	4.3
aol.com	11	4.7	libero.it	9	4.1

connection. The localized versions of the international search engines are expected to have similar performance as their root counterparts, so the .com engines were used in this experiment.

The objective of these two calculations was to realize which search engine offers the faster searching mechanism. Google exhibited the best performance. Local search engines are as slow as, or slower than, the worldwide systems. So, one could argue that, from the time perspective, Google should dominate over the others in English and non-English queries.

Index Size

As explained, the index size attribute refers to the number of Web documents which a search engine has in its database. This number expands daily as Web robots continually scan the Web for new pages. Since we cannot have absolute numbers, at least for all search engines, we run three queries in Greek and three queries in Italian. These queries were provided by the users participating in our experiment and consisted of one - two-term query and two - three-term queries. Terms were in title case, that is, the first character of each word was in upper case and the remaining letters were in lower case. Diacritics were also used wherever needed. Tables 3 and 4 present these queries and their English translations.

The aim of the current experiment was to get an estimation of the number of pages indexed by international and local search engines. The more pages that are retrieved in these queries, the larger the index file that a search engine

Table 3. Greek sample queries

#	Query in Greek	Query in English
1	Οδυσσέας Ελύτης	Odysseus Elytis
2	Μορφές Ρύπανσης Περιβάλλοντος	Environmental Pollution Forms
3	Εθνική Πινακοθήκη Αθήνας	National Art Gallery of Athens

Table 4. Italian sample queries

#	Query in Italian	Query in English
1	Università Roma	University of Rome
2	Poesia Italiana Innamorato	Italian Poetry for people in love
3	Moderne Tecniche Acustiche	Modern Acoustic Techniques

maintains. Naturally, retrieval is influenced by the mining algorithms employed by the retrieval systems. However, by carefully examining Table 5, it is easily inferred that local search engines recall only a small number of documents, which means that they do not employ effective indexing mechanisms.

The queries run in this experiment were general enough so as to smooth the progress of the retrieval systems. For example, the first Greek query "Οδυσσέας Ελύτης" (Odisseas Elytis – A famous Greek Nobelist poet) and the first Italian user question "Università Roma". In.gr returned 3,251 pages, while Google.gr retrieved approximately 36,000 Web pages. In the query "Università Roma", Virgilio.it retrieved 200 pages, Google.it 4,100,000 pages, and Yahoo.it 7,090,000 pages. These numbers are approximations given by the search engines. Ask.com retrieved zero pages because, as explained previously, it does not support Greek queries.

Table 5. Average number of pages retrieved in Greek and Italian queries

Search engine	Avg. number of retrieved pages in Greek	Search engine	Avg. number of retrieved pages in Italian
google.gr	39,266.67	google.it	1,434,566.67
yahoo.com	3,003.33	yahoo.it	2,386,320
alltheWeb.com	1,530.67	alltheWeb.com	118,763.33
msn.com	1,753	it.msn.com	62,765.33
aol.com	2,130	aol.com	92,233.33
ask.com	0	it.ask.com	573,135.33
in.gr	1,726	virgilio.it	37,066.67
anazitisis.gr	115.67	libero.it	4,946.67

The index size is important, as it is an indication that "richer" search engines could retrieve more results, which would probably be more precise. Search engines like Anazitisis.gr retrieve only a few documents compared to Google. Clearly, the likelihood of satisfying user needs with Anazitisis.gr is fairly smaller compared to Google's odds.

Precision

For measuring the precision of the ranked set of documents, we asked our assistants to run each of the two - three-query sets. The relevance of the Greek queries was the mixture of the estimations of all the six Greek-speaking users. As mentioned, two of the users were fluent in Italian (along with the author of the present study), so the precision in the Italian quest was also estimated. Relevance was calculated in the first 10 results, which hold the highest possibility to be viewed by users (Silverstein et al., 1998). Table 6 presents the user estimates and clearly illustrates that the international search engines returned more relevant pages than the native Greek and Italian local searching systems.

Case Sensitivity

The next phase of the experiment was to rerun the same queries in capital letters. In Greek upper case queries, accents are not used, and thus

they were removed from the first set of queries. The number of retrieved documents in Greek was dramatically diminished in the worldwide search-enabling sites, while it was left unaffected in the domestic ones (see Table 7). As anticipated, in Italian queries the number of retrieved documents did not change, as seen by comparing Tables 5 and 7.

We also measured the precision in the Greek queries as in the previous experiment. Precision was affected too. In the first query the relevance increased, while in the other cases it dropped. The purpose of our evaluation methodology is to identify the factors which affect Web retrieval systems and "jeopardize" their quality. Therefore, we have not further studied the reasons behind the relevance's "ups and downs" at this point. However, it can be definitely argued that if search engines have been treating Greek queries as English and Latin queries, focusing only on their content and not on their form, then retrieval performance would be improved.

Diacritics Handling

Handling of diacritics refers to efficient handling of intonation and accent marks such as grave and acute accents. To form an idea of how search engines handle queries when diacritics are used and how they respond when they are not, we executed the Greek queries "δικαστήριο" and

Table 6. Precision in the first 10 results

Search engine	Number of relevant pages in Greek			Search engine	Number of relevant pages in Italian		
	Q1	Q2	Q3		Q1	Q2	Q3
google.gr	10	6	7	google.it	10	6	6
yahoo.com	10	5	7	yahoo.it	10	6	5
alltheWeb.com	9	5	6	alltheWeb.com	10	5	4
msn.com	8	5	6	it.msn.com	10	6	5
aol.com	8	5	7	aol.com	10	5	5
ask.com	0	0	0	it.ask.com	10	5	4
in.gr	8	4	5	virgilio.it	8	4	4
anazitisis.gr	4	3	3	libero.it	8	4	3

Table 7. Average number of pages retrieved in Greek and Italian upper-case queries

Search engine	Avg. number of retrieved pages in Greek	Search engine	Avg. number of retrieved pages in Italian
google.gr	17,864.67	google.it	1,389,700
yahoo.com	162.67	yahoo.it	2,371,520
alltheWeb.com	127,33	alltheWeb.com	118,694.33
msn.com	249.67	it.msn.com	56,724.67
aol.com	1,173.33	aol.com	49,633.33
ask.com	0	it.ask.com	570,083.33
in.gr	1,726	virgilio.it	10,400
anazitisis.gr	115.67	libero.it	1,833.33

"δικαστηριο" (court) and the queries "ευρωπαϊκό" and "ευρωπαικό" (european). The first two variations differ in intonation, and the second group of queries differs in umlaut.

Table 8 illustrates the results of these runs. Google.gr and In.gr made no differentiation between the queries. All the other search engines seem to be acting as simple "grep" utilities and do not base the retrieval process on the content. In other words, they focus on data retrieval (exact matching) and not on information retrieval, as Baeza-Yates and Ribeiro-Neto (1999) distinguish in their introductory section. AOL does not distinguish the results in the case of intonation, but it produces a different number of results when

the umlaut is omitted. We further examined this fact, and it proved to be the normal behavior of the AOL search engine.

The queries "Università" and "Universita" produce the same page rank in all Italian-supporting search engines. Again, it turns out that English and Latin retrieval is easier in terms of user effort and required knowledge.

Stemming, Lemmatization

Another factor that influences searching relates to the suffixes of the user request words. All the Greek phrases "Εθνική πινακοθήκη Αθηνών" or "Εθνική πινακοθήκη Αθήνας" or "Εθνική πινακοθήκη Αθήνα" mean "National Art Gallery of Athens". While they are morphologically different, they describe exactly the same information need. Each variation retrieves a different number of pages. For example, Google returned 49,400, 58,000 and 56,500 Web pages, respectively. Precision is different in these three cases as well, and the correlation among the first 20 results is less than 50%.

One could argue that such a difference is rational and acceptable as the queries differ. If we consider these queries solely from a technical point of view, then this argument is right. However, if the need for information is the focal point of the discussion, then these subtle differences in queries, which merely differ in one ending, should

Table 8. Number of retrieved pages in Greek queries which differ in accent marks

	δικαστήριο	δικαστηριο	ευρωπαϊκό	ευρωπαικό
google.gr	893,000	893,000	2,920,000	2,920,000
yahoo.com	498,000	11,500	1,560,000	18,700
alltheWeb.com	207,000	3,200	793,000	13,400
msn.com	28,930	943	133,686	3,959
aol.com	51,070	51,070	194,010	178,670
ask.com	0	0	0	0
in.gr	7,336	7,336	24,231	24,231
anazitisis.gr	1,090	121	2,432	240

have recalled similar Web pages with comparable precision. Stemming is an important feature of retrieval systems, and its application should be at least studied in spoken languages which have conjugations of nouns and verbs, like in Greek. Google partially supports conjugation of English verbs and nouns. These techniques are combinations of stemming and lemmatization. Although some Greek stemmers have been created, they have been tested only on their stemming accuracy (Kalamboukis, 1995). The effect of stemming and lemmatization in retrieving Greek Web documents is still an issue for research.

Unlike in the previous experiments, lemmatization is not supported in Italian Web searching. For example, the English query "Famous Poets" in Google, returns pages having as matching terms the words "Poetry" and "Poets". On the contrary, Italian users need to run all three queries "Famoso Poeta", "Famosi Poeti" and "Famosa Poesia" to discover Web documents containing these data. The same applies for all the Italian-supporting search engines.

Stopword Removal

Stopwords are the common words with low discriminatory power efficient to distinguish between documents. Usual candidates of the stopword list are articles, prepositions, and conjunctions, although specific nouns, verbs, or other grammatical types could be of low importance in terms of information retrieval in specific domains. English stopwords list have been constructed since the "ancient times" of IR (Fox, 1990; Salton & McGill, 1983; van Rijsbergen, 1979). Such catalogues have been engineered for the major European languages, including Italian (Savoy, 1999, 2001). A recent study attempts to construct a Greek stopword list (Lazarinis, submitted). In this study, the effect of stopword elimination from 20 Greek Web queries is discussed, and an increase in precision is reported when common words are deleted from user questions.

To our knowledge, the effect of stopword removal in Italian has been tested only in traditional stand-alone information retrieval systems (Savoy, 2001). In these experiments, stopword removal is beneficial in terms of speed and precision. In Google, the Italian queries "il famoso poeta" (the famous poet) and "famoso poeta" recall a different number of documents in Google. Relevance is slightly worse in the first case, that is, eight versus nine relevant documents in the two query instances, respectively. Relevance was calculated on the first 10 Web pages again.

These experiments demonstrate that stopwords affect retrieval of Greek and Italian Web pages more than in English Web queries, since search engines have not incorporated suitable common word lists for other languages than English. Nevertheless, search engines are not to blame, as it is only in the last few years that researchers have attempted to engineer stopword lists for some European and Asian languages (Lazarinis, submitted; Zou, Wang, Deng, & Han, 2006).

FUTURE TRENDS

As the Web population continues to grow, more non-English users will be added. Users from countries with a low penetration of Internet will be amassed online in the next few years. Search engines, and especially the big players like Google and Yahoo, should foresee the future and start supporting the new demands so as to get an even larger slice of the pie. Researchers should try to value the needs of users and the features of morphologically-complex natural languages and propose new, more effective retrieval techniques. Some of the research directions which should be followed have been identified in the previous sections (e.g., lemmatization) and have already been tested in English searching. These techniques should be studied in natural languages with declensions of nouns, adjectives, and verbs, and with complex intonation. In Greek, for example, the position of an accent mark may change the meaning of a word, and this should be dealt with efficiently by search engines.

Support for non-English queries, localization of all the offered services, improved searching mechanisms, and services possibly adapted on cultural differences are some of the techniques which could strengthen the quality of Web searching systems. Traditional information retrieval procedures such as stemming and stopword removal will probably improve the precision in the retrieved set of Web documents.

The shortcomings identified in this chapter are also critical in e-shop searching. Lazarinis (in press) reported that the most common reasons for "no result" queries in Greek e-shop catalogue searching originate from the fact that users type the queries in capital letters, or in lower case without accent, or in plural form, or they use stopwords. In other words, they type queries in a slightly different form than they are typed in the product database. Nevertheless, these subtle differences are capable of letting user queries fail.

Our methodology attempts to assemble a number of attributes capable of identifying the desired features of average non-English Web users. Additionally, it tries to adapt the criteria proposed in other studies to Web retrieval and analyze them in a number of well-defined attributes which are understandable by non-information retrieval experts and thus easier to measure. However, as many methodologies, it could not be considered complete, even though it attempts to view search engine evaluation under the perspective of the easy-to-use, fast, and effective triptych. Especially the effectiveness class cannot be possibly restricted in a small number of attributes. More criteria such as effective summaries or further analysis of the precision to correspond to each of the offered services (text retrieval, image retrieval, video retrieval, etc.) could be added.

CONCLUSION

In this chapter, the utilization of Greek- and Italian-supporting Web searching systems were evaluated with the aid of a user-centric model. The application of the model revealed that search engines have a better understanding of Latin languages, like Italian. In non-Latin languages, like Greek, many of their quality features are not supported. Interfaces are not adapted to Greek and even Google, which comes in a .gr version, does not localize all its services, as in Italian. The model also revealed the inferiority of native Greek and Italian searching systems, in terms of services, indexed documents, response promptness, recall, and relevance in the highly-ranked documents. Case insensitivity, proper handling of diacritics, lemmatization, and other techniques which are supported in English, negatively influence retrieval of Greek pages. Lemmatization could aid Italian users as well and reduce their required effort and knowledge.

Summing up, it can be argued that international and national search-enabling sites do not value most of the features of the Greek language and possibly other languages with unusual alphabets. Latin-based languages, like Italian, are more fairly treated although they are not first-class citizens like English. In both cases, Google is the only exception as it seems to be in a process of adapting to and assimilating the additional characteristics of other natural languages.

REFERENCES

Amitay, E., & Paris, C. (2000). Automatically summarising Web sites - Is there a way around it? *Proceedings of the 9th International Conference on Information and Knowledge Management* (pp. 173-179). USA.

Baeza-Yates, R., & Ribeiro-Neto, B. (Eds). (1999). *Modern information retrieval*. New York: Addison Wesley, ACM Press.

Bar-Ilan, J., & Gutman, T. (2005). How do search engines respond to some non-English queries? *Journal of Information Science, 31*(1), 13-28.

Berners Lee, T., Caillau, R., Groff, J., & Pollermann, B. (1992). World Wide Web: The information universe. *Electronic Networking: Research, Applications, and Policy, 2*(1), 52-58.

Chu, H., & Rosenthal, M. (1996). Search engines for the World Wide Web: A comparative study and evaluation methodology. *Proceedings of the Annual Conference for the American Society for Information Science* (pp. 127-135).

Chung, W., Zhang, Y., Huang, Z., Wang, G., Ong, T., & Chen, H. (2004). Internet searching and browsing in a multilingual world: An experiment on the Chinese business intelligence portal (CBizPort). *Journal of the American Society for Information Science and Technology, 55*(9), 818-831.

CLEF (2006). Cross-language evaluation forum (CLEF). Retrieved July 31, 2006, from http://www.clef-campaign.org/

Cleverdon, C. W., Mills, J., & Keen, E. M. (1966). *An inquiry in testing of information retrieval systems* (Aslib Cranfield Research Project). Cranfield, UK: College of Aeronautics.

Courtois, M., Baer, W., & Stark, M. (1995). Cool tools for searching the Web: A performance evaluation. *Online, 19*(6), 14-32.

Del Galdo, E. M., & Nielsen, J. (1996). *International user interfaces*. New York: Wiley.

Dunlop, M. D. (1997). Time, relevance and interaction modeling for information retrieval. *Proceedings of ACM/SIGIR, Philadelphia, PA* (pp. 206-213).

Fox, C. (1990). A stop list for general text. *ACM-SIGIR Forum, 24*, 19-35.

Global Reach (2004). Global Internet statistics (by language). Retrieved July 31, 2006, from www.global-reach.biz/globstats

Gordon, M., & Pathak, P. (1999). Finding information on the World Wide Web: The retrieval effectiveness of search engines. *Information Processing and Management, 35*, 141-180.

Gwizdka, J., & Chignell, M. (1999). *Towards information retrieval measures for evaluation of Web search engines*. Unpublished manuscript. Retrieved July 31, 2006, from http://www.imedia.mie.utoronto.ca/~jacekg/pubs.html

Hofstede, G. (1991). *Cultures and organizations - Software of the mind*. New York: Mc-Graw Hill.

Hsieh-Yee, I. (1998). The retrieval power of selected search engines: How well do they address general reference questions and subject questions? *The Reference Librarian, 60*, 27-47.

ISO 9126 (2001). Software engineering - Product quality. Part 1: Quality model. Retrieved July 31, 2006, from http://www.iso.org/

Jansen, B., & Spink, A. (2005). An analysis of Web searching by European AlltheWeb.com users. *Information Processing and Management, 41*, 361-381.

Kalamboukis, T. Z. (1995). Suffix stripping with modern Greek. *Program, 29*(3), 313-321.

Lazarinis, F. (2005). Do search engines understand Greek or user requests "sound Greek" to them? *Proceedings of the Open Source Web Information Retrieval Workshop, in conjunction with IEEE/WIC/ACM International Conference on Web Intelligence & Intelligent Agent Technology, France* (pp. 43-46).

Lazarinis, F. (2007a). Evaluating the searching capabilities of Greek e-commerce Web sites. *Online Information Review Journal, 31*(6), 881-891.

Lazarinis, F. (2007b). Engineering and utilizing a stopword list in Greek Web retrieval. *Journal of the American Society for Information Science, 58*(11), 1645-1652.

Moukdad, H. (2004). Lost in cyberspace: How do search engines handle Arabic queries? *Proceedings of the 32nd Annual Conference of the Canadian Association for Information Science, Winnipeg.* Retrieved July 31, 2006, from http://www.cais-acsi.ca/proceedings/2004/moukdad_2004.pdf

Moukdad, H., & Cui, H. (2005). How do search engines handle Chinese queries? *Webology, 2*(3). Retrieved July 31, 2006, from http://www.Webology.ir/2005/ v2n3/a17.html

Oppenheim, C., Morris, A., & McKnight, C. (2000). The evaluation of WWW search engines. *Journal of Documentation, 56*(1), 71-90.

Robertson, S. E. (1969). The parameter description of retrieval systems: Overall measures. *Journal of Documentation, 25*, 93-107.

Salton, G., & McGill, M. J. (1983). *Introduction to modern information retrieval.* New York: McGraw-Hill.

Savoy, J. (1999). A stemming procedure and stopword list for general French corpora. *Journal of the American Society for Information Science, 50*(10), 944-952.

Savoy, J. (2001). Report on CLEF-2001 experiments. In C. Peters, M. Braschler, J. Gonzalo, & M. Kluck (Eds.), *Results of the CLEF-2001, cross-language system evaluation campaign* (pp. 11-19). Sophia-Antipolis: ERCIM.

Silverstein, C., Henzinger, M., Marais, J., & Moricz, M. (1998). *Analysis of a very large Alta Vista query log* (Tech. Rep. No. 1998-014). USA: COMPAQ Systems Research Center.

Sroka, M. (2000). Web search engines for Polish information retrieval: Questions of search capabilities and retrieval performance. *International Information & Library Research, 32*, 87-98.

Su, L., Chen, H., & Dong, X. (1998). Evaluation of Web-based search engines from an end-user's perspective: A pilot study. *Proceedings of the 61st Annual Meeting of the American Society for Information Science, Pittsburgh, PA* (pp. 348-361).

Sullivan, D. (2005). Nielsen net-ratings: Search engine ratings. Retrieved July 31, 2006, from http://searchenginewatch.com/reports/article.php/2156451

van Rijsbergen, C. J. (1979). *Information retrieval, 2nd ed.* London: Butterworths.

Zou, F., Wang, F. L., Deng, X., & Han, S. (2006). Automatic identification of Chinese stop words. *Research on Computing Science: Special Issue on Advances in Natural Language Processing, 18*, 151-162.

KEY TERMS

Information retrieval: Information retrieval (IR) is the science of searching for information in documents, searching for documents themselves, searching for metadata which describe documents, or searching within hypertext collections such as the Internet or intranets. IR is further analyzed to text retrieval, document retrieval, and image, video, or sound retrieval. IR is an interdisciplinary scientific field based in computer science, library science, information science, cognitive psychology, linguistics, and statistics.

Data retrieval: Data retrieval is the retrieval of items (objects, Web pages, documents, etc.) which satisfy specific conditions set in a regular expression like query. While IR aims at satisfying a user information need usually expressed in natural language, data retrieval aims at determining which documents contain the exact terms of the user queries.

Search engine: Search engines are advanced searching systems operating on hypertext collections. Search engines act both as information retrieval and data retrieval systems trying to locate Web pages, images, video, and sounds. They additionally offer a number of specialized services such as book search, blog search, maps, e-shopping, and so forth.

Index: Index refers to a database containing the most important terms of each document which has been statistically analyzed by a retrieval system. Index terms or keywords contained in the index of each search engine are matched to the user query terms so as to retrieve the most relevant documents. Traditional retrieval systems keep only the terms carrying significant information in their indexes. Search engines store all the terms contained in Web pages to support "exact matching" and "all the words" queries.

Precision: Precision is an information retrieval performance measure that quantifies the fraction of retrieved documents which are known to be relevant.

Recall: Recall is an information retrieval performance measure that quantifies the fraction of known relevant documents which are effectively retrieved.

Query: A user query is the expression of the user information need, usually in natural lan-

guage. Some retrieval systems allow the use of Boolean connectives between the query terms.

Stemming: Stemming is the process of reducing a word to its stem or root form. For the purposes of IR, morphological variants of words have similar semantic interpretations and can be considered as equivalent. For example, the word "computation" might be stemmed to "comput". Stemming is either based on linguistic dictionaries or on algorithms.

Lemmatization: Lemmatization involves the reduction of words to their respective lemmas. For example, the lemma for the words "computation" and "computer" is the word "compute". Lemmatizers operate on single and compound terms and on phrases, while stemmers take as input single words only.

Stopwords: Stopwords are the common words with low discriminatory power efficient to distinguish between documents. Usual candidates of the stopword list are articles, prepositions, and conjunctions, although specific nouns, verbs, or other grammatical types could be of low importance in terms of information retrieval in specific domains.

Chapter XXX
Web Information Resources Vis–à–Vis Traditional Information Services

John D'Ambra
The University of New South Wales, Australia

Nina Mistilis
The University of New South Wales, Australia

ABSTRACT

This chapter considers the change in information seeking behaviour of tourists as a result of the increased use of the World Wide Web as an information resource in the context of information services provided by visitor information centres (VICs). The theoretical approach adopts the model of expectation-disconfirmation effects on Web customer satisfaction. The chapter proposes that visitor information centres are analogous to an information system and that the user experience of visiting the centre can partially be explained by users perception of the information quality of information resources used at the centre and a prior use of the Web. The research proposition explored in the reported research is that a priori usage of the Web may influence tourists' perceptions of the information services provided by visitor information centres. In order to investigate this proposition a survey was conducted at the Sydney visitor information centre resulting in 519 responses. The analysis of the data collected, using structural equation modeling, found that perceived information quality of staff and brochures used at the centre explained 63% of the variance of the user experience at the centre, a prior use of the Web did not explain any of the variance. The implications for VICs' strategic information resource management to meet visitor needs are discussed.

INTRODUCTION

As use of the World Wide Web (The Web) continues to grow exponentially, scholars have recognized the need to measure a number of important issues related to information and inter-active-service delivery via the Web (Hoffman & Novak, 1996; Straub & Watson 2001; Straub et al. 2002). Straub at al. indicate that when measuring the new technology, both new and old perspectives of measuring effectiveness and other issues of the Web need to be applied differentially. This chapter proposes that the Web is a new technology replacing traditional media, that many information based tasks that had previously been executed outside the mediation of technology are now being mediated by the Web. In addressing the need to develop metrics, specifically in evaluating the Web as an information resource for non-work based tasks this chapter considers information seeking behaviour in the domain of tourism, specifically perceptions of information quality of information resources used at the Sydney visitor information centre and a priori usage of the Web.

The application of the use of the Web in tourism has been well documented (Gretzel and Fesenmaier 2002). In parallel to this high level of adoption of the Web in the tourism domain there has been limited research investigating the change in the information seeking behaviour of travelers within the context of Web usage (Fodness & Murray 1999). It is generally acknowledged that tourism is information intensive and that tourists need information before, during and sometimes after their trip (Sheldon, 1997). Tourists use various types and amounts of information sources to respond to internal and external contingencies in vacation planning (Fodness and Murray, 1999). Although there are many traditional information resources, information and communication technology, particularly the Internet and the World Wide Web, has brought about a major shift in the information seeking behaviour of tourists. The Web now has made a major impact on the information seeking behavior of visitors and their perception of, and the impact of, information provided by a variety of media (D'Ambra and Wilson, 2004).

Visitor information centres (VICs), the focus for this chapter, are just one information resource for visitors. In Australia, VICs' core business is the promotion of local tourism through the provision of information, though their functions can include visitor servicing, local marketing, tourism industry development and operations and destination. In the context of VICs, management must assess the impact of new technologies, like the Web, on their visitors' perceptions of the traditional media used in VICS, namely staff and brochures - the proposition being that a priori usage of the Web before visiting the centre may influence visitors' perceptions of the quality of resources used at the centre. This chapter proposes to measure visitors' perceived quality of the information resources available at the Sydney VIC (staff and brochures) as well as a priori usage of the Web; it also aims to determine the relationship between that perceived quality of these information resources and the visitor experience at the VIC.

CONCEPTUAL FRAMEWORK

The Web and Information Quality

In order to address the basic proposition of this chapter the concept of "information quality" must be considered. Users of the Web must make judgements of the quality of the information that they access on the Web. For printed media quality is inferred from reviews, refereeing process, and the reputation of publishers (Janes & Rosenfeld, 1996). Users of printed media (a traditional information resource) have previous experience and accumulated knowledge on which they can assess information quality. However on the Web, in the current context of evolving content and usage, the above attributes of quality are not always perceived to be present. Consequently users have to assess the quality of the content without any indicators. The complexity of technology used to locate and retrieve the information adds to the density of this problem (Rieh 2002). When considering the quality of Web content the two issues of content and retrieval require a two pronged approach: the content and its inherent quality and the quality of the technology used to locate and access it. It follows then that two conceptual foundations emerge when considering the quality of Web content: information quality and system quality.

This dichotomy is a common theme in the information systems and Web-based systems evaluation literature (Delone & Maclean 1992, 2003; Eppler 2003; Mckinney et al. 2002; Moraga et al. 2006; Rieh 2002). Information quality for Web-based information is defined as the users' perception of the quality of the information presented on the Web site inlcuding: usefulness, currency, accurate, and adequacy (Moraga et al. 2006; Rieh 2002). Web quality is defined as perceptions of the websites performance with regard to: usability, accessibility, privacy/security, interaction (Moraga et al. 2006).

Visitor Information Centres

A visitor information centre (VIC) is a "clearly labeled, publicly accessible, physical place with personnel providing pre-dominantly free of charge information to facilitate travellers' experiences" (Pearce 2004. p.8). Pearce identifies the functions of VICs as: Promotion Function; Orientation and Enhancement Function; Control and Filtering Function and the Substitution Function.

The promotion function refers to the active promotion of a city, region, state or nation advising clients on destination attractions, visitor accommodation, activities and so on. Essentially this role is about stimulating tourist demand and often seeks to increase visitor expenditure in a defined area.

The orientation and enhancement function seeks to improve the quality of the visitor experience and engender an appreciation of local culture and features. This is achieved through provision of information through a variety of media and experiences.

The control and filtering function allows centres to control the flow of visitors so that resources and settings come under less pressure. Typically such centres act as gateways and central points for visitor use of an area. Information media used in this role can include guided tours, films, interactive kiosks and other media experiences to concentrate visitors away from fragile sights or viewing areas.

Centres emphasising the substitution function are centres which are attractions in themselves. These centres are established at sites where the resource is scattered or fragile and difficult to appreciate without some form of interpretation presented by the center. For example Kretschmer et al (2001) describe a virtual reality project that enhances the experience of visitors to the "olde town" and castle at Heidelberg, Germany.

In order to fulfill these functions a primary role of VICs is to disseminate information. In line with the complexity of the function and related requirements VICs use a range of information resources, including traditional and new media. Traditional media would include staff and brochures, while the new media would be information and communication technology based. In fact the core business of VICs, globablly, is still reliant on traditional media.

The context of this chapter is then: an information service, heavily reliant on traditional media operating in a global, information intensive industry where the fundamental information infrastructure for consumers is increasingly the Web. There is an urgent need to investigate the impact of the new technology on the quality of services offered by a traditional information service, visitor information centres.

THEORETICAL BACKGROUND

The proportion of visitors who use a VIC as a resource in their information search is considered important, though hard to quantify for all destinations and market segments (Parolin, 2001:21). Within the VICs, managers are faced with many alternate means of distributing information to tourists, including pamphlets and other printed material, personal client services (supported by the Web) and online touch screens for information and perhaps reservation. There is no doubt that information and communication technology is having a profound effect on information dissemination (Buhalis, 1998; 2003). In Australia, a growing number of visitors (domestic and international) are using the Internet to seek information and/or make a reservation. In 2003, about twenty-two percent of international visitors used the Internet (Australian Tourist Commission, 2004); this proportion continues to grow, along with that for domestic visitors. Further there are other challenges for VICs to identify the needs of all their stakeholders, to raise operating revenue and to conduct business in a more user friendly manner. However, a strategic planned approach to managing information resources in VICs is not yet evident. The theoretical approach adopted below may assist in the strategic management of information resources in VICs.

Information needs are generally represented as a stage in an information-processing or decision-making process for consumers, including tourists (Vogt and Fesenmaier, 1998). Fodness and Murray (1998 and 1999) present a model of the tourist information search strategy process, which is composed of three distinct strategies for information searching: spatial, temporal and operational. In investigating correlates of tourist information search behaviour within the context of the operational dimension, Fodness and Murray (1999) found that travellers used various types and amounts of information sources to respond to internal and external contingencies in vacation planning. From a marketing perspective Kotler (2003) considers consumers satisfaction with products and services as a consequence of their experience during various purchasing stages: 1) need recognition; 2) information search; 3) evaluation of alternatives; 4) purchase decision; 5) post-purchase behaviour. In terms of the above purchasing stages this chapter focuses on the information search stage and to a certain extent, the evaluation of alternatives stage. As outlined in the introduction tourists do engage in information searching before undertaking a trip and the Web has brought about a shift in the information seeking behaviour of tourists. The Internet offers extensive benefits to Web users by reducing their search costs and increasing shopping convenience, vendor choices, and product options (D'Ambra & Rice 2001).

It is a basic proposition of this chapter that a significant number of users of a VIC will have retrieved information from the Web on the destination/attraction that is promoted by the VIC that they visit to obtain further information. Therefore the information search may not be complete until after the end of their visit to the destination/attraction. The proposition is extended further in that the perceived quality of the information received in the centre will be evaluated by the consumer with reference to outcomes of previous Web searches undertaken before the visit to the centre. This evaluation will influence the visitors' perceived experience of the VIC.

Successful use of the Web as an information resource depends on Web site information to compensate for the lack of physical contact and causes users to rely heavily on technology and system quality to keep them interested and satisfied (Mckinney et al. 2002). So consumers make inferences about information and product attractiveness on the basis of 1) information provided by retailers 2) design elements of the Web site such as ease of use and fun and navigation (D'Ambra and Rice 2001).

Based on IS success literature Delone and McLean's highly cited technology and acceptance model (1992 & 2003) identified information quality, service quality and system quality as antecedents of user satisfaction and intention to use/use. A similar approach can be found in marketing. In modelling overall satisfaction, Spreng et al. (1996) identified attribute satisfaction (consumers level of contentment with a product) and information satisfaction (quality of information used in deciding to purchase a product) as important determinants in forming customer satisfaction with a product purchase. Mckinney et al. (2002) in considering the measurement of Web-customer satisfaction in an online purchasing context develop a two dimensional model of Web-customer satisfaction, the Web-customer Satisfaction Model. Consistent with the Delone and Maclean approach of their 1992 model, the two dimensions of the Web-customer satisfaction model are Web-information quality and Web-service quality satisfaction, with Web-customer satisfaction being the dependant variable. The two dimensions recognise that overall satisfaction is dependant on both the perceived quality of the information provided and the perceived quality of the service that delivers the information. Satisfaction has been an important area of research both within the information systems (IS) and marketing domains. Mckinney et al. enhance the Delone & Maclean model further by considering Web users expectations (formed by their experiences and exposure to vendors marketing efforts) possible discrepancies (e.g. disconfirmation) between such expectations and perceived performance of a Web site. Expectations and disconfirmation for both IQ and SQ are operationalised in the Mckinney et al study.

MAIN FOCUS OF THE CHAPTER

The current research proposes that the VIC is analogous to an information system. The VIC

Figure 1. Information Quality (IQ) Effects on VIC Visitor Experience

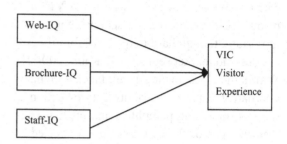

is a service (a system) that provides information (via a number of media: staff and brochures and perhaps touch screens/online kiosks) to satisfy the information need of its users (visitors). Therefore user satisfaction with their experience of the VIC may be explained by the users perceptions of the information quality (IQ) of the resources used at the centre to meet their information needs vis a vis their visit to Sydney as well as their prior use of the Web to obtain information for their Sydney visit. To test this proposition we adopt a modified Mckinney et al model, presented in figure 1.

In Figure 1 the researchers adopt the Web-information quality dimension of the Mckinney et al. model considering users perception of the quality of information resources used. Web-IQ is the construct to measure the perceived quality of information on visiting Sydney obtained through usage of the Web before using the VIC. Brochure-IQ and Staff-IQ are the perceived information quality of the information resources used at the centre. Web-IQ is for a priori usage of the Web, while Brochure-IQ and Staff-IQ measure the perceived information quality of the resources used at the VIC. VIC visitor experience is the user's overall satisfaction with the VIC as an information service. The model hypothesises that the visitor experience at the VIC is related to the perceived quality of information resources used at the VIC and a prior usage of the Web for the same information task. Information quality is a complex and multidimensional construct. The approach adopted here is that of Mckinney at al. where five dimensions of information quality are identified: relevance; timeliness; reliability; scope; perceived usefulness. These five dimensions were reduced to three (through analysis by Mckinney at al.): understandability; reliability; usefulness.

METHOD

To measure perceived quality the chapter uses scales derived from models considering the process by which Web-customer satisfaction is formed at the information search stage (Mckinney et al. 2002). The scales have been calibrated to measure the quality of non-Web based resources as well as the Web. This exploratory research will seek to answer the following research questions:

1. What is the perceived quality of electronic and other information resources used by visitors to the Sydney VIC in terms of meeting their information needs?
2. What is the efficacy of the proposed model in measuring the relationship between the perceived quality of information resources used at the VIC as well as the Web a priori on the one hand and the visitor experience at the VIC on the other?
3. What are the implications for VIC's strategic information resource management to meet visitor needs?

Based on the research model a questionnaire was developed, including questions on the following constructs:

- individual visitor socioeconomic, computer and Web usage attributes;
- the sources which were used by the visitors (the Web a priori and various media while visiting the VIC) and the level of usage of each resource;

- the perceived quality of the information resources used at the centre;
- the visitor experience at the VIC.

The Mckinney et al. scales to measure information quality were adopted. To measure information quality Mckinney et al. used three dimensions: understandability, reliability and usefulness. In the current research these constructs were calibrated to measure the visitors perceptions of Web_iq, brochure_iq and staff_iq on one dimension only. All items were measured on a continuous 11-point semantic differential scale, where 0 = very poor and 10 = very good.

The construct of visitor experience at the VIC was operationalised by the following three items:

- How would you rate the standard of service you received?
- How would you rate the range of products available?
- How would you rate your experience in the VIC?

These items were measured on a continuous 11-point semantic differential scale, where 0 = poor and 10 = excellent.

The data were collected at the major VIC for Sydney, which is located in one of the main tourist destinations of Sydney, The Rocks - the Sydney Tourist Centre. It has an average 2000 visitors/day and up to 6000 visitors/day at busy time for example when a cruise ships docks nearby. It installed touch screens for visitors in 2002 and also updated its computer information systems. The centre manages and distributes information 'to make the visit memorable' for planning trips within Sydney, to Sydney and from Sydney to other parts of the state; it also takes bookings, both electronic and commission-based. It is self funded so it must raise funds.

The study was undertaken with the full cooperation of the VIC. The authors discussed the research instrument with the VIC senior managers and pre-tested it; they then trained the research assistants who pilot tested the instrument under supervision. Modifications were made at each step. The data were collected in face to face interviews daily over a two-week period in January 2004; 519 usable responses were collected. Two alternating pairs of research assistants were placed in the VIC. Each research assistant approached visitors seeking their consent to take part in the study. If consent was given the research assistant then administered the survey.

The approach taken in analysing the results is as follows:

- The derivation of descriptive statistics.
- Structural equation modelling was used to test the basic proposition of this chapter.

RESULTS

In analysing the data the descriptive statistics of the sample were derived and then to test the strength of the theoretical model, a Structured Equation Modelling (SEM) technique was used, specifically Partial Least Squares (PLS). Gefen, Straub and Boudreau (2001) provide guidelines for use of SEM techniques. The current research satisfies the requirements for PLS analysis: the model is based on a set of path specific null hypothesis of no effect; the objective of the analysis is to confirm the variance of the dependent variable; the research is both exploratory and confirmatory; the sample size confidently meets the requirements of assumed distribution and required minimal sample size.

Table 1 provides the descriptive statistics for the sample. The visitor socioeconomic profile showed that most respondents (70%) were female – due to the female of the couple having made the travel arrangements and so preferring to be the respondent; their median age was 30-34 years. About one quarter were Australian in origin, the rest predominantly from the UK (27%), Europe (20%) and North America (18%), with a few (9%)

Table 1. Descriptive statistics of the visitor sample

	%	Mean
Country of origin *(n = 519)*		
Australia	23	
UK	27	
Europe	20	
Nth America	18	
New Zealand	3	
Asia	9	
Others	2	
Web usage *(n = 519)*		
Australia	75	
International	84	
Hours per week using the Web *(n = 425)*		
Australia		7hrs
International		9hrs
Years of computing experience *(n = 425)*		
Australia		9yrs
International		11yrs
Computing expertise *(n = 519)*		
None		
Australia	5	
International	2	
Novice		
Australia	11	
International	5	
Somewhat familiar		
Australia	20	
International	22	
Familiar		
Australia	34	
International	39	
Very familiar		
Australia	30	
International	32	

from Asia. Although all were quite familiar with computer use, more international visitors (84%) than Australian visitors (75%) reported Web usage, hours per week using the Web, years of computing experience, and computer experience,

Table 2. Sources of Sydney Information (n = 519)

Information Source	%
Internet	66
Travel book/guide	54
Friends or relatives	49
Travel agent	30
Tourist office/VIC/GTO	11
Airline	11
Newschapter, magazine, TV, radio advert.	10
Travel article in newschapter or magazine	9
Films or TV/radio program	6
Tour operator	6
Other	3
Information kiosk	3
Motoring association	2

Table 3. Australian and international visitors who collected brochures, asked staff for information (n = 519)

	Brochures %	Asked staff %
Australian	85	28
International	88	41

Table 4. Perceived quality of Web, Brochure and Staff (scale 0–10)

	Web	Brochure	Staff
Overall mean	7.78	8.53	8.95
Clear in meaning	7.75	8.5	8.93
Easy to comprehend	7.9	8.66	9.02
Easy to read	8.14	8.74	-----
Trustworthy	7.4	8.51	9.03
Accurate	7.6	8.42	8.96
Credible	7.57	8.48	9.06
Informative to purpose	.95	8.46	8.96
Valuable to making visit	7.84	8.5	8.71
In general, useful to visit	7.84	8.54	8.87

though they knew similar proportions of people using the Web (Table 1). Web usage diminished markedly with age.

Table 2 shows the information resources used in planning the trip. The top three sources of information for their trip were internet (two thirds), guide books and friends and relatives (each about one half); about one tenth used a VIC or tourist office. Table 3 indicates the use of brochures and the counter staff at the centre. Most of both cohorts equally tended to collect brochures whilst fewer Australian than international visitors asked staff for information.

Table 4 ranks the three resources, the Web, brochures available in the centre and centre staff, and provides the overall mean for each resource. In terms of perceived quality of information resources, all ranked quite highly with an average of seven on a scale of eleven (0-10), though the Web was slightly lower than the others, especially relative to staff in the trustworthy, accurate and credible criteria. The kiosk was discarded in the analysis as very few visitors used it. The mean visitor experience at the VIC was rated very highly (8.6 on a scale of 0-10).

Table 5 presents the confirmatory factor analysis (loadings and T-statistics) for the observed variables (scales) used to determine the constructs of Web-IQ, Brochure-IQ and Staff-IQ. The construct reliability for the three constructs is high with all loading above 0.70 (Segars, 1997; Hair et al., 1998).

In order to determine if visitors perception of the quality of brochures and/or staff may be influenced by their country of origin (international or local). The hypothesis being that local visitors, having more local knowledge may be more discriminating in the utility of information received at the centre than those visitors with less local knowledge. Analysis of variance was conducted on the constructs of brochure quality and staff quality controlling for origin of visitors and whether visitors used the Web to obtain information on Sydney before their visit to the centre. No significant difference in the means was reported.

Table 5. Confirmatory Factor analysis of observed variables: Staff-IQ, Web-IQ, Brochure IQ and Experience

	loading	T-statistic
Staff_iq		
Staff's performance: clear in meaning	.85	12.92
Staff's performance: easy to comprehend	.87	30.40
Staff's performance: trustworthy	.89	35.43
Staff's performance: accurate	.88	29.46
Staff's performance: credible	.87	29.36
Staff's performance: informative to the purpose of your visit	.85	21.77
Staff's performance: valuable to making visit decisions	.86	19.88
Staff's performance: in general, useful in visit decisions	.91	37.93
Web_iq		
Web's performance: clear in meaning	.85	30.54
Web's performance: easy to comprehend	.85	31.24
Web's performance: easy to read	.85	39.54
Web's performance: trustworthy	.76	29.90
Web's performance: accurate	.76	23.15
Web's performance: credible	.83	33.15
Web's performance: informative to the purpose of your visit	.85	42.57
Web's performance: valuable to making visit decisions	.81	32.01

	loading	T-statistic
Web's performance: in general, useful in visit decisions	.85	39.66
Brochure_iq		
Brochure's performance: clear in meaning	.86	26.70
Brochure's performance: easy to comprehend	.86	43.67
Brochure's performance: easy to read	.84	25.98
Brochure's performance: trustworthy	.80	24.08
Brochure's performance: accurate	.83	31.32
Brochure's performance: credible	.85	35.29
Brochure's performance: informative to the purpose of your visit	.81	24.14
Brochure's performance: valuable to making visit decisions	.79	20.92
Brochure's performance: in general, useful in visit decisions	.87	40.30
Experience		
How would you rate the standard of service you received?	0.88	46.29
How would you rate your experience in the SVC?	0.91	14.76
How would you rate the range of products available?	0.79	67.00

Figure 2 presents the structural results of fitting the model in figure 1 to the data. To be consistent with the objectives of the study, only data from those respondents who had indicated that they had used the Web to obtain information on Sydney before their visit to the centre, were entered into the PLS analysis. The multiple r2 for experience is 0.63. The significant paths are Brochure-IQ, (p < 0.05) and Staff-IQ (p < 0.01). The path for a prior usage of the Web is not significant, confirming that users' perceptions of their overall satisfaction with the centre were not influenced by previous Web usage. It should be noted, though, that staff at the centre do use the Web to assist with visitor enquiries. This may indicate a significant finding in terms of human mediation and information provision via the Web.

Figure 2. Path coefficients

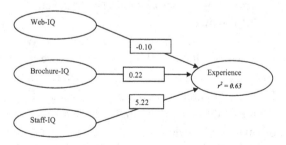

FUTURE TRENDS

It should be noted that the type of information resources visitors used will vary according to certain visitor characteristics and market segment (or visitor population); further the visitors' perceived quality of information resources in terms of fulfilling the information needs for their trip, will also vary for these and other reasons. So results may well differ in other visitor centres according to their visitor population, the resources available and used, and their delivery of customer service. Indeed, as the distribution of visitors to the Sydney VIC changes according to the tourist season, major tourist events or VIC promotion, so too will the resources used by visitors and their perceived quality. However there is strong evidence to suggest the efficacy of the model, so that it may be applied in other VICs and contexts successfully – to determine the precise relationship between perceived quality of information resources and the visitor experience in the VIC.

There are several implications for VIC's strategic information resource management to meet visitor needs. First, in spite of increasing use of the Web as an a priori information resource for visitors, VICs still make a significant contribution to the overall visitor experience at the VIC in terms of perceived quality of traditional information resources (staff, brochures). Second staff in this study used the Web to provide information to visitors. This may be a significant finding in terms of human mediation and interpretation between the visitor and the Web as an information resource - an issue for further research. Third the perceived information quality is a significant factor in explaining the visitor experience at the VIC - therefore managers must invest resources in maintaining the quality of information delivered by staff and brochures.

This exploratory research has developed a model, which determines the perceived quality of information resources used by visitors a priori and at the Sydney VIC. The model developed can be applied to any VIC in order first to determine the nature and extent of its visitors' resource use and the perceived quality of information; these results then inform its strategic information resource management. The implication for VIC's is that the perceived quality of information is an important determinant, or at least factor, to consider in its strategic information resource management. The ultimate reason of course for strategic management of these information resources lies in enhancing the visitor stay and yield.

DISCUSSION

The chapter has presented a model capable of determining the relationship between the perceived quality of information resources used at the VIC as well as a priori Web usage on the one hand and the visitor experience at the VIC on the other. The resources analysed included a priori Web usage and mainly the staff and brochures available at the VIC. The results demonstrate that the Web is a significant resource in the information seeking behaviour of international visitors to the Sydney VIC, though not so significant for domestic visitors. However an important finding is that traditional resources have higher perceived levels of information quality for most visitors.

This exploratory study has demonstrated that visitors to the Sydney VIC do differentiate between a priori use of the Web and the use of other information resources at the VIC. The structural model does demonstrate some efficacy for the theoretical approach in assessing the relationship between the perceived quality of information resources used at the centre and the visitor experience at the VIC, with the model explaining 63% of the variance. That is, the visitor experience at the VIC is partially determined by the quality of the information provided by its staff and brochures. This has important implications for managers of VICs in their strategic information resource management.

The research presented in this chapter explores the impact of a priori usage of the Web on user's perception of satisfaction with the overall experience of a visitor information centre. In a broader context the study considers the changing information seeking behaviour of tourists and what impact that change may have on information services provided by a VIC. To the knowledge of the authors such a study has not been undertaken before.

A major limitation of the study is that Web usage, as measured within the study, was undertaken before the respondents visited the VIC. The Web is not available to visitors in the centre where the study was conducted but is an important information resource used by visitors to the centre. The questions related to the users perception of the information quality of the Web will suffer from a recency effect as the Web was used before their visit to the centre while the other resources, brochures and staff, were used immediately before respondents took part in the study. Data on when the Web was last used for information related to the visit to Sydney was not collected. Data on types of Web usage, information gathering or more task related, was also not collected. This to, could be a factor to consider when assessing the perceived information quality if the Web. There may be bias in the sample as the sample only includes those travelers who used the VIC. The sample does not include those travelers who were very satisfied with the information quality they found on the Web and as a consequence, did not visit the centre. Any replication of this study should address these limitations thereby ensuring that the perception of the information quality of the Web is based on a common task and need to that which is being met by the VIC using traditional information resources.

REFERENCES

Australian Tourist Commission. (2004). *Internet usage fact sheet.* Retrieved from http://www. tourism.australia.com

Buhalis, D. (2003). *eTourism.* Prentice Hall: United Kingdom.

Buhalis, D. (1998). Strategic use of information techno.logies in the tourism industry. *Tourism Management, 19*(5), 409-421.

DeLone, W. H., & Mclean, E. R. (1992). Information Systems success: The quest for the dependable variable. *Information Systems Research,* 3(1), 60-95

DeLone, W. H., & Mclean, E. R. (2003). The De-Lone and Mclean model of information systems success: A ten-year update. *Journal of Management Information Systems, 19*(4), 9-30.

D'Ambra, J., & Rice, R. E. (2001). Emerging Factors in Evaluation of the World Wide Web. *Information & Management* 38(6), 373-384.

D'Ambra, J., & Wilson, C. S. (2004). Use of the World Wide Web for International Travel: Integrating the Construct of Uncertainty in Information Seeking and the Task-Technology Fit (TTF) Model. *Journal of the American Society of Information Science and Technology,* 55(8), 731-742.

Eppler, M. J., Algesheimer, M. D. & Dimpfel, M. (2003). Quality Criteria of Content-Driven Websites and Their Influence on Customer Satisfaction and Loyalty: An Empirical Test of an Information Quality Framework, *Proceedings of the Eight International Conference on Information Quality.*

Fondness, D., & Murray, B. (1998, November). A typology of tourist information search strategies. *Journal of Travel Research, 37,* 108-120.

Fondness, D., & Murray, B. (1999). A model of tourist information search behaviour. *Journal of Travel Research,* 37, February, 220-230.

Gefen, D., Straub, D.W., & Boudreau, M. (2001). Structural equation modeling and regression: Guidelines for research and practice. *Communications of AIS. 4*(7)

Gretzel, U., & Fesenmaier, D. R. (2002). Building narrative logic into tourism information systems *IEEE Intelligent Systems*, 17(6), 59-61.

Hair, J. F., Jr., R. E., Anderson, R., Tatham, L., & Black, W. C. (1998). Mutlivariate Data Analysis with Readings, 5th. Edition. Englewood Cliffs, NJ: Prentice Hall.

Hoffman, D. L., & Novak, T. P. (1996). Marketing in hypermedia computer-mediated environments: Conceptual foundations. *Journal of Marketing*, 60(3), 50-68.

Janes, J. W., & Rosenfield, L.B., (1996). Networked information retrieval and organzation: Issues and questions. *Journal of the Americal Society for Information Science*, 47(9), 711-715.

Kotler, P., Bowen J., & Makens, J. (2003). *Marketing for Hospitality and Tourism. Pearson*, Upper Saddle River, NJ.

Kretschmer, U., Coors, V., Spierling, U., Grasbon, D., Scheider, K., Rojas, I., & Malaka, R. (2001). Virtual reality, archeology, and cultural heritage, Proceedings of the 2001 conference on Virtual reality, archeology, and cultural heritage, Glyfada Greece, isbn: 1-58113-447-9, 141-152.

Mckinney, V., Yoon, K., & Zahedi, F. (2002). The Measurement of Web-Customer Satisfaction: An Expectation and Disconfirmation Approach, *Information Systems Research*, 13(3), 296-315.

Moraga, A., Calero, C., & Piattini, M. (2006). Comparing different quality models for portals, *Online Information Review, 30*(5), 555-568.

O'Connor, P. (1999). *Electronic Information Distribution in Tourism and Hospitality*. CABI Publishing: UK

Parolin, B. (2001). Structure of Day Trips in the Illawarra Tourism Region of New South Wales. *The Journal of tourism Studies,* 12(1), 11-27.

Pearce, P. (2004). The functions and planning of visitor information centres in regional tourism. *The Journal of Tourism Studies, 15*(1), 8-17

Rieh, S. Y. (2002). Judgement of Information Quality and Cognitive Authority in the Web, *Journal of the American Society for Infromation Science and Technology*, 53(2), 145-161.

Segars, A. H., (1997). Assessing the Unidimensionality of Measurement: A Paradigm and Illustration within the Context of Information Systems Research, *Omega* 25(1), 107 – 121.

Sheldon, P. (1997). *Tourism Information Technology*. CAB International: New York.Spreng, R. A., Mackenzie, S. B., & Olshavsky, R. W. (1996) A reexamination of the determinants of consumer satisfaction. *Journal of Marketing*, 60(3), 15-32.

Spreng, R. A., Mackenzie, S. B., & Wolsavsky, N. (1996). A Re-examination of the determinants of consumer satisfaction. *Journal of Marketing*, 60(3) 15-37.

Straub, D. W., Hoffman, D. L., Weber, B. W., & Steinfield, C. (2002). Measuring e-commerce in net-enabled organizations: An introduction to the special issue. *Information Systems Research,* 13(2), 115-124.

Straub, D. W., & Watson, R.T. (2001). Research commentary: Transformational issues in researching IS and net-enabled organizations. *Information Systems Research,* 12(4), 337-345.

Vogt, C., & Fesenmaier, D. (1998). Expanding the functional search model. *Annals of Tourism Research*, 25(3), 551-578.

KEY TERMS

Web information resources: Information content managed on the World Wide Web to meet the information need of users within a variety of contexts.

Traditional information service: An information service that makes use of traditional information resources to meet the information needs of its users including: brochures, staff.

Visitor information centre: A traditional information services that promotes tourism in a specific region or location.

Tourists: People who are planning a trip for recreational purposes.

Information need: A need associated with a level of uncertainty. Information is required to reduce uncertainty.

Information infrastructure: Structures both ICT and traditional based to meet the information needs of consumers.

Information system: As systematic approach of the provision of information often using technology to meet the information needs of consumers.

World Wide Web: An application of the Internet providing content.

About the Contributors

Coral Calero has a PhD in computer science and is associate professor at the Escuela Superior de Informatica of the Castilla-La Mancha University in Ciudad Real. She is a member of the Alarcos Research Group in the same university, and specialized in information systems, databases, and software engineering. Her research interests include: advanced databases design, database quality, software metrics, and database metrics. She is the author of papers in national and international conferences on this subject. She has been published in *Information Systems Journal*, *Software Quality Journal*, *Information and Software Technology Journal*, and *SIGMOD Record Journal*. She has organized the Web services quality workshop (WISE Conference, Rome 2003) and database maintenance and reengineering workshop (ICSM Conference, Montreal 2002).

Mª Ángeles Moraga is a PhD in computer science. She received her MSc in computer science and her technical degree in computer science by the University of Castilla-La Mancha (UCLM). Nowadays, she is assistant professor at the Escuela Superior de Informática of the University of Castilla-La Mancha in Ciudad Real (Spain). She is a member of the Alarcos Research Group in the same university, and specialized in information systems, databases, and software engineering. Her research interests are: portals, portlets, software quality, and measures. Her e-mail is: MariaAngeles.Moraga@uclm.es

Mario Piattini has an MSc and a PhD in computer science (Politechnical University of Madrid) and a MSc in Psychology (UNED.). He is also a certified information system auditor and a certified information system manager by ISACA (Information System Audit and Control Association), as well as a full professor in the Department of Computer Science at the University of Castilla-La Mancha, in Ciudad Real, Spain. Furthermore, he is the author of several books and papers on databases, software engineering, and information systems. He is a coeditor of several international books: *Advanced Databases Technology and Design* (2000, Artech House, UK), *Information and database quality* (2002, Kluwer Academic Publishers, Norwell, USA), *Component-based software quality: Methods and techniques* (2004, Springer, Germany), and *Conceptual Software Metrics* (2005, Imperial College Press UK). He leads the ALARCOS research group of the Department of Computer Science at the University of Castilla-La Mancha, in Ciudad Real, Spain. His research interests are: advanced databases, database quality, software metrics, security and audit, and software maintenance.

***

Silvia Abrahão is tenure-track assistant professor at the Department of Computer Science and Computation of Valencia University of Technology (Spain), where she teaches Web quality and databases. She received a PhD in computer science from this same university (2004). Currently, she participates on the board of the Spanish Association of Software Metrics and in the management committee of the COST Action 294 "Towards the Maturity of IT Usability Evaluation." Her current research focuses on Web quality, functional size measurement, integration of usability into model-driven development processes, and empirical software engineering.

Gustavo Aragón qualified as a computer science engineer at the University of Ciudad Real (1998). He worked as an analyst for various private organisations. He is currently writing his doctoral thesis in the Department of Computer Languages and Systems of the University of Seville (Spain). He has also worked as a senior consultant in Everis since 1999. His PhD thesis and his research work are oriented toward Web environments, specially development methodologies, and model driven Web engineering.

Fernando Bellas is an associate professor in the Department of Information and Communications Technologies at the University of A Coruña, Spain. His research interests include Web engineering, portal development, and data extraction and integration. He has a PhD in computer science from the University of A Coruña. In the past, he has held several professional positions in institutions such as CESAT (a telematic engineering company) and the University of Alfonso X el Sabio of Madrid.

Ignacio José Blanco is an assistant professor in the Department of Computer Science and Artificial Intelligence at the University of Granada. His research interests include deductive databases, fuzzy databases, and active databases. He received his PhD in computer science from the University of Granada.

Geraldo Bonorino Xexéo is a professor of computer science at the Graduate School of Engineering (COPPE) and Mathematics Institute of the Federal University of Rio de Janeiro (UFRJ) (Brazil). He has an electronic engineering degree from the Military Institute of Engineering (1988) and received his DSc in computer sciences from the UFRJ in 1994. His area of specialization is computer science with an emphasis in databases and software engineering, and he is involved in research in fields such as peer-to-peer, information retrieval, information quality, and fuzzy logic. He worked in many consultant projects for public and private organizations.

Sergiy Boroday received the diploma in applied mathematics from Donetsk State University, Ukraine, (1993), and the PhD from Saratov State University, Russia (1997). Since 1998, he has been a researcher at CRIM, Canada. From 1996 to 1998, he was a research assistant at the Institute of Applied Mathematics and Mechanics, Donetsk, Ukraine. He published more than 20 research papers. In 1999, Boroday received the best paper award of the IFIP FORTE/PSTV'99 Conference. His current research interests include formal methods, automata theory, distributed systems, and software testing and analysis.

Paloma Cáceres García de Marina is assistant professor at the Department of Computing Languages and Systems at the Rey Juan Carlos University, where she also received her PhD. She received her BSc and MSc in IT Systems from the Politechnical University of Madrid. Currently, she belongs to the Kybele Research Group. Her research interests include software engineering of web information systems.

Cristina Cachero Castro has a PhD in computer science. Currently she is assistant professor at the Universidad de Alicante (Spain), where she teaches software engineering and quality of Web applications. She is a member of the IWAD Research Group in the same university. Her research topics include Web engineering methodologies, automatic code generation techniques, model-driven development, Web application quality assessment, and empirical validation of Web quality models and measures. She has been visiting researcher at the Politecnico de Milano (Italy) and at the Gent Universität (Belgium), and she is a regular publisher in national and international conferences. She also regularly serves in the PC of several international conferences and workshops. Her e-mail is ccachero@dlsi.ua.es

Angélica Caro has a MSc in computer science and is assistant professor at the Departamento de Auditoría e Informática of the Bio University in Chillán, Chile. At moment she is student of a PhD program in computer science in the Castilla-La Mancha University, Spain. Her research interests include: data quality, Web portals, data quality in Web portals, and data quality measures. She is author of papers in national and international conferences on this subject.

Alejandra Cechich is an associate professor and head of GIISCo Research Group (http://giisco.uncoma.edu.ar) at the University of Comahue, Argentina. Her interests are centered on conceptual modeling, software quality, and component technology, and their use in the systematic development of software systems. She holds a European PhD in computer science from the University of Castilla-La Mancha, Spain, and an MSc in computer science from the University of South, Argentina.

Yao-Sheng Chang is a PhD student in the Department of Computer Science and Information Engineering (CSIE) at National Cheng Kung University, Tainan, Taiwan. He got his master's training in computer science from I-Shou University, Kaohsiung, Taiwan. His research interests include machine translation, data warehouse, and data mining.

Jengchung V. Chen is an assistant professor of telecommunications management at National Cheng Kung University (NCKU). He holds a doctoral degree in communication and information sciences from the University of Hawaii, and two master's degrees in computer science and management and policy from Polytechnic University and SUNY-Stony Brook, respectively. He has published 40 papers in refereed journals and conference proceedings and received the distinguished research award from Allied Academies (2003). His research interests include IT ethics, information assurance, IT impacts to work and organizations, and e-commerce.

Julio Córdoba is PhD student in University of Alicante. He received his MSc in software engineering by the Polytechnic University of Madrid, and his technical degree in computer science by the Technological Institute of Costa Rica. Nowadays, he is IT service manager of BAC Credomatic Network (private financial institution), based in Central America, Mexico, and Florida. He is a member of the Web Engineering and Datawarehousing Research Group in the University of Alicante. His research interests are: software quality, banking portals, measure, quality models, and IT services. His e-mail is jcordoba@dlsi.ua.es

Rebeca Cortazar is an associate professor in the Department of Software Engineering at the University of Deusto in Bilbao (Spain). Her interests include educational issues in software engineering, software measurement and effort estimation, and object orientation and distributed systems. She is currently lecturing on object-oriented design, patterns, and integration technologies. Cortazar received her PhD in computer science from the University of Deusto in Bilbao (1999).

John D'Ambra is an associate professor at the School of Information Systems, Technology and Management at the University of New South Wales, Sydney, Australia. John holds a PhD in information systems and is currently academic director of the Master of Business and Technology Program at UNSW. John has published extensively in the areas of computer-mediated communication and the evaluation of the World Wide Web as an information resource. In the last few years, John has collaborated with colleagues in the tourism discipline by applying his interest in evaluation of the World Wide Web to the study of the use of information within the tourism domain.

Óscar Díaz is full professor at the University of the Basque Country (Spain). His current interests include portlet-based portals, software product lines, and model-driven development. He leads a 15-member R&D group with focus on Web engineering and close partnership with industry. He has over 50 international publications that include *VLDB Journal, ACM TOIT, ACM Computing Surveys*, and *IEEE Software*, and conferences such as VLDB, ICSE, and WWW.

Eugenia Díaz received the MS and PhD in computer science from the University of Oviedo, Spain (1998 and 2005, respectively). Currently, she is an assistant professor in the Computing Department at the University of Oviedo. Her research interests are software engineering, especially software testing and its automation, developing tools to save time in the testing process.

María José Escalona obtained her PhD in computer science at the University of Seville (Spain) (2004). Since 1999, she has been a lecturer in the Department of Computer Languages and Systems of the University of Seville, where she is currently a full professor. Her current line of research is in the areas of requirement engineering, Web system development, model driven engineering, and quality assurance. She also collaborates with public companies like Consejería de Cultura or Servicio Andaluz de Salud in quality assurance.

Marta Fernández de Arriba works as an assistant lecturer in the Computing Department of the University of Oviedo. She has received the MS and PhD in computer science from the University of Oviedo. Her line of research is based on aspects related to the usability and accessibility of user interfaces, and also the search for practical solutions for communication problems which mobility disabilities present.

Joan Fons is assistant professor in the Department of Information Systems and Computation (DSIC) at the Technical University of Valencia, Spain. His research involves Web engineering, adaptive systems, conceptual modeling, model-driven development, and pervasive systems. He is a member of the OO-Method Research group, and he has published several contributions to well-known international conferences (ER, WWW, CAiSE, ICWE, AH, etc.), and he has contributed to some Web engineering books. His PhD is on OOS, a Web engineering method to automatically develop Web solutions from conceptual models.

Carlos García Moreno was born in Madrid (Spain) in 1977. He graduated with a degree in computer sciences at the "Universidad Politécnica de Madrid" (2000). Since 2000 he has been working as Software Engineer at Soluziona and Indra, two of the biggest Technological Consulting Companies in Spain and Europe. Since 2001 his work has been focused in Web accessibility, being involved in several innovation projects founded by the European Commission and the Spanish authorities. He also has performed several Web accessibility audits and reviews and has given several courses on this subject.

Ignacio García-Rodríguez de Guzmán received his MSc in computer science by the University of Castilla-La Mancha (UCLM) (2003). Currently, he is developing his PhD at the same university. He is a member of the Alarcos Research Group, at the School of Computer Science in Ciudad Real. His main research areas are legacy system reengineering, service oriented architecture, model driven engineering, and archtiecture driven modernization and Web Services.

Pascual González has a MSc and a PhD in computer science by the Polytechnic University of Madrid. Currently, he is associate professor at the Department of Computer Systems of the University of Castilla-La Mancha. He leads the Laboratory of User Interaction and Software Engineering (LoUISE) research group of the Computer Science Research Institute of Albacete. He is the author of several papers on software engineering and human computer interaction, and he is a member of several program committees of different conferences. His research interests are, among others, model-based user interface development, usability, quality models, and user interface adaptation. He can be reached at pgonzalez@dsi.uclm.es

Nicolas Guelfi is professor at the Faculty of Sciences, Technology and Communications of the University of Luxembourg. His main research activities concern the engineering and evolution of reliable and secure distributed and mobile systems based on semiformal methods and transformations. He is a leading member of the Laboratory for Advanced Software Systems (LASSY). He has made significant contributions on software engineering methods and tools for distributed systems. He has been involved in three European ESPRIT BRA projects, and is chair of the ERCIM working group on rapid integration of software engineering techniques (RISE), where he developed collaborations with the W3C consortium and with the Semantic Web working group.

May Haydar received a BS in computer science from the American University of Beirut, Lebanon (1996), and a masters in computer science from Concordia University, Montreal (2001). She is a PhD candidate at the Department of Computer Science and Operational Research at University of Montreal. Her research studies are sponsored by Centre de Recherche Informatique de Montreal (CRIM). She published several research papers on formal analysis of Web applications and linear temporal logic extensions at international conferences such as FORTE and ASE. Her current research interests include formal methods, analysis, and verification of Web applications, and temporal logic extensions.

Kuan-Yu He is a Master's student in the Department of Computer Science and Information Engineering (CSIE) at National Cheng Kung University, Tainan, Taiwan. His research interests include Web mining, information retrieval, and machine learning.

Winnie Hua is a Principal Consultant in CTS Inc. She has more than 15-year project and consulting experience on a broad range of leading-edge technologies. She holds a Master's degree in Computer Science. As a solution architect/lead, she has led lifecycle design and development of large-scale e-commerce systems on diverse platforms using a variety of cutting-edge technologies and unified/agile methodologies. She has initiated/participated in advanced research on various emerging Web technologies, and published numerous research papers. She is a member of various professional associations, a regular speaker in conferences/seminars, and also a cofounder of the Charlotte Architecture and Technology Symposium (CATS).

Pankaj Kamthan has been teaching in academia and industry for several years. He has also been a technical editor and participated in standards development. His professional interests and experience include software quality, markup languages, and knowledge represenation.

Fotis Lazarinis is currently a final year PhD student and a part-time lecturer at a Greek Technological and Educational Institute. He is the author of more than 30 papers in refereed journals, conferences, and workshops, 2 book chapters, and more than 15 papers in national journals and conferences. He has also published 16 computer science educational books in Greek.

Chad Lin is a Research Fellow at Curtin University of Technology. Dr Lin has conducted extensive research as in the areas of: IS/IT investments evaluation and benefits realization, IS/IT outsourcing, electronic commerce, e-health, virtual teams, and strategic alliance. Dr Lin has published more than 80 refereed journal (e.g., *Information and Management*, *International Journal of Electronic Commerce*, *Information Technology and People*, *Industrial Management and Data Systems*, and *Journal of Research and Practice in IT*) and conference papers, as well as book chapters. Dr Lin has also served as a member of editorial review board for several prestigious international journals.

María Dolores Lozano Has a MSc and a PhD in computer science by the Technical University of Valencia, Spain. Currently, she is associate professor at the Department of Computer Systems in the University of Castilla-La Mancha. She belongs to the Laboratory of User Interaction and Software Engineering (LoUISE) research group of the Albacete Research Institute of Informatics. Her teaching and research areas concern software engineering and human computer interaction. She is author of numerous papers and member of several program committees of different national and international conferences. Her research interests are, among others, Model-based user interface development, software engineering, usability, CSCW, and collaborative working environments. She can be reached at mlozano@dsi.uclm.es.

Wen-Hsiang Lu is an assistant professor in the Department of Computer Science and Information Engineering (CSIE) at National Cheng Kung University, Tainan, Taiwan. Dr. Lu received the BS, MS, and PhD in computer science and information engineering from National Chiao Tung University, Hsinchu, Taiwan. His current research focuses on Web mining, information retrieval, natural language processing, and medical informatics.

Francisco J. Lucas has an MSc in computer science and is a PhD student at the Facultad de Informática of the Murcia University (Spain). His current research interest includes model-driven engineering, model consistency, models verification and validation, and formal methods. He is developing his PhD in these areas in the Software Engineering Research Group at the University of Murcia (Spain). Contact him at fjlucas@um.es

Ghazwa Malak is a PhD student at the Department of Computer Science and Operational Research at the University of Montreal, Canada. She received the master's degree in computer science from Laval University, Quebec, (2002). She published several research papers on the quality modeling of Web-based applications in several international conferences as EC-WEB and WISE. Her current research interests include graphical models, fuzzy logic, and Web applications quality assessment.

Thomas Mandl studied information and computer science at the University of Regensburg, Germany, and at the University of Illinois at Champaign/Urbana. Thomas Mandl has worked as a research assistant at the Social Science Information Centre in Bonn, Germany, and as assistant professor at the University of Hildesheim, Germany, where he is teaching in the program, International Information Management. He is currently working toward a post doctoral degree (Habilitation) on Web retrieval. His research interests include information retrieval, human-computer interaction, applications of machine learning, and international information systems.

Esperanza Marcos obtained her computer science engineer degree, as well as her PhD at the Technical University of Madrid. She also graduated in computer science at the Valladolid University. Nowadays, she is associate professor at the Rey Juan Carlos University, where she is the head of the Kybele Research Group, whose research topics are mainly focused on information systems engineering, especially on model-driven methodologies, Web information systems, and so forth. She has given several courses and specialization masters. At present she collaborates on the software engineering master at the Technical University of Madrid. She is also author of a vast amount of books, book chapters, and national and international articles. Finally, she has also led several research projects, and has participated in others as well.

Yolanda Marhuenda García has a degree in computer science and is PhD in computational statistics by the University Miguel Hernández of Elche (UMH), Alicante, (Spain) in the Department of Statistics, Mathematics and Computer Science. She is assistant professor in this department and is member of the Computational Statistics Research Group in the Operations Research Center of the UMH. Her research interests are: Web quality models, measures, goodness of fit tests, and small area estimation. Her email is y.marhuenda@umh.es

Adriana Martín is an adjunct professor and member of the GIISCo research group (http://giisco.uncoma.edu.ar) at the University of Comahue, Argentina. Her interests are focused on Web engineering, Web reengineering, and Web quality. She holds a Masters in software engineering from the University of La Plata, Argentina, and she is currently a PhD student at the same university.

Carmen Martinez-Cruz is an assistant professor in the Department of Computers at the University of Jaen (Spain). She is also a PhD student at the Intelligent Databases and Information Systems Research Group at the University of Granada. Her research interests include database design, fuzzy data representation, and knowledge representation using ontologies.

Maristella Matera is assistant professor at Politecnico di Milano, where she teaches databases. Her research interests focus on design methods and tools for Web applications, and in particular concentrate on conceptual modeling quality, Web usage analysis, adaptive and context-aware Web applications, and Web application usability and accessibility. She is author of more than 50 papers on the above topics and of the book "Designing data-intensive Web applications," published by Morgan Kaufmann in December of 2002. She regularly serves as program committee member in several conferences and workshops in the field of Web Engineering. A more detailed curriculum vitae and the list of publications can be found at http://www.elet.polimi.it/people/matera.

Emilia Mendes is a senior lecturer in computer science at the University of Auckland (New Zealand), where she leads the WETA (web engineering, technology and applications) research group. She has active research interests in the areas of empirical Web and software engineering, areas in which she has published widely. Dr. Mendes has been on the program committee of more than 70 conferences and workshops, and is on the editorial board of the journals *IJWET, JWE*, and *The Journal of Software Measurement*. Dr. Mendes worked in the software industry for 10 years before obtaining her PhD in computer science from the University of Southampton (UK), and moving to Auckland.

Xiannong Meng is a professor in the Department of Computer Science at Bucknell University in Lewisburg, Pennsylvania, USA. His research interests include distributed computing, data mining, intelligent Web search, operating systems, and computer networks. He received his PhD in computer science from Worcester Polytechnic Institute in Worcester, Massachusetts, USA. He is a member of ACM and IEEE.

Nina Mistilis is senior lecturer in the tourism and hospitality management group, School of Marketing, University of New South Wales, Sydney, Australia. She publishes in tourism policy and planning, knowledge management for tourism crises and disasters, and ICT and tourism management, and has a PhD in political science from the Australian National University. She is a foundation board member and vice president of the Australasian Chapter of the International Federation of Information Technology and Tourism (IFITT). Her earlier industry experience includes senior appointments in a global banking corporation, where she drove the development of strategic information systems to meet business needs.

Fernando Molina is MSc in computer science and PhD student at the Facultad de Informática of the Murcia University (Spain). His current research interest include model-driven engineering, Web engineering, models verification and validation, formal methods, and precise modeling. He is developing his PhD in these areas in the Software Engineering Research Group at the University of Murcia (Spain). Contact him at fmolina@um.es

Francisco Montero Simarro is assistant professor and researcher at the University of Castilla-La Mancha since October, 2001. He obtained his Masters in computer sciences at the Technical University of Valencia (1997). He obtained his PhD in computing sciences, Laboratory of User Interfaces and Software Engineering (LoUISE), University of Castilla-La Mancha, 2005. He is researching around software engineering (design patterns, unified process and software development methods based on transformations) and human-computer interaction (usability, interaction patterns, and model-based user interface development environments). He can be reached at fmontero@dsi.uclm.es.

Jano Moreira de Souza is a professor of computer science at the Graduate School of Engineering (COPPE) and Mathematics Institute of the Federal University of Rio de Janeiro (UFRJ) (Brazil). His area of specialization is databases, and he is involved in research in fields such as CSCW, DB, DSS, KM, and GIS. He received his Bachelor's degree in mechanical engineering (1974), his Master's degree (1978) in system engineering from UFRJ, and his PhD in information systems (1986) from the University of East Anglia (England). He has published more than 200 papers in journals and conference proceedings and supervised around 50 theses and dissertations.

Ricardo Oliveira Barros is a doctorate candidate at the Computer Science Department of the Federal University of Rio de Janeiro. He received his MSc in computer systems engineering from Military Institute of Engineering (1996), and his accounting bachelor's degree from Oswaldo Aranha Foundation (1982). His current research focuses on information quality, cooperative work and ontologies, information retrieval, and fuzzy logic. He worked in many consultant projects at home and abroad for public and private organizations.

Alberto Pan is a senior research scientist at the University of A Coruña (Spain) and a consultant for Denodo Tehnologies. He received a BS in computer science from the University of A Coruña (1996), and a PhD in computer science from the same university (2002). His research interests are related to data extraction and integration. Alberto has authored numerous publications in scientific magazines and conference proceedings. Furthermore, he has held several positions in institutions such as CESAT (a telematic engineering company), the University Carlos III of Madrid, and the University Alfonso X el Sabio.

Iñaki Paz is a PhD student finishing his thesis on the ONEKIN Research Group, which belongs to the University of the Basque Country, Spain. His research interests include Web engineering, portal and portlet development and integration, data extraction and integration, and application adaptation and evolution. He is currently working in LKS S.Coop. as a technology consultant, previously holding several research positions in the ONEKIN Research Group.

Vicente Pelechano is an associate professor in the Department of Information Systems and Computation (DISC) at the Technical University of Valencia, Spain. His research interests are Web engineering, conceptual modeling, requirements engineering, software patterns, web services, pervasive systems development and model driven development. He received his PhD from the Technical University of Valencia (2001). He has published in several well-known scientific journals (*Information Systems, Data & Knowledge Engineering, Information and Software Technology, International Journal of Web Engineering* and *Technology,* etc.), book chapters for Springer and IGI Global, and international conferences. He is a member of scientific committees of well-known international conferences and workshops as CAiSE, ICWE, ICEIS, WWW, EC-WEB, ACM MT, and IADIS.

Asier Perallos is associate professor in the Department of Software Engineering at the University of Deusto in Bilbao (Spain), where he currently teaches courses on distributed systems design and software integration technologies. Perallos received his PhD in computer science (2007) (University of Deusto). His research interests focus on distributed systems and methods for evaluation of web application quality. He is active in several research projects in the scope of usability evaluation of Web sites and development of software middleware for remote control and supervision of real-time systems.

Alexandre Petrenko received the PhD in computer science from the Institute of Electronics and Computer Science, Riga, USSR. He has joined Centre de Recherche informatique de Montreal (CRIM) in 1996, where he is currently a senior researcher and team leader. He has published over 150 research papers and has given numerous invited lectures worldwide. He serves as a member of the program committee for a number of international conferences and workshops. His current research interests include formal methods and their application in distributed systems.

Wallace A. Pinheiro is a doctorate student of computer science at the Federal University of Rio de Janeiro. He has an electronic engineering degree from Federal University of Rio de Janeiro, where concluded his graduation (1998). He received his master's in science from Military Institute of Engineering (2004). His recent works involve information quality, autonomic computing, cooperative work, and ontologies. His current research focuses on ontologies, fuzzy logic, and information quality.

Cédric Pruski is a PhD student in the LASSY of the University of Luxembourg and in the IASI-GEMO joint team of the LRI and INRIA-Futurs at Paris-Sud University (France). He received his master's from the University of Nancy I (France) in September 2005. He also worked for 2 years as a R&D engineer in the SE2C group at the University of Luxembourg on research projects that dealt with security and trust management. His research interests include the use of ontologies for information management, ontologies evolution and Web information retrieval.

Chantal Reynaud is professor of computer science in the Laboratory of Computer Science (LRI) of the University of Paris-Sud. Her research areas include ontology engineering and information integration. In particular, she works on: Information extraction from semistructured data (e.g., XML documents), mappings between ontologies, discovery of mappings in peer to peer data management systems, and ontology evolution. She is involved in several projects combining artificial intelligence and database techniques for information integration. She is the head of the Artificial Intelligence and Inference Systems Group of the LRI and member of the INRIA-Futurs Gemo group.

Francesca Rizzo is a junior researcher at Politecnico di Milano, where she is a lecturer for the Human Computer Interaction Laboratory. In 2003, she obtained her PhD in telematics and information society from the University of Siena. In the last years, she has taught human computer interaction and interaction design at the University of Siena and at Politecnico di Milano. Her research interests focus on human-computer interaction, user-centered design, usability evaluation, and activity analysis. She is author of about 20 papers on the previous topics.

Jesús Rodríguez Pérez is a computer science technical engineer from the University of Oviedo. Since 1994, he has worked for a software development company, formerly as a developer and application architect in software projects for an enterprise client and since 2001 as a research and development department member, undertaking tasks such as designing and developing productivity tools for company developers, components to be deployed as part of the company's runtime platform, new products and services design, assessment and application of new technologies, software and prototype development, technological transference, and technical training.

Gustavo Rossi is a full professor and head of the LIFIA computer science research lab. His research interests include Web design patterns and frameworks. He coauthored the object-oriented hypermedia design method (OOHDM) and is currently working in separation of design concerns in context-aware Web applications. He holds a PhD in computer science from Catholic University of Rio de Janeiro (PUC-Rio), Brazil. He is an ACM member and IEEE member.

Houari A. Sahraoui is a professor at the Department of Computer Science and Operational Research (GEODES software engineering group) at University of Montreal. His research interests include the application of artificial intelligence techniques to software engineering, object-oriented metrics, software quality, software visualization, and software reverse- and re-engineering. He has published around 100 papers in conferences, workshops, and journals, and edited three books. He served as steering, program, and organization committee member in several major conferences (ECOOP, ASE, METRICS, ICSM, etc.) and as member of the editorial boards of two journals. He was the general chair of the IEEE Automated Software Engineering Conference in 2003.

Mohamed Salah Hamdi was born on April 1, 1967, in Sidi Bouzid, Tunisia. He received a diploma degree (Diplom-Informatiker Univ.) in computer science from the Technical University of Munich, Germany (1993), and a PhD (Dr. rer. nat.) in computer science from the University of Hamburg, Germany, (1999). From 1994 to 1999, he was a lecturer at the Department of Computer Science of the University of Hamburg, Germany. In September 1999, he joined the National Institute of Applied Sciences and Technology of the University of Tunis, Tunisia, as an assistant professor. From 2001 to 2005, he was working as an assistant professor at the Department of Mathematics and Computer Science of the United Arab Emirates University in Al Ain. Since September 2005, he has been an assistant professor at the

University of Qatar in Doha. His research interests are focused on intelligent autonomous agents, e-learning, information customization, machine learning, and on artificial intelligence in general.

Soonhwa Seok's research interests include: (a) digital inclusion, (b) developing traditional/nontraditional teaching programs for teacher education using universal design for learning and differentiated instruction, (c) staff development/teacher education in technology integrated inclusive settings, (d) new uses of technology in multicultural, special education, and (e) assessment of the effectiveness of one's own teaching strategies and curriculum plans. His research interests also include the implementation of universal design for learning. Currently, he teaches three courses in education to preservice teachers. They are classroom inclusion, diagnostic assessment, and theoretical perspectives in the education of individuals with mild disabilities.

Tony Shan is a SOA Strategist/Architect in Bank of America, the largest commercial bank in the United States, and adjunct professor at the University of Phoenix. He has been working on computing technologies for 20+ years, with extensive experience in a variety of technologies and programming languages in different industries. Holding three advanced degrees in engineering and science majors, he is a Sun-certified enterprise architect & Java 2 programmer, IBM-certified eBusiness solution designer, and Sun-certified faculty instructor. He has initiated/directed advanced research on emerging technologies, resulting in an invention patent and award-winning IT solutions, as well as several methodologies and platform models for adaptive system development. He has led establishing IT strategies and architecture blueprints, coupled with pragmatic technology roadmaps and enterprise architecture standards/policies, for Fortune 100 international organizations. He serves as a mentor/advisor on leading-edge technologies, architecture, and engineering in various technical committees, and teaches a wide variety of courses as an adjunct professor and professional trainer. In addition to dozens of top-notch technical publications, he authored multiple books on asynchronous Web services and heterogeneous business integration. He is a member of numerous professional associations and honorary societies, a frequent speaker and chair/program committee member in conferences/workshops, an editor/editorial advisory board member of IT research journals and books, and also a founder of Greater Charlotte Rational User Group and Architecture & Technology Symposium.

Stefan Siersdorfer is a research fellow at the IR Group of the University of Sheffield, UK. His research interests include probabilistic models and automatic tuning of ensemble-based meta methods for machine learning and personalized information management. In 2005, he did his PhD at the Database and Information Systems Group of the Max Planck Institute for Computer Science, Germany, under Gerhard Weikum.

Sergej Sizov is the research fellow in the ISWeb group (Information Systems & Semantic Web) at the University of Koblenz-Landau, Germany. He holds PhDs in applied mathematics and computer science. In the past, he held positions as researcher, project leader, and lecturer at the University of Saarland, Germany, and the Max-Planck Institute for Computer Science, Germany. In his prior work, he substantially contributed to the methodology of thematically focused Web exploration, collaborative IR methods in decentralized environments, and meta methods for Web-based machine learning applications. His research interests include thematically focused Web search, self-organizing folksonomies, peer-to-peer search, and retrieval.

Rosemary Stockdale is a senior lecturer in Information Systems at Massey University in New

Zealand. She completed her PhD at Edith Cowan University, Australia, where she worked in the School of Management Information Systems. More recently, she was a member of a research group in IT and Tourism at the School of Management, University of Innsbruck, in Austria, before moving to Massey in early 2006. Her research interests include mobile technology use in the health sector, online communities, and the use of IT in tourism. Dr Stockdale has published in a range of information systems journals, including the *European Journal of Operational Research* and the *Journal of Enterprise Information Management*.

Victoria Torres is a PhD student in the Department of Information Systems and Computation (DSIC) at the Technical University of Valencia, Spain. Her research interests include Web engineering, model-driven development, business processes, and Semantic Web. She is a member of the OO-Method Research group, and she has published several contributions to international workshops and conferences (BPM) and she has contributed in some Web engineering books. Her PhD work focuses on the automatic development of business process driven Web applications.

Juan M. Vara obtained his BSc and MSc in computer science engineering at the Rey Juan Carlos University, where he did the doctoral courses on the computer science and mathematical modeling program. Currently, he works as assistant professor at the Department of Informatics Languages and Systems of the Rey Juan Carlos University and he is a member of the Kybele Research Group, where he is doing his PhD Thesis focused on model-driven engineering for the development of Web information systems. He is coauthor of several publications at national and international events and he has participated in several regional, national, and European research projects.

Index

A

absolute scale of measurement 6

abstraction, polymorphism, inheritance, and encapsulation(A-PIE) 441, 453, 454, 456

accessibility 105, 109, 110, 145, 146, 148, 151, 153, 154, 155, 156, 158, 159, 160

accessible barriers 202

adaptability 204, 207

adaptive hypermedia system (AHS) 284, 287, 292, 294

algorithmic techniques 28, 55, 28, 55, 28

Americans with Disabilities Act (ADA) 205, 206, 216

annotations 202, 300

application program interface (API) 421, 422, 437

artificial intelligence techniques 28, 30

assistive technologies 151, 156, 163, 174, 177, 207, 212

automatic evaluation tools 236

averaged search length (ASL) 496, 497, 498, 499, 500, 504

B

banking portal quality model (BPQM) 121, 122, 123, 124, 125, 126, 127

basic combined programming language (BCPL) 444

Bayesian networks 85, 87, 93, 100

business process (BP) 247, 251, 254, 262, 265, 248, 250, 251, 254, 260, 261, 262

business process (BP) driven Web applications 247, 251, 265

business to business (B2B) 70, 71, 81

business to business electronic commerce (B2BEC) 83, 84

C

case-based reasoning 26, 30, 35, 36, 37, 51, 55, 30, 32, 34, 35, 37, 53, 54

classification, restrictive 404, 405, 406, 409, 412, 413, 419

classification trees 31

click-through data 478, 480, 481, 478, 482, 478, 480, 481, 482, 484, 485, 484

clients 62

clustering, collaborative 410

clustering, distributed 403, 411, 416, 418

clustering, meta 409, 412, 415, 416, 417

clustering, restrictive 406, 409

cognitive impairments 154

cognitive processing models 208, 209, 213, 216

collaborative classification 410

computation 6

computer based assistive technology 157

content 326, 331, 339

context 322, 324, 327, 328, 329, 330, 331, 333, 336, 337, 338

context of use 145, 146, 147, 148, 153, 158, 159, 160

cosine similarity 490, 491

cost estimation 32, 33, 34, 38, 52, 53, 54. *See* effort estimation

cross-validation 32, 47

cultural environment 148

X

Y